Competency	Chapter
Competency 1: Demonstrate Ethical and Professional Behavior	
Behaviors	
Make ethical decisions by applying the standards of the NASW Code of Ethics, relevant laws and regulations, models for ethical decision-making, ethical conduct of research, and additional codes of ethics as appropriate to context.	1, 7, 13, 14
Use reflection and self-regulation to manage personal values and maintain professionalism in practice situations	1, 4, 5
Demonstrate professional demeanor in behavior; appearance; and oral, written, and electronic communication	1, 6, 7
Use technology ethically and appropriately to facilitate practice outcomes	1, 6, 14
Use supervision and consultation to guide professional judgment and behavior	1, 4
Competency 2: Engage Diversity and Difference in Practice	
Behaviors	
Apply and communicate understanding of the importance of diversity and difference in shaping life experiences in practice at the micro, mezzo, and macro levels	3, 5, 6, 7, 8, 9, 10, 11, 12
Present themselves as learners and engage clients and constituencies as experts of their own experiences	1, 5, 8, 14
Apply self-awareness and self-regulation to manage the influence of personal biases and values in working with diverse clients and constituencies	1, 4, 5, 7, 8
Competency 3: Advance Human Rights and Social, Economic, and Environmental Justice	
Behaviors	
Apply their understanding of social, economic, and environmental justice to advocate for human rights at the individual and system levels	4, 5, 8, 9
Engage in practices that advance social, economic, and environmental justice	3, 4, 5, 9
Competency 4: Engage In Practice-informed Research and Research-informed Practice	
Behaviors	
Use practice experience and theory to inform scientific inquiry and research	2, 3, 8, 14
Apply critical thinking to engage in analysis of quantitative and qualitative research methods and research findings	2, 4, 8, 10, 14
Use and translate research evidence to inform and improve practice, policy, and service delivery	1, 2, 3, 4, 5, 6, 9, 10, 11, 12, 13, 14
Competency 5: Engage in Policy Practice	
Behaviors	
Identify social policy at the local, state, and federal level that impacts well-being, service delivery, and access to social services	1, 4, 5, 11, 12

CSWE EPAS 2015 Core Competencies and Behaviors in This Text

Competency	Chapter
Assess how social welfare and economic policies impact the delivery of and access to social services	1, 5, 10, 12
Apply critical thinking to analyze, formulate, and advocate for policies that advance human rights and social, economic, and environmental justice	1, 5, 8, 12
Competency 6: Engage with Individuals, Families, Groups, Organizations, and Communities	
Behaviors	
Apply knowledge of human behavior and the social environment, person-in-environment, and other multidisciplinary theoretical frameworks to engage with clients and constituencies	2, 3, 6, 7, 9, 10, 11, 12
Use empathy, reflection, and interpersonal skills to effectively engage diverse clients and constituencies	4, 5, 6, 7, 9, 11
Competency 7: Assess Individuals, Families, Groups, Organizations, and Communities	
Behaviors	
Collect and organize data, and apply critical thinking to interpret information from clients and constituencies	4, 7, 8, 12, 14
Apply knowledge of human behavior and the social environment, person-in-environment, and other multidisciplinary theoretical frameworks in the analysis of assessment data from clients and constituencies	2, 3, 4, 5, 6, 8
Develop mutually agreed-on intervention goals and objectives based on the critical assessment of strengths, needs, and challenges within clients and constituencies	6, 7, 8, 9, 14
Select appropriate intervention strategies based on the assessment, research knowledge, and values and preferences of clients and constituencies	3, 4, 5, 8, 9, 10, 11
Competency 8: Intervene with Individuals, Families, Groups, Organizations, and Communities	
Behaviors	
Critically choose and implement interventions to achieve practice goals and enhance capacities of clients and constituencies	1, 4, 5, 7, 8, 9, 10, 11, 12, 13
Apply knowledge of human behavior and the social environment, person-in-environment, and other multidisciplinary theoretical frameworks in interventions with clients and constituencies	2, 3, 4, 5, 8, 9, 10, 11, 12, 13
Use inter-professional collaboration as appropriate to achieve beneficial practice outcomes	8, 9, 10, 11, 12
Negotiate, mediate, and advocate with and on behalf of diverse clients and constituencies	5, 8, 9, 10, 12
Facilitate effective transitions and endings that advance mutually agreed-on goals	13
Competency 9: Evaluate Practice with Individuals, Families, Groups, Organizations, and Communities	
Behaviors	
Select and use appropriate methods for evaluation of outcomes	6, 8, 11, 14
Apply knowledge of human behavior and the social environment, person-in-environment, and other multidisciplinary theoretical frameworks in the evaluation of outcomes	1, 4, 5, 6, 8, 14
Critically analyze, monitor, and evaluate intervention and program processes and outcomes	5, 6, 8, 14
Apply evaluation findings to improve practice effectiveness at the micro, mezzo, and macro levels	14

Adapted with permission of Council on Social Work Education. These competencies and behaviors also appear in the margins throughout this text.

EIGHTH EDITION

An Introduction to Group Work Practice

Ronald W. Toseland
University at Albany, State University of New York

Robert F. Rivas
Siena College, Emeritus

PEARSON

Boston Columbus Indianapolis New York San Francisco Hoboken
Amsterdam Cape Town Dubai London Madrid Milan Munich Paris Montreal Toronto
Delhi Mexico City São Paulo Sydney Hong Kong Seoul Singapore Taipei Tokyo

VP and Editorial Director: Jeffery W. Johnston
Executive Editor: Julie Peters
Program Manager: Megan Moffo
Editorial Assistant: Pamela DiBerardino
Executive Product Marketing Manager:
    Christopher Barry
Executive Field Marketing Manager: Krista Clark
Team Lead Project Management: Bryan Pirrmann
Team Lead Program Management: Laura Weaver
Procurement Specialist: Deidra Skahill
Art Director: Diane Lorenzo

Art Director Cover: Diane Six
Cover Design: Carie Keller, Cenveo
Cover Art: Fotolia/Monkey Business
Media Producer: Michael Goncalves
Editorial Production and Composition Services:
    Lumina Datamatics, Inc.
Full-Service Project Manager: Doug Bell, Raja Natesan
Printer/Binder: RR Donnelley/Harrisonburg
Cover Printer: RR Donnelley/Harrisonburg
Text Font: Dante MT Pro 10.5/13pt

Library of Congress Cataloging-in-Publication Data
Names: Toseland, Ronald W., author. | Rivas, Robert F., author.
Title: An introduction to group work practice / Ronald W. Toseland,
  University at Albany, State University of New York, Robert F. Rivas, Siena
  College.
Description: Eighth edition. | Boston : Pearson, [2017]
Identifiers: LCCN 2015046267 | ISBN 9780134058962 (alk. paper) | ISBN
  0134058968 (alk. paper)
Subjects: LCSH: Social group work.
Classification: LCC HV45 .T68 2017 | DDC 361.4—dc23 LC record available at http://lccn.loc.gov/2015046267

5 2019

Student Edition
ISBN 10: 0-134-05896-8
ISBN 13: 978-0-134-05896-2

eText
ISBN-10: 0-13-408871-9
ISBN-13: 978-0-13-408871-6

Package
ISBN-10: 0-13-429014-3
ISBN-13: 978-0-13-429014-0

PEARSON

To our parents, Stella and Ed, Marg and Al

Contents

Preface

We are gratified by the wide use of this text by professionals, as well as by educators and students in undergraduate and graduate courses in schools of social work throughout the United States and the world.

Because we are committed to presenting a coherent and organized over-view of group work practice from a generalist practice perspective, the eighth edition continues to include typologies illustrating group work practice with task and treatment groups at the micro-, meso-, and macro-level. Our research and practice focuses primarily on treatment groups, and the eighth edition continues to present our interest in improving practice with many different types of treatment groups.

New to This Edition

- Research on Virtual Groups. In recent years, we have done research on the uses of virtual group formats (teleconference and Internet groups) and have included an updated and expanded section on virtual groups in the 6th chapter of this edition.
- Additional case examples throughout this edition illustrate practice with a wide variety of groups. These were added based on feedback from our students, reviewers of the book, instructors, and others who have contacted us about the importance of illustrations of evidence-based practice examples.
- Updated and deeper content of the middle stage chapters on practice with treatment and task groups. The latest evidence-based treatment and task group research is incorporated throughout Chapters 9 through 12, and content has been added, deleted, and changed to reflect current practice.
- Incorporated the most current literature on working with reluctant and resistant group members in specific sections of Chapters 7 and 9 and throughout the text.
- We find that our students face many situations with individuals who have encountered multiple traumas in their family lives and in the larger social environment, making them understandably reticent to engage group workers and fellow group members, and trust in the power of group work to heal. There-fore, we have updated and expanded sections on working with individuals who have difficulty engaging in and sustaining work in groups and have added additional information about conflict resolution skills as it pertains to both treatment and task groups.

- Thoroughly updated Chapter 5 on leadership and diversity as social group workers practice in an increasingly pluralistic society.
- Now available as an Enhanced Pearson eText. The Pearson eText platform has embedded multiple-choice quizzes at the end of each major section of the text to test students' knowledge of the chapter content and mastery of the competencies. These questions are aligned with new Learning Outcomes and are constructed in a format that will help to prepare students for the ASWB Licensing exam. (Third party eTexts such as Kindle and Nook do not contain the quizzes.)
- Thoroughly updated reference material and new content from evidence-based practice sources.

About Group Work

Over the years, we have been especially pleased that our text has been used by educators who are dedicated to improving task group practice within social work. Group work is a neglected area of social work practice, especially practice with task groups. Most social workers spend a great deal of time in teams, treatment conferences, and committees, and many social workers have leadership responsibilities in these groups. Group work is also essential for effective macro social work practice, and therefore, we have continued to emphasize practice with community groups. The eighth edition also continues our focus on three focal areas of practice: (1) the individual group member, (2) the group as a whole, and (3) the environment in which the group functions. We continue to emphasize the importance of the latter two focal areas because our experiences in supervising group workers and students and conducting workshops for professionals have revealed that the dynamics of a group as a whole and the environment in which groups function are often a neglected aspect of group work practice.

Connecting Core Competencies Series

This edition is a part of Pearson's Connecting Core Competencies series, which consists of foundation-level texts that make it easier than ever to ensure students' success in learning the nine core competencies as stated in 2015 by the Council on Social Worker Education. This text contains:

- Core Competency Icons throughout the chapters, directly linking the CSWE core competencies to the content of the text. Critical thinking questions are also included to further students' mastery of the CSWE's standards.
- For easy reference, a matrix is included at the beginning of the book that aligns the book chapters with the CSWE Core Competencies and Behavior Examples.

Instructor Supplements

The following supplemental products may be downloaded from pearsonhighered.com/educator.

Instructor's Resource Manual and Test Bank. This manual contains a sample syllabus, chapter summaries, learning outcomes, chapter outlines, teaching tips, discussion questions, multiple-choice and essay assessment items (different from those in the Pearson eText) and other supportive resources.

PowerPoint Slides. For each chapter in the book, we have prepared a PowerPoint slide deck focusing on key concepts and strategies.

Acknowledgments

The ideas expressed in this book have evolved during many years of study, practice, and research. Some of the earliest and most powerful influences that have shaped this effort have come about through our relationships with Bernard Hill, Alan Klein, Sheldon Rose, and Max Siporin. Their contributions to the development of our thinking are evident throughout this book. The ideas in this book were also influenced by Albert Alissi, Martin Birnbaum, Leonard Brown, Charles Garvin, Alex Gitterman, Burton Gummer, Margaret Hartford, Grafton Hull, Jr., Norma Lang, Catherine Papell, William Reid, Beulah Rothman, Jarrold Shapiro, Laurence Shulman, and Peter Vaughan. Our appreciation and thanks to the reviewers of the seventh edition who gave us valuable advice for how to improve this new eighth edition: Tom Broffman, Eastern Connecticut State University; Daniel B. Freedman, University of South Carolina; Kim Knox, New Mexico State University; Gayle Mallinger, Western Kentucky University; John Walter Miller, Jr., University of Arkansas at Little Rock. We are also indebted to the many practitioners and students with whom we have worked over the years. Reviewing practice experiences, discussing group meetings, and providing consultation and supervision to the practitioners with whom we work with during research projects, supervision, staff meetings, and workshops has helped us to clarify and improve the ideas presented in this text.

We would also like to acknowledge the material support and encouragement given to us by our respective educational institutions. The administrative and support staff of the School of Social Welfare, University at Albany, State University of New York, and Siena College have played important roles in helping us to accomplish this project. Most of all, however, we are indebted to our spouses, Sheryl Holland and Donna Allingham Rivas. Their personal and professional insights have done much to enrich this book. Without their continuous support and encouragement, we would not have been able to complete this work. A special note of thanks also goes to Rebecca, Stacey, and Heather for sacrificing some of their dads' time so that we are able to keep this book current and relevant for today's practice environment.

Ronald W. Toseland
Robert F. Rivas

1

Introduction

This text focuses on the practice of group work by professional social workers. Group work entails the deliberate use of intervention strategies and group processes to accomplish individual, group, and community goals using the value base and the ethical practice principles of the social work profession. As one prepares to become an effective social work practitioner, it is important to realize the effect that groups have on people's lives. It is not possible to be a member of a society without becoming a member or leader of groups and being influenced by others without direct participation. Internet groups are also becoming more popular as people choose to meet others in virtually as well as face-to-face. Although it is possible to live in an isolated manner or on the fringes of face-to-face and virtual groups, our social nature makes this neither desirable nor healthy.

Groups provide the structure on which communities and the larger society are built. They provide formal and informal structure in the workplace. They also provide a means through which relationships with significant others are carried out. Participation in family groups, peer groups, and classroom groups helps members learn acceptable norms of social behavior, engage in satisfying social relationships, identify personal goals, and derive a variety of other benefits that result from participating in closely knit social systems. Experiences in social, church, recreation, and other work groups are essential in the development and maintenance of people and society. Putnam (2000) points out that there has been a sharp decline in participation in clubs and other civic organizations and that social capital is not valued in contemporary society. At the same time, web-based social network and self-help group sites continue to grow enormously in popularity, enabling users to keep up contacts with more and more people. One goal of this book is to underscore the importance of groups as fundamental building blocks for a connected, vibrant society.

ORGANIZATION OF THE TEXT

Group work is a series of activities carried out by the worker during the life of a group. We have found that it is helpful to conceptualize these activities as being a part of six developmental stages:

1. Planning
2. Beginning
3. Assessment
4. Middle
5. Ending
6. Evaluation

Groups exhibit certain properties and processes during each stage of their development. The group worker's task is to engage in activities that facilitate the growth and development of the group and its members during each developmental stage. This book is divided into five parts. Part I focuses on the knowledge base needed to practice with groups. The remaining four parts are organized around each of these six stages of group work practice. Case studies illustrating each practice stage can be found at the end of Chapters 6 through 14.

THE FOCUS OF GROUP WORK PRACTICE

Social work practitioners use group work skills to help meet the needs of individual group members, the group as a whole, and the community. In this text, group work involves the following elements.

Group Work Practice
- Practice with a broad range of treatment and task groups
- Generalist practice based on a set of core competencies described in the Education Policy and Accreditation Standards (EPAS) of the Council on Social Work Education (2015)
- A focus on individual group members, the group as a whole, and the group's environment
- Critical thinking and evidence-based practice when it exists for a particular practice problem or issue
- Application of foundation knowledge and skills from generalist social work practice to a broad range of leadership and membership situations
- Specialized knowledge and skills based on a comprehensive assessment of the needs of particular members and groups
- Recognition of the interactional and situational nature of leadership

Intervention

Behavior: Critically choose and implement interventions to achieve practice goals and enhance capacities of clients and constituencies

Critical Thinking Question: Generalist social work practice involves many systems. How is group work related to generalist social work practice?

This text is firmly grounded in a generalist approach to practice. To accomplish the broad mission and goals of the social work profession, generalist practitioners are expected to possess core competencies based on the Council on Social Work Education's (2015) Educational Policy and Accreditation Standards (EPAS) that enables them to intervene effectively with individuals, families, groups, organizations, and communities. This text highlights the importance of the generalist practitioner's acquisition of the core competencies defined in the EPAS standards.

This text is designed to help generalist practitioners understand how group work can be used to help individuals, families, groups, organizations, and communities function as effectively as possible. Most group work texts are focused on the use of groups for clinical practice, and many focus only on therapy or support groups with little attention paid to social, recreational, or educational purposes. Scant is made of committees, teams, and other task groups that all social workers participate in as members and leaders. Despite the distinctive emphasis of the social work profession on the interface between individuals and their social environment, in most group work texts, even less attention is paid to social action groups, coalitions, and other community groups. This text examines work with a broad range of groups in generalist practice with individuals, organizations, and communities.

This text is also grounded in a critical thinking and evidence-based approach to practice. Whenever possible, suggestions made in this text are based on evidence accumulated from research studies in the literature. Although quantitative evidence from research studies is important, qualitative case studies of group work are also a part of this evidence base. Critical thinking and practice experience are essential on especially when a solid base of empirical evidence is lacking.

Macgowan (2008) points out that group workers using evidence-based group practice principles incorporate critical thinking skills such as challenging assumptions and questioning what is taken for granted. They evaluate sources of evidence for their rigor, impact, and applicability. Macgowan (2008) suggests a four-step process: (1) formulating answerable questions, (2) searching for evidence, (3) critically reviewing the evidence, and (4) applying and evaluating the evidence. Although this rigorous process cannot be done while in the midst of practicing with a group, practitioners can follow this advice when planning for a group and in-between sessions. Social group workers can also use evidence-based protocols in their area of interest. For example, LeCroy (2008) has edited a book of evidence-based treatment manuals for children and adolescents, and many similar publications exist for other populations. Part of the *art of practice* is using critical thinking skills, evidence, practice skills, and accumulated experiences in similar situations to achieve the very best outcomes for group members and others who are affected by the work of the group.

Regarding group work practice with individuals, the group as a whole, and the group's environment, some prominent group workers such as Gitterman and Shulman (2005) focus on the whole group as the unit of intervention and place less emphasis on working with individuals. Others place greater emphasis on changing individual group members and less on group as a whole dynamics (Boyd-Franklin, Cleek, Wofsy, & Mundy, 2013; Rose, 2004; Walsh, 2010). Both perspectives are useful. Whatever approach is used when leading groups, workers should direct their attention to individuals, the group as a whole, and the environment in which the group functions. The worker focuses on in-dividual members to help them accomplish their goals. The worker intervenes with the group as a whole to achieve an optimal level of group functioning and to ensure that the group accomplishes its purposes. The worker also assesses the group's environment and decides whether to help the group adapt to it or change it. During these interventions, it is especially important to focus on group processes as well as the content of the interaction. This dual focus has been referred to as the half-and-half principle (Chen & Rybak, 2004).

The purpose of the group helps determine the emphasis that each focal area should receive. For example, in a support group for recently separated people, the worker might focus on the development of mutual aid among all members of the group. Individual members might also need help developing plans for dealing with specific problems. Sim-ilarly, in the group for recently separated people, the worker might focus on developing individualized treatment plans, but also on enhancing group cohesion, mutual aid, and other beneficial group dynamics. The worker might also focus on factors outside the group that might have an impact on its members. This fits with a person-in-environ-ment perspective that is essential to generalist group work practice. For example, a close examination of the environment in which members of the support group for recently separated people functions might reveal a need to make community services, such as support for single parent dads, more responsive to members of the group. This may, in turn, lead to the development of a social action group to address this problem. Later, this text examines in detail the three focal areas of the individual, the group as a whole, and the group's environment.

Another aspect of group work practice is that workers draw on a broad base of knowledge and skills from generalist practice that they apply to their work with a broad range of groups. The generalist approach emphasizes that social workers perform many roles in their professional lives. It suggests that there are foundation knowledge and skills that transcend specific roles. For example, in-depth knowledge about human develop-ment and skill in empathic responding are essential for effective work with individuals, families, groups, and communities. Although foundation knowledge and skills are de-scribed throughout this text, specialized knowledge and skills are often needed when practicing with children, adolescents, adults, and elders with a wide variety of problems. Therefore, this text also presents specialized knowledge and skills useful for practice with these populations and problems. In keeping with an evidence-based approach to group work practice, the specialized knowledge and skills presented in this book are based on empirical findings in the literature when they are available or critical thinking and prac-tice experience when there is little or no empirical evidence.

Most experienced practitioners continue to learn by exposure to different approaches to group work. Aspects of different approaches, such as humanistic, behavioral, and em-powerment, can often be integrated in a particular practice situation to meet the multi-level needs and preferences of members. A major tenet of the generalist approach is that practice should be based on a comprehensive assessment of the needs of each member in their unique, complex situations.

An integration of practice approaches is often preferable to using a single approach. Exclusive adherence to one approach may work well for a group with a particular set of needs, but it may not work well when leading a group with other needs. Critical thinking skills should always be employed as workers make decisions about the best approach to take. Rigid adherence to one approach tends to make workers oblivious to other potentially useful methods. It can also distort workers' assessments of situations. Workers might mistakenly attempt to fit data from a situation to a particular practice approach rather than choosing the practice approach that best fits the situation. For these reasons, group workers can be most effective when they are familiar with several approaches to group work and when they apply specialized knowledge and skills differentially and critically depending on the particular group work endeavor.

The approach used in this book also recognizes the interactional nature of the helping process. A static, prescriptive approach to group work practice often appeals to novice practitioners because of its simplicity, but this often does not match the complexity and diversity of the real world of group work practice. The leadership model presented in Chapter 4 presents some of the factors that workers should consider when deciding how to proceed with a group.

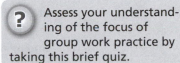

? Assess your understanding of the focus of group work practice by taking this brief quiz.

VALUES AND ETHICS IN GROUP WORK PRACTICE

Practice Values

Group work practice is influenced by a system of personal and professional values. These values affect workers' styles of intervention and the skills they use when working with group members. Values also affect members' reactions to workers' efforts. Despite the emphasis on ethics and values in the Education Policy and Accreditation Standards published by the Council on Social Work Education (2015), Strozier (1997) found that few social group work course syllabi gave much emphasis to the topic of values or ethics in group work practice.

Values are beliefs that delineate preferences about how one ought to behave. They refer to a goal that is worth attaining (Rokeach, 1968). There is no such thing as value-free group work practice. All group workers operate with certain specific assumptions and values regarding the nature of human beings, the role of members, and the role of the group leader. Values influence the methods used to accomplish group and individual goals. Even a leader who is completely permissive and nondirective reveals the values embodied in such a stance.

A worker's actions in the group are affected by contextual values, member value systems, and the worker's personal value system. Levine (2012) has identified values that are dominant in American society.

American Values
- Judeo–Christian doctrine with its emphasis on the dignity and worth of people and people's responsibility for their neighbor
- Democratic values that emphasize equality and participation, including men's and women's rights to life, liberty, and the pursuit of happiness
- The Puritan ethic that emphasizes men's and women's responsibility for themselves and the central role of work in a moral life
- Social Darwinism that emphasizes the survival of the strongest and the fittest in a long-term evolutionary process

The context in which the group functions affects the values exhibited in the group. Contextual values include the values of organizational sponsors, funders, communities, accrediting bodies, regulatory agencies, the social work profession, and the larger society. All of these entities have a direct or indirect effect on the group.

Before beginning a group, the worker should become familiar with the agency's formal and informal values. These are embodied in its mission statements, goals, policies, procedures, and practices. Are treatment groups a preferred method of delivering therapeutic services? Are decisions often made in task groups consisting of staff members, or are most decisions made by agency administrators without staff input? Becoming aware of the policies, procedures, and practices regarding the use of groups in a particular agency can help the worker prepare for possible resistance and evaluate and use sources of support within the agency.

The community where the group conducts its business can also influence the functioning of the group. For example, community standards and traditions, as well as racial, ethnic, and socioeconomic composition, differ widely among communities. When planning a group, the worker needs to consider how these aspects of communities are likely to influence the group and its members.

The worker and the group are also affected by professional values. These include respecting the worth and dignity of the individual, respecting a person's autonomy and self-direction, facilitating a person's participation in the helping process, maintaining a nonjudgmental attitude, ensuring equal access to services and social provisions, and affirming the interdependence of the individual and society.

Beyond the values held by all professional social work practitioners, group workers share a special concern and interest in values that are basic to group work practice. Some of the key values of group work have been stated by Gisela Konopka (1983). She suggests that all group workers should agree on the importance of the following values.

Group Work Values
- Participation of and positive relations among people of different color, creed, age, national origin, and social class in the group
- The value of cooperation and mutual decision making embodied in the principles of a participatory democracy
- The importance of individual initiative within the group
- The importance of freedom to participate, including expressing thoughts and feelings about matters of concern to individual members or the group as a whole, and having the right to be involved in the decision-making process of the group
- The value of high individualization in the group so that each member's unique concerns are addressed

These values are not absent in other aspects of social work practice, but in group work, they are of central importance. In addition to these five core values, we have found four additional values to be fundamental to practice with any type of task or treatment group.

Four Key Values
- Respect and dignity—The worth and dignity of all group members no matter how devalued or stigmatized they may be by society. This includes valuing members' contributions to the life of the group and adhering to all aspects of the National Association of Social Workers (NASW) code of ethics.

- Solidarity and mutual aid—The power and promise of relationships to help members grow and develop, to help them heal, to satisfy their needs for human contact and connectedness, and to promote a sense of unity and community.
- Empowerment—The power of the group to help members feel good about themselves and to enable them to use their abilities to help themselves and to make a difference in their communities.
- Understanding, respect, and camaraderie among people from diverse backgrounds—The ability of groups to help enrich members by acquainting them with people from other backgrounds. Members' respect and appreciation for each other grow as their relationships deepen over the life of a group. Thus, one powerful aspect of social group work is that it helps to decrease ignorance, misunderstanding, and prejudice among people from diverse backgrounds.

In addition to these core values, the worker and the members bring their own unique set of values to the group. Part of the worker's task is to help members clarify their values and to identify and resolve value conflicts between the leader and members, among members, and among members and the larger society. More information about resolving conflicts is discussed in Chapters 4 and 11.

The worker should be especially sensitive to the effect that cultural diversity has on valued behavior in groups. For example, in Native American culture, although cooperation is an important value, it is considered impolite to offer advice, help, or opinion to someone unless it is solicited (McWhirter, & Robbins, 2014; Ratts & Pedersen, 2014). At the same time, workers should be careful not to stereotype members by assuming that particular backgrounds are always associated with particular values (Sue & Sue, 2013).

Workers' personal value systems also affect how they practice. If workers are uncomfortable discussing certain value-laden topics, or if they impose their own values on the group, their work will be seriously impaired. Similarly, if they are not aware of the implications of their values, they are likely to get into conflicts with members who have different values.

Workers who are not aware of their own values will also have difficulty when faced with ambiguous and value-laden situations. Sometimes, the goals of the worker, the agency, the community, and the group members differ (Rothman, 2013). This often occurs with involuntary clients who are receiving the service of a worker at the request of law-enforcement officials or others in the community who find the client's behavior unacceptable. The clearer workers are about their own values and their own purposes and stances in relation to working with the group, the easier it will be for them to sort through conflicting goals and make their own purposes known to group members.

One of the best ways for workers to become aware of their own values and their own stance in working with a group is to obtain supervision. Although workers will never become value-free, supervision can help them become aware of the values they bring to the group. Supervision can help workers modify or change values that are not consistent with those of the social work profession or helpful in their practice with groups of people. Value-clarification exercises can also help workers identify personal and professional values that might influence their work with a group (Dolgoff, Harrington, & Loewenberg, 2012; Rothman, 2013).

Diversity and Difference in Practice

Behavior: Present themselves as learners and engage clients and constituencies as experts of their own experiences

Critical Thinking Question: Members bring their communication styles to the group. How can the leader support effective group communication among members with different styles?

Practice Ethics

The National Association of Social Workers (NASW) has developed a code of ethics to guide the practice of its members. The code of ethics is an operational statement of the central values of the social work profession. Social workers who lead groups should be thoroughly familiar with it. The code is available directly from NASW and is reproduced in many social work practice textbooks.

Corey, Corey, and Corey (2014) point out that a code of ethics specifically for group workers would be a helpful adjunct to the more general codes of ethics developed by professional associations. Although a code of ethics specifically for social group work practice has not been developed, the Standards for Social Work Practice with Groups that are reprinted in Appendix A1 contain core values (Association for the Advancement of Social Work with Groups, 2013).

Ethical practices with groups include (1) informed consent, (2) leader competence and training, and (3) the appropriate conduct of group meetings. Informed consent encompasses being clear with members about the purpose and goals of the group; giving them information about screening and termination procedures; the potential risks of participation; the cost, timing, and duration of sessions; whether participation is voluntary; what is expected of them during meetings; and procedures to ensure confidentiality. A written or verbal statement should also be included about what information the worker and the organization may have to disclose. Depending on the type of members, this might include the following situations: (1) child abuse or neglect, (2) harm to self or others, (3) diagnostic codes, utilization reviews, and other information for reimbursement from mental or physical health care providers, (4) courts, probation, or parole, and (5) family or legal guardians.

Social workers who provide services to groups face special confidentiality challenges when attempting to comply with standard 1.7 of the NASW code of ethics that focuses on privacy and confidentiality issues. Workers should inform members that they cannot guarantee that group members will not share confidential material outside the group (Fallon, 2006; Lasky & Riva, 2006). Nevertheless, workers should be aware that breaches of confidentiality in groups increase their liability (Reamer, 2001; Whittingham & Capriotti, 2009). They should guard against breaches of confidentiality by having all members of the group pledge that they will adhere to confidentiality policies. Reamer (2006) also suggests that workers have a firm policy not to talk individually about group members outside of the group context except during supervision. This policy builds trust and avoids perceptions of favoritism or special alliances with certain members. Some ethical dilemmas faced by group workers are described cogently by Bergeron and Gray (2003), Kirschenbaum (2013), and Rothman (2013).

In a survey of 300 group psychotherapists, Roback, Ochoa, Bloch, and Purdon (1992) found that the limits of confidentiality are rarely discussed with potential group members even though breaches of confidentiality by members are fairly common.

Group leaders may also be required to report certain information, such as child abuse, even without the permission of a group member. To avoid ethical and legal problems associated with a group leader's failure to provide sufficient information about the limits of confidentiality, Roback, Moore, Bloch, and Shelton (1996), Reamer (2006),and Fallon (2006) suggest having members and the leader sign an informed consent form (Table 1.1).

Table 1.1   Informed Consent Form

1. All verbal and nonverbal information mentioned before, during, and following group meetings is to remain confidential. It is not to be mentioned to anyone outside the group including your spouse, significant other, or others that are close to you, even if you think you can trust these individuals with the information without it being shared. There are no exceptions to this rule.

2. The law requires me to notify the authorities if you reveal that you are abusing children or if you express intent to harm yourself or to harm other people. In addition, I may share information with colleagues internally in this organization during supervision or consultation meetings about this group. Generally, no last names will be used when this information is shared, and the members of the staff of this organization are bound by confidentiality and will not share the information with others.

3. If you reveal confidential information in the group, this information may be spoken about outside the group by other members of the group, even though confidentiality has been requested of all group members. You could be hurt emotionally and economically if your confidences are told outside the group. Group leaders like myself, and this organization, may not be able to prevent other members' breaking the confidentiality agreement.

4. Other members of this group may tell confidential information to you. If you repeat these confidences outside the group, the member whose confidential information you tell may have legal grounds to sue you for telling the confidential information to someone outside the group.

5. If you violate the confidentiality rules of the group, you promise to tell the group leader and the members of the group. In certain circumstances, the group leader may expel you from the group.

I have read and understand the information about the risks of confidentiality in treatment groups. I have discussed the risks with the group leader, and I have had the chance to ask all the questions that I wish to ask about the matter and about all other matters pertaining to my participation in the group. The group leader has answered all my questions in a way that satisfies me. I understand that I can leave the group at any time. By signing this document, I agree to accept the risks to my confidentiality explained to me by the group leader.

_____	_____
SIGNATURE OF GROUP MEMBER	DATE
_____	_____
SIGNATURE OF GROUP LEADER	DATE
_____	_____
SIGNATURE OF WITNESS	DATE

The second area of ethics includes ensuring that workers have the proper education, training, and experience to lead a particular group. Practitioners should not offer a group, or use a procedure or technique within a group, without sufficient education, experience, and supervision to ensure that it is implemented properly. Practitioners should seek out additional supervision when they anticipate or encounter difficulties with a particular group.

As they continue to practice, group workers have the additional responsibility to engage in ongoing professional development activities, including workshops, seminars, and other professional educational opportunities. They should also keep up with current clinical and empirical findings that relate to their ongoing work with group members.

The third broad area in both codes of ethics focuses on ethical principles for the conduct of group meetings.

Ethical Principles
- Screening procedures lead to the selection of members whose needs and goals can be met by the group
- Workers help members develop and pursue therapeutic goals
- Workers discuss whether the proceedings of the group are confidential and make provisions so that they are kept confidential
- Members are protected from physical threats, intimidation, the imposition of worker and member values, and other forms of coercion and peer pressure that are not therapeutic
- Members are treated fairly and equitably
- Workers avoid exploiting members for their own gain
- Appropriate referrals are made when the needs of a particular member cannot be met in the group
- The worker engages in ongoing assessment, evaluation, and follow-up of members to ensure that the group meets their needs

Violations of these ethical principles can be damaging to group members. For example, it has been found that both unsolicited aggressive confrontation and passive abdication of authority are associated with damaging group experiences (Forsyth, 2014; Smokowski, Rose, & Bacallao, 2001). Overall, a safe, low-conflict environment is related to positive outcomes in treatment groups (Kivlighan & Tarrant, 2001).

Lakin (1991) suggests that even well intentioned, enthusiastic group workers can subtly violate ethical principles and that these violations can be harmful to members. He presents evidence, for example, that pressures to conform can lead members to suppress particular opinions, thoughts, or points of view simply because they clash with the dominant ideology expressed in the group. To guard against this, he suggests that all group workers should consider the extent to which (1) workers' values are consonant with the needs and problems of group members, (2) workers carefully consider members' needs, wants, and wishes instead of pushing their own agendas, and (3) each member's needs are individualized rather than treated as identical to the needs of other members.

In 2010, the Association for the Advancement of Social Work with Groups adopted a revised set of standards for social work groups. The standards include (1) the essential knowledge and values that underlie social work practice with groups, (2) the tasks that should be accomplished in each phase of group work, and (3) the knowledge that is needed to carry out the tasks in each phase. The standards provide social workers with needed guidance for the effective and ethical practice of social group work, and they help group workers to avoid unintended ethical violations. The standards have been reprinted in Appendix A1 and can be found in booklet form on the IASWG website (formerly AASWG). There are two other very helpful and detailed standards for group work practice from other organizations: Association for Specialists in Group Work (ASGW) and American Group Psychotherapy Association (AGPA).

> **?** Assess your understanding of values and ethics in group work practice by taking this brief quiz.

DEFINITION OF GROUP WORK

Although there are divergent approaches to group work within the social work profession and allied disciplines, a generalist approach suggests that each approach has its merits and particular practice applications. The broad definition offered in this chapter allows beginning practitioners to understand the boundaries of group work, specialized approaches, and many practice applications. *Group work* can be defined as

> Goal-directed activity with small treatment and task groups aimed at meeting socio-emotional needs and accomplishing tasks. This activity is directed to individual members of a group and to the group as a whole within a system of service delivery and a larger community and societal environment.

The definition describes group work as goal-directed activity that refers to planned, orderly worker activities carried out in the context of professional practice with people. Goal-directed activity has many purposes. For example, group workers may aim to support or educate members, help them socialize and achieve personal growth, or provide treatment for their problems and concerns.

Workers help members of a group develop leadership skills so that they can take increasing responsibility for the group's development. Workers enable their groups to change the social environment by focusing on group dynamics internally and focusing on external issues when necessary. This can include, for example, helping members gain greater control over the organizations and communities that affect their lives. This is advocated in a person-in-situation view of practice (Glassman & Kates, 1990; Shulman, 2016). Others focus on techniques of individual change within small groups (Boyd-Franklin, Cleek, Wofsy, & Mundy, 2013; MacKenzie, 1990, 1996; Rose, 1998; Rose & LeCroy, 1991, Walsh, 2010). Both approaches are valuable when groups set their goals.

The next component of the definition of group work refers to working with small groups of people. In this text, the term *small group* implies the ability of members to identify themselves as members, to engage in interaction, and to exchange thoughts and feelings among themselves through verbal, nonverbal, and written communication processes. Members can meet face-to-face, by telephone or video, or through computer networks.

The definition of group work also indicates that workers practice with both treatment and task groups. For example, workers help members of treatment groups to work on problems and personal goals. They are also expected (1) to work on behalf of clients in teams, treatment conferences, and other groups, (2) within their organizations in staff meetings and other groups that conduct the business of the organization, and (3) in community groups and interagency task forces.

Our definition of group work also emphasizes that the worker should have a dual focus within any group: goal-directed activities with individual members and with the group as a whole. It also emphasizes that attention should be paid simultaneously to individual members and group dynamics. The final portion of the definition of group work emphasizes that groups do not exist in a vacuum. They exist in relation to a community that sponsors, legitimizes, and purposes as they relate. Even self-help groups and groups conducted in private practice are influenced by organizational and community support, sponsorship, and sanction.

There is an exchange of influence between a group and its sponsoring agency. A group is often influenced by its sponsoring organization's resources, mission, goals, and policies. At the same time, a group may be the catalyst for a needed change in agency policies or procedures.

In the case example, the agency influences the composition of the group by limiting the parents attending to a specific geographical area. At the same time, the group influences the agency by ensuring that childcare is available during meetings.

Case Example   A Support Group for New Parents

A Catholic Family Service agency decided to form a group for new parents. However, because of the large number of parents that could possibly attend, the agency decided to limit membership in the support group for new parents to a specific geographic area served by the agency. It was also determined that a large number of single parents would be interested in attending the group meetings. The agency decided to respond to this interest by offering childcare during meetings to make it easier to reach these individuals and enable them to participate in the group.

? Assess your understanding of the definition of group work practice by taking this brief quiz.

CLASSIFYING GROUPS

To understand the breadth of group work practice, it is helpful to become familiar with the variety of groups in practice settings. Because there are so many kinds of groups that workers may be asked to lead, it is helpful to distinguish among them. In the following two sections, distinctions are made among groups based on whether they are formed or occur naturally and whether they are treatment- or task-oriented.

Formed and Natural Groups

Formed groups are those that come together through some outside influence or intervention. They usually have some sponsorship or affiliation and are convened for a particular purpose. Some examples of formed groups are therapy groups, educational groups, committees, social action groups, and teams. *Natural groups* come together spontaneously based on naturally occurring events, interpersonal attraction, or the mutually perceived needs of members. They often lack formal sponsorship. Natural groups include family groups, peer groups, friendship networks, street gangs, cliques, and groups created by peers within social media platforms.

This text is primarily concerned with formed groups. Natural groups, such as families, are neither planned nor constructed by a group worker. Often, natural groups have a longer developmental history that has unique implications for the relationships among members and the interventions used by workers. For these reasons, a separate body of knowledge has been developed for work with natural groups, such as families.

Despite the differences between formed and natural groups, many of the skills and techniques presented in this text are readily applicable to work with natural groups, and we encourage group work practitioners to use them. Some efforts have already been made in this regard, such as attempts to use group work skills in working with the family unit (Bell, 1981), working with gangs (Berlastsky, 2015; Howell & Griffiths, 2016), and enhancing the social networks of persons who are socially isolated (Maguire, 1991). Group work skills can also be used in phone and computer-mediated groups as described in Chapter 6.

Purpose and Group Work

Formed groups can be classified according to the purposes for which they are organized. The term *purpose* can be defined as the general aims of a group. The importance of purpose in group work cannot be overemphasized. According to Wilson (1976), "the nature of the framework for the practice of group work depends on the purpose of the group [that is] served" (p. 41). A group's purpose identifies the reasons for bringing members together. As Klein (1972) notes, "purpose guides group composition" (pp. 31–32). It also helps guide the group's selection of goal-directed activities and defines the broad parameters of the services to be provided.

In this text, the term *treatment group* is used to signify a group whose major purpose is to meet members' socio-emotional needs. The purposes for forming treatment groups might include meeting members' needs for mutual aid, support, education, therapy, growth, and socialization. In contrast, the term *task group* is used to signify any group in which the overriding purpose is to accomplish a goal that is neither intrinsically nor immediately linked to the needs of the members of the group. Although the work of a task group may ultimately affect the members of the group, the primary purpose of task groups is to accomplish a goal that will affect a broader constituency, not just the members of the group.

Treatment and Task Groups

In classifying groups as either treatment- or task-oriented, it is important to consider how the two types differ. Table 1.2 points out some of the major differences between treatment and task groups in terms of selected characteristics. These include the following:

- The bond present in a group is based on the purpose for which it is convened. Members of treatment groups are bonded by their common needs and common situations. Task group members create a common bond by working together to accomplish a task, carry out a mandate, or produce a product. In both types of groups, common cultural, gender, racial, or ethnic characteristics can also help to form bonds among members.

Table 1.2   A Comparison of Task and Treatment Groups

Selected Characteristics	Type of Group	
	Treatment	Task
Bond	Members' personal needs	Task to be completed
Roles	Develop through interaction	Develop through interaction or are assigned
Communication patterns	Open, back-and-forth interaction based on members' needs	Focused on a task to be accomplished
Procedures	Flexible or formal, depending on the group	Formal agenda and rules
Composition	Based on common concerns, problems, or characteristics	Based on needed talents, expertise, or division of labor
Self-disclosure	Expected to be high	Expected to be low
Confidentiality	Proceedings usually private and kept within the group	Proceedings may be private but are sometimes open to the public
Evaluation	Success based on members' meeting treatment goals	Success based on members' accomplishing a task or mandate, or producing a product

- In treatment groups, roles are not set before the group forms, but develop through interaction among members. In task groups, members may take on roles through a process of interaction, but roles are more likely to be based on members' positions within the organization. In addition, roles are frequently assigned by the group based on the tasks to be accomplished. Roles that may be assigned include chair or team leader, secretary, and fact finder.

- Communication patterns in treatment groups are open. Members are usually encouraged to interact with one another. Task group members are more likely to address their communications to the leader and to keep their communication focused on the task to be accomplished. In some task groups, the amount that members communicate on a particular agenda item may be limited by the worker. In other task groups, members may limit their own communication because they believe they will not be well received by the group.

- Treatment groups often have flexible procedures for meetings, including a warm-up period, a period for working on members' concerns, and a period for summarizing the group's work. Task groups are more likely to have formalized rules, such as parliamentary procedures, that govern how members conduct group business and reach decisions.

- Treatment groups are often composed of members with similar concerns, problems, and abilities. Task groups instead tend to be composed of members with the necessary resources and expertise to accomplish the group's mission.

- In treatment groups, members are expected to disclose their own concerns and problems. Therefore, self-disclosures may contain emotionally charged, personal concerns. In task groups, member self-disclosure is relatively infrequent. It is generally expected that members will confine themselves to discussions about accomplishing the group's task and will not share intimate, personal concerns.

- Treatment group meetings are often confidential. Some task group meetings, such as the meetings of treatment conferences and cabinets, may be confidential, but the meetings of other task groups, such as committees and delegate councils, are often described in minutes that are circulated to interested persons and organizations.
- The criteria for evaluating success differ between treatment and task groups. Treatment groups are successful to the extent that they help members meet their individual treatment goals. Task groups are successful when they accomplish group goals, such as generating solutions to problems and making decisions or when they develop group products, such as a report, a set of regulations, or a series of recommendations concerning a particular community issue.

Case Example   Treatment and Task Group

In one group, the worker meets with adults who have recently become parents for the first time. The purpose of this parenting group is to provide a forum for discussion about their adjustment to parenthood. In a second group, the worker brings together community representatives from several different social service agencies and school districts to study day-care resources and make recommendations to a government agency regarding changes in government support for day-care for low-income children. Here, the aim of the worker is to bring together representatives of the community to study day-care resources and make recommendations.

In the case example, the parents' group is classified as a treatment group because it is convened to meet the personal needs of its members. The group is bonded by its common purpose and the common needs and concerns of its members. It is expected that friendships may develop among group members and that members will help each other in their adjustment to parenthood. It is also expected that the feeling level and the level of self-disclosure will be high because of the similar circumstances of the members and the problems they face. Because members may self-disclose about personal issues, the proceedings of the group are confidential. Roles develop based on how members assist in accomplishing the purpose of the group and how members meet each other's needs.

Because parenting is a developmental phenomenon involving constant discovery and change, the procedures of the group are flexible to allow members to share any pressing concerns. The parents' group is composed with the similarity of members' needs in mind. Patterns of communication focus on members' needs, such as adjusting to parenthood and becoming effective parents. Procedures include an educational component, problem solving, and discussions of parenting issues and concerns. Self-disclosure is high, with members discussing difficult and emotionally charged parenting issues. Parents are asked to keep discussions of these issues strictly confidential. Success is evaluated by asking members about their satisfaction with participation and by evaluating individual outcomes.

In the case example of the group working on day-care services, the focus is task-oriented, and the purpose is external to the personal needs of the members. Members are bonded by the common cause of improving day-care services. Roles are assigned by the worker based on members' preferences. For example, members are appointed to subcommittees to collect needed data. Patterns of communication focus on the task rather than on members' personal concerns. Communication and interaction are based on the task of developing recommendations about day-care for low-income children. To facilitate an organized approach to the task, the group works from an agenda that is published in advance to give participants time to prepare for the proceedings. To facilitate a division of labor and encourage different perspectives, the group is composed by selecting members who have some knowledge of day-care programs and other needed areas of expertise, such as zoning restrictions, local, state, and federal child-care regulations, and financing.

Members are expected to reveal their personal viewpoints only to the extent that they contribute to the group's task. Personal feelings are occasionally shared, but factual data are given greater weight. The group is publicized. It seeks out experts to contribute to its deliberations. Confidentiality is impractical because it would hinder the accomplishment of the group's task. To evaluate the effectiveness of the group, the worker examines the group's decisions, actions, written reports, and recommendations for clarity, thoroughness, and feasibility.

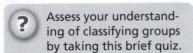

? Assess your understanding of classifying groups by taking this brief quiz.

GROUP VERSUS INDIVIDUAL EFFORTS

There are several advantages and disadvantages to using a group rather than an individual effort to meet individual, organizational, and community needs. In describing these advantages and disadvantages, it is important to distinguish between the effectiveness and efficiency of treatment and task groups.

Advantages and Disadvantages of Treatment Groups

There are many advantages of social group work. The advantages of group treatment stem from the fact that in addition to the worker, members can be helpful to each other. Members provide opportunities for socialization and for validation and normalization of problems and concerns. The presence of others also gives members an opportunity to learn from the experience of peers, to receive feedback, and to have role models and practice partners who can help with efforts to change. Feedback from peers is often seen as more grounded and less coercive than when it is received from a paid professional worker who may not have experienced similar concerns or who may be viewed as an authority figure by reluctant or involuntary clients. Coining the term *helper-therapy principle*, Riessman (1965) noted that those who provide help derive therapeutic benefit themselves. Mutual aid gives members an opportunity to share experiential knowledge and to gain insights vicariously.

Advantages of Group Treatment
- Empathy from multiple sources—vicarious identification with and understanding of members' situations by peers and the worker
- Feedback—multiple points of view shared by group members
- Helper-therapy—providing help and mutual support to other group members, therapeutic for the member who shares experiences and knowledge

- Hope—instillation of hope by other group members who have coped effectively with similar situations
- Mutual aid—members both giving and receiving help
- Normalization—removal of stigma from problems seen as socially unacceptable by the larger society
- Practice of new behaviors—opportunities to try out new behaviors in the safe environment of the group
- Reality testing—sharing ways of being and getting feedback about whether they are realistic and socially acceptable
- Recapitulation—working through previously unsatisfactory relationships with family members, peers, and friends with the help of group members
- Recreation of the family of origin—group members serving as surrogate family and symbolically representing family members
- Resources—a wide pool of knowledge about concerns and the resources and services to help with these concerns
- Role models—members and the leader serving as models
- Solidarity—connectedness with other members
- Socialization—opportunities to overcome isolation and learn social skills from others
- Social support—support from other members of the group
- Transcendence—members sharing how they adapted to and compensated for disabilities
- Validation—group members confirming similar experiences, problems, and concerns
- Vicarious learning—learning by hearing about other members' coping responses

Although these advantages provide justification for using group work in treatment, several potential disadvantages of group treatment should be considered. Groups can encourage member conformity and member dependency (Forsyth, 2014). When members open themselves to other members through self-disclosure, they are vulnerable to breaches of confidentiality and other harmful responses (Corey, Corey, & Corey, 2014). Groups can scapegoat individual members. Groups sometimes focus on a few particularly assertive or talkative members. This creates a danger that these members' problems will receive attention while other, less

Research-Informed Practice

Behavior: Use and translate research evidence to inform and improve practice, policy, and service delivery

Critical Thinking Question: Group work has benefits over casework. What research supports the effectiveness of treatment groups?

assertive or less talkative members will receive little help (Yalom, 2005). The best way to avoid these problems is to make sure that each member has time to speak in a group. This will be discussed in greater detail in Chapter 3.

Members can benefit from treatment groups when they have some ability to communicate with others and when their concerns or problems lend themselves to group discussion. To the extent that certain group members, such as autistic children and schizophrenic adults, cannot communicate effectively, group work must be modified to include nonverbal program activities and, where appropriate, simple, brief verbal activities that are consistent with those members' skill levels. People who have an extreme need for privacy or confidentiality may also be unable to take part in group treatment without considerable support or reassurance. Groups are contraindicated for people whose behavior is so alien to others' that it results in negative rather than positive interactions or when it leads to the failure of others to continue with the group.

Empirical studies tend to support clinical reports of the effectiveness of treatment groups. In a comprehensive review of well-designed studies comparing group and individual treatment, Toseland and Siporin (1986) found that group treatment was more effective than individual treatment in 25 percent of the studies that were reviewed, but individual treatment was not found to be more effective than group treatment in any of the studies. Group work was also found to be more efficient than individual treatment and to produce fewer dropouts from treatment. Most reviews confirm the effectiveness of group treatment for many types of client needs (Barlow, 2013; Burlingame, Whitcomb, & Woodland, 2014; Burlingame, Fuhriman, & Mosier, 2003; Burlingame, MacKenzie, & Strauss, 2004; Kosters, Burlingame, Nachtigall, & Strauss, 2006; McRoberts, Burlingame, & Hoag, 1998; Saksa, Cohen, Srihari, & Woods, 2009). For example, Burlingame, Straussm and Joyce's (2013) review of the literature reveals that group treatment is equally as effective as individual treatment for most problems, and more effective for some problems—especially those that involve interpersonal skill deficits.

Although the empirical literature does not yet yield a clear pattern of the types of problems most effectively treated in groups, there is some evidence that groups may be more effective than individuals for enhancing social support and less effective for dealing with intense, highly personal, psychological problems (Toseland, Rossiter, Peak, & Smith, 1990). Groups may also be more effective for interpersonal problems (Barlow, 2013). Overall, findings from both the clinical and the empirical literature suggest that social workers should consider recommending group treatment for individuals who suffer from isolation or who have other difficulties with interpersonal relationships, and individual treatment for those who do not want to be in a group. Individuals with difficult emotional problems, such as those of borderline personality disorder, suicidal ideation, and the effects of trauma, can be seen in groups using dialectical behavior therapy and acceptance and commitment therapy, which will be described later in this book.

Advantages and Disadvantages of Task Groups

A group approach, as compared with an individual effort, has advantages in helping individuals, organizations, and communities accomplish tasks. In working with groups of people in organizations and communities, free flowing participation is often highly desirable (Forsyth, 2014). Participation through group interaction helps members feel they have a stake in their organization or community. In addition, resistance to change is minimized when those who are to be affected are given the opportunity to participate in the change through group discussion and shared decision making.

Group discussion, deliberation, and decision making can have other benefits. The increased quantity of information available in groups can be beneficial for generating alternative action plans, for problem solving, and for making decisions. Certain tasks are complex, requiring a pool of talented and diverse expertise for them to be completed in a satisfactory manner (Forsyth, 2014). The division of labor that occurs in well-run groups can help members complete tasks quickly and efficiently (Tropman, 2014).

Some disadvantages should be kept in mind when considering selecting a group approach for accomplishing tasks. For example, group problem solving may take more time than individual problem solving, and the presence of others may interfere with the effectiveness of best member's problem-solving abilities (Forsyth, 2014). Poorly run groups can cause members to feel frustrated, bored, or unappreciated, and they often accomplish little (Tropman, 2014). Groups are also sometimes used to make simple decisions or solve simple problems that could be dealt with more easily by individuals. Under these conditions, group meetings can be costly for an organization.

Findings about the effectiveness of group versus individual problem solving and decision making suggest that groups are more effective than the average individual, but rarely more effective than the best individual (Forsyth, 2014; Hare et al., 1995). Groups tend to be more effective than individuals when dealing with problems with known solutions rather than with problems where there is no clear right or wrong answer, what Forsyth refers to as *intellective* versus *judgmental* tasks (Forsyth, 2014, p. 302). Groups also tend to be more effective than individuals when working on difficult and complex tasks requiring participation from many people (Forsyth, 2014).

Overall, the advantages and disadvantages of using a task group for problem solving and decision making should be evaluated within the context of a particular situation and in reference to the types of goals to be achieved. For example, shared decision making may be more important than the time it takes to make a decision or even the quality of the decision.

Although this text suggests that group work methods have a fairly wide applicability for many different types of individual, organizational, and community problems, these problems are sometimes best approached by using several practice methods. Thus, although group work is a valuable method by itself, within a generalist practice framework, it is also valuable as part of a larger, planned change effort that may use additional methods such as social casework or community organization to achieve particular goals.

> **?** Assess your understanding of group versus individual efforts by taking this brief quiz.

A TYPOLOGY OF TREATMENT AND TASK GROUPS

The broad distinctions between formed and natural groups and between treatment and task groups can be further refined and developed into a classification system of the many types of groups workers may encounter in practice settings. One way to develop a classification system is to categorize treatment and task groups according to their primary purpose. According to Klein (1972), a number of group purposes are possible.

Group Work Purposes
- Rehabilitation—restoring members to their former level of functioning
- Habilitation—helping members grow and develop
- Correction—helping members who are having problems with social laws or mores
- Socialization—helping members learn how to get along with others and do what is socially acceptable
- Prevention—helping members develop and function at an optimal level and helping them prepare for events that are likely to occur

- Social action—helping members change their environment
- Problem solving—helping members resolve complex issues and concerns
- Developing social values—helping members develop a humanistic approach to living

The rest of this chapter presents typologies of treatment groups and task groups that social workers encounter in practice. The typologies are based on the primary purposes of each type of treatment and task group. Although groups with only one purpose rarely exist in practice, developing pure categories—that is, groups with a single purpose—is useful in illustrating differences between groups and in demonstrating the many ways that groups can be used in practice settings.

TREATMENT GROUPS

Six primary purposes for treatment groups are (1) support, (2) education, (3) growth, (4) therapy, (5) socialization, and (6) self-help. In practice settings, there are innumerable variations of treatment groups that combine these six primary purposes. For example, a group for parents of children with Down syndrome might be oriented toward both education and growth. A group for alcoholics might have all six primary purposes. Table 1.3 is designed to show clearly the similarities and differences among groups with different purposes. Table 1.3 can be used as a guide by workers who are planning to lead groups with only one purpose or to lead groups that combine several purposes.

Support Groups

The description of the treatment typology begins with support groups because support is a common ingredient of many successful treatment groups. Support groups can be distinguished from other groups using supportive intervention strategies by their primary goals: to foster mutual aid, to help members cope with stressful life events, and to revitalize and enhance members' coping abilities so they can effectively adapt to and cope with future stressful life events. Examples of support groups include the following:

- A group of children meeting at school to discuss the effects of divorce on their lives
- A group of people diagnosed with cancer, and their families, discussing the effects of the disease and how to cope with it
- A group of recently discharged psychiatric patients discussing their adjustment to community living
- A group of single parents sharing the difficulties of raising children alone

Leadership of support groups is characterized by a facilitative approach that emphasizes helping members share their collective experiences in coping with a stressful event. The group worker helps members share their experiences and empathically respond to each other. Simply recounting events, ventilating feelings, and reflecting on efforts to cope can promote self-understanding and help overcome loneliness, isolation, and despair. The group worker also helps members overcome feelings of alienation, stigmatization, and isolation by validating, affirming, and normalizing their experiences.

Table 1.3 A Typology of Treatment Groups

Selected Characteristics	Purpose of the Group					
	Support	Education	Growth	Therapy	Socialization	Self-Help
Purpose	To help members cope with stressful life events and revitalize existing coping abilities	To educate through presentations, discussion, and experience	To develop members' potential, awareness, and insight	To change behavior Correction, rehabilitation, coping, and problem solving through behavior change interventions	To increase communication and social skills Improved interpersonal relationships through program activities, structured exercises, role plays, etc.	To help members solve their own problems
Leadership	A facilitator of empathic understanding and mutual aid	Leader as teacher and provider of structure for group discussion	Leader as facilitator and role model	Leader as expert, authority figure, or facilitator, depending on approach	Leader as director of the group's actions or programs	Leader is often a lay person with the problem shared by the other group members, but can sometimes be a professional who shares the problem
Focus	The ability of the individual to cope with a stressful life experience Communication and mutual aid	Individual learning Structuring of the group for learning	Either member or group focus, depending on the approach Individual growth through the group experience	Individual members' problems, concerns, or goals	The group as a medium for activity, participation, and involvement	Members working together to help each other solve their own problems
Bond	Shared stressful experience, often stigmatizing	Common interest in learning, and skills development	Common goals among members Contract to use group to grow	Common purpose with separate member goals Relationship of member with worker, group, or other members	A common activity, enterprise, or situation	Acceptance that all members are equal and valued and can help each other
Composition	Based on a shared life experience Often diverse	Similarity of education or skill level	Can be diverse Based on members' ability to work toward growth and development	Can be diverse or can be composed of people with similar problems or concerns	Depending on location of group and purpose, can be diverse or homogeneous	Based solely on shared problem or concern
Communication	Much sharing of information, experiences, and coping strategies Frequent self-disclosure of emotionally charged material	Frequently leader-to-member, didactic Sometimes member-to-member during discussions Self-disclosure low	Highly interactive Members often take responsibility for communication in the group Self-disclosure moderate to high	Leader-to-member or member-to-member, depending on approach Self-disclosure moderate to high	Often represented in activity or nonverbal behavior Self-disclosure low to moderate and often nonverbal	Diverse and open membership welcoming to all who share the problem Member-to-member communication with high level of self-disclosure

A major role of the worker is to facilitate hope in the future and motivate members to improve coping skills through self-help and mutual aid (Hyde, 2013; Kurtz, 2014; Steinberg, 2014). The worker fosters group norms that encourage members to share information and suggestions for more effective coping and to try out new coping strategies. Because support is basic to many types of groups, these strategies for assisting members are also used, to varying degrees, in other treatment and task groups.

Strong emotional bonds often develop quickly in support groups because of members' shared experiences. Emotional bonding may also occur because members are stigmatized by the larger community and find comfort and power in their association with each other. Frequently, there is a high level of self-disclosure of emotionally charged material in support groups.

In addition to directly facilitating support groups, workers are often called on to provide indirect assistance to support groups led by lay leaders. A worker might be asked to consult with the lay leader, serve as a referral source, or provide material assistance. Consultation may take the form of speaking at a meeting, helping the group resolve a problem in its functioning, or assisting members with specific problems or issues. The worker may be asked to refer appropriate individuals to a support group, provide a meeting place, or offer other support, such as help with printing a newsletter or distributing publicity.

Some writers have pointed out that professionals might interfere with the effective functioning of lay-led, self-help support groups (Kyrouz, Humphreys, & Loomis, 2002). The potential does exist for professionals to dominate, interfere with, or take over the functioning of such groups. Members of self-help groups are sometimes wary of professional involvement because they fear it will compromise the autonomy and confidentiality of the group. This is particularly true of self-help groups, such as Parents Anonymous, in which members share concerns about child abuse or neglect—situations often considered socially stigmatizing.

Most evidence, however, suggests that there are strong connections between self-help support groups and professionals and that both professionals and lay leaders benefit by cooperating with each other (Kurtz, 2004, 2014; Powell, 1987; Toseland & Hacker, 1982, 1985). Professionals gain an additional treatment resource that is often more flexible and responsive than the formal service system. Lay leaders have someone to turn to when they need particular types of expertise, resources, or assistance. Both can join forces when lobbying for additional community resources and services.

Educational Groups

The primary purpose of educational groups is to help members learn new information and skills. Educational groups are used in a variety of settings, including treatment agencies, schools, nursing homes, correctional institutions, and hospitals. Examples of educational groups include the following:

- An adolescent sexuality group sponsored by a family planning agency
- A wellness-in-the-workplace group designed by a social worker directing an employee assistance program
- A group for prospective foster parents sponsored by a child welfare agency
- A group sponsored by a community planning agency to help board members become more effective

All educational groups are aimed at increasing members' information or skills. Most groups routinely involve presentations of information and knowledge by experts. They also often include opportunities for group discussion to foster learning. When leading educational groups, workers concentrate on both individual members and whole groups, as vehicles for learning, reinforcement, and discussion.

Members of educational groups are bonded by a common interest in the material to be learned and by common characteristics, such as being an adolescent, a prospective foster parent, a union worker, or a board member. In composing educational groups, workers consider each member's knowledge of the subject matter and level of skills and experience so that all members can derive the most benefit from the learning process.

Some educational groups seek members with different levels of exposure to the subject matter so that beginners can learn from advanced members. When the group is small, there are usually opportunities for member-to-member communication and group discussion. Depending on the norms of the group and the subject matter, member self-disclosure varies from low to moderate. In general, a relatively low level of self-disclosure is expected in an educational group because the group is often structured around a presentation of material by the worker, a guest speaker, or a member. Usually, the material to be learned is seen as more important than the needs of members to self-disclose. However, workers often use a personalized approach to learning that emphasizes the developmental learning needs of individual members. This is especially true in residential and institutional settings in which members' emotional or social functioning is impaired.

Other approaches to leading educational groups emphasize learning as a social experience. Workers who use this approach focus on group discussion and group activities rather than on didactic methods. Community center workers often use this approach to attract and hold the interest of members who participate in educational groups for personal enjoyment and enrichment.

Growth Groups

Growth-oriented groups offer opportunities for members to become aware of, expand, and change their thoughts, feelings, and behaviors regarding themselves and others. The group is used as a vehicle to develop members' capabilities to the fullest. Growth groups focus on promoting socio-emotional health rather than remediating socio-emotional illness. Examples of growth groups include the following:

- An encounter group for married couples
- A values-clarification group for adolescents
- A consciousness-raising group sponsored by a women's community center
- A gay-pride group sponsored by a community health clinic serving the gay community in a large urban area

Growth groups generally stress self-improvement and the potential of human beings to live a full and rewarding life, especially through improved relationships with others. They provide a supportive atmosphere in which individuals can gain insights, experiment with new behaviors, get feedback, and grow as human beings. The bond in growth groups stems from members' commitment to help one another develop and maximize their potential.

When composing growth groups, workers often select members who have diverse backgrounds and the potential to enrich and broaden each other's experiences. However, some growth groups are composed of members with similar characteristics to enhance empathy and support within the group. In most growth-oriented groups, self-disclosure is moderate to high.

Communication in growth groups is member-centered and highly interactive. In-depth self-disclosure is expected, with members encouraged to reveal more about themselves as they become comfortable with their participation in the group.

Therapy Groups

Therapy groups help members change their behavior, cope with and ameliorate personal problems, or rehabilitate themselves after physical, psychological, or social trauma. Although there is often an emphasis on support, therapy groups are distinguished from support groups by their focus on remediation and rehabilitation.

In group work practice, particular importance is often accorded to leading therapy groups, even to the exclusion of other types of group work, possibly because of the traditional importance attributed to the medical model that stresses therapy and treatment to bring sick or dysfunctional people back to health. Konopka (1983) noted that the high status of psychiatry on the North American continent helped to make the term *therapy* more precious and more important than the terms *casework* and *group work* (terms used by the social work profession). Thus, therapy groups are often associated with the professionalism of group work as a method of practice. Examples of therapy groups include the following:

- A psychotherapy group for outpatients at a community mental health center
- A group, sponsored by a voluntary health association, for people who want to stop smoking
- A first-offenders group in a juvenile diversion program sponsored by a probation department
- A hospital-sponsored group for people addicted to drugs

In therapy groups, members come together to solve their problems. The group leader is often viewed as an expert, an authority figure, and a change agent. Members' problems are assessed and treatment goals are developed with the help of the worker. Although the group has a common purpose, each member may have a different problem with different symptoms. In addition, the etiology and development of each member's problem is unique. Therefore, to achieve individual goals, the worker often focuses on one member at a time. Depending on the approach or stance of the worker, the members of a therapy group may be expected to help each other work on problems. The level of member self-disclosure is usually quite high but can depend somewhat on the types of problems experienced by group members.

Members of therapy groups have much to gain: relief from symptoms, loss of emotional pain, or resolution of a problem. Still, to ensure that members' needs are met, much planning usually takes place before the beginning of a therapy group. Therapeutic interventions are selected after a careful assessment of individual members and the group is composed in relation to the members' problems. Often, members participate in an intake procedure so the worker can assess their interest in participating in the group, determine their suitability for group treatment, and explain the purpose of the group. Although these procedures are also used with other types of groups, they are often given greater emphasis in therapy groups.

Socialization Groups

Socialization groups help members learn social skills and socially accepted behavior patterns so they can function effectively in the community. Socialization groups frequently use program activities, such as games, role plays, or outings, to help members accomplish individual goals (Cheung, 2014; Drews & Schaefer, 2010; Harpine, 2008; Miller, 2012; Misurell & Springer, 2013; Nash, 2011; Springer, Misrell, & Hiller, 2012).

The personal needs of members and the goals of the group are often met through program activities rather than exclusively through group discussion. Thus, socialization groups feature a learning-through-doing approach in which members improve their interpersonal skills by participating in program activities. Examples of socialization groups include the following:

- A Catholic Youth Organization (CYO) activity group
- A social club for outpatients of a psychiatric center
- A monthly Vietnam veterans evening social at a rural Veterans of Foreign Wars (VFW) post
- A Parents Without Partners group that includes picnics, dances, and other social activities

Leadership of socialization groups can be directive or nondirective, depending on the complexity of program activities and the competencies of group members. Member participation is the key to successful individual and group outcomes. The group is a medium for activity, participation, and involvement, and members are bonded to each other through these activities. The composition of socialization groups can be based on the similar interests and needs of members or on the common experiences offered by a particular program activity.

There are at least three common forms of socialization groups: (1) social skills groups, (2) governance groups, and (3) recreation groups. Some social skills groups, such as assertiveness training groups, are formed for adults who wish to improve their existing skills. Unlike the other types of groups in our typology, social skills groups can be particularly useful for individuals who are unable or unwilling to communicate effectively and for those who have difficulty engaging in satisfying social relationships. Young children, shy adolescents, and adults with mild autistic spectrum disorders are examples of client populations that can benefit from social skills groups. Program activities can help draw out these types of group members by helping them form meaningful relationships and learn social skills. Activities provide the basis for interaction and communication without the need for direct, verbal communication. Thus, by using program activities, group work can take place through nonverbal means.

In other cases, role plays, psychodrama, and other activities requiring both verbal and nonverbal communication can be used to increase members' skills and promote socialization. The behavior displayed during these activities can help a worker assess members' problems and plan effective interventions.

Governance groups are often found in residential settings, such as group homes, psychiatric hospitals, and congregate housing. The purpose of these groups is to involve residents (of the unit, ward, floor, or house) in the daily governance of the institution. Although governance groups are closely related to task groups because they solve problems and make decisions, they have been classified as treatment groups because their primary focus is on the needs of their members.

Through their participation in the governance process, members learn advocacy, communication, conflict resolution, and empowerment skills. They also learn to share with others, take responsibility for their actions, and participate in decision-making processes. The concept of a governance group is borrowed, in part, from the idea of the therapeutic community in which members have input into the rules that govern their behavior. Examples of governance groups include house meetings, ward meetings, resident councils, family meetings, and patient-rights meetings.

Participation in governance groups provides a method for members to identify with and become committed to the goals of the therapeutic community. It helps clarify members' roles, responsibilities, and rights within the community. All members of therapeutic communities are encouraged to attend meetings so that they have a voice in the way the community functions. In some settings, such as residential treatment centers, attendance may be required.

A third type of socialization group focuses on recreational activities. Much of the recent group work literature has understated the importance of recreational groups in meeting members' personal needs. The roots of group work can be traced to recreational groups like scouting, camping, sports, and club groups (Boyd, 1935; Slavson, 1945, 1946; Smith, 1935). Recreation can be both an end and a means to an end. As an end, recreation can be a desirable leisure time activity. As a means, recreation can help a particular population become involved in an activity that has therapeutic benefits, such as increasing social skills.

Recreational groups are particularly important for working with children, adolescents, and older adults in neighborhood centers. Because the groups are enjoyable, they are often helpful in engaging resistant clients, such as gang members and pre-delinquent, latency-age children. They can help members learn community values and accepted norms of behavior. They can also help members develop interpersonal skills and feel a sense of belonging. In addition, recreational groups foster members' confidence in their ability to function as part of a group in other social situations. To carry out these important purposes, recreation groups require leaders who are skilled in both group work and the featured recreational mode or program activity.

Self-Help Groups

Although they share many characteristics with support, educational, and socialization groups, the distinguishing characteristic of self-help groups is that they are led by members who share the problem experienced by the other members of the group. Self-help groups have been developed for a wide variety of problems, and they are readily available online (Norcross et al, 2013). Because professionals often play vital roles in self-help groups, this type of group is included in the treatment group typology. Although it is often thought that self-help groups are led by lay people, in practice, many self-help groups are actually led by professionals who have experienced the problem shared by the other members of the group (Kurtz, 2004; White & Madara, 2002). There is also mutual aid group work that is closely related to empowerment and self-help (Hyde, 2013).

Examples of self-help groups include the following:

- Alcoholics Anonymous, groups for people trying to get sober and those trying to remain sober
- Mended Hearts, a group for patients who have undergone bypass or other heart surgery procedures
- Make Today Count, a group for cancer survivors
- Gamblers Anonymous, groups for people who are trying to stop gambling or who are trying to remain free of a gambling addiction

Although there is no accurate estimate of the number of self-help groups in the United States or throughout the world, they are very numerous. For example, the *Self-Help Group Sourcebook* alone lists over 1,000 national and international headquarters of self-help groups in the United States and Canada (White & Madara, 2002) and includes 33 separate clearinghouses for self-help information in 22 different countries. These organizations, in turn, sponsor many self-help groups in local communities. Online support groups are also an important resource, serving individuals with many different kinds of concerns (Norcross et al, 2013).

Leadership patterns can be quite diverse in self-help groups. In some self-help groups, leadership is rotated among members whereas in other self-help groups, a few members share responsibility for leading the group. There are also some self-help groups where one or two members take leadership responsibility. Some self-help groups, such as Alcoholics Anonymous, are very explicit that the groups are composed and run by lay leaders who are chosen from the membership. Such groups welcome professional members but treat professionals as ordinary members. These self-help groups may seek the assistance of professionals outside of the context of meeting as needed, but accord professional social workers no special status within the Alcoholics Anonymous fellowship. Other self-help groups welcome professional involvement as leaders and as speakers, and the role between professional and layperson may be blurred.

Self-help groups may be focused on helping members change or on social change and advocacy, although many groups combine different foci. Kurtz (2004), for example, organized self-help groups into five categories: (1) groups that are peer-led and oriented to individual change, such as Alcoholics Anonymous, (2) groups that are peer-led and social change-oriented that focus on support, education, and advocacy, such as the National Alliance for the Mentally Ill, (3) groups that are support-oriented, advocacy-oriented, and professionally led that are part of national organizations, such as the Alzheimer's Foundation, (4) smaller, local, professionally led groups that are held in hospitals, social service organizations, or other community organizations, and (5) change-oriented groups that have peer leadership combined with professional involvement as independent sponsors or coleaders, such as Parents Anonymous. Clearly, self-help groups are so diverse and numerous that they almost defy any simple classification system.

Most self-help groups are characterized by an open membership policy. Anyone can attend a group meeting who shares the problem or concern being addressed. Because of their policy of open membership, self-help groups often have set formats that are repeated each meeting. For example, there may be a brief statement of the purpose of the group at the beginning followed by a speaker and then a time for members to share concerns and issues. This set structure enables members to feel comfortable attending quickly, even if they are new to the group or if they have missed meetings. New members quickly learn the structure and feel comfortable with what is going to happen during the meeting and what is expected of them. The focus of self-help groups is on members helping members. Members are seen as equals who share similar problems and concerns. Self-help groups place a great deal of emphasis on de-stigmatizing the problems shared and faced by members. There is a strong sense of empathy and support accompanied by a sense of empowerment that members can help themselves to overcome problems, issues, and concerns and lead better, more fulfilled lives through their own efforts to help each other. Usually there are no special requirements for attendance except that members share the problem that is the focus or purpose of the group and that members limit what they say in the group to the purpose of the group. Members, therefore, may come and go freely, deciding when they would like to attend. Most self-help groups are self-supporting, although they may receive some support from a sponsoring organization that may provide a meeting room or may help with guest speakers or refreshments.

? Assess your understanding of treatment groups by taking this brief quiz.

TASK GROUPS

Task groups are common in most agencies and organizations. They are used to find solutions to organizational problems, to generate new ideas, and to make decisions. Task groups can have three primary purposes: (1) meeting client needs, (2) meeting organizational needs, and (3) meeting community needs.

Task groups with the primary purpose of serving client needs include teams, treatment conferences, and staff-development groups. Task groups with the primary purpose of serving organizational needs include committees, cabinets, and boards of directors. Task groups with a primary purpose of serving community needs include social action groups, coalitions, and delegate councils.

Selected characteristics of each type of group are presented in Table 1.4. As with the typology for treatment groups, there is often some overlap between different types of task groups in actual practice situations. Thus, instead of a rigid classification system, the typology is intended as a guide for workers who may be called on to lead different types of task groups.

Groups to Meet Client Needs

Teams

There is a growing body of evidence about the effectiveness of teams in social service and business settings (Abramson, 2002; Abramson & Bronstein, 2004; Gort, Broekhuis, & Regts, 2013; Greenberg, Feinberg, Meyer-Chilenski, Spoth, & Redmond, 2007; Hackman, 2002; Heinemann & Zeiss, 2002; Klein et al., 2009; Lemieux-Charles & McGuire, 2006; Levi, 2014; Perkins et al., 2011; Ramirez, 2014). By bringing together the knowledge and

Table 1.4   A Typology of Task Groups

Client Needs		
Selected Characteristics	**Teams**	**Treatment Conferences**	**Staff Development**
Purpose	To engage in collaborative work on behalf of a client system	To develop, coordinate, and monitor treatment plans	To educate members for better practice with clients
Leadership	Appointed by sponsoring agency	Neutral chair or chaired by member with most responsibility	Leader, supervisor, consultant, or educator
Focus	Build team to function smoothly High member focus	Decision-oriented Low member focus High client focus	Focus on staff members' needs and their performance with clients
Bond	Team spirit Needs of organization and client	Client system Treatment plan Inter- or intra-agency agreement	Continuing education needs Interest in client welfare Professional development
Composition	Often heterogeneous	Diversity by function, specialty, and expertise	Individuals with similar educational needs
Communication	Theoretically close, sometimes artificial or inspirational Low to moderate self-disclosure	Consideration of all points of view about the client system High disclosure	Leader-to-member Didactic and experiential instruction Member-to-member

Organizational Needs		
Selected Characteristics	**Committees**	**Cabinets**	**Board of Directors**
Purpose	To discuss issues and accomplish tasks	To advise an executive officer about future directions or current policies and procedures	To govern an organization
Leadership	Appointed or elected	Appointed by chief executive officer of an organization	Officers designated by bylaws are nominated by subcommittee and approved by vote of the membership
Focus	A specific task or charge	The development of procedures and policies for organizational management	Policy making Governance Monitoring Fiscal control Fundraising
Bond	Interest in a task	Loyalty to the organization and the chief executive officer	Commitment to the mission of the organization and its service orientation
Composition	Diversity to aid decision making and division of labor	Appointment based on administrative responsibilities and expertise	Diverse members often selected for their status, power, influence in the community, expertise, representation of particular interest groups and constituencies
Communication	Relative to task Low member selfdisclosure	Members present points of view based on their position in an organization To build a power base	Formal communication Parliamentary procedures Less formal in subcommittees Low member self-disclosure

Table 1.4   (*Continued*)

	Community Needs		
Selected Characteristics	Social Action Groups	Coalitions	Delegate Councils
Purpose	To devise and implement social change tactics and strategies	To exert greater influence by sharing resources, expertise, and power bases of social action groups with common goals	To represent different organizations, chapters, or other units
Leadership	Indigenous leadership emerging from the groups Practitioner often is staffer or adviser	Often a charismatic or dedicated individual leading by consensus or elected by vote of the membership	Representatives appointed by the sponsoring organization
Focus	Consumer, community, social justice	Building consensus and a partnership for maximum influence	Collective input and action Equality of representation Focus on larger issues, concerns, and positions
Bond	Perception of injustice, inequity, or need for change	Interest in an issue Commitment to an ideological position	Larger purpose or community concern, rather than individual or agency concern
Composition	Based on common interest, shared purpose, and investment in community	Loose, temporary confederation of groups or organizations working in partnership to achieve a common goal	Diverse by definition Represents interest of sponsoring organization
Communication	Informal member-to-member discussion Formulation and implementation of tactics and strategies for change High member self-disclosure in relation to social problems	Formal or informal, depending on type of coalition Less formal in caucuses and subgroups Moderate member self-disclosure representing group interests	Provides a forum for communication among organizations Delegates are communication links between council and the sponsoring organization Low member self-disclosure

skills of different categories of professionals and paraprofessionals, team work is often considered the most effective method of delivering comprehensive social and health services to those in need (Abramson & Bronstein, 2004; Levi, 2014; Scholtes, Joiner, & Streibel, 2003). A *team* can be defined as a group of staff members with varied backgrounds who work collaboratively, and, on a regular basis, develop and implement care plans for a designated group of clients.

Team members coordinate their efforts and work together on behalf of a particular client group. Examples of teams include the following:

- A group of professionals working with stroke victims and their family members in a rehabilitation hospital
- A group of professionals who deliver home-based hospice care

- Professional and paraprofessional helpers trained in crisis intervention sponsored by a county mental health agency
- A group of professionals and aides who work with patients in a psychiatric hospital

According to Abramson and Bronstein (2004), social workers have not always done a good job communicating their role on the team. Social workers need to make a strong case for their roles in resource procurement, counseling, advocacy, and coordination of service delivery. They also need to make a strong case for their skills in maintaining and building the smooth functioning of teams.

The functioning of the team is the responsibility of the team leader. Team leaders are often appointed by an administrator from the agency employing the worker, but in some settings, they are elected or nominated by team members. The team leader is a facilitator and coordinator for the group and is accountable to the agency for the actions of the team. The team leader is responsible for conducting meetings, motivating team members, coordinating individual efforts, and ensuring effective team functioning.

In most, if not all, cases, an agency sanctions the mutual involvement of team members on behalf of a particular client population. Often, the team is composed of members with different professional orientations, such as social work, nursing, physical and occupational therapy, and medicine. The team might also be composed of paraprofessionals, such as mental health therapy aides. Evidence suggests that there is value in involving clients and family members as members of the team (Abramson & Bronstein, 2004), yet this does not often happen in practice.

Meetings should avoid focusing solely on service delivery—some time should be devoted to how members function as a group (Bruner & Spink, 2011; Toseland, Palmer-Ganeles, & Chapman, 1986), a process known as *team building*. Neglecting team functioning can lead to a variety of problems, such as interpersonal conflict and rivalry, duplication of effort, and uncoordinated or incomplete service (Levi, 2014). In a comprehensive investigation into the effectiveness of team building, Klein et al. (2009) reviewed the impact of four specific team-building methods including improving: (1) goal setting, (2) interpersonal relations, (3) problem solving, and (4) role clarification. They found that all were moderately effective but that goal setting and role clarification had the largest effect. Thus, it is important to have clear goals for what the team is trying to accomplish and to make sure that each member of the team knows his or her role and is comfortable with the overlapping and complementary roles of his or her colleagues. It has also been found that trust and cohesion are important elements to enhance for building effective teams (Haines, 2014; Penarroja, Orengo, Zornoza, & Herandez, 2013).

Members are bonded by a team spirit that assists them in their work as a group rather than being a collection of individuals representing disparate concerns and professional agendas. When building and maintaining an effective team, the worker must foster the organization's support of teamwork, encourage members' personal and professional orientations toward collaboration and help members to develop skills to clarify roles and negotiate conflicts (Levi, 2014).

Ideally, team members should meet regularly to discuss their service delivery efforts and their functioning as a team (Abramson, 1989; Gruenfeld, 1998). In recent years there has been increasing emphasis on teams meeting virtually, online (Haines, 2014;

Penarroja, Orengo, Zornoza, & Herandez, 2013). More information is provided about online meetings in Chapter 6.

Communication among team members varies according to the working situation of the team (Levi, 2014). Sometimes team members work independently of each other. For example, within a residential program for children, child-care workers might be considered important team members although they work different shifts. To promote adequate communication and a coordinated team effort in such situations, meetings can be scheduled when shifts overlap.

Treatment Conferences

Treatment conferences meet for the purpose of developing, monitoring, and coordinating treatment plans for a particular client or client system. Members consider the client's situation and decide on a plan for working with the client. Examples of treatment conferences include the following:

- An interdisciplinary group of professionals planning the discharge of a patient in a mental health facility
- A group of child-care workers, social workers, nurses, and a psychiatrist determining a treatment plan for a child in residential treatment
- A parole board considering testimony regarding the release of a prisoner from a correctional facility
- A group of community mental health professionals considering treatment methods for a young man experiencing severe depression

Although treatment conferences may appear similar to team meetings, they differ in five respects:

1. Members of a treatment conference might not all work together as do members of teams. They may be employees of different organizations who come to a treatment conference to discuss ways to coordinate their efforts on behalf of a particular client.

2. Participants may not have the same close working relationship and shared sense of purpose that is essential in teamwork. Members may not work together from day to day. In fact, they may never have met before the treatment conference.

3. Treatment conference groups often meet less frequently than teams; they gather as the need arises in particular situations.

4. The composition of teams is relatively stable, but the composition of treatment conference groups varies depending on the clients being discussed.

5. The plan of action might be carried out by only one member who is entirely responsible for the client's care. For example, during a treatment conference in a family service agency, a worker gets advice from colleagues about how to help a group member with a particularly difficult issue. The other members of the treatment conference have no direct contact with the client. In contrast, all members of a team usually have some contact with clients served by the team.

In treatment conferences, participants generally focus on one client at a time. Members who are familiar with the client contribute information that may be helpful in developing or improving a treatment plan. Other members, who might not be familiar with the client, can also contribute their expertise about how to treat most effectively the type of problem the client is experiencing. Because of this information, the group discusses the client's overall circumstances and considers alternative treatment plans. The group decides on one plan that all members agree will be the most helpful for the client.

Treatment conferences are oriented toward decision making, problem solving, and coordinating the actions of members. The group focuses its attention on the needs of the client rather than on the needs of the group members. The bond that group members feel is based on their concern for a client and their commitment to an agreed-on treatment plan.

Treatment conferences usually include all helping professionals who are working with a client. The group can also include consultants or experts who do not work directly with the client but who can contribute to the treatment plan by offering insight, resources, or advice. Treatment conference membership is diverse by design. Participants are invited because they have new insights and treatment opportunities based on their area of expertise and their unique experiences with a client.

It is the policy of some agencies to have clients and their spouses, parents, guardians, or significant others participate in treatment conferences. However, the staffs of many agencies believe that inviting clients to treatment conferences may inhibit open discussion. In addition, some staffs believe that the conflicting facts, multiple options in treatment planning, or emotionally charged issues that are sometimes discussed during treatment conferences can confuse or upset clients. These agencies sometimes invite the client and significant others to the portion of the treatment conference that occurs after treatment staff have had a private discussion about the client's situation. However, these agencies are in a minority. Most agencies simply opt not to have the client present at treatment conferences (Toseland, Ivanoff, & Rose, 1987).

No data are available to address when, or even if, it is best to invite clients and their significant others to treatment conferences, but there is a growing consensus that it is important to do so (Abramson & Bronstein, 2004). Because a client's right to self-determination is an important part of the value base of social work practice, careful consideration should be given to soliciting clients' input into the treatment-planning decisions that will affect their lives.

Treatment conference leadership can be determined in a variety of ways. In some agencies, the conferences are always led by the same person. This person might be the program director or a member of the staff, such as the social worker whose job includes responsibility for treatment coordination. Commonly, the designated leader is the worker with the most responsibility for, or involvement with, the client's care. In some agencies, leadership is rotated or a supervisor leads the meeting. In these situations, the leader can lend objectivity to the proceedings because he or she does not work directly with the client.

Staff Development Groups

The purpose of staff development groups is to improve services to clients by developing, updating, and refreshing workers' skills. Staff development groups provide workers with an opportunity to learn about new treatment approaches, resources, and community services; to practice new skills; and to review and learn from their previous work with clients. Examples of staff development groups include the following:

- A group of professionals who attend a series of seminars about pharmacology offered by a regional psychiatric center
- An in-service development seminar on codependency for the staff of an alcoholism treatment agency
- Group supervision offered by an experienced social worker for social workers who work in school districts in which there are no supervisors
- A program director who conducts a weekly supervisory group for paraprofessionals who work in a community outreach program for isolated elderly people

Ideally, leaders of staff development groups are experts in a particular field. Often, they also possess extensive experience and knowledge gathered through specialized training, study, and reflection on difficult practice issues.

The focus of staff development groups is on improving workers' skills so they can perform more effectively on behalf of their clients. The trainer or leader can use many methods to aid learning, such as lectures, discussions, audio- and videotape presentations, simulations, and live demonstrations. Members may be given the opportunity to practice new skills in the group and to receive feedback from the trainer and the other members.

Members are bonded by their desire to improve their skills. Often they share an interest in a similar client population or treatment method. They may also share in the camaraderie that comes from being at similar stages in their professional development.

In some staff development groups, the leader takes primary responsibility for the content of each session. The leader may make presentations, arrange for guest speakers, or prepare and conduct simulations and other staff development exercises. In other groups, members are responsible for structuring the group by taking turns presenting their work with particular clients.

Members are expected to risk opening their work to the scrutiny and critique of the rest of the group and to participate in staff development exercises and discussions. They are also expected to learn from their own mistakes and the mistakes of others in the group. Honest, frank, constructive communication and feedback among members is valued, as is a high level of self-disclosure.

Groups to Meet Organizational Needs

Committees

The most common type of task group is the committee. A committee is made up of people who are appointed or elected to the group. Their task is to accomplish a charge or mandate that is delegated to the committee from a higher authority, such as a sponsoring organization or an administrator. Committees may be temporary creations (*ad hoc* committees) or more permanent parts of the structure of an organization (standing committees). Examples of committees include the following:

- A group of young people responsible for recommending activities for the local community center
- A group of employees assigned the task of studying and recommending changes in the agency's personnel policy

- A group of social workers considering ways to improve service delivery to pregnant teenagers
- A group of staff members developing recommendations for an employee-assistance program

In these examples, members are concerned with producing reports, accomplishing tasks, issuing recommendations, or making decisions. In each example, the committee's work requires the collective wisdom of a number of people with varied viewpoints, expertise, and abilities.

Although members are expected to share their personal views during deliberations, the level of self-disclosure in committees is frequently low. In some cases, however, there are variations in the level of self-disclosure, depending on the norms that have developed in the committee and on the nature of the issues being discussed. For example, when the subject matter is of a sensitive nature, discussing personal viewpoints may require a high level of members' self-disclosure.

Most committees tend to follow a standard set of procedures. Sometimes, committees rely on parliamentary procedure to conduct their meetings. In other cases, committees develop their own rules and regulations that control how members introduce and discuss issues and how decisions are reached.

It is useful for each meeting to have an agenda so committee members can follow the activity of the group and know what to expect during the rest of the meeting. The agenda provides structure, focus, and direction for the group. The chairperson is responsible for seeing that the agenda and the formalized procedures are carried out. The chairperson may be appointed by an executive of the organization or elected by committee members.

Committees frequently deal with complex issues, requiring the group to divide large tasks into a series of smaller subtasks. To deal with these subtasks, a committee often authorizes the formation of one or more subcommittees from its membership. Subcommittees report to the larger committee periodically or when their work is completed. The composition of subcommittees is sometimes the responsibility of the chairperson, who considers the qualifications and abilities of each committee member and selects subcommittee members based on their ability to complete a particular task. The chairperson may also ask for volunteers rather than appoint members. This is especially true when the subcommittee deals with a particularly onerous task and highly motivated members are needed. In other cases, subcommittee members are elected by members of the full committee.

Committees are generally accountable to an administrator or other individual or group who gave the committee its charge. The power vested in a committee depends on the group's mandate and the extent to which its actions are binding. It is common, however, for committees to be given the power to make recommendations rather than issue binding decisions.

The importance of the committee as a type of task group cannot be overemphasized. Most other types of task groups mentioned in our typology use elements of committee structure to complete their tasks. It can be argued that other forms of task groups, such as cabinets and treatment conferences, are special forms of committees.

Cabinets

Cabinets are designed to provide advice and expertise about policy issues to chief executive officers or other high-level administrators. Policies, procedures, and practices that affect the entire organization are discussed, developed, or modified in cabinets before being announced by a senior administrative officer. Cabinets enable formal communications among senior administrators in an organization and help garner support for particular policies and procedures among senior and midlevel administrators. Examples of cabinet groups include the following:

- A meeting of section heads in a large state health department to discuss long-term care reimbursement policies
- A weekly meeting of supervisory social work staff and the director of social services in a large municipal hospital
- A series of meetings of senior United Way staff to discuss potential changes in methods of allocating money among member agencies
- A meeting of department heads in a county social services department

Cabinets focus their efforts on administrative and policy issues that may have important implications for the entire organization or subdivisions within it. Although committees often make recommendations to a high-level administrator who is not part of the group, cabinet members often give advice about developing and changing policies and procedures directly to the chief executive officer or other administrator who leads the meeting. In some organizations, cabinets are delegated the authority to make decisions by the chief executive officer.

Unlike committee members, who may be elected or appointed, cabinet members are often appointed by the chief executive officer. Cabinet members are typically supervisors, department heads, or senior managers with powerful positions within the organization. Occasionally, the executive might ask an outside consultant to join the group because of that person's background and knowledge.

Authority and power are particularly important in cabinets. Members often vie for the chief executive's attention and for the chance to influence policy decisions. Members sometimes take stances on policy issues that will benefit the program or section they lead within the larger organization.

The proceedings of cabinet meetings are often kept confidential. Self-disclosure is typically low, with members thinking strategically about how they might influence current and future policy decisions while simultaneously maintaining or enhancing their own power and status within the group. In this manner, cabinets are often highly political groups that wield a great deal of influence within organizations.

Boards of Directors

There are two primary types of boards: the governing board and the advisory board (Conrad & Glenn, 1976). Under the articles of incorporation and the bylaws of not-for-profit organizations, governing boards—sometimes referred to as boards of trustees—are legally and financially responsible for the conduct of the organization.

The members of governing boards are stewards of the public trust and are accountable to the state government that granted the organization its charter; to the federal government that granted their tax-exempt status; and, ultimately, to the public whom the organization serves (Jaskyte, 2012; Tropman & Harvey, 2009). Members of advisory boards provide counsel and guidance to the management of an organization. However, they have no official power to make policy or fiscal decisions. Examples of board groups include the following:

- Trustees of a large public hospital
- Members of the governing board of a family service agency
- Individuals on the citizens' advisory board of a county department of social services
- Members of the board of a corporation that includes several affiliated social service and health agencies

The primary functions of boards of directors are policy-making, oversight of agency operations, ensuring the financial integrity and stability of the organization, and public relations (Callen, Klein, & Tinkelman, 2010; Jaskyte, 2012; Tropman & Harvey, 2009). Boards of directors determine the mission and the short- and long-range goals of the organization. They set personnel and operating policies. They offer counsel and advice to the chief executive officer and monitor the organization's operations. They establish fiscal policy, set budgets, and install monitoring and auditing mechanisms. They also engage in fundraising, hire the chief executive officer, and manage public relations (Howe, 2002). Boards, however, are not supposed to engage in the day-to-day operations of the organization, the hiring of staff (other than the executive director), or the details of programmatic decisions.

The position and duties of the president, vice president, secretary, treasurer, and any other officers of a board of directors are generally specified in the articles of incorporation and bylaws of the organization. The terms of these officers and how they are selected are specified in the board's operating procedures. Usually, officers are nominated by a subcommittee of the board and are elected to specified terms by the entire membership.

It was once estimated that 11.5 million people sit on the boards of not-for-profit agencies in the United States (Waldo, 1986) and this number has surely grown in the past three decades. Board members are bonded by their commitment to the mission and goals of the organization and by their commitment to community service. They are often a diverse group of individuals who are selected because of their power, status, and influence in the community; their expertise; and their representation of particular interest groups and constituencies. For example, a board might contain lawyers who can provide advice on legal matters, accountants or bankers who can provide advice on fiscal matters, businesspeople who can assist with fundraising and advertising, other media experts who can help with public relations, and policy experts and consumers who can provide guidance on programmatic and service issues.

Written agendas are usually circulated before board meetings. Communication is often formal, following the rules of parliamentary procedure. Much of the actual work, however, is often conducted in less formal subcommittee meetings (Pelletier, 2012). Boards often have several standing and *ad hoc* committees that report at board meetings and recommend actions in the form of motions. For example, the finance committee might recommend that the board approve the annual budget of the agency, the personnel committee might recommend a change in health benefits for employees of the organization, or the nominating committee might present a slate of new officers for board approval. For more information about boards, see Hughes, Lakey, and Bobowick (2007), Jaskyte (2012), or Tropman & Harvey (2009).

Groups to Meet Community Needs

Social Action Groups

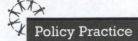

Policy Practice

Behavior: Assess how social welfare and economic policies impact the delivery of and access to service delivery

Critical Thinking Question: Group workers help to plan social policy. How can groups assess changing community trends and needs?

Social action groups empower members to engage in collective action and planned change efforts to alter some aspect of their social or physical environment (McKnight & Plummer, 2015; Pyles, 2013; Staples, 2004; Walls, 2015). They are often referred to as *grassroots* organizations because they arise from the concerns of individuals in the community who may have little individual power or status. Although the goals of social action groups are frequently linked to the needs of the individual members of the group, goal achievement generally also benefits people outside the group. Thus, social action groups serve the common good of both members and nonmembers. Examples of social action groups include the following:

- A citizens' group advocating increased police protection on behalf of the elderly population in a neighborhood
- A group of social workers lobbying for increased funding for social services
- A tenants' group seeking support for a playground area in their housing complex
- A group of community leaders working to increase the access of African Americans to a mental health agency

Hardina (2013), McKnight and Plummer (2015), Pyles (2013), and Walls (2015) all point out that there are varieties of ways that small groups take on social action efforts. These include organizing committees composed of well-respected opinion leaders who come together to organize a social movement; house meetings when a group of individuals get together to recruit others and to discuss controversial issues; issue committees that identify, prioritize, and select issues for action; lobbying committees that bring issues to elected officials; and negotiating teams that work at the bargaining table to bring about a change. Small groups are also used for many other social action purposes, such as fund raising and developing and coordinating special events.

A worker involved in a social action group can assume one of many leadership roles, depending on the nature of the change effort and the needs of the group. A worker assumes an enabler role to help the group acquire information or resources, determine priorities and procedures, and plan a strategy for action. For example, in working with tenants concerned about their rights, the worker might help organize a tenant-rights group to help the individuals pursue their common goals.

Alternatively, workers might take a directive role because of their expertise regarding the change effort. In a lobbying effort, for example, a worker might be particularly knowledgeable about techniques for influencing legislators. In this instance, the worker might be asked to speak for the social action group or might encourage the group to examine particular issues or use particular strategies, such as collaboration, bargaining, or conflict.

Although directive approaches to leading social action groups are sometimes useful and appropriate, the worker should be guided by the purpose of the group and the preferences of group members. The worker should make sure that a directive approach does not inhibit indigenous leadership from developing among members. The ultimate goal of the worker should be to help social action groups function effectively and independently (McKnight & Plummer, 2015; Pyles, 2013).

The bond that holds members of action groups together is a shared perception of injustice, inequity, and a need for a change in the current social structure. Yet, Mondros and Wilson (1994) point out that less than 2 percent of a potential constituency ever becomes involved in a social action group and that large numbers of individuals drop out after their initial enthusiasm fades. Five factors that help people stay involved in social action groups are (1) the importance of the work of the group, (2) the group's effectiveness, (3) a sense of community and peer support, (4) interest in the task, and (5) the feeling of contributing (Mondros & Wilson, 1994). Methods to enhance and sustain membership based on these and other factors are described in Chapters 3 and 12.

The composition of social action groups can vary depending on the nature and circumstances of the change effort. Sometimes, workers take a leadership role in composing social action groups; in other cases, groups may form because of the interests of one or more concerned citizens. In the latter case, the worker is often asked to be a facilitator, an enabler, or a consultant to lend expertise to the change effort without necessarily influencing the composition of the group.

When the worker does have a role in composing the group, consideration should be given to the level of support for the change effort among key community leaders. In some instances, the worker may seek members who can exert influence in the environment or who have the diverse skills and resources needed to empower the group.

Communication patterns in social action groups vary with the circumstances of the group. The worker helps the group develop open communication patterns so that all members have a chance to become involved. The worker also helps the group establish communication links with its environment. Good communication helps avoid misunderstandings and promotes a cooperative atmosphere among all those who may have some stake in the change effort (Hardina, 2013).

Coalitions

Coalitions—or alliances, as they are sometimes called—are groups of organizations, social action groups, or individuals that come together to exert influence by sharing resources and expertise. Coalition members agree to pursue common goals, which they believe cannot be achieved by any of the members acting alone.

Examples of coalitions include the following:

- A group of family planning and community health-care clinics who have formed a pro-choice coalition to influence state and federal legislation on abortion
- Not-for-profit home-care agencies who gather to lobby for greater access to community care for the chronically ill elderly
- Community agencies that want to bring public attention to the need for a community teen center
- Business, community, and civic leaders who team up to explore ways to reduce racial tensions in a large urban area

The formation of coalitions as political and social forces to improve the responsiveness of the social environment to human beings has a long tradition in social group work. For example, Newstetter (1948) described principles for interagency collaboration that have formed the basis for more recent writings on the formation and development of coalitions (Brown, Feinberg, Shapiro, & Greenberg, 2015; Feinberg, Bontempo, & Greenberg, 2008; Meyer, 2013); Pyles, 2013; Winer & Ray, 2009; Yang, Foster-Fishman, Collins, & Ahn, 2012; Zakocs & Edwards, 2006).

Coalitions are often formed by a charismatic or dedicated individual who has high visibility and respect within the community. This individual helps organizations, groups, and individuals understand that they have common goals and purposes that could be better served by working together.

Because members of coalitions are often concerned about preserving their autonomy while joining with others in the group, coalitions sometimes experience conflict in establishing mutual goals, working agreements, plans of action, and equitable ways of sharing resources and accomplishments. Therefore, a primary task throughout coalition formation and development is building and maintaining consensus and a smooth partnership in which efforts can be focused on the goals to be achieved rather than on intragroup rivalry. Charismatic leaders are helped in their efforts by the coalition members who are bonded by their ideals, common ideology, and interest in a particular issue or set of issues.

Coalitions can take many forms. Freewheeling interaction often occurs during caucuses and in subgroup and one-to-one discussions between coalition meetings. Informal procedures are also frequently used in *ad hoc*, single-issue coalitions that do not have a long history of operation. Frequently, coalitions are loose, temporary confederations of organizations or social action groups that coalesce to share resources and gain strength in numbers. In such informal coalitions, the autonomy of the individual members is strictly protected. Over time, however, some coalitions become stable, long-term organizations with centralized staff and resources. These types of coalitions often have one or more elite decision-makers who have considerable influence on decision making and operations.

Meetings of coalitions are often characterized by ideologically fervent speechmaking and position taking. Much emphasis is placed on developing strategies to accomplish specific goals and coordinating activities involved in the action plan. Sometimes, coalition meetings are characterized by formal interactions following the rules of parliamentary procedure. Although parliamentary procedures are often not as strictly adhered to as they are in board meetings or delegate councils, they are used in coalitions to promote a sense of inclusion and belonging so that members feel they have the opportunity to fully participate in collective deliberations and decision making.

Delegate Councils

Delegate councils are composed for the purposes of facilitating interagency communication and cooperation, studying community-wide social issues or social problems, engaging in collective social action, and governing large organizations. Members of delegate councils are appointed or elected by a sponsoring unit. The members' primary function is to represent the interests of their sponsoring unit during council meetings. A variation of the delegate council is the delegate assembly, which is usually larger. Examples of delegate councils include the following:

- A number of agency representatives who meet monthly to improve interagency communication

- A group of elected representatives from local chapters of a professional organization who meet to approve the organization's budget
- A state task force to study family violence composed of members appointed from each county
- A yearly meeting of representatives from family service agencies throughout the county

Representation is an important issue in delegate councils. A member represents a group of people, an agency, or another system. The member is often given authority to speak for the represented unit. Because the unit has agreed to participate by sending a representative, the represented unit generally agrees to abide by decisions made by the delegate council.

There are differing ways to achieve representation. The number of representatives for each sponsoring unit can vary with the size or importance of the unit. For example, legislative bodies frequently determine the number of representatives by considering the population of each voting district, county, or state, and apportioning an appropriate number of representatives for each district.

Other councils' representation may be dictated by a sanctioning authority to ensure control over policy decisions. For example, a consumer council for a large department of social services may have more employees than clients to ensure departmental control over the decisions made by the group.

Delegate councils are usually concerned with broad issues that affect several agencies, a large segment of a population, or a group of people in a wide geographic area. Delegate councils provide an effective communications link among groups of people who otherwise might not be able to communicate in a formal way. For example, delegate councils frequently serve as a forum for communication among diverse human service agencies within a city, state, or nation. Such agencies might not otherwise communicate effectively with each other. They may also form part of the governance structure of unions or professional organizations that represent a diverse and geographically dispersed membership.

Delegate councils can be either discussion-oriented or action-oriented, or they may have components of both orientations. The White House Conferences on Aging, for example, involve a series of delegate councils that discuss issues of concern to older U.S. citizens and make recommendations for government action.

Delegate councils are formed in a number of ways. Some councils are the product of ad hoc task forces or coalitions that have been meeting informally for some time. Other councils begin with the support and sponsorship of a particular agency and gradually establish their own identities, rules and procedures, and sources of funding. Representatives to delegate councils are either elected or appointed, and leadership is usually determined through an election.

Because council members are responsible for representing the views, interests, and positions of their sponsors to the delegate council, members often act formally on behalf of their constituencies. Delegates communicate with their sponsors regarding the proceedings of the council. The effectiveness of the delegate council depends on the ability of each delegate to achieve two-way communication between the council and the represented unit. The individual delegates are not expected to engage in a high level of personal self-disclosure because they are bound by a mandate to present the collective views of the group of people they represent.

 Assess your understanding of task groups by taking this brief quiz.

SUMMARY

This introductory chapter provides a framework for studying and working with groups. Group work is a broad field of practice conducted by professional social workers with, and on behalf of, many different client groups in many different settings. A definition of group work is offered that encompasses the breadth of group work practice and is sufficiently flexible to allow specialized approaches and objectives. To understand the types of groups that exist in practice, a distinction is made between treatment and task groups. Although some functions and objectives of task and treatment groups overlap, they are distinguished by a variety of characteristics.

This chapter also helps clarify the kinds of task and treatment groups often encountered in practice and illustrates the commonalities and differences among these groups. The typology of treatment groups distinguishes among those with six primary purposes: (1) support, (2) education, (3) growth, (4) therapy, (5) socialization, and (6) self-help.

The typology of task groups distinguishes among nine types of task groups that are organized to serve three primary purposes: (1) meeting client needs, (2) meeting organizational needs, and (3) meeting community needs. Types of task groups that serve client needs include teams, treatment conferences, and staff development groups. Types of task groups that serve organizational needs include committees, cabinets, and boards of directors. Types of task groups that serve community needs include social action groups, coalitions, and delegate councils.

Historical and Theoretical Developments

To develop a broad perspective concerning the potential uses of groups in practice settings, it is helpful to understand the developments that have occurred in the study of groups and in the practice of group work over the years. This historical perspective gives group workers a firm foundation on which to build a knowledge base for effective group work practice.

Two general types of inquiries have enhanced the understanding of groups. One type has been made for over 100 years by group work practitioners and scholars from disciplines including, but not limited to, adult education, counseling, psychology, psychiatry, recreation, and social work. The other type has come from social scientists who have experimented with groups in laboratories. This inquiry has led to social science findings about basic properties and processes of groups. The results of both inquiries have led to improved methods for working with groups.

KNOWLEDGE FROM GROUP WORK PRACTICE AND PRACTICE RESEARCH: TREATMENT GROUPS

Although casework began in England and the United States in charity organizations in the late nineteenth century, group work grew up mainly in British and American settlement houses. Jane Addams founded the first settlement house in Chicago in 1889 to address issues of assimilation (Singh & Salazar, 2010). Most of the life and self-advocacy skills were taught in groups. Other early pioneers were Joseph Pratt, who worked in asylums for tuberculosis patients, and Jessie Davis who worked in the schools. Both pioneered social justice through group work using empowerment and advocacy skills (Singh & Salazar, 2010).

The use of group work in settlement houses and casework in charity organizations was not by accident. Group work, and the settlement houses in which it was practiced, offered citizens the opportunity for education, recreation, socialization, and community involvement. Unlike the charity organizations that focused on the diagnosis and treatment of the problems of the poor, settlement houses offered groups as an opportunity for citizens to gather to share their views, gain mutual support, and exercise the power derived from their association for social change. Groups were a central component of clubs and social settlements. The focus was on promoting the well-being of individual members through acceptance, companionship, and solidarity, while at the same time promoting democratic participation, social justice, and social action in civic, industrial, and social institutions. For example, Grace Coyle's *Studies in Group Behavior* (1937) presented case studies of five club groups.

There were some exceptions to this trend. For example, as early as 1895, some people in the charity organization movement realized there was a need to organize the poor for social change as well as to work with them one to one (Brackett, 1895). Boyd (1935) reported how social group work was used for therapeutic purposes in state mental institutions.

Contributions to social group work also have been made by many other disciplines. For example, Dr. Pratt, a physician who worked with tuberculosis patients in 1905, is often attributed with being the first to use a group as a treatment modality. Early contributors with mental health backgrounds include Lazell (1921) who reported using psycho-educational methods in the treatment of inpatients, Marsh (1931, 1933, 1935) who reported using milieu therapy, and Syz (1928) who reported using a here-and-now focus on patients with dementia. There were also early psychodynamic group therapists, such as Wender (1936), Schilder (1937), and Slavson (1940), who reported the results of their clinical work.

Interest in group work also stemmed from those who had led socialization groups, adult education groups, and recreation groups in settlement houses and youth service agencies (McCaskill, 1930). In fact, during these early years, the term *club work* was often used interchangeably with the term *group work* (Slavson, 1939a, p. 126).

It is often believed that group work is considerably younger than casework, but group work agencies actually started only a few years after casework agencies. There were courses for group workers in schools of social work in the early 1900s (Maloney, 1963), and both casework and group work were used by social workers in the early twentieth century.

Casework soon became identified with the social work profession, but group work did not become formally linked with social work until the National Conference of Social Work in 1935. The identification of group work with the social work profession increased during the 1940s (American Association of Group Workers, 1947), although group workers continued to maintain loose ties with recreation, adult education, and mental hygiene until 1955, when group workers joined with six other professional groups to form the National Association of Social Workers.

Differences Between Casework and Group Work

Compared with caseworkers, who relied on insight developed from psychodynamic approaches and on the provision of concrete resources, group workers relied on program activities to spur members to action. Program activities of all types were the media through which groups attained their goals (Addams, 1909, 1926; Boyd, 1935, 1938; Smith, 1935). Activities such as camping, singing, group discussion, games, and arts and crafts were used for recreation, socialization, education, support, and rehabilitation. Unlike casework, which was mainly focused on problem solving and rehabilitation, group work activities were used for enjoyment as well as to solve problems. Thus, the group work methods that developed from settlement house work had a different focus and a different goal than did casework methods.

Differences between casework and group work can also be clearly seen in the helping relationship. Caseworkers sought out the most underprivileged victims of industrialization and diagnosed and treated worthy clients by providing them with resources and acting as examples of virtuous, hardworking citizens.

Although group workers also worked with the poor and impaired, they did not focus solely on the poorest people or those with the most problems. They preferred the word *members* rather than *clients* (Bowman, 1935). They emphasized members' strengths rather than their weaknesses. Helping was seen as a shared relationship in which the group worker and the group members worked together for mutual understanding and action regarding their common concerns for their community. As concerns were identified, group members supported and helped one another, and the worker mediated between the demands of society and the needs of group members (Schwartz, 1981).

Shared interaction, shared power, and shared decision-making placed demands on group workers that were not experienced by caseworkers. The number of group members, the fact that they could turn to one another for help, and the democratic decision-making processes that were encouraged meant that group workers had to develop skills different from those of caseworkers. Group workers used their skills to intervene in complex and often fast-paced group interactions but remained aware of the welfare of all group members. Schwartz (1966) summed up the feelings engendered by the new group work method very well in the statement, "there are so many of them and only one of me" (p. 572).

Unlike the early writings of caseworkers that emphasized improving practice outcomes by careful study, diagnosis, and treatment (Richmond, 1917), the early writings of group workers (Coyle, 1930, 1935) emphasized the processes that occurred during group meetings. For example, Grace Coyle, one of the first social workers to publish a text on groups, titled her 1930 work *Social Process in Organized Groups*, whereas the first text on casework, published in 1917 by Mary Richmond, was called *Social Diagnosis*.

The emphasis on group processes has remained throughout the history of group work. Group workers have always been concerned with how best to use the unique possibilities offered by the interaction of different people in a group. Thus, workers focus on the group as a whole as well as on individual members.

Intervention Targets

The importance of group work for enlightened collective action (Follett, 1926) and democratic living (Slavson, 1939b) was an essential part of social group work's early roots. Grace Coyle's work, for example, focused heavily on social action, social change, and social justice (Coyle, 1935, 1938). Thus, social group work has its roots in both the individual change focus of early group therapists and the educational and social change foci of group workers with educational, recreational, club, and settlement house settings. Today, group work in the settlement house tradition is best seen in community centers, especially in developing countries (Yan, 2001).

During the 1940s and 1950s, group workers began to use groups more frequently to provide therapy and remediation in mental health settings. Therapy groups were insight-oriented, relying less on program activities and more on diagnosis and treatment of members' problems (Konopka, 1949, 1954; Redl, 1944; Trecker, 1956).

The emphasis on the use of groups for therapy and remediation was the result, in part, of the influence of Freudian psychoanalysis and ego psychology and, in part, of World War II, which created a severe shortage of trained workers to deal with mentally disabled war veterans. It was also spurred on by Fritz Redl and Gisela Konopka who helped make group services an integral part of child guidance clinics. Interest in the use of groups in psychiatric settings continued into the 1950s, as can be seen in the proceedings of a national institute on this topic in 1955 (Trecker, 1956).

Although there was an increased emphasis in the 1940s and 1950s on using groups to improve the functioning of individual members, interest remained in using groups for recreational and educational purposes, especially in Jewish community centers and in youth organizations, such as the Girl Scouts and the YWCA. During the 1950s and 1960s, groups were also used for community development and social action in neighborhood centers and community agencies. At the same time, there was an increase in the study of small groups as a social phenomenon. For example, in 1947, Kurt Lewin and others founded the National Training Laboratories (NTL) that focused on group dynamics, using t-groups (training groups) to help executives and other group leaders understand the power of group dynamics and to learn how to facilitate groups more effectively. NTL flourished during the 1950s and 1960s and, after a period of decline during the 1970s, is effectively carrying out its mission today.

The Weakening of Group Work

During the 1960s, the popularity of group services declined. This can be seen in accounts of well-known projects, such as the Mobilization for Youth experiment (Weissman, 1969). Weissman stated, "The planners of Mobilization for Youth did not accord group work services a major role in the fight against delinquency" (p. 180). Work training programs and educational opportunities were viewed as more significant than group work services—except in the area of community organization, in which the skill of group workers played an important role in organizing youths and adults around important social concerns.

In addition, during the 1960s, the push toward a generalist view of practice in schools of social work and the movement away from specializations in casework, group work and community organizations tended to weaken group work specializations in professional schools and reduce the number of professionals trained in group work as their primary mode of practice. Taken together, these factors contributed to the decline of group work starting in the 1960s. The emphasis on generalist practice has unintentionally favored individual work over group work and community organization.

During the 1970s, interest in group work continued to wane. Fewer professional schools offered advanced courses in group work, and fewer practitioners used it as a practice method. To increase awareness among practitioners about the potential benefits of groups, group workers throughout the United States and Canada came together in 1979 for the First Annual Symposium for the Advancement of Group Work. Each year since then, an annual group work symposium has been convened. The symposia bring together social group workers from the United States and other countries, who present clinical findings, research results, and workshops based on the work they have done with groups in their own communities.

During the last several decades, attempts to revitalize group work within social work have continued unabated. The Association for the Advancement of Social Work with Groups (AASWG) has expanded into an international association with many affiliated local chapters. In addition to the annual symposia it sponsors, the AASWG has a person who is a liaison to the Council on Social Work Education to promote group work curriculum in schools of social work. The AASWG has also developed standards on group work education and has submitted testimony to the Commission on Educational Policy of the Council on Social Work Education.

Despite the attempts at revitalization, Putnam (2000) points out that the decline of civic engagement in voluntary associations and participation in formed and natural groups of all sorts has continued into the twenty-first century. Putnam (2000) attributes this to a number of factors, including (1) time and money pressures, (2) mobility and sprawl, and (3) the availability of technology and the mass media. In describing the harm that this has caused, he stresses the importance of human capital and reengagement in all of our social institutions.

Some schools of social work are having trouble finding qualified group work instructors even though agencies still rely heavily on all of the treatment group types described in Chapter 1. Task groups, such as teams and treatment conferences, have also remained important in practice. Their use may be growing because of the emphasis on care management and the increased demand for coordinated services from funding sources. The emphasis on Total Quality Management and other efforts to involve all members of organizations in participatory rather than hierarchical management has led to greater use of committees and other types of task groups (Johnson & Johnson, 2013). Therefore, more should be done to revive the teaching of group work in schools of social work and allied disciplines.

Current Practice Trends

Treatment Groups

In an article that has had a profound effect on social work practice with groups, Papell and Rothman (1962) outlined three historically important models of group work practice, shown in Table 2.1. These are the (1) social goals, (2) remedial, and (3) reciprocal models. Although these three models have been expanded to include many others in recent years, they still form the basis for group work practice with treatment groups.

Research-Informed Practice

Behavior: Use and translate research evidence to inform and improve practice and service delivery

Critical Thinking Question: Three historical models of group work are identified. How are these models used in groups that exist today?

Table 2.1   Three Models of Social Group Work

Selected Characteristics	Social Goals Model	Remedial Model	Reciprocal Model
Purpose and goals	Social consciousness, social responsibility, informed citizenship, and informed political and social action	To restore and rehabilitate group members who are behaving dysfunctionally	To form a mutual aid system among group members to achieve optimum adaptation and socialization
Agency	Settlement houses and neighborhood center settings	Formal agency setting, clinical outpatient or inpatient settings	Compatible with clinical inpatient and outpatient settings and neighborhood and community centers
Focus of work	Larger society, individuals within the context of the neighborhood and the social environment	Alleviating problems or concerns Improving coping skills	Creating a self-help, mutual aid system among all group members
Role of the group worker	Role model and enabler for responsible citizenship	Change agent who engages in study, diagnosis, and treatment to help group members attain individual treatment goals	Mediator between needs of members and needs of the group and the larger society Enabler contributing data not available to the members
Type of group	Citizens, neighborhood, and community residents	Clients who are not functioning adequately and need help coping with life's tasks	Partners who work together sharing common concerns
Methods used in the group	Discussion, participation, consensus, developing and carrying out a group task, community organizing, and other program and action skills to help group members acquire instrumental skills about social action and communal living and change	Structured exercises, direct and indirect influence, both within and outside of the group, to help members change behavior patterns	Shared authority where members discuss concerns, support one another, and form a cohesive social system to benefit one another

Social Goals Model

The social goals model focuses on socializing members to democratic societal values. It values cultural diversity and the power of group action. It was used, and continues to be used, in settlement houses and in youth organizations, such as the Girl Scouts, the YWCA, and Jewish community centers. The social goals model has also been used by community organization and development agencies to change societal norms and structures and improve the social welfare of all citizens.

The worker acts as an enabler who uses program activities, such as camping, discussions, and instructions about democratic processes, to socialize members. The worker also acts to empower members by helping them make collective decisions and use their collective strength to make society more responsive to their needs. For example, Macgowan and Pennell (2001) demonstrate how they use the social goals model to empower family members to make a plan for change in a model they refer to as *family group conferencing.*

The writings of Klein (1953, 1970, 1972) and Tropp (1968, 1976) helped to refine the social goals model. Tropp focused on how group development can be used to empower members to achieve the goals they have set for themselves. He was strongly opposed to the worker's establishing goals for members, believing instead that groups could promote growth only when the worker encouraged group self-direction toward common goals. Klein's writings emphasized the importance of matching members' needs to environmental opportunities for growth. Like Tropp, Klein emphasized the autonomy of group members and their freedom to pursue their own self-defined goals. Middleman (1980, 1982) made important contributions to the model by emphasizing the importance of program activities. Breton (1994, 1995, 1999), Nosko and Breton (1997–1998), Cohen and Mullender (1999), Cox (1988), Cox and Parsons (1994), Lee (2001), Mondros and Wilson (1994), Mullender and Ward (1991), Parsons (1991), and Pernell (1986) have made significant contributions by focusing on empowerment strategies in social group work. The social goals model of group work is still being used in contemporary practice, particularly in agencies that engage in community organization, empowerment, and mutual aid groups (see, for example, Pyles, 2013; Western, 2013).

Remedial Model

The remedial model focuses on restoring or rehabilitating individuals by helping them change their behavior. The worker acts as a change agent and intervenes in the group to achieve specific purposes determined by group members, the group worker, and society. The remedial model uses a leader-centered approach to group work, with the worker actively intervening in the group's process, often using systematic problem solving and task-centered or behavioral methods. Garvin (1997), Rose (1998), and Vinter (1967) are often associated with this approach to group work. With the increased attention to time-limited, goal-directed practice and measurable treatment outcomes, this model has received increasing attention in the group work literature in recent years (Conyne, 2010; Delucia-Waack, Kalodner, & Riva, 2014; Kleinberg, 2012; LeCroy, 2008). It is used widely in inpatient and community-based settings with individuals who have severe behavioral problems and social skills deficits.

Time-limited, highly structured remedial groups are also being used with increasing frequency in managed care settings as cost-effective alternatives to long-term individual and group psychotherapy (Conyne, 2010; Delucia-Waak, et al, 2014; LeCroy, 2008). A survey of directors and providers in managed care companies suggests that this trend is likely to accelerate in future years (Taylor & Burlingame, 2001). Although the survey indicated that social workers were more familiar than psychologists and psychiatrists with short-term structured group work approaches, it also indicated that practitioners from all disciplines tended to be more familiar and more comfortable with traditional process-oriented, long-term group models, suggesting that more graduate and undergraduate education and more in-service training are needed about how to conduct short-term, structured, remedial model groups (Taylor & Burlingame, 2001).

Reciprocal Model

The third model presented by Papell and Rothman (1962), the reciprocal model, is sometimes referred to as the *interactional model* or the *mutual aid model* (Reid, 1997; Gitterman & Shulman, 2005; Shulman, 2016). The model derives its name from the emphasis on the reciprocal relationship that exists between group members and society. Members both influence and are influenced by the environment. The worker acts as a mediator, helping group members find the common ground between their needs and societal demands. The worker also acts as a resource person who facilitates the functioning of the group and helps members form a mutual-aid system and explore new ways of coping with and adapting to environmental demands.

As contrasted with the remedial model, in which the work of the group is often focused on helping individual members with specific problems, the reciprocal model encourages workers to use group processes to foster a therapeutic environment in the group as a whole. The reciprocal model also encourages the worker to help the agency and the wider community better understand and meet individual members' needs. Gitterman and Shulman (2005), Schwartz (1976), and Shulman (2016) are best known for the group-centered, process-oriented approach to group work practice, but other authors such as Brown (1991), Glassman and Kates (1990), Steinberg (2014), and Wasserman and Danforth (1988) have made important contributions to this model of group work practice.

Divergent and Unified Practice Models

The different foci of current practice models are equally valid, depending on the purposes, practice situations, and tasks facing the group. Group work practice has an eclectic base that developed as a response to diverse needs for educational, recreational, mental health, and social services. A remedial purpose, for example, may be particularly appropriate for some populations and in some settings, such as alcohol and drug treatment centers and residential centers for delinquent youth. In contrast, the reciprocal model is ideally suited for support groups designed to help members cope with distressing life events. It is also ideally suited to the facilitation of self-help groups in which reciprocal sharing of mutual concerns and the giving and receiving of support are central. For example, in Make Today Count, a medical self-help group for cancer patients to help each other cope with their illnesses, members are encouraged to share their concerns, experiences, and the reactions of their family and friends.

The usefulness and appropriateness of different practice models suggest that group workers should make differential use of group work methods, depending on the purposes, objectives, and goals of the groups they are leading. In a comprehensive review of the history of group work, Reid (1981) concluded that there has always been more than one model of group work operating in the United States and that there will continue to be several models in use to meet the many purposes and goals of group work.

There have also been attempts to integrate different models of group work practice (Papell, 1997). For example, Papell and Rothman (1980) proposed a "mainstream model" of group work practice that incorporates elements of many different practice models. They pointed out that the fostering of a mutual-aid system among members is a common ingredient of many seemingly polarized approaches to group work practice.

They suggested that group development and the creation of group structures for increasing the autonomy of members as the group develops are also common elements of most current conceptualizations of group work practice.

Alissi (2001) has described the central tenets of the mainstream model. These include a commitment to (1) democratic values, including voluntary group association, collective deliberation, decision-making and action, cultural pluralism, individual freedom and liberty, and social responsibility to promote the common good; (2) the welfare of the individual and the betterment of society; (3) program activities that reflect the needs, interests, and aspirations of members; (4) the power of small group processes; and (5) the influence of the group worker doing *with* rather than *for* the members of the group.

Similarly, in considering the past, present, and future of group work in social work, Middleman and Wood (1990) also concluded that in practice, there is a blending of models of group work. They suggested that a mainstream model of social work with groups should include the worker (1) helping members develop a system of mutual aid; (2) understanding, valuing, and respecting group processes as powerful dynamics for change; (3) helping members become empowered for autonomous functioning within and outside the group; and (4) helping members "re-experience their groupness at the point of termination" (p. 11). They concluded that some clinical work with groups that focused exclusively on one-to-one attention to individual members is excluded from the mainstream model of social work with groups because this type of work does not utilize the dynamics of the group as a whole to bring about therapeutic change.

Evidence-based Group Work Practice

Knowledge of group work practice does not only come from workers' experiences in field settings, published primarily as case examples or presented in workshops. It is also developed by group workers working cooperatively with practice researchers. Practice research has taken many forms including surveys of practitioners, qualitative research, and quantitative field trials of group work methods and programs. The gathering of data from practice ranges from easily implemented quick data gathering to sophisticated randomized controlled trials. For example, easily implemented methods include asking members about their experiences periodically, or during the last meeting of a group, whereas very rigorous, time-consuming methods include randomized field trials of group work practices. These methods are described in more detail in Chapter 14.

Some practice researchers have also developed ways of aggregating information from many different studies on the same or similar topics. These studies are referred to as "meta-analyses." They provide summaries of data from many studies on particular topics, such as treating depression or trauma in groups. As more data become available for and from meta-analyses, evidence-based practice guidelines will follow. These can be very useful to busy practitioners who are often not afforded the time to do their own literature reviews. Group workers are encouraged to use evidence-based practices and guidelines whenever they are available. When there is scant or conflicting evidence, and multifaceted problems, critical thinking and use of supervision can help reflective group workers to make the best use of whatever evidence is available.

If you work frequently with members with particular concerns, then you may want to do your own literature review both to judge the quality of the evidence yourself and to identify field-tested group work programs that you might be able to use in your own practice. Many searchable databases are available through libraries to help you obtain articles, books, and book chapters. If you do not have ready access to these databases, you can use Google Scholar. You can also search the databases of government agencies for other sources in your area of practice. For example, there are very helpful Treatment Improvement Protocols (TIPS) and other resources developed by the United States Substance Abuse and Mental Health Services Administration (SAMHSA). Evidence-based manuals have also been conveniently gathered in handbooks that are available in local libraries and through interlibrary loan systems (see, for example, LeCroy, 2008).

At the same time there continue to be barriers to the use of evidence-based data. Burlingame (2010), for example, notes that there has been little effort to aggregate and disseminate evidence-based information about group work practice to workers. Increasing demands for more practice and paperwork by funding agencies also interferes with group workers becoming evidence-based practitioners. Therefore, continuing efforts are needed to enable practicing group workers to use evidence-based practice methods.

The Popularity of Psycho-educational, Structured, Practice Models

In recent years there has been a growing emphasis on short-term structured groups for persons with specific problems, such as depression, eating disorders, and a variety of other problems (Barlow, 2013; Bieling, McCabe, & Antony, 2006; Conyne, 2010; DeLucia-Waack, et al., 2014; Kaduson & Schaefer, 2015; Kellner, 2001; Langelier, 2001; LeCroy, 2008; McFarlane, 2002; Riess & Dockray-Miller, 2002; Roffman, 2004; Rose, 2004; Velasquez, Maurer, Crouch, & DiClemente, 2001; Waterman and Walker, 2009; White & Freeman, 2000). Some authors such as Bieling and colleagues (2006) make a concerted effort to pay attention to how group dynamics can be used when working on individual problems. Others, however, do not fit into the mainstream model because they use the group only as a vehicle for treating multiple individuals, rather than making use of the group and its dynamics as a vehicle for change. It is also important to be aware that funders of practice research often prefer or require structured short-term intervention protocols, so the literature may underrepresent other group-centered, interactional, and longer-term approaches to group work practice.

In the first edition of this book, Toseland and Rivas (1984) had as a primary goal bridging the chasm between leader-centered, short-term structured approaches and member-centered, longer-term, less structured, interactional and reciprocal approaches to group work. The intent of the first edition, and this edition, is to elucidate a core body of knowledge, values, skills, and procedures that are essential for professional, competent group work practice, regardless of theoretical orientation. The intent of this book is also to show how the group as a whole can facilitate change. Working with individuals for a time on a one-on-one basis in the context of a group is sometimes desirable, but only when the worker pays attention to the group as a whole, and invites and encourages all the members to get involved in the work being done with a single individual.

It is also the intent of this book to present a broad range of groups and practice models and to emphasize that one model does not fit all. The choice of a model and the degree of structure should depend on the nature of the problem and many other factors presented in the interactional model of leadership in Chapter 4. It is clear that evidence bases are needed for ethical practice, for insurance reimbursement, and for many other purposes. Nevertheless, mutual aid, reciprocal, psychodynamic, strengths-based and other practice models that have less rigorous evidence for their effectiveness should not be ignored. It is essential to recognize that there is great merit to evidence gathered by clinicians from actual practice experiences. Many problems do not yet have a clear evidence base for a particular problem approach. More importantly, practicing clinicians recognize that the problems that people bring to group work can be very complex. They do not fall neatly into any diagnostic category. People may have adverse childhood events, adult trauma, attachment disorders, learning problems, medical conditions, coping skills limitations, cultural styles, environmental deprivations, and many other factors that can play a role in how to intervene effectively. Evidence-based interventions can help immensely, but they are often targeted to very specific, narrowly defined problems that have been deliberately limited by careful screening criteria in randomized intervention trials. Specificity is essential in intervention research, but group members often have multifaceted, complicated syndromes that are only partially amenable to a single approach. The art of practice for experienced group workers involves critical thinking to blend, match, and tailor intervention strategies for each member and for the specific group dynamics that arise during every group meeting. Therefore, individualized, interactive, and changing care plans that consider the uniqueness of every member and the group as a whole are often needed. Available evidence-based interventions are often only one part of excellent group work practice.

> **?** Assess your understanding of group work practice and practice research with treatment groups by taking this brief quiz.

KNOWLEDGE FROM GROUP WORK PRACTICE: TASK GROUPS

Task groups have operated in social agencies since settlement houses and charity organizations began more than 100 years ago. The distinction between task groups and treatment groups made today was not made in the earlier history of group work. Groups were used simultaneously for both task and treatment purposes. Earlier in the history of group work, the journals *The Group,* published from 1939 to 1955, and *Adult Leadership,* published from 1952 to 1977, devoted much space to articles about leading task groups.

With a few notable exceptions (Brill, 1976; Trecker, 1980) during the 1960s and 1970s, interest in task groups waned. However, interest was rekindled during the 1980s and 1990s with the renewed emphasis on the value of participatory management practices (Gummer, 1991, 1995). For example, Dluhy (1990), Ephross and Vassil (2005), Fatout and Rose (1995), and Tropman (2014) have all made outstanding contributions to the task group literature. Still, the current need for expertise and evidence bases for task group practices is becoming critical as more agencies are using participatory management practices and team approaches to service delivery. This text is designed, in part, to address this gap in the literature.

> **?** Assess your understanding of group work practice with task groups by taking this brief quiz.

KNOWLEDGE FROM SOCIAL SCIENCE RESEARCH

Practitioners sometimes criticize the findings of social scientists as not being generalizable to real-world practice settings. Some social scientists conducting their research in laboratory settings use analogue designs that may include short-term groups, artificial problems, and students who are not always motivated. Despite these limitations, the precision of laboratory studies enables social scientists to examine how different group dynamics operate. Findings from these studies increase practitioners' understanding of how helpful and harmful group dynamics develop.

Social scientists also use naturalistic observations to study the functioning of community groups. Some classic observational studies are those conducted by Bales (1955), Lewin (1947, 1948), Roethlisberger and Dickson (1939), Thrasher (1927), and Whyte (1943). Although not as precise as laboratory studies, naturalistic studies overcome some of the limitations of laboratory studies and provide many insights into the way groups develop.

According to Hare (1976), the scientific study of groups began at the turn of the century. A basic research question asked at that time, and continuing to receive much attention today, concerns the extent to which group participation influences individual members. Triplett (1898), for example, examined the effect that cyclists had on each other during races and found that a racer's competitiveness appeared to depend on the activities of others on the track. Taylor (1903) found that productivity increased among workers who were freed from the pressure to conform to the standards of other workers. Those early findings suggest that the presence of others has a significant influence on an individual group member. The presence of others tends to generate pressure to conform to the standards of behavior that are expected of those who belong to the group.

Other early social scientists also recognized the influence of groups on individual behavior. LeBon (1910) referred to the forces that were generated by group interaction as "group contagion" and "group mind," recognizing that people in groups react differently than do individuals. McDougall (1920) extended the concept of the group mind. He noted the existence of groups as entities and pointed out a number of group-as-a-whole properties that could be studied as phenomena separate and distinct from properties affecting individuals working outside of a group.

The concept of a primary group was also an important contribution to the study of groups. Cooley (1909) defined a *primary group* as a small, informal group—such as a family or a friendship group—that has a tremendous influence on members' values, moral standards, and normative behaviors. The primary group, therefore, was viewed as essential in understanding socialization and development.

Few studies of small-group processes were published between 1905 and 1920, but activity in this area increased after World War I (Hare, 1976). Several experiments conducted during that time illustrated the powerful effects of group forces on the judgments and behavior of group members. Allport (1924), for example, found that the presence of others improved task performance, and Sherif (1936) and Asch (1952, 1955) found that members were highly influenced by the opinions of others in the group. For more about these and other studies of group influence, see Forsyth (2014) or go directly to the previously listed original sources.

After World War I, social scientists began to study groups operating in the community. One of the earliest social scientists to study groups in their natural environments was Frederick Thrasher (1927). He studied gangs of delinquents in the Chicago area by becoming friendly with gang members and observing the internal operations of gangs. He noted that every member of a gang had a status within the group that was attached to a functional role in the gang. Thrasher also drew attention to the culture that developed within a gang, suggesting there was a common code that all members followed. The code was enforced by group opinion, coercion, and physical punishment. Thrasher's work and the works of Shaw (1930) and Whyte (1943) have influenced how group work is practiced with youths in settlement houses, neighborhood centers, and youth organizations. The naturalistic studies of boys in camp settings by Newstetter, Feldstein, and Newcomb (1938) were also influential in the development of group work services.

Later, Sherif and colleagues (Sherif, 1956; Sherif & Sherif, 1953; Sherif, White, & Harvey, 1955) relied on naturalistic observations of boys in a summer camp program to demonstrate how cohesion and intergroup hostility develop in groups. Groups of boys became more cooperative when they spent time together and had common goals, such as winning a tug-of-war. They developed a liking for one another and felt solidarity with their teammates. At the same time, antagonism between groups increased. Bringing boys from different groups together only increased the tension until tasks were assigned that required the joint efforts of boys from different groups.

Social scientists also learned more about people's behavior in groups from studies done in industry and in the U.S. Army. Perhaps the most famous of all industrial studies is the classic series of studies at Western Electric's Hawthorne plant in Chicago (Roethlisberger, 1941; Roethlisberger & Dickson, 1939, 1975). These studies were designed to test whether piece-rate wage incentives increased the output of workers who assembled telephone equipment. The incentives were designed in such a way that wage increases gained by one team member would also benefit other team members. Management believed such a system would encourage individual productivity and increase group spirit and morale because all team members would benefit from the increase in productivity.

It was found that an informal group had developed among team members. Despite the opportunity to improve individual and group wages, workers did not produce more under the new incentive system. Results of the studies suggest that informal norms of what constituted a fair day's work governed the workers' behavior. Members of a work group that produced too much were ridiculed as "rate busters" and those who produced too little were called "chiselers." Occasionally, more severe sanctions called "binging" were applied by team members when a worker did not conform to the team's notion of a fair day's work. Binging consisted of striking a fellow worker as hard as possible on the upper arm while verbally asking the worker to comply with the group's norms.

Studies conducted on combat units during World War II also helped identify the powerful effects that small groups can have on the behavior of their members. For example, in describing the fighting ability of combat soldiers, Shils (1950) and Stouffer (1949) found that the courage of the average soldier was only partially sustained by hatred of the enemy and the patriotic ideas of a democratic society. Their studies revealed that soldiers' loyalty to their particular unit strengthened their morale and supported them during periods of intense combat stress.

During the 1950s, an explosion of knowledge about small groups took place. Earlier experiments by Bales (1950), Jennings (1947, 1950), Lewin, Lippitt, and White (1939), and Moreno (1934) spurred interest in the study of both task and treatment groups. Some of the most important findings from this period are summarized in the work of Cartwright and Zander (1968), Forsyth, (2014), Hare (1976), Kiesler (1978), McGrath (1984), Nixon (1979), and Shaw (1976). Because these studies are reflected in the models of group dynamics and leadership in Chapters 3 and 4, they are not presented in detail here.

The major themes of small-group research that were initially developed in the first half of the twentieth century—that is, cohesion, conformity, communication and interaction patterns, group development, leadership, and social cognition and perception—continue to dominate the research efforts of social scientists investigating the dynamics of small groups today (Forsyth, 2014; McGrath, Arrow, & Berdahl, 2000). However, new themes have also emerged. These include an increased emphasis on the effects of gender and diversity on group development (Forsyth, 2014, Yuli & Brewer, 2014). There has been a greater emphasis on research on teamwork (see, for example, Levi, 2014). There has also been an increased interest in the use of computer technology both for decision support systems (Forsyth, 2014), as well as to form virtual groups through telephone, video, and the Internet, for people who do not get together in person (Toseland, Naccarato, & Wray, 2007).

> **?** Assess your understanding of social science research by taking this brief quiz.

INFLUENTIAL THEORIES

From knowledge about small groups accumulated over the years in laboratory and natural settings, investigators of group phenomena began to develop comprehensive theories to explain group functioning. An enormous variety of these theories exist (Douglas, 1979). This chapter considers six of the most important theories: (1) systems theory, (2) psychodynamic theory, (3) learning theory, (4) field theory, (5) social exchange theory, and (6) constructivist, narrative, and empowerment theories. Although a thorough knowledge of systems theory is basic to all group work practice, the text also summarizes five other theories that have had an important influence on group work practice. As they become more experienced, group workers should consider learning more about each of these theories to enrich their practice with group members with different backgrounds and needs.

Assessment

Behavior: Apply knowledge of human behavior and the social environment, person-in-environment, and other multidisciplinary theoretical frameworks in the analysis of assessment data from clients and constituencies

Critical Thinking Question: A good deal of theory exists about how people act in groups. What are the main theories and how do they differ?

Systems Theory

Systems theory attempts to understand the group as a system of interacting elements. It is probably the most widely used and broadly applied theory of group functioning (Anderson, 1979; Olsen, 1968). Several influential theorists have developed conceptualizations of groups as social systems.

To Parsons (1951), groups are social systems with several interdependent members attempting to maintain order and a stable equilibrium while they function as a unified whole. Groups are constantly facing changing demands in their quest to attain goals and to maintain a stable equilibrium. Groups must mobilize their resources and act to meet changing demands if they are to survive. According to Parsons, Bales, and Shils (1953), there are four major functional tasks for systems such as a group: (1) integration—ensuring that members of groups fit together; (2) adaptation—ensuring that groups change to cope with the demands of their environment; (3) pattern maintenance—ensuring that groups define and sustain their basic purposes, identities, and procedures; and (4) goal attainment—ensuring that groups pursue and accomplish their tasks.

Groups must accomplish these four functional tasks to remain in equilibrium. The work of carrying out these tasks is left to the group's leader and its members. The leader and members act to help their group survive so they can be gratified as the group reaches its goal (Mills, 1967). To do this, group members observe and assess the group's progress toward its goals and take action to avoid problems. The likelihood that a group will survive depends on the demands of the environment, the extent to which members identify with group goals, and the degree to which members believe the goals are attainable. By overcoming obstacles and successfully handling the functional tasks confronting them, groups strive to remain in a state of equilibrium.

Robert Bales, another important systems theorist, has a somewhat different conception of groups as social systems. Whereas Parsons was interested in developing a generalizable systems model to explain societal as well as group functioning, Bales concentrated his efforts on observing and theorizing about small task groups in laboratory settings. According to Bales (1950), groups must solve two general types of problems to maintain themselves. These include (1) instrumental problems, such as the group reaching its goals, and (2) socio-emotional problems that include interpersonal difficulties, problems of coordination, and member satisfaction. Instrumental problems are caused by demands placed on the group by the outside environment; socio-emotional problems arise from within the group.

The implications of Bales' work is that the worker should be concerned about group processes and outcomes, that is, members' social and emotional needs and the task accomplishments expected of the group. Exclusive attention to tasks leads to dissatisfaction and conflict within the group. Exclusive attention to members' socio-emotional needs leads to the group's failure to accomplish its objectives and goals.

Because instrumental and socio-emotional needs often conflict, it is usually impossible to attend to both sets of problems simultaneously. Therefore, the worker is placed in the precarious position of attending alternately to task and socio-emotional needs to maintain a group's optimal functioning.

In contrast with Parsons, who emphasized harmony and equilibrium, Bales' systems model emphasizes tension and antagonism. Groups tend to vacillate between adaptation to the outside environment and attention to internal integration. Bales (1950) calls this the group's "dynamic equilibrium." Swings in attention are the result of the functional needs of the group in its struggle to maintain itself.

To study this "dynamic equilibrium," Bales observed interactions in several different kinds of task groups, such as juries and teams (Bales, 1950, 1954, 1955). Bales found that, to deal with instrumental problems, group members asked for or gave opinions, asked for or gave information, and asked for or made suggestions. To handle socio-emotional problems, group members expressed agreement or disagreement, showed tension or released tension, and showed solidarity or antagonism. Through these interactions, group members dealt with problems of communication, evaluation, control, decision-making, tension reduction, and integration.

Bales (1954, 1955) also suggests that groups go through a natural process of evolution and development. Analysis of the distribution of interactions in each category in problem-solving groups suggests that typical task groups emphasize giving and receiving information early in group meetings, giving and asking for opinions in the middle stage, and giving and asking for suggestions in later stages (Shepard, 1964).

Bales (1950) developed a scheme for analyzing group interaction on the basis of his theory about how group members deal with instrumental and expressive tasks. This scheme is called Interaction Process Analysis. It puts members' interactions into 12 categories. Bales, Cohen, and Williamson (1979) have continued to develop and refine this system of analyzing group interactions. The newer system, Systematic Multiple Level Observation of Groups (SYMLOG), is explained in Chapter 8.

The final conception of systems theory relevant to our understanding of group dynamics has been presented in Homans' (1950) early work, *The Human Group*. It is also evident in the writings of Germain and Gitterman (2008) on ecological systems theory. According to these writers, groups are in constant interaction with their environments. They occupy an ecological niche. Homans suggests that groups have an external system and an internal system. The external system represents a group's way of handling the adaptive problems that result from its relationship with its social and physical environment. The internal system consists of the patterns of activities, interactions, and norms occurring within the group as it attempts to function.

Like Bales, Homans notes that the relative dominance of the internal system or the external system depends on the demands of the external and the internal environment of the group. Homans, however, denies the homeostatic idea of equilibrium proposed by Parsons and Bales, preferring to conceive of groups as ever-changing entities. Change and the constant struggle for equilibrium are always present.

The different conceptualizations of systems theory may at first appear confusing. However, when one considers the vast array of groups in modern society and people's different experiences in them, it becomes easier to understand how different conceptualizations of systems theory have developed. It is important to recognize that each conceptualization represents a unique attempt to understand the processes that occur in all social systems.

Concepts derived from these differing views of systems theory that are particularly relevant for group workers include the following:

- The existence of properties of the group as a whole that arise from the interactions of individual group members
- The powerful effects of group forces on members' behavior
- The struggle of groups to maintain themselves as entities when confronted with conflicts
- The awareness that groups must relate to an external environment as well as attend to their internal functioning
- The idea that groups are in a constant state of becoming, developing, and changing that influences their equilibrium and continued existence
- The notion that groups have a developmental life cycle

Workers can use these concepts to facilitate the development of group processes that help treatment and task groups achieve their goals and help members satisfy their socio-emotional needs.

Psychodynamic Theory

Psychodynamic theory has had an important influence on group work practice. In his work *Group Psychology and the Analysis of the Ego,* Freud (1922) set forth his theoretical formulations about groups and their influence on human behavior. Many of Freud's other works have also influenced group work practice. For example, commonly used terms such as *insight, ego strength,* and *defense mechanisms* originated in Freud's work. Although psychodynamic theory focuses primarily on the individual, and Freud did not practice group psychotherapy, many of his followers have adapted psychodynamic theory for working with groups (Bion, 1991; Kauff, 2012; Klein, Bernard, & Singer, 2000; Kleinberg, 2012; Leszcz & Malat, 2012; Marmarosh, Dunton, & Amendola, 2014; Piper, Ogrodniczuk, & Duncan, 2002; Redl, 1942, 1944; Rutan, 1992; Rutan, Stone, & Shay, 2014; Yalom, 2005). Psychodynamic theory has also influenced the founders of other practice theories used in groups, such as Eric Berne's transactional analysis, Fritz Perl's gestalt therapy, and Jacob Moreno's psychodrama.

According to psychodynamic theory, group members act out in the group unresolved conflicts from early life experiences. In many ways, the group becomes a reenactment of the family situation. Freud (1922), for example, describes the group leader as the all-powerful father figure who reigns supreme over group members. Group members identify with the group leader as the "ego ideal" (Wyss, 1973). Members form transference reactions to the group leader and to each other because of their early life experiences. Thus, the interactions that occur in the group reflect personality structures and defense mechanisms that members began to develop early in life.

The group leader uses transference and countertransference reactions to help members work through unresolved conflicts by exploring past behavior patterns and linking these patterns to current behaviors. For example, the group leader might interpret the behavior of two group members who are struggling for the leader's attention as unresolved sibling rivalry. When interpretations made by the group worker are timed appropriately, members gain insight into their own behavior. According to psychodynamic theory, insight is the essential ingredient in modifying and changing behavior patterns inside and outside the group.

Conceptions of psychodynamic group treatment (Kleinberg, 2012; Yalom, 2005) have adapted and modified classical psychodynamic theory to include a greater emphasis on the here-and-now experiences of group interaction. Because of this emphasis, this application is often referred to in the literature as *interpersonal group therapy* (Leszcz, 1992; Leszcz & Malat, 2012). Emphasizing the here-and-now experiences of group members is useful in ensuring that members deal with issues of immediate concern to them. From an analysis of here-and-now behavior patterns in the microcosm of the group, the leader can help members reconstruct unresolved childhood conflicts and have "corrective emotional experiences" (Leszcz, 1992, p. 48). Through direct, mutual interpersonal communications, members build interpersonal skills, adaptive capacities, and ego strength, as well

Research-Informed Practice

Behavior: Use and translate research evidence to inform and improve practice, policy, and service delivery

Critical Thinking Question: Many theories support group work. What empirical evidence supports psychodynamic theory?

as gaining insight into their behavior. The cohesiveness of the group encourages members to reveal intimate details about their personal lives and to describe and act out their conflicts in a safe, supportive environment. Closely related to the interpersonal model of group work is the functional group model that focuses on integrative, inter-subjective, and relationship-based group-centered processes (Schermer & Rice, 2012; Schwartzberg & Barnes, 2012).

Psychodynamic theory has also been influential in furthering our understanding of how individuals behave in groups. Wilfred Bion, who was psychodynamically trained, developed the Tavistock approach to help people understand the primitive emotional processes that occur in groups. He suggested that group members often avoid the work of the group by reacting to the leader's authority with flight-fight responses and dependency (Bion, 1991).

A thorough discussion of psychodynamic theory of group functioning is beyond the scope of this book. For additional information about modern adaptations of psychodynamic theory to group work practice, see Kauff (2012), Kleinberg (2012), Leszcz and Malat (2012), Marmarosh, Dunton, and Amendola (2014), and Rutan, Stone, and Shay (2014).

Learning Theory

Perhaps no theory has stirred more controversy within social group work than learning theory. As with psychodynamic theory, the primary focus of learning theory is on the behavior of individuals rather than on the behavior of groups. Thus, learning theory has generally ignored the importance of group dynamics. In addition, like the early emphasis on primitive drives in psychodynamic theory, the early emphasis on environmental contingencies and the de-emphasis of free will has led some group workers to conclude that learning theory is deterministic. For these reasons, some view learning theory as antithetical to the values and traditions of growth, autonomy, and self-determination that are so much a part of the heritage of group work practice.

Despite the controversy, learning theory has had an important influence on current methods of group work practice. The emphasis on clear and specific goal setting, contracting, the influence of the environment on the group and its members, step-by-step treatment planning, measurable treatment outcomes, and evaluation can be traced, at least in part, to the influence of learning theory. The importance of short-term, structured psycho-educational groups attests to the important influence that learning theory principles have had on group work practice (Antony & Roemer, 2011; Burlingame, Strauss, & Joyce, 2013; Kalodner, Coughlin & Seide, 2014; Kazdin, 2013; LeCroy, 2008; Raczynski & Horne, 2014).

According to social learning theory (Bandura, 1977), the behavior of group members can be explained by one of three methods of learning. In the classical approach to learning theory, behavior becomes associated with a stimulus. For example, a worker responds by making a negative verbal comment each time a member turns and speaks to another member while the worker or other group members are speaking. After several times, the mere stimulus of the member's turning, without speaking, will be enough to cue the worker to respond with a negative verbal comment.

A second and more common method of learning is called operant conditioning. In this paradigm, the behaviors of the group members and the worker are governed by the consequences of their actions. Thus, if member A acts in a certain way and member B reacts positively, member A is likely to continue the behavior. Similarly, if a group worker receives negative feedback from group members about a particular behavior, the worker will be less likely to behave that way in the future (Antony & Roemer, 2011; Kazdin, 2013).

In the group, the worker might use praise to increase member-to-member communications and negative verbal comments to decrease member-to-leader communications. To help a member with a problem he or she has experienced in the outside environment, such as being overweight, the group leader might ask the member to develop a plan that specifies self-imposed rewards for behavior that decreases caloric intake and self-imposed sanctions for behavior that increases caloric intake.

Several writers (Feldman, Caplinger, & Wodarski, 1983; Feldman & Wodarski, 1975; Rose, 1989, 1998, 2004; Rose & Edleson, 1987) use operant learning theory principles in their approach to group work. For example, Rose (1989) suggests that tokens, praise, or other reinforcers can be used to increase desired behavior and decrease undesired behavior in the group or in the external environment. Groups that focus on themes, such as social skills training, assertiveness, relaxation, and parenting skills, also frequently rely heavily on learning theory principles.

Bandura (1977) has developed a third learning paradigm called social learning theory. If group members or group workers were to wait for classical or operant conditioning to occur, behavior in groups would be learned very slowly. Bandura proposed that most learning takes place through observation and vicarious reinforcement or punishment. For example, when a group member is praised for a certain behavior, that group member and other group members reproduce the behavior later, hoping to receive similar praise. When a group member who performs a certain behavior is ignored or punished by social sanctions, other group members learn not to behave in that manner because such behavior results in a negative outcome.

In response to concerns that learning theory has not taken into consideration motivations, expectations, and other cognitive aspects of behavior, Ellis (1992) and others have described cognitive-behavioral approaches to treatment (Beck, 2011; Leahy, 1996; Sheldon, 2011). Although learning theorists have not attempted to explain the functioning of groups as a whole, learning theory principles have been shown to be useful in helping members make desired changes. All group workers should be familiar with the basic principles of learning theory and cognitive behavior modification. Because of their particular relevance to treatment groups, some principles of classical, operant, social learning theory and cognitive-behavioral approaches are used in the discussion of specialized methods for leading treatment groups in Chapter 10.

Field Theory

Kurt Lewin, more than any other social scientist, has come to be associated with the study of group dynamics. He conducted numerous experiments on the forces that account for behavior in small groups. For example, in an early study investigating leadership, Lewin, Lippitt, and White (1939) created three types of groups: authoritarian, democratic, and laissez-faire leadership. The results of this study are reported in Chapter 4. Lewin and his colleagues were the first to apply the scientific method in developing a theory of groups.

In 1944, he and his colleagues set up laboratories and formed the Research Center for Group Dynamics at the Massachusetts Institute of Technology.

The unique contribution of field theory is that it views the group as a *gestalt*, that is, an evolving entity of opposing forces that act to hold members in the group and to move the group along in its quest for goal achievement. According to Lewin (1947), groups are constantly changing to cope with their social situation, although there are times in which a "quasi-stationary equilibrium" exists for all groups. In all cases, however, the behavior of individual group members and the group itself must be seen as a function of the total situation (Lewin, 1946).

In developing field theory, Lewin introduced several concepts to aid in understanding the forces at work in a group. Among these are (1) roles, which refer to the status, rights, and duties of group members; (2) norms, which are rules governing the behavior of group members; (3) power, which is the ability of members to influence one another; (4) cohesion, which is the amount of attraction the members of the group feel for one another and for the group; (5) consensus, which is the degree of agreement regarding goals and other group phenomena; and (6) valence, which is the potency of goals and objects in the life space of the group.

Lewin sought to understand the forces occurring in the group as a whole from the perspective of individual group members. He did this mathematically and topographically, using vectors to describe group forces. Emphasizing the importance of properties of the group that act on the individual member, most field theorists have focused their research efforts on *cohesion,* which they define as the totality of forces acting on individual members to keep them in the group. Studies by field theorists have shown that cohesion is related to agreement on goals and norms, shared understanding, and similar demographic backgrounds of members, as well as to productivity, satisfaction, and cooperative interaction patterns (Cartwright, 1951; Cartwright & Zander, 1968; Lippitt, 1957).

Along with his interest in formulating a theoretical model of group dynamics, Lewin was interested in the effect of groups on individuals' psychological makeup. He developed the t-group as a way to observe the effects of group processes on group members and as a means to help individual group members change their own behavior. Although he was not directly involved, he helped found the first National Training Laboratory in Group Development in 1947. Since then, t-groups have been used extensively at the National Training Laboratories as an experiential means to train group facilitators, to teach individuals about the effects of group dynamics, and to help individuals examine and change their own behavior.

Relying on a principle in Lewin's field theory that suggests individuals will not change their own behavior unless they see their behavior and their attitudes as others see them, the t-group experience attempts to provide participants with extensive feedback about their own behavior. Members are confronted with the effects of their behavior on other group members and on the group's facilitator. Role plays, simulations, and other experiential program activities are often used to illustrate how group processes develop and how they affect members.

Lewin (1951) is considered the founder of the action research approach to practice and evaluation described in Chapter 14 (Lawson, Caringi, Pyles, Jurkowski, & Bozlak, 2015). Lewin believed that the most effective way to understand a phenomenon was to try to change it in naturally occurring contexts. Action research is a practice and a research method that engages community residents as partners in the process of developing programs to meet their needs. The action research process is cyclical, so that participants engage in an iterative process of trying out new ways of doing things in community settings, collecting data about the effects, and then going back and making changes in programming based on the data collected. In this way, people affected by problems are treated with dignity and respect by being invited to participate fully in the design and intervention team. They are also encouraged to become fully involved in the implementation of interventions to address their concerns and needs. As the cyclical process continues, information and feedback about the new methods and programs are collected, and adjustments are made based on the feedback of all who are involved (Lawson, et al., 2015). Thus, Lewin's scholarship many decades ago is still quite relevant to current day social work practice and research.

Social Exchange Theory

Although field theory emphasizes the group as a whole, social exchange theory focuses on the behavior of individual group members. Blau (1964), Homans (1961), and Thibaut and Kelley (1959) are the principal developers of this approach to groups. Deriving their theory from animal psychology, economic analysis, and game theory, social exchange theorists suggest that when people interact in groups, each attempts to behave in a way that will maximize rewards and minimize punishments. Group members initiate interactions because the social exchanges provide them with something of value, such as approval. According to social exchange theorists, because ordinarily nothing is gained unless something is given in return, there is an exchange implied in all human relationships.

In social exchange theory, group behavior is analyzed by observing how individual members seek rewards while dealing with the sustained social interaction occurring in a group. For an individual in a group, the decision to express a given behavior is based on a comparison of the rewards and punishments that are expected to be derived from the behavior. Group members act to increase positive consequences and decrease negative consequences. Social exchange theory also focuses on the way members influence one another during social interactions. The result of any social exchange is based on the amount of social power and the amount of social dependence in a particular interaction.

Guided Group Interaction (Empey & Erikson, 1972; McCorkle, Elias, & Bixby, 1958) and Positive Peer Culture (Vorrath & Brendtro, 1985) are two specialized group work methods that rely heavily on principles from social exchange theory. They are frequently used with delinquent adolescents in residential and institutional settings. In both approaches, structured groups are used to confront, challenge, and eliminate antisocial peer-group norms and to replace them with prosocial norms through guided peer-group interaction.

Social exchange theory has been criticized as being mechanistic because it assumes people are always rational beings who act according to their analysis of rewards and punishments (Shepard, 1964). For the most part, these criticisms are unfounded. Social exchange theorists are aware that cognitive processes affect how people behave in groups (Keller & Dansereau, 1995; Knottnerus, 1994). Group members' perceptions of rewards and punishments are influenced by cognitive processes, such as intentions and expectations. Thus, the work of social exchange theorists in psychology and of symbolic interaction theorists in sociology has helped to account for the role of cognitive processes in the behavior of individuals in groups and other social interactions. The influence of symbolic interaction theory and social exchange theory on social work practice with groups can be seen in the work of Balgopal and Vassil (1983) and Early (1992).

Constructivist, Empowerment, and Narrative Theories

Constructivist and narrative theories focus on how group members create and maintain their realities through life stories and subjective experiences. Empowerment is intricately related to narrative and constructivist theories because by understanding their own life stories, group members can be empowered to take on new ways of being and behaving (Western, 2013). Instead of focusing on problems and deficits, empowerment and strengths-based approaches focus on the positive aspects of members' coping skills and their resiliency in the face of difficult and often hostile social environments. We place these theories together in one category because they are based on the premise that humans attach unique meanings to life experiences based on their social experiences and dialogue with the world around them (Granvold, 2008).

Constructivist and narrative theories suggest that through language and experience, group members construct life stories or personal narratives. For members of treatment groups, these are often problem-filled stories (Walsh, 2013). The stories created shape members' lives and have a profound effect on their self-concept and self-esteem. Constructivists believe that members' self-conceptions are imbedded in the way they are socialized and experience life and that meaning is created out of these experiences in conjunction with biological and temperamental qualities (Granvold, 2008).

These theories place a great deal of emphasis on understanding group members' unique, subjective realities. This is basic to the long-held social work practice of "starting where the client is." Once these realities are understood, the transformational and interactional leadership approaches discussed in Chapter 4 can be used to reframe stories, to empower members, and to bring out their strengths, resiliencies, and capacities. Members can then be helped by the leader and other group members to create new life stories, viewing their oppressive and negative life stories with more positive frames of reference that build on the opportunities, capacities, and strengths available to them. The worker helps members view how they might be vulnerable to narratives of diminished status from oppression, such as sexism, homophobia, and racism. Other techniques that are described in this book that fit with narrative therapy are journaling, letter writing, mutual aid, visualization, cognitive imagery, and mindfulness mediation. When these are done in groups, members help empower each other and reframe each other's life stories particularly working on the way members used strengths and resiliency to go on living after surviving trauma.

Constructionist and narrative theories are newer approaches to group work practice than are the other theories already mentioned in this text. They are compatible with empowerment and strengths-based approaches to social group work because they are based on helping members to overcome restrictive life narratives and social constructions of reality that not only are negative, but keep members oppressed and in low-status positions. By telling their stories verbally, keeping diaries, and journaling, members are helped to understand adverse childhood and adult experiences as products of an unsupportive environment rather than as personal limitations and flaws. Ventilation, affirmation, and support help members gain new perspectives on their experiences, especially the damage done to their self-esteem. Then, members are empowered to help each other to get in touch with their resiliency and ways to overcome marginalization and oppression.

There is some research-based evidence for the theories, so in our view they are not antithetical to the evidence-based approach used in this text (see Buckman, Kinney, & Reese, 2008; Walsh, 2013). Although the theories do not view quantitative empirical methods in a favorable light, they rely on qualitative approaches (Buckman, Kinney, & Reese, 2008). For example, Teaching Empowerment through Active Means (TEAM) is a research-based group program that helps members build stories of competency and resiliency (Redivo & Buckman, 2004).

The notion of liberating members from externally imposed constraints, helping those who are oppressed to come to terms with socially imposed restrictions, and reframing and redefining their lives through empowerment and strengths-based approaches, these approaches are in keeping with the objectives of this text and the history of social group work. Although Acceptance and Commitment Therapy (ACT) and dialectical behavior therapy (DBT) are based on cognitive behavior theory (learning theory), they borrow some strategies from these perspectives as well. We will learn more about ACT and DBT in Chapter 10.

There are also some limitations to these approaches for social group work because they tend to avoid attempts to universalize experiences, emphasizing instead the unique stories and socially constructed realities of members. In addition, the externalization of problems as socially constructed may not be helpful for mandated and acting-out group members who have violated social norms and conventions and are at risk of reoffending (Walsh, 2013). At the same time, narrative, constructivist, and empowerment approaches are particularly helpful for survivors of incest, sexual abuse, and other types of adverse childhood and adult experiences leading to trauma. They also work well with identity issues and prejudice faced by lesbian, gay, bisexual, and transgendered members, those with low self-esteem and denigrated self-concepts, and those with mental and physical disabilities who view themselves as outsiders who carry destructive labels that keep them in oppressed roles and out of touch with their strengths and resiliency.

 Assess your understanding of influential theories by taking this brief quiz.

SUMMARY

This chapter describes historical developments in the practice of group work and in the social sciences. A historical perspective is presented to help workers develop a broad understanding of the uses of groups in practice settings and develop a knowledge base they can use to practice effectively with different types of groups.

The historical overview of group work practice presented in this chapter suggests that throughout the twentieth century, groups were used for a variety of purposes, such as education, recreation, socialization, support, and therapy. The early emphasis on the use of groups for education, recreation, and socialization has waned in recent years in favor of an increased interest in the use of groups for support, mutual aid, and therapy. This trend parallels the gradual transition during the 1930s and 1940s away from group work's amorphous roots in adult education, recreation, and social work to its formal incorporation into the social work profession during the 1950s.

Currently, social group work is being revitalized in schools of social work and in practice settings. As current trends indicate, in recent years there has also been an increased recognition of the roots of social group work and the multiple purposes group work can serve.

This chapter also briefly explores historical developments in social science research that have relevance for understanding group processes. Findings from these studies emphasize the powerful influence that the group as a whole has on individual group members. The chapter closes with a review of six theories: (1) systems theory, (2) psychodynamic theory, (3) learning theory, (4) field theory, (5) social exchange theory, and (6) narrative and constructivist theories, all of which have had an important influence on group work practice.

3

Understanding Group Dynamics

The forces that result from the interactions of group members are often referred to as *group dynamics*. Because group dynamics influence the behavior of both individual group members and the group as a whole, they have been of considerable interest to group workers for many years (Coyle, 1930, 1937; Elliott, 1928).

A thorough understanding of group dynamics is useful for practicing effectively with any type of group. Although many theories have been developed to conceptualize group functioning, fundamental to all of them is an understanding of groups as social systems. A system is made up of elements and their interactions. As social systems, therefore, task and treatment groups can be conceptualized as individuals in interaction with each other. Groups are more than the sum of their parts (Forsyth, 2014). Group dynamic processes arise out of the interaction of the individual members of the group.

THE DEVELOPMENT OF HELPFUL GROUP DYNAMICS

One of group workers' most important tasks is to guide the development of dynamics that promote the satisfaction of members' socio-emotional needs while facilitating the accomplishment of group tasks. Some years ago, Northen (1969) reminded group workers that this is not an automatic process.

Inattention to group dynamics can have a negative effect on the meeting of members' socio-emotional needs and on goal attainment. Groups can unleash both harmful and helpful forces. The Hitler youth movement of the 1920s and 1930s, the Ku Klux Klan, the religious groups in Jonestown and at the Branch Davidians' ranch in Waco, Texas, and other harmful cults are familiar examples of group dynamics gone awry. Studies over the past 30 years have clearly shown that harmful group dynamics can be very traumatic for group members, with some emotional effects lasting years after the group experience (Galinsky & Schopler, 1977; Lieberman, Yalom, & Miles,

1973; Smokowski, Rose, & Bacallao, 2001; Smokowski, Rose, Todar, & Reardon, 1999). Two extremes of group leadership, aggressive confrontation and extreme passivity, seem to have particularly pernicious effects on members (Smokowski, Rose, & Bacallao, 2001; Smokowski et al., 1999). In contrast, appropriate development of group dynamics can lead to positive outcomes for the group and its members (Forsyth, 2014).

This chapter's purposes are to help (1) group workers recognize and understand the dynamics generated through group processes in all types of treatment and task groups, (2) workers establish and promote group dynamics that satisfy members' socio-emotional needs, and (3) groups to achieve goals consistent with the humanistic value base of the social work profession. Some strategies for doing this follow.

Strategies for Promoting Helpful Group Dynamics
- Identify group dynamics as they emerge during ongoing group interaction
- Assess the impact of group dynamics on group members and the group as a whole
- Assess the impact of current group dynamics on future group functioning
  - Examine the impact of group dynamics on members with different backgrounds
  - Facilitate and guide the development of group dynamics that lead to members' satisfaction with their participation and that enable members and whole groups to achieve their goals

> **?** Assess your understanding of the development of helpful group dynamics by taking this brief quiz.

GROUP DYNAMICS

In this text, four dimensions of group dynamics are of particular importance to group workers in understanding and working effectively with all types of task and treatment groups:

1. Communication and interaction patterns
2. Cohesion
3. Social integration and influence
4. Group culture

In-depth knowledge of group dynamics is essential for understanding the social structure of groups and for developing beginning-level skills in group work practice.

Communication and Interaction Patterns

According to Northen (1969), "social interaction is a term for the dynamic interplay of forces in which contact between persons results in a modification of the behavior and attitudes of the participants" (p. 17). Verbal and nonverbal communications are the components of social interaction. Communication is the process by which people convey meanings to each other by using symbols. Communication entails (1) the encoding of a person's perceptions, thoughts, and feelings into language and other symbols, (2) the transmission of these symbols or language, and (3) the decoding of the transmission by another person. This process is shown in Figure 3.1. As members of a group communicate to one another, a reciprocal pattern of interaction emerges. The interaction patterns that develop can be beneficial or harmful to the group. A group worker who is knowledgeable about helpful

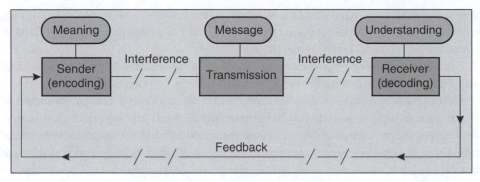

Figure 3.1
A Model of the Process of Communication

communications and interactions can intervene in the patterns that are established to help the group achieve desired goals and to ensure the socio-emotional satisfaction of members.

Communication can be verbal, nonverbal, or written. Whereas members of face-to-face groups experience verbal and nonverbal communications, members of telephone groups experience only verbal communications, and members of computer groups experience only written messages. Communication can also be synchronous, that is, back and forth in real time, or asynchronous, that is, not within the same period. Asynchronous communications occur in computer groups where members may respond to messages after they are posted on bulletin boards or in chat rooms.

Communication as a Process

The first step in understanding and intervening in interaction patterns is for the worker to be aware that, whenever people are together in face-to-face groups, they are communicating. Even if they are not communicating verbally, they are communicating nonverbally, their behaviors sending intended and unintended messages.

As shown in Figure 3.1, all communications are intended to convey a message. Silence, for example, can communicate sorrow, thoughtfulness, anger, or lack of interest. In addition, every group member communicates not only to transmit information but also for many other reasons. Kiesler (1978) has suggested that people communicate with such interpersonal concerns as (1) understanding other people, (2) finding out where they stand in relation to other people, (3) persuading others, (4) gaining or maintaining power, (5) defending themselves, (6) provoking a reaction from others, (7) making an impression on others, (8) gaining or maintaining relationships, and (9) presenting a unified image to the group. Many other important reasons for communication could be added to this list. For example, Barker and colleagues (2000) highlight the importance of relational aspects of communication, such as cooperation, connection, autonomy, similarity, flexibility, harmony, and stigmatization.

Workers who are aware that group members communicate for many reasons can observe, assess, and understand communication and interaction patterns. Because patterns of communication are often consistent across different situations, group workers can use this information to work with individual members and the group as a whole. For example, a worker observes that one member is consistently unassertive in the group. The worker might help the member practice responding assertively to situations in the group. Because the pattern of a lack of assertiveness is likely to occur in situations outside the group, the worker suggests that the member consider practicing the skills in situations encountered between meetings.

In addition to meanings transmitted in every communication, the worker should also be aware that messages are often received selectively. *Selective perception* refers to the screening of messages so they are congruent with one's belief system. As shown in Figure 3.1, messages are decoded and their meanings are received. Individual group members have a unique understanding of communications because of their selective perception. Selected screening sometimes results in the blocking of messages so that they are not decoded and received. Napier and Gershenfeld (1993) suggest that the perception of a communication can be influenced by (1) life positions that result from experiences in early childhood, (2) stereotypes, (3) the status and position of the communicator, (4) previous experiences, and (5) assumptions and values. Thus, what might appear to a naive observer as a simple, straightforward, and objective social interaction might have considerable hidden meaning for both the sender and the receiver.

Case Example: Selective Perception in a Parenting Group

In a parenting group, one member began to talk about the differences between her son and her daughter. The member mentioned that her daughter was much more difficult for her to handle than her son. Another member of the group said in an angry voice, "You just never think your daughter can do anything good." The group became silent and the original member said that even though her daughter was difficult it was not true that she "could never do anything right." The worker asked the other members about their reactions to the interaction but no one volunteered. The worker then asked the second member to talk about her own relationship with her mother and her daughter. As the member talked, it became clear that she had a lot of resentment about the way her mother had treated her as a child, and now as an adult, she had compensated for that in her interactions with her own daughter. The worker then asked the member if the way she perceived the first member's interaction with her daughter could have anything to do with how she was treated by her own mother. Before the member could answer, other members of the group began to talk about how they were treated by their own parents and how it made them especially sensitive to the way they interacted with their own children. Later, in the same session, the member who had gotten angry said to the member that she had confronted that she apologized if she had overreacted. The member who had been confronted said that she had learned a lot from the discussion and was going to think of some new ways that she could interact with her daughter when her daughter "pushed her buttons." This led to a discussion of the things that triggered members to act in angry ways toward their children and what they might do differently to avoid getting angry.

It is not possible, or even desirable, for workers to analyze each interpersonal communication that occurs in a group. However, with a little practice, workers can develop a "third ear," that is, become aware of the meanings behind messages and their effect on a particular group member and on the group as a whole. Group workers are in a much better position to intervene in the group when they have a full understanding of the meanings of the messages being communicated and received by each member.

It is particularly important for the worker to pay attention to the nonverbal messages that are communicated by members. Body language, gestures, and facial expressions can provide important clues about how members are reacting to verbal communications. Members may not want to verbalize negative feelings, or they may just not know how to express their feelings. When workers are attuned to nonverbal messages, they can verbalize the feelings conveyed in them. This, in turn, may encourage members to talk about issues that they were previously only able to express nonverbally. For example, without identifying particular members who may be uncomfortable being associated with a particular sentiment, the worker might say, "I noticed some tension in the group when we began to talk about. . . . I am wondering if anyone would like to share their feelings about this." Similarly, the worker might say, "I thought I noticed a little boredom when we began talking about. . . . Has that topic been exhausted? Would you like to move on to the other issues we were going to discuss?"

Communications can also be distorted in transmission. In Figure 3.1, distortion is represented as interference. Among the most common transmission problems are language barriers. In the United States, workers frequently conduct groups with members from different cultural backgrounds and for whom English is a second language. In addition to problems of understanding accents and dialects, the meanings of many words are culturally defined and may not be interpreted as the communicator intended. Special care must be taken in these situations to avoid distorting the meanings intended by the communicator.

Noise and other distortions inside or outside the meeting room can interfere with effective communication. Similarly, hearing or eyesight problems can create difficulties in receiving messages. For example, approximately 10 percent of adults are visually impaired (American Foundation for the Blind, n.d.) and approximately 20 percent report at least some hearing impairment (Hearing Loss Association of America, n.d.). Thus, when working with groups, the practitioner should be alert to physical problems that may impair communication. Some strategies for working with members with visual impairments and hearing impairments are presented in Tables 3.1 and 3.2.

Diversity and Difference in Practice

Behavior: Apply and communicate understanding of the importance of diversity and difference in shaping life experiences in practice at the micro, mezzo, and macro levels

Critical Thinking Question: Members bring their communication styles to the group, and their styles are also affected by the nature of the group. How can the leader support and promote effective communications among members with different styles?

Table 3.1 Techniques for Communicating with Group Members Who Have Hearing Impairments

1. Position yourself so you are in full view of the person and your face is illuminated.
2. Speak in a normal voice.
3. Speak slowly and clearly. Stress key words. Pause between sentences.
4. Make sure no one else is talking when a group member is speaking to a hearing-impaired person or when a hearing-impaired person is speaking to a group member.
5. Make sure the room is free of background noises and has good acoustics.
6. Look for cues, such as facial expressions or inappropriate responses, that indicate the individual has misunderstood.
7. If you suspect that the individual has misunderstood, restate what has been said.
8. Speak *to* the individual, not *about* the person.

Table 3.2   Techniques for Communicating with Group Members Who Have Visual Impairments

1. Ask the individual whether assistance is needed to get to the meeting room. If the reply is yes, offer your elbow. Walk a half step ahead so your body indicates a change in direction, when to stop, and so forth.

2. Introduce yourself and all group members when the meeting begins. Go around the group clockwise or counterclockwise. This will help the group member learn where each member is located.

3. When you accompany a visually impaired person into a new meeting room, describe the layout of the room, the furniture placement, and any obstacles. This will help orient the individual.

4. Try not to disturb the placement of objects in the meeting room. If this is unavoidable, be sure to inform the person about the changes. Similarly, let the individual know if someone leaves or enters the room.

5. When guiding visually impaired individuals to their seat, place their hand on the back of the chair and allow them to seat themselves.

6. Speak directly to the visually impaired person, not through an intermediary.

7. Look at the individual when you speak.

8. Don't be afraid to use words such as *look* and *see*.

9. Speak in a normal voice. Do not shout.

10. Visually impaired people value independence just as sighted people do. Do not be overprotective.

11. Give explicit instructions about the location of coffee or snacks during program activities. For example, state, "The coffee pot is 10 feet to the left of your chair," rather than "The coffee pot is right over there on your left."

Messages also are simplified by the receiver for easier memory storage. Complex messages are made shorter and more concise by the listener. The receiver sharpens some parts of messages and ignores others for parsimony and perceived relevancy and saliency. Thus, messages sent from one member to others are affected by how they are communicated, how they are distorted in transmission, and how they are received. Although meaning is communicated in every verbal and nonverbal message, it is important for workers to be aware that problems in the sending, transmission, or receiving of messages can distort or obfuscate intended meanings.

Even when messages are clear, language barriers and cultural interpretations of the meaning conveyed in a message may mean that it is not received as intended (Anderson & Carter, 2003). This can be a particularly vexing problem for members from bilingual backgrounds for whom English is a second language (Sue & Sue, 2013). It has been pointed out, for example, that white Americans have a significantly higher rate of verbal participation in groups than Asian Americans, Native Americans, and Mexican Americans of similar educational background (Gray-Little & Kaplan, 2000). Because higher rates of verbal participation in groups are associated with reduced attrition and other therapeutic benefits, lower levels of participation by minority members of multicultural groups is troubling (Gray-Little & Kaplan, 2000). Therefore, care should be taken to ensure that all members feel comfortable contributing to the group discussion. Workers can help by ensuring that all members, including those who are marginalized and oppressed by society, have many opportunities to speak. The worker can point out and sharpen messages so that all members' points of view are carefully considered by the group.

To prevent distortions in communications from causing misunderstandings and conflict, it is also important that members receive feedback about their communications so that the true meaning of messages can be clarified. Feedback is a way of checking that the meanings of the communicated messages are understood correctly. For feedback to be used appropriately, it should (1) describe the content of the communication or the behavior as it is perceived by the group member, (2) be given to the member who sent the message as soon as the message is received, and (3) be expressed in a tentative manner so that those who send messages understand that the feedback is designed to check for distortions rather than to confront or attack them.

Examples of feedback are, "John, I understood you to say . . ." or "Mary, if I understand you correctly, you are saying. . . ." Feedback and clarification can help to prevent communications from being interpreted in unintended ways. Feedback can also help members who were not paying attention for various reasons to get back into the communication processes and reconnect as contributing participants. For example, workers who observe members of trauma recovery groups' loss of focus can tentatively point out the possible loss and invite members to refocus. There is no need to speculate about the reason for the lack of focus, unless members bring up issues like dissociation that might be beneficial for all members of a trauma recovery group to explore.

Interaction Patterns

In addition to becoming aware of communication processes, the worker must also consider patterns of interaction that develop in a group.

Patterns of Group Interaction

- Maypole—when the leader is the central figure and communication occurs from the leader to the member and from the member to the leader
- Round robin—when members take turns talking
- Hot seat—when there is an extended back-and-forth between the leader and one member as the other members watch
- Free floating—when all members take responsibility for communicating, taking into consideration their ability to contribute meaningfully to the particular topic

The first three patterns are leader-centered because the leader structures them. The fourth pattern is group-centered because it emerges from the initiative of group members. The four patterns provide convenient and parsimonious ways to describe the overall communications taking place in groups.

In most situations, workers should strive to facilitate group-centered rather than leader-centered interaction patterns. In group-centered patterns, members freely interact with each other. Communication channels between members of the group are open. In leader-centered patterns, communications are directed from members to the worker or from the worker to group members, thereby reducing members' opportunities to communicate freely with each other.

Group-centered communication patterns tend to increase social interaction, group morale, members' commitment to group goals, and innovative decision-making (Carletta, Garrod, & Fraser-Krauss, 1998). However, such patterns can be less efficient than leader-centered patterns because certain communications may be superfluous or extraneous to group tasks (Shaw, 1964), and sorting out useful communications can take too much group time. Therefore, in task groups that are making routine decisions, when time constraints are important and there is little need for creative problem solving, the worker may deliberately choose to encourage leader-centered rather than group-centered interaction patterns.

Leader-centered patterns may also be useful at times in psycho-educational groups, but workers should always take care not to present too much information without interaction or applied learning experiences. For example, in support groups for family members of people with serious and persistent mental health problems, the worker may want to provide information about housing or care management resources. During such a presentation, the worker should invite members to talk about their experiences and thoughts about using these types of services and resources.

To establish and maintain appropriate interaction patterns, the worker should be familiar with the factors that can change communication patterns, such as:

- cues and the reinforcement that members receive for specific interactional exchanges
- the emotional bonds that develop between group members
- the subgroups that develop in the group
- the size and physical arrangements of the group
- the power and status relationships in the group

Workers can change interaction patterns by modifying these important factors.

Cues and Reinforcers. Cues, such as words or gestures, can act as signals to group members to talk more or less frequently to one another or to the worker. Workers and members can also use selective attention and other reinforcements to encourage beneficial interactions. For example, praise and other supportive comments, eye contact, and smiles tend to elicit more communication, whereas inattention tends to elicit less communication. So that all members may have a chance to participate fully in the life of a group, workers may want to reduce communication from particularly talkative members or encourage reserved members to talk more. Often, pointing out interaction patterns is all that is needed to change them. At other times, verbal and nonverbal cues may be needed.

Sometimes, even more action is needed. For example, reserved members may benefit from group go-rounds when they are provided an opportunity to speak when it is their turn. Similarly, directing communication to others may help to reduce the amount of time dominant group members talk. When these strategies do not work, other strategies may be used with the permission of members. For example, to ensure that a dominant member does not monopolize all the group time, the worker may seek permission to interrupt any member who talks for more than two or three minutes and to redirect the communication to other members. This can be done with the understanding of giving all members a chance to participate. The worker can say things like, "Your thoughts are important, but other members need time to share their thoughts as well. If it is okay with you, I would like to find out who else has something they would like to talk about," or "That's a good thought, but you have been talking for a while. Can you hold that thought for later and let someone else have a turn to share their thoughts now?" When this is done consistently by the worker, it is often sufficient to reduce the dominance of a single member.

Emotional Bonds. Positive emotional bonds, such as interpersonal liking and attraction, increase interpersonal interaction, and negative emotional bonds reduce solidarity between members and result in decreased interpersonal interaction. Attraction and interpersonal liking between two members may occur because they share common interests, similar values and ideologies, complementary personality characteristics, or similar demographic characteristics (Hare et al., 1995).

Hartford (1971) calls alignments based on emotional bonds *interest alliances*. For example, two members of a planning council might vote the same way on certain issues, and they may communicate similar thoughts and feelings to other members of the council because of their common interests in the needs of the business community. Similarly, members of a minority group might form an interest alliance based on similar concerns about the lack of community services for minority groups.

Subgroups. Subgroups also affect the interaction patterns in a group (Forsyth, 2014). Subgroups form from the emotional bonds and interest alliances among subsets of group members. They occur naturally in all groups. They help make the group attractive to its members because individuals look forward to interacting with those to whom they are particularly close. The practitioner should not view subgroups as a threat to the integrity of the group unless the attraction of members within a subgroup becomes greater than their attraction to the group as a whole.

There are a variety of subgroup types, including the dyad, triad, and clique. In addition, there are isolates, who do not interact with the group, and scapegoats, who receive negative attention and criticism from the group. More information about these roles, and other roles, is presented in Chapter 8.

In some situations, the worker may actively encourage members to form subgroups, particularly in groups that are too large and cumbersome for detailed work to be accomplished. For example, subgroup formation is often useful in large committees, delegate councils, and teams because they lead to more effective meetings of the whole group (Tropman, 2014). Members are assigned to a particular subgroup to work on a specific task or subtask. The results of the subgroup's work are then brought back to the larger group for consideration and action.

Regardless of whether the worker actively encourages members to form subgroups, they occur naturally because not everyone in a group interacts with equal valence. The formation of intense subgroup attraction, however, can be a problem in some cases. Subgroup members may challenge the worker's authority. They may substitute their own goals and methods of attaining them for the goals of the larger group. They can disrupt the group by communicating among themselves while others are speaking. Subgroup members may fail to listen to members who are not a part of the subgroup. These types of subgroups can negatively affect the performance of the whole group (Forsyth, 2014).

When intense subgroup attraction appears to be interfering with the group as a whole, a number of steps can be taken to better integrate members into the life of the whole group.

Strategies for Addressing Intense Subgroup Attraction
- Examine whether the group as a whole is sufficiently attractive to members
- Promote the development of norms that emphasize the importance of members' listening to and respecting each other
- Promote the development of norms restricting communication to one member at a time
- Change seating arrangements
- Ask certain members to interact more frequently with other members
- Use program materials and exercises that separate subgroup members
- Assign tasks for members to do outside of the group in subgroups composed of different members

If intense subgroup loyalties persist, it can be helpful to facilitate a discussion of the reasons for them and their effect on the group as a whole. A frank discussion of the reasons for subgroup formation can often benefit the entire group because it can reveal problems in the group's communication patterns and in its goal-setting and decision-making processes. After the discussion, the worker should try to increase the attraction of the group for its members and help them reach out to one another to reopen channels of communication.

In some cases, the worker may wish to use subgroups for therapeutic purposes. For example, Yalom (2005) suggests that the worker can use relationships between members to recapitulate the family group experience. Transference and countertransference reactions among members may be interpreted to help members gain insight into the impact of their early development on their current way of relating to others in the group and their broader social environment. Such here-and-now interventions are hallmarks of modern psychodynamic theoretical approaches to group work briefly described in the previous chapter. For more about interpersonal, relational, and integrative psychodynamic approaches to therapy groups see Kleinberg (2012), Yalom (2005), or some of the other sources of information mentioned in the psychodynamic section of the previous chapter. Because these approaches are specialized, group workers will need additional education and training. They will also need assessment and critical thinking skills to identify for whom this approach might be helpful.

Size and Physical Arrangements. Other factors that influence interaction patterns are the size and physical arrangement of the group. As the size of the group increases, the possibilities for potential relationships increase exponentially. For example, with three people, there are six potential combinations of relationships, but in a group with seven people, there are 966 possible combinations of relationships. Thus, as groups grow larger, each member has more social relationships to be aware of and to maintain, but less opportunity to maintain them.

With increased group size, there are also fewer opportunities and less time for members to communicate. In some groups, the lack of opportunity to participate might not be much of a problem. Members who are not actively participating may be actively listening and engaged in the group process. It is the worker's responsibility to assess whether all members are actively engaged in the group and to consider how to intervene when members appear not to be engaged.

Some group members welcome a chance for active involvement but speak only when they have an important contribution that might otherwise be overlooked. For these members, non-intervention may be the best worker option. For others, however, a reduced chance to participate leads to dissatisfaction and a lack of commitment to decisions made by the group. In these situations, workers should consider breaking large groups into smaller subgroups of members working together and then reporting the results of their work back to the larger group.

The physical arrangement of group members also influences interaction patterns. For example, members who sit in circles have an easier time communicating with each other than do members who sit in rows. Even members' positions within a circular pattern influence interaction patterns. Members who sit across from each other, for example, have an easier time communicating than do members on the same side of a circle who are separated by one or two members.

Because circular seating arrangements promote face-to-face interaction and are one sign of equality of status and participation, they are often preferred to other arrangements. There may be times, however, when the group leader or members prefer a different arrangement. For example, the leader of a task group may wish to sit at the head of a rectangular table to convey his or her status or power. The leader may also wish to seat a particularly important member in proximity. In an educational group, a leader may choose to stand before a group seated in rows, an arrangement that facilitates members' communications with the leader and tends to minimize interactions among members of the group.

Physical arrangements can also be used to help assess relationships among members and potential problems in group interaction. For example, members who are fond of each other often sit next to each other and as far away as possible from members who they do not like. Similarly, members who pull chairs out from a circle, or sit behind other members, may be expressing their lack of investment in the group. Effective group workers pay attention to the symbolism that is expressed by different seating arrangements.

An interesting physical arrangement that often occurs in groups results from members' tendency to sit in the same seat from meeting to meeting. This physical arrangement persists because members feel secure in "their own" seat near familiar members. To maintain and enhance comfort, security, and trust, these seating arrangements should not be modified by workers unless they are trying deliberately to change interaction patterns or other group dynamics. Thus, by monitoring physical arrangements, and intervening when necessary, the worker can improve both the socio-emotional climate and the ability of the group to accomplish its goals.

Power and Status. Two other factors affecting communication and interaction patterns are the relative power and status of the group members. Initially, members are accorded power and status because of their position and prestige in the community, their physical attributes, and their position in the agency sponsoring the group. As a group develops, members' status and power change, depending on how important a member is in helping the group accomplish its tasks or in helping other members meet their socio-emotional needs. When members carry out roles that are important to the group, their power and status increase.

Members who come to groups feeling marginalized and oppressed are likely to have cognitive schema from the start that tell them they have little status or power in groups. Workers should be sensitive to status differentials among members and help those who may feel disenfranchised and powerless to play important roles in the group. The importance of equality within groups should be emphasized at the very beginning. Workers should continue to monitor how power and status are distributed within the group as it progresses and make interventions when necessary to ensure that each member feels like an important part of the group.

Principles for Practice

With basic information about the nature of communication and interaction patterns in groups, workers can intervene in any group to modify or change the patterns that develop. Workers may find the following principles about communication and interaction patterns helpful:

- Members of the group are always communicating. Workers should assess communication processes and patterns continually to help members communicate comfortably and effectively throughout the life of a group.
- Communication patterns can be changed. Strategies for doing this start with identifying patterns during the group or at the end of group meetings during a brief time set aside to discuss group process. Workers then can reinforce desired interaction patterns; increase or decrease emotional bonds between members; change subgroups, group size, or group structure; or alter the power or status relationships in groups.
- Members communicate for a purpose. Workers should help members understand each other's intentions by clarifying them through group discussion.
- There is meaning in all communication. Workers should help members understand and appreciate the meaning of different communications.
- Messages may not be clearly communicated. By clarifying messages and providing or soliciting feedback, workers can help to reduce distortions in how messages are sent.
- Messages may be distorted in transmission. Workers should help members clarify verbal and nonverbal communications that are unclear or ambiguous.
- Messages are often perceived selectively. Workers should help members listen for accurate and intended meanings and encourage dialogue and open communication patterns when there is a chance that distortions or misunderstandings are taking place.
- Feedback and clarification enhance accurate understanding of communications. The worker should educate members about how to give and receive effective feedback and model these methods in the group.
- Open, group-centered communications are often, but not always, the preferred pattern of interaction. The worker should encourage communication patterns that are appropriate for the purpose of the group.
- Special attention should be paid to marginalized and oppressed members of groups. The worker should ensure that all members have sufficient power and status so that they feel they are an important and valued part of the group.

Workers who follow these principles can intervene to help groups develop patterns of communication and interaction that meet members' socio-emotional needs while accomplishing group purposes.

Group Cohesion

Group cohesion is the result of all forces acting on members to remain in a group (Festinger, 1950). According to Forsyth (2014), cohesion is made up of three components: (1) member-to-member attraction and a liking for the group as a whole, (2) a sense of unity and community so that the group is seen as a single entity, and (3) a sense of teamwork and *esprit de corps* with the group successfully performing as a coordinated unit.

People are attracted to groups for a variety of reasons. According to the group dynamics experts Cartwright (1968) and Forsyth (2014), the following interacting sets of variables determine a member's attraction to a group.

Reasons for Members' Attraction to a Group
- The need for affiliation, recognition, and security
- The resources and prestige available through group participation
- Expectations of the beneficial and detrimental consequences of the group
- The comparison of the group with other group experiences

Cohesive groups satisfy members' need for affiliation. Some members have a need to socialize because their relationships outside the group are unsatisfactory or nonexistent. For example, Toseland, Decker, and Bliesner (1979) have shown that group work can be effective in meeting the needs of socially isolated older persons. Cohesive groups recognize members' accomplishments and promote members' sense of competence. Members are attracted to the group when they feel that their participation is valued and when they feel they are well liked. Groups are also more cohesive when they provide members with a sense of security. Schachter (1959), for example, has shown that fear and anxiety increase people's needs for affiliation. It has also been found that when group members have confidence in the group's ability to perform a specific task, the group is more cohesive and performs more effectively (Gibson, 1999; Pescosolido, 2001, 2003; Silver & Bufiano, 1996). Similarly, feelings of collective self-efficacy have been shown to have an important impact on actual performance (Bandura, 1997a, 1997b).

The cohesion of a group can also be accounted for by incentives that are sometimes provided for group membership. Many people join groups because of the people they expect to meet and get to know. Opportunities for making new contacts and associating with high-status members are also incentives. In some groups, the tasks to be performed are enjoyable. Other groups might enable a member to accomplish tasks that require the help of others. Prestige may also be an incentive. For example, being nominated to a delegate council or other task group may enhance a member's prestige and status in an organization or the community. Another inducement to group membership may be access to services or resources not otherwise available.

Expectations of gratification and favorable comparisons with previous group experiences are two other factors that help make groups cohesive. For example, members with high expectations for a group experience and little hope of attaining similar satisfactions elsewhere will be attracted to a group. Thibaut and Kelley (1959) have found that members' continued attraction to a group depends on the "comparison level for alternatives"—that is, the satisfaction derived from the current group experience compared with that derived from other possible experiences.

Members' reasons for being attracted to a group affect how they perform in the group. For example, Back (1951) found that members who were attracted to a group primarily because they perceived other members as similar or as potential friends related on a personal level in the group and more frequently engaged in conversations not focused on the group's task. Members attracted by the group's task wanted to complete it quickly and efficiently and maintained task-relevant conversations. Members attracted by the prestige of group membership were cautious not to risk their status in the group. They initiated few controversial topics and focused on their own actions rather than on those of other group members.

High levels of cohesion can affect the functioning of individual members and the group as a whole in many ways. Research and clinical observations have documented that cohesion tends to increase many beneficial dynamics.

Effects of Cohesion
- Expression of positive and negative feelings (Pepitone & Reichling, 1955; Yalom, 2005)
- Willingness to listen (Yalom, 2005)
- Effective use of other members' feedback and evaluations (Yalom, 2005)
- Members' influence over each other (Cartwright, 1968)
- Feelings of self-confidence, self-esteem, personal adjustment, and collective efficacy (Pooler, Qualls, Rogers, & Johnston, 2014; Seashore, 1954; Yalom, 2005)
- Satisfaction with the group experience (Widmeyer & Williams, 1991)
- Perseverance toward goals (Cartwright, 1968; Spink & Carron, 1994)
- Willingness to take responsibility for group functioning (Dion, Miller, & Magnan, 1971)
- Goal attainment, individual and group performance, and organizational commitment (Bulingame, McClendon, & Alonso, 2011; Evans & Dion, 1991; Gully, Devine, & Whitney, 1995; Mullen & Cooper, 1994; Wech, Mossholder, Steel, & Bennett, 1998)
- Attendance, membership maintenance, and length of participation (Prapavessis & Carron, 1997)

Although cohesion can have many beneficial effects, workers should be aware that cohesion operates in complex interaction with other group properties. For example, although cohesive groups tend to perform better than less cohesive groups, the quality of decisions made by cohesive groups is moderated by the nature of the task (Gully, Devine, & Whitney, 1995) and by the size of the group (Mullen & Cooper, 1994). Cohesion has more influence on outcomes, for example, when task interdependence is high rather than when it is low (Gully, Devine, & Whitney, 1995). Cohesion also varies over the course of a group's development. For example, Budman, Soldz, Demby, Davis, and Merry (1993) have shown that what is viewed as cohesive behavior early in the life of a group may not be viewed that way later in the group's development.

Although cohesion often leads to higher levels of performance, Forsyth (2014) points out that it does not always have this effect. In groups with a culture of accepting mediocre or low standards of performance, high levels of cohesion can lead to the continuation and sustainment of these performance levels. Cohesion can have other negative effects on the functioning of a group when it results in too much control (Hornsey, Dwyer, Oei, & Dingle, 2009). It can suppress personal expression and minority opinions. It can also deter any dissent or conflict, even though these can be positive signs of growing trust in maturing groups. Members should feel safe to express themselves, take risks, and disagree without the threat of sanctions or being ostracized. Deeper self-disclosure and improved idea generation and problem solving processes occur in groups where cohesion does not suppress members' creativity or openness.

Cohesion is a necessary, albeit not sufficient, ingredient in the development of "group think." According to Janis (1972), *group think* is "a mode of thinking that people engage in when they are deeply involved in a cohesive group, when the members' strivings for unanimity override their motivation to realistically appraise alternative courses of action" (p. 9). When group think occurs, groups become close-minded and the pressure for conformity limits methodical search and appraisal procedures (Forsyth, 2014).

In addition to encouraging pathological conformity, cohesion can lead to dependence on the group. This can be a particularly vexing problem in intensive therapy groups with members who started the group experience with severe problems and poor self-images. Thus, while promoting the development of cohesion in groups, the worker should ensure that members' individuality is not sacrificed. Members should be encouraged to express divergent opinions and to respect divergent opinions expressed by other group members. It is also important to adequately prepare members for group termination and independent functioning. Methods for this preparation are discussed in Chapter 14.

Reasons for Lack of Attraction to a Group

Group workers are often asked to lead groups with members who are disinterested, reluctant, or mandated. Those who abuse alcohol, drugs, or their spouses are just some examples of members who may not want to attend groups. Even in task groups, members may feel pressured to attend.

There are many sources of pressure to attend. For example, in groups for children or adolescents, parents, school officials, and legal systems may urge attendance, and members may face stiff penalties for not attending. There are many in society who are marginalized, oppressed, ignored, or targets of bigotry and intolerance. These individuals may be particularly apathetic or hostile about attending groups sponsored by systems that they perceive as perpetuating or abetting their diminished status and power in society. It is difficult enough to work on personal issues when members have supportive environments, but many individuals have little emotional, social, or material support within their families and communities. This also makes participation in treatment groups more difficult.

To attain high cohesion in groups with members who do not view the group as attractive before it begins, workers should focus on building caring and warm relationships as early as possible. Workers should strive to build trust between themselves and group members. They should also work to build trust among all members. In this way, the worker cannot only begin to help members, but can also encourage members to help each other. Building trust can take many forms. Examples include screening interviews that include careful attention to orientation issues, and direct talk with group members about their reluctance to attend using stages of change (Prochaska, DiClimente, & Norcross, 1992) and motivational interviewing strategies (Hohman, 2012; Miller & Rollnick, 2013) described later in this text. Exposure of reluctant group members to successful group experiences of past members can also be a very effective strategy, but this involves workers staying in touch with alumni and asking them to come in to talk about their experiences with potential members prior to the first group meeting, or during the first session.

It is important for group workers to recognize challenges to engagement as early as possible in the life of a group. Continued focus on engagement should also be a priority during subsequent group sessions. Workers can use a measure of engagement by Macgowan (2000) described in Chapter 14 or other measures described by Macgowan (2008) to measure engagement and cohesion.

Trust and Self-Care

There is no substitute for building trust. Trust is at the heart of engagement. Sometimes workers are "forced" because of short stays in inpatient and other settings to move quickly to therapeutic goals. In situations such as these, some intervention goals, such as disseminating information, can be done despite lacking full trust of members. Still, retention and use of this information will not be as good as it would be for committed, trusting members. It should also be recognized that it is very difficult, if not impossible, to engage members in highly emotional, psychological, and interpersonal issues without the formation of trusting relationships.

Trust takes time to build but frequently workers do not have a lot of time. Short inpatient stays for health and mental health problems are just one example. In these situations, workers can find themselves in an unsolvable conundrum because they want to establish trust, but short lengths of stay and many other reasons can block or diminish their attempts to accomplish worthy goals. In such situations, workers should try to be easy on themselves and engage in self-care, recognizing that some of the exigencies of the situation, such as agency policy or funding requirements, may limit what they can accomplish. It is important to be realistic about possible accomplishments while still doing as much as one can to engage members who are not initially attracted to the group. In teams and treatment conference meetings, workers can talk with their colleagues about what might help to engage those who are reluctant to attend groups. Teams and treatment conferences often come up with innovative ideas for engagement and they also can be source of support for workers. Workers can also join with their colleagues to advocate for changes in agency policies or practices that may be making it difficult for people to attend groups. They are also encouraged to engage in self-care practices alone and with colleagues.

Principles for Practice

Because cohesion has many benefits, workers should strive to make groups attractive to members. Workers may find the following principles helpful when trying to enhance a group's cohesiveness:

- A high level of open interaction promotes cohesiveness. The worker should use group discussions and program activities to encourage interaction among members.

- When members' needs are met, they want to continue participating. Therefore, the worker should help members identify their needs and how they can be met in the group.
- Achieving group goals makes the group more attractive to its members. The worker should help members focus on and achieve goals.
- Noncompetitive intragroup relationships that affirm members' perceptions and points of view increase group cohesion. The worker should help group members to cooperate rather than compete with each other.
- Competitive intergroup relationships help to define a group's identity and purpose, thereby heightening members' cohesion. The worker can use naturally occurring intergroup competition to build intragroup bonds.
- A group that is large can decrease members' attraction to the group by obstructing their full participation. The worker should compose a group that gives all members the opportunity to be fully involved.
- When members' expectations are understood and addressed, members feel as if they are part of the group. The worker should help members clarify their expectations and should strive for congruence between members' expectations and the purposes of the group.
- Groups that offer rewards, resources, status, or prestige that members would not obtain by themselves tend to be attractive. Therefore, workers should help groups to be rewarding experiences for members.
- Pride in being a member of a group can increase cohesion. The worker should help the group develop pride in its identity and purpose.
- Trust is essential for cohesion and engagement. The worker can use stages of change theory, motivational interviewing, and many other strategies to engage apathetic, reluctant, and resistant group members.

If the costs of participation in a group exceed the benefits, members may stop attending (Thibaut & Kelley, 1954). Although workers cannot ensure that all factors are present in every group, they should strive to make sure that the group is as attractive as possible to each member who participates.

Social Integration and Influence

Social integration refers to how members fit together and are accepted in a group. Groups are not able to function effectively unless there is a high level of social integration among members. Social order and stability are prerequisites for the formation and maintenance of a cohesive group. Social integration builds unanimity about the purposes and goals of the group, helping members to move forward in an orderly and efficient manner to accomplish work and achieve goals.

Norms, roles, and status hierarchies promote social integration by influencing how members behave in relationship to each other and by delineating members' places within the group. They lend order and familiarity to group processes, helping to make members' individual behaviors predictable and comfortable for all. Norms, roles, and status dynamics help groups to avoid unpredictability and excessive conflict that, in turn, can lead to chaos and the disintegration of the group. Too much conformity and compliance resulting from overly rigid and restrictive norms, roles, and status hierarchies can lead to the suppression of individual members' initiative, creativity, and intellectual contributions. At the same time, a certain amount of predictability, conformity, and compliance is necessary to enable members to work together to achieve group goals. Therefore, it is important for workers to guide the development of norms, roles, and status hierarchies that achieve a balance between too little and too much conformity.

The extent of social integration and influence varies from group to group. In groups with strong social influences, members give up a great deal of their freedom and individuality. In some groups, this is necessary for effective functioning. For example, in a delegate council in which members are representing the views of their organization, there is generally little room for individual preferences and viewpoints. Norms and roles clearly spell out how individual delegates should behave. In other groups, however, members may have a great deal of freedom within a broad range of acceptable behavior. The following sections describe how the worker can achieve a balance so that norms, roles, and status hierarchies can satisfy members' socio-emotional needs while simultaneously promoting effective and efficient group functioning.

Norms

Norms are shared expectations and beliefs about appropriate ways to act in a social situation, such as a group. They refer to specific member behaviors and to the overall pattern of behavior that is acceptable in a group. Norms stabilize and regulate behavior in groups. By providing guidelines for acceptable and appropriate behavior, norms increase predictability, stability, and security for members and help to encourage organized and coordinated action to reach goals.

Norms result from what is valued, preferred, and accepted behavior in the group. The preferences of certain high-status members might be given greater consideration in the development of group norms than the preferences of low-status members, but all members share to some extent in the development of group norms.

Norms develop as the group develops. Norms develop directly as members observe one another's behavior in the group and vicariously as members express their views and opinions during the course of group interaction. As members express preferences, share views, and behave in certain ways, norms become clarified. Soon it becomes clear that sanctions and social disapproval result from some behaviors and that praise and social approval result from other behaviors. Structure in early group meetings is associated with increased cohesion, reduced conflict, and higher member satisfaction (Stockton, Rohde, & Haughey, 1992). The emergence of norms as the group progresses, however, reduces the need for structure and control by the worker.

Because norms are developed through the interactions of group members, they discourage the capricious use of power by the leader or any group member. They also reduce the need for excessive controls to be imposed on the group from external forces.

Norms vary in important ways. Norms may be overt and explicit or covert and implicit. Overt norms are those that can be clearly articulated by the leader and the members. In contrast, covert norms exert important influences on the way members behave and interact without ever being talked about or discussed. For example, a group leader who states that the group will begin and end on time, and then follows through on that "rule" each week, has articulated an explicit group norm in an overt fashion. In contrast, a covert, implicit norm might be for members of a couples group to avoid any talk of intimate behavior or infidelity. The implicit norm is that these topics are not discussed in this group.

Case Example   A Couples Group

In the fourth meeting of a couples group, the leader noticed that the members had not mentioned anything about their sexual lives. At one point during the group meeting, the leader observed that although members had talked about the conflicts that they were having in their lives about money, household chores, and other issues, no one had brought up the topic of sex. The leader asked if they would like to talk about their satisfaction or dissatisfaction with their sex lives. After a pause, one woman volunteered that she and her husband had not had sex for several months and that her husband seemed to be resentful about that. Her husband did not respond at first, but other members of the group began to talk about their sex lives and eventually, the husband who had not responded talked about his feelings. Later in the group, the leader used the taboo topic of sex to lead a productive discussion of how safe and secure members of the group were feeling about bringing up difficult topics in the group and what could be done to make members feel more comfortable. One agreement that came out of this discussion was that members would try not to get angry at each other between meetings for things said in the group and instead would bring any feelings they had back into the group during the next meeting.

Norms vary according to the extent that people consider them binding. Some norms are strictly enforced whereas others are rarely enforced. Some norms permit a great deal of leeway in behavior, whereas others prescribe narrow and specific behaviors. Norms also have various degrees of saliency for group members. For some members, a particular norm may exert great influence, but for others it may exert little influence.

Deviations from group norms are not necessarily harmful to a group. Deviations can often help groups move in new directions or challenge old ways of accomplishing tasks that are no longer functional. Norms may be dysfunctional or unethical, and it may be beneficial for members to deviate from them. For example, in a treatment group, norms develop that make it difficult for members to express intense emotions. Members who deviate from this norm help the group reexamine its norms and enable members to deepen their level of communication. The worker should try to understand the meaning of deviations from group norms and the implications for group functioning. It can also be helpful to point out covert norms and to help members examine whether these contribute to effective group functioning.

Because they are so pervasive and powerful, norms are somewhat more difficult to change than role expectations or status hierarchies. Therefore, a worker should strive to ensure that the developing norms are beneficial for the group. Recognizing the difficulty of changing norms, Lewin (1947) suggested that three stages are necessary for changing the equilibrium and the status quo that hold norms constant. There must first be disequilibrium or unfreezing caused by a crisis or other tension-producing situation. During this period, group members reexamine the current group norms. Sometimes, a crisis may be induced by the worker through a discussion or demonstration of how current norms will affect the group in the future. In other cases, dysfunctional norms lead to a crisis.

In the second stage, members return to equilibrium with new norms replacing previous ones. According to Lewin (1947), the second stage is called *freezing*. In the third stage, called *refreezing*, the new equilibrium is stabilized. New norms become the recognized and accepted rules by which the group functions. Norms can be changed in many ways.

Changing Norms
- Discussing, diagnosing, and making explicit decisions about group norms
- Directly intervening in the group to change a norm
- Deviating from a norm and helping a group to adapt a new response
- Helping the group become aware of external influences and their effect on the group's norms
- Hiring a consultant to work with the group to change its norms

Assessment

Behavior: Select appropriate intervention strategies based on the assessment, research knowledge, and values and preferences of clients and constituencies

Critical Thinking Question: Role theory helps explain some aspects of people's behavior. How do important roles in the group help members accomplish goals?

Roles

Like norms, roles can also be an important influence on group members. Roles are closely related to norms. Whereas norms are shared expectations held, to some extent, by everyone in the group, roles are shared expectations about the functions of individuals in the group. Unlike norms, which define behavior in a wide range of situations, roles define behavior in relation to a specific function or task that the group member is expected to perform. Roles continue to emerge and evolve as the work of the group changes over time (Forsyth, 2014).

Roles are important for groups because they allow for the division of labor and appropriate use of power. They ensure that someone will be designated to take care of vital group functions. Roles provide social control in groups by prescribing how members should behave in certain situations. Performing in a certain role not only prescribes certain behavior but also limits members' freedom to deviate from the expected behavior of someone who performs that role. For example, it would be viewed as inappropriate for an educational group leader to express feelings and emotional reactions about a personal issue that was not relevant to the subject material being taught.

Case Example   A Cancer Survivors Group

In a group for cancer survivors, one member, Mary, took on the role of socio-emotional leader, comforting members when they brought up difficult topics and drawing out quiet members who seemed like they were feeling particularly down or vulnerable. Joe, on the other hand, took on the role of task leader making sure that the group stayed on topic when the conversation moved away from issues dealing with cancer or how to cope with the effects of the disease. Jenny was the humorist, making positive remarks and seeing the bright side of things when the tone of the group became somber. June took on the role of the indigenous leader, offering to help the leader Dorothy set up the meeting room, bringing in baked goodies and other treats for the group, and helping members between meetings when they needed transportation to medical appointments or someone to talk to when they were feeling down.

Changes or modifications of roles are best undertaken by identifying roles, describing and discussing alternative roles, clarifying the responsibilities and the privileges of existing roles, asking members to assume new roles, and adding or modifying roles according to preferences expressed during the group's discussion.

Status

Along with norms and role expectations, social controls are also exerted through members' status in a group. Status refers to an evaluation and ranking of each member's position in the group relative to all other members. A person's status within a group is partially determined by his or her prestige, position, and recognized expertise outside the group. To some extent, however, status is also dependent on the situation. In one group, status may be determined by a member's position in the agency sponsoring the group. In another group, status may be determined by how well a member is liked by other group members, how much the group relies on the member's expertise, or how much responsibility the member has in the group. It is also determined by how a person acts once he or she becomes a member of a group. Because status is defined relative to other group members, a person's status in a group is also affected by the other members who comprise the group.

Status serves a social integration function in a rather complex manner. Low-status members are the least likely to conform to group norms because they have little to lose by deviating. For this reason, low-status members have the potential to be disruptive of productive group processes. Disruptive behavior is less likely if low-status members have hopes of gaining a higher status. Medium-status group members tend to conform to group norms so that they can retain their status and perhaps gain a higher status. Therefore, workers should provide opportunities for low-status members to contribute to the group so that they can become more socially integrated and achieve a higher status. High-status members perform many valued services for the group and generally conform to valued group norms when they are establishing their position. However, because of their position, high-status members have more freedom to deviate from accepted norms. They are often expected to do something special and creative when the group is in a crisis (Forsyth, 2014). If medium- or low-status members consistently deviate from group norms, they are threatened with severe sanctions or forced to leave the group. If high-status members consistently deviate from group norms, their status in the group is diminished, but they are rarely threatened with severe sanctions or forced to leave the group.

Case Example   A Psychiatric Team in an Inpatient Setting

In a psychiatric team in an adolescent ward of a state mental hospital, the psychiatrist was clearly viewed as the highest-status member of the team. Of the other team members, the social worker and the nurse held middle-status positions, and the mental health therapy aides and the student intern held lower-status positions. Gradually, over time, however, the status of the social worker and one of the mental health therapy aides rose because they seemed to be able to develop a special rapport with some of the adolescents with the most difficult problems. At the same time, the status of the psychiatrist diminished somewhat as he was called away from meetings and missed some meetings entirely and also was perceived as rather rigid in his theoretical perspectives and demanding in his views of what he expected of other team members. The nurse's role on the team also increased somewhat because she became the person who could meet with the psychiatrist and make needed adjustments to medications. One of the mental health therapy aides continued to maintain a rather low status on the team, as he seemed not very engaged in his work, often talking disparagingly about patients and contributing little that was positive to the overall team meeting.

Status hierarchies are most easily changed by the addition or removal of group members. If this is not possible or desirable, group discussion can help members express their opinions and feelings about the effects of the current status hierarchy and how to modify it. Changing members' roles in the group and helping them to achieve a more visible or responsible position within the group can also increase members' status. Program activity roles that are associated with higher status, appointments to leadership or other positions within the whole group or subgroups, and requesting that members take on certain roles, are among the many other strategies that workers can use to change status hierarchies, and empower members who are in lower-status rankings in the group.

Overall, norms, roles, and status are important components of the social influence groups have on members. Pioneering studies by Sherif (1936), Newcomb (1943), Asch (1952, 1955, 1957), and Milgram (1974) clearly demonstrated the power influence that the group has on the individual. It has also been shown, however, that individual group members with minority opinions can influence the majority (Moscovici, 1985, 1994; Moscovici & Lage, 1976; Moscovici, Lage, & Naffrechoux, 1969). Some methods that members with minority opinions can use to get their opinions heard and paid attention to follow.

Expressing and Getting Minority Opinions Adopted by the Majority
- Offer compelling and consistent arguments
- Ask the group to carefully listen to and consider your thoughts
- Appear confident
- Do not rigidly cling to a viewpoint or be close-minded about other points of view
- Take a flexible stand; consider compromise
- Use uncertainties and flawed logic in the majority's opinions to inform your own approach

Principles for Practice

Norms, roles, and status are interrelated concepts that affect the social integration of individuals in the group. They limit individuality, freedom, and independence, but at the same time stabilize and regulate the operation of the group, helping members to feel comfortable and secure in their positions within the group and with each other. Therefore, in working with task and treatment groups, workers should balance the needs of individuals and of the group as a whole, managing conformity and deviation, while ensuring that norms, roles, and status hierarchies are working to benefit rather than hinder or limit individual members and the whole group. Workers may find the following principles about these dynamics helpful when facilitating a group.

- The worker should help group members to assess the extent to which norms, roles, and status hierarchies are helping members feel engaged and socially integrated while helping the group to accomplish its goals.
- The worker should facilitate norms, roles, and status hierarchies that give the group sufficient structure so that interaction does not become disorganized, chaotic, unsafe, or unduly anxiety producing.
- The worker should avoid facilitating norms, roles, and status hierarchies that restrict members' ability to exercise their own judgment and free will and to accomplish agreed-on goals. The worker should ensure that there is freedom and

independence within the range of acceptable behaviors agreed on by the group. Empowerment of members should always be a fundamental goal.

- Norms, roles, and status hierarchies develop slowly in a group but are difficult to change once they are established. Therefore, workers should carefully attend to the development of helpful social integration mechanisms and should be vigilant about working to change unhelpful norms, roles, and status hierarchies as soon as they are observed to be developing in groups.

- Members choose to adhere to norms, roles, and status hierarchies in groups that are attractive and cohesive. Workers should help make the group a satisfying experience for members.

- Members choose to adhere to norms, roles, and status hierarchies when they consider the group's goals important and meaningful. Therefore, workers should emphasize the importance of the group's work and the meaningfulness of each member's contributions.

- Members choose to adhere to norms, roles, and status hierarchies when they desire continued membership because of their own needs or because of pressure from sources within or outside the group. Therefore, workers should consider the incentives for members to participate in a group.

- Rewards and sanctions can help members adhere to norms, roles, and status expectations. Workers should assess whether rewards and sanctions are applied fairly and equitably to promote healthy social integration that benefits each member and the group as a whole.

By following these principles, workers can ensure that the norms, role expectations, and status hierarchy that develop in a group satisfy members' needs while helping to accomplish individual and group goals.

Group Culture

Although it has often been overlooked in discussions of group dynamics, group culture is an important force in the group as a whole. Group culture refers to values, beliefs, customs, and traditions held in common by group members (Yuki & Brewer, 2014). According to Levi (2014), culture can be viewed as having three levels. At the surface, symbols and rituals display the culture of the group. For example, in Alcoholics Anonymous groups, members usually begin an interaction by saying their first name and by stating that they are an alcoholic. At a deeper level, culture is displayed in the way members interact with one another. For example, the way conflict is handled in a group says much about its culture. The deepest level of culture includes the core beliefs, ideologies, and values held in common by members.

Multicultural differences within the group can have an important impact on the development of group culture and the social integration of all members. For example, individualism, competitiveness, and achievement are more valued in American and European cultures than are humility and modesty, which are more prevalent in some non-Western cultures. Similarly, experiences of group survival, social hierarchy, inclusiveness, and ethnic identification can powerfully influence the beliefs, ideologies,

Human Rights and Justice

Behavior: Engage in practices that advance social, economic, and environmental justice

Critical Thinking Question: Many people have firsthand experiences with injustices and human rights violations. How can the group address these issues?

and values that are held by racially and ethnically diverse members, but these same experiences may have little salience for members of majority groups who have long been acculturated to dominant societal values (Burnes & Ross, 2010; Hopps & Pinderhughes, 1999; Matsukawa, 2001). Insensitivity to these values, however, can isolate and alienate minority members and reduce their opportunity for social integration within the group.

When the membership of a group is diverse, group culture emerges slowly. Members contribute unique sets of values that originate from their experiences as well as from their ethnic, cultural, and racial heritages. These values are blended through group communications and interactions. In early meetings, members explore each other's unique value systems and attempt to find a common ground on which they can relate to each other. By later meetings, members have had a chance to share and understand each other's value systems. As a result, a common set of values develops, which becomes the group's culture. The group's culture continues to evolve throughout the life of the group.

Case Example   A Caregivers' Group for Latinos

In a caregiver support group for Latinos sponsored by a community agency, the worker, who was experienced in leading many caregiver groups, mostly for non-Latinos, noticed that when the members of this group talked about their elders, there was even more respect accorded to the elders' status in the family than was true in groups of Anglo caregivers. The group leader also noticed that members were reluctant to volunteer comments unless specifically invited to do so by the leader. The leader decided to ask members about this, and she learned that among some Latinos the traditional norm of respect for the leader precluded them from volunteering comments. The leader explained to the group that in this context, spontaneity was welcome, and they should feel free to voice their opinions about caregiving issues and needs. The worker also noticed that the members would sometimes use Spanish-language words to describe their feelings to one another even though the group was being conducted in English. The worker had a discussion with the members about what to do when this happened because she was afraid that not all the members might understand what was being said between two members. The group decided that this practice was acceptable and came to an agreement about how this would be handled. In this particular group, because some of the members did not speak fluent Spanish, it was decided that any member could ask for a translation of what was being said between members when they lapsed into Spanish.

Group culture emerges more quickly in groups with a homogeneous membership. When members share common life experiences and similar sets of values, their unique perspectives blend more quickly into a group culture. For example, members of groups sponsored by culturally based organizations, such as the Urban League or Centro Civico, and groups that represent a particular point of view, such as the National Organization for Women (NOW), are more likely to share similar life experiences and similar values than are groups with more diverse memberships. One of the attractions of these homogeneous groups is that they provide an affirming and supportive atmosphere.

Culture is also influenced by the environment in which a group functions. As part of the organizational structure of an agency, a community, and a society, groups share the values, traditions, and heritage of these larger social systems. The extent to which these systems influence the group depends on the degree of interaction the group has with them. For example, on one end of the continuum, an administrative team's operational procedures are often greatly influenced by agency policies and practices. On the other end, gangs tend to isolate themselves from the dominant values of society, the community, and local youth organizations. Group workers can learn a great deal about groups by examining how they interact with their environment.

Groups that address community needs often have much interaction with their environment. When analyzing a change opportunity, building a constituency, or deciding how to implement an action plan, groups that set out to address community needs must carefully consider dominant community values and traditions. The receptivity of powerful individuals within a community will be determined to some extent by how consistent a group's actions are with the values and traditions they hold in high regard. Whenever possible, groups attempting to address community needs should frame their efforts within the context of dominant community values. The practitioner can help by attempting to find the common ground in the values of the community and the group. When a group's actions are perceived to be in conflict with dominant community values, it is unlikely to receive the support of influential community leaders. In these situations, the group may rely on conflict strategies (described in Chapter 12) to achieve its objectives.

Once a culture has developed, members who endorse and share in the culture feel secure and at home, whereas those who do not are likely to feel isolated or even alienated. For isolated members, the group is often not a satisfying experience. It is demoralizing and depressing to feel misunderstood and left out. Feelings of oppression can be exacerbated. Those who do not feel comfortable with the culture that has developed are more likely to drop out of the group or become disruptive. More extreme feelings of alienation can lead to rebellious, acting-out behavior. Subgroups that feel alienated from the dominant group culture may rebel in various ways against the norms, roles, and status hierarchies that have developed in the group. This can be avoided by providing individual attention to isolated members and by stimulating all members to incorporate beliefs, ideologies, and values that celebrate difference and transcend individual differences. The worker can also help by fostering the full participation and integration of all group members into the life of the group.

Principles for Practice

The culture that a group develops has a powerful influence on its ability to achieve its goals while satisfying members' socio-emotional needs. A culture that emphasizes values of self-determination, openness, fairness, and diversity of opinion can do much to facilitate the achievement of group and individual goals. Sometimes members bring ethnic, cultural, or social stereotypes to the group and thus inhibit the group's development and effective functioning. Through interaction and discussion, workers can help members confront stereotypes and learn to understand and appreciate persons who bring different values and cultural and ethnic heritages to the group.

In helping the group build a positive culture, the worker should consider the following principles:

- Group culture emerges from the mix of values that members bring to the group. The worker should help members examine, compare, and respect each other's value systems.

- Group culture is also affected by the values of the agency, the community, and the society that sponsor and sanction the group. The worker should help members identify and understand these values.
- Group members and workers can hold stereotypes that interfere with their ability to interact with each other. Workers should help members eliminate stereotypical ways of relating to each other and develop an awareness of their own stereotypes.
- Value conflicts can reduce group cohesion and, in extreme cases, lead to the demise of the group. The worker should mediate value conflicts among members and between members and the larger society.
- Group culture can exert a powerful influence on members' values. The worker should model values, such as openness, self-determination, fairness, and acceptance of difference that are fundamental to social group work and the social work profession.
- Groups are most satisfying when they meet members' socio-emotional and instrumental needs. Therefore, the worker should balance members' needs for emotional expressiveness with their needs to accomplish specific goals.

? Assess your understanding of group dynamics by taking this brief quiz.

Research-Informed Practice

Behavior: Use and translate research evidence to inform and improve practice, policy, and service delivery

Critical Thinking Question: Understanding that groups go through stages helps the worker understand the behaviors and actions of members at different points in time. What evidence supports stage theory in group development?

STAGES OF GROUP DEVELOPMENT

According to Northen (1969), "a stage is a differentiable period or a discernible degree in the process of growth and development" (p. 49). The rest of this text is organized around the skills that workers can use during each stage of a group's development. A group's entire social structure, its communication and interaction patterns, cohesion, social controls, and culture evolve as it develops. Therefore, an in-depth understanding of group development is essential for the effective practice of group work. This section reviews some of the ways that group development has been conceptualized by other group work theoreticians.

Many attempts have been made to classify stages of group development. Table 3.3 lists some of the models of group development that have appeared in the literature. Most are based on descriptions of groups that the authors of each model have worked with or observed. Most models propose that all groups pass through similar stages of development. As can be seen in Table 3.3, however, different writers have different ideas about the number and types of stages through which all groups pass. For example, Bales' (1950) model of group development has only three stages, but the model presented by Sarri and Galinsky (1985) has seven stages.

Relatively few empirical studies have been conducted of particular models, and little empirical evidence exists to support the notion that any one model accurately describes the stages through which all groups pass. The studies that have been conducted suggest that groups move through stages, but that the stages are not constant across different groups (Shaw, 1976; Smith, 1978). MacKenzie (1994), Wheelan (1994), and Worchell (1994) point out that both progressive and cyclical processes exist in groups; that is, although

Table 3.3   Stages of Group Development

Development Stage	Beginning	Middle	End
Bales (1950)	Orientation	Evaluation	Decision-making
Tuckman (1965)	Forming	Storming Norming Performing	Termination
Northen (1969)	Planning Orientation	Exploring and testing Problem solving	Pretermination
Hartford (1971)	Pregroup planning Convening Group formation	Disintegration and conflict Group formation and maintenance	Termination
Klein (1972)	Orientation Resistance	Negotiation Intimacy	Termination
Trecker (1972)	Beginning Emergence of some group feeling	Development of bond, purpose, and cohesion Strong group feeling Decline in group feeling	Ending
Sarri & Galinsky (1985)	Origin phase Formative phase	Intermediate phase I Revision phase Intermediate phase II Maturation phase	Termination
Garland, Jones, & Kolodny (1976)	Preaffiliation Power and control	Intimacy Differentiation	Separation
Henry (1992)	Initiating Convening	Conflict Maintenance	Termination
Wheelan (1994)	Dependency Delusion	Counter dependency and flight Trust and structure Work	Termination
Schiller (1995)	Preaffiliation	Establishing a relational base Mutuality and interpersonal empathy Mutuality and change	Separation

groups often move through stages of development from beginning to end, they also often come back to readdress certain basic process issues in a cyclical or oscillating fashion. For example, there is often a cyclical movement of group members from feeling (1) invested in the task to emotionally divested from the task, (2) part of the group to autonomous, (3) defended to open, and (4) isolated to enmeshed.

There is some evidence that stages of group development may be affected by the needs of the group members, the type of group, the goals of the group, the setting in which the group meets, and the orientation of the leader (Shaw, 1976; Smith, 1978). For example, a study of open-membership groups (Schopler & Galinsky, 1990) revealed that few moved beyond a beginning stage of development. *Open-membership* groups that are able to move beyond a beginning level of development are those that have a membership change less frequently than every other meeting and those with less than a 50 percent change in membership (Galinsky & Schopler, 1989). Most Alcoholics Anonymous groups would qualify under these criteria.

Groups with frequent and extensive membership changes usually remain at a formative stage. Such groups cope with problems in continuity and development by following highly ritualistic and structured procedures for group meetings. For example, a group in a stroke rehabilitation unit in a large teaching hospital in which a patient's typical stay is three to four weeks might be structured to begin with a half-hour educational presentation, followed by a half-hour discussion. The group would meet three times a week. At least nine different topics could be presented before they are repeated. Therefore, patients with typical hospital stays of three to four weeks could learn about all nine topics, yet begin and end their participation at any time. However, the intimacy that can be achieved during the middle stage of groups with closed memberships is rarely achieved in groups in which members are continually entering and leaving the group.

Despite the variable nature of the stages of group development described by different writers, many of the models contain similar stages. As can be seen in Table 3.3, the various phases of group development can be divided into three stages: beginning, middle, and end. Each model of group development is placed in relationship to these three broad stages.

Most writers suggest that the beginning stages of groups are concerned with planning, organizing, and convening. The beginnings of groups are characterized by an emergence of group cohesion, but it may not emerge without a struggle. There is a desire by members to get to know each other and share in a fellowship, but also to maintain autonomy. Garland, Jones, and Kolodny (1976) identified this tendency as an approach–avoidance conflict. As the beginning stage progresses, norms and roles are differentiated, and members explore and test the roles they are beginning to assume in the group. Conflict may emerge. The leader can help by pointing out that encountering conflict and dealing with it are normal steps in the development of smooth-working relationships in preparation for the work that characterizes the middle stage.

Although some work is accomplished in all stages of a group's development, most occurs in the middle stage. At the beginning of this stage, the conflicts over norms, roles, and other group dynamics found in the later part of the beginning stage give way to established patterns of interaction. A deepening of interpersonal relationships and greater group cohesion begin to appear. After this occurs, groups concern themselves with the work necessary to accomplish the specific tasks and goals that have been agreed on. The terms used to describe this stage include *problem solving*, *performing*, *maintenance*, *intimacy*, *work*, and *maturity*. Task accomplishment is preceded by a differentiation of roles and accompanied by the development of feedback and evaluation mechanisms.

The ending stage of a group is characterized by the completion and evaluation of the group's efforts. Bales's (1950) model of group development suggests that during this stage, task groups make decisions, finish their business, and produce the results of their efforts. Treatment groups, which have emphasized socio-emotional functioning as well as task accomplishment, begin a process of separation, during which group feeling and cohesion decline. Often, members mark termination by summarizing the accomplishments of the group and celebrating together.

Models of group development provide a framework to describe worker roles and appropriate interventions during each stage of a group. They also help workers organize and systematize strategies of intervention. For example, in the beginning stage, a worker's interventions are directed at helping the group define its purpose and helping members feel comfortable with one another. Models of group development can also prepare the leader for what to expect from different types of groups during each stage of development. For example, models, such as the one by Schiller (1995) shown in Table 3.3, help the worker to focus on the development of dynamics in women's groups.

The usefulness of theories of group development for group work practice, however, is limited by the uniqueness of each group experience. Narrative and constructionist theories would echo this point. The developmental stages of groups vary significantly across the broad range of task and treatment groups that a worker might lead. It should not be assumed that all groups follow the same pattern of development or that an intervention that is effective in one group will automatically be effective in another group that is in the same developmental stage. Nevertheless, organizing content into specific developmental stages is a useful heuristic device when teaching students and practitioners how to lead and be effective members of treatment and task groups.

The model of group development presented in this text includes four broad stages: (1) planning, (2) beginning, (3) middle, and (4) ending. The beginning stage includes separate chapters on beginning groups and assessment. The middle stage includes four chapters focused on generic and specialized skills for leading task and treatment groups. The ending stage includes chapters on evaluating the work of the group and on terminating with individual members and the group as a whole. The rest of this text is organized around the skills, procedures, and techniques that help groups function effectively during each stage.

> **?** Assess your understanding of the stages of group development by taking this brief quiz.

Principles for Practice

The worker should be knowledgeable about the theoretical constructs that have been proposed about the stages of group development. Knowing what normative behaviors are for members at each stage can help the worker to assess whether the group is making progress toward achieving its goals. It can also help workers to identify dysfunctional behavior in an individual group member and problems that are the responsibility of the group as a whole. The following practice principles are derived from an understanding of group development:

- Closed-membership groups develop in discernible and predictable stages. The worker should use systematic methods of observing and assessing the development of the group and should teach group members about the predictable stages of group development.
- The development of open-membership groups depends on member turnover. The worker should help open-membership groups develop a simple structure and a clear culture to help new members integrate rapidly into the group.
- Groups generally begin with members exploring the purpose of the group and the roles of the worker and each member. The worker should provide a safe and positive group environment so that members can fully explore the group's purpose and the resources available to accomplish the group's goals.
- After the initial stage of development, groups often experience a period of norm development, role testing, and status awareness that results in expressions of difference among members and the leader. The worker should help members understand that these expressions of difference are a normal part of group development.

- Structure has been demonstrated to increase member satisfaction, increase feelings of safety, and reduce conflict in early group meetings. A lack of structure can lead to feelings of anxiety and insecurity, and can lead to acting out and projection. Therefore, the worker should provide sufficient structure for group interaction, particularly in early group meetings.
- Tension or conflict sometimes develops from differences among members. The worker should help the group resolve the conflict by helping the group develop norms emphasizing the importance of respect and tolerance and by mediating the differences and finding a common ground for productive work together.
- Groups enter a middle stage characterized by increased group cohesion and a focus on work and task accomplishment. To encourage movement toward this stage, the worker should help members stay focused on the purpose of the group, challenge members to develop an appropriate culture for work, and help the group overcome obstacles to goal achievement.
  - In the ending stage, the group finishes its work. The worker should help members review and evaluate their work together by highlighting accomplishments and pointing out areas that need further work.
- Groups sometimes experience strong feelings about endings. The worker should help members recognize these feelings, review what they accomplished in the group, and help members plan for termination.

> **?** Assess your understanding of the practice principles that support effective group development by taking this brief quiz.

SUMMARY

Groups are social systems made up of people in interaction. This chapter describes some of the most important forces that result from the interaction of group members. In working with task and treatment groups, it is essential to understand group dynamics and be able to use them to accomplish group goals. Without a thorough understanding of group dynamics, workers will not be able to help members satisfy their needs or help the group accomplish its tasks.

Group workers should be familiar with four dimensions of group dynamics: (1) communication and interaction patterns; (2) the cohesion of the group and its attraction for its members; (3) social controls, such as norms, roles, and status; and (4) the group's culture. Communication and interaction patterns are basic to the formation of all groups. Through communication and interaction, properties of the group as a whole develop, and the work of the group is accomplished. This chapter presents a model of the communication process.

Groups are maintained because of the attraction they hold for their members. Members join groups for many reasons. The extent to which the group meets members' needs and expectations determines the attraction of the group for its members and the extent to which a group becomes a cohesive unit. As cohesion develops, group structures are elaborated and norms, roles, and status hierarchies form. Norms, roles, and status hierarchies are social integration forces that help to form and shape shared expectations about appropriate behavior in the group. Conformity to expected behavior patterns results in rewards, and deviation results in sanctions. Social controls help to maintain a group's equilibrium as it confronts internal and external pressure to change during its development. However, social controls can be harmful if they are too rigid, too stringent, or if they foster behavior that is contrary to the value base of the social work profession.

As the group evolves, it develops a culture derived from the environment in which it functions as well as from the beliefs, customs, and values of its members. The culture of a group has a pervasive effect on its functioning. For example, a group's culture affects the objectives of the group, which task the group decides to work on, how members interact, and which methods the group uses to conduct its business.

Although properties of groups are often discussed as if they were static, they change constantly throughout the life of a group. Many writers have attempted to describe typical stages through which all groups pass. Although no single model of group development is universally accepted, some of the major characteristics that distinguish group process during each stage of group development are discussed in this chapter. These characteristics can be a useful guide for group practitioners in the beginning, middle, and ending stages of group work, which are described in later portions of this text.

This chapter points out the power of group dynamics in influencing group members and in contributing to or detracting from the success of a group. As workers become familiar with properties of groups as a whole, their appreciation of the effects that natural and formed groups have on the lives of their clients is enhanced. In addition, workers can use their understanding of group dynamics to enhance their ability to work effectively with both task and treatment groups.

4

Leadership

Leadership is the process of guiding the development of the group and its members. The goals of effective leadership are to help the group and its members to achieve goals that are consistent with the value base of social work practice and to meet the socio-emotional needs of members. Task leadership includes defining a structure for the group, setting standards, identifying roles, being goal-focused, planning and coordinating activities, working on solutions, monitoring compliance, and stressing the need for efficiency and productivity (Yukl, 2012). Relationship leadership includes giving support and encouragement, boosting morale, establishing rapport, showing concern and consideration for members, and reducing tension and conflict (Yukl, 2012).

There is also process leadership. This is not a goal in itself, but rather an essential ingredient for the accomplishment of the two previously described goals. Process leadership contributes by ensuring that group dynamics facilitate both goal-directed activities and the socio-emotional satisfaction of members. Workers guide group processes that help members feel that they can trust the worker and all members of the group. Workers use group processes to ensure that members are safe and secure during their participation. They help all members to build a supportive norm, where each member knows all members have their best interests in mind. There is a large literature on the importance of therapeutic group dynamics on members' attachment and engagement with the leader and other group members (Barlow, 2013; Burlingame, Whitcomb, & Woodland, 2014; Harel, Shechtman, & Cutrona, 2011; Joyce, Piper, & Ogrodniczuk, 2007; Kivlighan & Tarrant, 2001; Lieberman & Golant, 2002; Marmarosh, Dunton, & Amendola, 2014; Marshall & Burton, 2010; Ogrodniczuk, Joyce, & Piper, 2007; Tasca & Lampard, 2012). This literature also emphasizes the importance of therapeutic group dynamics on positive outcomes (Joyce, Piper, & Ogrodniczuk, 2007). Therefore, the first task of leadership is to ensure that members feel safe and supported in the group (Barlow, 2013).

Leadership is not a static process performed only by one person. Rather, leadership is a reciprocal, transactional, transformational, cooperative, and adaptive process involving members (Forsyth, 2014). Leadership is reciprocal, because the leader does not just influence the members, but rather leaders and members influence each other. Leadership is transactional because leaders and members work together exchanging ideas, skills, and effort to increase rewards and attain goals. Leadership is transformational because effective leaders motivate members, build their confidence and trust in one another, and unite them in common beliefs, values, and goals. Leadership is also a cooperative process during which leaders do not use their power but gain the cooperation and mutual respect of members in shared goal-seeking activities. Leadership is an adaptive goal-seeking process whereby the leader helps members to change course and adapt to new situations to attain personal and group goals.

Although the leadership role is most often associated with the designated leader—that is, the worker—it is important to distinguish between the worker as the designated leader and the indigenous leadership that emerges among members as the group develops. Leadership is rarely exercised solely by the worker. As the group unfolds, members take on leadership roles. Workers should do as much as possible to stimulate and support indigenous leadership. Encouraging indigenous leadership helps to empower members. Members begin to feel that they have some influence, control, and stake in the group situation. Exercising leadership skills in the group increases members' self-esteem and the likelihood that they will advocate for themselves and for others outside of the group context.

Encouraging indigenous leadership also helps members to exercise their own skills and abilities. This, in turn, promotes autonomous functioning and ensures that members' existing skills do not atrophy. Thus, this chapter emphasizes both the importance of the worker as group leader and the importance of members sharing in leadership functions as the group develops.

There is an increasing amount of evidence that gender roles play an important role in emerging leadership. In studies of emerging leaders, males are generally viewed more positively than females but this may change as women's roles in society change (Forsyth, 2014). Currently, the same leadership behaviors are often viewed more positively when attributed to males than to females (Forsyth, 2014). These differences are entangled with societal role expectations and cultural stereotypes in the United States and many other countries. Traditionally in groups, men are rewarded for dominant, nonconforming ways whereas women are rewarded for acting in cooperative, communal ways (Forsyth, 2014). Group leaders who are aware of this evidence will be better prepared to provide female members with opportunities to assert their leadership abilities and to guard against male dominance of leadership roles. As societal attitudes change, gender norms and roles are changing. The ways that men and women participate in groups is a complex subject. Women and men have different styles of relating in some areas and the way that these styles interact with leadership and participation in groups is very complex and multifaceted. For more information about the complexity of gender in group dynamics, see Forsyth (2014).

LEADERSHIP, POWER, AND EMPOWERMENT

Workers who are new to the leadership role are sometimes uncomfortable with their power and influence and react by denying their power or by trying to take too much control. These strategies are rarely effective. Especially in early group meetings, members

Ethical and Professional Practice

Behavior: Make ethical decisions by applying the standards of the NASW Code of Ethics, relevant laws and regulations, models for ethical decision-making, ethical conduct of research, and additional codes of ethics as appropriate to context.

Critical Thinking Question: Social group workers should use the power bases mentioned in this chapter in a positive manner to facilitate individual member and group goal attainment. What ethical dilemmas could arise as a result of using the power bases available to the worker?

look to the leader for guidance about how to proceed. Experienced leaders are comfortable with their power and influence. They use it to empower members, which gradually enables them to take increasing responsibility for the group as it develops.

Workers use their influence as leaders within and outside the group to facilitate group and individual efforts to achieve desired goals. Within the group, the worker intervenes by guiding the dynamics of the group as a whole or by helping individual members reach a goal. Goal-directed activity takes many forms. The worker has to be flexible when helping members to decide on goal-directed activities. Sometimes members' goals correspond to what others want, but often, members' goals are not coordinated with agency, community, or larger societal goals and expectations. In these situations, it is important for workers to respect and validate members' goals, as long as they are not illegal or self-destructive. The worker has the delicate task of letting members know that their points of view about goals are valid, while at the same time helping members understand the expectations of others.

Workers should never impose goals on members or try to force members to accept the goals that others have for them. Instead, they should help members to be clear about the goals that others have for them and any consequences for not adhering to them. Workers should enable members to express their feelings and thoughts about this in the presence of attentive and supportive members. This does not mean that the worker has to accept members' points of view. Encouraging and enabling members to tell their story and share their viewpoints builds trust and understanding. Validation demonstrates that workers and other group members genuinely hear and understand members' experience, not that they necessarily agree with a particular point of view.

The worker's job is to explore members' points of view and get background information for later attempts to be as helpful to all group members as possible. After this has occurred, workers might use the reciprocal model to help mediate any conflict between members' expressed desires and goals and the goals that others have for them. This should occur only after members begin to feel comfortable that they can express their opinions without penalty. A warm, supportive, affirming environment where trust is built-up is the key to any change effort. At the same time, workers should encourage members to speak about their abilities, capacities, coping skills, dreams, and resiliency. Gradually, in the trusting environment built in the group, workers can use what members say about their ambivalence about changing, discrepancies in their goals or viewpoints, and previous behavioral consequences as motivational levers to help members grow and change in ways that are consistent with their own hopes and dreams for themselves. The overall goal is for workers to help members change in self-directed ways that are congruent with the healthy living expectations that they have for themselves and that others have for them.

In exercising leadership outside the group, the worker intervenes to influence the environment in which the group and its members function. For example, the worker might try to change organizational policies that influence the group or obtain additional resources from a sponsor so the group can complete its work. In exerting leadership inside or outside the group, the worker is responsible for the group's processes, actions, and task accomplishments.

In considering a worker's power, it is helpful to distinguish between attributed power and actual power. *Attributed power* comes from the perception among group members or others outside the group of the worker's ability to lead. Workers who take on the responsibilities inherent in leading a group are rewarded by having attributed to them the power to influence and the ability to lead. Group members, peers, superiors, the sponsoring agency, and the larger social system attribute power to the leader.

The attributed power of the worker comes from a variety of sources. Among these sources are professional status, education, organizational position, years of experience, defined boundaries between worker and group members' roles, fees for service, and the commonly held view that a group's success or failure is the result of its leadership. Workers should recognize that attributed leadership ability is as important as actual power in facilitating the development of the group and its members.

Workers can increase the power attributed to them by group members. Studies have shown that members' expectations about the group and its leader influence the group's performance (Bednar & Kaul, 1994; Karakowsky & McBey, 2001; Piper, 1994). Preparing members with films, brochures, or personal interviews that offer information about the group, its leader, and the success of previous groups has been shown to be effective in increasing the change-oriented expectations of members and in helping individuals and groups accomplish their goals (Bednar & Kaul, 1994; Karakowsky & McBey, 2001; Kaul & Bednar, 1994). When formal preparation is impossible, informal preparation by word of mouth or reputation can be used.

As their attributed power increases, workers are more likely to be regarded with esteem by group members and to be looked to as models of effective coping skills whose behaviors are emulated and whose guidance is followed. Workers should not, however, attempt to gain power for its own sake or unilaterally impose their own values, standards, and rules concerning conduct inside or outside the group.

Actual power refers to the worker's resources for changing conditions inside and outside the group. Actual power depends on the sources of a worker's influence. The power bases first described by French and Raven (1959) follow.

Power Bases
- Connection power—being able to call on and use influential people or resources
- Expert power—having the knowledge or skill to facilitate the work of the group
- Information power—possessing information that is valuable to and needed by others
- Legitimate power—holding a position of authority and the rights that accrue to that position in the organization or larger social system
- Identification power—being liked and admired; the group members want to be identified with the worker
- Reward power—being able to offer social or tangible rewards
- Coercive power—being able to sanction, punish, or deny access to resources and privileges

Use of power can have both negative and positive consequences. For example, coercive power is sometimes used to compel clients to receive treatment. However, coercion can have negative effects, such as hostility, anger, rebellion, and absence from group meetings. Therefore, the worker should exercise power judiciously, in a manner consistent with personal, professional, and societal values.

At the same time, the worker's power as leader cannot, and should not, be denied, which sometimes occurs when suggestions are made that members should take total responsibility for leading the group. Groups need leaders to avoid disorganization and chaos; leadership and power are inseparable (Etzioni, 1961).

Anyone who has attended the first meeting of a new group recognizes the power the worker has as the designated leader. This power can be illustrated most vividly by examining members' behaviors and feelings during the initial portion of the first group meeting. Members direct most of their communications to the worker or communicate through the worker to other group members. Members are often anxious and inquisitive, wondering what they can expect from the group and its leader. They comply readily with requests made by the worker. Although members may wonder about the worker's ability to help them and the group as a whole, they usually give the worker latitude in choosing methods and procedures to help the group achieve its objectives.

It is essential that workers move as rapidly as possible to share their power with members and the group as a whole, starting right from the first group meeting. This encourages members to begin to take responsibility for the group and makes members more potent. It empowers members to bring out their capacities, strengths, and resiliencies (Saleebey, 2013). Some methods for sharing power are presented here.

Human Rights and Justice

Behavior: Engage in practices that advance social, economic, and environmental justice

---

Critical Thinking Question: Sharing power and empowering members are important for effective group leadership. How can a leader contribute to the empowerment of members?

Methods for Sharing Power with the Group

- Enable members to tell their own story.
- Affirm and validate members' experiences of reality
- Focus on members' coping abilities, capacities, resilience, strengths, and their own motivations and goals
- Foster an atmosphere of trust and cohesion where members can help each other by emphasizing members' role in the power of the group to create change.
- Encourage member-to-member rather than member-to-leader communications.
- Ask for members' input into the agenda for the meeting and the direction the group should take in future meetings.
- Support indigenous leadership when members make their first, tentative attempts at exerting their own influence in the group.
- Encourage attempts at mutual sharing and mutual aid among members.
- Model and teach members selected leadership skills early in the life of the group.
- Use naturally occurring events in the life of the group to "process" information about leadership skills and styles and to empower members.
- Encourage members to take leadership roles in struggling with the difficulty of making changes and resolving difficult problematic situations.

Leadership, Empowerment, and the Planned Change Process

Whether in task groups or in treatment groups, one of the major roles of the leader is to empower members so that they are willing participants in the planned change process.

In task groups, the leader should start from the very beginning to help members own the agenda and the work of the group. Workers, as leaders, should not view themselves as commanders but rather as advisors and facilitators who help the members get the job done. Members should feel that they own the tasks they are being asked to accomplish because they have had a hand in shaping them and in executing the steps in the planned change process necessary to accomplish them.

In treatment groups, empowerment means helping members to see the possibilities of growth and change. Throughout the leadership of treatment groups, the worker should emphasize members' choices, their resiliency in the face of obstacles, and their strengths and abilities to change and to overcome adverse living conditions. The worker should provide new frames of reference and new ways of thinking about growth and change as opportunities for the members and those they love.

Theories of Group Leadership

Early theories about the best method to use in leading a group focused primarily on leadership style. Leadership was considered a trait rather than a cluster of behaviors that could be learned (Avolio, Walumbwa, & Weber, 2009). More recent evidence, however, clearly indicates that although certain personality factors may foster effective leadership, it can also be learned (Forsyth, 2014).

Three positions on a continuum of leadership behavior—laissez-faire, democratic, and autocratic—were the subject of early investigations (Lewin & Lippitt, 1938; Lewin, Lippitt, & White, 1939). The continuum can be seen in Figure 4.1. Findings from these studies indicated that there were more aggression, hostility, and scapegoating in autocratic groups than in democratic groups. There were no differences in the tasks

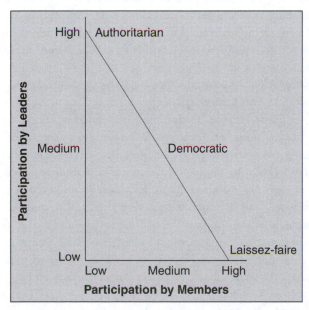

Figure 4.1
Participation in Decision Making by Leaders and Members in Groups Using Three Leadership Skills

completed by the groups, but there was some evidence that the quality of the products of democratic groups were superior to those of autocratic or laissez-faire groups. Group members also preferred the democratic group's process—that is, they liked the leader better and felt freer and more willing to make suggestions. These early findings seemed to suggest that allowing members to participate in the group's decision-making process was the preferred leadership style.

Factors Influencing Group Leadership

The early theories that focused on leadership styles were found to be too simplistic to explain leadership in most situations (Chemers, 2000). Gradually, contingency theories became more popular. These theories emphasized that situational factors helped to determine what skills and leadership style are most appropriate and effective for a particular group. For example, Nixon (1979) suggested considering seven factors before deciding on what leadership styles or behaviors are most effective.

Influences on Leadership
- The leadership expectations held by group members
- The way leadership has been attained
- Whether there is competition between designated leaders and the leaders that emerge as groups develop
- The needs, tasks, and goals of members and the group as a whole
- The task and socio-emotional skills of members
- The nature of authority within and outside of the group
- The environmental demands placed on the group and its leadership

To understand the dynamics of leadership in diverse treatment and task groups, several factors in addition to the personality and leadership style of the worker should be considered. In analyzing leadership in task groups, a number of investigators have shown that leaders develop different relationships with different members of a group (Dienesch & Liden, 1986; Graen & Schiemann, 1978; McClane, 1991). For example, an "individualized consideration" of each member is one of the central components of Bass's (1985, 1998) transformational leadership theory.

Others have suggested that leadership must be seen as a process within the context of the group and its environment. For example, Garvin (1997) emphasizes the role of the agency in influencing the work of treatment groups. When studying group leadership, Heap (1979) observed that the degree of activity of a worker is directly related to the social health of the group's members. Thus, a worker should be more active in groups in which members are "out of touch with reality" or "withdrawn or very aggressive" (p. 50). For example, a worker might need to be directive and structured in a remedial group for severely mentally ill inpatients of a state hospital. The worker, as "expert," may work with each member in turn for 5 or 10 minutes. Other members may be asked to offer opinions or provide feedback, but the primary focus is on helping an individual achieve particular treatment goals.

Similarly, Toseland (1995) noted that group workers have to be active when working with the frail elderly in groups. The energy level of these group members is often low, and they are often preoccupied with their own physical functioning. In addition, frail, older group members tend to relate to the group leader rather than to each other. Being energetic and working hard to establish connections among members can counteract these tendencies.

In contrast, when working with interested, eager, and less frail older members, the worker should take on a less active, enabler role. A group-centered leadership approach is more compatible with the goals of support, growth, and socialization groups in which members are eager to share their experiences and are not severely impaired. In using a group-centered method, the worker facilitates communication, interaction, understanding, and mutual aid and encourages members to help one another rather than to look to the worker as an expert who can solve their concerns or problems.

Overall, one conclusion that can be drawn from social science findings and from data accumulated from group work practice is that one method of leadership is not effective in all situations. The worker's leadership skills and intervention strategies should vary depending on the degree to which the group as a whole and its individual members can function autonomously. The less autonomous the group, the more the worker must play a central role in leading the group. Conversely, the more autonomous the group, the more the worker can facilitate the members' own self-direction and indigenous leadership abilities. In all groups, however, to accomplish goals most effectively, a secure, supportive, and trusting environment must underlie group interaction.

Effective Leadership

Although research on contingency theories of leadership has continued, research on "transformational" leadership has taken preeminence in recent years. A major contribution to leadership theory was made by Burns in 1978 when he distinguished between transactional (contingency-based) leadership and transformational leadership. Transformational leaders are those who (1) display high levels of competency and trustworthiness, (2) inspire and motivate members with their vision, (3) stimulate independent and creative thinking among members, and (4) individualize members by understanding their personal needs and goals (Avolio, Walumbwa, & Weber, 2009; Bass, 1998; Bass & Avolio, 1990a, 1990b, 1993). Transformational leadership models suggest that the leader should be a charismatic role model with vision who helps members to align their own goals with group and organizational goals (Avolio, Walumbwa, & Weber, 2009). Transformational leaders empower members by affirming and reinforcing their autonomy and individuality as they pursue individual, group, and organizational goals. Members are encouraged to question assumptions and to approach problems in new ways so that they are creative and innovative problem solvers (Alimo-Metcalfe & Alban-Metcalfe, 2001). Thus, transformational leaders use the power bases available to them, but the focus is on inspiring and empowering members rather than inducing compliance (Sosik & Jung, 2002). Transformations occur as members embrace group and organizational goals and view their own personal goals as a part of these larger goals.

In an attempt to unify contingency theories and transformational theories of leadership, Chemers (2000) suggests that effective leaders first have to establish the legitimacy of their leadership by being competent and trustworthy. He refers to this as "image management." Thus, effective leaders are highly respected individuals who have a vision. They promote safe, welcoming environments that avoid the extremes of aggressive confrontation of members or passive abdication of leadership to members who attempt to dominate groups (Kivlighan & Tarrant, 2001; Smokowski, Rose, & Bacallao, 2001). Next, leaders have to understand the abilities, capacities, values, and personalities of members. They use this understanding to encourage and guide members as they contribute to group goal attainment, while at the same time helping members to satisfy their own needs and achieve their own personal goals. Effective leaders skillfully deploy the resources they have at their disposal. This includes empowering members and reinforcing feelings of confidence and individual and group efficacy (Bandura, 1995, 1997b; Saleebey, 2013). It also includes making sure that the group engages in good information processing and decision making, so that when resources are deployed, the environmental demands on members and the group are carefully considered (Chemers, 2000). Overall, transformational leadership enables both workers and members to raise

> Assess your understanding of leadership, power, and empowerment by taking this brief quiz.

each other to higher levels of motivation and ethical conduct so that agreed upon goals can be achieved in a manner that is satisfactory to all (Forsyth, 2014). Transformational leadership has been positively associated with leadership effectiveness and better outcomes than traditional leadership (Avolio, Walumbwa, & Weber, 2009).

AN INTERACTIONAL MODEL OF LEADERSHIP

Unlike contingency and transactional leadership theories that focus exclusively on the leader, the model of leadership presented in this book focuses on the group, the worker as designated leader, the members, and the environment in which the group functions. This "interactional model" is presented in Figure 4.2. Because this model views leadership as being derived from the interactions of the group, its members, the designated leader, and the environment, the model is closely related to the ecological systems perspective of social casework proposed by Germain and Gitterman (2008) and Gitterman and Shulman (2005). Yet it also incorporates motivational interviewing, behavioral, cognitive, humanistic, interpersonal, psychodynamic, strengths-based, and transformational perspectives to enable members to work effectively together for change.

The interactional model represents leadership as a shared function that is not lodged solely in the designated group leader, but rather is empowering to members (Saleebey, 2013). In addition to the worker's role as designated leader, the model in Figure 4.2 clearly shows that leadership emerges from a variety of interacting factors as the group develops. These factors are (1) the purposes of the group, (2) the type of problem the group is working on, (3) the environment in which the group works, (4) the group as a whole, (5) the members of the group, and (6) the leader of the group.

Purposes of the Group

When one considers how leadership emerges in a group, it is essential to consider the purposes of the group. According to Browning (1977), a group may be formed (1) to perform tasks that require more than one or two people, (2) to meet individual needs, (3) to bring people together who are involved in the same or similar problems, (4) to represent a larger collection of people, (5) to form the largest collection of people that can be managed together, (6) to help maintain an organization more economically than individuals,

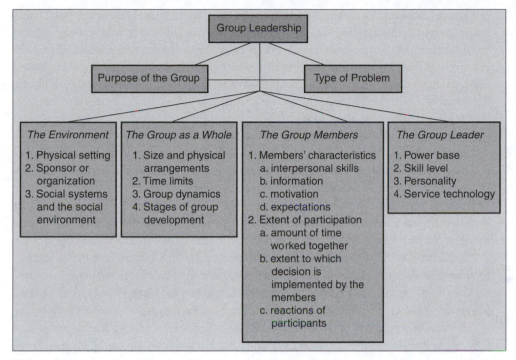

Figure 4.2
An Interactional Model of Group Leadership

(7) to increase motivation, or (8) as a result of physical factors, such as working together in the same office. Added to this list can be the purpose of using the group to change conditions or situations outside the group in an organization, a service delivery system, or an entire social system.

A group may have a single purpose or several purposes. The worker should consider how a group's purposes are interpreted by all systems that interact with it. The worker should ensure that the purpose of the group and the type of problem to be worked on are consistent. For example, if the purpose of a group is to meet the needs of socially isolated individuals, the types of problems on which the group works should be related to group members' needs for increased social interaction; that is, the group should not be working on problems of housing or finances unless they are linked to the primary purpose of decreasing isolation.

The purpose of a group helps determine how workers guide group processes. For example, in a group whose purpose is solely to complete a task or solve a problem, a worker might choose to encourage members to structure and focus the interactions more than in a group whose purpose is to have members share common concerns and ideas about an issue.

Type of Problem

The type of problem or task a group works on also has important implications for leadership. It has been found that groups do better than individuals on certain types of tasks, but individuals working alone do better on others (Forsyth, 2014; Hare et al., 1995). Generally, groups do better when the task is additive, such as collecting information. Thus, it would be better to form a treatment conference group to collect information about a client from all the professionals working with the client rather than to get the information from each professional separately. Groups are also more effective when they are choosing between clearly delineated alternatives. For example, Toseland, Rivas, and Chapman (1984) found that groups were more effective than individuals working alone when making decisions about funding priorities for medically underserved counties.

Groups also do better on tasks requiring a wide range of responses (Thorndike, 1938). For example, it is preferable to have group members and the leader generate alternative solutions with a woman who is having trouble expressing her anger rather than to have the woman generate the alternatives with just the leader. For these kinds of tasks, the leader should promote interaction, input, and feedback from all group members so that a wide range of responses is generated and evaluated, and members feel empowered in the process.

Individuals working alone solve some problems or accomplish some tasks faster and better than they would working in a group. Individuals working alone more readily solve technical and complex problems requiring expert knowledge. In these cases, an individual working alone may make a better decision than the whole group working together (Forsyth, 2014).

Several other aspects of problems should be considered when leading a group. One is whether the problem is of concern to the group as a whole, to a subgroup, or to an individual. Not all members of the group might be affected to the same extent by a particular problem or task being considered by a group. For example, when leading a group to teach parenting skills to foster parents, the worker should try to get all members involved in discussing parenting problems that are of interest to everyone in the group. When a member raises a problem unique to his or her particular situation, many responses are generated. The worker should try to develop generalized principles of child rearing of interest to all group members from the responses to the specific problem. This technique is often called *universalizing*.

When considering the type of problem confronting a group, workers should also be aware of where their legitimate influence ends. It may not be appropriate for the worker to encourage discussion of certain topics. For example, a worker leading a task group planning for an emergency housing shelter may not want to encourage a group member to talk about his or her personal family life or his or her need for housing. In other situations, however, workers may want to encourage discussion of taboo areas. For example, when the problem being discussed is child abuse, it might be helpful for the worker to encourage all members to talk about how they were disciplined during their early childhood.

Case Example   Individual and Group Problem Solving

In preparing a countywide plan for distributing emergency allocation funds to communities affected by a recent tornado, a worker decided to use a nominal group procedure that encouraged members to work alone before sharing their ideas with the group. In addition, the worker formed subgroups to work on specific ideas generated by the individual before they were considered in formal group discussion. By using both individual work and group interaction, the worker helped the group deal with a complex problem more efficiently.

The Environment

The environment in which the group conducts its work has a profound effect on how leadership emerges in the group. Environmental influences come primarily from three interrelated sources: (1) the physical setting, (2) the sponsor, and (3) the community and larger social environment.

Setting

The worker should ensure that the setting facilitates the group's work. The decor and comfort of the waiting room and meeting area and the availability of equipment and supplies, such as tables, blackboard, or newsprint, all influence the group's leadership. It is important for the worker to match group members' needs and preferences to a setting that facilitates the group's work. For example, sitting around a table may facilitate the work of a task group because members can spread out papers and write more easily. In contrast, a table may interfere with the observation of nonverbal communication in a therapy group and hamper role playing and engagement in other program activities.

Policy Practice

Behavior: Assess how social welfare and econimic policies impact the delivery of and access to social services

Critical Thinking Question: Groups are partially the products of their environments. In what ways do sponsoring organizations influence groups?

Sponsor

In addition to the physical environment, the organization sponsoring the group influences it in several ways. The worker, for example, must be aware of organization policies, rules, and regulations that apply to the work of the group. Funding, accrediting, and regulatory organizations can play an important role in the organization's mandate for the group service. The worker is given legitimate authority by the organization to help the group perform its tasks. The organization's delegation of this authority to the worker often assumes the worker will use the method of service delivery that currently exists in the agency. For example, two group workers trying to help pregnant women stop abusing alcohol may use quite different means, depending on the type of program sponsored by each agency. One group leader may use a reality-therapy group approach; the other may use a group format based on cognitive-behavioral self-control procedures.

Community and Social Environment

The third way the environment influences group leadership is through the community and larger social systems. The worker's leadership is influenced by the norms of behavior in the community and the larger society. For example, in a group for abusive parents, the worker intervenes to help members comply with societal norms and values concerning appropriate parenting behaviors. Smaller social systems can also affect a group's work. For example, an agency committee might hesitate to become involved in a search for additional emergency housing if a delegate council formed by a community planning agency is already looking at ways to develop additional emergency housing resources.

The Group as a Whole

At least four properties of the group as a whole influence how leadership emerges. These are (1) size, (2) time limits, open and closed membership, and turnover, (3) group dynamics, and (4) the stage of a group's development.

Size

As the size of a group increases, the opportunity for member participation decreases. The number of rules may increase as workers use them to maintain order and control in the group. Subgroups are more likely to form. The leader is more likely to be in the front of a large group, and leader-to-member and member-to-leader interactions are more likely than member-to-member interactions to occur.

Time Limits, Open and Closed Membership, and Turnover

Time limits may be voluntary or mandatory. A treatment group, for example, might decide to use a time-limited method, such as a behavioral group approach or a task-centered group approach. A task group, such as a delegate council, might feel responsible for making a speedy decision on an issue for an upcoming statewide meeting. In either case, time limits affect leadership behavior. Generally, time limits are associated with greater structuring of interactions, an increase in task-focused behavior, and fewer opportunities for indigenous leadership to emerge.

Closed and open membership has an important impact on group leadership. In closed membership groups, the original members stay with the group until completion or dropout, and the worker is able to get to know each person well. In these groups, workers are able to facilitate the growth and development of the group through the stages mentioned in Chapter 3. In open membership or rolling admissions groups when individuals come and go, the worker does not know members well and is more likely to rely on a structured format to help members feel welcome.

Membership turnover also makes a difference. Leadership varies based on whether there is a core group of members along with other members who come and go, and the duration of members' participation. For example, the leadership of a group that is open to all members of a 28-day rehabilitation program in a hospital would be quite different from the leadership of a group in a rehabilitation program with an average length of stay of 7 days. This is especially true if there were a core group of attendees of the open group in the 28-day rehabilitation program.

Group Dynamics

Another property that can influence leadership is the dynamics that operate in a group. As discussed in Chapter 3, these include communication and interaction patterns, cohesion, social control, and group culture. Workers should use their skills to foster the development of group dynamics that help the group accomplish its tasks and contribute to members' satisfaction. Interventions to change the dynamics of the group as a whole are described throughout this book.

Stage of Development

The stage of a group's development also affects leadership behavior (Brabender & Fallon, 2009). If the group is to develop successfully, the worker must be aware of the developmental tasks that face the group during each stage. A large portion of this text focuses on the specific skills and methods that workers can use during each stage of a group's development.

The Group Members

Group members influence how leadership emerges in three important ways: (1) through the unique characteristics and life experiences they bring to the group, (2) by the extent that they participate in the group, and (3) by the extent that they share in leading the group.

Member Characteristics

Several characteristics of members affect their ability to influence the group. These include members' interpersonal skills, access to information, perceived responsibility for the work of the group, motivations, and expectations about the process and outcome of the group. The importance of these characteristics should not be overlooked when considering how leadership develops in a group. It has been shown, for example, that member expectations influence outcomes in treatment (Gelso & Harbin, 2007) and task groups (Forsyth, 2014) and that interpersonal skill level and knowledge about a particular problem also help determine how well a group functions (Barlow, 2013).

Case Example   Group Activities for Children with Autism

In a self-contained classroom with eight children with autistic spectrum disorders, in order to help the children understand others' feelings, a school social worker might use feelings charades. For example, the worker might first show pictures of people with different feelings and then act out or model the feelings. Then the social worker would ask for volunteers to role play a person with a feeling and to have another child guess the feeling. The worker might also play a movement game called the mirror to help students pay attention to each other and to practice following the lead of another child in a social situation. In this game, the worker might bring in a mirror and show the children how it reflects whatever action is performed in front of it. Then the worker asks the children to form pairs and for one child to follow or *mirror* the movements of the other. Next, the children reverse roles, and the child who initially was the mirror acts out or *mirrors* what the first child does.

Because members' attributes differ, one member who is knowledgeable about a particular topic may become the task leader while that topic is being discussed. Another member may serve as the group's socio-emotional leader by expressing feelings and responding to other members' feelings. This suggests that the worker should remain aware of each member's leadership potential as the group progresses and help members to take on appropriate leadership roles that match their interests and skills. This is in keeping with the transformational leadership model mentioned earlier in this chapter in which the leader individualizes and empowers members, helping them to use their unique interests and strengths and to view personal goals within the context of the larger group goal (Avolio, Walumbwa, & Weber, 2009).

Extent of Participation

The extent of members' participation also influences how a worker leads a group. Some members' lack of interpersonal skills or motivation may prevent them from participating fully. In these situations, the worker may want to take on a more active stance by encouraging members to interact by using go-rounds to get each member's feedback about particular topics and by using program activities and other expressive therapies, such as music, movement, or art, to involve and draw out members. In some groups, for example in school settings, members may also have developmental disabilities that limit their ability to participate.

Sharing Leadership

Members' willingness to share leadership responsibilities is determined by their feelings of competency, their previous leadership experiences, and their perceptions of the openness of the designated leader to sharing leadership functions. It is also affected, in part, by the amount of time the member has been a part of the group. A new group member often has difficulty exerting leadership in a group in which the relationship among members has been established. Similarly, a member of a street gang that has been together for several years has more influence with the gang than a worker who is just beginning to interact with the gang.

The Group Leader

When one examines how leadership emerges in a group, the power base, skill level, personality, and choice of service technology of the designated leader all play important roles. As indicated earlier, seven types of power bases can be used to influence a group: connection, expert, information, legitimate, identification, reward, and coercive. Most workers draw on a variety of power bases; workers should realize the power bases at their disposal when they are considering leading a group.

Case Example   A Group of Persons with Alcoholism

A worker planning to lead a group of individuals referred from the court for driving-while-intoxicated offenses has several power bases to draw on in leading the group. The leader can present information about the harmful effects of alcohol, can connect the members of the group to other treatment resources, such as Alcoholics Anonymous (AA), and may even be able to connect members to sponsors within the AA program. The leader can also use some other power bases, such as the role of an expert who can certify if the person has completed the group successfully, which may have implications for the person getting their license back or on their probation status.

The level of skill that workers possess also influences their ability to lead. Experience and training of workers have been correlated with effectiveness in working with individuals and groups (Barlow, 2013; Brown, 2010).

A worker's personality, interpersonal style, and preferences for how to lead all influence how leadership emerges in the group (Bauman, 2010; Trotzer, 2010). For example, a worker who is shy and sensitive about others' feelings is less likely to use confrontation as a technique when leading a group. Therefore, it is important for workers to be aware of how their interpersonal style affects their attempts to analyze objectively what the group needs as they attempt to exert effective leadership. This is often referred to as *effective use of self* in social work practice. Some methods for becoming aware of leadership styles and how to modify them are described later in this chapter.

The service technology that workers use also affects how they conduct their groups. *Service technology* refers to particular theories or methods of intervention used by a worker. Three leaders of groups for alcoholics, for example, may intervene in quite different ways— by using transactional analysis or behavior therapy or, perhaps, reality therapy. Workers' choice of service technologies may be influenced by their personal preferences, their training, or the ideology of the agency in which they work.

A worker's technological and ideological stance often helps in organizing interventions. Workers may wish to receive specialized instruction in a particular service technology, such as behavior modification; however, it is essential that they become familiar with basic practice principles of leading groups before they receive specialized training.

> **?** Assess your understanding of an interactional model of leadership by taking this brief quiz.

GROUP LEADERSHIP SKILLS

Group leadership skills are behaviors or activities that help the group achieve its purpose and accomplish its tasks, and help members achieve their personal goals. Both workers and members use leadership skills, although workers ordinarily use them more than other group members. Leadership skills are combined when conducting group meetings. For example, in using a problem-solving method, a worker calls on numerous leadership skills to help a committee arrive at a decision concerning personnel practices in a family service agency. Similarly, in an aftercare treatment group for recovering drug addicts, a worker relies on many different skills to help members remain drug free.

There has been long-standing interest in the *skillful use of self* in social work practice (Goldstein, 1983). Most evidence concerning the effect of skill level on desired outcomes has been gathered from the evaluation of work with individuals rather than from work with groups (Dies, 1994). Reviews of the literature suggest that skills can be learned and that skill level makes a difference in performance (Barlow, 2013). There is some evidence that specific skills leading to therapeutic factors, such as attending intently and responding empathically, are directly connected to positive outcomes in therapy groups (Egan, 2013; Luke, 2014; Kivlighan & Kivlighan, 2014; Marmarosh, Dunton, & Amendola, 2014; Paquin, Kivlighan, & Drogosz, 2013). Results are tentative, however, because it is difficult to design studies to assess the independent effect of one particular skill.

Group leadership skills are somewhat different from skills used in working with an individual. Both members and the worker have greater choices regarding the level and focus of their interactions. For example, they may choose to be active or passive, and they may decide to interact with some members more than others. There is also a greater possibility of shared leadership and the delegation of various leadership responsibilities.

Some of the basic skills necessary for group leadership are categorized in Table 4.1. The skills are listed in three categories: (1) facilitating group processes, (2) data gathering and assessment, and (3) action. Skills are classified based on their most likely function within the group. Skills listed under one category may, however, be used in another category, particularly if they are combined with other skills. For example, responding is classified as a skill in facilitating group processes. Although responding to another group

---

Table 4.1   A Functional Classification of Group Leadership Skills

Facilitating Group Processes	Data Gathering and Assessment	Action
1. Involving group members	1. Identifying and describing thoughts, feelings, and behaviors	1. Supporting
2. Attending to others		2. Reframing and redefining
3. Expressing self	2. Requesting information, questioning, and probing	3. Linking members' communications
4. Responding to others		4. Directing
5. Focusing group communication	3. Summarizing and partializing information	5. Giving advice, suggestions, or instructions
6. Making group processes explicit	4. Synthesizing thoughts, feelings, and actions	6. Providing resources
7. Clarifying content	5. Analyzing information	7. Disclosure
8. Cuing, blocking, and guiding group interactions		8. Modeling, role playing, rehearsing, and coaching
		9. Confronting
		10. Resolving conflicts

---

member's actions or words facilitates communication, responding may also lead to additional data gathering, assessment, or action.

Facilitating Group Processes

Table 4.1 lists several different skills in the category of facilitating group processes. All of these skills can be used by workers differentially, depending on their intentions when attempting to influence various group processes. In general, however, skills in facilitating group processes contribute to positive group outcomes when they improve understanding among group members, build open communication channels, and encourage the development of trust so that all members are willing to contribute as much as they can to the problem on which the group is working.

Involving Group Members

Ideally, all members should be involved and interested in what is being discussed in the group. Yalom (2005) has called this universalizing a group member's experience. Involving members who have been silent helps identify commonalities and differences in their life experiences. As members become involved, they realize how particular problems affect them and how a solution to one member's problem can directly or indirectly help them. Involving others is also essential for building group cohesiveness, developing a sense of mutual aid, and encouraging shared decision-making.

Involving group members also means helping them take on leadership roles within the group. The worker should be cautious about doing too much for members and thereby stifling individual initiative. Instead of jealously guarding the leadership role, workers should encourage members to contribute to the content of group meetings and help shape group dynamic processes. This can be done by providing members with opportunities for leadership roles during program activities, by praising members for their leadership efforts, and by inviting and encouraging members' participation and initiative during group interaction. For example, the worker might say, "Mary, I know that you are knowledgeable about that; do you have anything to add to what Tom has said?" Similarly, the worker might say, "Tom, you did such an excellent job in the role play last week. Would you be willing to play the part of the angry storekeeper?"

Attending Skills

Attending skills are nonverbal behaviors, such as eye contact and body position, and verbal behaviors that convey empathy, respect, warmth, trust, genuineness, and honesty. Attending skills are useful in establishing rapport as well as a climate of acceptance and cohesiveness among group members. Egan (2013) suggests that, in addition to body position and eye contact, skills that indicate that a worker has heard and understood a member are part of effective attending. Research has shown that effective attending skills are an important characteristic of successful leaders (Luke, 2014). Effective attending skills include repeating or paraphrasing what a member says and responding empathically and enthusiastically to the meaning behind members' communications. They also include what Middleman (1978) has referred to as "scanning" skills. When scanning the group, the worker makes eye contact with all group members, which lets them know that the worker is concerned about them as individuals. Scanning helps reduce the tendency of workers to focus on one or two group members.

Expressive Skills

Expressive skills are also important for facilitating group processes. Workers should be able to help participants express thoughts and feelings about important problems, tasks, or issues facing the group and to reiterate and summarize them when necessary. Members should also be helped to express their thoughts and feelings as freely as possible in an appropriate and goal-oriented manner. Members of task and treatment groups can often benefit from an open discussion of formerly taboo areas that affect the group or its members. Self-disclosure is an expressive skill that can be used effectively for this purpose. Although self-disclosures should be made judiciously, according to their appropriateness for particular situations, they can often be useful in helping the worker promote open communication about difficult subjects. For example, a worker might say, "I just lost my mother, who also had been ill for a long time. I know what you mean, Bea, when you say that watching a loved one slowly decline right before your eyes is so hard. Your situation is different from mine, because it is your husband, but I can just imagine how terribly difficult it is for you. Do you want to share with us how you have been coping?"

Responding Skills

Skillful responses help the group as a whole and individual members accomplish tasks. The worker might, for example, amplify subtle messages or soften overpowering messages (Luke, 2014). The worker can also redirect messages that may be more appropriate for a particular member or the group as a whole.

Workers can use responding skills selectively to elicit specific reactions that will affect future group processes. For example, if a worker's response supports a group member's efforts, the member is more likely to continue to work on a task or a concern. If the worker disagrees with a member's statement or action, the member is likely to react either by responding to the worker's statement or by remaining silent. The member is not likely to continue to pursue the original statement. Thus, by responding selectively to particular communications, the worker can exert influence over subsequent communication patterns.

Focusing Skills

The worker can facilitate group processes by focusing them in a particular direction. This can be done by clarifying, asking a member to elaborate, repeating a particular communication or sequence of communications, or suggesting that group members limit their discussion to a particular topic. Helping the group maintain its focus can promote efficient work by reducing irrelevant communications and by encouraging a full exploration of issues and problems. Tropman (2014), for example, describes the importance of focusing on task groups agendas.

Making Group Processes Explicit

The skill of making group processes explicit helps members to become aware of how they are interacting. For example, a worker may point out implicit group norms, particular member roles, or specific interaction patterns. The worker may ask members whether they observed a particular pattern or type of interaction, whether they are comfortable with the interaction, and whether they would like to see changes in the ways members interact. Ward (2014) points out that it is important for the worker to verbalize therapeutic group norms and to encourage the development of traditions and rituals. For example, point out that at the beginning of each meeting members seem to take turns "telling their story" and receiving feedback about how they handled a particular situation. This encourages members to consider whether they want to continue this pattern of interaction.

Case Example   Pointing Out Group Dynamics

In order to help members understand how their interactions affected the group-as-a-whole, the leader of a support group for recovering alcoholics often took time out from the discussion of members' issues to bring up group dynamics and processes. He noted that members sometimes ignored nonverbal reactions of other members and often asked members to observe what was going on with the group-as-a-whole. Eventually, members became more skilled at observing this and other communication dynamics within the group. The leader frequently asked members to evaluate the leadership behavior of other members, using this "processing" time to discuss both member and group strengths. As the group progressed, the leader and members structured these discussions into the final few minutes of the session, giving them time each week to discuss group processes.

Pointing out the here-and-now of group interaction is an underused skill (Ward, 2014). Sometimes, workers are so caught up in the content of interaction that they forget to pay attention to group processes. Other workers are reluctant to make their observations public. Workers who have difficulty directing the group's attention to group processes should consider practicing this skill by setting aside a few minutes at the beginning or end of each meeting for a discussion of group processes or by making a conscious effort to point out group processes in brief summary statements at intervals during meetings. Clinical and supervisory experience suggests that the process of pointing out here-and-now group interaction becomes easier with practice. A brief example of how to point out here-and-now interactions during group meetings is presented in the case example.

Clarifying Content

Just as it can be beneficial to make group processes explicit, it can also be beneficial to point out the content of members' interactions. The worker's purpose in clarifying content is to help members communicate effectively. The skill of clarifying content includes checking that a particular message was understood by members of the group and helping members express themselves more clearly. It also includes pointing out when group interaction has become unfocused or sidetracked by an irrelevant issue.

The skill of clarifying content can also be used to point out the possible avoidance of taboo subjects. For example, in a support group for caregivers of the frail elderly, the worker might point out that the subject of nursing home placement has not arisen.

Cuing, Blocking, and Guiding Group Interactions

To help a group accomplish the goals it has set for itself, the worker will often find it helpful to guide the group's interaction in a particular direction. To start this process it is helpful to scan the group to look for verbal and nonverbal cues about group processes. The worker should avoid getting too caught up in the content of the group and instead should focus on the processes that are occurring among members. Cuing can be used to invite a member to speak so that the group stays focused on a topic. It can also be used when the worker wants to move the group in a new direction by focusing on or cuing a member who has brought up an important new topic for the group to discuss. Blocking can also be used when a member is getting off topic or is saying something that is inappropriate. By encouraging a member to speak or by limiting or blocking a group member's communication, the worker can guide the group's interaction patterns. Thus, blocking can both protect and energize members (Barlow, 2013). Blocking and drawing out members can be used to select communications patterns purposely to help groups to work with purpose and stay on goal (Barlow, 2013; Luke, 2014).

Case Example   A Bereavement Support Group

In a support group for recently widowed persons, members are talking about what to do about the personal belongings of their loved one who has died. One member, John, starts to talk about giving things to the Salvation Army. However, the worker scanning the group notices that two of the other members, Mary and Helen, are having strong personal reactions to the topic of disposing of their loved ones' personal belongings. The worker turns to John who had started to talk about the Salvation Army, mentions that that is a good resource, but asks if he would mind holding on to that thought until later in the group. The worker then asks if Mary, Helen, or anyone else would like to share what they are feeling or thinking before getting into the specifics of how to dispose of the belongings.

The skill of guiding group interactions has many uses. For example, the worker may want to correct a dysfunctional aspect of the group's process, such as the development of a subgroup that disrupts other members. A worker who can skillfully guide group interaction patterns can limit the communication between subgroup members and increase their communication with other group members. The worker may also want to use guiding skills to explore a particular problem or help members sustain their efforts in solving a problem or completing a task. At other times, the worker may want

Engagement

Behavior: Use empathy, reflection and interpersonal skills to effectively engage diverse clients and constituencies

Critical Thinking Question: Group leaders continually gather information in the group. What skills are particularly important for gathering data about the group?

to encourage open communication. For example, by redirecting a communication, the worker can help members speak to one another. The worker might say, "John, your message is really intended for Jill. Why don't you share your message directly with her rather than through me?"

Data-Gathering and Assessment

Data-gathering and assessment skills are useful in developing a plan for influencing communication patterns as well as in deciding on the action skills to use to accomplish the group's purposes. These skills provide a bridge between the process-oriented approach of facilitating group processes and the task-oriented approach of using action skills to achieve goals and satisfy members' needs. Without effective data-gathering and assessment skills, workers' interventions are not grounded in a complete understanding of the situation. This can result in the use of premature, oversimplified, or previously attempted solutions that have not been carefully analyzed and weighed.

Identifying and Describing Skills

Perhaps the most basic data-gathering skill is helping members identify and describe a particular situation. This skill allows elaboration of pertinent factors influencing a problem or task facing the group. In using this skill, workers should attempt to elicit descriptions that specify the problem attributes as clearly and concretely as possible. To understand the problem, it is often useful for the worker to identify or describe historical as well as current aspects of the problem. It may also be helpful to share alternative ways of viewing the situation to obtain diverse frames of reference, alternative interpretations of events, and potential solutions to a problem. For example, the worker might say, "You have given us a pretty complete description of what happened, Amy, but I wonder, what do you think Jim would say if I asked him to give an account of the same situation? How do you think he would view this?"

Requesting Information, Questioning, and Probing

The skills of identifying and describing a situation are essential to workers' attempts to gather data by requesting information, questioning, and probing. Using these skills, workers can clarify the problem or concern and broaden the scope of the group's work by obtaining additional information that may be useful to all members. The worker should be careful to ask questions that are clear and answerable. Double questions or value-laden questions may be met with resistance, passivity, anger, or misunderstanding. For some issues and for some group members, questioning or probing may be seen as a confrontation or a challenge to what has already been stated, particularly in areas in which the member is reluctant to give additional information, because the information is perceived as emotionally charged or potentially damaging to the member's status in the group. The worker should be particularly sensitive to these concerns when seeking additional information from a member. Helping the member explore fears or concerns about the potentially damaging effect of a disclosure can be a helpful intervention. Another is asking for feedback from other members about the realistic basis of personal fears.

Summarizing and Partializing

When information about the problems or concerns facing the group has been discussed, a worker can use summarizing or partializing skills. Summarizing skills enable a worker to present the core of what has been said in the group. It also provides members an opportunity to reflect on the problem. Summarizing skills give members and the worker an opportunity to consider the next steps in solving the problem and allow members to compare with the worker's summary their perceptions about what has gone on in the group. Partializing skills are useful for breaking down a complex problem or issue into manageable bits. Partializing is also helpful in determining group members' motivation to work on various aspects of the problem. For example, the worker might say, "John, I heard you talk a lot about your frustration with the group's not sticking to its purpose here. Would you tell us briefly, what you would like to see the group do that we are not doing right now? . . . Okay, so you are suggesting that we could take three steps to stay on track better during future discussions. . . . Am I paraphrasing you correctly? Are these the three things you think would keep us on track?"

Case Example	A Single Parents Group

In a single parents group, the worker asks John, a member of the group with partial custody of an 11-year-old son who has attention deficit hyperactivity disorder, to elaborate on his feelings about his son who has many behavior problems both at school and at home. In response, John says spontaneously, "Sometimes I get so frustrated I just feel like bashing his head in," but then immediately says he would not do such a thing. Sensing that John feels awkward about what he just said, the worker asks other members if they have had similar feelings in dealing with their own children. Several members talk about their frustrations and how they sometimes feel like they are about to lose control. A good interaction follows when members talk about how they handle situations when they fear they may lose control. The worker decides to join in and self-disclose a particular occasion on which she became so frustrated with her child that she had to leave the room before she did or said something she would regret later. In this way, John and the other members were able to disclose strong feelings without fear of how they would be perceived in the group.

Synthesizing

Another useful data-gathering and assessment skill is synthesizing verbal and nonverbal communications. Examples of synthesizing skills include making connections among the meanings behind a member's actions or words, expressing hidden agendas, making implicit feelings or thoughts explicit, and making connections between communications to point out themes and trends in members' actions or words.

Synthesizing skills can be useful in providing feedback to members about how they are perceived by others. Because these skills often involve a considerable amount of judgment and conjecture about the facts available to the worker, they should be used cautiously, and all members should have the opportunity for input into the synthesis. Ideally, when the worker synthesizes a number of interactions or points out similarities in group problem solving or in group communication patterns, all members should be able to give feedback about their perceptions of the situation. For example, during a weekly staff meeting of an adolescent unit in a state mental hospital, a worker might mention the patterns of interactions that have developed among team members. In describing these patterns, the worker would ask members for feedback on how they perceived the group's interaction.

Analyzing Skills

Once the data have been gathered and organized, the worker can use analyzing skills to synthesize the information and assess how to proceed (Ward, 2014). Analyzing skills include pointing out patterns in the data, identifying gaps in the data, and establishing mechanisms or plans for obtaining data to complete an assessment (Tropman, 2014). For example, in a treatment conference at a group home for adolescents, the worker can use analyzing skills to point out patterns used by staff members in previous work with a particular youngster. The group can then explore new methods and techniques for future efforts to work with the youngster. In an educational treatment group for potentially abusive parents, the worker can use analyzing skills to link parents' behavior patterns to the onset of physical abuse of their children.

Action Skills

Supporting Group Members

Action skills are most often used by the worker to help the group accomplish its tasks. Perhaps the most basic skill in this area is supporting group members in their efforts to help themselves and each other. There is also evidence that providing support to others increases one's own meaning and self-esteem (Sarason & Sarason, 2009) and mutual aid in the whole group (Shulman, 2014). Skills to support group members will not be effective unless members perceive the group to be a safe place in which their thoughts and feelings will be accepted. Thus, it is essential to begin by helping the group develop a culture in which all members' experiences and opinions are valued. The worker supports members by encouraging them to express their thoughts and feelings on topics relevant to the group, by providing them the opportunity to ventilate their concerns, by soliciting their opinions, and by responding to their requests and comments.

Support also means helping members respond empathically to each other, validating and affirming shared experiences. Skills in supporting members often involve pointing out their strengths and indicating how their participation in the group can help to resolve their problems. It also means providing hope for continued progress or success.

Ventilation and support are the primary goals of some groups. For example, support groups are sometimes formed for the staff of neonatal intensive care units and burn units of regional hospitals. Such groups give staff a chance to talk about and reflect on the emotionally draining situations they frequently face. Medical social workers who form and facilitate these groups encourage staff to ventilate pent-up emotions and provide peer support for one another. Similarly, the therapeutic elements of a treatment group for recently widowed people include the ventilation of feelings about the loss of a loved one, the affirmation of similar feelings and experiences, and the encouragement to cope effectively with the transition despite feelings of grief.

Reframing and Redefining

Often, one of the greatest obstacles to the work of a group or an individual is failure to view a problem from different perspectives to find a creative solution (Forsyth, 2014;

Tropman, 2014). Redefining and reframing the problem can help members examine the problem from a new perspective. Thus, a worker may want to reframe or redefine an issue or concern facing the group. For example, in a group in which one member is being made a scapegoat, the worker might help members redefine their relationship to that member. Redefining can be done by having members talk about how they relate to the person who is being scapegoated and how they might improve their relationship with that person. In this case, reframing the problem from one that focuses on the scapegoated member to one that is shared by all members is a useful way to change members' interactions with this particular member. As the problem is redefined and group members change their relationship with the member being scapegoated, the problem often diminishes or disappears.

Linking Members' Communications

The skill of linking members' communications involves asking members to share their reactions to the messages communicated by others in the group. Middleman and Wood (1990) refer to this skill as reaching for a feeling link or an information link. Members have a tendency to communicate with the worker rather than with other members, especially in early group meetings. The worker can prevent this from becoming a pattern by asking members about their reactions to a particular communication. For example, in a group in a psychiatric inpatient setting designed to prepare the members for independent living, the worker might say, "Mary, how do you feel about what Joe just said? I recall that during our last meeting, you expressed feeling anxious about living on your own." Alternatively, the worker might say, "Have any of you had the same feeling?" When members of the group validate and affirm each other's experiences and feelings, they develop a sense of belonging. Members no longer feel isolated or alone with their concerns. They stop questioning and doubting their own interpretations of a situation and their own reactions to it.

The skill of linking members' communications also involves asking members to respond to requests for help by other members. Helping members respond to each other fosters information sharing, mutual aid, and the building of a consensus about how to approach a particular problem. For example, in response to a query from a group member about whether the worker knows of a resource for helping him or her take care of his or her frail father while he or she is at work, the worker might ask whether any other members have used adult day care or respite care. Workers find that members are often more receptive to using a service or a resource when they hear positive reports about it from other members of the group.

Particularly when working with mandated and reluctant clients, workers who suggest the use of a particular resource may be viewed with skepticism. Members sometimes believe that the worker has a stake in getting them to use a particular service. In contrast, the testimonials of one or more group members about the benefits of a particular service are often viewed with less skepticism. Workers should also be aware that once they provide a response, other members are less likely to provide their own perspective. Thus, although a direct response to a member's communication is often warranted, it is often a good practice for workers to turn to other members of the group for their input before jumping in with their own responses.

Directing

Whether the worker is clarifying the group's goal, helping members participate in a particular program activity, leading a discussion, sharing new information, or assessing a particular problem, the worker is directing the group's action. Directing skills are most effective when coupled with efforts to increase members' participation and input (Chen & Rybak, 2004; Saleebey, 2013). The worker should not use directing skills without obtaining members' approval or without involving them in decisions about the direction the group should take to accomplish its goals. The worker should be aware of how each member reacts to being directed in a new component of the group's work. For example, when directing a role play in a remedial group designed to help teenagers learn how to handle angry feelings more effectively, the worker should be aware of how the action will affect each member. Depending on the way they express their anger, some group members may benefit more than others from playing certain roles.

Advice, Suggestions, and Instructions

Workers give advice, suggestions, and instructions to help group members acquire new behaviors, understand problems, or change problematic situations. Advice should only be given, however, after a careful assessment of what the member has tried in a situation. This avoids awkward situations when the worker provides advice or suggestions only to find that it has been tried without success. Advice should also be given in a tentative manner, such as "have you considered . . ." This type of phrasing enables members to express their opinion about the advice and whether they are ready to accept it. Group work experts have suggested being cautious about giving advice, especially if it is not solicited by a member (Kottler & Englar-Carlson, 2015), and process analyses of treatment and support groups indicate that it is not given often by professionals (Smith, Tobin, & Toseland, 1992). Nonetheless, advice is expected and wanted by many clients, especially those of lower socioeconomic status (Aronson & Overall, 1966; Davis, 1975; Mayer & Timms, 1970). Further, these skills appear to have some beneficial effect in helping clients formulate new ideas and approaches to resolving problems (Davis, 1975; Ewalt & Kutz, 1976; Fortune, 1979; Reid & Shapiro, 1969; Smith, Tobin, & Toseland, 1992). For example, in a review of studies of various therapeutic mechanisms of change, Emrick, Lassen, and Edwards (1977) reported that advice giving was strongly associated with positive changes in clients. Effective ways to give advice, suggestions, and instructions follow.

Giving Advice, Suggestions, and Instructions
- Should be appropriately timed
- Should be clear and geared to comprehension level of members
- Should be sensitive to the language and culture of members
- Should encourage members to share in the process
- Should facilitate helping networks among members

Advice, suggestions, and instructions should be timed appropriately so that group members are ready to accept them. They should also be clear and geared to the comprehension level of the members for whom they are intended. A group of teenage parents who have not completed high school requires a presentation of ideas, advice, suggestions, and instructions quite different from a presentation to a group of highly educated women who have delayed child rearing until their early thirties.

Workers should also be sensitive to the language and culture of the members of their groups. Certain words in English might not translate appropriately or with the same meaning in another language. Further, the cultural heritage of a population may influence how such individuals receive and decode messages sent from the worker.

The worker should not act alone in giving advice, suggestions, and instructions. This sets the worker off as an expert who may be seen as too directive. The worker should encourage members to share information, advice, and instructions with each other. Shulman (2014, 2016) refers to this as the worker's reaching for feelings and information that members may be hesitant to disclose. The aim is to deepen the level of disclosure in the group, thereby enhancing cohesion. It is also to empower members so that they get in touch with their own strengths and resiliencies and take ownership of the change process.

To encourage members to share information and advice with each other, the worker should facilitate the development of helping networks where members feel free to share their life experiences, information, and resources, as well as their opinions and views. One of the distinct advantages of group work over individual work is the ability of group members to rely on one another for help in solving problems and accomplishing goals. Experience suggests that well-established helping networks often continue outside the group long after the group experience has ended. For example, a worker who formed a support and parenting skills education group for single parents in an inner city later helped the group members form a child-care cooperative that flourished for years after the 12-week parenting skills group ended. Similarly, the members of a support group for family members of patients recently discharged from inpatient settings in the inner city were helped by a worker to form a local chapter of a national welfare rights organization.

Providing Resources

Organizations that sponsor groups have access to a wide variety of resources, such as medical treatment, home health care, financial assistance, job and rehabilitation counseling, family planning, and financial management consultation that the worker can make available to members. Making skillful use of these resources through accurate assessment and referral can be helpful to members. The worker can also encourage members to talk about the resources and services they have found to be effective. In this way, the cumulative knowledge of all group members can be used for mutual aid. Members who talk enthusiastically about a resource or service can be more convincing than a worker providing the very same information.

In task groups, workers can also provide a variety of resources for members. They can influence the environment in which a group works, either directly or indirectly, to make it easier for the group to accomplish its tasks. Workers may have access to important people or action groups that can give the group's work proper consideration. In addition, because task groups are often composed of members with a variety of skills and resources, members can also help one another achieve the group's goals.

Disclosure

Disclosure is an action skill that should be used sparingly by the worker for the specific purpose of deepening the communication within the group. Too often, novice workers disclose to join in and be a part of the group. Workers should remember, however, that their main role is to facilitate communication among members. Therefore, it is often more important to pay attention to the processes that are occurring in the group among members rather than to get involved directly in the content of the discussion. Being pulled into the content can have negative consequences, as the worker can be seen to be taking sides. It also distracts the worker from focusing on the verbal and nonverbal interaction occurring among members. The value of disclosure is in deepening communication occurring in the group, empathizing with members, and letting the members know that the worker understands their situation. Disclosure can also model openness and risk-taking, demonstrating that the group is a safe place to talk about difficult emotional issues.

Modeling, Role Playing, Rehearsing, and Coaching

The action skills of modeling, role playing, and rehearsing situations in the group can be helpful in both task and treatment groups. *Modeling* refers to the worker or a member demonstrating behaviors in a particular situation so that others in the group can observe what to do and how to do it. For example, the worker in an assertion training group might demonstrate how to respond to a spouse who has become quite angry. In another group, the worker might model caring and concern by going over to a group member who has begun to cry and placing an arm around the member's shoulder.

Case Example   Disclosure in a Couple's Group

During the interaction in a couple's group, members began to talk about how difficult it was for them to take responsibility for their own actions within their marriage and how it was easier to blame their partner for situations. Members went on to talk about how they could carry around anger at their spouse for hours and even days at a time. At one point, the worker stepped in and said that he had had similar experiences in his own relationship with his wife and how hard it was for him to step back and think about his role in the situation. The worker then asked the members to think about what happened when they stepped back and examined the situation and their role in it. This led to a productive discussion of how to step back from situations when one blamed one's partner for a situation and how this could be done without holding the anger in for hours or even days.

Role playing refers to having group members act out a situation with each other's help. The two primary purposes of role playing are to assess members' skill in responding to an interpersonal situation and to help members improve particular responses. Responses can be improved through feedback, rehearsal of a new response, or coaching.

Role playing can be a very useful tool when trying to help members improve their responses to stressful situations. For example, in a group for couples trying to improve their relationships, the worker might ask each couple to role play an argument they had during the past week. During the role play, the worker asks each couple to switch roles so that each partner could experience how the other felt, thought, and acted in the situation. Role plays can help members understand their partner's behavior in relationship to their own behavior. The couples can use the feedback they received to experiment with new and better ways to communicate during an argument. In this way, the couples learn new communication skills and begin to use improved ways of responding to each other during disagreements.

Rehearsing refers to practicing a new behavior or response based on the feedback received after a role play. Because it is difficult to learn new behaviors or to diminish less adaptive but habituated behavior patterns, a member may have to practice a new response several times.

Coaching is the use of verbal and physical instructions to help members reproduce a particular response. For example, members of a group for the mentally retarded might practice expressing their feelings during interpersonal interactions. As members practice, the worker coaches them by giving instructions and demonstrating how to improve their responses. Additional information about different role-playing techniques is presented in Chapter 9.

Confrontation Skills

Confrontation is a useful action skill for overcoming resistance and motivating members. Confrontation is the ability to clarify, examine, and challenge behaviors to help members overcome distortions and discrepancies among behaviors, thoughts, and feelings (Chen & Rybak, 2004; Egan, 2013). Confrontation skills should be used only when the worker has carefully assessed the situation and decided that what is said will not be rejected by a member. If a member is not ready to examine thoughts, behaviors, or feelings, the member may react negatively to a confrontation by becoming passive, angry, or hostile.

Because confrontations are potent and emotionally charged, workers should be prepared for strong reactions. In certain circumstances, workers may want to make gentle or tentative confrontations to explore a member's reactions before making direct, full-scale confrontation. Although confrontations are often associated with pointing out a member's flaws or weaknesses, they can be used to help members recognize strengths and assets. For example, in a remedial group for psychiatric inpatients, a depressed group member who is self-deprecating might be confronted and challenged to begin to recognize his or her strengths and assets. Similarly, a member of a growth group might be confronted by pointing out how her words differ from her actions.

Resolving Conflicts

One of the most important action skills is helping resolve conflicts among the members of the group and with individuals and social systems outside the group. Group members may conflict with one another for a variety of reasons. For example, in a delegate council, members may represent constituencies that have quite different concerns, interests, and goals. In a treatment team, group members' responsibilities for different work functions and tasks may cause conflict or competition, particularly if resources for accomplishing a task are limited.

Many of the models of group development described in the previous chapter indicate that conflict may arise among members as the group develops. The worker should help the group view conflict as a healthy process that can clarify the purposes and goals of the group and the way members can work together.

Although conflicts inevitably arise, skillful group facilitation can help avoid unnecessary conflicts and resolve disagreements before they turn into hostile disputes. To help avoid unnecessary conflicts, workers can suggest that the group develop and maintain rules for participation. These rules are frequently expressed in early contractual discussions with members. Sometimes these rules, which should be developed with the participation of all

I, the undersigned, agree to:

1. Attend each group session or call one day before the group meeting to explain my absence.

2. Not talk about anything that occurs in the group to anyone outside the group, unless it applies only to me and no other group member.

3. Carry out all assignments agreed to in the group between group sessions.

4. Speak in turn, so that everyone gets a chance to talk.

5. Give the group two weeks' notice before terminating my participation.

_____   _____
            Name   Date

Figure 4.3
Rules for Group Participation

group members, are stated in a written agreement that all members sign at the beginning of a new group. An example of such a written agreement is shown in Figure 4.3. Having agreed-on rules clearly written and displayed on a blackboard or flip chart is particularly helpful in children's groups. Children enjoy setting rules for their group, and, with the guidance of a leader, they can help each other follow rules they have made.

When conflicts arise among members, the worker may also use moderating, negotiating, mediating, or arbitrating skills to resolve disagreements before they turn into hostile disputes. Moderating skills help workers keep meetings within specified bounds so that conflict is avoided. Negotiating skills are used to help members come to an agreement or an understanding when initial opinions differ. Mediating skills are used when two or more members are in conflict, and action is necessary to help them reach an agreement and resolve the dispute. Arbitration skills involve having an authoritative third person meet with the group. This person listens to the dispute and binds the members to a settlement. Arbitration is sometimes used in task groups that have reached an impasse when working on a labor contract. Specific methods that workers can use to help resolve conflicts in groups are described in detail in Chapters 9 and 11.

Members may also come into conflict with forces outside the group. The members of therapy groups, for example, often expect workers to provide guidance about how to resolve conflicts with spouses, other family members, friends, fellow workers, and acquaintances. In attempting to be more assertive, a member of a therapy group might receive hostile, angry, or aggressive responses from family members or friends. In such a case, the worker might attempt to reduce the conflict by intervening directly in the situation or by helping the member develop the skills necessary to overcome the conflict alone. When the conflict is an inevitable by-product of a change the member wishes to make outside the group, the worker can help the member feel comfortable with the conflict until a new state of equilibrium is achieved.

Sometimes it is helpful for the worker to meet with people outside the group to resolve a member's conflict. For example, a worker might meet with the parents of an adolescent group member to discuss how the parents set limits and rules for their child.

In other cases, workers can prepare members for the reactions they may encounter outside the group. For example, a worker can help members learn how to respond to potential rejection or hostility when they are more assertive than usual with a particular person. Preparing members for what to expect in a wide range of situations and settings also helps ensure their success when they are using newly learned behaviors in unfamiliar settings or situations.

Workers may also need to resolve conflicts between the group as a whole and the larger society. For example, workers may help resolve conflicts between tenants' associations and housing authorities, welfare rights groups and county departments of social services, or support groups for individuals with chronic illnesses and health-care providers. Moderating, negotiating, mediating, and arbitrating skills can often be used successfully in these situations. However, in some situations, mobilization and social action skills (described in Chapter II) may have to be used to resolve a conflict.

Learning Group Leadership Skills

Persons who are training to become group workers should begin by becoming thoroughly familiar with the theoretical knowledge about groups as a whole and the way members and leaders function in groups. However, to integrate theoretical knowledge about group dynamics with practical experience, trainees should (1) participate in exercises and role plays illustrating how group dynamics operate, (2) observe others leading and being members of groups, (3) examine their participation as members of natural or formed groups, and (4) lead or colead a group in a supervised field practicum. It is also essential for trainees to have excellent supervision (Riva, 2014b).

In the classroom, trainees can learn to lead groups under a variety of conditions and circumstances by combining didactic and experiential methods of learning. Didactic material should expose trainees to the array of groups they may be called on to lead. Therefore, lectures, discussions, and examples should include groups in several settings with different purposes and clientele. Lecture material can be supplemented with films and videotapes of different social work groups in action.

Cognitive knowledge is, by itself, insufficient for effective group work practice. Training should include exercises and role plays to illustrate and demonstrate the material presented during lectures. Often laboratory groups can be formed to help trainees practice the material that has been presented. Lab groups give trainees a sense of what it is like to be a member of a group. In addition, leadership can be rotated in a lab group so that all members are responsible for leading a group at least once.

Laboratory group experiences can be enhanced by the use of video and audio equipment. These devices give trainees feedback about their verbal and nonverbal behavior as they participate in or lead a meeting. Tapes made during labs can be reviewed by trainees and the lab leader during supervisory sessions to help members develop their leadership skills.

Trainees can also learn how to lead a group by observing a group or by becoming a member of an existing group in the community. The trainee learns vicariously by observing the leader's behavior. The leader acts as a model of leadership skills for the member.

Learning also occurs through critiques of the group's process. Analyzing the group helps ensure that trainees do not accept all the activities of the group's leader without question. It gives trainees an opportunity to examine the development of a group over time and to observe the effects of leadership skills in action. It is relatively easy to structure lab groups so that part of the group's time is spent analyzing the group process, but trainees may not have this opportunity in community groups. Therefore, to achieve maximum benefit from participation in a community group, trainees should have an opportunity to discuss their experiences in supervisory sessions or in the classroom.

When trainees become familiar with basic skills in leading a group through these experiences, they are ready for a field practicum. The field practicum may include leading several sessions of a group, coleading a group, or leading an entire group while receiving supervision. For purposes of learning about group leadership skills, group supervision is preferable to individual supervision because the supervisor models group leadership skills while reviewing a trainee's work with a group. Rivas and Toseland (1981) have found that a training group is an effective way to provide supervision. Methods for conducting group supervision are discussed by Rose (1989). If not enough practicum sites are available, trainees can form their own task or treatment groups by providing group services to students or community residents (Rivas & Toseland, 1981).

Before leading a group, it is helpful for trainees to discuss their concerns about the first meeting. Lonergan (1989) reports that these concerns can include (1) unmanageable resistance exhibited by members, such as not talking; (2) losing control of the group because of members' excessive hostility or acting out; (3) inability to deal with specific behaviors, such as a member dropping out of the group capriciously, members dating each other, or individuals making sexual advances within the group or between group meetings; (4) overwhelming dependency demands by members; and (5) lack of attendance and the disintegration of the group. Because trainees react differently to their first group experience, supervisors should explore each individual's concerns and help them deal with their anxiety by discussing likely group reactions and reviewing what could be done in the unlikely event that a trainee's worst concern is realized. For additional information about effective methods for learning group leadership skills, see Riva, (2014a) and Stockton, Morran, & Chang (2014).

Leadership Style

It is important to recognize that, although leadership skills can be learned, they are not applied in a mechanical, objective fashion. Group work is a subjective encounter among the members of the group, all of whom have distinct personalities, viewpoints, and methods of relating to objective reality. Workers and members bring expectations, preferences, and styles of relating to the group (Bauman, 2010). Although these may be modified during the course of interaction, they continuously color and shape the evolving interaction and the skills that workers use to facilitate the group. For example, a feminist approach to group work with abused women would emphasize power differentials, identity formation, and equality of participation more than other approaches to the same problem (Pyles, 2013).

As Goldstein (1988) states, "As people enter into a group and take part in shaping its purpose and goals, the underlying premises that they bring to the encounter and their ways of perceiving, thinking and interpreting will inexorably determine how the process unfolds" (p. 25). Reid (1997) aptly points out that in therapy groups, "Each [person] brings to the [group] experience a history of relating to others, sometimes with success and at other times without. In this therapeutic alliance group, members may react to the therapist as if he or she were a significant figure from their own family. Similarly, the leader may react in exactly the same way, projecting onto others his or her own unresolved feelings and conflicts" (pp. 105–106). In the psychoanalytic tradition, the projection of feelings by members onto the leader is called *transference*. Projection of feelings onto members by the leader is called *countertransference*.

To become an effective group leader it is not sufficient, therefore, to learn group leadership skills without paying attention to how they are applied. It is essential for leaders to become self-reflective practitioners who consider carefully the meaning of their interactions with all members of the group. One of the hallmarks of an effective leader is the ability and willingness to examine the effect of personal beliefs, expectations, preferences, personality, style of relating, and subjective experience of reality on a particular group. Effective leaders are not afraid to explore with members, supervisors, or colleagues the possible ramifications of their behavior in a group (Okech, 2008). They observe carefully and think deeply about the meaning of members' reactions to a particular interaction.

The first step in helping leaders become more aware of the effect of their style of interaction is for them to do a self-assessment of their strengths and weaknesses as a leader. One way to do this is by asking participants to complete the Leadership Comfort Scale (LCS) shown in Figure 4.4. The LCS allows participants to rate their degree of comfort with 10 situations that group leaders frequently experience. Participants are also asked to write down their responses to a series of open-ended questions, such as:

- Describe what you perceive to be your major strengths and weaknesses as a leader.
- What types of group members make you feel uncomfortable?

Indicate your feelings when the following situations arise in the group. Circle the appropriate feeling.

1. Dealing with silence	Comfortable	Uncomfortable
2. Dealing with negative feelings from members	Comfortable	Uncomfortable
3. Having little structure in a group	Comfortable	Uncomfortable
4. Dealing with ambiguity of purpose	Comfortable	Uncomfortable
5. Having to self-disclose your feelings to the group	Comfortable	Uncomfortable
6. Experiencing high self-disclosure among members	Comfortable	Uncomfortable
7. Dealing with conflict in the group	Comfortable	Uncomfortable
8. Having your leadership authority questioned	Comfortable	Uncomfortable
9. Being evaluated by group members	Comfortable	Uncomfortable
10. Allowing members to take responsibility for the group	Comfortable	Uncomfortable

Figure 4.4
Leadership Comfort Scale

- What situations or events during group meetings do you find particularly difficult to deal with?
- What feedback have you received from others about your leadership skills?
- What steps have you taken to improve your leadership skills? What steps have you considered but not taken?

Participants' anonymous answers to the LCS are tabulated, and the aggregate answers are presented on a flip chart or blackboard. Volunteers are asked to share their answers to the open-ended questions, which inevitably lead to a lively discussion of difficult leadership situations and participants' strengths and weaknesses in dealing with them. The discussion also helps point out the diversity of responses to challenging leadership situations.

Completing the Beliefs About Structure Scale (BASS), shown in Figure 4.5, can further the process of self-assessment. When completing the BASS, participants sometimes state that their answers depend on the purpose of the group, the types of group members, and so forth. Leadership is interactive, but individuals have preferences about the degree of structure with which they are most comfortable. Participants should be asked to respond to the inventory in a way that best describes their natural tendencies and preferences.

After completing the BASS, participants can be asked to total the number of items they circled in column A and column B and to form two groups—one for those who had higher column A scores favoring a higher level of structure and one for those who had higher column B scores favoring a lower level of structure. Participants in each group are asked to discuss why they preferred a higher or lower level of structure. They may also

Circle the statement in Column A or B that best describes your preference when running a group.

Column A	Column B
Time-limited group	Open-ended group
High structure/rules	Low structure/rules
Formal contract	Informal contract
Leader sets group purpose	Members decide purpose
Focus on member goals	Focus on group process
Leader-centered authority	Shared authority
Closed membership	Open membership
Homogeneous membership	Heterogeneous membership
Use of program activities	Use of open discussion
Focus on member behavior	Focus on meaning of communication
Directive leadership	Nondirective leadership

Summarize what you have learned about your style from the above choices. What are the major themes that emerge about your preferences for a particular level of structure within a group?

Figure 4.5
Beliefs About Structure Scale (BASS)

be asked to prepare for a debate with members of the other group about the benefits of their approach to structuring the work of the group.

Participants can also be asked to complete the How Members Achieve Change Scale, which is presented in Figure 4.6. Once this scale is completed, different approaches to helping members change are discussed. For example, the importance of insight in psychoanalytic group psychotherapy is contrasted with the importance of identifying here-and-now feelings in gestalt therapy. Similarly, the importance of cognition in cognitive therapy is contrasted with the importance of action in behavior therapy. Participants can also be asked to provide examples of the methods they use to help members change. For example, participants who prefer to help group members change through action strategies might describe role-playing or psychodrama procedures that they have found to be particularly effective.

Group leadership style is partly a function of how one believes members achieve change in their lives and how one believes the group should take responsibility for helping members change. Answer the following questions about these dynamics. Avoid using the term "it all depends." Instead, choose the answer that best expresses your natural preference or inclination.

1. Do people achieve change best through insight or action?

2. Do people achieve change best by focusing on their affect (feelings) or their cognition (thoughts)?

3. When helping a member to achieve change, would you concentrate on changing the member's behavior or the member's thoughts?

4. When evaluating whether a member was making progress in the change efforts, would you assess whether the member did what the member wanted, what you wanted, or what society wanted?

5. Is it more important to give your attention to group content or group process?

6. Do you think the responsibility for the functioning of the group rests with the leader or the members?

Choose the statement that best characterizes your opinion. (circle one)

7. The purpose for group work is:
   a. Raising social consciousness, social responsibility, informed citizenship, and social and political action.
   b. Restoring and rehabilitating group members who are behaving dysfunctionally.
   c. Forming a mutual aid system among members to achieve maximum adaptation and socialization.

8. The role of the worker is to be a:
   a. Role model and enabler for responsible citizenship.
   b. Change agent, problem solving with members to meet their goals.
   c. Mediator between the needs of the members and the needs of the group and larger society.

9. Which methods would you tend to use in the group?
   a. Discussion, participation, consensus, group task
   b. Structured exercises, direct influence in and out of group
   c. Shared authority, support, building a positive group culture

Based on your responses to the previous nine questions, summarize your preferences for how to help members change.

Figure 4.6
How Members Achieve Change Scale

Participants can also discuss preferences for process-oriented or outcome-oriented leadership styles and preferences for member-centered or leader-centered leadership styles. Discussion is not intended to promote a particular style of leadership or even to help leaders identify what style of leadership they prefer. Rather, the aim is to encourage participants to become more self-reflective, to consider their natural tendencies and preferences, and to gain greater insight into how their natural tendencies and preferences affect their interaction with group members.

> **?** Assess your understanding of group leadership skills by taking this brief quiz.

CO-LEADERSHIP

Co-leadership presents a dilemma for the practicing group worker. Do the benefits of co-leadership exceed its potential disadvantages? Although there is little empirical evidence to suggest that two leaders are better than one (Luke & Hackney, 2007; Yalom, 2005), there are many clinical reports of the benefits of having two leaders (Luke & Hackney, 2007; Okech, 2008).

Co-leadership allows greater coverage of the dynamics of the groups, especially if co-leaders sit opposite each other. Because it is hard to see what is going on with members to your immediate right and left, co-leaders who sit across from each other can more easily monitor members on both sides of the group. In addition, co-leaders can specialize in attending to some facets of group behavior over others. For example, co-leaders can take turns focusing on process and content issues. Some of the other most frequently cited benefits of having a co-leader follow.

Benefits of Co-leadership
- Leaders have a source of support.
- Leaders have a source of feedback and an opportunity for professional development.
- A leader's objectivity is increased through alternative frames of reference.
- Inexperienced leaders can receive training.
- Group members are provided with models for appropriate communication, interaction, and resolution of disputes.
- Leaders have assistance during therapeutic interventions, particularly during role plays, simulations, and program activities.
- Leaders have help setting limits and structuring the group experience.

This list suggests several ways in which co-leadership can be helpful. For the novice worker, probably the greatest benefit of co-leadership is having a supportive partner who understands how difficult it is to be an effective leader. As Galinsky and Schopler (1981) point out, "The support of a compatible co-leader lessens the strains of dealing with difficult and often complicated group interactions" (p. 54). During group meetings, co-leaders help each other facilitate the work of the group. Between group meetings, they share their feelings about the group and their roles in it. In addition to supporting each other's efforts at group leadership, co-leaders can share feedback with each other about their mutual strengths and weaknesses and thereby foster each other's professional growth and development.

Co-leadership can also be helpful because it allows workers to share alternative frames of reference regarding the interaction that has taken place in the group (Okech, 2008). This helps fill in gaps in each worker's memory of events and helps each view the interaction from a different perspective. This process, in turn, may lead to a more complete and accurate assessment as well as to more adequate planning when the co-leaders prepare for future group meetings.

Co-leadership provides a group with the benefit of having two workers who can help with problem solving. It provides two models of behavior for members to identify with and helps in role plays, simulation, and program activities engaged in by the group. Co-leaders can increase workers' abilities to establish and enforce limits as long as they share common goals. Co-leaders also have the opportunity to structure their roles to meet the needs of members. For example, one worker can focus on members' socio-emotional needs and the other worker can focus on members' task needs. In its most refined form, co-leadership can be used strategically to promote therapeutic goals in a powerful and effective fashion. For example, when describing the benefits of male and female co-leadership of spouse abuse groups, Nosko and Wallace (1997) point out that male and female co-leaders who are perceived as different but equal can be effective at structuring their leadership and interactions to promote the resolution of faulty gender socialization among members. Effective co-leaders use their relationship with each other to model effective interpersonal interactions that members can emulate both within and outside of the group.

Despite the benefits, co-leadership has some potential disadvantages.

Disadvantages of Co-leadership
- Can be more expensive than solo leadership
- Coordination needed for planning meetings
- Leaders not functioning well together are poor role models
- Training new leaders by placing them in groups with experienced leaders may create conflict and tension
- Conflict between leaders can negatively affect group outcomes

Because it requires the time of two leaders, co-leadership is expensive. Leaders must coordinate their actions in planning for the group. Between group sessions, communication can be a problem if workers do not make a concerted effort to find the time to discuss their work together (Luke & Hackney, 2007; Miles & Kivlighan, 2010). If leaders do not function well together, they may not serve as therapeutic role models for members (Davis & Lohr, 1971). Yalom (2005) recommends that co-leaders have equal status and experience. He suggests that the apprenticeship format—that is, training new group leaders by placing them in groups with experienced leaders—may create conflict and tension.

Conflict between co-leaders can have detrimental effects on the outcome of a group (Miles & Kivlighan, 2010; Yalom, 2005). Members may be able to side with one leader against the other or avoid working on difficult issues. When co-leaders experience conflict with one another, it can be helpful to resolve the conflict in the group. This lets members know that the leaders are comfortable with conflict and are able to work together to resolve it. It also enables the co-leaders to act as models by demonstrating appropriate conflict-resolution strategies. In some situations, it may not be helpful to resolve a conflict between co-leaders in the group. For example, when conflicts are deep-seated and when there is little hope of a successful resolution, they may be better handled in supervisory sessions. The decision about whether to resolve a conflict in a group should depend on its potential effect on members. Because members are usually aware of conflicts between co-leaders, it is generally preferable to resolve them within the group, especially if the resolution process is amicable and not too distressing for members. When conflict is resolved outside the group, some members may not be aware that a resolution has occurred, and it does not model conflict-resolution skills for them.

Because of the lack of empirical evidence about its effectiveness, the benefits and drawbacks of co-leadership should be carefully considered before two leaders are used in a group. Wright (2002) points out that the decision to have co-facilitators should be based on the needs of the group rather than on worker preferences for solo or co-leadership. In situations in which it is especially important to have models that represent different points of view, it may be important to have co-leaders. For example, in a group of couples, it can be useful to have both male and female leaders. In other situations, however, the expense of co-leadership or the incompatibility of potential co-leaders may negate any potential benefits.

When the decision is reached to colead a group, it is essential that co-leaders meet together regularly to plan for the group and to discuss group process issues that arise as the group develops (Okech, 2008). To avoid co-leaders becoming too busy to meet together, it is helpful if they schedule a specific time to meet after each group meeting. During these meetings, co-leaders should review what they did well in working together, what difficulties they experienced, how they plan to work together during the next meeting, and how members and the group as a whole are progressing. In particular, they should discuss their reactions to members and their perceptions of any difficulties or resistance that members may be experiencing. They should review the overall development of the group as it moves through the phases of group development to hopefully more cohesive and productive forms of interaction. Co-leaders should also discuss their own relationship, such as their division of responsibility in the group and their feelings about their equitable contributions in the group. This type of reflective co-leadership practice is essential for making the experience successful and productive (Okech, 2008).

Okech and Kline (2006) point out that competency concerns strongly influence co-leaders' relationship and performance in a group. Therefore, it is essential for co-leaders to talk about their respective roles in the group between meetings. Co-leaders should be particularly aware of any attempts to divide their effort that could result in working toward different purposes or on behalf of different group factions. Co-leaders should schedule their review meeting soon after a group meeting because they are more likely to remember what has occurred, and they have more time to prepare for the next meeting.

Experience has shown that it is worse to have a co-leader with whom one does not agree than to lead a group alone. Therefore, group workers should be cautious in choosing a co-leader. Difficulties may arise when workers agree to colead a group without carefully considering whether they can work together effectively. Potential co-leaders

1. Describe your leadership style. Discuss whether your style is characteristically nurturing or confrontational, whether you tend to be a high-profile or a low-profile leader, and to what extent you are comfortable with spontaneity as contrasted with sticking with a planned agenda.

2. Describe your strengths and weaknesses as a leader. What makes you feel uncomfortable when leading a group?

3. Describe your beliefs about how people change and grow, and how you will intervene in the group. For example, discuss your favorite interventions, and whether you typically intervene quickly or slowly, waiting for members of the group to engage in mutual aid.

4. Share your expectations for group accomplishments.

5. Discuss your respective roles in the group. Discuss specifically (1) where you will sit, (2) starting and ending group meetings, (3) how you will divide responsibility for any content you will be presenting, (4) what you will do about talkative and silent members, (5) scapegoating and gatekeeping, and (6) what you will do about lateness and absenteeism.

6. Discuss where, when, and how you will deal with conflict between you, and between either of you and the members of the group.

7. Discuss how you will deal with strong expressions of emotion such as crying and anger.

8. Is there anything that is nonnegotiable regarding your co-leadership of a group?

Figure 4.7
Issues to Talk Over with a Potential Co-leader

may want to examine each other's styles while leading a group or during team meetings before agreeing to colead a group. Figure 4.7 presents some issues to discuss before deciding to colead a group.

 Assess your understanding of co-leadership by taking this brief quiz.

SUMMARY

This chapter focuses on leading task and treatment groups effectively. Although leadership is sometimes viewed as a function executed exclusively by the worker, leadership functions should be shared with group members. In this regard, the text distinguishes between the worker's role as the designated leader of the group and the leadership roles of group members that emerge as the group develops.

Leadership is the process of guiding the development of the group and its members to achieve goals that are consistent with the value base of social work practice. A worker's ability to guide group members depends on the power attributed to the worker by group members, by the supporting agency or organization, and by the larger society that sanctions the work of the group. It also depends on workers' abilities to use an interactional model of leadership described in the chapter. This model creates transformational possibilities, empowering members to use their own capacities, resiliencies, and strengths to accomplish group and individual goals.

Leadership is affected by a variety of situational factors that act in combination. Thus, there is no one correct way to lead all groups. Rather, leadership methods should vary according to the particular group a worker is leading. This chapter reviews the remedial, social goals and reciprocal models of group leadership and examines several variables that affect group leadership. To help workers examine situational variables, the text describes an interactional model of group leadership. The model includes (1) the purpose of the group, (2) the type of problem the group is working on, (3) the environment in which the group is working, (4) the group as a whole, (5) the members of the group, and (6) the leader of the group.

It is essential that workers be familiar with a range of leadership skills that can be applied in many different types of groups and in many different settings. Skills include (1) facilitating group processes, (2) data gathering and assessment, and (3) action. Together, these skills constitute the core skills needed for effective leadership of task and treatment groups.

It is also essential that workers be aware of their leadership styles. A number of exercises are presented to help workers identify their preference for a particular leadership style and understand how their preferences influence their practice with treatment and task groups.

The chapter ends with an examination of co-leadership. The benefits, drawbacks, and pitfalls of co-leadership are described.

5

Leadership and Diversity

Group leaders often work with people from a wide range of backgrounds. Diversity within the group can be based on a variety of characteristics, such as culture, disability, ethnicity, gender, national origin, race, religion, sexual orientation, and social class. When differences exist among members or between the leader and members, leadership can be particularly challenging. There is some empirical evidence that training in diversity and multicultural competence helps group leaders to be more effective, but more is needed (Barlow, 2013).

When working with diverse members, workers should try to identify with each one, always seeking a fuller appreciation of the combined effects that adverse childhood events, lack of resources, marginalization, oppression, social stigmatization, trauma, victimization, and other factors may have had on them (Hays, 2007). At the same time, it is equally important to identify the accomplishments, capabilities, resiliency, resources, and strengths of each member. This is especially true in early group meetings when trust has not been established, and assessments of members' abilities and strengths have only just begun.

An empirically based approach to learning about issues of race, gender, and class in groups was presented by Davis and Proctor more than 25 years ago (1989). Although knowledge about issues of race, gender, and class has continued to expand since then (Forsyth, 2014), evidence-based group work practices with diverse populations remains very limited. For example, the number of studies about groups for women is increasing (Holmes, 2002; Kurtz, 2014; Pure, 2012; Western, 2013), but more evidence-based research on the effectiveness of these groups is needed. Similarly, there is literature on group work with lesbian, gay, bisexual, transgendered, questioning, and intersex members (LGBTQI) (Debiak, 2007; dickey & Loewy, 2010; Horne, Levitt, Reeves, & Wheeler, 2014; Pure, 2012; Ritter, 2010), but evidence about the effectiveness of these groups is needed. Group work practice research with other vulnerable populations, such as immigrants, is also limited (Akinsulure-Smith, 2009; McWhirter & Robbins, 2014; Weine et al., 2008). This chapter presents a framework for leading diverse groups that can be used by practitioners and researchers to address these limitations.

APPROACHES TO MULTICULTURAL GROUP WORK

Because there is at least some diversity in all groups, it is essential for group workers to develop a perspective on how to work with people whose backgrounds are different from their own. Many perspectives have been offered: (1) social justice (Finn, & Jacobson, 2008; Hays, Arredondo, Gladding, & Toporek, 2010; Ratts, Anthony, & Santos, 2010; Ratts & Pedersen, 2014; Smith & Shin, 2008), (2) racial/cultural identity (D'Andrea, 2014), (3) anti-oppressive (Brown & Mistry, 1994), (4) ethnic-sensitive (Devore & Schlesinger, 1999), (5) process stage (Lum, 2003, 2011), (6) cross-cultural and multiethnic (Green, 1999; Pinderhughes, 1995; Sue & Sue, 2013), and (7) cultural/multicultural competence (Diller, 2015).

Common Elements of Multicultural Approaches
- Personal comfort with differences
- Openness to new information about members' backgrounds and willingness to change or modify ideas and behaviors based on it
- Perceiving others through their own cultural and social lens rather than through workers' perspectives
- Seeking information and understanding about the specific beliefs and values members hold that may affect their behavior in groups
- Flexibility and adaptability when working with members who have backgrounds that are unfamiliar to workers
- Sorting through and synthesizing diverse information about specific communities to understand how it might apply to particular members of a group

Social Justice and Empowerment

Ratts, Anthony, and Santos (2010) and Barlow (2013) argue that social justice should pervade group work practice because many members experience oppressive environmental conditions. The goal of social justice is to ensure that every member has an equal opportunity to be a contributing members of society. Group work should help members to cope more effectively with oppressive situations, but also to change oppressive situations whenever possible. When describing skills for social justice practice, Hays, Arredondo, Gladding, and Toporek (2010) suggested identifying a common struggle among members that they all can work on in the group and in advocacy outside the group. For example, this might include focusing on the just and equitable allocation of resources and advocating for the greatest good for the whole society (Crethar, Torres, and Nash, 2008). It might also include consciousness raising and empowerment for those who have been traumatized by social injustices. Recovery groups for women who are battered or who have suffered adverse childhood experiences and adolescent and adult traumas are examples of this approach (Kurtz, 2014). Ratts, Anthony, and Santos (2010) have developed a social justice model for group work that includes five dimensions: (1) naiveté, (2) multicultural integration, (3) libratory critical consciousness, (4) empowerment, and

(5) social justice advocacy. Each dimension describes the degree to which social justice is actualized in a group, from complete naiveté to social justice advocacy. In the naiveté dimension, context and cultural variables are ignored when considering members' problems. In the multicultural integration dimension of the model, members are encouraged to consider each other's cultural backgrounds and worldviews. The libratory critical consciousness dimension of the model goes one step further by helping members understand how their experiences have historical, political, and social roots. Members' stories are reframed so that the problem is not the person but the environment. In this dimension, members can externalize and reframe problems, such as bullying, incest, rape, and family and community violence as environmentally caused. In the empowerment and strengths dimension of the model, members are helped to find their voice, identify and build on strengths, and develop self-advocacy skills. In the last dimension of the model, members and workers are asked to step out of their roles within the group to advocate for a social justice cause or issue.

Burns and Ross (2010) have developed some strategies to implement the social justice tenets of empowerment. These include:

Social Justice Tenets of Empowerment
- Be intentional about having a diverse group membership whenever possible by avoiding having only a token member of a marginalized community participate.
- Separate socially constructed biases from actual psychological problems.
- Facilitate consciousness raising about social justice by addressing and processing issues of oppression as they arise during meetings.
- Use structured program activities to highlight issues of privilege and oppression.

Understanding the dynamics of race, ethnicity, and culture is essential for effective group work practice, but people also differ from each other in gender, social class, geographic background, educational and disability level, language, sexual orientation, level of acculturation and assimilation, age, and many other factors. Thus, in addition to learning practice principles for use with particular groups such as Native Americans (McWhirter, & Robbins, 2014; Ratts & Pedersen, 2014; Weaver, 1999), African Americans (Aponte, Rivers, & Wohl, 2000; McRoy, 2003; Ratts & Pedersen, 2014; Steen, Shi, & Robbins, 2014), Latinos (Rivera, Fernandez, & Hendricks, 2014); persons with disabilities (Brown, 1995; Ellis, Simpson, Rose, & Plotner, 2014), and other groups that are more likely to experience oppression and privilege (Delucia-Waack, Kalodner, & Riva, 2014; Lum, 2004, 2005; Ratts & Pedersen, 2014; Sue & Sue, 2013), leaders can benefit from using a broader conceptual framework about diversity within groups.

> **?** Assess your understanding of the approaches to group work that promote social justice and culturally sensitive practice by taking this brief quiz.

A FRAMEWORK FOR LEADING DIVERSE GROUPS

The following framework is useful for leading diverse treatment and task groups:

- Developing cultural sensitivity
- Assessing cultural influences on group behavior
- Intervening with sensitivity to diversity

Developing Cultural Sensitivity

The terms *identity* and *culture* are often used to refer to the many ways people can differ. To develop a perspective on effective work with people of diverse cultural backgrounds, the group leader should engage in a process of self-exploration that leads to cultural competence (Diller, 2015; Sue & Sue, 2013). Workers who are culturally competent have an awareness of their own cultural limitations, are open to cultural differences, and acknowledge the integrity of other cultures. Steps in the process of developing cultural sensitivity follow.

> **Developing Cultural Sensitivity in Groups**
> - Explore your own cultural identity.
> - Learn how members define and identify themselves culturally.
> - Frame discussions of differences by emphasizing the strengths of various cultures.
> - Provide members with opportunities to describe how they experience their cultural backgrounds and identities.
> - Become familiar with the backgrounds of client groups with whom you frequently work.
> - Gain knowledge about particular cultural communities.
> - Become immersed in a particular culture.
> - Model acceptance and a nonjudgmental attitude about the values, lifestyles, beliefs, and behaviors of others by recognizing the value of diversity.
> - Acknowledge the effect of societal attitudes on members of diverse groups.
> - Honestly explore prejudices, biases, and stereotypical assumptions about working with people from diverse backgrounds.

Workers can become more culturally sensitive by exploring their feelings about their own identity. Sometimes leaders fail to take into account how they experience their identity and how this might affect their interactions with members from other backgrounds. Among both leaders and members, there may be little acknowledgment of identity issues and how these issues affect values, beliefs, and skills, perhaps because of discomfort with the subject of identity or because leaders fear that raising identity issues may reduce cohesion within the group. However, to ignore differences within the group denies the background and self-identity of each member. Davis, Galinsky, and Schopler (1995) note, for example, that "whenever people of different races come together in groups, leaders can assume that race is an issue, but not necessarily a problem" (p. 155). This can be expanded to include not only race, but disability, sexual orientation, and other forms of difference in groups. Diversity should be celebrated in all its forms, and workers should welcome all the different perspectives that it brings to group interaction.

Group workers benefit from knowledge about how members define and identify themselves. Because the manifestation of racial, cultural, ethnic, and other identity variables is the prerogative of the member rather than of the leader, the leader should provide opportunities for members to discuss their identities. For example, the leader can ask, "How do our cultural backgrounds affect how assertive we are in our daily lives?" or "How can we use our differing ethnic backgrounds to brainstorm some innovative solutions to the problem we are discussing here?" It is also essential for group workers to appreciate the context in which members grew up, and how that affects their identities. For example, are they from a privileged background or one fraught with oppression and social injustice?

Acculturation and assimilation are two other important factors to consider when developing cultural sensitivity. The theory of assimilation views minority status as temporary, with everyone living in the United States, regardless of ethnicity or race, gradually acquiring the cultural values of the mainstream culture. Although the assumption that everyone eventually assimilates is deeply rooted in U.S. society, it is clear that some minority groups continue to practice traditional, culturally bound norms for generations. Therefore, cultural pluralism theory may provide a better theoretical framework for culturally competent workers (Pillari, 2002). Cultural pluralism's main premise is that different ethnic and racial groups can interact in the larger society while maintaining their cultural distinctiveness and integrity (Parrillo, 2014). The cultural pluralism framework encourages workers and members to view differences in attitudes, norms, structures, and values positively as distinctive and defining elements of a person's identity. Workers can also read about the struggles of immigrants to acculturate, and how to work with them in groups (Akinsulure-Smith, 2009; McWhirter & Robbins, 2014; Weine et al., 2008).

It is often helpful for the worker to frame the discussion of differences in ways that help members see the strengths in their backgrounds. Diversity should be viewed as an asset to the group. After reviewing the empirical evidence about the performance of homogeneous versus heterogeneous groups, Forsyth (2014) pointed out that "diverse groups may be better at coping with changing work conditions, because their wider range of talents and traits enhances their flexibility" (p. 364). McLeod, Lobel, and Cox (1996) found that groups that included Asian Americans, African Americans, Latinos, and whites outperformed groups that included only whites. Similarly, Watson, Johnson, and Merritt (1998) found that diverse teams performed better than non-diverse teams. Forsyth (2014) noted that organizations should take steps to minimize the potential negative effects of diversity and maximize its benefits. Diverse teams need time to work through superficial first impressions based on gender, skin color, age, and other factors. Leaders should help members to appreciate and harmonize differences in values and principles by emphasizing how different perspectives can be an asset. The whole organization may need a culture shift to encourage collectivist values that minimize distinctions and distractions based on surface-level characteristics. Leaders should help members to engage, listen to, and respect each other, replacing competitive or denigrating interactions with cooperative working alliances.

Members may also have a variety of self-identity issues that affect their participation in groups (Forsyth, 2014). For example, some members may clearly identify with a single racial or ethnic background whereas others may identify with more than one, or none. It can be helpful if the leader provides members with opportunities to describe how they experience their background and whether they experience any identity conflicts.

Self-identity may be especially important when working with LGBTQI group members. Groups can provide an important support network and can be helpful in consciousness raising and problem solving regarding issues such as isolation, marginalization, oppression, prejudice, stereotyping, and coming out (Mallon, 2008). There is a substantial body of information for working with LGBTQI individuals in groups that group workers may find helpful to review (see, for example, Debiak, 2007; dickey & Loewy,

2010; Lev, 2009; Mallon, 2008; Nystrom, 2005; Pure, 2012; Ritter, 2010; Rothman, 2008); Walters, Longres, Han, & Icard, 2003).

Although it is not possible to know all the complexities of diverse cultures and backgrounds, it is helpful to become familiar with the cultural and racial backgrounds of members who are seen frequently by group workers. Listing characteristics of particular racial and cultural groups has been avoided here because members who may be thought of by others as coming from a single group often have unique, blended identities and may be acculturated to different degrees. Among Hispanic Americans, for example, there are wide differences in life experiences of people from Mexican American backgrounds and people from Puerto Rico (Moreno & Guido, 2005). Similarly, there are differences among African Americans with ancestry from different regions of Africa and African Americans with ancestry from different regions of the Caribbean and South America. Even members with similar backgrounds can differ significantly on the valance of certain normative attitudes. For example, many Latinos may agree on the importance of familism, but differ when it comes to other concepts, such as fatalism or a sense of extended family hierarchy. Still, it is helpful for group workers to become familiar with the broad cultural heritages of client groups with whom they frequently work.

Knowledge can be gained in a variety of ways. For example, the leader can research literature and other information to develop a personal knowledge base about people from different cultures. Even better, when working with groups composed of members from a particular culture, workers can visit that cultural community, interview community leaders and key informants, or become participant observers in the community. This knowledge can be quite helpful to group workers, but it is also essential to attend to how members self-identify because this individualizes members, and avoids stereotyping them.

It is also important to assess social class and status hierarchies, especially the extent to which members have experienced exclusion, marginalization, and oppression (Rothman, 2008). These are sensitive topics that members may not want to talk about, particularly in early group meetings where trust is lacking. Therefore, it is important to take time to get to know members individually, and it is often best to start out without preconceived notions, trying to build trust within the group at every opportunity. Opening a dialogue among members about any value-laden interactions that may reduce trust and understanding in the group is essential. Workers can also use these interactions as teachable moments, gently exploring and getting feedback from members about how they perceive their own identity and their experiences in society. In this way, workers become role models for open dialogue and the exploration of core issues at the heart of members' identities and cognitive schema. The following case example illustrates one worker's attempt to model cultural sensitivity through open dialogue and exploration of self-identity.

Case Example   Cultural Sensitivity

The group worker was concerned about a member's participation in a support group for women preparing to return to the workforce. The member often showed up for the meetings late and appeared tired. The worker suspected that the member was stressed by family responsibilities, but she also wondered whether other factors affected her participation. During a group meeting, the leader asked members to discuss how their cultural backgrounds influenced their return to work. The previously mentioned member explained that her family duties posed considerable time constraints on her ability to look for work, and she was unsure how her family would react to her holding a full-time job. She explained that as a Latina, there were specific expectations placed on her by her cultural upbringing. These included putting her family first in all of her activities and adhering to specific role expectations about what women should do within and outside the home. The member's disclosure to the group of this aspect of her self-identity and the subsequent discussion facilitated by the worker helped other members to explore their own cultural identities and the impact that these had on their job-seeking behavior. The discussion provided new insights for members about how their cultural identities affected their job readiness.

The leader can also gain knowledge about a particular cultural community through the process of *social mapping*, in which formal and informal relationships among members of a community are systematically observed and analyzed. For example, a leader assigned to conduct an after-school group that included several Latina members visited the local parish priest serving the Hispanic community and interviewed several members of the parish to gain a better understanding of the needs of young people in the community. In addition, the leader attended several social functions sponsored by the church and met with parents and other community members who provided the worker with new insights into the needs of Latina and Latino youth.

Devore and Schlesinger's (1999) community profile provides a helpful tool to complete the social mapping of a community. Lum's (2004) "culturagram" can be used to individualize social mapping by diagramming group members' individual experiences, their access to community resources, and their support networks. Rothman (2008) points out that assessments are also more productive and beneficial when they are conducted using a strengths and needs perspective rather than a problems and deficits perspective.

It is particularly important for leaders to demonstrate, verbally and nonverbally, that they are accepting and nonjudgmental about the values, lifestyles, beliefs, and behaviors that members express as the group progresses. Recognition and acknowledgment of the value of difference and diversity is a key ingredient in building trust and cohesion in the group as it progresses (Diller, 2015). By taking opportunities throughout the group experience to encourage members to share their self-identities, leaders express their interest in members and their desire to get to know them individually.

Similarly, it is also important to continually acknowledge the effect of societal attitudes on members as the group progresses and they become more open about sharing experiences of marginalization and oppression. Leaders should keep in mind that members of minority groups continually experience prejudice, stereotyping, and overt and institutional discrimination. The reality of ethnic and racial superiority themes in society, as well as classism, sexism, and the history of depriving certain groups of rights and resources, should all be considered when attempting to develop greater cultural sensitivity. The following case example illustrates how one worker attempted to help a group discuss discrimination and develop a positive perspective on diversity.

Case Example   Discrimination and Diversity

During an educational group for parents of children with developmental disabilities, the worker asked members to discuss the effects on themselves and their children of societal attitudes toward children with disabilities. Members were very willing to discuss examples of prejudice and incidents of discrimination. The worker used these discussions to help members share experiences about other forms of discrimination based on race, ethnicity, culture, and sexual orientation. These discussions helped members understand the universality of these experiences in the group and the dynamics behind prejudice and discrimination. The worker helped the group examine the strengths in their backgrounds and how negative experiences had helped them to grow strong and cope more effectively. The discussion also helped to empower members who began to talk about how they could best confront stereotypes and challenge discriminatory practices when they encountered them outside of the group.

Williams (1994) suggests that leaders themselves may go through stages of ethno-cultural development in which they experience cultural resistance and "color blindness" before acknowledging the importance of cultural influences and achieving cultural sensitivity. Attending workshops on cultural sensitivity, doing self-inventories, researching one's own cultural heritage, attending specific cultural activities in the community, and joining cultural associations and organizations can help group workers gain greater cultural self-awareness and a better sense of their strengths and weaknesses when working with diverse members. McGrath and Axelson (1999) and Hogan-Garcia (2013) also present helpful exercises that can be used to increase leaders' awareness, knowledge, and sensitivity when working with multicultural groups.

> **?** Assess your understanding of guidelines for developing cultural sensitivity in groups by taking this brief quiz.

Diversity and Difference in Practice

Behavior: Apply and communicate understanding of the importance of diversity and difference in shaping life experiences in practice at the micro, mezzo, and macro levels

Critical Thinking Question: Group workers are advised to consider the cultural influences on members' behaviors. How do workers use this information during the planning stage of the group?

Assessing Cultural Influences on Group Behavior

Assessing cultural influences on group behavior requires constant vigilance throughout the life of a group. Diversity among members from differing cultural backgrounds as well as among members from the same cultural background requires careful consideration. Rothman (2008, p. 45) suggests using a "cultura-gram" and considering four items in additon to the traditional biopsychosocial assessment: (1) immigration history, (2) acculturation, (3) school adjustment, and (4) employment. Some issues that should be considered when assessing cultural influences on group behavior are described below.

Factors to Consider When Assessing Cultural Influences on Group Behavior

- The match between member and leader backgrounds
- The influence of member backgrounds on group participation
- Members' views of the agency sponsoring the group
- The cultural sensitivity of outreach and recruiting efforts
- The formation of relationships among persons from diverse backgrounds
- The influence of the larger environmental context where members live on their behavior in the group
- Preferred patterns of behavior, values, and languages within the group
- Members' experiences with oppression and their feelings about themselves, their group identity, and the larger society
- Members' acculturation and the way they have fit into the society through work and school

Early in the planning stage of a group, the benefits of matching member and leader backgrounds should be considered. There is some evidence that minority clients express a preference for ethnically similar workers (Atkinson & Lowe, 1995; D'Andrea, 2004), but there is mixed evidence about whether matching client and worker backgrounds actually leads to more effective treatment (Hays, 2007; Yuki & Brewer, 2014). Also, there are often practical difficulties with matching workers and members in real-world settings (Forsyth, 2014; Yuki & Brewer, 2014).

Regardless of whether matching is attempted, some differences in the backgrounds of members and between members and the leader are likely. Therefore, when one plans a group, it is important for the leader to consider how members' backgrounds are likely to affect their participation in it. For example, it is helpful to assess how potential members' differing cultural backgrounds and levels of acculturation and assimilation affect their understanding of the purpose of the group. Members with different backgrounds bring differing expectations and experiences, and that can affect how they view the group's purposes and the way work is conducted in the group. Confusion about the purpose of the group can lead to members' frustration and anxiety in the group's early stages. Similarly, the level of written materials to achieve educational objectives or when engaging in program activities should be carefully assessed not only for members who speak English as a second or third language, but also when working with those from poor socioeconomic backgrounds who may have dropped out of school for economic or other reasons.

The leader should also consider how members' backgrounds are likely to interact with the sponsorship of the group. The worker should consider, for example, how the sponsoring agency is viewed by members from different backgrounds. It is also important to consider how accessible the agency is, both physically and psychologically, to potential members. As Davis, Galinsky, and Schopler (1995) note, ethnic and socioeconomic boundaries of neighborhoods may be difficult for members to cross. When the sponsoring agency is perceived as being in a neighborhood that does not welcome persons from differing cultures, the leader may need to hold meetings in welcoming communities. Key community members, such as clergy, political leaders, and neighborhood elders, may play an important part in helping the worker to gain support for the group and to reach potential members.

When composing a diverse group, the worker should consider how members from differing cultural groups are likely to relate to each other. A marked imbalance among members with one type of characteristic can cause problems of subgrouping, isolation, or domination by members of one particular background (Burnes & Ross, 2010). For example, Pure (2012) has noted that same-sex groups have advantages when the group task is associated with issues of personal identity, social oppression, empowerment, and issues of personal and political change.

A complete assessment of group members should consider the larger environmental context in which members live and how that context might influence behavior within the group (Ramos, Jones, & Toseland, 2005; Ratts, Anthony, & Santos, 2010; Rothman, 2008). The direct experience of racism, sexism, and other forms of oppression can have profound effects on members' behavior,

Assessment

Behavior: Apply knowledge of human behavior and the social environment, person-in-environment, and other multidisciplinary theoretical frameworks in the analysis of assessment data from clients and constituencies

Critical Thinking Question: Members are influenced by the environments where they live. How can group workers gain an appreciation and understanding of these environments?

but social impact theory suggests that minorities cluster together in groups, thereby up-lifting and empowering themselves in the face of a dominant culture (Forsyth, 2014). The following case example describes the impact of one type of experience on open communication and self-disclosure among a group of resettled refugees from Myanmar.

Case Example   Communication and Self-Disclosure

Despite his efforts to model the skills of open communication and self-disclosure, the leader of a group for resettled refugees from Myanmar often encountered members who were silent when discussions turned to conditions in their homeland. During these discussions, several members had difficulty talking about their experiences and seemed unable to confide in other members of the group. Through encouragement and honest interest, the worker helped several quiet members identify that they had been exposed to a variety of extreme conditions in their homeland, including torture, civil unrest, and government-sponsored violence. One member bravely told her story of watching members of a different ethnic and religious group kill her parents. Her courage in disclosing this to the group helped other silent members to develop trust in the group and to gradually share their own stories. The worker learned how external oppression can profoundly influence communication and interaction within a group.

When problems such as member dissatisfaction or conflict among members occur, the leader should keep in mind that the problems may be caused by cultural differences, not by an individual member's characteristics or flaws in group processes. For example, some members of a group became upset when two African American group members became animated when talking about oppression. The other members talked about their reactions to the anger expressed by these two members. The worker helped the group discuss what it was like to live with racism and prejudice on a daily basis and the anger that this causes. She acknowledged the white members' difficulty in knowing how to react when this anger is expressed. The worker also helped the group to see that, in some ways, the group reflected difficult and unresolved issues in the community. The interaction that followed the worker's intervention helped all members to become more empathic and understanding almost immediately, and it gradually increased group cohesion.

Several factors can interfere with the process of learning about how cultural background affects members' behavior in the group. The leader may fail to recognize that cultural differences exist or may diminish their importance. Facing difference is a difficult process. Leaders may think recognizing and expressing difference among members will cause conflict within the group. The leader may also fail to recognize differences among members of the same cultural group by assuming that all members of that culture have common behavioral characteristics and thereby overgeneralize and stereotype members with a common cultural heritage. Even if members share a common cultural background, major differences in acculturation, economic status, and other factors influence members' group experiences (Lum, 2011; Ratts & Pedersen, 2014; Sue & Sue, 2013). Information on how members' cultural backgrounds can influence group dynamics follows.

Diversity and Difference in Practice

Behavior: Apply and communicate understanding of the importance of diversity and difference in shaping life experiences in practice at the micro, mezzo, and macro levels

Critical Thinking Question: Group work involves work with people from many cultural backgrounds. How do cultural factors influence group dynamics?

Cultural Influences on Group Dynamics

Communication and Interaction
- Language, symbols, and nonverbal communication patterns of persons from different cultural backgrounds
- Language sensitivity and knowledge of words appropriate to various cultural contexts
- Stylistic elements of communication among diverse groups
- Nonverbal communications and how cultural groups differ in their use of space and distance
- Interaction patterns specific to different cultural groups

Cohesion
- Subgroup patterns among various cultural groups
- Expectations and motivations among persons from diverse backgrounds
- Cultural characteristics that influence common group goals
- Level of openness and intimacy that is comfortable for various cultural groups

Social Integration
- Culturally determined normative behavior
- Influence of culture on task and socio-emotional role development in groups
- Influence of discrimination and oppression on how members experience norms, roles, status, and power within groups

Group Culture
- Shared ideas, beliefs, and values about the dominant culture held by members from diverse cultural backgrounds
- Level of group feeling expressed by members as influenced by cultural norms that are a part of their identity
- World views about the value of material wealth and spiritual practices by members from diverse cultures

The leader should assess how members' backgrounds are likely to affect the way they experience communication and interaction patterns, cohesion, social integration, and the overall group culture. To assess communication and interaction patterns, it is important for the leader to understand the language, symbols, and nonverbal communication patterns of people from different cultural backgrounds (Lum, 2011; Ramos, Jones, & Toseland, 2005). For example, in leading her first group with Chinese American members, a worker learned that some members felt uncomfortable with the type of attending behaviors she had learned in her social work education. Through some gentle probing and consultation with persons from that community, she learned that her direct eye contact, forward body position, and open body position could be perceived as intimidating and disrespectful by these members.

D. W. Johnson (2014) suggests that assessing communication and interaction patterns requires language sensitivity and knowledge of words and expressions that are appropriate and inappropriate in communicating with diverse groups. The leader should also have an awareness of the stylistic elements of communication, including how members of diverse cultural backgrounds communicate. For example, because of their respect for the authority of the leader's status and position in the group, some Asian Americans relied heavily on the group leader, especially in the first few sessions. Some groups of Native Americans may consider it impolite to give opinions in the group, and such attitudes may be mislabeled as resistance by the leader or by non-Native American members.

The group leader should strive to become aware of the nuances of messages sent by members, including how nonverbal messages differ across various cultures (Ramos, Jones, & Toseland, 2005). People from different backgrounds use body language, gestures, and expressions to accompany and define the meaning of the verbal messages they send. In addition, the leader should consider how cultural groups differ in their use of space, that is, whether distance or closeness is the norm, and what other nonverbal communication norms govern interaction in the culture. It is also helpful for leaders to learn the language of members from diverse cultures. Earnest attempts to learn even rudimentary language skills are often respected by group members, an important factor in developing a trusting, professional, helping relationship with members.

The leader should be aware that culture can affect interaction patterns. Members from some cultural backgrounds favor member-to-leader patterns of interaction while others favor member-to-member patterns. The following case example illustrates how culture can influence interaction in a group.

Case Example   Culture and Group Interaction

A committee in a community center in a Chinese American section of the city was charged with planning a fundraising event. The leader observed that the Chinese American members of the group hesitated to criticize the behavior of an elderly gentleman who was monopolizing the group. The leader, who was not Chinese American, asked a member after a group meeting about this behavior. The leader learned that the Chinese American members were hesitant to bring up their feelings because the monopolizing member was a person of advanced age and status in the community. According to Chinese American cultural heritage, interactions with older, high-status persons require respect. Criticism was not an acceptable behavior. The leader asked the member for advice about how to handle the situation, and it was suggested that using go-rounds and an agenda that designated other members to give reports could help to reduce the elderly member's dominance, because he would then not feel that he had to fill voids or take the lead in loosely structured group discussions. This was tried successfully in subsequent meetings.

Cohesion can also be influenced by the cultural background of members. For example, in a support group for caregivers, some members with Hispanic backgrounds did not expect to divulge private family matters or publicly complain about their role as caregivers, and this affected how they bonded with other group members. If the cultural characteristics of members differ widely and are not explicitly taken into consideration, a climate of togetherness and a common sense of group goals can be difficult to achieve, and the overall cohesion of the group is affected.

Group workers should assess how members' cultural characteristics may affect norms, roles, status hierarchies, and power within the group. Group norms are often the result of the expectations that members bring to the group from previous experiences. The leader should assess how members' cultural backgrounds influence the norms that are developed in the group. For example, in many African American communities there is a strong belief in the power of spirituality and the "good" Christian life as antidotes to problems, such as substance abuse, marital disharmony, difficulties in child rearing, depression, and alienation (Diller, 2015). Members' role expectations, developed within their particular cultural context, also often guide their behavior within the group. Gender-specific role expectations, for example, are prominent among certain ethnic groups. Thus, the leader should consider how members' cultures influence their role expectations.

Workers should be sensitive to how members from diverse backgrounds experience power and control within the group. Many members of minority groups have had direct experience with oppression, discrimination, and prejudice, which can affect how they feel about the use of power within the group, and how they react to it.

Group workers should also assess how the backgrounds of individual members contribute to the overall group culture. Shared ideas, beliefs, and values held by group members are, in part, a reflection of what experiences individual members bring to the group. The group culture can include, for example, a heightened sense of spirituality when the group is composed of Native Americans or Hispanic Americans. The strengths of some cultural backgrounds can reinforce other important aspects of group culture. For example, in a caregivers group composed of African Americans, the cultural strength of the extended family as a natural helping network can help create a group culture of networking and mutual aid among members.

The expression of affect may also be a function of the cultural background of members. In a group composed of Latinas, a higher level of expression of group feelings and emotions may occur than in a group composed of Asian Americans, because in the latter group, members may be more likely to believe that strong expressions of emotion outside the family are not appropriate (Gray-Little & Kaplan, 2000). However, acculturation and many other factors should be considered along with this possibility, as workers experience members' actual interactions during meetings.

In addition to having an impact on group dynamics such as the culture of the group, it is important for workers to be aware that members' backgrounds can have a profound impact on group development and how leadership emerges in the group. Consider, for example, the impact of gender. Regarding group development, Schiller (1997) points out that affiliation and intimacy often appear earlier in women's groups and that conflict occurs later. Using Garland, Jones, and Kolodny's (1976) model of group development, Schiller (1995, 1997) proposes that the first and last stages of group development—preaffiliation and termination—remain the same, but that the three middle stages of group development—power and control, intimacy, and differentiation—would be conceptualized better as establishing a relational base, mutuality, interpersonal empathy, and challenge and change. Schiller (1997) goes on to describe the implications for practice of this alternative conceptualization of group development, which she refers to as the *relational model*.

Forsyth (2014) points out that women's leadership skills are often undervalued because they are viewed as socio-emotional experts rather than as instrumental experts. Because of gender stereotypes and leadership prototypes, men are often viewed by both genders as having more leadership potential, and men more often emerge as leaders of groups, even in groups that are composed largely of women (Forsyth, 2014). There is evidence, however, that by pointing out these dynamics in task and treatment groups, workers can provide greater opportunities for women to take on leadership roles (Forsyth, 2014).

> **?** Assess your understanding of cultural influences on group behavior by taking this brief quiz.

Intervening with Sensitivity to Diversity

There are many ways for a group leader to intervene with sensitivity to issues of diversity in the group. Many of these are based on established principles of social work practice. Others are culturally specific practices that can be especially helpful in culturally competent group work practice. Some of these methods follow.

Intervening with Sensitivity to Diversity
- Using social work values and skills
- Using a strengths perspective
- Exploring common and different experiences among members
- Exploring meanings and language
- Challenging prejudice and discrimination
- Advocating for members
- Empowering members
- Using culturally appropriate techniques and program activities
- Raising members' awareness and consciousness about social justice issues
- Developing a liberation critical consciousness by understanding the deeper political, social, and historical roots of exclusion, marginalization, and oppression

Using Social Work Values and Skills

Developing a culturally sensitive approach to group leadership means using social work values to guide interventions. The values of being nonjudgmental, genuine, and accepting can often compensate for wide differences in cultural backgrounds between the leader and members. These and other therapeutic factors described elsewhere in this text are essential for a culturally competent approach to group work.

Effective communication skills can also make a big difference. For example, good questioning skills, which stress open, nonjudgmental questions, can encourage members to respond in their own cultural styles. Similarly, the leader should be aware that for listening skills to be effective, the skills should be tailored to the cultural background of members. This is illustrated in the following case example.

Case Example   Culture and Communication

A leader in a group for substance abusers used active listening skills with a Native American member, often paraphrasing and summarizing the content of the member's statements. When the member's participation became less frequent, the leader wondered if the member was experiencing a relapse of his substance abuse. Despite these initial impressions, the leader learned from his supervisor that his paraphrasing and summarizing might be viewed as offensive by the Native American member. Recognizing that his leadership style might not be the most effective in this situation, he used non-verbal listening skills such as attention and head nodding that conveyed to the member that he was being heard and that his participation was being carefully considered. The member's participation in the group increased. The leader learned that depending on the cultural style of the member, the leader might use verbal listening skills for some members and non-verbal listening skills for others.

Using a Strengths Perspective

The leader should explore and use the strengths inherent in the cultural backgrounds of members (Appleby, Colon, & Hamilton, 2011; Saleebey, 2013). All cultures have strengths that can be tapped to empower members. Assessments and interventions should be focused on members' strengths and needs rather than on their problems and deficits (Rothman, 2008). A case example of a leader using a strengths-based approach with a group of older adults follows.

Case Example A Strengths-Based Approach

In a group for adults who care for relatives with Alzheimer's disease, the leader discussed the strong natural helping networks of several African American members and how these networks supported the efforts of the caregivers. The African American members acknowledged that their networks were resources that were used for respite care. As other members learned about some of the strengths of the African American extended family, some became more willing to call upon family members and other relatives for respite care.

In the same group, a woman of Latino background was criticized by another member for passively accepting the sole responsibility for caregiver in her family. The leader intervened, stressing that the role of caregiver was a culturally assigned one, usually given to a female in the household. The leader pointed out that the commitment to the care of family members by Latinas was viewed as a core value in Latino culture. Such strong familism is viewed as a strength both within and outside the Latino community (Flores, 2000; Rivera, Fernandez, & Hendricks, 2014). Other group members agreed with the leader's perspective. Because she felt her cultural heritage had been acknowledged positively, the woman became more active in the group.

In both task and treatment groups, it is important to point out how the group is strengthened by having members with diverse experiences and perspectives. It can be helpful for workers to mention to members the accumulating evidence supporting the positive effects of diverse perspectives on problem solving in groups (Forsyth, 2014). The worker can then go on to encourage members to express diverse perspectives and to help the group to consider fully the implications of each perspective. The worker's ultimate aim is to ensure that the alternative perspectives that diversity brings to the group are viewed as benefiting all members.

Exploring Common and Different Experiences Among Members

When working with members from diverse backgrounds, it is often useful to acknowledge and explore the differences and commonalities among members. This process can begin in orientation sessions and first group meetings by acknowledging diversity in the group and exploring how the cultural backgrounds of members may contribute to that diversity. For example, in a support group for parents who have experienced the death of a child, the leader began by self-disclosing that she was of Irish American background. She explained that, in her family, death was characteristically dealt with by planning large family gatherings that sometimes took on a festive atmosphere. She said that having a party after a person's death might seem strange to some members and she encouraged them to talk about the practices in their own families. The members then proceeded to explore their own cultural reactions to death and grieving.

Exploring common and different experiences can also help overcome barriers to members' self-disclosure. Members are sometimes reluctant to disclose when they believe others may be judgmental about their cultural values, behavior, or lifestyle. As described in the following case study, exploring cultural differences and fostering cultural appreciation can help members feel more secure in disclosing their thoughts and feelings.

Case Example   Exploring Cultural Differences

In a support group for parents, it seemed particularly difficult for participants who came from a Chinese American background to share intimate details of their family life. The worker tried to model self-disclosure and also encouraged other members to openly discuss difficult issues that they faced with their children. The developing norm of high self-disclosure continued to be difficult for the Chinese American parents. After one meeting, the father met briefly with the worker and noted that in his culture, certain family matters were considered private, to be discussed only among close family members. The worker acknowledged this and promised to help members show sensitivity to this cultural difference during the meetings. The Chinese American family felt more comfortable after that and participated more frequently.

There are also invisible and chosen affiliations that should be carefully considered by the group worker (Rothman, 2008). Although some group affiliations, such as gender and race, are obvious, others may be much less obvious. Some group affiliations, such as sexual orientation, religious and political affiliations, and certain disabilities such as AIDS, are not easily recognized in a group unless they are self-reported (Ellis, Simpson, Rose, & Plotner, 2014). Disclosure of these identities varies from group to group based on trust level, cohesion, subgroup size, and many other variables. The worker should be sensitive to the fact that hidden group affiliations may exist and strive to ensure that all members feel welcome and are helped by the group (Rothman, 2008).

Exploring Meanings and Language

Meaning is expressed through language. Many cultures do not attach common meanings to certain phenomena, such as social problems or medical diseases (Dinges & Cherry, 1995). There may be no clear equivalent in the Spanish language, for example, for some psychiatric diagnoses. Likewise, an illness, such as Alzheimer's disease, may be defined in Spanish using nonmedical terms. The leader should help group members explore the differences in meaning reflected in different languages. Some rudimentary knowledge of other languages is an asset, and the leader should realize that language helps to shape reality. There are instances in which common terms and idiomatic expressions in English have no clear equivalent in another language. Members who speak English as a second language can define social situations, problems, and other conditions in culturally bound ways. It can be very helpful and interesting for all group members to discuss and explore culturally bound definitions, as the following case example indicates.

Case Example   The Impact of Language

In a socialization group for new parents, one of the members had a mobility disability that required her to use a wheelchair. Although other members seemed to be sensitive to the needs of the member with the mobility disability, they used a variety of terms to refer to her during group discussions, including "the handicapped person" and "the disabled person." The leader asked the members to consider using a "person-first" formulation when referring to the member. She suggested that the member was a person with a disability, rather than a disabled or handicapped person. In group discussions, the leader noted that most persons with disabilities are offended when language suggests that they should be primarily defined by the nature of their disability rather than as people first, with all of the same strengths, capabilities, and potential as others. Through this intervention, members became more sensitive to the meanings inherent in language and how language can promote the strengths or weaknesses of people with disabilities.

The leader can help members interpret the significance of certain aspects of their culture to members of the group. In some instances, members may not understand the reasoning behind a cultural practice or phenomenon, which can lead to criticism or insensitivity among members. For example, in a rehabilitation group for spine-injured people, a member from Central America noted that he had visited the local *curandero* who prescribed native herbs and other remedies. The initial reaction of several members was to discount this practice and accuse the member of going outside the traditional medical establishment. However, the leader and other members explained the importance of folk medicine and traditional healing in the member's culture and how the local healer contributed to the member's mental and physical well-being. Members learned the importance of this cultural practice and the significance of different sources of folk healing for some members (Koss-Chioino, 2000).

Similarly, spirituality may contribute significantly to the well-being of members of a group. It is important to acknowledge the importance of spirituality for particular members of a group and to explain the significance of different religious orientations. Group workers sometimes ignore spirituality because of the belief that it is linked to a specific religious denomination. It is important to take an ecumenical view and emphasize how spirituality transcends organized religion. The worker should avoid proselytizing about a particular religion but should acknowledge the importance of spirituality in the lives of many members (Abernethy, 2012).

Diversity and Difference in Practice

Behavior: Present themselves as learners and engage clients and constituencies as experts of their own experiences

Critical Thinking Question: Many members have experience with discrimination and oppression. How can the worker explore these issues in the group?

Challenging Discrimination, Oppression, and Prejudice

Because the realities of discrimination, oppression, and prejudice experienced in the larger society can be expressed in the group, challenging biases, prejudice, and stereotypes is an important leader skill (Burnes & Ross, 2010). Everyone has some prejudicial attitudes that they may not be aware of holding. Some members may deny their biases. Members may come from backgrounds with very different levels of social privilege and oppression and beliefs about social justice that vary considerably. It can be difficult to find a common ground among members who have only known social privilege and members who have experienced a lifetime of oppression, inadequate resources, and dominance by a privileged group. Socially privileged members may be completely oblivious or actively hostile to other worldviews and realities, and oppressed group members may be hypervigilant about real and perceived slights by more privileged members. Group leadership can be very challenging in these situations, even when leaders are aware of the chasm.

There are many hurdles to overcome as groups begin to meet and workers guide members to develop trust in each other and group processes. Workers should start where members are, being careful not to bring members along so quickly that they reject views that they perceive as too radical. It is important for the leader to challenge all members to more realistically understand how they feel about people who are different from themselves, but in these situations workers must take special care to hear what is being said with empathy and openness.

Ultimately, workers aim to help members develop a liberator's critical consciousness by understanding the deeper political, social, and historical roots of marginalization and oppression and how these factors may have a significant impact on fellow group members (Hays, Arredondo, Gladding, & Toporek, 2010; Ratts, Antony, & Santos, 2010). To do this, the leader helps members understand the discrimination that members have experienced in the past, and continue to experience. Almost all minority groups have experienced discrimination. Burwell (1998) notes that extermination, expulsion, exclusion, and assimilation have all been used against minority group members. On a more subtle level, society often ignores the views of minorities and marginalizes their contributions. Schriver (2011) and Rothman (2008) indicate, for example, that minorities do not partake of the privileges often accorded to members of the majority group. Access to a privileged status results in unearned advantages accruing to a particular group because of race, gender, socioeconomic status, or some other characteristic. In the United States, for example, white males have a more privileged status than do African American males, which has profound consequences for both groups.

The leader can help members understand the effects of privilege and discrimination by asking members to identify a situation in which they felt discriminated against and to discuss the experience with other group members. After this exercise, members are often better able to appreciate each other's experiences in dealing with discrimination and the effect it has had on their views of themselves, others, and their life position.

The process of challenging discrimination, oppression, and prejudice continues as needed throughout the life of treatment groups. Experience suggests that it is important to take a gentle but firm stand, assuming that members who hold stereotypical ideas about other members need to be educated about the realities that these members have faced, and continue to experience. Attitudes are difficult to change, but workers must persist in an understanding manner to help members grow more open and accepting. Group interaction and program activities with diverse members can promote greater understanding, and workers should always be looking for new opportunities to help members better understand each other.

Experience also suggests that task groups can help to overcome prejudice. Differences in cultural beliefs (Maznevski & Peterson, 1997; Diaz, 2002), attitudes toward interpersonal interactions (Goto, 1997), differences in attitudes and judgments about the self and others (Earley & Randel, 1997), and language differences (Orasanu, Fischer, & Davison, 1997) can all be addressed in task groups. The following case example focuses on attitudes toward and judgments about group members based on age stereotypes.

Case Example   Overcoming Prejudice

In a coalition planning a homeless shelter for teenagers and young adults, several of the younger members seemed to discount or ignore the suggestions made by older members.

This developed into a pattern over the course of the early meetings of the group. Noting this, the leader asked members at the end of the third meeting to spend time giving attention to the group's processes, particularly asking members how age differences might be inhibiting the group's work. By discussing what she had observed in the group, the leader helped younger members confront their behaviors toward the older members. Initially, the younger members professed unawareness of their behavior. They said that it was not their intention to ignore the views of older members. They said they valued older members' views and welcomed them. As the coalition continued its work, the interaction changed and the group became more cohesive and appreciative of everyone's viewpoints.

Advocating for Members

Members from minority groups may need special assistance in negotiating difficult service systems. Also, they may need help obtaining benefits and services. In a parenting skills group, for example, the leader became concerned about the absence of several Native American members. In investigating the reasons for their absence, she noted that these group members felt guilty about leaving their child-care duties to attend group sessions. The leader secured the support of her agency in providing child care at the agency during group meetings. Because of her efforts, members attended more regularly, and their commitment and bond to the parenting group was greatly enhanced.

Leaders may wish to consider engaging in other advocacy activities on behalf of group members, such as working with family members and community support systems. For example, in a socialization group for the frail elderly at a senior citizens center, absenteeism was high although members seemed to enjoy the group. The worker surveyed the membership and found that many members depended on transportation from family or friends who were often busy. The leader used this information to advocate on members' behalf, with the local Office for the Aging and the county, for transportation to and from group meetings. Funding was in short supply so the worker also enlisted the support of local businesses. Eventually, with the help of all the partners, a senior van was bought and assigned to provide transportation for group members, and for other events sponsored by the senior citizens center. In another instance, a worker built a coalition of members from various gay, lesbian, and bisexual support groups to bring political pressure on city officials to pass adequate antidiscrimination legislation.

Advocating for group members, within and outside the group, is especially important for populations and groups who experience prejudice and discrimination. Persons who are diagnosed with AIDS, for example, often have difficulty obtaining housing, health care, social services, and other community-based services to which they are entitled. Leaders of groups for members experiencing high levels of discrimination should be prepared to spend time outside group sessions to help members gain access to needed services.

It is also important to facilitate consciousness raising in the group and helping members to feel better about their identities and affiliations (Burnes and Ross, 2010). In some groups, especially those used in community organization practice, workers can also encourage members to be self-advocates outside the group. This can be done either by individual members or by the group as a whole. Ratts, Anthony, and Santos (2010, p. 165) suggest that in addition to helping members develop a liberator's consciousness, members should also be empowered to go outside the group and "advocate with and on behalf of a cause or issue."

Empowering Members

Group intervention can help empower members by raising their cultural consciousness and by developing mutual aid within the group. Personal, interpersonal, and political power can be fostered by constructive dialogue among all members and by discussions that foster cultural identity and consciousness (Rothman, 2008). The leader can help members gain greater personal power and self-worth by reinforcing positive feelings about their identity and encouraging all members to interact with each other. Through consciousness raising, members can also be encouraged to advocate for themselves (Burnes & Ross, 2010; Rothman, 2008). All levels of system intervention, including larger systems such as institutions and communities, should be included in these efforts. The following case example provides a brief illustration of how a social support group engaged larger systems.

Case Example   Engaging the Community

A social support group sponsored by Centro Civico decided to sponsor a "senior expo" featuring the contributions of Latino elderly to the local community. The senior expo included ethnic foods, arts and crafts, exhibitions, workshops, and volunteer opportunities. Two other important aspects of the senior expo were a voter registration drive and an opportunity for members of the community to discuss their concerns about public transportation and safety with city council members.

Using Culturally Sensitive Techniques and Program Activities

Culturally sensitive techniques and program activities value diversity within the group, acknowledge how members of minority groups have unique sets of experiences, and allow members to appreciate both minority and majority cultural contexts (Burnes & Ross, 2010). The use of culturally sensitive program activities and intervention techniques helps members to develop mutual respect for each other. When members have ethnicity or some other characteristic in common, they often feel understood by each other and gain validation for a similar heritage and a similar experience.

Developing culturally sensitive intervention skills can be fostered by reviewing specialized formats reported in the literature for groups composed of members from specific cultures. Pearson (1991), for example, suggests that leadership skills need to reflect a more structured approach for some Asian and Asian American people. Adopting a traditional Western style, with less structure and reliance on members to take responsibility for group interactions, would cause discomfort for these types of members. In contrast, feminist group workers suggest encouraging unstructured out-of-group contact, the minimization of the power distance between leader and member, and a focus on the societal and political factors that contribute to members' problems (Holmes, 2002; Pure, 2012; Western, 2013). Other writers have also developed culturally sensitive formats for particular minority groups. For example, Misurell & Springer (2013) have developed a culturally sensitive program for working with sexually abused children. Similarly, Shea and colleagues (2012) have developed a cultural adaptation of a cognitive behavior therapy program for Mexican American women with binge eating disorders.

Overall, group interventions should be directed at helping members enhance ethnic consciousness and pride, develop ethnic resource bases and sources of power, and develop leadership potential. The following case example provides a brief illustration of how one agency adapted treatment services for Native Americans.

Case Example   Culturally Sensitive Treatment Services

Despite many years of working with persons who experienced alcohol and substance abuse, a substance abuse treatment agency recognized that it was less effective when working with persons from Native American backgrounds than with persons from other backgrounds. The executive director of the agency contacted a Native American social worker who had experience in leading a culturally oriented group experience called "The Red Road." This program employed an intensive three-day experience for participants using many aspects of Native American traditions and spirituality, including traditional talking circles, prayers and discussions, traditional drumming and music, and other spiritual aspects, such as smudging, pipe ceremonies, and participating in a sweat lodge. In addition, members were able to discuss their people's history of oppression and discrimination, including United States social policy toward Native Americans and the effects of the boarding school experience and the reservation system on various Native American nations. This turned out to be a powerful experience for participants, and later qualitative evaluations supported the effectiveness of this culturally relevant treatment method.

Principles for Practice

The group worker has a dual responsibility with regard to diversity. The worker should differentiate among members and individualize each member's strengths but also universalize members' common human characteristics and goals. The worker should help to ensure cultural pluralism, that is, the right of persons from all cultures to adhere to their practices and worldviews. In addition, the worker should seek to promote harmony among members who are different from each other.

The research literature on working with persons from diverse backgrounds is characterized by suggestions for working with particular categories of persons. Group work practitioners can benefit from studying this body of knowledge and applying specific suggestions to their practice with particular groups of people. More broadly, however, workers should challenge members to acknowledge, understand, and celebrate diversity. Often, members are the best source of teaching and learning about diversity. Although this should not be seen as the sole responsibility of members who are from different backgrounds, they can be invited to share their experiences.

To understand diversity and be sensitive to working with persons who come from different backgrounds, group workers should consider the following practice principles:

- Some form of diversity is always present in groups. Workers should acknowledge the diversity in the groups they lead and help members to explore the differences they bring to the group experience.
- Sensitivity to diversity is important for both workers and members of groups. Workers who engage in their own process of self-assessment and an exploration

of feelings about their own identity are in a better position to deliver culturally sensitive interventions than are those with less self-awareness.

- The process of becoming culturally sensitive is an ongoing obligation of all group workers. Thus, it is important for workers to continuously seek knowledge about how members define themselves and how their identities affect their participation in the group.

- Being culturally sensitive requires an open mind. Workers should be nonjudgmental about the differences they encounter among group members and should welcome the richness and positive potential that diversity offers to the group as a whole.

- Workers should be aware that exclusion, oppression, entitlement, power, and privilege operate in covert, subtle ways as well as openly, and that these phenomena occur on both individual and institutional levels.

- Persons from diverse backgrounds often have firsthand experience with prejudice, stereotyping, discrimination, and oppression. Workers should understand and acknowledge the effects of these phenomena and help members understand how such treatment can affect group participation.

- Diversity and difference can have a profound effect on how groups function. Workers should recognize that the dynamics of groups vary because of differences in the identities and backgrounds of their members and should consider how diversity is likely to affect the development of groups.

- Member identity and background affects how members work toward their goals. A complete assessment—of group members, the group as a whole, and the group's environment—should consider the diverse characteristics of members and the cultural context in which they have developed.

- Differences in communication styles and language affect the members' overall ability to communicate. Workers should monitor the effects that language and communication have on the conduct of the group and attempt to understand how members from differing cultural groups communicate.

- On the basis of their experiences with environments outside the group, certain members may lack power and may be denied access to society's resources. Empowering members on both an individual and a community-wide basis by using empathy, individualization, support, and advocacy is an important group work skill.

- Persons from different cultures are often sustained by their cultural and spiritual practices and traditions. It is important for workers to acknowledge and support these traditions.

- There are members of groups whose identities are not always obvious and may be hidden (e.g., gay, transgendered, HIV infected). The worker should build a trusting group climate where these identities can be revealed if members choose to do so. The worker should also keep in mind that members have multiple identities that may not all be revealed in the group.

- It is important to empower members of the group by doing consciousness raising and other transformational leadership activities. The ultimate goal is for workers to help members develop a liberation critical consciousness that frees them to understand the effects of exclusion, marginalization and oppression, to examine the internalization and externalization of these experiences, and to embrace the capacities, resilience, and strengths of all participants.

- Members who stereotype each other or discriminate against each other should be challenged to confront their biases, prejudices, and stereotypes. These behaviors should not be allowed to continue within the group.
- There are a variety of specialized cultural formats appropriate for use in groups. It is helpful for workers to develop a repertoire of intervention techniques and program activities relevant to particular cultural groups with whom they are likely to work.

> **?** Assess your understanding of intervening with sensitivity to diversity by taking this brief quiz.

SUMMARY

This chapter focuses on leading task and treatment groups with members from diverse backgrounds. It is important for the group leader to develop a perspective from which to work effectively with members from differing backgrounds. The group leader should develop cultural sensitivity through a process of self-exploration. The leader can also benefit from exploring the identity of others and by gaining knowledge about differing cultural and ethnic groups. An important prerequisite to these activities is openness to differences exhibited by diverse cultures. In planning and composing groups, the leader should consider how persons of differing backgrounds will experience the group and how the group will be affected by their membership. The cultural backgrounds of members can have a profound effect on how members participate in the group. A complete assessment of the group and its members should consider the larger environmental context in which members live and how that context can influence group dynamics.

This chapter also discusses how leaders can intervene with sensitivity to diversity. Suggestions developed in this regard include using social work values and skills, emphasizing a strengths perspective, exploring common and different experiences among members, exploring meanings and language, challenging prejudice and discrimination, advocating for members, empowering members, and using culturally appropriate techniques and program activities. The chapter ends with a description of practice principles to assist leaders working with diverse groups of people.

Planning the Group

PLANNING FOCUS

Planning marks the beginning of the worker's involvement in the group endeavor. The planning process has two distinct parts. The first is directed at forming the group, the aspect with which this chapter is primarily concerned. The second part of planning includes the ongoing adjustments and forward-looking arrangements that are made by the leader and the members as the group progresses through its beginning, middle, and ending stages.

In forming the group, the worker focuses on the individual member, the group as a whole, and the environment. In focusing on individual members, the worker considers each person's motivations, expectations, and goals for entering the group. The worker focuses on the group as a whole by considering the purpose for the group and the dynamics that may develop because of the members' interaction. The worker also focuses on the environment of the group by considering the likely influence on the group of the sponsoring organization, the community, and the larger society.

The second aspect of planning is carried out throughout the life of the group. During the beginning stage, the worker and the members plan in more detail how to accomplish the overall group purpose. The worker carries out detailed assessments of individual members of the group. These assessments lead to additional planning activities in the middle and ending stages of the group. For example, in treatment groups, the worker and the members engage in an ongoing assessment of the extent to which the group is helping members accomplish their goals. This assessment, in turn, leads to the refinement, adjustment, and reformulation of treatment plans, as well as contracting with individual members for modified treatment goals.

In task groups, the worker uses data collected during assessments to formulate procedures for accomplishing the group's work. This includes selecting members with the right expertise for the group, developing session agendas, dividing labor and responsibility, and determining methods to be used in making decisions and solving problems. For example, when helping to select members for boards, a worker might consider inviting a lawyer, fund-raiser, accountant, and member who have expertise in the services offered by the organization.

Although this chapter emphasizes the need for pregroup planning, there are many times when the worker's ability to plan a group is constrained. It is common, for example, for the recruitment process to yield a pool of potential group members that is large enough to form only a single group. In this case, a worker faces the choice of accepting all applicants, delaying the group for additional recruitment, or screening out some applicants and beginning a group with few members. It is also common for workers to inherit leadership of existing groups or to form a single group from all clients of a particular program or residential setting. In this case, the worker has little choice about the membership.

The planning of task groups may be constrained for a variety of reasons. For example, recruitment may be constrained by organizational bylaws or dictated by administrative structure. Likewise, the members of a delegate council are often selected by the organizations that are represented by the council, thereby constraining pregroup planning about the composition of the group. Despite constraints, workers still have the responsibility to think carefully about how they will guide the group's development to ensure that it is productive and that it provides a satisfying experience for members. Workers should plan for the group as carefully as possible within any existing constraints. Such planning helps foster the achievement of positive group and member outcomes and avoids unanticipated difficulties later in the life of the group.

Case Example   Planning for an Advisory Group

The First Methodist Church of River Falls decided to begin an initiative to resettle refugees fleeing from the crime and harsh living conditions in El Salvador. Although church members had a strong desire to help and a good knowledge of the resources in their community, they had little knowledge about professional helping methods or the administration of a volunteer program. Further, they had very little knowledge about El Salvador and the persons who were fleeing from there to seek refuge in the United States.

Members of the church decided to develop a committee to assist in carrying out the resettlement initiative. Members began by spending a good deal of time deciding on the specific goals of the committee. They decided that the group's goals would include the following: (1) providing the church with advice on how to set up and administer a volunteer program, (2) locating persons who could provide culturally appropriate consultation about refugees from El Salvador, and (3) assisting the church in securing funding for the initiative through grants and other fund-raising activities.

Next, church members spent time discussing who should be invited to join the committee. They decided that the group would need a membership that had diverse resources at its command. For example, it was suggested that some of the members be recruited from social work organizations, particularly those that had volunteer programs. Other members should have knowledge of persons from El Salvador who speak Spanish and are familiar with the Catholic religious traditions that are dominant in this country. They also decided that the committee should have members with experience in writing grants and in fund-raising for refugees.

In addition to these planning considerations, church members discussed what would occur during the first meeting. They agreed on a meeting agenda and a list of resources that the group would need to conduct its work.

> **?** Assess your understanding of the focus of important planning elements that lead to successful group outcomes.

PLANNING MODEL FOR GROUP WORK

We have developed a model of planning that can be used for both treatment and task groups. This model includes the following:

- Establishing the group's purpose
- Assessing the potential sponsorship and membership of the group
- Recruiting members
- Composing the group
- Orienting members to the group
- Contracting
- Preparing the group's environment
- Reviewing the literature
- Selecting monitoring and evaluation tools
- Preparing a written group proposal
- Planning distance groups

This planning model describes an orderly set of procedures to guide workers. In actual practice, however, workers may not plan for the group in a systematic fashion. Instead, the worker may find that it is necessary to engage in several aspects of planning simultaneously. For example, recruiting, contracting, and preparing the environment can occur at the same time. Similarly, determining purpose and assessing potential membership can sometimes be done together. Carrying out one step may also influence how another step is handled. For example, in assessing the potential membership of a committee, the worker may realize that a budget item for travel is required for certain members of the group. Thus, the information gained in carrying out one procedure (assessing membership) influences action taken in another (securing financial arrangements).

Establishing the Group's Purpose

The first and most important question that can be asked about a proposed group is "What is the group's purpose?" A statement of the purpose should be broad enough to encompass different individual goals, yet specific enough to define the common nature of the group's purpose. A clear statement of purpose helps members answer the question, "What are we doing here together?" It can help prevent a lack of direction that can be frustrating for group members and can lead to an unproductive group experience.

A brief statement of the group's purpose generally includes information on the problems or issues the group is designed to address, the range of individual and group goals to be accomplished, and how individual members and the group as a whole might work together.

Some examples of statements of purpose follow.

- The group will provide a forum for discussing parenting skills; each member is encouraged to bring up specific issues about being a parent and to provide feedback about the issues that are brought up.
- The group will study the problem of domestic violence in our community, and each member will contribute to a final task force report on how to address the issue.
- The group will review and assess all proposals for improving services to youth from minority communities and decide what projects to fund.

These statements are broad, but they provide information that will help members understand the nature of the group endeavor. As discussed in Chapter 7, the members of the group usually discuss and clarify the group's purpose in early group sessions and produce more specific aims and goals through their interactions with each other and with the worker. It is nonetheless helpful for the worker to prepare for the first meeting by anticipating questions that members might raise, identifying potential agenda items, clarifying the roles that the members and the worker will play in the group, and identifying potential obstacles to effective group functioning.

The purpose of a group can frequently be clarified by considering how the idea for establishing it was generated. The idea may have come from several sources, such as the group worker, agency staff members, potential clients, or the larger community. The following examples illustrate how ideas for groups are generated.

Group Worker-Generated

- The worker proposes an educational group for children based on the worker's perception of the need for adolescent sex education.
- The worker proposes an advising delegate council in a hospital based on a survey of employees' job satisfaction, which indicates the need for better communication among professional departments.

Agency Staff-Generated

- Several agency caseworkers, concerned with rising rates of family violence, suggest that clients from their caseloads participate in a remedial group for child abusers.
- The chairperson of the agency board of directors requests that a committee be established to study and suggest alternative sources of funding for the agency.

Member-Generated

- The parents of children in a day-care center request a series of educational group meetings to discuss concerns about their children's behavior at home.
- Several clients receiving subsidized housing suggest to the director of the agency that a social action group be formed to combat poor housing conditions in a neighborhood.

Community-Generated

- A group of ministers representing community churches approaches a community center about developing an after-school program for children of the working poor.
- A coalition of community groups requests a meeting with the administrator of a community center to explore ways to reach out to young people before they are recruited by gangs.

Assessing Potential Sponsorship and Membership

Although assessment of potential sponsorship and membership for the group might be seen as separate, in reality, the agency and its clients are intrinsically linked. The worker must assess both the sponsoring agency and the potential membership base to plan for the group. Agency sponsorship determines the level of support and resources available to the group. The assessment of potential membership helps the worker make an early estimate of the group's potential viability.

Assessing Potential Sponsorship

The nature of the sponsoring organization has a significant effect on the formation of the group. The following aspects of the potential sponsor should be considered when planning a group.

Elements in Assessing the Potential Sponsorship of a Group

- The mission, goals, objectives, and resources of the organization
- The fit between the policies of the organization and the goals of the proposed group
- The level of potential support for the group within the organization
- The nature of the unmet and ongoing needs of the group
- The costs and benefits of the group in relation to the sponsoring organization
- The level of community need for the group and the level of community interest and support
- The role that federal, state, and local funding mandates and regulatory bodies play in the focus of the group

In treatment groups, the sponsoring organization may be affected by federal, state, and local funding mandates, licensing bodies, or other entities. It is important for workers to understand that funding and legal mandates, medical necessity, and other factors may come into play, especially when potential members are severely impaired. For example, treatment groups rely on agency administrators and staff for financial support, member referrals, and physical facilities. Funding mandates often play a part in both who can be served and the shaping of the purpose of the group.

Task groups are intrinsically linked to their sponsoring organizations and must continually refer to the organization's mission, bylaws, and policies for clarification of their task, charge, and mandate. In assessing an organization as sponsor for the group, the worker should pay careful attention to the fit between the organization's policies and goals and the purpose of the proposed group. The proposed group should fit within the overall operating goals of the organization. If the group represents a new form of service or suggests a problem area or a population that has not been the focus of the potential sponsor, the worker will have to be prepared to justify the request to begin a group.

The worker's assessment of the sponsoring organization is carried out to determine the overall level of support for the proposed group service and to garner any additional support that may be needed to begin the group. It is essential to identify key areas of mutual interest and perceived need within the organization and the community where the group will be held. This includes funding and regulatory agencies that may have subtle but strong influences on how a new group service should operate.

An early step that is often helpful is to meet with line staff and program administrators to obtain their ideas about the need

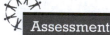

Assessment

Behavior: Apply knowledge of human behavior and the social environment, person-in-environment, and other multidisciplinary theoretical frameworks in the analysis of assessment data from clients and constituencies

Critical Thinking Question: The sponsoring organization can greatly influence a group's purpose and goals. What organizational factors should be considered in planning?

for a particular group service. In interdisciplinary settings, it is important to test the idea for a new group service beyond the social work staff. The idea for a new group service should be presented through appropriate channels to staff from other disciplines. Highlighting common perceptions of unmet needs and pointing out how the new group service could support and enhance the work of other disciplines can be useful ways of garnering support. This process has the added benefit of reducing interdisciplinary competition, fostering a sense of mutual mission, and developing a bond with staff on which the new group program may depend for referrals or other assistance. For example, a new group service in an outpatient health clinic for those with post-traumatic stress disorder should seek the support of psychologists who may be asked to do testing, physicians who may be asked to prescribe medications, and other allied health professions who may be asked to be guest speakers or referral resources.

The worker may wish to carry out a needs assessment or gather data to document unmet needs. Workers can identify public and private funding sources for the effort by searching the Internet, speaking with representatives of private foundations, and local, state, and national nonprofit and public agencies. Administrators and boards of directors may be particularly interested in the costs and potential benefits of the proposed group service. A brief review of similar group work efforts can help clarify the possible costs and benefits associated with a new group program. An organization may decide to offer the group service on a trial basis while conducting a cost analysis, such as the one described in Chapter 14.

It is also helpful to gather support for the idea for a new group service from the larger community. This can be done by encouraging consumers within a geographical region to express their interest in a new group service or by urging community leaders and others who have influence within community social service organizations to express their interest in and support for the new service. The relevance of the proposed group program to the sponsoring organization's mission and the visibility it could bring to the organization should also be highlighted.

In some instances, the potential sponsoring organization may decide that the proposed group is not central enough to its core mission. In a county-funded rape crisis center, for example, a worker proposed a group service for battered women who had been victims of family violence but who have not been raped. Such an expansion of services, although appropriate and related to the agency's purpose, may be viewed as beyond the scope of the agency's mission, beyond staff resources, or not reimbursable within the agency's current funding sources.

When workers encounter a lack of support they should determine whether the proposal can be modified to increase support and alleviate the concerns that have been expressed or whether a different sponsor should be sought. For example, with the previously mentioned domestic violence group, the worker joined with her supervisor and met with other agency administrators to highlight the need for the group and to seek additional funding for it. Together the group decided to explore the idea for the group service with a family service agency that had expressed interest in providing service for domestic violence victims.

Garnering support for the idea of a new group service both within and outside the organization helps ensure the success of the group when it is implemented. A summary of how to gather support follows.

Gathering Support for a New Group

- Identify the extent to which the problem or issue that the group intends to work on fits the mission and goals of the sponsoring organization.
- Identify the extent to which a resolution of the problem or issue to be addressed by the group is valued by the sponsoring organization and the larger community.
- Obtain the support of the administration of the organization to explore the possibility of a new group service.
- Find out if the need is being met, or should be met, by any other organization in the community and contact that organization to avoid any possible duplication of service and to check the possibility of joining forces for co-sponsoring a group service.
- Identify and resolve any differences in perspectives among staff that may lead to hidden agendas and thereby jeopardize the group service being planned.
- Obtain staff consensus about the goals of the program and the group work methods that will be used to achieve them.
- Assess the willingness of the sponsor to provide external support, such as transportation, childcare, or supplies needed to conduct the group.
- Identify sources of funding and regulatory requirements for the new group service.

Assessing Potential Membership

Along with assessing agency sponsorship and garnering support for a new group work endeavor, the worker should begin to assess the potential membership of the group. Such a beginning assessment does not involve extensive procedures, such as arriving at goals for members or agreeing on individual contracts. Rather, in this early assessment, the worker thinks about who should be recruited by considering the following elements for developing harmonious, hardworking groups.

Elements in Assessing the Potential Membership of a Group

- The extent of the problem or need addressed by the group
- Members' recognition and shared perceptions about the purpose of the group
- Cultural and other differences that could influence perceptions about the purpose of the group
- Members' perceptions of the sponsoring organization
- Potential effects of ambivalence, resistance, or the involuntary nature of the group on members' participation
- Specialized knowledge needed for understanding and working with members
- Demographic differences and commonalities of potential members
- Potential benefits to members of participating in the group
- Barriers, obstacles, and drawbacks to member participation
- Resources needed from the organization and community to ensure members' interest and participation
- Guidelines and mandates from funding sources about who is eligible to participate

When planning treatment groups, workers should start by collecting data about the extent of the problem and the need for a new group service. If possible, the worker can also collect data about potential clients by observing or interviewing them directly, by phone, or by talking with collateral contacts, such as family members or agency staff. The permission of the potential member has to be obtained for this to occur. Making collateral contacts is sometimes neglected in practice but can be a rich source of data about how to tailor the group to meet members' needs.

When planning task groups, the worker considers potential members according to their interest in the task, their expertise, and their power and position to help the group accomplish its purposes (Tropman, 2014). Members might also be sought because of their importance to the sponsoring agency, their status in the community, or their political influence.

An important aspect of assessing potential membership is determining whether potential members share the worker's perception of the tasks facing the group. Shared perceptions lead to group cohesion and increase members' satisfaction with group functioning. In addition, the worker spends less time overcoming obstacles and resistance to accomplishing the group's goals when members share similar perceptions of the concerns facing the group.

Information should be gathered about the extent to which potential members recognize the need for the group, its purpose, tasks, and goals. This process helps workers anticipate the degree of member commitment to the group. It also helps to coalesce divergent views of the purpose of the group and the methods used to accomplish the work of the group. Shulman (2016) refers to this as "tuning in" to the members of the group.

It is also important to assess potential members' views of the sponsor. Is there any stigma attached to receiving service from a particular organization? Is the organization known to the potential client group? What is the organization's reputation with the group to be served? The worker should carefully consider what qualities of the potential sponsor are likely to attract clients and what obstacles may interfere with the successful initiation of a group program. For example, a family service agency may have the resources to sponsor a group for African American single mothers but may have difficulty recruiting members because potential members perceive the staff of the agency to be culturally insensitive. If the agency sponsoring the group is perceived to be unable to relate to particular segments of the community, it will encounter considerable resistance when trying to initiate a group service.

Case Example   A Parenting Group for Single Mothers

The previously mentioned family service agency contacted local community leaders, a community center, and a health clinic serving primarily African Americans. The family service agency also reached out to a coalition of ministers from Baptist churches in the area serving the African American community. After meeting with individuals from these organizations separately, a series of three planning meetings was held. It was decided to host the group for single mothers in the health clinic and that each of the organizations at the meeting would publicize the group and encourage single mothers to attend. A worker from the family service agency led the group, but speakers on educational topics related to health and nutrition came from the health care clinic, and a worker from the community center provided childcare while the members attended the group.

Engagement

Behavior: Use empathy, reflection, and interpersonal skills to effectively engage diverse clients and constituencies

Critical Thinking Question: Workers often work with involuntary members. What techniques can the group worker use to involve them in the group?

Often, the worker must plan for leading a group of reluctant participants. The extent of reluctance can range from ambivalence about seeking assistance to active resistance. The term *involuntary* is often applied to individuals who are ordered by the courts to receive treatment. Working with involuntary clients requires special expertise. During the planning stage, the worker should become thoroughly familiar with the legal statutes and ethical issues that apply. The dignity and rights of individuals who find themselves in these situations must be protected while the individual is in the care of the worker (Rooney, 2009).

Workers may also be called on to plan groups for reluctant members who are given the choice between treatment and a negative alternative, such as incarceration, probation, or the suspension of driving privileges. In these situations, the worker should become thoroughly familiar with the specialized methods developed to motivate clients to make productive use of the group experience (Rooney, 2009). For example, in a residential program for substance abusers, information and techniques to confront denial may be used in combination with powerful incentives, such as the return of driving privileges. Within the residential setting, information about the damaging effects of alcohol, peer interaction focused on sobriety, and access to certain privileges may be combined to help members make productive use of a group program. More information about working with reluctant and resistant clients is presented later in this text.

Workers planning a group for a new population are unlikely to have information readily available about what strategies are most effective for working with individuals who have specialized problems. Gathering information by reviewing the literature and from practitioners experienced with the population can be invaluable in preparing for a group. Obtaining information about specialized groups is particularly important when planning groups for people from diverse cultural backgrounds and when the worker's background differs significantly from that of group members. Such information helps workers recognize their own biases, develop tolerance for their own and others' perceptions, and enhance their abilities to perceive clients' needs accurately. It is also good evidence-based practice.

In assessing potential membership, the worker should consider the demographic differences and commonalities of potential members and how these affect other steps in the planning process. For example, when planning a support group for Latino caregivers of elderly parents, the worker might print announcements in Spanish, post announcements in newspapers for speakers of Spanish, contact civic and social service organizations serving Latino communities, and reach out to Latino community and religious leaders.

To prepare for recruiting and orienting members in both voluntary and mandatory groups, the worker may list the potential benefits of participating and share them with potential members. Some workers are reluctant to describe the potential benefits of participating in a group because they fear they will be perceived as boasting about their own skills or because they fear raising the expectation for service among members of vulnerable groups. However, individuals who are considering whether to participate in a group welcome a clear description of the potential benefits of participation. A worker's enthusiasm and optimism can be contagious, increasing members' motivation to participate and their enthusiasm for what might be accomplished. Yalom (2005) refers to this process as the "instillation of hope."

Workers should also identify barriers, obstacles, and drawbacks to group participation. In their zest to recruit members, workers sometimes minimize the difficulties individuals can encounter when joining a group. Experience suggests that it is better to acknowledge barriers to participation and try whenever possible to resolve them so they do not prevent individuals from participating. Often, discussing disadvantages with potential members during an orientation interview and planning ways to resolve them can be helpful. For example, practical barriers are overcome if the sponsoring agency can provide transportation, childcare, or a sliding fee scale.

Case Example   Planning for Resistant and Reluctant Members

Although she was enthusiastic about starting a new group for college students who had violated the college dormitory's alcohol policy, Beth was worried about how members would feel about being mandated to attend this short-term group. During preparations for the group, she became familiar with the college policies that prohibited alcohol use in the dorms. She hoped that knowledge of the policies would prepare her to answer members' questions about why they needed to attend the group. She prepared a clear statement about her role in the group and the expectations for attendance and participation. In addition, Beth prepared a list of group goals for members' consideration during the first meeting. Beth also consulted the literature about how to deal with involuntary group members. Based on what she learned, she prepared what she would say during the opening of the first meeting. The statement acknowledged the mandatory nature of the group and members' ambivalence about participating. She noted that it was ultimately up to members to decide how they would participate in the group and whether the group would be a positive and productive experience for each of them. She hoped that these beginning preparations, along with her enthusiasm and genuine desire to help, would overcome some of the resistance she anticipated from the members during the beginning stage of the group. Beth also asked a willing former member to be available to answer any questions that potential members might have about the benefits of participating in the group.

Recruiting Members

Recruitment procedures should ensure an adequate number of potential members for the group. In recruiting members, the worker considers sources from which potential members can be identified and referred to the group. Members can be recruited within the worker's agency, other organizations, or the community.

Within a social service agency, potential members can be identified from the caseloads of colleagues, from records, or from mailing lists. In some groups, current members may be able to identify potential members. Potential members might also introduce themselves to the worker, individually or in a group, to suggest that the agency initiate a particular group service. Finally, the worker might consider reviewing the agency's waiting list to determine whether any persons waiting for service would benefit from group treatment.

For certain treatment groups, such as for men who batter, the worker's own agency may not have a large enough potential

Engagement

Behavior: Apply knowledge of human behavior and the social environment, person-in-environment, and other multidisciplinary theoretical frameworks to engage with clients and constituencies

Critical Thinking Question: Recruiting members requires creative community action. What methods can workers use to recruit members for a group?

membership base. In planning for these groups, the worker can contact other social service and health agencies to obtain referrals. The worker should also become familiar with the community to locate concentrations of potential members. Talking to community and religious leaders, politicians, police officials, and schoolteachers may be helpful to identify ways to contact potential members.

For task groups, the type of group and its purpose often determine the best sources for recruiting members. For example, members of a committee to study an agency's employee benefit package can be recruited from employees of the agency and from the agency's board of directors. A task force to study the problem of refugee resettlement can recruit members from all agencies serving that population in the community. Similarly, team members can be selected for their specific expertise and professional background. Boards recruit members from community constituents because the board "stands in" for the community and is accountable to the community for the services the agency provides.

Methods of Recruiting Members

When the worker has identified recruitment sources, decisions must be made about how to reach them. A variety of recruitment techniques will help potential members understand the purpose of the group and help them decide whether to join.

> **Methods of Recruiting Members**
> - Contacting potential members directly through interviews and phone contacts
> - Contacting key people in the networks of potential members
> - Sending announcements through direct mail
> - Posting announcements in community organizations
> - Using websites to advertise the group
> - Speaking at public meetings and appearing on radio and television shows
> - Issuing press releases, publishing announcements in organizational and association newsletters, and working with reporters to prepare feature newspaper articles

Direct personal contact with potential members is often the most effective recruitment method. When potential group members can be identified from agency records or from caseloads of colleagues, the worker may wish to set up initial appointments by letter, email, or phone. The worker can then interview prospective members in the office or at home. However, person-to-person contact, particularly in-home contact, can be quite expensive in terms of the worker's time and therefore may not be feasible.

Workers can also recruit members by contacting key people in the informal networks of a particular population. For example, in recruiting for a group composed of Native Americans, the worker may first discuss the idea with important Native American community elders to gain their acceptance for the group. When recruiting Chinese Americans, the worker might identify cultural associations that provide support for this population, which could provide the worker with a means for assessing the viability of the group and the potential for recruiting members. Since trust is a key issue when recruiting members of culturally diverse groups, workers also should spend time getting to know the community and to become known to its members before attempting to organize and lead a group.

Brief, written announcements can be an effective recruitment tool. However, care must be taken to ensure that announcements are sent to the correct audience. To be effective, mailed and posted announcements must be seen by potential members or potential referral sources. Therefore, careful targeting of the pool of potential group members is essential. Too often, workers rely on existing mailing lists developed for other purposes or post announcements where they will not be noticed by the target group. Computerized record systems and Internet list serves are becoming more widely available and can be useful in identifying and targeting individuals who may need a particular service.

If the worker has a list of potential members, announcements can be mailed directly to them. The worker may also mail announcements to workers in other social service agencies who are likely to have contact with potential group members. Experience suggests that a follow-up phone call to those who have received announcements increases the probability that referrals will be made. Announcements can also be posted on community bulletin boards, in housing projects, public gathering places, and local businesses. In rural locations, announcements can be posted at firehouses, church halls, schools, general stores, and post offices. Such locations are usually the best places to post announcements because people gather in those places to discuss information about their community. The worker also can ask that announcements be read at meetings of community service groups, church groups, business associations, and fraternal organizations.

The increase in computer literacy, the availability of local area networks, and the Internet have improved accessibility for potential members. Group announcements can be posted on local area networks or community computer bulletin boards or be sent to targeted users of particular computing services. It is also possible for local organizations as well as nationally federated groups to create their own web pages that are accessible to millions of persons who may be interested in learning more about particular services.

Appendix B contains two examples of announcements for groups. An announcement should include a clear statement of the group's purpose. The proposed meeting place, dates, times, length and frequency of meetings, and any service fees should also be clearly specified. The sponsoring agency and the group leader's name should be listed along with phone numbers for potential members to call for more information. It is sometimes helpful to list any special arrangements that are planned, such as childcare services, transportation, or refreshments.

The worker might also want to make information about the group available through public speaking and through local television or radio stations. Many civic and religious organizations welcome guest speakers. A presentation on the need for the group, its purpose, and how it would operate can be an effective recruitment tool. Commercial television and radio stations broadcast public service announcements deemed to be in the public interest, and the proposed group program might be eligible for inclusion in such broadcasts.

Commercial television and radio stations frequently produce their own local public interest programs, such as talk shows, public discussions, special news reports, and community news announcements. Although public access cable television channels generally have smaller audiences, they can also be used by the worker to describe a group service and to invite members to join.

Press releases and newsletter articles are another way to recruit members. Many local newspapers publish a calendar of events for a specified week or month; brief announcements can be placed in the calendar. An article in the features section of a local newspaper can reach many potential members. Online and print-based newspapers frequently publish stories about new group services or particular social problems. The worker should consider whether the group is newsworthy and, if so, contact a local editor and request an interview with a reporter. We have found that feature newspaper stories are the single most important source for recruiting new members to groups in community settings.

Composing the Group

Rolling admissions, sponsor organizations' missions, funding sources, and other factors may make it difficult or impossible for workers to select members. When workers are able to select members, they should consider member and group needs and goals, as well as their own capacity to work with those who may be in the group. Sometimes, the Group Selection Questionnaire or other measures can be helpful when deciding whom to include (Burlingame, Cox, Davies, Layne, & Gleave, 2011). For example, in therapy groups, the Group Therapy Questionnaire may be helpful for selecting appropriate members (MacNaire-Semands, 2002). In general, however, three broad principles should guide workers' selections.

Principles of Group Composition
- Homogeneity of members' purposes and certain personal characteristics
- Heterogeneity of member coping skills, life experiences, and expertise
- Complementary overall structure that includes a range of the members' qualities, skills, and expertise to achieve the right balance of members who can work well together and help each other achieve individual and group objectives

In addition to these principles, the worker should consider demographic and sociocultural factors, group size, and whether the membership will be open or closed.

Homogeneity

The principle of homogeneity suggests that members should have a similar purpose for being in the group and have some personal characteristics in common. Homogeneity facilitates communication and bonding and helps members to identify and relate to each other's concerns.

Members should accept and identify with the major purpose for the group so they can use the meetings to their full advantage. The worker should assess the extent to which members' purposes coincide with one another and with the purpose of the group. Without some common purposes for being in the group, members will have little basis for interacting.

Members should share some personal characteristics, such as age, level of education, cultural background, and expertise relative to the group task, communication ability, or type of problem. The worker should determine that all members have enough characteristics in common to facilitate the work of the group. The extent to which members should possess common characteristics varies with the type of group. In an educational group for new parents, it might be important that all members be able to read English at a sixth-grade level to understand program materials recommended for reading at home. In a program-oriented group for youngsters in a treatment center, the most important common characteristic may be their living situation. Groups of alcoholics, drug abusers, and delinquents all have a problem in common.

In a study of selection criteria for new members of treatment groups, Riva, Lippert, and Tackett (2000) found that a national sample of leaders mentioned compatibility with the group theme as the most important variable, followed by the client's motivation for personal change, enthusiasm about being in the group, and expectations that the group would help. Other important selection criteria included clients' (1) reality testing, (2) self-awareness, (3) ability to express feelings, (4) ability to tolerate anxiety, (5) ability to self-disclose, and (6) sensitivity to others' needs. In studies that compared those who dropped out of group treatment to those who completed, it was found that the ability to express oneself and the ability to trust and relate to others were the important predictive factors (Blouin et al., 1995; Oei & Kazmierczak, 1997). Thus, personality factors are important in screening and selecting members. Forsyth (2014) provides evidence that extroversion, agreeableness, and openness are three particularly desirable personality traits.

Heterogeneity

For most groups, there should be some diversity of members' coping skills, life experiences, and levels of expertise. This helps members to learn about new options, different alternatives, and varying perspectives, which they may choose to adapt to their own circumstances. In support groups, for example, it is helpful for members to learn what coping skills other members have found to be effective and what strategies they have used to solve problems.

In some groups, the worker chooses members with differing life experiences or diverse characteristics to foster learning among members. A growth group, for example, might be composed of members from different cultures, social classes, occupations, or geographic areas to expose individuals to the benefits of differing viewpoints and lifestyles. Differences among members can provide multiple opportunities for support, validation, mutual aid, and learning.

Workers should also consider building heterogeneity into the membership of task groups to ensure an adequate range of resources and provide an efficient division of labor when dealing with complex tasks. For example, agency boards of directors are usually composed of members who represent a variety of professions, agencies, and occupations. These members bring legal, financial, marketing, and other kinds of expertise to the board. Other task groups, such as delegate councils, are also often composed of members who represent differing constituencies with diverse interests and needs. For example, a coalition formed to study the problem of juvenile delinquency might be composed of members from diverse parts of a city, that is, members from the business district, the inner city, and suburban neighborhoods. Such heterogeneity can be an important asset to the group in accomplishing its tasks.

Complementary Group Structure

Workers should also consider selecting members who have complementary attributes that can lead to group synergies when working on accomplishing goals (Forsyth, 2014). Guidelines include selecting members who:

- Have the ability and desire to communicate with others in the group
- Can accept each other's behavior

- Can get along with each other despite differences of opinions, viewpoints, or positions
- Have some capacity to understand one's own behavior
- Are open to sharing their experiences and listening to others

In treatment groups, members who are ineffective in communicating with peers can engender more antagonism than support from fellow members. These individuals fare better if they are seen individually to begin with or are placed in groups with others who have similar communication difficulties. Similarly, people who cannot accept or use feedback and those who are highly opinionated and unwilling to consider other viewpoints are poor candidates and may be better served in individual treatment until they gain greater awareness of how their behavior affects others. In task groups, the same principles apply, but there is greater emphasis on recruiting members who have the expertise and dedication to accomplish specific goals (Tropman, 2014).

It is desirable to recruit members who are able to put the needs of the group or the requirements of the task before their own personal needs. The worker also should seek members who demonstrate the ability to cooperate with one another. No matter what the level of expertise or ability of members, task groups can be hampered by a lack of cooperative effort. Although it is not always possible to predict how people will work together, it is helpful to consider personality characteristics, such as agreeableness, cooperative spirit, and openness, when workers have the ability to compose task groups.

Demographic and Sociocultural Factors

When selecting members, the worker should pay particularly close attention to three major characteristics: age, gender, and sociocultural factors.

It is not sufficient to consider only age when composing a group. The worker should seek members who are similar in their stage of development and their life tasks. The level of maturity, self-insight, and social skills can vary considerably within age groups. Neither children nor adults acquire these characteristics solely because of age, but rather through multiple experiences with their environment, family, peer group, and culture. For example, in composing a children's group, it is helpful to consider the level of members' social and emotional development as well as the children's ages.

Research suggests that the behavior of members varies with the gender composition of the group (Forsyth, 2014). In a men's or women's support group, for example, an atmosphere of support and openness can often be enhanced through homogeneity of gender composition. In a remedial group for children, a mixed-gender group may interfere with interaction because of the tendency of children at certain ages either to impress or ignore members of the opposite sex.

In other situations, mixed groups are more effective. For example, in a task group, such as a teen-club planning meeting, a mixed group is most appropriate to help members of one sex learn to relate to those of the opposite sex. Similarly, an assertiveness group might include both men and women so that members can realistically role-play exercises.

The importance of the sociocultural background of potential members has already been described in Chapter 5. When planning a group, the worker should assess differences and commonalities among members in sociocultural factors and should be sensitive to the needs of each member as well as to the overall needs of the group. The level of support and interaction is often increased when members have a common socio-cultural background. The worker may decide that similar backgrounds will help members deal with certain problems or issues better when they share them with members from similar backgrounds. For example, a worker may restrict membership in a cultural awareness group to members of a single ethnic group. Similarly, in a support group for parents of terminally ill children, the worker may restrict membership to people from the same cultural background to ensure that members will have similar belief systems and values about death, loss, and grieving.

In other situations, the worker may deliberately plan a group composed of members with diverse sociocultural backgrounds. Diversity can foster mutual understanding and learning among members. For example, socialization groups in neighborhood centers and youth organizations might be composed by the worker so they encourage members from different ethnic, cultural, and racial groups to interact. Sometimes, differences among members can be a real source of strength. For example, in planning for a social action group concerned with increasing neighborhood police protection, membership drawn from people of different cultural backgrounds can demonstrate a broad base of support for the group's cause. Some writers, however, suggest not having only a single minority member in a group to avoid token representation (Burnes & Ross, 2010). Common mistakes in composing a group are presented in the following case example.

Case Example   Composing a Group

David, a new school social worker, was asked by the assistant principal to compose a group for seventh-grade students who were having trouble at school because their parents were in the process of separation or divorce. Students were identified by teachers, the school nurse, and the school guidance counselor as potentially benefiting from a group experience. After the first meeting, David did not understand why the group was such a disaster. The members did not want to follow his directions and would not work on the tasks and activities he had prepared for them. Members teased each other and failed to follow the group rules. In addition, the group divided into subgroups that interfered with meaningful discussion. David had followed all of the rules of composition, as far as he could tell. Nevertheless, the group just was not cohesive. He assumed that members would have a common bond based on their home situation. He also felt that since they were in the same grade that they would have sufficient homogeneity to work well together. Their ages were all within one year of each other, and they all lived in the same affluent suburban community. After thinking more about it, he realized his mistakes. He had composed a co-ed group, without considering the differences that might be influential between girls and boys at that grade, age, and stage of life. Same sex groups are often preferable for middle school students. He failed to ask students if they wanted to be in the group. He also failed to screen out two verbally and physically aggressive students who had really acted out in the group and who were much better behaved when they were seen individually by David. By way of a solution, David planned shorter program activities that would engage and interest members more effectively than the activities used in the first session.

Size

The worker determines the size of the group according to several criteria. The worker should consider how many members are needed to accomplish purposes and tasks efficiently and effectively. When determining the size of treatment groups, the worker should consider how the members might be affected. Will members feel satisfied with the attention given to their concerns or problems? This is an issue for workers leading treatment groups because members may need time to get to know one another and share personal information. In general, the literature indicates that about seven members are ideal, but absents should be considered so that group meetings do not become too small (Yalom, 2005).

In large treatment groups, members have greater potential for learning because of the presence of additional role models. Members have more opportunity for support, feedback, and friendship, yet there is also less pressure to speak or to perform. Members can occasionally withdraw and reflect on their participation. In addition, in larger groups, fewer difficulties arise when one or more members are absent. There is also less danger that the group will fall below the size needed for meaningful interactions (Yalom, 2005).

Larger groups, however, also have disadvantages. The larger the group, the less individualized attention each member can receive. Close, face-to-face interaction is more difficult. There is more danger of harmful subgroups forming. Large groups also encourage withdrawal and anonymity by silent members. They create less pressure to attend because members' absence is less conspicuous than in smaller groups. Larger groups are also more difficult for the worker to manage. They frequently require more formalized procedures to accomplish their meeting agendas. Large groups have more difficulty achieving cohesiveness and more difficulty reaching consensus (Forsyth, 2014).

In task groups, workers should consider the advantages and disadvantages inherent in different group sizes. Larger groups offer more ideas, skills, and resources to members than do smaller groups, and they can handle complex tasks (Forsyth, 2014). Overall, decisions about the number of members to include in a treatment or task group should be based on the purpose of the group, the needs of the members, their ability to contribute to the work of the group, practical considerations, such as whether a potential member will be able to attend meetings, and any constraints imposed by the sponsor. Following is a summary of some of the major planning considerations related to deciding on the size of the group.

Group Size: Large Versus Small

Large Groups

- Offer more ideas, skills, and resources to members
- Can handle tasks that are more complex
- Offer members greater potential for learning through role models
- Provide members with more potential for support, feedback, and friendship
- Allow members to occasionally withdraw and reflect on their participation
- Help to ensure that there will be enough members for meaningful interaction even if some members fail to attend

Small Groups

- Provide members with a greater level of individualized attention
- Enable closer face-to-face interaction
- Present less opportunity for the formation of harmful subgroups
- Present fewer opportunities for members to withdraw from participation
- Allow for easier management by the worker
- Tend to have more informal operating procedures

- Provide more opportunities for achieving cohesiveness
- Can achieve consensus more easily

Open and Closed Membership

Often, the choice between open or closed membership is affected by the purpose of the group or by practical considerations. Some groups have rolling admissions where the worker does not have the opportunity to decide if the group should be open or closed to members. A treatment group based in a residential treatment facility, for example, adds members as they are admitted. In many situations, open membership is the only practical alternative. Because of rapid patient turnover in hospitals, for example, workers would find it impractical to form a group and expect the same patients to attend a fixed number of meetings and then be discharged all together.

In some open membership groups, it is possible to add members periodically on a planned basis. For example, a committee formed to study the deinstitutionalization of psychiatric patients might discover it needs to add representatives from local community group homes to make recommendations that are more comprehensive, but it can do so at a time that is not disruptive to the ongoing business of the groups. In treatment groups, it may be possible to add members once each month. This gives members a chance to bond before new members are added.

When workers have the opportunity to determine whether the group will be open or closed to new members they have to carefully consider the benefits of each type of group. Open groups maintain a constant size by replacing members as they leave (Yalom, 2005). Members enter and terminate throughout the life of the group, ensuring the group's continuance.

Often, closed groups are preferable to open groups because they can attain greater cohesion and move through the group development stages to the middle stage of work more quickly. For this reason they can often get more accomplished. In treatment groups, there is more privacy, trust can be developed, and members are often able to disclose emotionally charged and potentially stigmatizing experiences within a supportive environment (Yalom, 2005). An anger management group, for example, might find it helpful to begin and end with the same membership so that new members will not impede the progress of the original members. A closed group might also be helpful for teenage mothers learning parenting skills so that a prescribed curriculum that covers the content in a competency-based, systematic manner can be followed.

A disadvantage of closed groups is that when members drop out or are absent, the number of members in the group may become too small for meaningful group interaction. Without the benefit of new ideas, viewpoints, and skills from new members, a closed group runs the risk of engaging in what Janis (1982) refers to as "group think," or what Kiesler (1978) calls "the avoidance of minority or outside opinions" (p. 322). Such avoidance can create an extreme form of conformity within the group that can reduce its effectiveness (Forsyth, 2014).

Therefore, in some situations open group membership is preferable. Open membership allows new ideas and new resources to be brought to the group through new members. New members can change the entire character of the group. The difficulties involved in adding new members to an already functioning group are surmountable. Yalom (2005), for example, notes that members can join a group, learn the group norms, and participate in meaningful ways without requiring the group to regress to an earlier stage of its development. Members of Alcoholics Anonymous (AA), for example, are comforted by the knowledge that they can attend, without notice, any open AA meeting in the community. Open-membership groups provide people who are experiencing crises in their lives with a timely alternative to treatment. They do not have to wait for a new group to form.

There are, however, potential disadvantages to open group membership. Members of open groups may experience less cohesion because the stability of roles, norms, and other social integration mechanisms have not been firmly established. There may be less trust and willingness to disclose and less commitment to regular attendance or work during meetings (Forsyth, 2014). The instability of membership also makes it more difficult for the worker to plan effective group meetings.

What modifications should the worker consider when planning for an open-membership group? If the worker can control when members begin and leave a group, the worker should consider during the planning process when it is optimal to add new members. For example, the worker may decide it is best to add new members during the first few sessions and then close group membership. Alternatively, the worker might plan to add no more than one or two new members in any given meeting.

In Chapter 3, it was mentioned that when membership change is frequent and extensive, group development is adversely affected. To cope with the effects of a changing membership, planners of open groups should consider ensuring that there is a well-publicized, fixed structure for every group meeting (Galinsky & Schopler, 1989; Keats & Sabharwal, 2008; Schopler & Galinsky, 1984, 1990; Turner, 2011). Each meeting, for example, might feature a guest speaker followed by small-group discussion. It is helpful to publicize the topic for each meeting and to stress that meetings are open to new members. In groups with high turnover, each meeting should be independent; that is, an individual should not need to have attended a previous meeting to understand or participate in a current meeting. In addition, consideration should be given to rotating a cycle of topics in a fixed period so that all clients or patients who have an average length of stay in inpatient or outpatient programs can attend a full cycle of meetings before their discharge. Overall, workers should plan structured activities for open groups while at the same time enabling members to adapt and modify them to their preferences and needs (Turner, 2011; Keats & Sabharwal, 2008).

There is only a little evidence about the effectiveness of open as compared to closed membership treatment groups. Clinical experience suggests that workers prefer closed groups, but what evidence exists suggests that open groups are as effective as closed groups (Tourigny & Hebert, 2007; Turner, 2011). Therefore, more evidence is needed because many groups in practice settings are open membership when members come and go as their treatment plans are completed and new members are added on a rolling basis. Renewing the group in this manner can also be cost efficient since it is easier than starting an entirely new group (Tasca et al., 2010).

> **?** Assess your understanding of guidelines for recruiting members and composing the group by taking this brief quiz.

Orienting Members

After potential members have been recruited, the worker should screen them for appropriateness and orient them to the group. The primary orientation method for treatment groups is the intake interview. Generally, intake interviews are conducted individually. Intake interviews are important because they offer workers and members their first impressions of each other.

Alternatively, members of treatment groups can be oriented by listening to streaming or DVD recordings of a previous group, through didactic instruction or by rehearsal of membership skills, such as how to communicate effectively one's thoughts and opinions. Role-induction strategies can take a single half-hour session or several sessions lasting several hours. They can enhance group outcomes, reduce dropout rates, and increase members' satisfaction with the subsequent group experience (Barlow, 2013; Conyne, 2010).

Orientation for new members of task groups is sometimes done in small groups. For example, new board members may be asked to participate in a board training program that consists of several small group sessions on governance and the bylaws of the organization, fiduciary responsibilities, fund-raising, and public relations.

Orientations may be designed for many purposes, but three primary ones are (1) explaining the purpose of the group, (2) familiarizing members with group procedures, and (3) screening members for appropriateness.

Explaining the Purpose of the Group

The worker should begin orienting members by stating the group's purpose. The statement should be specific enough to allow members to ask questions about the group and clarify what will be expected of them. However, the statement should also be broad enough and tentative enough to encourage input and feedback. This can help potential members discuss and work through any ambivalence they might have about participating in the group.

Familiarizing Members with Group Procedures

Group members frequently have questions about how the group will work. Through these questions, members try to understand some of the general rules of group functioning. During the orientation interview, it is helpful for the worker to explain procedures for member participation and for how the group will conduct its business.

Leaders of both treatment and task groups often establish routine procedures for meetings during either the planning stage or the beginning stage of the group. Some treatment group meetings, for example, use a short review period for the first few minutes to discuss the major points of the last session. Time is then allotted for identifying particular member concerns to be discussed during the current session. Some groups use the final few minutes to summarize, to discuss between-meeting assignments, or to talk about the group's progress.

Task groups frequently follow routine procedures, such as reading the minutes of the previous meeting; having reports from officers, like the treasurer; discussing old business; and bringing up new business. Many of these procedures are decided on by the group in its early meetings, but discussion of group procedures during the planning stage helps members see how they can participate in and contribute to the group.

Screening Members for Appropriateness

During the orientation, the worker screens members to ensure that their needs are matched with the purposes of the group. The worker observes members and collects

Diversity and Difference in Practice

Behavior: Apply and communicate understanding of the importance of diversity and difference in shaping life experiences in practice at the micro, mezzo, and macro levels

Critical Thinking Question: The worker should consider how diversity in demographic characteristics can affect the group. What does diversity contribute to groups?

impressions and information about them. Workers also apply any criteria developed for inclusion or exclusion of potential members. Members with impaired functioning can often be identified during the orientation interview, which gives the worker a chance to decide whether their membership in the group is appropriate.

Factors that may render people inappropriate for group membership include (1) problems with scheduling transportation or other practical considerations, (2) personal qualities, such as level of social skills, that are extremely dissimilar to those of other group members, and (3) needs, expectations, or goals that are not congruent with those of the other group members. Such factors have been linked to members' dropping out of treatment prematurely (Barlow, 2013; Brabender & Fallon, 2009; Conyne, 2010; Yalom, 2005).

Contracting

During the planning stage, the worker begins the contracting process. Contracts usually result from the dynamic interaction of the worker and the members during the beginning stage of the group, but certain contracting procedures are initiated before the group begins.

A *contract* is a verbal or written agreement between two or more members of a group. In a legal contract, each party agrees to provide something, although what is provided by each does not have to be equal, and penalties are specified if either party does not fulfill the contract.

Two forms of contracting take place during the planning stage: contracting for group procedures and contracting for individual member goals. The worker should make some preliminary decisions about group procedures before beginning. These decisions include the duration and frequency of group meetings, attendance requirements, procedures to ensure confidentiality, and other considerations, such as time, place, and any fees for meetings. The worker should also begin the process of contracting for individual member goals, although most of this type of contracting takes place during the beginning stage of group work.

In most task and treatment groups, contracts are verbal agreements. For example, the leader of an educational treatment group for foster parents may agree to meet with the group for five two-hour sessions to explain the process of becoming a foster parent and parents' ongoing responsibilities. The leader may also agree to explain the help that the agency can offer and how the legal rights of foster children can be safeguarded. Members may agree to attend each session and use the information that is provided to become effective foster parents. Similarly, the leader of a treatment conference may verbally agree with group members about the procedures for reviewing cases, the responsibility of each staff member in the review process, and the ways in which the information presented during the meeting will be used in case planning.

At times, a written contract may be used. A written contract helps to clarify the group's purpose. It also helps members clarify expectations about the worker and the agency and allows the worker to specify what is expected of group members (Figure 6.1).

As a group member I agree to:

1. Attend all group sessions.
2. Arrive on time for each group session.
3. Refrain from repeating anything that is said during group sessions to anyone outside of the group meeting.
4. Complete any readings, exercises, treatment plans, or other obligations that I agree to in the group before the next group session.
5. Participate in exercises, role plays, demonstrations, and other simulations conducted during group meetings.

As the group leader I agree to:

1. Be prepared for each group session.
2. Begin and end all group sessions on time.
3. Provide refreshments and program material needed for each session.
4. Discuss the group only with my colleagues at work and not outside of the work context.
5. Evaluate each group session to ensure that the group is helping all members resolve their problems and is personally satisfying to all group members.
6. Provide members with appropriate agency and community resources to help them resolve their problems.

_____   _____
Group member   Date

_____   _____
Group leader   Date

Figure 6.1
Example of a Treatment Group Contract

A written contract can be referred to in group meetings if either the members or the worker needs to be reminded of the purpose, expectations, or obligations to which they agreed. Generally, written contracts specify ground rules for participation that do not change during the life of the group. However, contracts can be renegotiated by mutual agreement at any time during the group's life.

Written contracts are rarely used in task groups. The meeting agenda and the bylaws or other governance structures under which the task group operates is usually the only written agreements binding group members. Ordinarily, task groups rely on verbal contracts about the tasks to be accomplished, the roles of group members, and the division of labor in the group.

Contracting for Group Procedures

The worker begins to determine group procedures by deciding on the duration and frequency of meetings. These decisions are closely related to the group's purpose and the needs of its members. In treatment groups, the optimal length of time for each meeting varies. Meetings of groups of individuals with dementia in a nursing home may last only 30 to 45 minutes, but meetings of outpatient support groups may last for one hour or longer. Some groups, such as encounter or sensitivity training groups, meet for even longer periods and within a short time frame to achieve high communication levels and reduce member defensiveness.

The frequency of group meetings should also be considered when contracting for group procedures. In general, weekly sessions are recommended for treatment groups, although this does not preclude meeting more often when needed. The frequency of task group meetings depends on the requirements of the task and any time limits or deadlines that need to be considered. The worker must also consider how much time each member can devote to the group.

Specification of other group procedures should also be considered. The worker can specify attendance requirements, confidentiality of discussions, or other rules governing behavior in the group, such as how discussions will take place and how decisions will be made. Additional details include the time and place for meetings, any attendance fees involved, and the monitoring and evaluation procedures to be used by the worker.

Contracting for Member Goals

During the planning stage, workers also begin contractual arrangements with individual members. During orientation meetings, workers should help members describe what they would like to accomplish through group participation. Workers should describe the broad goals they have for the group and invite members to do the same. Questions such as "What do you hope to accomplish through your participation in the group?" can stimulate members to think about their roles in a group, what goals they want to accomplish, and how the goals fit with the broad purposes described by the worker. Methods that can be used when contracting with members of both treatment and task groups are explained in more detail in Chapter 7.

> **?** Assess your understanding of guidelines for orienting and contracting with members by taking this brief quiz.

Preparing the Environment

Three factors that should be considered when preparing a group's environment are the physical setting, arrangements to accommodate members who have special needs, and financial support. The extent of worker control over these factors is sometimes limited, but incorporating them into the planning process whenever possible enhances the chances for successful group development. Environmental factors to consider are presented in the following checklist.

Checklist for Preparing the Environment
- Room size: adequate for size of group and activities associated with meetings
- Furnishings: seating requirements, work and activity spaces, population-specific needs
- Technology: audiovisual, computer, and telecommunications needs
- Atmosphere: lighting, heating and air conditioning, overall effect created by the meeting space
- Special needs: physical accessibility of meeting space, assistive technology, childcare, transportation, interpreter
- Financial support: cost of group activities and materials, technology, duplicating, advertising, mailing, hospitality (food, beverages), other special arrangements

Preparing the Physical Setting

The setting for the group can have a profound effect on the behavior of group members and the conduct of group meetings. Room size, space, seating arrangements, furnishings, and atmosphere should all be considered. Difficulties encountered in early meetings, inappropriate behavior by members, and unanticipated problems in the development of the group can sometimes result from inadequate attention to the group's physical environment.

Room size can influence how active or involved members become with the business of the group. Generally, a small room engenders positive feelings of closeness among members and limits potential distractions. A large room can put too much distance among members and thus may encourage some members to tune out. A small group of people meeting in a large room may be distracted by the open space around them and have difficulty concentrating on the group process.

On the other hand, a room may be too small and doesn't allow enough space between members, which can lead to discomfort, irritability, anxiety, or acting out. Certain populations are particularly reactive to the size of the meeting room. Young children, for example, often benefit from a large, open area in which to engage in activities. Similarly, disabled older adults benefit from a room with wheelchair access; comfortable, high-back chairs that are not difficult to get in and out of; bright, glare-free lighting; and good acoustics (Toseland & Rizzo, 2004).

Comfortable seating should be available. Sometimes, group members prefer to sit on the floor to create an informal atmosphere. Carpets, lamps, worktables, and other furnishings can also help create a comfortable atmosphere. A comfortable physical environment conveys a message to group members about the agency's regard for them as clients.

Overall, the worker should consider the total effect of the physical setting on a group's ability to accomplish its tasks. If a group is to engage in informal discussion, the worker can create an informal atmosphere with comfortable couches or pillows for sitting on the floor. If a group is to work on formal tasks, such as reviewing priorities for a five-year plan, the worker should create a more formal atmosphere. For example, a room in which the group can sit around a well-lighted table may be most appropriate.

Making Special Arrangements

The worker should be particularly sensitive to any special needs of group members and should be sure that special needs will not prevent members from being able to attend meetings. For example, when working with the physically challenged, the worker should plan a barrier-free location for meetings or should consider phone or computer groups as an alternative to face-to-face meetings. When planning a group for parents, the worker should consider childcare arrangements. For a children's group, the worker should discuss transportation arrangements and obtain parental consent for the children's involvement in the group. When working with individuals for whom English is a second language, the worker may wish to arrange for the services of an interpreter or may wish to co-facilitate the group with a bilingual worker.

The worker should pay particular attention to the resources needed by members who experience specific forms of disability. For example, the worker might want to ensure that persons who have hearing impairments have access to interpreters. In an educational group, it might be necessary for a person with severe physical disabilities to include his or her personal care attendant in meetings to ensure the member's full participation in discussions and activities. Members who have visual impairments may need reading materials converted to Braille.

The worker may not know that a potential member experiences a particular disability. For example, certain hidden disabilities, such as asthma, might preclude a member from participation in certain group activities or in certain environments. Insofar as possible, the worker should assess all potential members of a group during the intake process to determine their special needs.

Securing Financial Support

The worker should be concerned about how the expenses associated with the group will be met. For this reason, the worker should explore the financing arrangements with the group's sponsoring agency, beginning with an assessment of the agency's total financial statement. The costs associated with treatment and task groups vary, but major items include the salary of the worker, the use of the meeting room, and the expense of supervision for the worker. Other expenses may include duplicating, phone, mailings, refreshments, and transportation.

Using information about costs and income, the worker can determine what financial support must be obtained for the proposed group. Expenses, such as the worker's salary and the meeting room, are often routinely paid by the agency. For expenses requiring an outlay of cash, the worker should submit a budget request to the sponsoring agency. A petty-cash fund can provide a flexible means to cover expenses incurred by the group.

For some treatment groups, income may be generated by fees collected from members, or it may be produced from contracts or grants. Although most task groups do not usually generate income, some are formed specifically to generate money for new programs or to raise funds for the agency. Others generate financial savings for their sponsoring organization through creative problem solving or decision-making.

Reviewing the Literature

When planning a treatment group, it is important to review the literature. An essential part of evidence-based group work is to search the literature about the group that is being planned. There are at least four bodies of literature that should be searched by anyone planning a group. The first type is articles and book chapters that present case examples or qualitative studies of similar groups. These can be helpful in providing experiential information about what it might be like to lead a similar group and what issues and themes should be considered during the planning process.

A second type of literature is the empirically based article or book chapter that presents findings about a similar group. These articles not only present evidence for certain approaches to the problem or issue to be addressed by the planned treatment group but also can point out measures that might be used to evaluate the group being planned. There may also be literature reviews or meta-analytic studies that summarize the literature on empirically based approaches to similar groups. These summary articles present accumulated evidence for different approaches to the planned group and can let the worker know if similar groups have already been conducted and evaluated. If there is strong evidence for a particular approach, the worker planning the group should give the findings of this literature strong consideration in formulating the way they will conduct their own planned group.

Third, the worker can go to the World Cat and other database sources to see if books have been written about similar group work efforts focused on the planned topic of the group. Even if the worker does not find books on group work with the population planned for the group, there may be books addressing individual, family, or other treatment approaches that may be helpful. There may also be psychological and sociological books that may be helpful in conceptualizing the problem and formulating a treatment strategy for the planned group.

Fourth, the worker can search for field-tested and evidence-based manuals and curricula that may exist about how to conduct a similar group. Sometimes, these evidence-based manuals and curricula even include workbooks for participants. Frequently, field-tested curricula are found in catalogues and other printed material from for-profit publishing companies that specialize in work with certain populations, for example, children or adolescents. Searching the web or asking colleagues if they know about these catalogues are ways to find curricula so that the worker does not have to start planning a treatment group without any background information. The curricula that are found can be modified to fit the needs of the particular situations and agency-based needs confronting the worker. Another approach is to email or call lead authors of articles who have conducted a similar group to see if they have an agenda and curricula for the group they led. There are also compendiums of group treatment manuals for children and teens (LeCroy, 2008), and government agencies, such as the Substance Abuse and Mental Health Services Agency, that offer free treatment improvement protocols for many different substance abuse and mental health problems.

Selecting Monitoring and Evaluation Tools

It is never too early to consider how to monitor and evaluate the progress of a group. Therefore, during the planning stage, the worker should consider how the progress of the group will be monitored and evaluated. Monitoring the group can be as simple as the worker using a recording form to take notes on the main features of what occurred during sessions. A group recording form is shown in Figure 14.1. Members can also self-monitor their progress toward treatment or task goals, and they can give their feedback on individual sessions. Methods for doing this are described in Chapter 14.

Monitoring the group's change process and progress can help it stay on track and make sure agreed-upon goals are explicit and being accomplished. It is our experience, from listening to hundreds of group tapes and CDs in clinical research studies, that goals can often be lost or forgotten by well-meaning workers who do not make explicit attempts to refocus the group when it is getting off track. This causes the whole group to drift from its stated purpose or to completely lose its focus. We were surprised, when listening to tapes and CDs of groups, how often this occurred. There is a socio-emotional aspect to groups that should not be neglected. We are not trying to insinuate that groups always have to remain on task and simply focus on goals. Balancing socio-emotional and task needs is essential to the proper functioning of a group. At the same time, getting off track because the group is drifting aimlessly should be avoided and monitoring the group's progress is an important way to keep this from happening.

The worker should also decide during the planning phase in what way goal accomplishment will be ascertained. In treatment groups, the worker may simply want to check in with members at the beginning or end of each session to find out how they are progressing toward their goals. At the end of a group, members can be asked to rate their goal attainment and what aspects of their goals remain to be accomplished. In task groups, this might mean reviewing at each group meeting what the group has accomplished and what tasks remain. Workers may want to do a more formal evaluation by giving a measure at the beginning of the group and then again at intervals or at the end of the group to see if goals are being accomplished. These more ambitious plans for evaluating the effectiveness and efficiency of treatment and task groups are discussed in detail in Chapter 14. The primary point that we are trying to make here during the planning phase is not to leave monitoring and evaluation tasks until the last group meetings. Monitoring and evaluation are ongoing processes that should happen throughout the life of a group. They are often more useful and effective when planned early than when left to later group meetings.

Preparing a Written Group Proposal

In planning for a group, the worker might find it useful to prepare a written proposal. Such a proposal is sometimes required for obtaining agency sponsorship or for obtaining funding from various sources. A written proposal can also inform potential members about the group. Spending time to organize and write a group proposal can also aid the worker in preparing for meetings. For most groups, a brief summary of one or two pages, following the outline presented in Appendix C, is sufficient. Two sample proposals, one for a treatment group and one for a task group, are presented in Appendices D and E.

Planning Distance Groups

Distance groups are those where members do not meet face-to-face. Instead, they meet over the phone or through the Internet. Phone groups and Internet groups are becoming more and more popular as we move further into the twenty-first century.

Distance groups are an important alternative to face-to-face groups for many reasons. In some situations, it is just not possible for people who could benefit from social group work to meet face-to-face. For example, people who suffer from debilitating illnesses, such as the frail elderly and persons with terminal illnesses, often are not able to attend group meetings. In addition, it is often very difficult for those with rare diseases to find face-to-face support groups composed of people with the same illnesses.

Transportation and distance can also be barriers to attending face-to-face meetings. In many rural and suburban areas, public transportation is poor, and people who lack private transportation find that it is difficult or impossible to attend face-to-face group meetings. Others find it difficult to avail themselves of a group service because they live such a long distance from the organization offering the service. For example, in rural communities, health and social service agencies often serve large geographic areas. Even in urban and suburban communities, some health and social service agencies, such as regional hospitals, serve the needs of special populations dispersed over a large area. The inconvenience of the meeting location along with time pressures and transportation costs can make attending face-to-face meetings difficult.

There are also many situations when it is possible for individuals to attend face-to-face groups, but they prefer not to attend. For example, some issues are socially stigmatizing, and members may not want to take the risk of disclosing their concerns in a face-to-face group. Hectic schedules and time constraints can make attending face-to-face groups unattractive for potential members (McKenna & Green, 2002). For others, social anxiety and high levels of introversion can make attending face-to-face groups excruciatingly difficult. Some also see distance groups as safer, because such groups offer greater control over the timing and pace of written and verbal interactions and direct physical contact (McKenna & Bargh, 1999, 2000).

Contrary to what is commonly expected, some research suggests that distance groups may actually be more cohesive than face-to-face groups, and they exert greater influence on members' behavior (McKenna, Green, & Gleason, 2002; Postmes, Spears, & Lea, 1999; Postmes, Spears, Sakhel, & de Groot, 2001; Smith & Toseland, 2006). Because members are not present, there are no visual cues to distract them from the core issues that motivated them to participate in the group (McKenna & Green, 2002). Members no longer focus on personal features, such as skin color, or social status cues, such as the way members are dressed (McKenna & Bargh, 2000). They focus more on the shared issues that bring them into contact. For example, a research project studied the impact of psycho-educational phone support groups on caregivers to frail and disabled older adults. It was found that adult children caregivers from very different socioeconomic backgrounds were able to interact easily with each other. Bonds were formed because of similar caregiving issues and concerns, rather than because of personal appearance or socioeconomic status (Smith & Toseland, 2006).

Although there are many advantages to distance groups, there are also disadvantages that should be carefully considered. Some research suggests that there may be greater hostility and aggression in distance groups (Siegel, Dubrovsky, Kiesler, & McGuire, 1986; Weinberg, 2001). For example, the term *flaming* is often used by Internet users to describe the activity of sending emotionally charged, hostile messages without clear provocation or advance warning (Oravec, 2000). It may be that the anonymity of these groups encourages this type of behavior. Text-only messages without nonverbal cues in Internet groups and tonal inflections and verbal messages without visual cues in phone groups enable group members to project negative meanings onto messages that were intended to have more positive connotations (Smokowski, Galinsky, & Harlow, 2001).

Privacy can also be an issue, particularly in online interactions that are open to the public (Oravec, 2000; Smokowski et al., 2001). Even in groups that use passwords, "lurkers" may sign up, but not interact. Active members may leave computer messages on screens that are open to public viewing. It is also easier for members of distance groups to conceal or mask their identities in order to form relationships with vulnerable group members who are seeking interaction with those who have similar life experiences.

Another concern is the quality of the information and services offered during distance group interaction (Glueckauf & Noel, 2011). Information shared on the Internet is not subject to the same standards as information printed in scientific journals. Online and phone counseling and support can be given by individuals without professional degrees who have not agreed to abide by the professional standards of accrediting bodies.

Distance group leaders may respond too quickly to text messages with little context or background. Exacerbating this problem, some members of distance groups may expect quick fixes. Because of the open nature of the medium, it is not always feasible to prevent harmful interactions or to provide valid information that tempers or contradicts bad advice.

Another potential disadvantage of distance groups is the problem of making sure the site for phone and online groups is secure. Members will need to be careful about viruses and other security issues that are the result of previous use of their computers as well as ongoing security threats from hackers from outside the site. Spyware and other viruses must be cleaned from members' computers. Passwords should be hard to hack and kept secure. There also should be a packet of information provided to members with clear instructions about how to use the online site. This includes screen captures of computer settings to ensure privacy (Page, 2010).

Another issue is how to provide emergency care. Page (2010) presents several steps that should be taken to ensure enough information is available in an emergency. First, it is recommended that potential members send a photos to the leader with signed forms with emails, physical addresses, and phone numbers. Second, have each member send two emergency contacts who can be easily reached. Third, a form should be developed that contains the names and contact information of members' physicians, medicines taken, and any chronic or acute illnesses that may affect participation. Fourth, a written safety plan should be prepared by members, and an emergency care document should be prepared by workers with specific local resources tailored to each member's situation and community and national resources, such as hotlines, that all members can benefit from possessing. Fifth, workers should make sure that appropriate releases of information are in place so that the worker can share information with emergency service providers, if necessary (Page, 2010).

Despite the disadvantages and the changes in practice needed to conduct distance groups, phone and Internet services providing help for group members have experienced a surge in popularity in recent years. For many members and leaders of treatment and task groups, the advantages of distance groups outweigh their disadvantages. The following sections describe specific issues when working with phone and computer-mediated distance groups.

Special Considerations: Phone-Mediated Groups

Technological advances have made it possible to have phone conversations among a number of individuals. This has been referred to as *teleconferencing* or making a *conference call* (Kelleher & Cross, 1990). Until recently, the use of this technology was largely limited to task group meetings in large organizations with members who were geographically dispersed, but it is being used more widely now in social service agencies who are trying to reach out to individuals who either cannot get to in-person groups or prefer phone groups to other forms of service.

Some of the special considerations in setting up a phone group are (1) teleconferencing capacity of the organization's phone system or sufficient funds to purchase the service, (2) a speaker phone if there will be more than one leader, (3) teleconferencing equipment, and (4) a willingness of participants to stay on the phone for a long duration. One of the authors has explored the use of hands-free headsets and ear buds for participants, but we have found that these are not necessary, and some participants find purchasing and using them difficult. Many phones have speakers, but there are issues of sound quality for other members, and the privacy of members who are using them when other family members are at home.

A review of the literature reveals that there are phone support groups for people with many types of disabilities, ranging from those with AIDS to those with visual impairments. Although few rigorously controlled studies are reported in the literature, the results of our review indicate that outcome studies are overwhelmingly positive. There are a number of advantages of phone groups, some of which follow.

Advantages of Phone Groups
- Convenience and accessibility of meeting in one's own home
- Reduced time needed to participate because there is no travel time
- Reduction of stigma because of greater privacy
- Ability to reach persons living in rural areas and those who lack transportation
- Ability to reach people who are homebound or caring for someone who cannot be left alone
- Greater willingness to share issues that might be taboo in in-person groups

At the same time, phone groups have potential disadvantages. One disadvantage can be the cost of conference calling, which can be quite expensive if the group is using a major landline provider. Costs can be reduced substantially by using low-cost voice-over-Internet teleconference providers, such as Skype. It is also possible to purchase equipment called a teleconference bridge necessary to make conference calls, but then an agency needs to have sufficient phone lines to run a call center. This is cost effective for very large organizations because the costs can be spread over many employees who may use the technology for administrative and clinical purposes as well. To help defray costs, teleconferencing capabilities can also be rented to other organizations and private practitioners. The following is a list of potential disadvantages of phone groups.

Disadvantages of Phone Groups
- Difficulties in assessing members' needs and the impact of interactions without the benefit of facial expressions and other nonverbal cues
- The difficulty of including members with hearing problems
- Distortions caused by technological problems, call waiting, or background noises from other persons in the household
- Concerns about confidentiality because of a lack of privacy within callers' households
- Changes in group dynamics caused by the lack of visual and nonverbal cues
- The difficulty of using program activities, flip charts, and other visual media
- Expressions of hostility or insensitivity that can sometimes be greater when members are not meeting face to face

Some disadvantages of phone groups are not inherent in the technology itself, but rather in how it is used. For example, phone groups that last over an hour can lead to fatigue, especially when members are frail (Stein, Rothman, & Nakanishi, 1993; Wiener, Spencer, Davidson, & Fair, 1993). For this reason, and because the amount of time for a phone conference is often predetermined by arrangements with the teleconference provider, leaders must be vigilant about preparing members properly for the duration of the meeting. Although one hour is ideal for most treatment group meetings, we have been able to have successful treatment group meetings for 75 minutes and even as long as 90 minutes depending on the membership of the group. For example, members of support groups can often meet for 90 minutes without a problem as long as they are not too frail. There is a need for additional research on the ideal length of group meetings, but it is noteworthy that task group conference call meetings often last for 90 or 120 minutes or even longer without members becoming too tired to continue.

Another disadvantage of phone groups is that they do not offer informal time for members to get together with each other before or after the meeting. With members' consent, swapping phone numbers for between-session contact is one solution. In our current research on phone support groups for caregivers, members have gotten together between meetings, after the time-limited groups ended over coffee at a diner, and in members' homes. There is also the possibility of having an informal time before or after meetings where members can call in to talk to other members before or after the official start of the meeting.

Because members lack visual cues during phone meetings, the worker must be particularly attentive to tone of voice, inflection, silences, and other cues, such as members becoming less responsive or completely dropping out of the discussion over time. It is helpful to have members (1) identify themselves each time they communicate, (2) anticipate frustrations, such as missed cues or interruptions during group meeting times, while at the same time appreciating the benefits of the medium, (3) clarify statements and give clear feedback to each other, and (4) check on emotional reactions and make these clear to all group members (Schopler, Galinsky, & Abell, 1997). In general, leaders of phone groups should plan to be more active than in in-person groups, helping members communicate effectively without visual cues. Despite these limitations, phone groups offer a promising alternative to face-to-face interacting groups for frail or isolated individuals.

Workers who are planning phone groups may also consider some of the following things that we have learned from our experiences with phone groups (Smith & Toseland, 2006; Toseland, Naccarato, & Wray, 2007). For example, it works better for the worker to call each member than to have members call in to the group using an access code. When members call in, they are more apt to call late or call from inconvenient locations. If members know we are going to call at a certain time, the chances of starting a group on time with all members present are enhanced. The Internet provider that we use enables us to set amplification levels for each caller so that the voices of callers with soft voices can be amplified and those with loud voices can be softened. However, we still occasionally have to remind members not to use speaker phones, cordless phones, and cell phones with poor voice quality. Although it is a good practice for members to identify themselves each time they speak, members get to know each other's situations and voices quickly and can frequently identify each other without the need for self-identification. Our experience also suggests that the leader has to take a more active role in directing the action than in face-to-face groups. For example, in an opening go-round, the leader has to indicate who should introduce themselves next, because the physical cues that indicate a particular member is next in line are not present in phone groups.

Leaders of phone groups have to be active in directing questions from one member to another member. Repeating or paraphrasing questions is often useful because members may not realize they are expected to respond. It is a good practice to meet with each member of a phone group at least once before the start of the group. Sometimes, however, this is not practical because of the long distances separating members. In these cases, we have found that it is helpful to mail each member of a phone group a workbook with all the handouts, worksheets, and other materials that will be used during meetings. In that way, members can follow along in their workbook when the leader is speaking about a particular topic or asking the members to engage in an exercise. This helps to overcome the inability to use flip charts or other visual media that are commonly used in in-person groups. We have also found that members of phone groups like to get together in person after the group has been meeting for a while. Therefore, if a series of phone group meetings is planned, it is a good idea to try to have members from similar geographic locations in the same group. This enables them to get together in person more easily. It also helps the leader to link members to convenient community services when needed. We have not found distractions within members' home environments to be a major problem. Most members are good about explicitly stating when they have to stop their participation for a brief period when they have to deal with an interruption or a chore that could not be avoided, and they readily let the group know when they have returned and are reengaged in the teleconference. Overall, we have found that participants really enjoy phone groups, and few have experienced any problems with being on the phone for the hour and fifteen minutes it takes us to start and conduct a group session.

Phone groups are still not widely used and there are some issues that will need to be resolved in coming years. For example, reimbursement for phone group services is not widely available, and practitioners will have to check prior to starting a group whether private or public insurers will reimburse for the service. There has also been little discussion in the literature about the professional standards for delivering phone services (Glueckauf, Pickett, Ketterson, Loomis, & Rozensky, 2003; Maheu, Whitten, & Allen, 2001; Nickelson, 2000). The American Psychological Association has developed an ethics statement about phone psychotherapy (Haas, Benedict, & Kobos, 1996), but the focus of it is more on one-on-one phone therapy with patients with mental health problems than on group intervention focused on support, education, or coping skills for dealing with chronic illnesses. Recently, however, some standards for distance services have been developed, and these can help those who lead phone, video, and other computer-mediated groups (National Board For Certified Counselors, 2012). For more information about phone groups, see Glueckauf and Ketterson, (2004); Glueckauf and Loomis, (2003); Glueckauf, Nickelson, Whitton, and Loomis, (2004); Martindale-Adams, Nichols, Burns, and Malone, (2002); Rosswurm, Larrabee, and Zhang, (2002); Toseland et al., (2007).

Special Considerations: Computer-Mediated Groups

There has been a sharp increase in the popularity of computer-mediated groups in recent years. There are now literally thousands of computer-mediated groups for persons with many different types of health, mental health, and social concerns. Research on the outcomes of computer-mediated groups has also increased but there are not yet any evidence-based standards (Page, 2010).

Workers must have access to a computer and an online service to become a developer, leader, or member of a computer-mediated group. The online service is used to access search services, such as Bing, Google, or Yahoo, which, in turn, are used to find desired sites on the Internet. For example, Alcoholics Anonymous groups can be accessed online.

Some computer-assisted group meetings occur in real time; that is, everyone participates at a specific time and the discussion is interactive. Other group meetings require members to post messages to which other members can respond at any time. Although the terminology can vary and is frequently updated, there are three distinct and broad ways to plan and conduct computer-mediated groups: (1) email/list serves, (2) instant messaging, chat rooms, and other forums, and (3) discussion boards. Email/list serves allow groups of individuals to receive messages, information, and news. The posting of new messages and information may be limited to certain members, and communications occur whenever people with permission post new information. Instant messaging enables the formation of real time, synchronous, interactive groups that are typically limited to a specific time period, for example, every Friday from 1PM to 2PM. Discussion boards are usually open 24 hours a day. They enable individuals to post and answer messages at any time, i.e., asynchronously.

Sites on the Internet are also excellent sources of information and education for group members who may be meeting in-person or at a distance. For example, members of a computer-mediated, synchronous communication support group for cancer patients might be encouraged to visit a site sponsored by a reputable source, such as the National Cancer Institute, to obtain current information about diagnoses and treatment options.

In recent years, social networking sites, such as Alliance Health Networks, Cure Together, Diabetic Connect, Health Central, Inspire, Ning, PatientsLikeMe, and Wetpaint, have brought together people who have similar chronic health problems. They can connect with one another and get the latest information on treatments, and living with chronic illnesses. Some of these sites encourage the formation of new groups to meet the needs of people with health problems who are not being served by support groups.

Video groups can also be created. Members all must have web cameras attached to their computers and have access to Skype, Google Hangouts, Go To Meeting, or similar technological platforms. Using this technology, the image of the person speaking lies in the middle of the computer screen and images of participants are on the edges of the screen in boxes so that everyone can be seen at the same time. When new members speak, their image moves to the center of the screen and that of the person who was in the center of the screen moves to the side. This allows nonverbal cues to be observed, unlike when using phone group technology. Video conferencing technology is in its infancy in social group work, but it will grow in coming years.

Computer-mediated groups offer many advantages to participants. Like phone groups, they offer a variety and diversity of support, especially for frail group members and persons with very specialized concerns who may not be sufficiently numerous in any one geographic area to form a group (Page, 2010). They also offer the same anonymity as phone groups but have particular appeal to those who enjoy written communication or the convenience of 24-hour access. Although they require an initial investment in hardware and software, some online service charges are less expensive than some phone conferencing services. In addition, they eliminate time and distance barriers even more effectively than do phone groups.

There are numerous reports that members of computer-mediated support groups experience many of the same therapeutic factors commonly associated with face-to-face support groups (Barlow, 2013; Glueckauf & Loomis, 2003; Page, 2010). There is also a growing body of empirical evidence about the effectiveness of computer-mediated groups (Coulson & Greenwood, 2011; Fukkink & Hermanns, 2009; Golkaramnay, Bauer, Haug, Wolf, & Kordy, 2007; Haberstroh & Moyer, 2012; Owen, Goldstein, Lee, Breen, & Rowland, 2010; Riper et. al., 2011; Spek et al., 2007; Spek, Nyklicek, Cuijpers, & Pop, 2007). Still, this literature is in its infancy, and there is more outcome research on some types of groups, such as breast cancer and self-injurious behaviors, than for other problems (Haberstroh & Moyer, 2012; Merchant & Yozamp, 2014; Page, 2010).

There are potential disadvantages to computer-mediated groups. Computer-mediated groups sometimes lack clear and accountable leadership. This, in turn, has the potential to lead to destructive interactions, superficial self-disclosure, and the compounding of isolation by persons with interpersonal difficulties (Barlow, 2013). Other problems such as unsecured sites, blurred boundaries leading to ethical issues, and lack of access to emergency services have also been mentioned (Barlow, 2013; Page, 2010). Computer-mediated groups tend to limit access by individuals in lower socioeconomic groups who have less access to computer hardware, software, and high-speed services. In addition, certain types of distance group services may not be covered by private, nonprofit, or government health plans.

There are a number of other issues besides reimbursement that should be considered by workers who plan to lead computer-mediated groups. There can be a lack of formal facilitation by social workers and other trained helping professionals that may make referring to certain types of computer-mediated groups risky. There is also a lack of professional standards regulating how to conduct groups at a distance or how to bill for services privately or through social and health service agencies (Glueckauf et al., 2003). The previously mentioned standards for distance professional services by the National Board For Certified Counselors are one important step to address this problem, but more needs to be done by national organizations of social workers and allied health professionals.

Overall, more research is needed about the benefits and limitations of computer-mediated groups before any definitive conclusions can be drawn about their effectiveness. Also needed are ethical and practice standards about service accountability, legal requirements, record keeping, reimbursement, and other aspects of computer-mediated group work.

> **?** Assess your understanding of how various aspects of the environment affect the planning process by taking this brief quiz.

Case Example

Cathy worked for a university counseling center that stressed preventive services. She perceived that there were an increasing number of women being referred to her by the university's health center with symptoms of depression and anxiety. Many had successfully raised children and were seeking further education to start a new career after their children left home. In addition to having concerns about returning to school as nontraditional-aged students, many did not receive much encouragement from their spouses or partners, rendering their efforts to seek a new career even more difficult. Cathy wondered if a support group would be the best way to help these women. She conveyed her plans for a possible group to her supervisor in the form of a group proposal and began planning for the group.

She talked with colleagues in the counseling center and the health center about their experiences with older students to assess the need for a support group. She found that they too had been seeing a number of women who were beginning second careers and who were in need of supportive services. To learn more about the types of problems older students might be encountering, she called the local community college and discussed the group with several academic advisors from Start Again, an educational program designed to assist nontraditional-aged students. In addition, she spoke with a few women on her caseload to see if they shared her perception of the need for a support group. They seemed very interested. Cathy also spoke to her supervisor and discussed her preliminary ideas about the group. Her supervisor said that a support group would fit the mission and goals of the organization. She thought the group could help Cathy's clients with the transition back to school. It could also prevent more serious psychological, social, and physical problems later, as the women pursued life changes associated with starting a second career.

Informed by her initial assessment, Cathy concentrated on defining the purpose of the group. She recognized that the initial statement of purpose should provide basic information that would help members understand the nature of the group and how it would work. She decided that the purpose would be to bring women together to discuss issues about starting a second career, going to college as a nontraditional-aged student, and dealing with family issues related to life changes. Members would share their experiences and support each other through discussion and social activities. Cathy hoped that the group would help eliminate or reduce members' depression and anxiety and increase their coping skills.

Cathy developed a two-pronged recruitment plan that she hoped would ensure the group had an adequate number of members. She described the purposes of the proposed group during weekly staff meetings in both the counseling center and the health center and asked her colleagues to refer potential members to her. In addition, she wrote a short article about the group for a monthly student newsletter that was widely distributed on campus. In it, she listed the purpose of the group and suggested that potential members call her at the office to discuss their interest in attending.

Despite these efforts, only a few persons contacted her about the group. In her phone conversations with potential members, she learned that many felt overwhelmed by the demands of returning to school. Despite their perception that the group could be helpful, they seemed reluctant to commit their time to another new endeavor. Cathy suggested that potential members meet once to assess whether the group would meet their needs and be worth attending. Twelve women agreed to a first meeting, but the most convenient meeting time for the majority accommodated only nine women's schedules.

During the first orientation meeting, Cathy took notes on the women's individual situations. She noted that all potential members were over 40 years old, and all but one had children who were in either high school or college. All seemed to be having some difficulty balancing the academic demands of college with the time demands of their families. They displayed an interesting range of diversity based on income level as well as racial, ethnic, and cultural backgrounds. They also seemed to use differing coping strategies for dealing with their spouses, or partners' lack of supportiveness, suggesting that they could learn much from each other. Cathy also felt that all potential members were articulate, had good insight into their personal and family situations, and had potential for helping others in the group. Despite having only eight members attending the orientation session, Cathy felt that the composition of the group would promote the development of therapeutic group processes.

Cathy described the purpose of the group, answered members' questions about how the group would work, and helped members discuss and shape how the group would function. After this discussion, members seemed genuinely interested in attending more sessions, and they seemed relieved to meet others who were experiencing similar life transitions. Cathy and the members agreed that the group could be an open one, adding members from time to time, but that the size of the group should not exceed eight members. In addition, members discussed some initial thoughts about attendance, confidentiality, length and time of meetings, and Cathy's role in the group. After this discussion, Cathy noted that they had started to form the elements of an informal contract that could be discussed more fully in the next meeting of the group. She added that in the early sessions, members could also begin to work on their individual goals and contracts with the group and with each other. Overall, the orientation session seemed quite successful.

Behind the scenes, Cathy spoke with the counseling center that was supporting the new group. She identified a comfortable meeting space for the group, one that was accessible and private. Although members had no special childcare or transportation needs, she asked the counseling center to provide some funds for refreshments.

Cathy also considered carefully how she would monitor the progress of the group, deciding to ask members at the beginning of each session about their goals and the progress toward them. She decided that she would make notes immediately after each session about the progress of members and asked members to evaluate the group using a session evaluation form (see Chapter 14). She also planned on spending time, at the end of the group, asking group members what they had accomplished, what remained for them to do, and what plans they had to accomplish these, as of yet, unaccomplished goals.

SUMMARY

This chapter stresses the need for planning in group work. Workers consider many variables and exercise control over as many of them as possible. The planning process should be guided by the purposes of the group, the needs of the members, and the requirements of the task.

The chapter presents a model for planning treatment and task groups. Steps in the model include (1) establishing the group's purpose, (2) assessing the potential sponsorship and membership, (3) recruiting members, (4) composing the group, (5) orienting members, (6) contracting, (7) preparing the group's environment, (8) planning of distance groups, and (9) preparing a written group proposal. The model can be useful in planning for the many different types of groups a worker may lead. All planning models represent an idealized, systematic set of procedures that may vary, depending on the realities of agency practice, but following a logical planning model can assist workers in helping groups meet members' needs and accomplish established goals.

The Group Begins

The beginning of a group is often characterized by caution and tentativeness. The members have certain expectations about the group based on experiences in other groups. They may have met with the worker before the first group meeting or received information on the purpose of the group through other agency workers or from other group members. Nevertheless, at the beginning of any group, members are not fully certain about its purposes. Members wonder about what will be expected of them and what the leader and the other members will be like. Thus, from the very first contact, participants assess each other, mainly based on nonverbal cues, such as dress and personal appearance. The first interchanges are often stereotypical conversations in which participants attempt to become familiar with one another through mutual interests in places, people, events, leisure and work pursuits, and other common experiences.

As the group meeting progresses, an approach-avoidance conflict often becomes more evident (Garland, Jones, & Kolodny, 1976). Members approach each other in their striving to connect with one another, but they avoid getting too close because they fear the vulnerability that such intimacy implies. Members are concerned about the way they present themselves early in a group and often prefer to proceed with caution. Members often do not feel secure about what they can expect from the group or their own ability to perform in the group. Therefore, they are often cautious about what they reveal.

Discussion of emotionally charged issues can be detrimental in the beginning of a group. When a member self-discloses emotionally charged issues very early in the group's development, other members sometimes feel threatened and may disclose little for a time. This occurs because few norms have developed about how to behave, and members are unsure about how to respond. Members may feel threatened if they think they will be asked to self-disclose at similar levels. They may not be ready to do so, or they may think others will not be receptive or supportive.

Through their initial interactions, members attempt to find their places within the group. As the group develops norms, members begin to find out what is acceptable and unacceptable behavior. The tentative interactions found at the beginning of most groups are a testing ground for developing re-lationships. Group members attempt to reach out to find whom in the group they can trust with their thoughts and feelings and with whom they can form continuing relationships.

Members' experiences can affect their reactions in a new group. A useful exercise that can be done early in the group's life is to have all members describe an experience they had in a previous group and emphasize how that group experience affects their participation in the current group.

Members react in different ways to groups. Some remain silent, taking a wait-and-see stance. Others try to reduce their anxiety by engaging in conversation or by asking questions to help them clarify their position in a group. Those with mental health problems, social relationship problems, or other disabilities may feel that their symptoms worsen at the beginning of the group because of performance anxiety. Gradually, a pattern of relating develops within the group, and the pattern crystallizes as the group develops.

Workers should try to remain aware of the patterns of relating as the group develops. The worker can point out patterns of relating as they form and can encourage the development of patterns that will help to accomplish group and individual goals. For example, the worker may want to model and reinforce open-interaction patterns that encourage all members to participate.

OBJECTIVES IN THE BEGINNING STAGE

The beginning stage is often considered, by both novice and experienced workers, to be a difficult stage of group work because members often seek direction about how to proceed but are ambivalent about following any suggestions. Members struggle to maintain their autonomy but, at the same time, to fit in and get along with others in the group. The worker's primary goals are to help members feel comfortable in the group, to work together in a cooperative and productive manner, and to feel that their unique contribution to the group is respected and appreciated. To accomplish these goals it is helpful to:

- Ensure a secure environment where members begin to bond with the leader and with each other
- Facilitate member introductions
- Clarify the purpose and function of the group, as it is perceived by the worker, the members, and the sponsoring organization
- Discuss and clarify the limits of confidentiality within the group
- Help members to feel that they are an important part of the group
- Guide the development of the group
- Balance task and socio-emotional aspects of the group process
- Set goals
- Contract for work
- Facilitate members' motivation and ability to work in the group
- Address ambivalence and resistance
- Work with involuntary members
- Anticipate obstacles to achieving individual and group goals
- Monitor and evaluate the group as the change process begins

In the following pages, these tasks and the corresponding skills necessary to carry them out are presented sequentially. In actual practice, of course, the group worker should be concerned about these tasks simultaneously.

Ensuring a Secure Environment

No work can be accomplished in groups unless members feel secure when participating. Therefore, a fundamental and essential role for the worker in the beginning stage is to make sure that members are feeling comfortable, safe, and secure with their participation in the group. New workers should recognize that members of groups might come from environments that are not comfortable, safe, or secure. In fact, some members may be hypervigilant, expecting the worst in all or most environments. This could be because of any number of adverse childhood events, or current bio-psycho-social-environmental assaults on their integrity. For example, members could have witnessed or experienced repeated trauma during childhood, such as neglect, or emotional and physical abuse. They could have experienced severe poverty, racism, or violence. They may have been bullied as a child or adolescent or learned that the way to survive in their neighborhood was to become a gang member. As adults they may continue to experience violence, marginalization, exploitation, oppression, or other factors that make them wary of participating in a group.

Workers should display patience and equanimity, gradually demonstrating to these traumatized members that the group is a positive place for support, healing, and rejuvenation where they can trust the worker and fellow members to work together to accomplish meaningful goals. Workers have to spend time to build security and trust before proceeding with agendas and goals. Workers who do not build a secure and safe environment early in the group will not be successful over the long-term. It is a mistake to pursue mandated goals without physical and emotional safety and security assured to members. Proceeding without safety and security also violates ethical principles.

There are too many settings where workers are expected to work on mandated goals before members are ready. Workers should keep in mind members' rights to self-determination and social justice. There are limits to what can be accomplished with some members. Workers need to recognize and be comfortable with the limits of what they are able to accomplish in some situations and engage in self-care. The goal should be engagement and respect, using a positive, relaxed pace where members are encouraged to gradually share their stories, and reveal what help they would like from the group. Workers should listen intensely, learning all they can while encouraging members to use their resilience, skills, and strengths to overcome adversity and move toward healthier lifestyles. Group leaders may have an immediate or delayed impact on some members, and may not be able to help others. It is often difficult for workers to know what if any impact they have had on members. Therefore, they should remain positive and self-soothing even when they question whether they are having a positive impact.

There are many ways to build a safe and secure environment. First, the worker should acknowledge that members might not feel secure or be ready to self-disclose. In some families and cultures, showing vulnerabilities, such as insecurity, may not be acceptable. Therefore, members may not want to risk sharing feelings at first, and this should be acknowledged by the worker. Workers can begin by asking members to present whatever information about themselves they are willing to share. Workers can be role models sharing information about themselves first. After this occurs, members can be encouraged to talk about their aspirations, goals, and dreams. Workers can tie these aspirations to what the group may be able to help them accomplish.

Another step is to take every opportunity to support members' goals, paying close attention to both their immediate and longer term needs and wants. Workers should be role models, describing their previous positive experiences in similar groups and how they might be able to help members have better lives. They can ask for members help to make the group a safe, enjoyable place to heal and grow.

In the early stages, conflict, criticism, and other forms of negative feedback should be avoided. If any verbal or nonverbal interactions occur that are not supportive or encouraging, workers should intervene, gently modeling supportive interactions that are uplifting and self-esteem building. Workers should remember that time will be available later in the development of the group to focus on problems and issues and to use confrontation or other strategies that are more appropriate in later group meetings when respectful, trusting relationships have been established.

The beginning of groups should be reserved for pointing out and building on members' strengths and resiliencies, helping them to become empowered and vital contributors to the success of the group. A positive, upbeat, and warm manner that praises and encourages members for their unique contributions is essential in early group meetings, especially when working with members who are reluctant, resistant, or mandated participants. As members tell their stories, and have them affirmed, they begin to grow more trusting and open with their fellow group members. By affirming and validating members' experiences, workers show that they are attentive and understanding, starting with the members and staying with them. This, in turn, can help to form therapeutic alliances with members, where trust grows. As genuine and warm interactions continue, members begin to bond with the worker and each other, and can begin to feel safe to tackle some of the difficult issues they face as they move forward. Building a base of trust, and feelings that the group can be helpful, is of utmost importance when reluctant members first begin to participate and engage in beginning group meetings.

> **?** Assess your understanding of the objectives and skills that are useful in the beginning stage of group work by taking this brief quiz.

Introducing New Members

When the participants have arrived and the group is ready to begin, the first task of the worker is to introduce members to one another. Introductions help members share their mutual concerns and interests, and they develop trust. The worker should decide what information is important for members to share with the group. Beyond each member's name, the information revealed by each member should depend on the purpose of the group. For example, if the group is an interagency task force to study the problems of battered women, members might be expected to share their position in their agency, their experiences with services for battered women, and their reasons for becoming involved in the task force. If the group is for parents with children who have behavior problems, in addition to information about themselves, members might briefly describe their children and the behavior problems they are experiencing.

Introductions can give members a starting point for interaction. Therefore, the information that is shared should attempt to bring out commonalities. The worker can facilitate this process by noting common characteristics and shared concerns disclosed by different members. Rather than proceeding through the introduction mechanically, the worker should encourage members to discuss commonalities. This process helps members feel at ease with one another. It also helps develop group cohesion and demonstrates to members that they are not alone with their problems and concerns.

Case Example   A Support Group for Caregivers of Persons with Dementia

The worker asked each member in turn to talk about themselves, the person for whom they were caring, and the problems they were experiencing. One member, Mary, mentioned how concerned she was about her husband driving even though he refused to give it up. The worker stopped the group introductions at this point and asked if anyone else had experienced a similar problem and how they handled it. Several members began to talk about the problem and their concerns about it. The worker suggested that since this seemed to be a concern for many members that they continue with the introductions, but take up the topic of driving later during the group meeting. Later during introductions, another member brought up the topic of her husband's agitated behavior and how he paced and followed her from room to room. Again, the worker asked if any other group members had experienced that problem, and several said they had. The worker said that they would also talk about that behavior later in the group meeting or during the next group meeting if there was not time to get to it in today's meeting.

The opportunity for members to share common concerns and issues with one another is one of the unique aspects of social group work practice. Yalom (2005) has called this phenomenon *universality*. People who come to treatment groups often believe that they are alone with their problems. In reality, although they may have been experiencing their problems in isolation, other people experience similar concerns. The first group meeting provides them with feelings of support and comfort as they realize they are not alone.

A similar process occurs in task groups. For example, workers from different community agencies often experience the same frustrations and problems in serving clients with particular social service needs. Alone, workers may think they can do little to make the system more responsive to clients. Together, in a task force, a treatment conference, or in any other task group, workers can share their concerns, coordinate their efforts, and work to change problematic situations.

Round Robin

The most common method of introducing members to one another is to have them speak in round robin fashion. If this method is used, it is helpful for the worker to go first. In the early stages of the group, members take many of their cues from the worker who can serve as a model by disclosing personal characteristics. Once members hear the worker's introduction, they are likely to focus on the disclosures as they introduce themselves.

Sometimes, the worker may want members to disclose information about areas of concern that the worker does not share. For example, in a group of parents, the worker may not have children. Workers should note the absence of this characteristic in their own lives, state how it might affect their work in the group, and ask members to comment on this factor in their introductions. For example, the worker might say, "I don't have any children of my own, but I've worked with children in the past at summer camp, in foster care, and for the past four years in my current position."

When they introduce themselves, members rarely disclose more than the worker has disclosed. In fact, they initially tend to disclose less than the worker. Therefore, if workers expect a certain level of self-disclosure or want to foster disclosures in a certain area, their introductions should reflect what is expected. This is not to suggest that the introductions should call on members to reveal in-depth, personal life experiences. Pressing for such disclosures at the beginning of a group is likely to increase rather than decrease barriers to open communication.

Communication styles and expectations about self-disclosure are influenced by our cultural heritage. Pearson (1991) suggests, for example, that clients who identify with the cultural imperatives in Chinese society may believe that close, personal relationships are usually reserved for family and that high levels of self-disclosure are not as desirable as a "balance and restraint in the experience and expression of emotions" (p. 51).

Variations on Round Robin

Several variations on the round robin may be useful in opening different types of groups. To increase interaction, for example, members can be divided into pairs. One member of each pair interviews the other for five minutes by asking for details specified by the worker. When time is up, members reverse roles and continue for another five minutes. When the group reconvenes, members introduce their partners to the group by recalling the facts learned during their conversation. In addition to helping members develop a relationship with a partner, group workers find that this method of introduction sometimes leads to a greater depth of self-disclosure than round robin because new group members are likely to reveal more about themselves on a one-to-one basis than when they face the entire group.

A variation on this opening is what Shulman (2016) has called "problem swapping" (pp. 428–429). Members volunteer to discuss their problems or concerns openly before the group. This opening promotes group interaction, leads to the identification of shared problems and concerns, and helps members consider how they might proceed.

An opening that is useful in growth-oriented groups is known as *top secret*. Members are asked to write down one thing about themselves that they have not or would not ordinarily reveal to new acquaintances. The leader collects the top secrets and reads them to the group. Members attempt to identify the person who made each revelation, giving a reason for their choice. This exercise can be repeated in a later group session to illustrate the extent to which trust and cohesion have increased in the group. Members often reveal more intimate or personal top secrets after they come to know and feel comfortable with the members of their group. Variations on this opening exercise are *my most embarrassing experience* and *my greatest success*.

Another opening exercise that can help members disclose something about themselves or their family of origin is called *my name*. Members can be asked to discuss how they got their names and what meaning the name has for them and for their family of origin. For example, a member might state that his father felt strongly that he should be named Samuel, after an uncle who had died. The member goes on to discuss the uncle and other facts about his family of origin. He might also mention that he disliked being called Sam by his parents and decided at age 13 to insist that his parents and friends call him by his middle name, Allen. This exercise can often lead to interesting discussions of members' feelings about themselves now and in the past. It also helps members learn each other's names, which is important for open and personal interaction.

Other openings, such as *treasure hunt*, can be useful. Members are asked to find two or three facts about each of the other group members. This activity offers much structured but informal interaction, helping members overcome initial anxieties and shyness about participating. The facts obtained are shared when the group reconvenes.

Program activities can also be used in opening a group. Such activities help members share important information about themselves while working on an assigned task or activity. In addition to increasing members' self-disclosure, program activities can build cohesion in the group. For example, in children's groups, members may be asked to pick an animal that represents them. When introducing themselves, members can name the animals they have selected and state what characteristics of the animal they identify with. Another program activity for children or adolescent groups is to have members stand in a circle and hold hands with two members who are not next to them. Members are then asked to untangle themselves and form a circle without letting go of each other's hands.

Variations in Group Beginnings

A number of factors can change the way a worker begins a group. Sometimes workers become involved with groups of people who have known each other before the group was formed. This can occur when the members are clients of a neighborhood center, a residential treatment facility, or are friends in the community. Similarly, in task groups, members may be familiar with one another as coworkers in the same agency or as coworkers in a network of agencies working with similar clients or a similar social problem. When members know one another, the challenges for the worker are different from the challenges that occur in a group of strangers.

Members who have had previous contact with one another are more likely to relate in ways that are characteristic of their previously established patterns. Roles and relationships established earlier may be carried into the new group, regardless of their functional or dysfunctional nature in the current group situation. In groups in which only a few members know one another or in which previous relationships between members vary from friendly to neutral or unfriendly, subgroups are likely to develop more often than they would in groups composed of strangers. There is also a natural tendency for friends or acquaintances to interact with one another and exclude strangers.

When it is possible to obtain information about potential group members, the worker should try to find out about any relationships that may exist among them. This will give the worker some indication of what form members' relationships are likely to take as they begin the group. It also gives the worker an opportunity to plan strategies to intervene in dysfunctional relationship patterns. The worker may wish to use information about members' previous relationships to reconsider the composition of the group and to understand members' interactions as the group unfolds. For example, a worker in a group home might use knowledge about the relationships that have developed among residents when deciding how to intervene to change communication patterns in a group that has just been established within the facility.

Another common variation in beginning a group occurs when the worker becomes involved in a previously formed group (see, for example, the following case example). This can happen when a worker (1) reaches out and works with a gang of adolescents, (2) is a consultant for a self-help group, (3) is asked to staff a previously formed committee, or (4) is asked to replace the leader of an intact treatment group. These situations are different from one in which all members are new to the group. Instead of members looking to the leader for direction, as in a new group, the worker in a previously formed group is the newcomer in a group with established patterns of relating. Members of previously formed groups are concerned with how the worker will affect the group, what they will have to do to accommodate the worker, and what the worker will expect of them. Members may also act on feelings resulting from termination with a previous worker. This is demonstrated in the following case example.

Case Example   Dealing with Feelings About a Worker Leaving the Group

In assuming leadership for an existing substance abuse prevention group, the new worker began the meeting by asking members to discuss how they felt about her replacing their former worker. Because the group had been meeting together for over a year, members freely discussed their concerns about changing group leaders. They also asked very direct questions about the new worker's credentials, experiences, and leadership style. During these discussions, the new worker listened carefully to what members were saying. She chose to be less verbal so that members had more opportunities to talk. By encouraging members to be more verbal, the worker was able to make a preliminary assessment of the group's structure and was able to identify the informal leadership structure that had previously developed in the group.

In working with previously formed groups, the worker should become familiar with the group's structure and its current functions and processes. It is especially important that the worker become familiar with the formal and informal leadership of the group, with members' relationships with one another, and with the tasks that face the group. Information obtained from a previous leader or from agency records may offer some indication of how to approach the group. In working with gangs or other community groups for which little information is available, the worker may find it helpful to gather information about the group. Any information obtained before contact with the group should be considered tentatively, however, because it is difficult to predict how an ongoing group is likely to react to a new worker. The worker may also want to observe the group before attempting to intervene.

The worker's presence in a previously formed group will cause adjustments. A process of accommodation to the new worker and assimilation of the worker into the culture of the group will occur. In general, cohesive and autonomous groups that have functioned together for some time will find it difficult to accommodate a new worker and will expect the worker to become assimilated into the ongoing process of the group. For example, a worker from a neighborhood center who is interested in working with a closely knit gang of adolescents who grew up together may have to spend a considerable amount of time developing trust and rapport with the group before members will seriously consider participating in a recreational activity at the neighborhood center.

Defining the Purpose of the Group

Opening Statement

After introductions, the worker should make a brief statement about the group's purpose and the worker's function in the group. When members are not clear about the purpose of the group or the motives of the worker, their anxiety increases, and they are less likely to become involved in working toward group goals. Evidence suggests that workers often fail to define the purposes of the group they are leading (Fuhriman & Burlingame, 1994). Even if the purpose has been explained to members during pregroup intake interviews, the worker should be sure to restate the purpose during the first meeting and in subsequent meetings.

Workers should take the lead and make a broad but concise statement of purpose to members. These statements help members to become aware and focus on goals enabling them to reflect on, and determine, whether they want to become involved in the group. When stating purposes, workers should be clear about the role of the sponsoring organization, legal and funding mandates, and any other factors that may affect group members' participation. Members should be fully informed about what their participation entails. Workers should use simple straightforward language, interpreting complicated mandates in terms of what they mean for members' participation in a group.

Demonstrating that workers are open and willing to inform members fully is one way to build trust and a working alliance. Encouraging members to have input is also essential because it enables members to feel that they are partners with the worker in deciding how to proceed. Workers should do as much as possible to develop a climate that helps members feel that they "fit in" and are welcome in the group (Paquin, Kivlighan, & Drogosz, 2013). This includes fostering complementary interactions, when members are helped to identify with their fellow members' situations rather than contrasting or comparing their situations to those of other members. Identification with other members' situations helps everyone to feel that they have commonalities that build cohesion, whereas contrasting or comparing situations can lead to alienation, competition, or the enhancement of perceptions of difference (Maxwell, et al., 2012).

Case Example   Statement of Purpose in a Domestic Violence Group

The following statement of purpose was made by a worker in a new group for female victims of domestic violence at a shelter: "*This group will provide support, empowerment, and resources to all of you who have experienced domestic violence and homelessness as a result of having to flee from the person who abused you. This domestic violence shelter has a long history of helping people like you in similar situations. Here we encourage you to keep confidential all that is shared while at the same time being supportive and empathic as we help one another heal and transition to a better life path. Remember, this is a safe space where you can share whatever you want, to the extent that you want. It is expected that you will help each other and that we will also do our part to support you in your path to a better life.*"

Notice how this statement of purpose encourages members to trust that the worker and fellow members will engage in a process of healing and growth through mutual aid and support in the safe environment of the group. The statement illustrates the worker's attempt to foster a therapeutic alliance among all participants. It emphasizes safety, security, freedom to participate, and mutual aid, and explicitly acknowledges members' rights to share only as much as they are comfortable with disclosing. The worker can then go on to discuss confidentiality and the safety features in the sponsoring organization that protect anonymity, which are so important to members of these kinds of groups.

Helping the Group Define Its Purpose
- Construct a brief statement of purpose and clearly articulate it to the group.
- Present the purpose as a positive statement that includes what members can accomplish.
- When possible, have members present and discuss their views of the group's purpose, especially when orienting new members to the group.
- State the purpose in a manner that enhances members' "fit" within the group.
- Mention the importance of members feeling secure and safe during emotional disclosures.
- Emphasize the importance of identifying with members' situations.
- Encourage mutual aid and complementary interactions that build camaraderie and dispel distrust.
- Do not focus on differences and conflicting viewpoints in early group meetings
- Highlight commonalities and shared visions for a better future.
- Discuss the role of the group in relation to its sponsoring agency, stressing the mutual contributions that can be made by both the group and the agency.
- Involve members by asking for feedback, and use this feedback to refine or modify the purpose.

The group's purpose should be presented in a positive and hopeful manner. In a classic book, Frank (1961) pointed out the importance of persuasion, expectancy, and placebo effects in psychotherapy. These factors are also present in group work practice. Presenting a positive, hopeful image of what can be accomplished in the group makes use of the beneficial effects of these cognitive expectancies. Rather than focusing on members' problems or concerns, the worker can express the group's purpose in terms of members' strengths and resiliency and the goals to be accomplished. Thus, statements that focus on positive objectives and goals, such as "Through this group experience you can learn to build on your. . .," "With the assistance of fellow group members you can get in touch with your strengths to overcome. . .," or "Through all of our efforts in this task force we can. . .," are preferable to statements that focus on the negative aspects of problems or concerns.

If the worker has successfully led a previous group that focused on similar concerns, the worker can mention this success. In treatment groups, such as a statement by the leader offers members the hope that the group will help them to achieve their goals. In task groups, members are more likely to be motivated and to persist in goal achievement.

In open-ended treatment groups, when new members replace old ones, it is often helpful to have those who have been in the group for some time state how the group has been helpful to them. Professional group workers can learn from the way that self-help groups, such as Alcoholics Anonymous, rely on the testimony of successful members as a major component of their group program. In task groups, members who have had some experience in the group can be asked to orient new members.

The opening statement about the group's purpose should include a brief description of the functions of the agency sponsoring the group. Notice, for example, in the previous example of the domestic violence group, there was a very brief mention of the agency's purpose. In treatment groups, the opening statement should define the limits of service so that members will have a clear notion of what services they can expect and what services are beyond the scope of the agency. There is nothing more frustrating for members than having their expectations go unfulfilled. The opening statement should include a brief statement about how the worker will help the members accomplish their goals.

In task groups, relating the agency's function and mission to the group's purpose helps members understand why they were called together to participate in the group. The opening statement allows members to see how the agency's functions are related to the group's task. It is not uncommon, for example, for members of task groups to ask about how the results of their work will be used. Task group members may be interested, for example, in the extent to which their group can make permanent changes in policies, procedures, and practices through its findings and recommendations.

Involving Members

The opening statement focuses the group on considering the purposes for meeting. It should be presented as a starting point for further discussion rather than as an immutable definition that is not open to negotiation, modification, or change. Attempting to impose a definition of the group without input from members tends to reduce their commitment and motivation and to increase their suspicions that their autonomy may be threatened.

The stated purposes and goals should be broad enough that members can formulate their own purposes and their own goals, but not so broad that almost any purpose or goal can be contained within it. Statements about improving members' social functioning or coping ability may be too abstract for members to comprehend. Opening statements should be presented in clear, jargon-free language. However, the leader should avoid being overly specific. Instead, the worker should solicit members' ideas and suggestions about how to operationalize particular purposes and goals.

In the beginning stage, members are often reluctant to risk their own tentative position within the group by expressing opinions that differ from those expressed by the worker or other members. Therefore, in addition to providing members with opportunities to express their opinions and concerns regarding the group's purpose and goals, the worker should actively reach out for members' input. This can be done in a variety of ways. In treatment groups, the worker should state clearly that the group is meant to serve the needs of its members, who ultimately determine the group's purpose and goals. Members can then be asked to state their own purposes and goals and to comment on the broad purposes and goals articulated by the worker. During this process, workers can encourage feedback by taking comments seriously and praising the members for sharing their feelings and thoughts. In task groups, the worker should encourage members to comment on the group's charge from the sponsoring organization, and discuss with members how any suggested changes will be brought to the attention of administrators or others who formulated the initial charge.

Members can sense whether the worker's call for feedback is genuine or perfunctory. If the worker makes a continuous effort to solicit feedback by encouraging all members to express their thoughts and feelings, members are more likely to feel that their input is welcome. For example, members can be asked to make a statement about how the group's purposes and goals meet their needs and to suggest how the group could be improved. Members can also simply be asked about their goals, as illustrated in the following example.

Case Example   A Mandated Group for Men Who Batter

During the opening statement the worker mentioned that one of the primary goals of the group was to help the men in the group control their tempers. The worker asked the members what else they wanted to accomplish. This was first met by silence. The worker did not say anything, and after a minute, one member stated that he wanted to get back together with his girlfriend. Another member began to talk about how he had done things that he regretted and wanted to "make things right." At the same time, several members said that they felt backed into a corner by their partners and finally "exploded." They had tried to get out of the situation but their partner kept at them. The worker acknowledged these statements and indicated that the group was there to give them the tools to help them deal with these situations.

Ethical and Professional Behavior

Behavior: Make ethical decisions by applying the standards of the NASW Code of Ethics, relevant laws and regulations, models for ethical decision-making, ethical conduct of research, and additional codes of ethics as appropriate to context

Critical Thinking Question: Group rules often have ethical implications. How can the group worker help members to observe confidentiality in groups?

Confidentiality

In treatment groups and certain task groups, it is important for the worker to lead a discussion of confidentiality during the opening portion of the group meeting. This will be the first time that many of the members may have been asked to keep the proceedings of a group meeting confidential. Therefore, it is important for workers to emphasize the need for confidentiality and the harmful and destructive effects that can result when breaches occur. Trust among group members is essential for cohesion and the smooth functioning of the group. When workers reassure members that the group is a safe haven, a place where they can discuss emotionally charged issues in confidence and without fear of reprisal, trust deepens and cohesion develops. In treatment groups, members are often concerned about how information they share with the group will be used outside the group meeting by the worker and other group members. Members cannot be expected to disclose intimate concerns or develop a sense of trust unless they can be assured that discussions within the group will not be shared outside of meetings. It can be helpful to remind members about the confidentiality of meetings periodically throughout the life of the group. This is particularly important in residential settings because frequent interaction outside the group may promote violations of confidentiality.

As mentioned in Chapter 1, in some cases, the worker may be obligated to share information discussed in the group with law-enforcement officials. Workers are also likely to share information with supervisors and fellow staff members during treatment conferences. Therefore, workers have an ethical obligation to be clear about the limits of confidentiality and with whom and under what circumstances data may be shared.

Confidentiality is also an important issue in many task groups. Members are often unsure about what issues, proposals, and facts can be shared with colleagues and others outside of the group. Because sensitive personal information is usually not discussed in task groups, it is especially important for the leader to mention if the content of group meetings should be kept confidential or if it can be shared with others outside the group to get their input, as illustrated in the following example.

Case Example   A State-Level Task Force

A state-level task force designed to study ways to improve services to older people trying to live independently in the community deliberated for six months about a single-point-of-entry system that could be used to assess all individuals who might need long-term care services in the community or in a nursing home. The leader of the task force emphasized the confidential nature of the proceedings, letting members know that premature or partial release of the information discussed in the task force could hinder its work and upset various stakeholders who now screened older people for long-term care services. The leader pointed out that another reason for keeping the report of the task force confidential was because it was preliminary and advisory. It would not be released by the governor until it was approved after extensive deliberation and hearings by the legislature in consultation with the governor's office.

The time set aside for the discussion of confidentiality also provides an ideal opportunity for the worker to bring related value issues to the attention of the group. For example, the worker might engage the group in a discussion of how social group work values, such as democratic participation, respect for the individuality of each member, self-determination, cooperation, mutual decision making, and the importance of individual initiatives will be operationalized in the group. Depending on the type of group, workers might also talk about the problems that may arise when group members form intimate relationships outside of group meetings. These dangers include (1) distraction from the group's purpose, (2) side conversations, alliances, and other effects of being a couple on group dynamics, and (3) dealing with conflict and the breakup of relationships that developed in earlier group sessions.

It is helpful for the worker to assist the group in formulating a set of principles—a code of behavior for its operation—to which each member agrees to adhere. These are sometimes referred to as *group rules*. For example, members might agree to the following group rules.

Group Rules
- Come to the group on time.
- Give the worker prior notice if you are unable to attend.
- Listen without interruption when another group member is talking.
- Avoid dominating the group discussion.
- Be respectful of each other's thoughts and feelings.
- Be sincere and honest when communicating thoughts and feelings.
- Make positive, cooperative, helpful, and trustworthy contributions in response to each other's comments.

Group rules should not be imposed unilaterally by the worker. Instead, members should help formulate the rules so that they take ownership of them. Group rules should not be confused with norms. They may become norms if they are adhered to by the group over time. However, norms develop gradually, and it is the workers' roles to guide group development to embrace norms that foster socio-emotional well-being and task accomplishment. Rules may be a first step in this process but they need to be gently enforced and followed if they are to become the norms that govern the group's work.

? Assess your understanding of the the techniques used to introduce members and to begin the group by taking this brief quiz.

Helping Members Feel a Part of the Group

When a group begins, there is little sense of belonging or cohesion. As members begin to feel secure and safe, an important early objective is to help a diverse collection of individuals, who may be apprehensive and ambivalent, begin to identify themselves as a collective of supportive partners in a common enterprise. The worker aims to build a fellowship where mutual aid and respect are normative.

To empower members and build self-esteem, it is important to ensure that the demands of participating in the group do not exceed members' abilities. Thus, workers may have to tone down expectations for intimate disclosures implied by a member's early disclosure or scale back unrealistic expectations about what can be accomplished in a given period. In Acceptance and Commitment Therapy (ACT) (Hays, Strosahl, & Wilson, 2011) and Dialectical Behavior Therapy (DBT; Linehan, 2015), for example, no expectations or judgments are made about a person's disabilities. The member is helped to practice acceptance of past and current events.

Pointing out shared interests and common goals among members helps them to feel that they are a part of the group. Members are comforted by the familiar. Knowing that they are not alone with their concerns or issues helps them feel closer to other participants in the group. There is also a growing body of evidence that members from similar backgrounds, who share complementary life views and values, develop trust faster than members with clashing backgrounds, interests, and values (Forsyth, 2014). Careful planning can help, but workers also need to draw out members, helping them to identify with each other and emphasizing commonalities and complementary skills, while simultaneously steering clear of comparisons that focus on difference or conflict.

Differences and conflicts should be acknowledged rather than ignored. Workers can reframe them as opportunities to understand how other members see the problems or issues facing the group. They can also encourage members to postpone discussions of differences and conflicts until they have gotten to know one another more fully and developed enough trust to tackle these more difficult issues in a productive manner.

In early group meetings, the leader can use several techniques to help members acknowledge and begin to appreciate differences that can be addressed more fully later in the group. For example, the leader can point out the contributions that different backgrounds and different perspectives make to the group. They can encourage members to welcome or at least be open to new perspectives and to explore differences gradually as therapeutic alliances and member-bonding occur as the group progresses. The leader can ask nonthreatening, direct questions that help members explore, understand, and appreciate the different perspectives that are present within the group.

The leader can also use program activities or exercises to help members explore differences in an entertaining and lively fashion. For example, a leader might help the group plan a dinner to which members would bring a dish representative of their culture, ethnicity, or nationality. Another activity is for each member to design a coat of arms that represents something about his or her personal background and to present the coat of arms to the group for discussion. The leader might also ask each member to create a *self-disclosure collage* that artistically represents elements of them not known to other members of the group. Overall, differences among members in their backgrounds and life experiences should be neither magnified nor ignored. Instead, the worker's task is to help members appreciate and respect differences in early group meetings and explore them in more depth as the group meets and becomes more comfortable.

The worker also helps members feel that they are a part of the group by protecting them from injury. Thus, misinformation should be corrected, and personal attacks should not be condoned. In addition, the worker should continually scan the group to ensure that the content of the meeting is not having an adverse emotional effect on members. Empowering members by fostering active participation in group decision making can also help members feel that they have an important and meaningful role to play in the group.

> **?** Assess your understanding of the techniques used to help members feel a part of the group by taking this brief quiz.

Guiding the Development of the Group

Different theoretical writings suggest a range of possibilities for guiding the development of a group. Some writers suggest that the worker should provide little or no direction at the beginning of a group and prefer an approach that encourages members of the group to struggle with purposes and goals until mutual agreements about them can be achieved. Unstructured approaches to group beginnings are often used in *t-groups* (group dynamic training groups) and other growth groups when the purpose of meeting is to learn about group dynamics and one's own interpersonal interaction style. The process of struggling to develop purposes and goals without any direction from the leader, however, is often anxiety provoking. Therefore, workers should be cautious about using unstructured approaches with members who are not functioning at optimal levels, when time to achieve particular outcomes is limited, and when exploration of one's interpersonal style is not a primary goal.

Structure in Treatment Groups

Humanistic and mutual aid approaches to group work practice often have limited structure. They aim to empower members in early group meetings by ensuring that consensus building is used during the decision-making processes about how groups will operate. Techniques can be used to shape interaction and self-expression processes, but these approaches should take care not to manipulate, coerce, or control members (Glassman & Kates, 1990; Steinberg, 2004). Humanistic and mutual aid approaches to leadership during the beginning stage is especially appropriate in support, self-help, social action, and coalition groups in which the empowerment of members and the mobilization of their collective energy and wisdom are primary goals (Saleebey, 2013). However, elements of humanistic and mutual aid approaches, such as respect for the dignity and individuality of each member and the belief in each member's potential for growth and development, are essential in all group work efforts.

Writers within the humanistic tradition point out that techniques such as "directing" and making a "demand for work" can help members develop and implement mutually agreed-on purposes (Gitterman & Shulman, 2005; Shulman, 2014, 2016). Yet, few writers within the humanistic and mutual aid traditions spend time addressing issues of limit setting, socialization, and structure in groups of severely impaired individuals and in groups with members who have been ordered into treatment because of delinquent or criminal behavior. Yet there are many practice situations in which the sponsoring organization and the larger society expect that workers will use their authority to help members function as more productive members of society. Yalom (1983), for example, points out the need for limit setting and a clear structure when working with psychiatric inpatients. Levine and Gallogly (1985) suggest methods for dealing with challenges to the worker's authority when working with groups of alcoholics in inpatient and outpatient settings. Similarly, DBT and other practice methods described in Chapter 10 designed for work with individuals who have borderline personality disorders, suicidal behavior, and other severe psychiatric disabilities prescribe active structuring of the work of the group by the leader.

Intervention

Behavior: Critically choose and implement interventions to achieve practice goals and enhance capacities of clients and constituencies

Critical Thinking Question: Group workers use multiple skills during the life of the group. What skills are used by group work practitioners during the beginning stage?

In many practice settings, short-term psychoeducational groups, such as social skills for children, life skills training groups for psychiatric inpatients, groups to help new parents learn parenting skills, and anger control groups, are offered because workers have specific information and specific skills they think will benefit members (see, for example, Walsh, 2010). In these groups, the worker is designated by society and the sponsoring organization as an expert who provides direction and structure so that the members can learn new skills. Of course, even in these groups, members should have the opportunity to shape individual goals, group goals, and meeting agendas, and to share their concerns and learn from one another. Too often novice group workers try to stick to structured psycho educational group agendas without first taking the time to build trust and to help members feel comfortable and safe in the group.

An example of a session agenda for a time-limited, structured, psychoeducational parenting group is presented in Figure 7.1. The agenda provides the organizing framework for the first meeting. It indicates the goals for the session, the material to be covered during the group meeting, and the reading assignments and tasks required of each parent during the following week. Similar session agendas are prepared by the worker for each of the 10 sessions in the time-limited parenting group.

In structured, time-limited groups, it is quite common for the agenda to be developed before the group session. As compared with less structured, process-centered approaches, structured group approaches give the worker greater responsibility for group goals and the way the group conducts its work. In process-centered approaches, members are encouraged to take informal leadership roles and develop their own goals, agendas, and contracts, whereas in time-limited psychoeducational groups, members' input is sometimes limited to modifying goals, agendas, and contracts that the worker has already developed.

There are many types of time-limited, structured groups for acquiring skills, managing anxiety, coping with life transitions, and learning parenting skills (see, for example, Bauer & McBride, 2003; Bieling, McCabe, & Antony, 2006; Garvin, Guterrez, & Galinski, 2004; LeCroy, 2008; McKay & Paleg, 1992; Passi, 1998; Rose, 1989, 1998; Shapiro, Peltz, & Bernadett-Shapiro, 1998; White & Freeman, 2000). These groups often use evidence-based manuals or field-tested curricula, specifying agendas for 6 to 20 meetings. Structured psychoeducational groups using manuals and field-tested curricula usually contain a mixture

AGENDA

Date_____

Session I

Goals

By the end of this session, each parent will be able to

1. Describe the purpose of the group program
2. State how behavior is learned
3. Describe specifically one behavior of his or her child
4. State the behavior he/she will monitor during the next week
5. Describe how each behavior will be monitored

Agenda

1. Introduction
   A. Leader introduces self to group
   B. Each member introduces self to group (name, number of children, current problems you would like to work on)
2. Orientation to the group program
   A. Purpose of the group session
      1. Goals
      2. Why should parents be trained in parenting skills?
      3. Who is responsible for what?
   B. Group contracts—read, modify, sign
3. Introduction to behavior modification—lecture
   A. Behavior is learned
      1. Reinforcement
      2. Extinction
      3. Punishment
   B. Role-play demonstration
4. Break
5. Assessment
   A. Discuss behavior checklist
   B. Describe one behavior of your child
   C. Develop monitoring plan: what, who, how, when
6. Buddy system
   A. Description
   B. Choose buddy, exchange numbers, arrange calling time
7. Assignment
   A. Monitor chosen behavior and begin to chart it
   B. Call buddy
   C. Read units 1 and 2 (exercises at the end of each chapter are optional)
8. Evaluation

Figure 7.1
Sample Session Agenda for a Time-Limited, Structured Parenting Group

of (1) educational materials; (2) exercises to help members practice the material; (3) discussions of the material and the problems members are experiencing outside the group; (4) weekly assignments for members to do outside the group; and (5) a very brief evaluation of the meeting. The following case example illustrates one type of psychoeducational group.

Case Example A Healthy Heart Group in a Medical Setting

A medical social worker decided to form a group for patients who had recently undergone heart bypass surgery. Family members were invited. This six-session daily group meeting was structured so that there was a speaker followed by a discussion period. Topics included nutrition, diet, exercise, keeping a positive mood, engaging in sexual activity, and other lifestyle issues, such as a moderation in drinking alcoholic beverages and stress reduction techniques. After the speaker's presentation, each meeting provided the members with a chance to talk about their specific concerns and issues and to practice stress reduction techniques.

Studies about the efficacy of group work found that groups with specific purposes, homogeneous concerns, clear agendas, and structured group meetings were more effective than groups with less structure (Bauer & McBride, 2003). Members reported appreciating that the leader provided specific information and effective strategies to help them with their concerns as the case example illustrates. Workers should keep in mind, however, that members' concerns and needs are not always most appropriately served by a time-limited, structured group approach. In support groups, for example, a flexible structure that maximizes member input may be more effective than a structured approach in helping members to ventilate their concerns and to give and receive help from fellow group members. In these groups, members are encouraged to reach out to one another as much as possible. Goals and specific agendas for each meeting are determined based on feedback and mutual agreement among all members during meetings.

It is unfortunate that there is not more dialogue among scholars who promote short-term, structured, behavioral, and task-centered approaches to treatment groups and those who promote long-term, process-oriented, humanistic approaches. Scholars who promote one approach over another often fail to acknowledge the value of alternative approaches, actively dismiss important contributions of alternative approaches, and ignore the core skills that form the base for all group work. It is the thesis of this text that both approaches have much to offer and that social work practice situations fall along a continuum. At the ends of the continuum, pure approaches may be effectively applied, but in most practice situations, a blending of approaches makes the most sense. Structure should be viewed as a tool to be used differentially in practice situations to help members and the group as a whole achieve agreed-on objectives. The work of McKay and colleagues (2011) is one encouraging attempt to bridge the divide.

To find protocols for leading specific types of groups for individuals with the types of concerns you encounter in practice settings, it is best to search databases, subscribe to book publishing catalogues, and search for websites with the latest information in your area of group work expertise. For example, World Cat can help to identify books and chapters that contain evidence-based manuals and field-tested protocols, and Psych Info, Medline, and Google Scholar can be used to identify articles that describe evidence-based interventions, programs, and practices. Macgowan (2008) and Barlow (2013) have written books that can also help group workers to conduct evidence-based group work.

Structure in Task Groups

Written agendas are frequently used in task groups to keep groups focused on the work that is to be accomplished. Figure 7.2 shows an example of an agenda for a meeting of a delegate council. The example agenda shown in the figure follows a standard outline as shown in the following:

Meeting Agenda Outline
- Approve the minutes of the previous meeting
- Call for new agenda items
- Make announcements
- Receive reports from standing committees and administrative officers
- Work on current business
- Discuss any new agenda items that might have been introduced earlier in the group meeting
- Adjourn

Agenda items can be divided into three categories: information, discussion, and action. Often, agendas are accompanied by attachments to explain the agenda items. Agendas with their attachments are usually given to all group members several days before the meeting so they can become familiar with the business that will be discussed during the meeting.

In task groups, feedback is encouraged in several ways. Members might be encouraged to submit formal agenda items before group meetings. The items are then placed

Order of Business	Information	Discussion	Action
CYPRUS HILLS DELEGATE COUNCIL Meeting date _____			
1. Call to order			X
2. Approval of the minutes of the previous meeting			X
3. Call for new agenda item			X
4. Announcements	X		
5. Treasurer's report	X		
6. Program committee's report	X		
7. Director's report	X		
8. Emergency housing proposal		X	
9. Proposed changes in bylaws (see attachment A)			X
10. Election of members of the women's issues task force (see attachment B for slate of candidates)		X	
11. Proposal to develop an ad hoc committee on community health care		X	
12. New business		X	

Figure 7.2
Sample Agenda for a Delegate Council

on the agenda. When the item is considered by the group, it is often helpful for the member who submitted the item to present it to the group. During meetings, members' feedback is usually limited to a discussion of the specific task or agenda item currently being discussed. Members have a chance to add new agenda items during a meeting only if the group's predetermined order of business can be concluded in time to discuss new business at the end of the meeting. For additional information about leading task groups in the beginning stage, see Levi (2014) and Tropman (2014).

Balancing Task and Socio-emotional Foci

Another objective of the worker in the beginning stage is to balance the task and socio-emotional aspects of the group process. Through systematic observation of leadership training groups, committees, juries, classes, therapy groups, and labor relations teams, Bales (1950) established a set of 12 categories to describe group interactions. Half the categories are in problem solving or task-focused areas and the other half pertain to socio-emotional areas. Bales' scheme for observing a group is instructive because it points out that in all groups the worker must be conscious of both the task and socio-emotional aspects of group process.

In task groups, it has been found that about two-thirds of group interactions are focused on task accomplishment and one-third on socio-emotional aspects, such as giving support and releasing tension (Bales, 1955). Evidence concerning treatment groups suggests that they often spend more time on socio-emotional aspects than on task-focused discussion (Munzer & Greenwald, 1957). Despite the difference in emphasis, pioneering studies by Bales (1950, 1955) and more recent studies by other researchers (Forsyth, 2014) suggest that in both task and treatment groups, neither the task nor the socio-emotional aspects of group process should be neglected. An exclusive focus on tasks in any group may lead to members' dissatisfaction with their social and emotional interaction in the group. An exclusive focus on the social and emotional aspects of group interaction can lead to a group whose members will be satisfied with their relationships with one another but will be dissatisfied about what has been accomplished. Thus, a balance between the task and the socio-emotional aspects of group process is essential. No magic formula exists for achieving the appropriate balance between task and socio-emotional aspects of the group. Only through careful, ongoing assessments of group and member needs can the worker determine the appropriate balance.

Goal Setting in Group Work

In the first few meetings, groups often spend a considerable amount of time discussing goals. When the worker discusses the group's purposes, the process of goal formulation begins. Goals emerge from the interaction of individual members, the worker, and the system in which the group functions.

Workers' goals are influenced by the values and aims of the social work profession. As members of social service organizations, workers are aware of the aims and the limitations of the services they provide. Workers should also be cognizant of their function in the larger society that sanctions and supports their work. Workers' formulation of goals reflects what they believe can be accomplished with the support, resources, and limitations within the environment where the group operates.

Workers' goals also are affected by what they know about the group members. In treatment groups, workers often have an opportunity to meet each member during the planning stage. Potential members are selected, in part, because of their compatibility with the purposes and goals developed for the group. Workers make preliminary assessments of members' needs and the capacities of each group member, as well as the tasks that face them. Goals are formulated based on the assessment process.

In task groups, a similar process occurs. Goals are formulated by the worker in relation to the charge of the group from the sponsoring organization and the roles and status of the members who compose the task group. The following case example of a task group illustrates that the roles and the status of committee members limit their ability to make binding recommendations.

Case Example   Task Group to Examine Interdepartmental Coordination

A worker is charged with leading a committee to examine interdepartmental coordination of client services. Representatives from various departments throughout the agency are represented, but not the department heads. The committee meets a number of times and comes up with a series of goals and recommendations for better coordination. However, given the status and the roles of the members of the committee, the recommendations about improving coordination between departments are not adopted. Instead, a report is prepared and sent to the executive committee of the agency for additional action, because the members of the committee do not have the authority to implement the recommendations without approval from top-level management.

Goals are formulated by individual group members who have their own perspective on the particular concerns, problems, and issues that affect them and their fellow group members. In previously formed or natural groups, members have the advantage of knowing more than the worker does about the concerns of the other group members.

In formed groups in which members do not know each other before the first group meeting, members' goals are based on a variety of factors.

Factors Affecting Members' Goals
- An assessment of their own needs
- Their previous attempts to accomplish a particular goal
- The environmental, social, and familial demands placed upon them
- Their assessment of their own capacities and capabilities
- Their impressions or experiences of what the social service agency sponsoring the group has to offer

Goals for the group are formulated through a process of exploration and negotiation in which the worker and the group members share their perspectives. In this process, members and the worker should communicate openly about the goals they have formulated individually.

The extent to which common goals can be developed for all group members varies from group to group. In some groups, members have one, overriding concern in common. For example, a group of cigarette smokers suffering from chronic lung disease may be able to move quickly to a discussion of a specific contract to reduce cigarette smoking. In groups that are more diverse, such as outpatients in a mental health setting, it is often more difficult to develop common goals. In these groups, common goals are often formulated on a general level, for example, to improve the interpersonal social skills of members. Goals for individuals in the group are formulated at a more specific level. For example, an individual goal might be "To improve my skills when confronting others about behaviors I find unacceptable."

The process of goal setting, therefore, is one in which the goals of the worker and the members are explored and clarified. Three types of goals emerge from this process: (1) group-centered goals that focus on the proper functioning and maintenance of the group; (2) common group goals that focus on the problems, concerns, and tasks faced by all group members; and (3) individual goals that focus on the specific concerns of each group member. In an educational treatment group for parents of young children, a group-centered goal might be to increase the group's attraction for its members. A common group goal might call for the parents to learn about the normal growth and developmental patterns of young children. An individual goal for the parents of one child might be to reduce their son's temper tantrums.

In task groups, three levels of goals can also be identified. For example, in a committee mandated to review intake procedures in a family service agency, a group-centered goal might be to establish open, member-centered interaction patterns. A common group goal might be to make several recommendations to the program director to improve admission procedures. An individual goal for a committee member might be to interview workers in two other agencies about different approaches to intake procedures that can be shared with the committee at the next meeting.

The worker should help members develop clear, specific goals. Early in the process, members formulate general goals they would like to achieve. Examples include statements such as "I would like to be less depressed" or "The group should try to reduce the paperwork involved in serving our clients."

After members have stated their goals for the group, workers can help to clarify them and make them as specific as possible. Workers help members identify objective and subjective indicators of their goals and the criteria that will be used to evaluate them. The case example that follows illustrates this process.

Case Example   Clarifying Goals and the Criteria for Evaluating Them

For the goal statement "I would like to be less depressed," a member might be helped by the worker and the other group members to define indicators of depression, such as sleeplessness, lack of appetite, lack of energy, depressed affect, and so forth. The worker can then lead the group's efforts to help the member identify criteria that would indicate goal achievement. For the depressed member, this might include (1) sleeping through the night and not waking up early in the morning, (2) eating three meals a day, (3) having the energy to do things, and (4) smiling and laughing more often.

Defining goals clearly helps both workers and members focus on what they are attempting to achieve in the group. Developing clear goals is a prerequisite for entering the middle stage of group work. Before goals can be prioritized and a contract between worker and members developed, goals should be stated as clearly as possible. All members should have input into the development of goals and an opportunity to influence the direction the group will take to accomplish them.

In previously formed groups with preexisting goals, the worker has a different role in goal formulation. In some groups, goals may not have been clearly defined, and the worker's task is to help members clarify their goals. This is often the case with groups of teenagers and children who have not carefully considered their goals. In other previously formed groups, clear goals may exist. The worker's task in these groups is to help members achieve the goals that can be accomplished and modify or abandon those that are not likely to be achieved.

Achieving consensus about purposes and goals can be particularly difficult with involuntary members who are often pressured into participating in a group. Still, there is usually some common ground on which mutually agreed-on goals can be developed. For example, youthful offenders are sometimes given the choice of participating in group treatment or being sentenced through the juvenile court system. The worker can begin by stating the conditions and standards for continued participation and then encouraging members to develop their own goals within these minimally acceptable conditions and standards. Trust takes longer to develop in such groups, but if the worker consistently shows interest in the members' goals, concerns, and aspirations, the group can be a useful treatment modality (Bauer & McBride, 2003).

Assessment

Behavior: Collect and organize data, and apply critical thinking to interpret information from clients and constituencies

Critical Thinking Question: Helping members articulate their goals is important. How can the group worker help members state goals so that they are measurable?

Contracting

In group work, *contracts* are mutual agreements that specify expectations, obligations, and duties. The types of contracts that can be developed are presented in the following list. Contracts involving the group as a whole are usually developed around group procedures. Individual members' contracts are usually developed around individual treatment goals or individual task assignments.

Types of Contracts
- The group as a whole and the agency
- The group as a whole and the worker
- The worker and the group member
- Two or more group members
- The group as a whole and a member

The most common form of an individual-member contract is between a member and the worker. For example, a member may contract with the worker to stop smoking, to become more assertive, or to make more friends.

Contracts can also be developed between two or more group members to help each other achieve particular goals. For example, in an assertiveness training group, one member might decide to practice being assertive in two situations during the group meeting and in one situation during the week. The member may ask another member to praise her if she is assertive in the group and to telephone her during the week to see if she has been assertive in a situation outside the group. In return, she agrees to help the other member achieve a particular goal.

A third form of individual contracting occurs between a member and the group. The member, for example, can agree to obtain information about a resource for the group or can promise to report to the group about the results of a particular meeting. In a cohesive group, member-to-group contracts can be quite effective because members do not want to let each other down by failing to follow through on the contract.

When contracting with individual members for goals or tasks, it is important to be as specific as possible about formulating behaviorally specific outcome goals. Goals specified in a written or verbal contract should state briefly who will do what, under what circumstances, and how results will be measured.

Facilitating Members' Motivation

After an initial clarification of the purposes and goals of the group, the worker helps members increase their motivation for accomplishing the goals that have been mutually agreed on. Motivation is the key to the successful achievement of group and member goals. To a large extent, motivation is determined by members' expectations about (1) the worker's role in the group, (2) the processes that will occur in the group, and (3) what can be accomplished through the work of the group. Members bring a set of expectations to any group experience, and the expectations have a powerful influence on the way the members behave in the group. For example, if a member expects the worker to tell him or her how to proceed, it is unlikely that the member will take much initiative in the group. If the member has been involved in a previous group experience in which little was accomplished, the member's expectations and motivations to work hard to achieve individual and group goals are likely to be diminished.

As the worker and the members begin to explore how they can work together, the worker should help members identify their expectations and motivations. The worker can do this by asking members direct questions about what they think they can accomplish in the group and how they expect the group to function. These questions often uncover ambivalence about giving up old ways of doing things and fear about what new and unknown changes may bring. At the same time, they can empower members, helping them to feel that they are a vital part of the group and have an important stake in the agenda (Saleebey, 2013).

Addressing Ambivalence and Resistance

Sometimes members respond evasively to direct questions about their motivations and expectations, particularly when the worker has made an early and clear "demand for work" before assessing members' expectations and motivations (Schwartz, 1971, p. 11). Members may be reluctant to state ambivalent feelings about their ability to accomplish the goals for which they have contracted because they fear that the worker will disapprove. Mandated members may not be prepared to acknowledge problems others have identified. The following list summarizes some techniques for dealing with ambivalence and resistance.

Addressing Ambivalence and Resistance in the Group
- Pay attention to overt and covert messages about accomplishing the group's work.
- Acknowledge members' ambivalence and provide a realistic appraisal of members' chances for accomplishing successful change.
- Help members work through their ambivalence and resistance.

- Assist members to recognize the range of choices they have for participating in the group.
- Help members work with each other to recognize where points of resistance may occur and to overcome challenges to their full participation.

Before the worker states expectations about what members need to do to accomplish their goals, the worker should notice the overt and covert messages members give about accomplishing the group's work. If the worker picks up signals indicating a lack of motivation to accomplish goals, the worker should check the perception of the meaning of the message with the group members.

Ambivalent feelings about change are common and should not be viewed as an obstacle to accomplishing the group's work. It is rare for changes to be proposed and worked on without ambivalent feelings, and it is often difficult and painful to change problematic areas of one's life. At the very least, it requires giving up the security of old ways of doing things. Rather than ignoring, playing down, or attacking the ambivalence, workers should help members work through it. Acknowledging a member's ambivalence is a helpful way to get members to recognize their reactions to change. A frank discussion of a member's ambivalence about change and the perceived ability to achieve a goal helps all members see that this is a common reaction to the changes they are planning to make. In addition, a realistic appraisal of the chances for success is much preferred to covering up barriers to task achievement.

One exercise that can help uncover ambivalence is to have each member focus on a goal and list psychological, social, and environmental factors that hinder and promote its achievement. A variation on this exercise done with individual clients has been called a "force field analysis" (Egan, 2013). In task groups, all members focus on one group goal. In treatment groups, it is more common for members to focus on one member's goal, but occasionally it is possible to select a common group goal on which to focus. The exercise can be done by all group members, in pairs, or at home between sessions.

In a force field analysis, the worker helps members list on paper or a blackboard the positive and negative aspects of attaining a goal and displays the results before all group members. This process facilitates an organized discussion of the factors that can help members achieve goals and the factors that may hinder them. Such a visual display helps members to realize that many factors may be detracting from their motivation.

An example of a list of positive and negative factors that could influence a group member's decision is shown in Figure 7.3. The decision involves whether the member should separate from her husband. An examination of a list of factors can help group members decide whether there are sufficient positive motivations for achieving a particular goal.

If a member reaches a decision to pursue a goal despite numerous factors that reduce motivation, the task of the worker and the other group members is to suggest ways to decrease the negative factors and increase the positive factors. For example, in the situation in Figure 7.3, the member decides to separate from her husband. To change some of the factors that reduce her motivation, the group helps the member to (1) overcome her fear about the effects of the separation on her children by suggesting that the children may be harmed more by seeing mom and dad constantly fighting than by experiencing their parents' separation; (2) examine her finances, her plans for child care, and other

Problem: Whether to separate from my husband

Factors Increasing Motivation	Factors Decreasing Motivation
1. Tom drinks too much.	1. Concern about what breaking up will do to the kids.
2. Tom has been physically abusive twice in the last year.	2. Worried about whether I can live on only my salary.
3. There is almost daily verbal conflict between Tom and me.	3. Wonder if I can care for three kids and keep working 40 hours a week.
4. Staying in the relationship causes me to feel angry and depressed.	4. Feeling as if I would be breaking my commitment to Tom.
5. My relationship is interfering with the quality of my work at my job.	5. I'll have to explain the separation to my parents, friends, etc.
6. Tom and I have infrequent sexual relations.	
7. The kids are being affected by our constant fighting.	

Figure 7.3
Analysis of Factors that Increase and Decrease the Motivation of a Member of a Treatment Group

practical needs that she may have as she considers living independently; and (3) build her self-confidence and self-esteem by providing support and positive feedback during the separation process. Through this process, the group helps the member become motivated to achieve her goal with as little ambivalence, fear, and anguish as possible.

In some groups, workers encounter members who feel pressured or coerced into coming to the group. Members who feel pressured or coerced often are not ready to engage in the work of the group. They may delay or obstruct other members' work.

In an excellent text on working with resistant group members, Rooney (2009) suggests that the worker can point out that the members chose to participate in the group. Although some individuals may have chosen to participate in the group to avoid other less desirable choices, the choice was an agreement made with a referring agency. For example, in the case of being found guilty of driving while intoxicated, the member may have agreed to participate in a group treatment program instead of losing his driver's license. The worker should acknowledge that the member might not want to be in the group, but also note that the person freely chose the group over an alternative. The worker should also state that members are free to terminate their participation at any time, but their decision to participate implies that they will adhere to the group norms and contractual obligations agreed to during the intake interview or the first group session.

As the group progresses, it may be necessary to remind members that it was their choice to participate rather than experience a serious consequence, such as going to jail or being put on probation. The group also needs to help reluctant and resistant members to find reasons to participate. For example, the leader can encourage members to help each other to figure out what is positive and negative about their current lifestyle and what they want to change. Then, members can decide how they want the group to support them and help them to accomplish these changes. This type of empowerment helps members feel that they have a stake in the group and that their views are being considered and acted on. At the same time, the worker can point out members' strengths and resiliencies, helping them to feel that they have the power to grow and to change (Saleebey, 2013). It can also be helpful for the worker to use "I" statements and to make a clear demand for work, as the following case example illustrates.

Case Example Use of "I" Statements

I have a problem. Some of you do not seem to want to be here. If you do not want to be here, you do not have to be here. I do not want you to get the wrong impression—I'd rather you stay. However, if you don't like being in the group, you can take it up with the agency that sent you and deal with the consequences of not continuing your participation. My job is to help you use your time in this group productively. Therefore, I would like those of you who choose to stay to think now about how you will use the group—what you want to accomplish. Think about the problems and issues in your life and what you'd like to work on in this group. I'll give you a few minutes. Then, let's go around and see what we can do together. I suggest that we begin the go-round by saying what we like and do not like about our current lifestyles and what changes we want to make. Then, later, we can focus on creating a plan to make these changes, what strengths you bring to the process, and how the group can help you to accomplish the changes you want to make.

Expectations About Role Performance

In addition to ambivalence about changing a way of doing things, members often are concerned at the beginning of the group that they will not be able to contribute in the way they think is expected of them. For example, members of a committee may think they will be asked to do too much to prepare for group meetings, or they may fear they have nothing to contribute. Similarly, members of educational groups are often apprehensive about their ability to learn new material, and members of support groups are fearful that members will not understand or share their concerns. Because expectations about role performance can interfere with a member's participation in the group, it is helpful for workers to describe their expectations of members and solicit feedback and input. Role clarification is a key leadership skill in working with mandated members (Trotter, 2015). This process provides a forum for members to air their fears about the challenges they face. It also helps clarify any mistaken or distorted expectations that members may have and provides an opportunity for workers to modify or change their own expectations.

Role clarification also helps members to understand the dual role of the worker as an agent of social control as well as a helper (Trotter, 2015). With respect to members' behavior inside and outside of the group, the worker can clarify what is negotiable and what is not negotiable. Workers can also help members to think about their own expectations versus the expectations held by other constituencies, such as the referral source that suggested members attend the group as an alternative to a harsher punishment, the worker, the member's family, and so forth. Clarifying roles in this way can create greater empathy and understanding, and it will ensure that all parties are clear about what goals are shared in common and what goals are not. Work can then proceed based on tackling shared goals. The worker might also discuss the consequences, if any, of not working on the goal expectations of the referring agency, the worker, or the member's family. This helps to clarify the choices members are making and the likely consequences in their lives.

Authentic Communication About Purposes and Goals

Ambivalence about changing and fears about the demands that may be placed on them may lead members to be less than candid in early group meetings. Shulman (2016) points out that members of treatment groups may begin by sharing problems that do not directly address some of the more difficult and hard-to-talk-about issues they are experiencing. Building trust involves enabling members to talk about "safe" problems to gauge the reaction of the leader and other members before sharing more emotionally charged problems. In task groups, members may bring up peripheral issues that could potentially sidetrack the group. The worker may also want to view these as safe problems that can be addressed without getting into difficult or controversial issues.

To increase authentic communication as the group develops, the worker can take several steps:

- Always treat members' suggestions and ideas about how to proceed with respect. The worker should not dismiss or ignore what a member says or treat it as a smoke screen or a red herring. This will only alienate members and certainly will not encourage them to open up and reveal the issues that are more meaningful. Instead, the worker should strive to understand the deeper issues implied by the member's message.
- Link the member's statements with the larger purposes of the group. The worker can do this by asking members how the suggestions or ideas fit in with the agreed-on purposes of the group.
- Place the relevant parts of the member's message in the context of themes or issues that have been previously discussed in the group.
- Support the initiative the member demonstrated by speaking up without endorsing the message. Statements such as "I'm glad to see that you are thinking about what you want to accomplish in the group" or "I'm happy to see that you care enough about the direction of the group to make that suggestion" lets members know that their perspectives are welcome and valued without indicating that the worker supports the content of the message.

Promoting Prosocial Behaviors

Trotter (2015) also points out that it is important to promote prosocial behavior when working with mandated members. He suggests doing this by (1) pointing out prosocial comments made during group interaction, (2) praising prosocial comments, suggesting that others emulate these comments and rewarding prosocial comments in other ways, (3) acting as a model by using problem-solving skills and coping skills that are prosocial, and (4) identifying and challenging antisocial comments or behaviors.

Prosocial comments can be rewarded, for example, by sending a note to members' probation officers about how well they are doing in the group. Members can also be encouraged to discuss their attempts at engaging in prosocial behaviors between meetings,

Engagement

Behavior: Apply knowledge of human behavior and the social environment, person-in-environment, and other multidisciplinary theoretical frameworks to engage with clients and constituencies

Critical Thinking Question: Groups sometimes have involuntary members. How can the worker engage involuntary members in the group?

the successfulness of these attempts, and obstacles to engaging in prosocial behaviors outside of the group. Both ACT and DBT use homework assignments and experiential exercises extensively to promote prosocial behaviors and self-statements between meetings (see, for example, Linehan, 1993; Neacsiu, Bohus, & Linehan, 2014; McKay, Wood, & Brantley, 2007).

Working with Involuntary Members

There are many situations when group workers are called upon to work with involuntary members who are mandated to attend groups. Involuntary members are those who are pressured or required to attend a group in lieu of some worse punishment, such as going to jail, losing a driver's license, or as a condition of probation. Involuntary members may also be those who are forced into a group by a school system, a therapeutic community, or some other entity with the notion that it will do them some good to participate. In these latter situations, the consequences of not following through by attending the group may not be clear, although the members know that they simply have to attend the group. Involuntary and mandated members put workers in an awkward position, because they are being asked to help members make changes that they may not want to make.

One of the first steps in working with involuntary members is to assess their readiness for change. Prochaska, DiClimente, and Norcross (1992) have developed a five-part model of change: (1) pre-contemplation, (2) contemplation, (3) preparation, (4) action, and (5) maintenance. Mandated members often start in the pre-contemplation stage that may take on many forms. According to Goldstein (2001), there are reluctant pre-contemplators who do not want to consider change because they do not have sufficient information about what change might mean or simply because of inertia. There are also rebellious pre-contemplators who are motivated to avoid change and maintain the status quo. This may be because of peer pressure or fear that change will make things even worse for them. There are resigned pre-contemplators who have given up hope that change is possible. They are demoralized and lack the energy to make changes. There are also rationalizing pre-contemplators who either do not see the problem or view the problem as a problem for someone else but not for them. When working with groups of mandated members, the worker should carefully assess whether group members are reluctant, rebellious, resigned, or rationalizing pre-contemplators. Reluctant pre-contemplators may simply need information or a heightened sense of the consequences of their actions to move to the next stage of change. Rebellious pre-contemplators actively resist change because of peer pressure or feeling that their lifestyle is the better alternative. Resigned pre-contemplators are those who have tried and failed. They lack the motivation and the feelings of self-efficacy to do anything about their situation. Rationalizing pre-contemplators are those who blame others for their problems. Although each of these group members may respond to somewhat different approaches, there are some common strategies that the worker can use to help all members of mandated groups begin to make changes.

In order to determine where members are at on the continuum of change, the worker can start by asking members how they feel about attending the group and what they hope to get out of it. By reflective and skillful listening, the worker seeks to understand members' feelings without being judgmental, critical, or blaming (Lynch & Cuper, 2010; Miller & Rollnick, 2013; Waltz & Hays, 2010). Rooney and Chovanec (2004) point out that in the early stages of the group the members may express their hostility at the worker. The worker should not be put off by this but instead may want to make statements early in the group that acknowledge the members' feelings about being pressured or coerced to attend and their wary, noncommittal approach to the group. The worker should also look for nonverbal signs about the members' motivation. Peer pressure, despair, hopelessness, and other factors that hold members back from contemplating change may not come out directly, but instead may be expressed in silence or rebellion. Workers who are aware of these nonverbal cues should acknowledge them, feeding them back to the members of the group, and letting them know that the worker is aware of their feelings. The worker should avoid arguing or disputing what members are saying verbally and nonverbally and instead should roll with the resistance, acknowledging it and letting the members know that they are at best ambivalent about their participation and, at worst, unwilling participants in the change process (Miller & Rollnick, 2013).

After acknowledging the resistance to change, the worker has to figure out what can motivate members to engage in the work of the group. There is no easy way to accomplish this, and for each member the motivation may come from different sources. Miller and Rollnick (2013) suggest trying to develop a discrepancy between members' current behaviors and their long-term personal goals. The problem in some groups is that members have not thought about their long-term goals, or their long-range goals have become distorted by dysfunctional home lives and impoverished neighborhood environments. Poverty, despair, abuse, and neglect are often the root causes of these problems. Peer pressure, repeated failure, a lack of self-efficacy, or other issues may also work against developing the discrepancy between current dysfunctional behavior patterns and the positive long-range goals that the worker is seeking to help members achieve. When this is the case, the worker should acknowledge these issues with empathy and concern. The worker should show a genuine concern for members' long-term well-being and realistically mention some of the consequences of continuing on the same path of dysfunctional behavior. Members may not buy into the worker's view, so a portion of the group's time may need to be spent on acknowledging these feelings and asking members to discuss their own worldview and to describe where they think their current patterns of behavior will lead. Although at first members may rage against persons, situations, or systems that are unfair, gradually the worker can reframe the discussion into how they can negotiate the system and get what they need to live better lives. This discussion can also heighten the discrepancy between members' current behavior patterns and future desired behaviors. The worker can use these discrepancies to motivate members to make the changes they find desirable.

Gradually, the worker sets expectations for the group but at the same time tries to maximize choice and minimize demand, helping the members themselves come up with what they would like to do in the group (Welo, 2001). Rooney (2009) noted that it is helpful to point out what choices members have within mandates. For example, workers can point out that members have the choice not to follow mandates and accept the consequences, or to use mandated group time to work on goals of value to themselves while acceptable to the authority that mandated their treatment. In this way, members are able to see that change is under their control and is possible despite the operation of coercive forces.

At some point during this process, it can be helpful for the worker to bring a guest speaker to the group with whom the members can identify. By relating his or her story about being a mandated client and overcoming obstacles to change, the speaker may help members see a path out of their current situation and open possibilities that the members may not have contemplated. The worker may also have some members in the group who are further along on the change continuum, such as those who are actively contemplating change or who have moved beyond contemplation to take some action. The worker can help these members become a catalyst for those who are still in the pre-contemplation stage by encouraging them to describe how they moved from pre-contemplation to contemplation or action. Through dialogue and interaction members can be encouraged to form a peer support network to help everyone move to the next stage of change, and to overcome any obstacles they face as they attempt to change.

Those who work regularly with involuntary and mandated members recognize that change does not come easily or without setbacks. Working with involuntary members is one of the most difficult challenges a worker can face, but seeing members becoming motivated to make changes is also one of the most rewarding experiences a worker can have. It is very important to keep in mind that change has to come from within each member and that the workers' roles are to foster a group climate where members can feel comfortable enough to talk about change and begin to attain their aspirations for themselves. External incentives, such as getting a driving license back, getting out of the therapeutic community sooner, or reduced probation time will not lead to change over the long term unless the members can see a better future for themselves and develop the feelings of self-efficacy that are necessary for them to become self-motivated. Workers can be ready by being empathic about the difficulties the members face but at the same time offering the encouragement and the resources that are needed to help motivate members to make a better life for themselves. For more about working with mandated members, see Edelwich and Brodsky (1992); Goldstein (2001); Miller and Rollnick (2013); Rooney (2009); Rooney and Chovanec (2004); Schimmel and Jacobs (2011); Welo (2001); and Chapter 9 of this text.

Anticipating Obstacles

In the beginning stage of group work, it is important for workers to help members anticipate the obstacles they may encounter as they work on specific goals and objectives. It is useful to ask members to describe the obstacles they foresee in accomplishing individual and group goals. Sometimes it is useful to encourage members to engage in a time-projection program activity. In this exercise, members are asked to imagine what it will be like for them at the end of the group when they have accomplished their goals. Members can be encouraged to discuss how changes brought about in the group are likely to be received by those around them and to focus on what might prevent accomplishments in the group from being implemented in settings outside the group. As members share potential impediments to long-term, meaningful change, the worker can facilitate a discussion about overcoming the impediments.

Experience suggests that when members and the leader are aware of potential obstacles, they can often plan ways to overcome them before the middle stage of the group. Some workers' and scholars' research suggests that meditation, mindfulness, or other experiential exercises can help to bring about acceptance of one's past and present situation

(Hays, Strosahl, & Wilson, 2011; Linehan, 1993, 2015; Lynch & Cuper, 2010; Waltz & Hays, 2010). Chapter 9 describes a variety of methods that can be used during the middle stage of a group to help members overcome obstacles to accomplishing specific goals.

> **?** Assess your understanding of the possible challenges to member participation in the group by taking this brief quiz.

Monitoring and Evaluating the Group: The Change Process Begins

It is important to start the monitoring and evaluation process as soon as the group begins. In treatment groups, at the start of monitoring, the worker should carefully note the problems and concerns members state at the onset of the group and the tentative goals they wish to establish. Keeping careful notes of this is important because the worker can show members right from the beginning how their initial concerns and problems have been clarified, redefined, or adjusted as they get feedback and support from the group. This, in itself, can be useful because it demonstrates to members that the change process has already begun. The worker should point out positive changes as the group progresses and be liberal with their praise of members. Those who are not changing as rapidly can be reassured that change will come if they continue to work at it. Workers should encourage these members to avoid being critical of themselves. In the beginning, members need encouragement to forge ahead with change goals and to avoid slipping into self-defeating and self-critical statements that often accompany low self-esteem, and life-long living in an adverse environment. Being positive about change processes can help members grow and flourish, and it reassures them that the progress they are already making can continue even in the face of obstacles and setbacks.

Monitoring initial goals can also help to establish a purpose for the group and make clear to members what they are working toward achieving. In subsequent meetings, we have found it is often helpful to start with a check in when members are asked to present their tentative goals. This keeps them focused on what they are trying to accomplish and allows them to modify and reformulate goals they may have mentioned during the first meeting. It also provides an incentive for members who do not yet have goals to begin the process of formulating them. The second group meeting can be used to begin to partialize goals and to suggest what members may be able to do between meetings to clarify goals and begin to take the first tentative steps to accomplish them. It is never too early to have group members focus on goals and what they want to accomplish through their participation in the group. At the same time, some members may need time to formulate goals. The worker should make the group a safe place for members so that the demand for goal formulation is tempered by an understanding that the change process is a difficult one that takes time to take shape.

In task groups, monitoring should focus on the goals of the group as a whole. The worker should keep notes on each member's contributions to goal formulation. Sources of agreement and disagreement should be monitored, with the worker looking for common ground on which the task group can move forward. Just as in treatment groups, goal clarification is essential in task groups. It is also important for the worker to start the beginning of subsequent group meetings by describing agreements and common ground and where compromise or more work toward clarifying goals is necessary.

The beginning of a group is also the time for any evaluation processes to be put into place. In treatment groups, workers may want to distribute baseline measures that group members can take to monitor their progress. For example, in a group for members with depression, the worker may want to distribute a depression inventory or have members begin to monitor their depression in a chart, a diary, or a log book. As the group progresses, the worker can ask members to review their forms to see what progress, if any, is being made. Demonstrating progress builds cohesion and optimism that the group members are accomplishing their goals. Similarly, in task groups, in the initial meetings, members can be asked to take a baseline or a benchmark reading of where they are in relationship to the goal of the group. This baseline or benchmark can be used as a progress indicator throughout the life of the group.

Case Example

At first, Drew felt enthusiastic about being assigned to lead a group called "the Lunch Bunch." His enthusiasm was tempered when his field instructor told him that it would be composed of 10 fourth- and fifth-grade boys who were suspended from the school lunchroom because of acting-out behavior. The purposes of the group were to help members learn acceptable ways of dealing with their peers and to reintegrate each member into the main lunchroom milieu.

In addition to having no control over the composition of the group, Drew was concerned about what might happen when all of the "offending parties" would come together for the first session. He interviewed each of the members assigned to the group to introduce himself, to learn about their expectations, and to begin to orient them to the group's purposes and goals. During the interviews, he learned that various members were suspended from the lunchroom because they fought with other students and expressed their anger in inappropriate ways, such as yelling, cursing, and throwing food. Most of the youngsters he met seemed to act appropriately during the initial interview and appeared enthusiastic about meeting with the Lunch Bunch.

On the day of the first session, Drew came prepared. In addition to a written agenda, name tags, art supplies, and some CDs for music, he brought chocolate chip cookies, hoping that after members ate their lunch, dessert would be an incentive for them to act appropriately until the group ended. As members entered, most seemed to know each other from classes they took together. Drew chose to help members introduce themselves by playing a version of "Top Secret" in which each member wrote down something about himself that others would not ordinarily know. He read what each boy had written and had fun trying to figure out who had written each statement. Drew felt that this activity was moderately successful because it helped the members get involved with the group right away.

Next, Drew made an opening statement about the purpose of the group. He was careful to word the statement of purpose so that the boys could understand it and so that it gave them some guidance about what would happen in the group. He noted that the group's purpose was "to work together to learn safer ways of handling yourselves in the lunchroom and to have fun while learning." Two of the members stated that they thought the group was like detention and was punishment for their behavior. Drew clarified that it was true that their behavior had gotten them referred to the group, but that the group was not punishment. He noted that both he and the members could plan some of the activities, and these would take into account what members wanted to do during group sessions. The boys seemed skeptical about this, so Drew asked for more discussion. He clarified that his role was to help them explore how to act with each other and to help them plan activities in the group.

One of the most difficult discussions that took place early in the first session concerned confidentiality. One member wanted to know if Drew was going to tell the principal or his parents about what he might say or do in the group. Drew recognized that many of the boys frequently interacted with each other in settings outside the group, and this could easily compromise any promises of confidentiality. In addition, Drew was responsible for reporting the progress of members to his field instructor and, ultimately, to the school principal. Drew mentioned these two issues to the members and suggested a few ground rules about confidentiality that the group might discuss at their next meeting. He suggested that it would be appropriate for a member to discuss aspects of his participation with his parents, but members should not refer to group members by name. He emphasized that under no circumstances should members talk to other students about what went on inside the group. Finally, Drew said that he had to report on each member's progress to his field instructor, but that he would try to share what he would say with each boy individually before he discussed it with his field instructor.

After this, the group started to work on other rules for how the group should operate. During the first session, they agreed that they should all be good listeners, should wait their turn before speaking, and should try to help each other. Drew was satisfied that, in the time allotted, the group seemed to be making some progress on formulating a beginning contract. He suggested that members might think of other rules for the group and could bring these up in the next meeting.

Drew recognized that the time allotted for this first session was running out, and he wanted to provide the members with a fun experience before they left to return to their classes. During the remaining time, they played some music from Drew's collection. Drew asked members what they felt after listening to each song. This discussion was difficult for some of the members because they were not familiar with some of Drew's musical selections. Drew suggested that members could bring in some of their favorite music for the next session. The members received this news with enthusiasm. Drew said that when a member brought in a favorite musical selection, his responsibility would be to ask other members to identify what they felt after listening to it. Chocolate chip cookies for dessert tempered this early "demand for work."

SUMMARY

Although all aspects of group work are important for the successful functioning of a group, the initial stage sets the tone for the group's future development. In the beginning stage, the worker's central task is to ensure that a group develops patterns of relating and patterns of task accomplishment that facilitate functioning as the group moves toward its middle stage of development.

To accomplish this, workers should focus on achieving certain objectives in the beginning stage of task and treatment groups. These include (1) ensuring a safe environment where trust can develop; (2) introducing members of the group; (3) clarifying the purpose and function of the group as it is perceived by the worker, the members, and the sponsoring organization; (4) clarifying confidentiality issues; (5) helping members feel a part of the group; (6) guiding the development of the group; (7) balancing task and socio-emotional aspects of the group process; (8) setting goals; (9) contracting for work; (10) facilitating members' motivation and ability to work in the group; (11) addressing ambivalence and resistance; (12) working with involuntary members; (13) anticipating obstacles; and (14) beginning the monitoring and evaluation process.

Workers who are able to help their groups achieve these objectives in the initial stage will find themselves in a good position to help the group make a smooth transition to the middle stage of development. Any objectives that are not achieved early in the group's development will have to be reconsidered later as the group and its members encounter difficulties accomplishing agreed-on goals.

Assessment

Because of the complexity of human behavior and group dynamics, assessment is one of the most challenging aspects of group work practice. In this text, the term *assessment* rather than *diagnosis* is used because assessment is more compatible with a social work perspective and a generalist approach to practice. *Diagnosis* is a term borrowed from medicine. It refers to the identification of disease processes within an individual. In contrast, a thorough generalist assessment focuses on both the strengths and the problems encountered by individual group members and the whole group. This text assessment is viewed holistically, taking a bio-psychosocial, environmental perspective.

The worker makes assessments to understand particular practice situations, planning effective interventions for (1) individual group members, (2) the group as a whole, and (3) the group's environment. The distinguishing feature of group work as compared to casework is that assessments focus on group as well as individual functioning. Assessments of group process should be continuous as workers scan groups to make sure that interactions are helping members accomplish agreed-upon objectives and goals.

Workers begin their assessments during the planning stage and continue to assess and reassess the group's work until it ends. Although assessments are made in all stages of a group's life, the process dominates a worker's time in the beginning phase of group work. It is at this time that the worker is most actively engaged in understanding the functioning of the group and its members. It is also the time when interaction patterns of cohesion, norms, and other group dynamics are forming. In groups, workers have the opportunity to encourage the development of group processes that help groups accomplish their puposes in the most effective and efficient manner. Although leaders may be more attentive to assessment processes in early stages, assessment continues as group work progresses.

CONDUCTING EFFFECTIVE ASSESSMENTS

Assessments involve gathering, organizing, and making judgments about information from many sources. Assessments are ongoing, often requiring complex coordination. Workers may have to rely on colleagues, families, friends, and other sources of data, such as records, to make assessments as the group evolves. The process often calls for reaching out to many individuals, and using different information collection strategies, iteratively, over the life of a group. Gradually, as the group develops, a more complete picture emerges. Sources contribute information, then the worker reflects on it critically and attempts to collect additional information as needed. This iterative process of collecting data, reflecting on it, and collecting more data is repeated throughout the life of the group as new information is needed to reach specific goals and objectives.

During the assessment process it is important to obtain as reliable and valid information as possible. Information comes from a variety of sources. The accuracy and completeness of each source of information varies, so an important aspect of assessment is using critical thinking to judge the accuracy and adequacy of the information that is obtained from each source (Gambrill, 2009). It is also essential to determine if initial information is adequate or if more is needed to gain greater accuracy and understanding as the group develops. The goal is to gain as complete an understanding of the situation as possible in the time that is available. Workers have to use critical judgment about how much information is enough to intervene effectively.

Because of time pressures and ethical considerations, workers should be aware of being parsimonious during data collection, only collecting the information needed to help members achieve agreed-upon goals and plans. In treatment groups, workers make assessments to assist individual members, whereas in task groups, they help groups to achieve goals that have implications beyond the members. In both treatment and task groups, the goal, charge, or mandate may be formulated within the group or by an external source. Workers have to carefully assess if goals are clear and consistent among members and any other constituencies or if goals need to be clarified and harmonized before the assessment process can continue.

When conducting assessments, it is especially important that the information being collected remains aligned with agreed-upon goals. Because goals can change, workers should keep track of them and use check-ins or go-rounds at the beginning of meetings to make sure that members are clear about goals and remain focused on them. Check-ins and go-rounds enable members to modify goals as situations change. As goals change, new assessment data may be needed.

As with other aspects of social group work practice, assessment varies according to the type of group being conducted. In a treatment group, for example, the worker frequently focuses assessments on the problems experienced by individual members, but a task group leader's assessment is often focused on the ability of members to contribute to the group's productivity.

Despite differences in focus, there are many commonalities in the assessments made by workers leading different types of groups. For example, in both task and treatment groups, most workers assess the strengths and weaknesses of the group as a whole, the members, and the external environment in which the group and its members function.

Commonalities also can be found in the assessment of different groups that are at the same stage of development. For example, in the beginning stage, workers make a systematic assessment of the functioning of the group and its members. During the middle stage, workers test the validity of their initial assessments and modify their intervention plans on the basis of the success of early interventions. In the ending stage of the group, the worker makes an assessment of the functioning of the group and its members to highlight accomplishments, to focus attention on areas that still need work, and to ensure that achievements accomplished during the group will be maintained after the group ends.

Focus on Group Processes

Most readers are familiar with generalist social work practice approaches that rely on systems theory and take a holistic approach to assessment (Johnson & Yanca, 2010; Kirst-Ashman & Hull, 2012). Using a generalist approach, group workers are supposed to assess individual members, the group as a whole, and the group in relation to its environment. In practice, however, there is a tendency for group workers to focus on individual members rather than on the processes of group interaction or on the group in relation to its environment. This may be because they may have more experience working with individuals than with groups. Also, some workers do not have any formal education in group work. Data from analyses of the content and style of group leaders confirm the lack of focus on group processes (Barlow, 2013; Forsyth, 2014; Hill, 1965; Toseland, Rossiter, Peak, & Hill, 1990; Ward, 2014). Despite the lack of focus on group processes, there is evidence that it can make groups more cohesive and effective (Barlow, 2013; Forsyth, 2014; Ward, 2014). Based on the available evidence, we strongly recommend that group workers be especially vigilant about spending time during each group meeting on group processes. This can often be accomplished by making a conscious effort to point out processes in the here-and-now of group interaction.

Sometimes, however, stopping the action to identify, clarify, or discuss group processes can be disruptive to the content being discussed. One way to avoid disrupting group interaction is to reserve talk about important processes to a few minutes at the end of each group meeting. Workers and members can use the time to comment on and discuss the processes that were particularly helpful and those that could be improved. If this is done routinely near or at the end of each meeting it will reinforce helpful group dynamics. For example, a member might state that there seemed to be much member-to-member communication during the group meeting, the discussion included only a few members, or members did not seem to be considering the points of view of others. Similarly, the worker might comment on the norms developing in the group or the roles that members were playing. Workers can close meetings by asking if members would like to change any processes that might have been identified and suggest that the discussion could occur at the beginning of the next meeting if it is too extensive a topic for the group to resolve now. Workers could then review tasks for the next meeting and close the meeting. When setting aside a time at the end of meetings for discussing group processes, care should be taken not to use the time to discuss content. It is easy to slip into discussions of content when group processes are being discussed. The following case example is of a process discussion at the end of one type of group.

Case Example   Group Processing During Group Therapy

During a discussion of group interaction patterns in an early meeting of a therapy group in an outpatient mental health clinic, two members noted that the entire second session was spent focusing on one member's problem. Another member said, "John talked a lot because he is having a lot of problems with his wife." The worker pointed out that the issue was not John's problems with his wife, but whether the group wanted to spend an entire session focused on only one member's concern. The worker suggested that in all future meetings, a brief check-in period would occur, once the summary of the previous group meeting was made by the leader. The check-in period would be used to make sure that each member took a minute to remind the group of the goal they were working toward, a very brief statement of progress, and whether they wanted to do more work on some aspect of their mental health later in the group meeting. The worker then guided the group in a brief discussion of the pros and cons of focusing on one member for an entire session. The group decided after a few minutes to try to focus on at least two members' concerns during each meeting. They also decided to make sure that all members could identify with the issues being discussed by the members who would be the focus of work during any meeting.

External Constituencies and Sponsors

Workers often fail to pay sufficient attention to external constituencies and other aspects of groups' environments. External constituencies vary depending on the nature of groups but may include parents, courts, teachers, and others who have a stake in members' lives. Similarly, the expectations of sponsors for the conduct of groups and the outcomes achieved are important to consider during assessments. Periodically throughout the life of a group, workers and members should take time to identify, describe, and update their perceptions of the relationship of the group to significant others, the sponsoring organization, and the larger community sanctioning and supporting groups.

Overall, assessment in group work is more complex than assessment in practice with individuals. In addition to assessing the functioning of individual members, assessment in group work also means examining the processes that take place in the group as a whole and the support and opposition the group as a whole is likely to encounter in the larger social environment.

THE ASSESSMENT PROCESS

In the early stages of group work, the worker is confronted with amorphous and sketchy data about the group and its members. Initially, the worker fills in gaps by collecting missing data. As information is collected, the worker begins to sort through it and organize it systematically. The group members should be involved as much as possible in collecting and analyzing data. This will help them to be invested in the goals that are formulated and the way the group will be working to achieve desired outcomes.

Gradually, the assessment process narrows as data are collected and organized and judgments are made about how to intervene in, cope with, or alleviate whatever concern, problem, or task is facing the group. In a group for people getting a divorce, for example, the worker asked members to describe their feelings about their spouses. Information gathered from this preliminary assessment leads to a further assessment of members' feelings of loss and anger toward their spouses. The assessment might also involve the members and the leader in identifying coping skills and strengths to help with these feelings and to move forward in positive directions.

How Much Information?

Several issues arise when workers assess the functioning of the group and its members. One of the most basic issues is how much information to collect. Although it is often recommended that workers collect as much information as possible, increasing information beyond a certain point may not lead to more effective goal achievement. Also, workers are sometimes confronted with urgent situations that preclude extensive data collection. In these situations, workers should be guided by goals formulated during the planning and the beginning stages of group work. Workers also should be as clear as possible about the relevance of the information being collected. Extensive data collection that has little relation to the group's goals is a violation of members' right to privacy and of dubious value for accomplishing group and individual member goals.

No matter how much information is collected, workers should suspend their judgments about a problematic situation until they have reflected on all the data they have time to collect. A widespread and potentially damaging mistake of novice workers occurs when they make judgments and offer suggestions concerning intervention strategies before they fully understand a problem or have found out what the member has already tried. When making premature suggestions, the novice is often confronted by a group member who says, "I tried that and it didn't work." The result is that the worker is at a loss as to how to proceed, and the member's faith in the worker's ability to help is shaken.

Case Example   A Group of People Getting Divorced

Seeing that the members found it difficult to talk about how hard it was for them to deal with feelings about their spouses, the worker decided to do a group go-round, asking each member in turn to talk about their predominant feelings toward their spouse. Once the group go-round was completed, the worker helped the members talk about the feelings that they shared in common and how they were dealing with them. Members began to realize that they were not alone with the feelings they were having. They then began to talk about some ways to cope with their feelings and move beyond them. For extra support, members decided to exchange telephone numbers so that they could talk about their emotional reactions between group meetings.

Some helpful principles to guide workers in their data-collection efforts follow.

Principles of Data Collection
- Use more than one mode of data collection whenever possible.
- Distinguish between the problem, concern, or task about which information is being collected and the source of the information.

- Obtain relevant samples of data from several sources.
- Structure data collection so that relevant information can be obtained quickly and efficiently.
- Develop a system that will not place overwhelming demands on persons who are collecting information or on persons who are asked for information.
- Avoid biasing data despite the selectivity and subjectivity that are inherent parts of any effort at data collection and assessment.
- Involve all group members in the assessment process so that multiple viewpoints can help overcome limitations of the worker's subjectivity.
- Discuss assessment data with a co-leader or a supervisor between meetings.

Diagnostic Labels

Another issue that often arises when one makes assessments of the members of treatment groups is the use of diagnostic classification systems and labels. Diagnostic classification systems can be helpful in making differential assessments and arriving at effective treatment plans for group members. Classification systems such as the *Diagnostic and Statistical Manual of Mental Disorders* (DSM) are used in many mental health settings for assessment, intervention, and reimbursement purposes (American Psychiatric Association, 2013).

Diagnostic labels can result in social stigma. Members of a group may be at risk for harmful stereotyping when diagnostic labels are used indiscriminately or without attention to confidentiality. Also, some scholars believe that members may start to behave in ways that are consistent with the labels ascribed to them (Kirk, Gomory, & Cohen, 2013; Kirk & Kutchins, 1999). There are also many issues about what should be classified as a mental illness, with some scholars believing that some mood states, such as normal sadness and worry, have been erroneously classified as mental illnesses (Horwitz & Wakefield, 2007, 2012). Although group work practitioners should be wary of the indiscriminate use of diagnostic labels in mental health and other settings, our clinical experience suggests that group workers often encounter members with very serious, even life-threatening anxiety, depression, and other mental illnesses. Proper assessment of mental disorders can lead to appropriate group and other forms of treatment that can reduce or eliminate the terrible pain and suffering that these conditions cause. Treatment can also reduce or eliminate the risk of self-injury, suicide, and the suffering of caregivers and others who care deeply about the person. Also, organizations where group workers practice must be reimbursed for the services rendered, and private and government insurance funding often require assessments and diagnosis for payment. For all these reasons, although diagnostic labeling is not ideal, careful assessment leading to the right type of treatment is essential to enable persons with mental health disorders get the care they need, and a diagnostic label may be needed to obtain the necessary services. Although an in-depth examination of the applications of the DSM-V to group treatment is beyond the scope of this text, the following case example may help illustrate its usefulness. Also, there are books that focus on assessment and diagnosis and the DSM-V that can serve as helpful resources for group workers (see, for example, Corcoran & Walsh, 2015).

Case Example	The Diagnostic and Statistical Manual (DSM)

An 81-year-old man was misdiagnosed as having an organic brain syndrome. The diagnosis was based solely on the symptoms of confusion and disorientation that he exhibited. Based on that diagnosis, it was recommended that the man participate in a reality orientation group and an activity group designed for persons with Alzheimer's disease and other dementias. However, a more extensive assessment using criteria from the DSM revealed that the person was actually suffering from major depression compounded by dehydration, isolation, and malnutrition. Given this diagnosis, a quite different form of group treatment was recommended after the person's medical and nutrition needs were addressed. The man was encouraged to attend a therapy group for people suffering from problems of depression and to expand his personal friendship networks by becoming involved in an activity group at a senior center and a social group at his church.

Assessment Focus

A third issue that often arises in making an assessment is how to focus data-collection efforts. Workers should avoid becoming locked into one assessment focus. Premature allegiance to a particular view of a situation can result in ignoring important data or attempting to fit all data into a particular conceptualization of the situation.

Kottler and Englar-Carlson (2015) point out that almost all mental health professionals use the DSM in their work, even if they do not subscribe to the underlying assumptions of the medical model when people are labeled with diagnoses using the DSM. They do so for billing purposes and because the DSM enables group workers to communicate with others using a common language and also to be held accountable for clinical decisions based on assessing and intervening with individual members of a group. However, Kottler and Englar-Carlson (2015) also point out that there are other assessment approaches that are valuable. For example, in a developmental assessment process the worker is looking not for pathology or problems but rather for the current developmental functioning of a group member and where it places him or her in relationship to others at a given age or life situation. Thus, in a developmental assessment, the leader is looking at whether a person has reached an appropriate developmental level for his or her age and whether they are ready to move to and take on the tasks associated with the next developmental stage in their lives.

Kottler and Englar-Carlson (2015) also point out that behavioral assessments can be useful because they do not label pathology or what is normative during a particular developmental stage but rather what specific maladaptive behaviors need to be changed. For additional information see Corcoran and Walsh (2015) or Newhill (2015).

Two other assessment foci should also be kept in mind by leaders in the early stages of group work. One is to make a careful assessment of members' strengths and resilience (Corcoran & Walsh, 2013). Taking an empowerment approach takes the focus off of members' pathology and maladaptive behaviors and instead clearly focuses it on members' existing coping skills and what they bring to a situation to help them overcome the issues and problems they may face. Another is to make a systemic assessment of situations, focusing on the context of problems and issues that members face as they live in the larger environment. Therefore, although the DSM is widely used as a diagnostic tool, group workers should keep in mind that other assessment approaches are equally valid and may be more helpful than simply labeling a person with a particular disorder.

In focusing their assessments, workers should be guided by the unique needs and particular circumstances of each member and by the purposes of the group. In one group, for example, it may be important to focus on members' family situations, but in another group, it may be more beneficial to assess members' problem-solving skills. In other words, the focus of assessment should change with the changing needs of the group and its members.

To make an accurate assessment, workers should strive for objectivity. Although all observations contain some subjectivity, it is important to separate subjective impressions and opinions from more objective observations of behavior and events. Inferences should be based on logic, evidence, and critical thinking about the information and impressions workers observe and gather from members (Gambrill, 2009).

It can also be helpful to share observations and inferences with group members. They can confirm the validity of the worker's observations and inferences and provide an alternative perspective. It is also helpful to check the validity of assessments with supervisors. Obtaining alternative perspectives in this manner can help the worker make assessments and formulate intervention plans.

Relationship of Assessment to the Change Process and Problem Solving

In the last chapter, we mentioned that monitoring and evaluating goal formulation was essential to the beginning of the change process. Assessment is also essential to the change process because it helps members identify what individual and group goals have been accomplished and what work remains to be done. In early group meetings, an assessment provides a baseline that members can use to compare their progress as the group progresses. As the group progresses, assessments help to identify progress and success, but they also identify obstacles in the path of goals that remain unachieved.

In treatment groups, assessment helps members understand their concerns and problems, and it allows them to normalize them. It is very disconcerting, even frightening, not to know what is happening to you, and assessment helps members get a handle on the type and severity of their problems and effective treatment methods. An instillation of hope comes about as members begin to understand their problems in the context of others who have had them.

Members begin to feel that they are not alone with their problems, that similar problems have been experienced and overcome by others. Members can be encouraged to do their own research on their problems and the treatment methods for them, thereby being better-informed consumers of the services they are receiving from the social group worker. This is empowering to members as they begin to grapple with making changes to cope more effectively or alleviate their problems entirely. A strengths-based assessment also emphasizes members' resiliency and capacity to change, making the change process and problem solving easier to conceive.

For members of task groups, assessment gives the group a conceptualization of the problem confronting them. Facts and data that are needed are gathered and clarified. Assessment enables members to see what methods have already been tried to resolve the

? Assess your understanding of the assessment
process by taking this
brief quiz.

problem or issue facing the group and promising avenues for further work. It can also point out positive and negative aspects of group functioning so that problem-solving abilities can be enhanced. Overall, a thorough and comprehensive assessment is essential to problem solving in both treatment and task groups.

ASSESSING THE FUNCTIONING OF GROUP MEMBERS

During the assessment process, the worker should consider the current functioning of the members and, whenever possible, also examine members' functioning from a developmental perspective. A developmental perspective can help the worker assess whether a member's current functioning manifests itself in a transitory, acute pattern of behavior, or a longer-term, chronic pattern. It also helps the worker gain a greater understanding of their intensity, duration, and scope of particular concerns. Overall, developmental assessments are more likely to be accurate and complete.

Eco-maps and genograms are two well-known tools described in many social work practice textbooks that can be used during developmental assessments. They can be completed on members' current lives, or members can be asked to fill them out acting as if they were living in a specific age of interest. For example, one member of the trauma group was asked to fill out an eco-map that represented her life space when she was eight years old and being abused, while another member was asked to do the same while remembering back to when she was six years old.

Group workers also have to decide on what service technologies might be best suited to address members' concerns. For example, would a problem respond best if a cognitive behavioral approach were used and developmental issues were treated as cognitive schema, or would an ego psychology or interpersonal therapy approach be more effective? Whenever possible, evidence-based interventions should be selected (Barlow, 2010, 2013; Macgowan, 2008), but when problems are complex and evidence is lacking, critical thinking and practice experience often have to be applied along with available evidence to formulate effective intervention plans (Gambrill, 2009).

When conducting assessments, group workers also should consider other interventions that might be used in conjunction with group work. For example, a careful assessment might reveal that members could benefit from case management, housing, or medication. Before arranging for any services or resources, the group can be used to assess capacity, motivation, and readiness to receive needed services.

When making an assessment, workers should examine three broad aspects of a member's functioning:

1. The intrapersonal life of the member
2. The interpersonal interactions of the member
3. The environment in which the member functions

When assessing members' intrapersonal lives, workers rely on their own observations, members' self-reports, and collateral reports. To examine members' intrapersonal functioning, the worker may focus on members' perceived health status;

psychological and emotional well-being; and their cognition, beliefs, motivations, and expectations.

When assessing interpersonal functioning, workers focus on members' social skills, the extent and quality of their social support networks, and their role performance. The group provides a natural laboratory for the worker to observe the interpersonal functioning of each member, but it is also helpful to inquire about a member's interpersonal interactions with family and close friends because these relationships often have a significant effect on the member.

Workers should also examine the environmental context in which members function. Questions such as "Is the environment supportive or does it hinder members' ability to work on group and individual goals?" and "What resources can members draw on from their environment to help them achieve their goals?" are often pertinent.

In task groups, workers will also find it useful to assess the intrapersonal, interpersonal, and environmental functioning of members, but with a different focus. For example, leaders of task groups generally do not make in-depth assessments of members' physical, psychological, or emotional states. However, they are likely to examine a member's motivation for attending and the member's expectations about accomplishing the work of the group. Similarly, a task group leader would be unlikely to assess the extent to which members' families support their work in the group. The leader is more likely to consider what effect a controversial committee report might have on members' day-to-day interactions with their colleagues or on their interaction with the line staff they supervise.

Assessment

Behavior: Apply knowledge of human behavior and the social environment, person-in-environment, and other multi-disciplinary theoretical frameworks in the analysis of assessment data from clients and constituencies

Critical Thinking Question: The group worker assesses each member. What techniques help to understand the intrapersonal characteristics of members?

Methods for Assessing Group Members

A variety of methods exist to help workers assess the functioning of group members. Among the most commonly used methods for assessing functioning are (1) members' self-observations, (2) worker observations, (3) reports by others who have seen the member function outside the group, and (4) standardized assessment instruments.

Self-Observation

Self-observation refers to members' examination and assessment of their own behavior. Usually, members simply recall and describe their own behavior, then examine and reflect on it with the help of the worker and other group members (Ward, 2014). Self-observation and self-reflection are often helpful in developing insight about one's behavior, identifying patterns of behavior, and examining the effect of the environment. However, members' recollections may not be accurate; for a variety of reasons, recollections may be incomplete, vague, or distorted. Therefore, other methods of self-observation, such as self-monitoring, have been developed.

Because these methods are more intrusive and require more effort on the part of the member than simply recalling and reflecting on past behavior, workers should be sure

Research-Informed Practice

Behavior: Apply critical thinking to engage in analysis of quantitative and qualitative research methods and research findings.

Critical Thinking Question: Workers use multiple measures to assess group members. Why are multiple measures important for a thorough assessment?

that members are motivated to try the methods and have sufficient resources to implement them successfully. Workers should be aware that self-monitoring methods often presume members to be action-oriented, insightful, and sensitive; thus, the methods may not be useful for all members.

Self-Monitoring. Rather than relying on memory of past events, members may examine their own behavior outside the group in a prospective and systematic fashion by collecting data on the frequency, intensity, and duration of a particular behavior and its antecedents and consequences. This process is often referred to as self-monitoring. An assessment of a particular behavior and its antecedents and consequences can be useful in determining how particular problematic behaviors are maintained.

Awareness of behavior patterns is a prerequisite for changing behavior. For example, an assessment of the antecedents of the anxiety that a member experiences in social situations may reveal that the statements the member tells himself about his lack of anything interesting to say trigger his anxiety.

The act of self-monitoring may by itself increase desired behaviors and decrease undesired behaviors (Hopwood & Bornstein, 2014). Self-monitoring can also have therapeutic benefits by heightening members' awareness of behavior patterns and empowering them to make changes (Hopwood & Bornstein, 2014).

To begin self-monitoring, the worker should be sure that members are motivated to examine their own behavior and to record it. Then the worker should help members decide exactly what they are going to monitor. It is often helpful to have members monitor behaviors they would like to increase as well as behaviors they would like to decrease. This process can help members to replace problematic behaviors with desired ones, rather than only reducing problematic behaviors.

In deciding what to monitor, workers should help members determine what is feasible and realistic, given their life circumstances. Members often want to collect data about several problematic behaviors at the same time. However, members are rarely able to follow through on such ambitious plans. Therefore, initially, members should be encouraged to develop modest plans that they can realistically accomplish. Later, they may wish to develop more ambitious monitoring plans.

In deciding on a realistic plan, it should be clear where, when, and under what conditions a particular behavior will be monitored. For example, it is unrealistic for a single parent with four children to expect to monitor the behavior of one child just before dinner or in the morning when the children are preparing for school. However, there may be time during the afternoon or evening when the parent can observe the child's behavior for a short period without being interrupted.

In most groups, members make a mental note of what they have observed between meetings, and they share their observations with other members during the next group meeting. Because it is sometimes difficult for members to accurately recall the data they have monitored, methods for recording self-monitored data have been developed. These methods include charts, logs, diaries, problem cards, and self-anchored rating scales.

Charting. Some members find it useful to record monitored data on a chart because it provides an organized, visual display of the information. A chart allows members to see trends in the data—that is, whether a behavior is increasing or decreasing.

It also may serve as a reminder for members to perform tasks that they agreed to complete between meetings. For an example of charting, see the following case example.

Case Example   Charting

During the early sessions of an assertiveness training group for single parents, members were encouraged to discuss examples of their behavior they would classify as unassertive. Members identified instances of how difficult it was for them to be assertive in work and social situations. The group worker asked members to chart their behavior outside of the group, concentrating on recording the frequency of their nonassertive behavior. Members charted incidents each day for two weeks. After that, the worker helped members review their "problem" behaviors and convert these into "positive" goal statements, leading to the establishment of individual goals for members.

Workers should help members to be creative in designing charts. For example, in helping a parent develop a monitoring chart that will be shared with a young child, the worker can suggest using smiley faces, stars, or hearts instead of check marks to signify that a behavior was performed correctly.

The format of a chart depends on the method used to collect self-monitoring data. The simplest format uses a tally to measure the frequency of a behavior. More complicated formats are sometimes used to get an accurate assessment of the frequency of a behavior without having to count each occurrence. A chart divided into a number of time intervals can be used to count behaviors. For example, members can count the number of occurrences of a behavior in 10-minute intervals between 6 P.M. and 7 P.M. every evening. Charts can also be made that allow a member to record whether a behavior occurred at particular intervals during a designated period, such as at the beginning of every 30-minute time interval.

Members sometimes fail to follow through on charting self-monitored behaviors. For some, charting may require too much organization. Others find it inconvenient to monitor and record their behavior immediately after it occurs. Members sometimes prefer one of the methods described in the following sections.

Logs and Diaries.   Logs and diaries are often less accurate than monitoring charts because members rely on their memory of events to record behaviors at some convenient time after they occur rather than as they occur. However, because of their convenience, members sometimes prefer keeping a log or diary to keeping a chart.

Logs and diaries require members to record events in a descriptive fashion and can be a valuable source of qualitative data for the worker to gain valuable insights into the world of each member. Logs and diaries can also be used to help the worker understand other data reported in quantitative self-observations. To avoid logs and diaries that become too idiosyncratic, the worker can give members a clear indication of what data they are to record. For example, a worker may ask members to record problematic situations and their immediate cognitive, affective, and behavioral responses to situations. For examples of logs and diaries and more information about how to use them, see Bloom and colleagues (2009).

Very Depressed	Moderately Depressed	Not Depressed
1. Does not eat	1. Eats one meal a day	1. Has good appetite
2. Does not sleep	2. Has difficulty in sleeping	2. Sleeps well
3. Has suicidal thoughts	3. Has thoughts about not being a good father or husband	3. Has thoughts about being a good father and husband

Figure 8.1
Example of a Self-Anchored Rating Scale

Self-Anchored Rating Scales.   Members can also record their observations by using a self-anchored rating scale. This is a measurement device made by the worker and a group member specifically to record data about a problematic behavior that has been identified as the target of an intervention. To develop a self-anchored rating scale, the worker helps a group member identify behaviors, feelings, and thoughts that are associated with various levels of the problematic behavior. For example, in developing a scale to measure depression, a member suggests that severe depression occurs when he has suicidal thoughts and does not eat or sleep. Moderate depression occurs when he has thoughts that he is not a good father or husband, when he has little appetite and eats only one meal a day, and when he falls asleep only after lying awake for a long time. The member suggests that he is not depressed when he has a good appetite, can sleep well, and has thoughts that he is a good father and husband. An example of a self-anchored scale to rate depression is shown in Figure 8.1. For further information about developing self-anchored rating scales, see Bloom and colleagues (2009).

Worker Observation

Workers can assess the functioning of group members by observing them during meetings. In most practice situations, workers rely on naturalistic observations. However, specific activities, such as simulations and program activities to assess members' functioning in a particular area, can also be used.

Naturalistic Observation. As demonstrated in the following case example, workers can learn a great deal about members by observing their behavior in the group. Given free interaction within the group, members often display behaviors similar to behaviors exhibited outside the group. By scanning the group, the worker can stay aware of the reactions of all group members. The worker observes a member behaving in a certain manner, for example, and makes a mental note. Further observation, over time, helps the worker identify the member's behavior patterns and typical coping styles.

Case Example   Naturalistic Observation

The leader of a group to teach employment skills to teens spent the initial sessions of the group observing how members demonstrated interpersonal skills. Using these naturalistic observations, the worker was able to point out the interpersonal strengths of each member and how these could be used during the job-seeking process. The leader also asked members to give each other feedback, concentrating on identifying the positive interpersonal skills that could be useful. Using these assessment techniques, members were able to identify their strengths and work on skills that needed strengthening. Later in the group, the leader asked members to practice these skills by assigning role playing exercises that simulated the employment interview situation.

As the group develops, members can be asked to describe their behavior. This feedback can be used to determine whether members' self-perceptions are consistent with the worker's observations. The worker may also solicit other members' observations and reactions. The process of formulating an assessment on the basis of observations and perceptions of more than one individual is often referred to as *triangulation*. Triangulation can lead to assessments that are more accurate than assessments made by a single individual.

Although naturalistic observation offers the worker an opportunity to observe members' behavior in an unobtrusive fashion, its chief limitation is that group interaction may not offer the right opportunities to assess pertinent aspects of a member's behavior. For example, in a parenting skills group, a parent may describe how she sets limits on her child's behavior, but group interaction does not provide the worker with an opportunity to view the parent actually setting limits.

In addition, experience suggests that members may not always give accurate or sufficiently detailed accounts of their behavior. When the worker can actually observe the member engaging in a behavior, such as limit setting, for example, the worker may find that the member does not set limits in the way that is stated. For example, a member may appear angrier or more threatening than her self-report would indicate. Therefore, the worker may find other methods useful when observing members' behavior.

Role Playing.   Role playing, sociodrama, and psychodrama are as important for assessment as for intervention. They allow the worker and the other members of the group to observe a member acting out a situation. Role-play methods are described in detail in Chapter 10.

Simulations.   Simulations assess members' functioning in specific, predetermined role-play situations. The worker asks for one or more volunteers to simulate a specific, real-life situation. Simulations are developed by workers to teach particular skills. The member whose behavior is being assessed is asked to respond to the situation enacted by the volunteers as they would if they were confronted with the situation in their everyday lives.

Simulations can be developed for many situations. For example, in a parenting group, a simulation may involve having two members play the role of siblings in an argument about who gets to play with a toy truck. The parent whose behavior is being assessed is asked to act as she would if such a situation occurred in her home, and the other members of the group can give their feedback about the way the parent handled the situation and alternative ways of responding.

Assessments of a member's behavior during a simulation can be made by all group members. Scales to rate a member's response can be developed specifically for the objectives and goals of a particular group. For example, in the previously mentioned assertiveness training group all group members are trying to reduce their anxiety and improve their responses. Assessments might focus on (1) the anxiety level that a member demonstrates while making a response, and (2) the effectiveness of a response in asserting the member's rights in the situation.

Simulations have been developed for many different populations. New simulations can be developed by using the model described by Goldfried and D'Zurilla (1969). This model includes (1) analyzing a problematic situation and developing several realistic situations that members are likely to confront in their daily lives, (2) enumerating possible responses to these situations, (3) evaluating the responses in terms of their efficacy in handling the problematic situation, (4) developing a measurement format, and (5) evaluating the measure's reliability and validity. Workers can use this model to create simulations that address the needs of the populations with whom they work.

Simulations have the potential limitation that group members know they are acting rather than performing in real-life situations. In most cases, however, members appear to forget that they are acting and perform as they would in real life. The following case examples illustrates how a simulation can be created and used in a group.

Case Example   Creating a Simulated Situation in an Assertiveness Training Group

In an assertion training group, three members are asked to volunteer to role play standing in a line at a grocery store. The member whose behavior is being assessed is asked to stand at the end of the line. Then, another volunteer is asked to try to get ahead of the member who is in line when he is looking at a magazine in a rack next to the checkout counter. The worker and the other members observe how the member handles the situation both verbally and nonverbally and give the member feedback. The situation can be role played again with the same member or with additional members for additional practice using the improved strategies.

Program Activities. Many different types of program activities can be used to assess the functioning of group members. The selection of appropriate activities depends on the type of group the worker is leading. In children's groups, the worker can have members participate in play activities and games. For example, the game Charades can be used to assess how members act out particular situations. Games requiring cooperation can be used to assess the extent to which members are able to negotiate differences.

In adolescent groups, a party, a meal, or a sports activity can often help the worker make an assessment of members' social skills and their level of social development. In adult groups containing moderately or severely impaired members, preparing a meal together or going on an outing can help the worker assess daily living skills. Program activities should be age-appropriate and should give members the opportunity to demonstrate behaviors that they would like to improve through their participation in a group. For more information about using program materials in groups, see the section on program activities in Chapter 9.

Reports by Others

In addition to members' self-observations and workers' observations, leaders often rely on the reports of people who are familiar with members' behavior outside the group. When considering data reported by others, the worker should assess its reliability and validity, which can vary considerably from person to person and from one report to another. For example, some data may be based on rumors, assumptions, or the statements of unidentified third parties; other data may come from direct observations. Obviously, the worker should place less confidence in rumors than in direct observations.

The worker should also consider the relationship of the person reporting the data to the member about whom data have been collected. Is the person reporting the data interested in the well-being of the group member, or is the person motivated by ill feeling, personal gain, or rivalry? By examining a person's motivation for reporting data about a group member, the worker is in a better position to assess any potential bias in a report.

When a worker has an ongoing relationship with individuals who regularly report data about group members' behavior, such as mental health therapy aides, child care workers, and teachers, it is often worth the effort to help these individuals use reliable and valid data-collection systems. For example, a therapy group leader can offer to help a mental health therapy aide develop a chart to monitor the behavior of a group member at meals or during recreational activities. Similarly, a school social worker can offer an elementary school teacher assistance in using the Achenbach (1997) checklist, which is a standardized instrument to measure children's social behavior. In this way, the worker can build a relationship with persons who have daily contact with group members and ensure that accurate data are reported about members' behaviors outside the group.

Standardized Instruments

A fourth way that workers can assess the functioning of group members is by using standardized assessment instruments. Some instruments require lengthy personal interviews, but others are brief, paper-and-pencil measures known as *rapid assessment instruments*. The Beck Depression Inventory (BDI), for example, is a 21-item scale that assesses the presence and severity of depression. Rapid assessment instruments can be used in many ways in a group. For example, some members of an outpatient psychiatric group can be asked to spend a few minutes filling out the BDI during a group meeting or at home between meetings. Other members might be asked to fill out the Stait-Trait Anxiety Inventory (Spielberger, Gorsuch, Lushene, Vagg, & Jacobs, 1983) or other instruments that assess the particular symptoms individual group members are experiencing.

Despite the usefulness of standardized assessment instruments for understanding the problems and concerns experienced by group members, it should be kept in mind that these instruments may not be appropriate for use with all populations. For example, when administered to members of specific sociocultural groups or to developmentally disabled persons, such instruments may not be valid or reliable. In fact, they may give the worker a distorted impression of members' strengths. Thus, when considering the use of a standardized measure with a particular group of individuals, workers should check whether the description of the instrument includes information about its use with particular populations. If no information is available, workers should select another measure that has been found to be valid for use with the population of interest. A measure suspected of being culturally biased should never be used because even if caution is exercised in interpreting the results, others who have access to the results may draw erroneous conclusions.

Because rapid assessment instruments are focused on particular problem areas, the type of assessment instrument selected depends on the group's focus. Corcoran and Fischer (2013) present a wide variety of rapid assessment instruments for use with children, adults, couples, and families in a two-volume set. These volumes are a good desk reference for clinicians because they contain a wide variety of measures that can be used in many different situations.

> **?** Assess your understanding of assessing the functioning of group members by taking this brief quiz.

ASSESSING THE FUNCTIONING OF THE GROUP AS A WHOLE

In most practice situations, workers limit their assessment of the functioning of the group to simply reflecting on it during and between meetings. They may also meet with a supervisor or a consultant to help process their reactions to a group and to get suggestions to improve future group meetings. Nevertheless, it can be beneficial to use more formal structured assessments of group processes. These help workers and members become more aware of and involved in improving whole groups' functioning. Having a group with excellent communication, strong cohesion, inclusive and supportive social integration mechanisms, and an overall positive and efficacious culture, can make a great deal of difference in accomplishing individual and group goals. Therefore, the inconvenience of implementing some of the assessment measures we suggest in the following pages should be weighed against the potential benefits that accrue when groups have supportive, smooth, and efficacious group processes.

Assessment

Behavior: Apply knowledge of human behavior and the social environment, person-in-environment, and other multi-disciplinary theoretical frameworks in the analysis of assessment data from clients and constituencies.

Critical Thinking Question: Workers draw from many methods for assessing the group. What methods can be used to assess the group as a whole?

A careful assessment of group dynamics can lead to immediate intervention by the worker in the here-and-now work of the group. The worker can use many different skills to guide group dynamics, such as clarifying, changing direction, emphasizing, focusing, and reframing. There are many other skills as well, so there is a great deal of critical judgment that workers have to use about the choice of skills to employ and the timing of the intervention. The assessment measures described next should be viewed as methods that can be used selectively to augment the skillful use of self by the worker in the here-and-now of group process.

There is no single measure of group processes that is perfect for all situations. Therefore, it is important to become familiar with as many measures as possible to be able to select the ones that might be helpful in particular group assessment situations. Reviews of group measures are a helpful way to gain an overview of what measures are available (see for example, Anderson & West, 1998; Chapman, Baker, Porter, Thayer, & Burlingame, 2010; Delucia-Waack, 1997; Fuhriman & Barlow, 1994; Fuhriman & Packard, 1986; Johnson et. al., 2006; Macgowan, 2008; Strauss, Burlingame, & Bormann, 2008).

Assessing Communication and Interaction Patterns

Communication and interaction patterns are established early in the group. Therefore, the worker should be especially concerned about these patterns as they develop during the beginning stage of groups. A careful assessment of communication patterns can alert the worker to potential problems and prevent them from becoming established as a routine part of group functioning. It can also help facilitate member-to-member communication and disclosure of important information that may be helpful in attaining group or individual member goals.

At the beginning of a group, too many member-to-leader interactions and too few member-to-member interactions may be of concern. In newly formed groups, there is a natural tendency for members to look to the worker for direction. The worker may feel gratified by this and encourage it. Unfortunately, this pattern may undermine the mutual aid and group problem solving that occur when members direct their communication to everyone in the group rather than exclusively to the worker.

Other communication patterns may also alert the worker to potential problems. For example, one member may attempt to dominate group discussions and thus prevent other members from interacting. Another potential problem is a lack of communication by a member. Although it is not unusual for some members to communicate less frequently than others, the worker should be aware of the potential for isolation when a member says little or nothing for long periods during the beginning stage of the group. Go-rounds and check-ins are ways to include silent members without singling out those who may just be more comfortable listening.

If there is a concern that one or more members may not be engaged in the group, workers can use the Group Engagement Measure (Macgowan & Levenson, 2003; Macgowan & Newman, 2005). It is a brief measure that can be given to each member and scored in the group or between meetings. Another simple way to measure engagement is to list members' names on a pie chart, and place a check mark in the slice next to each member when they speak. This can be done for 5 or 10 minutes, and then the results can be discussed with the group.

To even out participation in children's groups, tokens can be used during a short game lasting 5 to 7 minutes. The worker can tell members that they will receive a token each time they talk until they reach a certain number, such as five, then they have to wait to participate until all the other members have received five tokens. Tokens can be redeemed for a small prize. Variations on this can be having a baton or a ball in order to talk. The ball or baton can be passed to the member who wants to talk. As with all children's groups, the length of these games should be short and should depend on the age of the children in the group.

Assessing Cohesion

Group cohesion takes longer to develop than communication patterns. Still it is important to intervene as early as possible to encourage a high level of cohesion. Group cohesion can be measured by using a sociometric scale or by using scales specifically designed to measure group cohesiveness (Budman et al., 1987, 1993).

Sociometry is a widely used method to measure interpersonal attraction. Originally developed by Moreno in the 1930s (Moreno, 1934), *sociometry* refers to the measurement of social preferences, that is, the strengths of members' preference or rejection of each other. Sociometric measures are obtained by asking about each member's preference for interacting with other members in relation to a particular activity or to one another (Crano & Brewer, 1973; Selltiz, Wrightsman, & Cook, 1976).

Case Example   Using Sociometric Ratings

During the assessment phase of a discharge planning group for teens in a residential treatment facility, the group worker administered a sociometric measurement to understand the patterns of member attraction for each other. Members were asked to identify, in order of preference, which members they would be most interested in seeing after discharge. Using the data from this assessment, the worker constructed a sociogram and "paired" members who indicated mutual attraction, creating a buddy system for work on tasks associated with individual member and group goals. The worker also used the data to identify members who were rated as less popular than most, allowing her to give special attention to these members during group sessions.

Sociometric ratings can be made concerning any activity of interest to workers or members. For example, a worker may want to assess members' preferences for other members in relation to socializing between group meetings or choosing a partner to complete a task. An additional example follows.

To obtain sociometric ratings, members are usually asked to write the names of the other members on one side of a sheet of paper next to a preference scale, for example, $1 =$ most preferred to $5 =$ least preferred. Members are then asked to rate everyone in the group except themselves in relation to a particular activity. For example, children in a residential treatment center might be asked, "If we were going on a day trip together, who would you like to sit next to during the bus trip?" and "Who would be your second choice?"

An index of preferences can be calculated for each member by dividing the total score a member receives from all group members by the highest possible score the member could receive. Members of attractive, cohesive groups have higher mean preference scores than do members of groups who are less cohesive and attractive.

Another way of presenting sociometric data is through a sociogram. As shown in Figure 8.2, solid lines represent attraction, dotted lines represent indifference, broken lines represent repulsion, and arrows represent the direction of preferences that are not reciprocal. For research purposes, sociometric data can be analyzed by more complicated methods, such as multidimensional scaling (Gazda & Mobley, 1981).

Several other measures of the relationships between individual group members and of overall group cohesion have been developed. Cox (1973), for example, developed the Group Therapy Interaction Chronogram, a graphic representation of interactions and relationships among group members that is similar to a sociogram but more complex. For assessments of the psychometric properties and utility of the Chronogram, see Fuhriman and Packard (1986) and Reder (1978). Budman and colleagues (1987, 1993) have also developed the Harvard Community Health Plan Group Cohesiveness Scale that can be used by trained clinical raters viewing half-hour, videotaped segments of psychotherapy groups.

A widely used measure of treatment groups' cohesion is The Group Environment Scale (GES) (Moos, 1986), described in Chapter 14. It can be used to examine cohesion in teams and other task groups (Carless & De Paola, 2000). The GES is now being used less frequently than the Group Climate Questionnaire – Short (GCQS), which is probably the most widely used measure of group climate. The GCQS includes three factors: "engaging," "avoiding," and "conflict" (MacKenzie, 1990). Cohesion is one aspect of the engagement factor of the GCQS. For a recent review of the GCQS and other measures, see Sodano, et al. (2014).

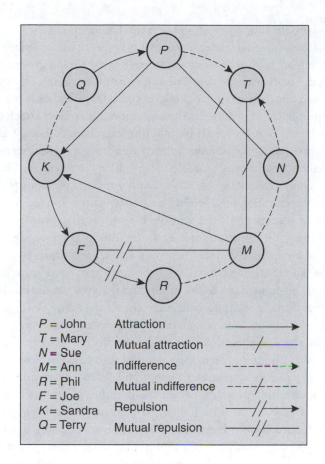

Figure 8.2
A Sociogram

Assessing Social Integration

Workers should also assess norms, roles, and status hierarchies through focused observations. The norms that develop are extremely important because they define acceptable and unacceptable behavior in a group. Norms have an important influence on members' satisfaction with their group experiences (Forsyth, 2014). Because norms take time to develop in groups and are difficult to change once established, it is important for leaders to monitor their development and guide them in directions that help members achieve individual and group goals starting in the first meeting. Workers should involve members by pointing out developing norms, asking for members' input, helping to modify norms that detract from individual and group goals, and promoting and protecting norms that are beneficial for goal achievement.

Members' roles also begin to develop early in the group. Initial role taking in a group is a tentative process and may not reflect the roles members will occupy later in the group. Members try out roles and often vacillate among them, such as the socio-emotional leader, task leader, and dominator. During this stage of the group, the worker can point out the functional and dysfunctional characteristics of the roles to members and help the members develop role behaviors that will facilitate the group's functioning and their own functioning in the group.

Focusing on problematic roles, Shulman (2016) has identified the scapegoat, deviant member, gatekeeper, internal leader, defensive member, quiet member, and talkative member as challenging roles that members frequently take on in groups. Most roles are not difficult for the worker to identify. The scapegoat, for example, receives much negative attention and criticism from the group because the member is blamed for a host of defects and problems. According to Shulman (2016), members attack the portion of a scapegoat's behavior that they least like about themselves. Although Shulman (2016) mentions that scapegoating is common, our experience suggests that scapegoating is relatively rare in adult groups. Scapegoating is more likely to occur in children's groups, but appropriate program activities, structured and timed to consider the developmental abilities and the concentration of different groups of children, can reduce or eliminate it.

In the case of a scapegoat, the worker may want to point out the pattern of interaction to the group without taking sides (Shulman, 2016). In doing so, the worker should be aware that sometimes groups use scapegoats to avoid talking about difficult, emotionally charged issues that may be catalyzed by the scapegoat's behavior. This pattern could be pointed out to the group, and the group could be asked to address the difficult, emotionally charged issue directly. At the same time, the scapegoat's behavior may be deviant and annoying to the average person, and the group's negative interactions with the scapegoat may simply be an effort to get the individual to stop the behavior. In this situation, the worker may want to help the group consider more appropriate ways to help the member change the behavior. In more extreme cases, the worker may want to consider whether the member is appropriate for the group or whether the member could be helped to change the annoying behavior with feedback and encouragement from the group. The scapegoat's behavior may also represent an inappropriate way to get attention. In this situation, the worker can help the scapegoat to lead an activity or in some other way get attention for prosocial rather than antisocial behavior. Malekoff (2014) suggests that it is also helpful to humanize scapegoats by helping members to understand them more fully, to help the group understand their struggle to fit in, and the reasons why they behave in a fashion that elicits negative feedback from the group.

When one or more members of a group assume dysfunctional roles, it is often a signal that the group as a whole is not functioning at an optimal level. For example, when an assessment reveals that a member is functioning as a gatekeeper, that is, one who does not allow the group to discuss sensitive issues, the worker should help the group as a whole examine how to change its overall functioning rather than focus on the member who has assumed the dysfunctional role. A quiet member may signal difficulties in the communication and interaction patterns established in the group as a whole. It is rare that a problematic group role is an expression of one individual rather than of group dysfunction. Guidelines that workers can use to help the group change dysfunctional member roles are presented in the following list.

Helping Members with Dysfunctional Role Behaviors
- Keep in mind that all behaviors have meaning.
- Point the behavior out to the group in a tentative fashion.
- Ask the member displaying the behavior to describe his or her own perception of it.

- Ask the other group members to describe how they experience the member's behavior.
- Identify feelings and points of view expressed by all members about the behavior.
- Ask the member displaying the behavior to consider the perceptions of other members.
- Help all members consider their reactions to the behavior and whether they wish to change the way they interact with others about it.
- Work with all members to change role behaviors so that they help the group to function effectively.

As shown above, the first step in helping groups to change dysfunctional member roles is to be aware that all behavior is meaningful and purposeful. Workers should consider what the member who is playing a dysfunctional role is trying to accomplish by behaving in such a fashion. For example, is the member attempting to gain attention or acceptance? Is the member fearful of what others may think? Pointing out and describing the member's behavior in a tentative manner helps all group members to be aware of the behavior and to think about the meaning of it. Asking a member who displays a dysfunctional behavior to describe how he or she perceives it enables the other members of the group to understand and empathize with the member's situation.

The next step, helping members to consider their reactions to the behavior and to consider whether they wish to change the way they interact about it, allows members the opportunity to think about the impact of the behavior on the whole group and their role in sustaining or changing it. In this way, the whole group begins to own and take responsibility for doing something about the behavior instead of leaving responsibility for the behavior with only the one member identified as playing a dysfunctional role. At this point, the group is often ready to talk together about role behaviors and how to change them in order to facilitate goal attainment. The worker can help by guiding the group to focus on group processes and goal-attainment strategies.

The steps presented previously are intended as a general guide that workers can use to address dysfunctional role behaviors. These steps, however, have to be adapted sensitively when working with members with specific dysfunctional role behaviors. For example, monopolizers may acknowledge their behavior, but may still not be able to change it. Therefore, when helping members who talk too much to change their behavior, it may be necessary to place time limits on communication by all group members or to seek one or more volunteers who will prompt the talkative member when he or she exceeds time limits. It may also be necessary for the worker to take an active stance, reminding talkative members that they have been talking for a while, that they should consider giving others a turn to talk, or asking members to hold onto a thought for a later group discussion. In contrast, when working with quiet members, it is important to find out if there is something about the group that is impeding their communication or if they tend not to talk much in groups. Experience suggests that most quiet members are good listeners who prefer to listen rather than to talk. Singling quiet members out by soliciting their opinions or pointing out their silence can make them uncomfortable. Instead, to ensure full participation from quiet members, workers can use go-rounds, program activities, or they can assign specific task roles that provide opportunities and encourage quiet members to participate.

Gatekeepers and rescuers are other common dysfunctional group roles that should be addressed sensitively. Gatekeepers and rescuers intervene when emotionally charged issues are raised in the group. They may change the subject, divert attention, make light of an issue, or become overly solicitous. These behaviors prevent discussion of emotionally sensitive issues that could make the work of the group more relevant and meaningful, because sensitive but important issues that members are confronting would be addressed. Gatekeepers and rescuers are often unaware that they are playing these roles. Workers can help by having all group members identify the fears they have about discussing particular emotionally charged issues. Gatekeeping and rescuing behaviors can then be viewed as attempts to avoid these feared discussions. The worker helps members to confront their fears while simultaneously ensuring that the group is a safe and supportive place where meaningful but emotionally charged issues can be openly discussed and addressed.

Case Example   A Gatekeeper in an Anger Management Group

In an anger management group, members began to talk about their own backgrounds. When the topic of childhood physical and sexual abuse came up on two occasions, one member of the group, Fred, kept changing the topic by talking about his own recent experiences of abusive behavior toward his wife. The second time this occurred the group leader mentioned that it was good that Fred was talking about his experiences with his wife and showing some empathy toward her. At the same time, the leader pointed out that childhood sexual abuse was an emotionally charged but important topic that should be talked about in the group, and that it might be relevant to what some members were experiencing regarding their own anger and abusive behavior. Therefore, the leader asked the members who had brought up the topic of sexual abuse to talk about their experiences, and they invited other members of the group to share their reactions and experiences. In this way, without explicitly mentioning that Fred was a gatekeeper who was not allowing the group to talk about an emotionally charged topic, the leader enabled group members to begin a discussion of an important issue they might not otherwise have had the opportunity to discuss.

The status of individual group members and the power that the leader and other group members have at their disposal also affect the development of social integration and influence dynamics within the group. For example, although high-status members are likely to adhere to group norms and procedures, they are also much more likely to influence the development of a group than are low-status members. Members in the middle of the status hierarchy are likely to strive for greater status within the group by adhering to group norms and upholding the status quo (Forsyth, 2014). Low-status members are less likely to conform to group norms than either high-status or middle-status members (Forsyth, 2014). An accurate assessment of the status hierarchy in the group can help workers understand and anticipate the actions and reactions of members when the worker intervenes in the group.

An accurate assessment of the power bases that the worker and the members have at their disposal can be important in the beginning stages of group work. Workers who understand the limits of their influence over group members are able to use their power effectively and avoid trying to use it when it will be ineffective. An accurate assessment of the sources of members' power can also help the worker in planning strategies for intervening in the group as a whole and for helping members to form a mutual-aid network of shared resources within the group.

The most fully developed method for assessing norms, roles, and status is Bales' Systematic Multilevel Observation of Groups (Bales, 1980; Bales, Cohen, & Williamson, 1979). SYMLOG can be used as a self-report measure or as an observational measure. Figure 8.3 presents a SYMLOG field diagram of one person in a group. The horizontal axis of Figure 8.3 represents the dimension friendly versus unfriendly, and the vertical axis represents the dimension instrumental versus emotionally expressive. The third dimension, dominant versus submissive, is represented by the size of the circles. Larger circles represent greater dominance and smaller circles represent greater submissiveness. For example, in Figure 8.3, Sharon perceives that Ann is the most dominant group member and Ed is the most friendly and emotionally expressive member. Members rate all other members and themselves in relation to the three-dimensional SYMLOG space. In addition to rating overt behaviors, members can rate their values by evaluating which behavior they would avoid, reject, wish to perform, and think they ought to perform (see circles marked "avoid," "reject," "wish," and "ought" in Figure 8.3).

SYMLOG field diagrams can be used for assessment in a variety of ways. One of the most basic ways is for members to compare their field diagrams. A composite of group field diagrams can be made from the field diagrams of individual members. The composite can be used to analyze the functioning of the group as a whole. For example, who are the most dominant group members? Which members are included in the dominant subgroup (in Bales' terminology, "dominant triangle" as illustrated in Figure 8.3)? Particular roles of individual group members can also be identified. For example, Figure 8.3 shows Bill isolated in the unfriendly, instrumental quadrant of the field diagram. Is he

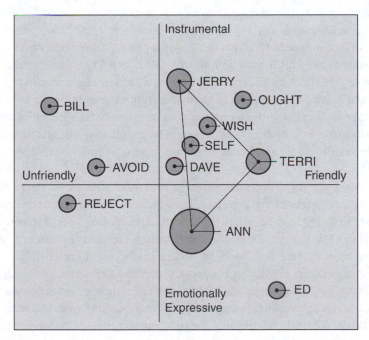

Figure 8.3
Sharon's SYMLOG Diagram of the Group

an isolate or perhaps a scapegoat? For a detailed discussion of these methods, see Bales, Cohen, and Williamson (1979) and Bales (1980).

The SYMLOG method has two limitations. First, the method is complex and takes time to learn. A more serious limitation is that a SYMLOG self-study takes about three hours to complete. Although this amount of time may be warranted for a team that functions together on a daily basis over a long period of time, it may not be justifiable for a short-term treatment group.

Assessing Group Culture

A fourth area that workers should assess when examining the functioning of the group as a whole is the group's culture. Ideas, beliefs, values, and feelings held in common by group members have a profound effect on the therapeutic benefits that can be achieved in the group. Just as some societal cultures promote the public expression of emotion and others do not, groups develop cultures that value certain ways of behaving.

In the beginning stage, the worker should examine the culture that is developing in a group. Does the culture help the group and its members achieve their goals? Because group culture develops more slowly than the other group dynamics, the worker's initial assessment of a group's culture should be viewed as a tentative indication about how the culture may develop. It is difficult to change a group's culture after it is well established, so the worker may wish to share initial impressions with members early. For example, in a group in which a worker observes that a negative, unsupportive culture is developing, it may be helpful to point out in the first or second meeting that most members' communications are problem-oriented rather than growth-oriented or that few supportive comments are made within the group. Methods to modify or change a group's culture are described in Chapter 9.

A number of methods to assess the group's culture have been developed. Some methods, such as the Hill Interaction Matrix (HIM) and SYMLOG, were designed to assess a variety of types of groups along several different dimensions. The HIM employs a 16-cell matrix to assess the content and style of group interaction. SYMLOG and the HIM can be used with all types of treatment and task groups. However, they are primarily used in long-term groups, such as teams, boards, and so on for long-term development and for addressing problems in group processes that are resistant to change.

There are a variety of other assessment measures that workers are able to use to assess culture in treatment groups. These include the Group Atmosphere Scale (Silbergeld, Koenig, Manderscheid, Meeker, & Hornung, 1975), Group Climate Questionnaire (MacKenzie, 1983), and the Curative Climate Instrument (Fuhriman, Drescher, Hanson, Henrie, & Rybicki, 1986). The previously mentioned Group Climate Scale (MacKenzie, 1983) is probably the most widely used measure of overall group climate, but other measures such as the Therapeutic Factors Inventory (Lese & MacNair-Semands, 2000) are also widely used (Joyce, MacNair-Semands, Tasca, & Ogrodniczuk, 2011; Strauss, Burlingame, & Borman, 2008). When working with task groups, the Team Climate Inventory (Anderson & West, 1998) is widely used.

? Assess your understanding of assessing the group as a whole by taking this brief quiz.

ASSESSING THE GROUP'S ENVIRONMENT

The worker's assessment of the environment's influence on the functioning of the entire group should be distinguished from the assessment of environmental factors that affect individual group members. In both cases, however, the environment in which group members and the group as a whole function has an important effect on group work practice.

When assessing the influence of the environment on the group, the worker focuses on the following levels.

Levels of Assessment
- The organization that sponsors and sanctions the group
- The interorganizational environment
- The community environment

The emphasis on the influence of the environment is a distinctive aspect of social work practice and is not found to any great extent in the writings of group workers from other professional disciplines.

Assessing the Sponsoring Organization

When assessing the influence on the group of the sponsoring organization, the worker examines how the group's purposes are influenced by the agency, what resources are allocated for the group's efforts, what status the worker has in relation to others who work for the agency, and how the agency's attitudes about service delivery influence the group work endeavor. Taken together, these factors can have a profound influence on the way the group functions.

Assessments

Behavior: Collect and organize data, and apply critical thinking to interpret information from clients and constituencies.

Critical Thinking Question: Group workers respond to multiple contexts that shape practice. How would you assess an organization's ability to sponsor group work services?

As Garvin (1997) points out, an organization always has a purpose for sanctioning a group work effort. An organization's purpose may be stated explicitly or may be implied in the overall program objectives. The organization administration's purpose for encouraging the development of a group may not correspond to the worker's or the group members' ideas about a group's purpose. The extent to which the organization, the worker, and the group members can agree on a common purpose for the group will determine, in part, the extent to which the group will receive the support it needs to function effectively and the extent to which the group experience will be judged as beneficial by all concerned.

It is helpful for the worker to clarify the organization's purpose for sponsoring the group. A written group proposal, such as the one described in Chapter 6 (also see Appendices C, D, and E), can clarify the worker's intentions and provide the organization's administration with an opportunity to react to a written document.

During the process of clarifying the organization's purposes for the group, the worker can help shape the purposes proposed for the group. For example, a nursing home administrator may decide to sponsor a group to help the residents "fit in better" with the nursing home's schedule of bathing, feeding, and housekeeping. The worker could help the nursing home staff and residents reformulate the group's purpose by considering the needs of both the group members and the organization. For example, the purpose of the group might be changed to have residents and staff work together to find a way to accomplish all the personal care tasks in the staff's busy schedules, while at the same time accommodating residents' needs for autonomy and individual preference.

An organization can also influence a group by its allocation of resources. As mentioned in Chapter 6, the worker should identify as early as possible the resources the group will need to function effectively. Once this is done, the worker can assess the likelihood that the organization will be able to allocate sufficient resources and can plan the best strategy to obtain any that may be needed. The worker's assessment may also include the extent to which resources, for example, a meeting room or some refreshments, can be obtained from alternative sponsors.

The worker's status in the sponsoring organization can also influence the group. If a worker is a low-status member of the sponsoring organization, there may be difficulty in obtaining resources for the group, in convincing the sponsor that the endeavor is a good use of his or her time, or in demonstrating that the group's purposes are consistent with the overall objectives of the organization. In this situation, the worker may want to consult with trusted colleagues who can give the worker some feedback about the feasibility of the proposed group. The worker might also ask these colleagues for their support for the development of the new group service.

The attitudes and practices of the sponsoring organization with regard to service delivery can have an important influence on the group work endeavor. The worker should assess whether the organization stresses individual or group work services. For example, in some organizations, the stated commitment to teamwork is not matched by the resources and reward structure to support effective team functioning (Levi, 2014; Ramirez, 2014). Where individual services are given priority, the worker may have to spend considerable time developing the rationale for the group and convincing the organization that it is important to undertake such an endeavor (Levi, 2014; Ramirez, 2014).

The organization's policies regarding recruitment and intake of potential members also can affect a group. The worker should assess whether the clients are receiving services voluntarily or whether they have been mandated to attend the group. Mandated clients are likely to be hostile or apathetic about becoming members of the group. It is also helpful to gather information about the extent to which individuals are prepared by intake workers to receive group work services.

The organization's commitment to a particular service technology, such as practice theories, ideologies, and intervention techniques, may also influence the group work endeavor. For example, if the organization is committed to a long-term psychodynamic treatment model, it may oppose the development of a short-term, behaviorally oriented group. When the service technology planned for a particular group runs counter to an organization's preferred service technology, the worker should develop a convincing rationale for the particular service technology that is planned. For a treatment group, the rationale might include the effectiveness and efficiency of a particular method for treating a particular problem. In the case of a task group, the rationale might include the effectiveness or efficiency of a particular method for generating ideas or making decisions about alternative proposals. The impact of service technology is illustrated in the following case example.

Case Example   A Psycho-Educational Group for Caregivers of Dementia

In a family service agency that relied primarily on a long-term psychodynamic treatment model including long-term groups, a worker proposed a six-week psycho-educational group for caregivers of persons with dementia. In proposing the group at a staff meeting, the worker pointed out that many of the clients coming to the agency were elderly and that a number of them had talked about their problems with dealing with spouses who were forgetful or who had been diagnosed with some form of dementia. The worker suggested that she research best practice models and come up with a short-term group that focused on education about memory loss and dementia, community resources for care for the person with dementia and support for the caregiver. The worker pointed out that the group could start out as a short-term, six-week, weekly meeting group. Then, if members were interested or if more short-term groups were formed, a longer-term support and mutual-aid group could be started with members who wanted to continue in a group. This latter group would be more in keeping with the family agency's traditional approach to its long-term group programs.

To help ensure continued organizational support for the group, workers should take every opportunity to describe the group's progress to clinical supervisors and other administrative staff. This tactic provides an opportunity for the worker to mention the helpfulness of organizational support and any additional resources that are needed. For example, a worker leading a parenting group could discuss the progress made by members and the importance of transportation to and from group meetings but also note that problems in attendance could be reduced if the agency provided child care services during group meetings. In the following chapters, guidelines are presented for choosing interventions and for formulating treatment plans on the basis of the needs of members and of the group as a whole.

Assessing the Interorganizational Environment

When assessing the group's environment, it is important for the worker to pay attention to anything happening in other organizations that may be relevant to the group. The worker can make an assessment of the interorganizational environment by asking several questions: Are other organizations offering similar groups? Do workers in other organizations perceive needs similar to those that formed the basis for the worker's own group? Do other organizations offer services or programs that may be useful to members of the group? Would any benefit be gained by linking with groups in other organizations to lobby for changes in social service benefits?

Unless the worker or others in the organization are already familiar with what is being offered by all other organizations in the community, the worker's primary task in making an interorganizational assessment is to contact other organizations to let them know about the group offering. In addition to generating referrals and making other organizations aware of the group, the assessment may uncover needless duplication of service or, conversely, a widespread need that is not being met or is being met by uncoordinated individual efforts within separate organizations.

Assessing the Community Environment

The worker should also assess the effect of the community environment on the group, the extent of support for the group from other community groups, and the community as a whole. When assessing the effect of the community on a group, the worker should focus on the attitude of the community concerning the problems or issues being addressed by the group. Within Hispanic and African American communities, for example, support groups for people with Alzheimer's disease are difficult to organize because of the stigma attached to the disease. These communities also attach great significance to handling such matters privately through family caregiving (Ramos, Jones, & Toseland, 2005).

In treatment groups, if the problem is one that violates basic community values, members of the group are likely to be stigmatized. Lack of community acceptance and the resulting stigma attached to the problem may have other consequences, such as discouraging potential members from reaching out for help. It may also increase the level of confidentiality of group meetings and may affect procedures used to recruit new members. For example, because of the stigma attached to persons who abuse their children, Parents Anonymous groups generally have confidential meetings, and the recruitment process occurs on a first-name basis to protect members from people who may be more interested in finding out their identities than in attending meetings. Similar recruitment procedures are used in other professionally led and self-help groups that deal with socially stigmatized problems, such as spousal abuse, alcoholism, and compulsive gambling.

The worker should also make an assessment of the support for the group from other community groups and the community as a whole. For example, ministers, priests, and rabbis might be receptive to a group for abusive or neglecting parents, alcoholics, or spouse abusers. The worker can get referrals from these sources or obtain a meeting room, such as a church basement. Similarly, a worker in a family service agency may find that several community groups—a women's civic organization, a battered women's shelter, a victim's compensation board, a council of churches, and a dispute resolution center—would welcome the development of a support group program for domestic violence victims. Workers who assess support from community groups are often in a better position to obtain new funding for a proposed group work service. This is demonstrated in the following case example.

Case Example   Making Interorganizational Assessments

An executive director of a small organization decided to do an interorganizational assessment after problems encountered in serving homeless people had been mentioned several times in monthly staff meetings. The director discovered a lack of sufficient space in shelters and a general lack of community interest in the welfare of the homeless. The worker called a meeting of professionals from several organizations to see what could be done. The interorganizational group contacted a local planning organization. In cooperation with the planning organization, the interorganizational group sought federal, state, local, and private funding to address the needs of the homeless. After much work, a social service program for the homeless was founded with a combination of federal, state, and local funding, and a new community shelter was opened.

Group workers interested in building social action groups and coalitions should find out about the problems that are important to individuals in a community, who has the capacity to make a change in a particular problem, and who has the capacity to prevent or delay change. Information may be gathered from persons affected by the problem and those who have the capacity to affect it through a variety of means, such as (1) focused individual interviews, (2) focus groups, (3) community needs assessments, and (4) state and national survey data and reports (see Chapter 14). The information gathered while interacting with and forming alliances with community members, community leaders, politicians, and community activists is also very important. It is essential for group workers who are interested in building social action groups and coalitions to get to know a community. To understand competing factions, uncover hidden problems, and form alliances often takes a considerable amount of time and commitment. Still, when the intent is to mobilize social action groups and coalitions, there is no substitute for taking the time necessary to get to know a community and to establish trusting relationships with as many different representatives as possible.

A worker's assessment of the community environment may lead to a coalition of forces to resolve a concern. According to Rubin and Rubin (2008), in assessing a community there may be a systematic gathering of information by people who are affected by a problem and who want to solve it. There may also be a fact-gathering endeavor to learn about the problem, a mobilization effort to become involved with the problem, and a capacity-building effort to solve the problem. For example, a community assessment may indicate that police officers have been asked increasingly to handle family disturbances. With the cooperation of the police force and local community leaders, a community organization might decide to reach out to persons experiencing family disturbances. In addition to casework service, these efforts could result in the development of several treatment groups, such as a couple's communication group, a parenting group, and a recreational group for adolescents. It also might result in a task force of community leaders to work on issues of concern to families in the community. This is illustrated in the following case example.

Case Example   Assessing the Community Environment

In a rural county, a community coalition formed to assess the need for a shelter for runaway and homeless youth. Members of county social service organizations, local church leaders, and educators from a local social work program met to discuss the need and to examine whether the community would support a shelter. Coalition members initially divided into separate subgroups that concentrated on collecting data about the extent of the problem. One subgroup met with the local police department to determine how many reports of runaway children were filed each year. Another subgroup conducted individual interviews with community leaders to determine if they would support a shelter. A third subgroup conducted a focus group with residents of the neighborhood that was a potential site for the shelter. The fourth subgroup explored state and national data about homeless and runaway youth. While all these subgroups collected important data establishing need, the coalition discovered that neighborhood residents were very strongly against the idea of a shelter, especially one that would be located in their neighborhood. The coalition reassessed the idea of establishing a shelter and decided to more fully explore how they could involve neighborhood residents in planning for the needs of this population.

? Assess your understanding of assessing the group's environment by taking this brief quiz.

LINKING ASSESSMENT TO INTERVENTION

In preparation for the middle stage of treatment groups, discussed in Chapter 9, workers should consider how they will use their assessment data to plan effective interventions. Few texts in group work or casework practice have addressed the way assessments are linked to intervention methods and treatment plans. This may, in part, account for findings from practice studies suggesting there is little correlation between workers' assessments or diagnoses and the interventions that are selected. Without guidelines about the interventions that are most appropriate for particular problems, workers will rely on interventions with which they are most familiar, regardless of their assessment of the group or its members.

Figure 8.4 illustrates a framework for developing treatment plans that result from an assessment of the individual group member, the group as a whole, and the group environment. Because problems are often multidimensional, several different interventions may be selected to become part of a comprehensive treatment plan. For example, in a couples group, the worker and each member may select specific interventions to meet individual needs. One member decides to use a cognitive restructuring intervention to help her stop getting defensive when confronted by her husband. As part of his treatment plan, another member decides to join Alcoholics Anonymous. At the same time, the worker helps the first member change her interaction patterns in the group and helps the second member to stop avoiding confrontation in the group.

Case Example

Jody conducted a Banana Splits group for fourth graders whose parents were in the process of separating or divorcing. The group had been meeting for four weeks. Its purpose was to help the children discuss their concerns about their changing family situation and to assist them in finding support from each other. The beginning phase of the group was going well. Members were becoming more comfortable with Jody and with each other. They seemed to be opening up a little more about their concerns. Jody used a number of program materials to help members get to know each other and identify their feelings.

As she conducted the group, Jody recognized that she was beginning to gather information about each of the members and about how the group was working as a unit. She was also learning a good deal about how important it was to work with others in the group's environment, such as teachers, guidance counselors, and school administrators. It was time to take some of this information and prepare a more formal assessment that would be useful for her future work with the members of the group. Also, she wanted to become more systematic in her understanding of the dynamics in the group as a whole because she recognized that the group's environment played an important part in the success of the group process. She designed several methods for collecting additional data to help her begin the formal assessment process.

She began by assessing the needs of the individual members of the group. The membership was fairly homogeneous—all the students were fourth graders and came from the same school district. Yet, she noted that members had very different home situations that could affect how they were coping with their changing family situations. She used several sources to collect data about how students were coping with their family situations. First, she contacted the parents of each child. She asked each parent to fill out a short rating scale on the child that identified eating, sleeping, and study habits while the child was at home. Second, she asked each child's teacher to write a paragraph that described the child's behavior in the classroom. Specifically, she asked each teacher to comment on his or her observations of the child's social interaction, school performance, and overall mood in the classroom. Third, Jody recorded her own observations of each child during group sessions, carefully documenting her observations by using excerpts from the child's dialogue in the group. She also recorded the major concerns that surfaced for each member during group sessions.

She organized this information in individual files for each member and added to the information as the group progressed. As she collected more data, Jody synthesized them and wrote a summary assessment of each member's situation that included information about the home environment, adjustment to the separation process, class behavior, connections to other members in the group, socialization patterns at school, and grades. She planned to use this information to work with each member in formulating individual goals to be worked on during later group sessions.

Although Jody observed that the group seemed to be progressing well, she decided to assess more formally how the group was functioning. She began by taking careful notes on the patterns of communication and interaction between members. She noticed that the group had several small cliques that had formed, and she wondered if this dynamic was reinforced by interaction among subgroup members that took place outside of the group. She administered a short sociometric exercise to the members to more fully assess interaction within the group. On further investigation, she learned that subgroups seemed to form based on how classes were organized for the fourth-grade students at the school. She also learned through observation that many members were communicating more to her than to other members. As a group goal for future meetings, she planned to promote member-to-member communication by encouraging students to talk to each other rather than to her. One way Jody assessed the group's cohesion was by asking members to end each meeting with a comment about what they liked or didn't like about the group that day. She noted that many members made positive comments. She also noted that the members were becoming more independent and responsible for deciding things in the group, and she felt that the group's culture was developing adequately for this stage of the process.

Jody also took a good deal of time planning for this group, especially by preparing the organizational environment. She felt it was a good time to reassess aspects of the group's environment, particularly in relation to how the group was being perceived by teachers, administrators, and parents. She designed a short evaluation instrument and sent it to these constituencies, asking for their perceptions and feedback about the Banana Splits group. In addition, she interviewed the principal to share information about the group and to assess how important the group was to members of the school. On interviewing the principal, Jody learned that the school board was interested in replicating Jody's group with students in other classes. To avoid behavior problems and school violence that might occur if family problems were not addressed, the board currently seemed to favor early intervention and increased services to children whose parents were separating or divorcing. As a goal, Jody planned to make a presentation to the school board about expanding group work services to students experiencing turbulent family environments.

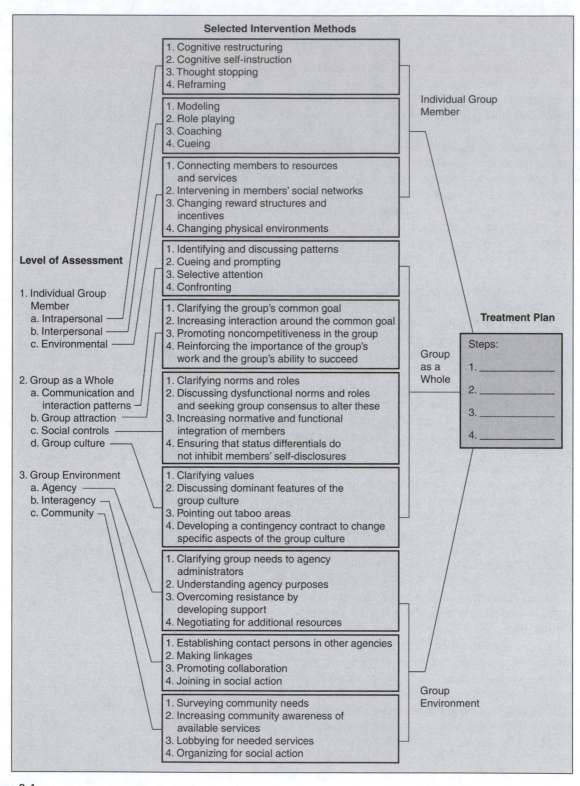

Figure 8.4
Linking Assessment and Intervention in Treatment Groups

SUMMARY

This chapter has suggested that the worker assess three areas of the functioning of individual group members, four areas of the functioning of the group as a whole, and three areas of the environment in which the group functions. Chapters 9 through 12 describe a variety of interventions that the worker can use when assessment indicates an intervention is warranted.

This chapter examines in detail the process of assessment. Although assessments are made throughout all stages of a group's development, they are often concentrated in the latter portions of the beginning stage and the initial portions of the middle stage. This is the time when the worker and the group members are planning intervention strategies to achieve the goals they have agreed on in the planning and beginning stages of the group.

In making assessments, the worker examines the functioning of individual group members, the group as a whole, and the group's environment. When assessing individual members, the worker examines intrapersonal, interpersonal, and environmental areas of each member's functioning. In addition, the worker examines each member's functioning in relation to what the member can contribute to the group, what needs the member brings to the group, and what intervention plans are most likely to be successful in helping the member alleviate concerns and problems. A number of methods that can be used separately or in combination for assessing the functioning of individual members are presented in this chapter.

To assess the group as a whole, the worker focuses on the four areas of group dynamics described in Chapter 3. These are (1) communication and interaction patterns; (2) cohesion; (3) social integration; and (4) the group's culture. Several methods for assessing the group as a whole are described.

Because group work practice occurs within the context of a larger service delivery system, it is important to consider the effect of the group's environment on its functioning. To make a thorough assessment of the group's environment, it is suggested that the worker assess the sponsoring organization, the interorganizational environment, and the larger community environment in which the group functions. After explaining the potential effects of each of these aspects of the environment on the group, the chapter describes the linkage between assessment and intervention.

Treatment Groups: Foundation Methods

During the middle stage, groups are focused on accomplishing the objectives, goals, and tasks developed earlier in the life of the group. It is assumed that by the middle stage, workers have already discussed the group's purposes; developed a group contract concerning confidentiality, attendance, and number of sessions; and developed individual contracts with particular treatment goals for each member. It is also assumed that the group as a whole has developed an initial set of dynamic processes, including a pattern of communication and interaction; a beginning level of interpersonal attraction and group cohesion, norms, roles, and other social control mechanisms; and a group culture. The primary task of the worker during the middle stage is to help members accomplish the goals they have contracted to achieve.

MIDDLE-STAGE SKILLS

The middle stage of treatment groups is characterized by an initial period of testing, conflict, and adjustment as members work out their relationships with one another and the larger group. Contracts are negotiated and renegotiated, members establish their positions in relation to one another, and the group develops a niche within the sponsoring organization.

The testing, conflict, and adjustment that occur in the group are signs that members are becoming comfortable enough to assert their own needs and their own vision of the group. During this period, members demonstrate their independence and abilities to engage in leadership activities. They may question the purposes and goals of the group or the methods that have been proposed to accomplish them. They may also express contrary opinions and concerns about group processes or their interactions with the leader or certain members. In the beginning stage, members are often glad to have the worker structure the group, but at the beginning of the middle stage, testing and conflict can signify that members are vying for a voice and some control of the direction of the group.

Informal leadership and control by members should be encouraged when it is contributing to socio-emotional comfort and goal achievement. Effective leaders welcome and encourage it. They know that it enhances their own status in the group because members view them as open, welcoming, and empowering.

In most situations when testing and conflict occur, acknowledging members' issues and concerns about group processes and goals and enabling them to have a discussion about how to move forward is all that is needed to help the group continue to function in a smooth and satisfying manner. In some situations, however, conflicts may escalate. In these situations, the conflict resolution skills and strategies presented in Chapter 11 can be quite useful.

Although some elements of testing and conflict will continue to emerge as a normal part of the life of a group, after an initial period of adjustment, the main focus of the middle stage turns to goal achievement. Members work together to achieve the goals expressed in the contracts they have made with the group's leader, other group members, and the group as a whole. During the middle stage, the worker makes modifications to these contracts based on an assessment of the group's development, the changing needs of members, and the changing demands of the social environment in which the group functions.

Although every group has a unique developmental pattern that calls for different leadership skills, workers are often expected to perform seven fundamental tasks during the middle stage of all treatment groups. These include:

- Preparing for group meetings
- Structuring the group's work
- Involving and empowering group members
- Helping members to achieve goals
- Using empirically based treatment methods
- Working with reluctant and resistant group members
- Monitoring and evaluating the group's progress

Preparing for Group Meetings

During the middle stage, the worker should continuously assess the needs of the group and its members and plan to meet identified needs in subsequent meetings. The cycle of assessment, modification, and reassessment is the method by which the leader ensures continued progress toward contract goals.

In structured, time-limited groups, the worker prepares the agenda between meetings. For example, for the fourth session of an educational group for prospective foster parents, a worker prepared (1) material on helping children develop values, (2) a handout on value clarification, (3) an exercise that helped the children develop their own values, and (4) questions that helped to organize the group's discussion of values. In preparing for the meeting, the worker tried to select material that led to a stimulating and interesting discussion. In addition, the worker estimated the time needed to complete each of these educational components and discussed this with members during the initial part of the meeting.

Engagement

Behavior: Apply knowledge of human behavior and the social environment, person-in-environment, and other multidisciplinary theoretical frameworks to engage with clients and constituencies

Critical Thinking Question: The worker engages members in the beginning of the group. How do program activities support the engagement of group members?

Preparation is also required when workers use *program activities* to achieve group goals. *Program activities* include exercises, games, play, social events, sports, drawing, music, dance, sculpture, and many other nonverbal and verbal activities. They are designed to provide fun, interesting experiences for members while achieving particular therapeutic goals. The use of program activities has a long and important place in the history of group work. They continue to be very widely used especially in children and teen groups (see, for example, Crenshaw, Brooks, & Goldstein, 2015; Crenshaw & Stewart, 2015; Kaduson & Schaefer, 2015; Kastner & May, 2009; Webb, 2015).

Workers sometimes make the mistake of thinking that program activities, such as arts and crafts or preparing for a dance, are not appropriate group work activities because they are not focused solely on therapeutic verbal interactions. However, when carefully selected, program activities can be very therapeutic. Program activities provide a medium through which the functioning of members can be assessed in areas such as interpersonal skills, ability to perform daily living activities, motor coordination, attention span, and the ability to work cooperatively. Although they are often used in children and teen groups (Webb, 2015), program activities can be very useful in many types of groups. Miller (2012), for example, used therapeutic program activities effectively in addictions groups. In addition to achieving specific goals, such as improving skills in interpersonal functioning, leadership, problem solving, and activities of daily living, program activities help build group cohesion, prosocial group norms, and a group culture that fosters continued member participation. Program activities can also be used to make the group more attractive for its members. For example, in a children's group, the worker may place a program activity, such as charades, between group discussions to maintain members' interest.

Less structured, process-oriented groups also require preparation. This is illustrated in the following case example.

Case Example   Preparing for Group Meetings

A worker leading a self-esteem support group for residents of an adolescent treatment center prepared for the next meeting according to her assessment of the efficacy of the previous group meetings and the current functioning of each group member assessed during weekly treatment review meetings. The worker decided to focus the next meeting on helping members improve how they expressed anger. When preparing for the group, the worker gathered examples of how anger had been expressed in the past by residents of the treatment center. She used these examples to prepare role-play exercises designed to improve members' expression of anger. During the next meeting, some of the role plays were enacted. The worker modeled appropriate ways of expressing anger and helped members to practice the new methods. Then, she encouraged the group to discuss factors that facilitated and hindered the use of these methods in real-life situations. She concluded by asking members how the newly learned skills might affect their self-esteem and overall self-concept.

Choosing appropriate program activities requires a careful assessment of the needs of group members. Characteristics of members should be matched with the characteristics of potential program activities. Effective group workers use their knowledge of human behavior to make sure that program activities are developmentally appropriate. The level of ability, attention span, interests, and motivations should all be considered carefully as workers choose therapeutic program activities that are both fun and helpful for each member. One of the mistakes of novice group workers is to choose program activities that are too challenging, lack interest, or, in some other way, lead to the disengagement of group members.

To avoid problems, use field-tested and evidence-based program activities if they are available. Also, try out activities beforehand and get feedback about potential activities from the members of the group or people who are similar to the members of the group. When activities do not seem to be catching members' interest, workers should not press forward in an inflexible manner. Instead, they should take a deep breath, relax, and adjust program activities on the spot. It is also a good practice to have alternative program activities ready just in case carefully thought-out activities either do not go as planned or do not capture the imagination of members. Creativity, flexibility, good humor, and knowledge of the members' interests are essential. Group workers have to get to know the likes, dislikes, and special interests of the individuals with whom they are working. Modifications may be needed on the spot to ensure that all members are involved and enjoying program activities, and workers have to use their knowledge of members' interests in thoughtful, creative ways while always being open to adjusting or completely changing the originally planned activities if members are not engaged. Workers should avoid blaming group members for a lack of attention or engagement and instead reflect on what they can do to make the activity more attractive and engaging.

Because of the great number of possible program activities for children, adolescents, adults, and the elderly, workers should keep a resource file of catalogued activities to draw on as they are called on to work with different types of groups. Such a resource file can be an asset in selecting specific program activities during the life of a group.

Figure 9.1 presents a procedure for evaluating program activities for specific group needs. Selection should be made on the basis of (1) the objectives of the program activity; (2) the purposes and goals of the group; (3) the facilities, resources, and time available for the activity; (4) the characteristics of the group members; and (5) the characteristics of particular program activities.

The procedure suggested in Figure 9.1 can be used to help workers select program activities for any type of treatment group. For example, when choosing activities for an inpatient group whose purpose is to help prepare members for community living, the worker should consider activities that stimulate members' interests in the outside world. In addition to the group's purpose and the objectives of particular program activities, the worker should consider the other factors shown in Figure 9.1 as illustrated in the following case example.

Case Example   Using Program Activities

An inpatient group meets in an occupational therapy room equipped with kitchen facilities, tables, blackboards, arts and crafts, and toys. All members are more than 70 years old. They are recovering from mental health problems, and the purpose of the group is to prepare them for discharge. The members' interests include cooking, gardening, playing certain card games, and talking about their children and grandchildren. Between meetings, the worker reflects on the selection of a program activity that will stimulate members physically and socially while preparing them to live in the community. Using Figure 9.1 as a guide, the worker rules out activities, such as a discussion of current events, and, in consultation with members, decides on an activity of preparing a noontime meal to be shared by all. During the next meeting, the worker asks members if they would like to plan, cook, and eat a meal together.

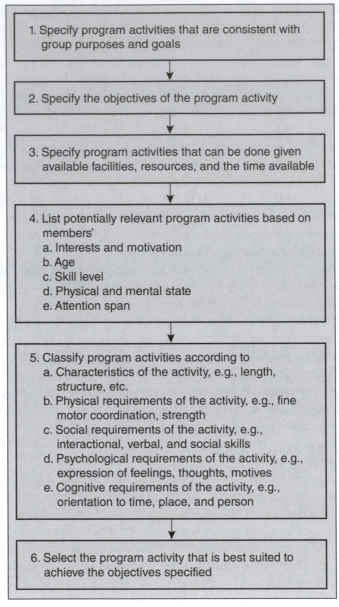

Figure 9.1
A Procedure for Selecting Program Activities

The members agree and the worker uses the remainder of the group to talk about what they would like to eat. The worker brings in the raw food the next day and, with the help of an occupational therapist, supervises their preparation of it. After eating, the worker asks members to share their feelings about preparing and eating the meal. To stimulate and organize the discussion, the worker asks the following questions: "Did the activity remind you of when you lived at home and cooked for your family?" How do you feel about living on your own again?" "What are your concerns about preparing meals when you leave here?" "Would you consider inviting your family or friends over for a meal?" The questions stimulated a therapeutic discussion that continued during the following day's meeting.

The therapeutic benefit of any program activity depends on how the activity is used by the worker. Activities provide little benefit if careful attention is not given to making sure they are directed toward therapeutic purposes. In the previous example, the program activity of preparing the meal stimulated the sensory awareness of members. During the activity, the worker encouraged social interaction. At the end of the meal, a discussion of the thoughts, feelings, and behaviors that members experienced during the activity was used to stimulate members' interests and desires to return to the community.

To prepare for meetings, workers should also review notes and ratings from previous meetings to make ongoing adjustments. Making effective use of feedback about the progress of a group is essential during the middle stage. The worker can use observations collected in summary recordings, for example, as the basis for determining that the interaction pattern of the previously described inpatient group should be changed to encourage participation from several members who have not been active in group discussions. In another case, a worker asked members to respond to a question about one thing they would change about the meeting of a single-parent support group. This question pointed out that members would welcome more information about adult educational opportunities in future meetings.

Preparation for the next group meeting may also include visualizing how the meeting should be conducted and, if necessary, rehearsing intervention procedures or techniques. This strategy is particularly important when a worker is using a new or unfamiliar procedure or exercise.

> **?** Assess your understanding of preparing for group meetings during the middle stage of group work by taking this brief quiz.

Structuring the Group's Work

Managed care and private health care insurance utilization reviews are giving greater impetus to the use of structured evidence-based approaches to group work (Boyd-Franklin, Cleek, Wofsy, & Mundy, 2013). Structure is especially essential in multicomponent group treatment programs, sometimes referred to as *psycho-educational* groups (Lefley, 2009; Walsh, 2010). The literature also increasingly points to the effectiveness of structured protocols and specific treatment modalities, such as group cognitive behavior therapy (GCBT) and behavioral activation (BA), for specific types of mental health problems, such as depression and anxiety (for a review, see Burlingame, Whitcomb, & Woodland, 2014). Cognitive behavioral and behavioral approaches have been used for many other problems ranging from hoarding (see, for example, Muroff, Underwood, & Steketee, 2014) to addictions treatment (Tuten, Jones, Schaeffer, & Stitzer, 2012; Wenzel, Liese, Beck, & Friedman-Wheeler, 2012). Other approaches, such as brief, structured, solution-focused therapy, are increasingly evidence-based (see, for example, Franklin, Trepper, Gingerich, & McCollum, 2012). The following case example describes one session of a psycho-educational group using a combination of cognitive behavioral and behavioral activation treatment approaches.

Case Example　A Psycho-educational Group for Depression

The third meeting of a psycho-educational group for persons with major depression began with a go-round check-in focused on an assignment from the previous meeting, which was to do one pleasurable thing each day. Members were asked what they did and were praised for their efforts. Members who were not able to complete the assignment were asked to describe briefly what obstacles they encountered. After the go-round, the worker presented a cognitive behavioral thought-monitoring workbook that enabled members to track particularly intrusive thoughts they have between meetings that lead to depressive feelings. Members were asked to monitor and write down in the workbook at least a few negative thoughts they have each day until the next meeting and also the immediate antecedents and consequences of each thought. Next, members were invited to select a partner and take 10 minutes to practice using the workbook. First, they were asked to reflect and write in silence, recalling a depressing thought they had earlier in the day, and then to discuss the thought, its antecedents, and the consequences with their partner. After the 10 minutes, members were asked to return to the whole group format and to briefly discuss their reactions to the exercise. After a coffee break, the leader asked members to talk more about the obstacles they encountered doing one pleasurable thing that was briefly mentioned during the check-in. She then facilitated a problem-solving discussion focused on ideas to overcome the particular obstacles that were described by two members of the group. The worker ended with a brief summary of the session, pointing out positive group dynamics, and reminded members to continue to do one pleasurable thing each day and write down a few thoughts in their workbooks. Members were also asked to write down what they liked most and least about the day's session. Subsequent sessions focused on other cognitive behavioral and behavioral activation strategies for depression, as well as preparing safety plans and discussing resources, such as suicide prevention hotlines, medication management, and relapse prevention.

In general, structure encourages the rapid learning of new responses. Therefore, one advantage of structured psycho-education and skills-building groups is that they provide an efficient means for members to learn new coping skills and educate themselves about the mental or physical problems they may be experiencing (Lefley, 2009; Walsh, 2010). There are now a wide variety of field-tested curricula, psycho-educational treatment manuals, evidence-based practices, and practice guidelines for many mental health problems experienced by children, youth, and adults. See, for example, LeCroy (2008) or the Treatment Improvement Protocols (TIP) available from the Substance Abuse and Mental Health Services Administration (SAMHSA) website. For example, TIP 41 contains in-service training for group therapy in substance abuse treatment (SAMHSA, 2012). One limitation of structured group approaches is that they often fail to individualize group treatment for each member. However, structured group approaches are becoming more sophisticated now, enabling workers to tailor interventions for individualized situations (see, for example, McKay, Gopalan, Franco, Dean-Assael, Chacko & Jackson, 2011).

Structured psycho-educational approaches can also be used to increase the knowledge and skills of family members of persons with problems. This is illustrated in the following case example.

Case Example   A Group for Caregivers of Persons with Alzheimer's Disease

The sixth group meeting of a psycho-educational support group for adult children caring for a parent with Alzheimer's began with a brief lecture and discussion about symptoms associated with the middle stage of the disease. This was followed by suggestions about effective communication strategies with people with cognitive and executive functioning impairments in that phase of the disease. Members were encouraged to talk about their own situations and the communication difficulties they were experiencing with their loved ones. After some role playing and practice, the leader invited members to talk about how they were dealing with agitation, apathy, and other common behavior problems that frequently occurred during the middle phase of Alzheimer's. After a coffee break, a couple of members took turns problem solving about the specific situations they were facing. In this particular group meeting, the problem-solving topics were how to deal with the difficult topic of stopping their loved one from driving and when to consider home care help or nursing home placement.

Despite the evidence for the effectiveness of structured short-term psycho-educational approaches to group work, some needs are clearly better served in long-term and less structured groups. For example, the popularity of self-help groups indicates that they provide important support through life transitions and life crises (Norcross, Campbell, Grohol, Santrock, Selagea, & Sommer, 2013; White & Madara, 2002). It may also be preferable to address some needs in groups that do not emphasize a time-limited structured format. For example, when members seek help in changing established personality characteristics, long-term rather than short-term group treatment approaches are often recommended (Rutan, Stone, & Shay, 2014; Seligman, 2014). During the middle stage of treatment groups, the worker can perform a variety of activities to structure the group's work. Some of these activities are listed here.

Structuring the Group's Work
- Inform members about beginning and ending the group on time.
- Give attention to apportioning time for ending meetings.
- Focus on and review goals.
- Establish and maintain orderly communication and interaction patterns.
- Attend to transitions between group activities.
- Focus on multilevel interventions: individual, group, and environmental.
- End with a review and evaluation.

One of the most basic activities is to let members know that each meeting will begin and end on time. Except for the first meeting, openings should not be delayed in anticipation of late members. Starting meetings late only reinforces members' future tardiness.

The worker should also structure the end of a meeting to summarize and conclude interactions. New concepts or activities should not be introduced near the end of a session. If a few minutes, remain the group can be ended early or the time used to discuss group dynamics or members, perceptions of how the group is progressing. Sometimes a group member will wait until the end of the meeting to disclose an important piece of information or to voice an important concern. Because these "doorknob" communications (Shulman, 2016) cannot be dealt with adequately in the short time remaining, the worker should ask the member to hold the new material until the next meeting. If the member's concerns cannot wait until the next group meeting, the worker may want to schedule an individual meeting.

Another important structuring activity is to ensure that members are working toward their goals. Experience from listening to hundreds of tape recordings of group sessions indicates that in the middle phase of treatment groups, even experienced group workers sometimes neglect to keep members attuned to and working on their individual goals. One way to accomplish this is to begin middle-session treatment groups with a brief review of the previous meeting, followed by a go-round when each member is asked to take a minute or two to mention the goal they are working on and their progress toward it. Although this sounds simple, many new and experienced group workers forget to check in with each member about their progress toward their goals during each meeting. When this happens, there is a perceived lack of commitment by leaders to encourage members to work toward goals. Instead of encouraging members and praising them for their efforts and accomplishments toward achieving what they have agreed to work on in the middle stage of the group, members are left feeling adrift or ignored. Focusing on goals each meeting empowers members to help each other to accomplish cherished goals and discuss frankly the challenges and obstacles they face when trying to change by overcoming obstacles to self-improvement.

The worker also can structure a group by establishing and maintaining orderly communication and interaction patterns. The structure of the interaction process should give all members an opportunity to participate. Some members, however, may receive more attention in one meeting and less in others. For example, in a remedial group in which members have individualized treatment contracts, the worker may decide to focus on one member at a time to help each one work on the personal treatment contract for an extended period. In other situations, such as an educational group, the worker may decide to present didactic material and then encourage all members to discuss the material. The worker may decide to structure the discussion so that each member is encouraged to participate, and no member is allowed to talk for longer than several minutes at one time. In either case, the worker will have made a planned effort to structure the group's use of communication and interaction patterns.

The worker structures a group's communication and interaction patterns by helping the group determine how much time should be spent on a particular issue or problem and by guiding members' participation in role plays, exercises, and other group activities. In these efforts, the worker balances the socio-emotional needs of individual members and the needs of the group as a whole to accomplish specific goals. The worker also should strive to foster members' initiative and leadership but should prevent the group from being dominated by a single individual or a subgroup. Sometimes workers are reluctant to assert themselves, for example, by guiding the group from a discussion of one issue to another or directing role plays or program activities. Workers should be aware, however, that group members expect them to provide guidance and leadership, particularly when the group is having trouble staying focused on its stated objectives. Workers are expected to use their professional knowledge and skills to guide members' progress toward the goals that have been set without dominating or suppressing members' initiatives. When the worker is unsure about whether the group needs more time to work on an issue or an exercise, he or she can ask members a direct question about their needs.

When guiding group activities, the worker should ensure that the transition from one activity to another is as smooth as possible. This can be done by summarizing what has been said, recommending how the group might pursue unresolved issues, and suggesting that the group move on to the remaining issues.

Focusing is another way to structure the work of a group. In any treatment group, the focus of an intervention, sometimes referred to as the level of an intervention, can be either the individual member, the group itself, or the group's external environment. The focus of the group should change with the changing needs of the group. An example taken from work with a group of men who assaulted their partners is presented in the following case.

Case Example   Focusing on Different Intervention Levels

A worker leading a group for men who abused their wives made an assessment that the group was failing to encourage members to express their feelings of anger, and this problem was inhibiting the group from achieving its goal of preventing further domestic violence. The worker decided to select the group as the target of an intervention designed to help members talk about their feelings. He had each member express two feelings about being a member of the group. Other exercises used in later group sessions helped members learn to identify their feelings of anger and to intervene before they escalated into violent outbursts. At the end of the first exercise, the group leader changed the focus of the group and concentrated on helping members work on individual treatment plans. In a subsequent group meeting, the leader again suggested a change in focus by asking group members if they would like to invite their partners to a meeting. The leader explained that this could help members appreciate the devastating effect that domestic violence had on their partners. By suggesting changes of focus, the leader helped the group to obtain new perspectives on problems and to tackle problems in multidimensional ways that add variety to the type of work that is done in the group.

For more information about groups for men who batter, see Black, Weisz, Mengo, and Lucero (2015); Corvo, Dutton, and Chen (2008); Fall and Howard (2012); Hamberger, Lohr, Parker, and Witte, (2009); Mills, Barocas, and Ariel (2013); Nason-Clark and Fisher-Townsend, (2015); Gondolf, (2011); Herman, Rtunda, Williamson and Vodanovich (2014); and Saunders (2008).

Another element of structure is to end groups with a brief summary of what occurred. The summary should include a brief review of the highlights and salient aspects of the group's discussion, concentrating on accomplishments and tasks still needing to be addressed. There should also be some attention given to perceptions of the group process, highlighting growth in group interaction, cohesion, and prosocial norms, roles, and other integration dynamics. The end can also be used to ask a few simple evaluation questions, such as an overall rating of the meeting on a 10-point scale, what was liked most and least, and suggestions for the future.

Degree of Structure

Reviews of the effectiveness of group interventions (Barlow, 2010, 2013; Burlingame, Strauss, & Joyce, 2013; Burlingame, Whitcomb, & Woodland, 2014) indicate that both structure and process are critical for effective group work. Therefore, a strong therapeutic alliance between the group worker and members, and a high level of group cohesion, are as important as the use of evidence-based structured protocols, such as group cognitive behavior therapy, in achieving effective outcomes in groups (Burlingame, Whitcomb, & Woodland, 2014). In her review of the group work literature, Barlow (2010, 2013) describes how important it is for group workers to be able to use a continuum of structure that matches the needs of members. Although some early structure is almost always helpful in reducing tension and providing some guidance and direction for members (Barlow, 2010, 2013), the degree of structure during the middle phase depends on many factors.

Research-Informed Practice

Behavior: Use and translate research evidence to inform and improve practice, policy, and service delivery

Critical Thinking Question: Groups can be structured or unstructured. What are some positive effects of a high degree of structure in the group?

Early group structure has a variety of beneficial effects on group processes and outcomes, such as reducing members' fears and anxieties, promoting members' involvement and self-disclosure, and increasing group cohesion and positive feelings about the group. As the group develops cohesion and social integration mechanisms, the need for structure to reduce members' initial anxiety wanes, and the worker has to decide how much structure is needed for the group to be as effective and efficient as possible.

Some factors that should be considered by workers are the capacity of members for independent functioning, the nature and severity of their problems, motivation levels, and homogeneity of concerns. Members who are highly motivated, functioning well, and sharing similar problems or concerns often can function effectively in less structured groups with higher levels of member-to-member interaction and more self-help than members who do not have these characteristics. For example, group leaders often have to be more active and use more structure in groups in inpatient mental health settings than in family caregiver support groups. Yet, in both types of groups, forming a strong therapeutic alliance and a cohesive group atmosphere is important for achieving therapeutic goals. Therefore, effective group workers have to pay attention both to the optimum degree of structure for the group as well as the process variables that lead to high levels of cohesion and strong therapeutic alliances.

Considerable controversy exists about just how *much* structure is useful for treatment groups. It has been argued, for example, that substantial structure may not be beneficial because it prevents members from exercising their own initiative (Glassman & Kates, 1990). Too much structure may decrease members' commitment to the group because they may feel structure has been imposed on them rather than selected by them to help them achieve their own goals (Saleebey, 2013; Shulman, 2016). Although much available evidence indicates that groups using structured, evidence-based protocols and treatment guidelines are effective for an increasingly wide range of mental health and other problems (see, for example, Burlingame, Strauss, & Joyce, 2013; Lefley, 2009; Walsh, 2010), the importance of cohesion and the therapeutic alliance in groups that are less structured has also been emphasized (see, for example, Barlow, 2010, 2013; Burlingame, 2010; Burlingame, Whitcomb, & Woodland, 2014).

Less structured, longer-term interventions may be more appropriate than highly structured interventions for some problems. For example, short-term, highly structured approaches may not be best for clients who are mandated to attend group treatment. These clients take time to develop relationships and to build trust in workers' efforts to help them. This may be especially true in groups for people with alcohol and substance abuse problems (Bowen, Chawla, & Marlett, 2011; Substance Abuse and Mental Health Services Administration, 2012; Wenzel, Liese, Beck, & Friedman-Wheeler, 2012), and for those who have experienced childhood and adult trauma (Courtois & Ford, 2013a, b). On the other hand, clients who are in crisis may need immediate short-term help and less time to build relationships with the worker and other members and therefore can profit from short-term treatment (Akinsulure-Smith, 2009; Yeager & Roberts, 2015).

The nature of clients' problems and needs should be carefully considered when deciding how to structure a group. Group work with antisocial adolescents, clients in residential treatment centers, severely impaired psychiatric patients, and street gangs often occurs in long-term groups. These groups focus on specific, narrowly defined concerns and objectives only in the context of broader, long-term objectives and goals.

For example, a short-term goal for a group of children in a residential treatment center might be for the patients to learn specific social skills. This goal may be accomplished in a short-term social skills group. However, the long-term goal for each member—to live independently in the community—may best be accomplished through a comprehensive treatment program that includes a series of short-term groups focused on specific skills and a long-term group integrating what is learned in the brief, focused groups.

Although it is important to plan meetings carefully, a worker must also recognize that at times it may be desirable or even necessary to abandon the agenda temporarily. Interpersonal interactions provide many opportunities for workers and members to achieve group goals. For example, it is better to use spontaneous opportunities during group interaction to teach appropriate assertiveness skills than to teach concepts in a structured module that does not draw on actual group experiences. Similarly, it may also be necessary to temporarily abandon the group agenda when a member is in crisis or an important point is raised by one or more members that should be addressed immediately. The "art" of effective group leadership is to identify opportunities to use group processes and content to help the group and its members achieve agreed-on goals. Agendas and structure are tools to help groups function effectively, but they should not be adhered to rigidly. Effective workers use their judgment, their clinical experience, and their knowledge of human behavior to intervene at appropriate times during group meetings to help the group and its members to achieve goals.

> **Case Example**   A Group of Parents of Children with Down Syndrome
>
> In forming a group for parents of children with Down's syndrome, the worker decided to use a semi-structured approach to group meetings. A portion of each meeting was devoted to an educational topic related to some aspect of Down's syndrome, such as variations in developmental delays; physical, occupational, and speech therapy; resources that might prove helpful; and helping parents and their children deal with other's reactions to Down's syndrome. After the brief educational portion of the group, plenty of time was left for parents to share and discuss their mutual concerns and their diverse efforts at being effective parents and advocates for their disabled children. In this way, a structured educational portion of the group meeting was combined with an unstructured portion.

> **?**   Assess your understanding of structuring the group's work during the middle stage of group work by taking this brief quiz.

Involving and Empowering Group Members

Another important activity in the work stage of treatment groups is to help members become fully involved in the work of the group. The ultimate goal of this process is to empower members so they can take charge of their lives both inside and outside the group. Workers who are insecure about their position often make the mistake of being overly directive. Instead of doing their utmost to help members take as much responsibility as they are able to for the direction of the group, insecure workers often think they have to be in control at all times. This view is often counterproductive and leads members to become rebellious or passive-aggressive.

An important first step in the process of involving and empowering group members is for workers to show their belief in members' strengths. Statements that express confidence in members' motivation and tenacity, point out their abilities, and describe their previous accomplishments help to foster therapeutic alliances and members' resolve to accomplish particular goals. Although strengths-based (Rapp & Goscha, 2012; Saleebey, 2013) and solution-focused (Cooley, 2009; Franklin, Trepper, Gingerich, & McCollum, 2012; Greene & Lee, 2011) approaches to group work practice are most frequently associated with involving and empowering group members, group workers often use these strategies in conjunction with other approaches, such as behavioral, cognitive behavioral, and interpersonal/psychodynamic.

Expressing belief in members' strengths does not mean that the worker should be unrealistic and ignore impediments to goal achievement. Thus, a second step in the process of empowering group members is to acknowledge the difficulties and obstacles they encounter as they attempt to reach particular goals and objectives and their efforts to overcome them. Statements such as "Ann, I really admire that you're not giving up—that you continue to confront this difficult issue with your daughter" or "Expressing yourself about this painful issue really shows your courage, Charlie" affirm and validate members' efforts to take charge of their own lives, even when the work is difficult.

A third way to empower group members is to help them know that they have a stake in the content and direction of the group. Statements such as "This is your group. What do you want to see happen in it?" help members overcome a tendency to expect the worker to take full responsibility for group content and process.

A fourth step to encourage involvement and empowerment is to praise members for reaching out to help each other. Statements such as "I really liked the way you shared how you felt about Ann's situation" or "This group is really making progress—it's wonderful to see how supportive you are of each other" demonstrate support of members' self-help efforts and foster the continued development of cohesion in the group as a whole.

Another way to empower group members is to encourage them to try out new behaviors and actions both within and outside the group. Members should be encouraged to begin by taking small action steps and carefully observing the results. Members can then report the results of their efforts to the group. They should be encouraged to acknowledge each other's accomplishments and to support each other when obstacles are encountered. Program activities can also be used to involve and empower group members. Activities should involve as many members as possible, and members should be encouraged to take leadership roles and support each other's efforts.

Involving and empowering members does not mean that the worker stops providing guidance and direction. However, when guiding the group interaction, workers should solicit members' input and feedback, as the following case example illustrates.

Case Example A Group Teaching Cognitive Behavioral Techniques
to Combat Depression

In a cognitive behavioral group for people experiencing depression, the group worker described the way members' internal dialogue sometimes led to increased depression. The worker mentioned such things as catastrophic thinking, either-or dichotomous thinking, and self-talk that inhibits positive thinking. One member of the group spoke up and said that she was not sure what the worker meant or how this contributed to her depression. The worker solicited feedback from other members of the group, some of whom seemed to understand the point the worker was trying to make but others who did not. The worker then said to the first member who spoke up that she was glad that the member had mentioned that she was unclear about what was being said and that maybe they were moving a bit too fast. The worker then went back and talked about inner dialogues, getting members to volunteer about what they say to themselves when they are in situations they are not feeling good about. The worker then used some of these internal dialogues to point out examples of catastrophic thinking, either-or dichotomous thinking, and other self-statements that added to members' feelings of depression.

Helping Members Achieve Goals

During the middle stage of the group, it is important for workers to concentrate on helping members achieve the goals they have agreed to accomplish. Contracting for treatment goals is an evolving process. A tentative agreement or contract is usually discussed while interviewing potential members during the planning stage of a group. The contract is reaffirmed and made more concrete and specific during the beginning stage of the group as members interact with one another for the first time. Although much of a treatment group's work during the middle stage is devoted to carrying out contracts developed during the beginning stage of the group, contracts continue to evolve as the group progresses during the middle stage.

Case Example Using Contracts to Achieve Goals

A member of a group for recently separated people contracted to reduce her angry feelings by taking deep breaths to avoid verbally abusive outbursts toward her former spouse when he picks up their children. A secondary contract was made to have the member discuss her feelings of anger with another member between meetings. The member reported back to the group on her discussion with the member during the next meeting. She also described the helpfulness of the deep breathing technique.

A variety of different primary and secondary contracts could be used to help the member in the above case example achieve the goals specified in her primary contract. Thus, primary and secondary contracts evolve as group members progress toward their treatment goals during the middle stage of the group.

Although a portion of a treatment group's work should be devoted to maintaining a group's optimal functioning, most of an effective group's time during the middle stage should be focused on helping members achieve their goals. This can be accomplished by helping members (1) maintain their awareness of their goals, (2) develop specific treatment plans, (3) overcome obstacles to members' work on treatment plans, and (4) carry out treatment plans.

Awareness of Goals

The first step in helping members achieve their goals is to maintain their awareness of the goals they identified and agreed to work on in earlier group meetings. It is a good practice to begin each meeting with a very brief review of what occurred during the previous meeting and then to review the goals that each member is working toward achieving. A brief go-round or check-in serves to keep members focused on their goals and lets members know that there is an expectation that they should be working toward specific goals. It also gives members a chance to talk about their accomplishments or any obstacles that they encountered that they might like to work on during the meeting.

Workers should not assume that members continue to be aware of these goals as the group progresses. Reconfirming members' commitment to the goals they decided to achieve in earlier meetings serves several purposes. It lets members know the worker remains interested in their progress. It checks for a continued mutual understanding of the contract. It helps ensure that the worker and members remain focused on the same issues. Confirming goals helps avoid confusion and promotes members' organized and systematic efforts to work on contracts.

Periodically confirming goals also gives the worker an opportunity to check whether any changes need to be made in the contract, and it gives members a chance to share their feelings and thoughts about what has been accomplished and what remains to be done. For example, the contract for a group of parents waiting to adopt children might include attending group meetings on (1) child development, (2) legal proceedings for adoption, (3) special issues and concerns of adopted children, and (4) supportive resources and services available for adoptive parents and their children. During each meeting the worker might ask members whether the content of the meeting was useful. Members can be given the opportunity to express their reactions to what has occurred and to make suggestions for improving future meetings or continuing the meetings as originally planned.

Maintaining members' awareness of and commitment to contract goals is essential in treatment groups that focus their work on individual contracts. At times, the worker may spend a considerable amount of time helping one member work toward a particular goal. For example, in a group for alcoholics, the worker might spend 30 minutes working with one member in relation to a secondary contract to help the member improve his methods of expressing anger. As a result, during the two-hour group meeting, only three or four members may have an opportunity to work intensively on their treatment goals. When this occurs, it is particularly important to generalize work with an individual to other members so that everyone feels involved in the group as the following case illustrates.

Case Example   An Anger Management Group

One member, John, just spent some time talking about his struggles with anger. He said that he finds it useful to take a time-out when he feels anger overwhelming him, taking a walk around the block or just getting out of the room for a few minutes. The leader asked to hear from others about this. He asked others to talk about their struggles with keeping their anger under control. How do they deal with anger? Several members spoke up, and the leader made connections between the similarities and differences in the ways members coped. For example, one member said that he took several deep breaths and told himself not to respond; another member said he also tried to get out of the situation but found it difficult to get away because his wife would pursue him into another room. Other members had experienced similar problems with trying to take a time-out when a situation was getting explosive, and this led to a productive discussion about making some rules ahead of time with spouses or others about getting them to back off and allow for space during confrontations. One member mentioned that he had tried this but that his spouse said that they then never got back to talking about the situation that led to the anger. The worker asked if this came up for other members, and one member said that he made an agreement with his wife that he would come back and talk about the situation without prompting after he had calmed down, but that it might not happen for a couple of hours or even until the next day. He said that when his wife realized that he would follow through and talk about the situation after he calmed down, their heated arguments had decreased substantially.

If extensive time is spent with only a few members during one meeting, the worker should spend a brief period of time checking on other members' progress. Members who did not have an extensive opportunity to participate in a meeting should be encouraged to participate more during the next meeting. This strategy helps prevent repeated and prolonged attention to a few members and reduces the possibility that some members will avoid working on their contracts.

During the middle stage, the worker should also help members to develop a process for reviewing their treatment goals and contracts. Although the review process may be idiosyncratic to the needs of a particular group, the worker should avoid haphazard or constantly changing review procedures. Without a clearly defined process that all members can expect, there is the danger that some members' progress will be carefully monitored but that of others will not. When monitoring is haphazard, members who are assertive and highly involved are more likely to be monitored, but members who are less assertive and those who are resistant will not receive the attention they require. That is why the brief go-round during the beginning of a meeting mentioned earlier in this section is an excellent way to start middle-stage meetings. It gives all members, in turn, a few minutes to describe their goals, what they accomplished since the last meeting, and what they plan to accomplish before the next meeting. In this way, systematic monitoring of goal progress is accomplished regularly throughout the middle stage of the group.

An important caution for beginning group workers using check-ins and go-rounds to assess progress toward goals is to make sure that each member only takes a minute or two to mention their goal and a recent accomplishment or obstacle. Otherwise the process can become cumbersome and take up the whole meeting. At the beginning of middle-stage group meetings, workers can mention time limits for the check-in and ask members who need more time to self-identify during the go-round. After the check-in, any members wanting more time can become the focus of the group.

Without systematic monitoring procedures, tasks that are to be completed between meetings might not receive proper follow-up. There is nothing more frustrating and disconcerting for members than to complete a task between meetings and then not be given the opportunity to report the results during the next meeting. In addition to creating an ambiguous demand for work, failure to follow up on tasks often gives members the impression that the worker is disorganized and that there is little continuity from one meeting to the next.

Once a systematic procedure for monitoring is established, it becomes normative for members to report their progress to the group. The expectation of weekly progress reports helps maintain members' motivation to work toward contract goals between sessions and reduces the need to remind members of their contract agreements. It also helps members gain a sense of independence and accomplishment as they assume responsibility for reporting their own progress.

Developing Treatment Plans

A second way to help members achieve contract goals is by facilitating the development of specific, goal-oriented treatment plans. When all members are working on the same contract goal, the

Assessment

Behavior: Develop mutually agreed-on intervention goals and objectives based on the critical assessment of strengths, needs, and challenges within clients and constituencies

Critical Thinking Question: Social workers develop treatment plans when working with individuals. How do group workers develop treatment plans with members of treatment groups?

worker develops and implements plans with the group as a whole. For example, in a weight-loss group, a medical social worker might help members prepare a method for monitoring their daily caloric intake, present material on good nutrition, and introduce methods for modifying eating habits. The worker might then help individual members discuss their special needs and help them modify what has been presented to fit their specific circumstances.

When helping a member develop and implement an individual treatment plan, the worker should enlist the support of all group members, as illustrated in the following case example.

Case Example   Developing a Treatment Plan

In an outpatient psychotherapy group, information gathered by a member who experienced depression suggested that negative, self-deprecating thoughts and self-statements were maintaining her depression. The negative thoughts and self-statements persisted despite the member's adequate performance in job- and family-related responsibilities. As a result of this information, the worker helped the member develop a treatment plan that would assist her to replace negative thoughts and self-deprecating comments with realistic thoughts and self-statements about her abilities, accomplishments, and positive qualities. The member contracted with the group to make a list of positive self-statements to be repeated each time an obtrusive, negative self-statement occurred. Secondary contracts included having the member ask other group members to describe how they perceived her during the interactions of the group, having the member get positive feedback from other significant persons in her life, making a gratitude list to hang on her refrigerator, and engaging in one pleasurable activity each day.

The worker should use every available opportunity to make connections among members, to point out parallel issues and concerns among members' situations, and to encourage all members to participate. As members become involved as helpers, the group's cohesion increases, and members feel satisfied that they have something to contribute. Known as the *helper-therapy principle* (Riessman, 1965), this strategy works in such a way that members who help others often benefit as much as those who are helped.

Before deciding on a treatment plan, the worker helps members explore and gather facts about their situations. A guided group discussion on the specifics of a situation, the alternatives that have been tried, and the possibilities that have not been explored is often sufficient to help members develop intervention plans. Sometimes, however, members try to grab at potential solutions without exploring alternatives, particularly when members are experiencing a great deal of stress or psychic pain from their problems. The worker should encourage members to explore alternatives thoroughly before deciding on an action plan.

An exploration of the situation may reveal a need for additional information. The member, with or without the help of the worker, might be asked to spend time between sessions gathering data. The process of members monitoring their own behavior and gathering additional facts about their situation is essential to the development of effective treatment plans.

Sometimes exploration of the problem may not immediately lead to a clear plan of action. The worker should help members consider alternatives before deciding on a final plan of action. Because of their professional training and knowledge, workers are often the primary generators of alternative intervention plans. Although the intervention plan that is selected may have been originally generated by the worker or another group member, members should be encouraged to refine alternatives and select the most appropriate plans for their own needs. When this occurs, they will not experience a plan as imposed by someone else. Members who experience their action plans as self-selected are more likely to follow through on them. A treatment plan can be quite complex. It may involve a sequence of actions suggested by different members of the group. These different sequences of actions occur simultaneously. As the following case example illustrates, a complex plan should be divided into a series of discrete steps that are defined as clearly and specifically as possible.

Case Example   A Complex Treatment Plan For Passivity and Explosive Anger

To become more assertive, a member who struggles with being passive for long periods and then occasionally explodes in angry outbursts might (1) clarify the difference between aggressiveness and assertiveness through group discussion and reading a book on assertiveness, (2) decide in what situations to become more assertive, (3) practice being more assertive in the group during role plays and group discussion, (4) practice being assertive outside the group with family members or a friend, and (5) practice being assertive in a real-life situation. After the member completes these steps, she may also be helped to develop a plan to control her explosive outbursts. This might include (1) identifying cognitive schema or long-held views about herself and others that might lead to the holding on to and building up of anger, (2) exploring coping skills learned in her family of origin that might mitigate against expressions of anger or that have modeled explosive expressions of anger, (3) identifying triggering events, (4) learning how others in the group cope with and manage anger, (5) reading about anger management strategies in a self-help book recommended by the leader, (6) keeping a feeling log or journal and sharing entries with the group, (7) asking for feedback from the group about these entries and her interpersonal behavior in the group, (8) describing anger management strategies used between meetings, (9) practicing anger management strategies in the group, and (10) deciding to attend an anger management workshop offered by a family service agency.

Ideally, each step of the treatment plan should specify (1) who, (2) does what, (3) when, (4) where, (5) how often, and (6) under what conditions. It is especially important to be clear and specific when there are several people responsible for different aspects of a comprehensive treatment plan. Treatment plans often require the involvement of the worker, the client, other agency personnel, and the client's family. The effective worker should make sure that all persons who are a part of the treatment plan are clear about their roles, their responsibilities, and their expected contributions.

In some groups, all work is completed during meetings, but it is often helpful to encourage members to complete tasks between meetings. Many different types of tasks can be developed to help accomplish treatment plans between meetings. There are (1) observational and monitoring tasks to gather information and to increase awareness of behaviors, emotions, or beliefs; (2) experiential tasks to arouse emotion and to challenge beliefs or attitudes; (3) incremental change tasks to stimulate change step by step; (4) mental or cognitive tasks to help group members change cognition and belief systems; and (5) paradoxical or two-sided tasks that result in changes no matter how they are carried out. For example, the treatment plan of a nonassertive group member includes the paradoxical task of having the member assert her right in a situation in which she would normally remain passive. If the member does the task, she is learning to be more assertive. If she does not do it, she is showing that she can assert herself in reference to her treatment plan.

Tasks can also be individual, reciprocal, or shared.. For example, an individual task for a member in a smoking-cessation group may be to keep a log of the number of cigarettes smoked each day. Workers may also agree to perform individual tasks. A worker in a rural county welfare agency, for example, might agree to find out whether there are any transportation services available to enable teenage parents to attend a parenting skills group. In a reciprocal task, if one person does something, another person will also do something. For example, if a member of an adolescent group does his assigned chore in his community residence each day for one week, the worker will help the member obtain a pass to see his parents the next weekend. A third type of task is shared by two or more people. For example, members of the group may form "buddy" systems or consulting pairs in which members are expected to remind each other to work on a specific task between group meetings.

When developing treatment plans and specific tasks, the worker should proceed by making sure that members are able to carry out each step successfully. It is especially important for members to have a successful experience in carrying out the first task they agree to accomplish. If they are successful with their first task, they are much more likely to successfully complete a second task.

Successfully completing an initial task gives members a sense that their goals are reachable. It also helps build self-confidence, feelings of self-efficacy, and a sense of control and mastery over the problem the member is attempting to alleviate. As members begin to feel self-confident, they are more likely to persist in their attempts at solving problems and concerns and are therefore more likely to be successful than when feelings of inadequacy limit their attempts to solve problems (Bandura, 1977). In this way, feelings of self-efficacy are reinforced and enhanced, which in turn can result in empowerment and more effective and persistent problem solving in the future (Greene & Lee, 2011; Rapp & Goscha, 2012; Saleebey, 2013).

The worker should assess a member's competencies and work with the member to plan an initial task that can be accomplished without an extraordinary amount of effort. Beginning group workers sometimes develop treatment plans that are unrealistic. Members may agree to a treatment plan to please a worker or another group member, only to find that they are not prepared to undertake the tasks contained in the plan. It is also helpful to ensure that tasks are paced appropriately so that they become progressively more difficult as the member gains confidence and skill.

Case Example   A Parenting Group Task

In a parenting group, members were asked to develop charts to reward their children for socially appropriate behaviors. The worker passed out cardboard paper, and each member made a chart following an example the worker presented. Members were asked to choose problems that they wanted to work on with their children. For example, one member chose the socially inappropriate behavior of "grabbing for a toy from his older brother." The parent then suggested that a socially appropriate behavior would be "using words to ask his brother for the toy." After each parent mentioned a behavior, the worker handed out gold stars. The worker mentioned that the parents, or their children, could put the stars on their charts to signify that their children had behaved appropriately. They were asked to use the charts at home during the following week to see if they would help to increase their children's socially appropriate behaviors. The parents talked about whether they should give their children prizes when they received a certain number of gold stars. They decided to give their children healthy snacks after getting two gold stars.

The worker can intervene to reduce the possibility that a member might have considerable difficulty in completing a task. Simulations, role plays, and other exercises can be performed in the group before the member tries the task at home, in the community, or in any other less hospitable environment. Members can be prepared for unreceptive or hostile environments by simulating these conditions during role plays in the group. One of the advantages of group treatment is that members can practice with other members of the group before they attempt to perform a task in the natural environment. Acting out roles also helps members become more aware of their own roles in a situation. An entire treatment method known as *psychodrama* is based on the benefits of acting out life experiences with others (Blatner, 1996).

Members should be encouraged to tackle one task at a time. In treatment planning, it is surprising to find how many clients with multiple problems suggest working on several different problems and their resulting tasks simultaneously. Although members often have good intentions in the group session, when they return home they may have less motivation to follow through on the multiple tasks they have agreed to accomplish. It is better to start with one carefully planned task than to encourage a member to work on a variety of tasks simultaneously. When members complete the initial task, they can take on another one.

At the end of a session, the worker should ask members to review the tasks that were agreed on during the session. It is not uncommon for members or the worker to forget tasks that were agreed to earlier in the midst of an active and interesting group session. A review can eliminate confusion, misconceptions, or discrepancies about specific tasks. This process ensures that everyone who has agreed to do some task leaves the group with a clear notion of what is to be done before the next meeting. A recording form, such as that shown in Figure 9.2, can be used to help the worker and the group members keep track of the tasks they have agreed to complete.

Overcoming Obstacles to Members' Work

It is important to help members work on their treatment goals when they encounter obstacles. Members need help to work on their goals because making changes in habituated behavior patterns can be difficult. For example, a member of a therapy group for substance abusers who contracted to stop drinking alcohol began drinking again after only two days of abstinence. In a different group, a member who contracted to become independent of her parents made excuses in subsequent meetings about why she has not had time to explore alternative living arrangements.

In both cases, members encountered obstacles to achieving their goals. To address this, the worker should begin by checking with the members to find out whether they

Date: _____

Session #: _____

Group: _____

Member's Name	Task	When	Where	How Often	Under What Circumstances

Figure 9.2
A Group Task Recording Form

acknowledge encountering obstacles. The worker should encourage the members to describe their feelings and thoughts about completing the tasks. Encouraging members to ventilate their feelings and listening carefully to what they have to say are strategies drawn from motivational interviewing (Hohman, 2013; Miller & Rollnick, 2013; Wagner & Ingersoll, 2013). Once members have done this, the worker can help them to examine both the positive and negative aspects of completing tasks and to make decisions that are consistent with their aspirations and goals for themselves. If there are discrepancies in what members say they want, and their actual behavior, workers can point these out and use them to help motivate members to make desired changes. Motivational interviewing has been used in group work to help members overcome obstacles when tackling many types of problems (see, for example, Wagner & Ingersoll, 2013).

Assuming the members remain motivated to work on a task, Shulman (2016) suggests that workers should make a clear and specific "demand for work." The initial demand for work is a gentle reminder to members that the worker and the other group members are interested in helping them achieve their personal goals. The demand for work should be accompanied by an offer to help the member overcome any obstacles to goal achievement.

With the members' agreement, workers can then encourage stuck members to explore what has been happening to prevent or block work on a particular treatment goal. Workers can also involve the group as a whole by having members participate in the analysis of the factors that may be inhibiting a particular member's goal achievement. This technique can help the member who is having difficulty following through on a treatment contract, and others who may be encountering ambivalence or resistance as they engage in their own change efforts.

Obstacles interfering with members' abilities to work toward treatment goals may be the result of an inappropriate contract. A careful analysis of the contract may indicate that it was poorly designed and should be renegotiated. A contract can be inappropriate for several reasons.

Problems with Contracts
- Goals in the contract are vaguely defined or too global to be achieved.
- Goals are too difficult to achieve at the current stage of treatment.
- The worker and the member focused on long-term goals rather than on more immediate, short-term goals that have a higher probability of being accomplished in a shorter period of time.
- There is a misunderstanding between the member and the worker about the nature of specific contract goals.
- Inappropriate goals were set without careful assessment of the member's situation.
- Changing problems and situations necessitate modifications in the treatment goals developed for a contract made earlier in the group's development.

For all these reasons, helping members work toward treatment goals often means helping them clarify, redefine, or renegotiate contracts.

Working toward goals also involves increasing members' motivation to take action to overcome the obstacles they have encountered. If a member agrees that action is important, the worker's task is to help the member believe that change is possible. Many group members are willing to act but refuse to do so because they do not believe in their own ability to change their situation. In such cases, self-instructional training (Beck, 2011; Ellis & Joffe-Ellis, 2011), described in Chapter 10, may be useful in increasing a member's willingness to attempt a new behavior. It can also be helpful to ask other members to share their experiences regarding behavior change. They often serve as convincing role models who inspire and motivate reluctant members.

When the lack of motivation is severe, the worker should consider renegotiating a contract, focusing the new contract on helping the member increase motivation to work on a specific issue or concern rather than to work on the concern itself. Such a contract may involve helping the member examine factors that affect motivation to work on a particular goal and to examine any potential consequences of not working toward the goal (Rooney, 2009; Trotter, 2015).

When helping members overcome obstacles, workers should not ask "why" questions. Group members often do not have the answers to "why" questions, and, if they do, the explanation may attribute causes to incorrect sources, which further complicates the problem. Instead, the worker should ask members "how" or "what" questions that encourage members to describe cognitive, affective, behavioral, or environmental circumstances that may be diminishing their ability to work on treatment goals.

"How" questions and "what" questions keep members focused on current behaviors that lead to or exacerbate existing problems. For example, the worker might ask: "What occurred just before you became angry?" or "How did you feel when _____ happened?" Such questions tend to elicit actual behavior and events, but "why" questions, if they can be answered at all, tend to elicit the opinion or judgments of members on the basis of their interpretations of the information. Thus, "how" questions are more likely than are "why" questions to elicit information that will help members make active behavior changes and achieve their treatment goals.

The final step is to help members decide what actions to take to overcome obstacles and renew their progress toward treatment goals. In making the plan, the worker helps members to get support for their efforts from as many sources as possible. This is demonstrated in the following case example.

Case Example   Overcoming Obstacles to Members' Work

In an alcoholism treatment group, the worker asked a member who had relapsed to go around the group and promise the other group members that he would not drink until the next group meeting. Members were encouraged to support the member, who emphasized that slips might occur for any member and that temporary relapses should not be viewed as insurmountable relapses. By making replies such as: "I admire your determination to work on this problem," group members' responses to the member displayed their support and empathy. Group members also helped by suggesting that the member think of cognitive self-statements that would support his sobriety and by suggesting strategies for home environment modification, such as removing all remaining alcohol from his house—a suggestion that the member had resisted before the relapse. The worker asked several members to give the member a call during the week to help him follow through on his verbal commitment. To enlist the help of his family and friends, the worker asked the member for permission to contact family and friends to gain their support and encouragement for the member's decision not to drink. To provide continued support during evening hours, the member was referred to an Alcoholics Anonymous group. In this way, the member received support from a variety of sources within and outside the group.

In summary, helping members work toward treatment goals is an important activity for any worker who plans to lead effective treatment groups. All treatment groups require effort from members if they are to be successful in achieving their goals. The worker's task is to help members mobilize their resources and maximize their use of the group to help them accomplish their goals. The worker should be constantly vigilant and point out inertia, ambivalence, and other psychological, social, and environmental barriers that block members' progress in the group. Because inertia, ambivalence, and reluctance to change are common, even among highly motivated clients, the strategies and techniques on working with reluctant and resistant group members, presented later in this chapter, may also be useful in helping members to work on their treatment plans.

Helping Members Carry Out Treatment Plans

Workers can use five intervention roles to help members carry out their treatment plans. These roles are (1) enabler, (2) broker, (3) mediator, (4) advocate, and (5) educator. Although other roles have been identified as appropriate for helping members carry out their treatment plans, these five roles are the most important and most frequently assumed by workers leading various types of treatment groups. These roles are summarized in the following list.

Treatment Plan Intervention Roles

- *Enabler:* Helps members utilize their own resources and strengths; encourages members to share their thoughts with the group; supports a culture of mutual aid among members
- *Broker:* Identifies community resources that may help members carry out their treatment plans; connects members with these resources
- *Mediator:* Resolves disputes, conflicts, or opposing views within the group or between a member and some other person or organization; takes a neutral stand and helps members arrive at a settlement or agreement that is mutually acceptable
- *Advocate:* Represents members' interests and needs; helps members obtain services and resources
- *Educator:* Presents new information to help resolve members' concerns; demonstrates and models new behaviors; leads role plays, simulations, and *in vivo* activities to help members practice new or different ways of behaving in problematic situations

Handling Crisis Situations

Whenever possible, all therapeutic issues should be handled during group meetings. However, in crisis situations, such as when members threaten to harm themselves or others, group workers may need to spend time outside of the group meeting helping the member with the crisis. After the situation has abated or been resolved, the worker should try to connect with any members who were in crisis to ascertain their plans for returning to the group. Before returning, workers should help members who have left the group because of a crisis or another reason to decide what can be said comfortably to all the other members about the situation. In this way, members are not left wondering about any member's well-being, and members who had crises or other unplanned absences can control the nature of the information that is shared. For additional information about crisis intervention see Yeager and Roberts (2015).

Using Empirically Based Treatment Methods in Therapy Groups

The skills we teach in this book are based on empirical findings in the literature. Our aim is to cover a wide array of skills needed to lead treatment groups of all types. In Chapter 10, we present some specialized skills for leading therapy groups. Whenever they are available, using empirically based treatment methods is the best way to lead therapy groups during their middle phase. There are many researchers and clinicians working on the best ways to treat members with specialized problems, such as sexual abuse, suicide, and depression. The practicing group worker working with therapy groups for people with specialized problems should try to get to know as many of the evidence-based treatment programs and guidelines as possible. In Chapter 10, we present a variety of therapeutic techniques that are broad enough to be used with members who have a variety of different problems. However, it is still important for the practicing group worker to look at the literature to see if a specialized treatment program for a particular problem has been developed.

There are always specialized problems that workers encounter in their practice. When workers encounter people with mental health problems or other problems they are unfamiliar with, finding an empirically tested program for the specific problem can often be done by maintaining access to search engines on the Internet that can identify literature on specific treatment problems. Macgowan (2008) provides a wide variety of resources that can be used to identify empirically based approaches to particular social group work practice problems.

One problem for the practicing group worker is that groups are often not made up of members with just one type of mental health or other problem. Members may have co-morbid mental health problems, mental health problems that do not fit nicely into a category of the DSM-V, or mental health problems that are comorbid with physical or developmental problems. Treatments for these problems can sometimes be difficult to locate using library resources.

In this book, we have attempted to provide basic skills in working with a wide variety of members' needs. In addition to these skills, social workers take practice courses that teach methods for handling specific mental health and other behavioral, cognitive, and emotional problems. In therapy groups, leaders must choose among many different approaches to treatment that they have learned in classes, workshops, conferences, and other continuing education programs. For example, Kazantzis, Reinecke, and Freeman (2010) present 10 different cognitive and behavioral evidence-based therapies for treating mental health problems. They are (1) Beck's Cognitive Therapy, (2) Problem-Solving Therapy, (3) Rational-Emotive Behavior Therapy, (4) Acceptance and Commitment Therapy, (5) Behavioral Activation Therapy, (6) Dialectical Behavior Therapy (DBT), (7) Cognitive Analytic Therapy, (8) Positive Psychology and Therapy, (9) Mindfulness-Based Cognitive Therapy, and (10) Emotion-Focused/Interpersonal Cognitive Therapy (Kazantzis, Reinecke, & Freeman, 2010). In addition to these theories that all come from the social learning perspective, there are numerous other evidence-based approaches that come from other theoretical perspectives. The worker should not just use a single theory for all problems, but should rather choose practice theories selectively based on the nature of members' problems.

A continuing assessment process during the middle phase of group work helps leaders to draw upon and select the right treatment methods for the problems being faced by the members of the group. Most treatment approaches in therapy groups use a multimodal or multi-module approach to build a group treatment program. A leader can select from a number of treatment strategies, described in Chapter 10, and build a treatment protocol. Alternatively, a leader can use a treatment approach, such as DBT, that is known to be effective with a certain client group, such as those with borderline personality disorder. This multicomponent treatment program may be used in its entirety, or because of the nature of the members of the group, the worker may have to adapt the program. Overall, to the extent possible, the worker should be using empirically based treatment interventions, combining them in such a way as they are most effective for the complex nature of the needs of the members of the group. Also see Chapter 14 for additional information about combining evidence, critical thinking, and practice experience when faced with multifaceted problems where a single evidence-based strategy may not be sufficient or even available.

? Assess your understanding of how to involve and empower group members to achieve their goals by taking this brief quiz.

Working with Reluctant and Resistant Group Members During the Middle Phase

We have already described working with involuntary members during the beginning phase of group development. When working with involuntary group members during the middle phase, it should be kept in mind that members always have the right to refuse to participate. It is important, however, for the worker to point out the consequences of refusal and to clarify nonnegotiable aspects of participation if involuntary members choose to participate in the group (Schimmel & Jacobs, 2011). Nonnegotiable aspects may include rules about attendance and participation, such as coming on time and not coming to the group intoxicated or high on drugs. It is also important to clarify members' rights and choices. The worker should attempt to maximize members' freedoms within the constraints of the legal pressures they are experiencing to be in the group and to change behaviors (Newhill, 2015; Rooney, 2009; Trotter, 2015).

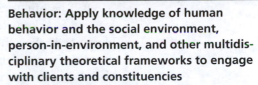

Engagement

Behavior: Apply knowledge of human behavior and the social environment, person-in-environment, and other multidisciplinary theoretical frameworks to engage with clients and constituencies

Critical Thinking Question: Involuntary members sometimes refuse to participate in the group. How can the worker use collaborative strategies to involve involuntary members?

Individuals in involuntary groups resist goal setting for many reasons. Some perceive their problems to be too embarrassing to work on them in a group. Some are angry that they have been considered incapable of handling their own problems. Some view themselves as failures or as incompetent and, consequently, find their personal problems too daunting to tackle. Some deny problems because to admit them would throw their view of themselves into chaos.

One of the first tasks of the worker, therefore, is to develop a nonjudgmental, accepting, and safe group environment in which members can feel free to express their own views of their problems (Hohman, 2013; Miller & Rollnick, 2013). This is illustrated in the following case.

Case Example   Creating a Safe Environment

Several members of a nursing home resident council were reluctant to participate in discussions about problems they were having in relation to their institutional environment. Some of the members were concerned that the group facilitator, who was also the staff social worker, would represent the viewpoints of the organization and its administration. In addition, this was the first formal group experience for several members, and they seemed to be anxious when they tried to share their views. The facilitator also knew that other members had been criticized by staff members for complaining about their care. The worker commented on her observations of members' reluctance to talk about their perceptions of care in the home and encouraged members to listen carefully to each other's suggestions. The worker modeled this skill by using strong active listening skills and by using positive body language when responding to members' comments. In addition, the worker encouraged members to develop a policy on confidentiality of group discussions about problems encountered in the nursing home. The worker also clarified her role of instructed advocate in which she was responsible for helping council members bring their suggestions for change to the administrative officers of the organization. After the worker modeled nonjudgmental behaviors, members became more involved in sharing their ideas for change.

As members express their views, it is important for the worker to assess members' motivation for being in the group and to identify how the group can be helpful to them (Rooney, 2009; Rooney & Chovanec, 2004).

It is helpful to adopt a position that maximizes members' sense of control and expertise. Acknowledging that members can help the leader understand what it is like to be in their shoes and that members are in the best position to help themselves demonstrates respect and can do much to help the worker join with members in their fledgling attempts to express and work on their concerns (Hohman, 2013; Miller & Rollnick, 2013).

It is also essential to acknowledge members' feelings and reactions to being in the group during the middle phase when the work gets harder and members are being asked to make changes in their lifestyles. Authentic and direct communication helps members express their feelings rather than hide them. Sometimes, paradoxical interventions can be combined with authentic and direct communication to help members express and begin to deal with their feelings of resistance. For example, the worker might state that he or she is aware that the members were ordered to attend the group or face more severe consequences and that they are not interested in what the group has to offer. This can sometimes have a paradoxical result in that often one or more members react by talking about how the group might be helpful.

The worker should try to uncover the feelings and thoughts that underlie members' resistant behavior. For example, are members scared or hurt? Are they trying to control the situation or to avoid confronting issues that they experience as too difficult to face? Once the underlying meaning of resistant behavior has been figured out, the worker is in a much better position to offer therapeutic assistance (Joyce, Piper, & Ogrodniczuk, 2007; Miller & Rollnick, 2013; Rutan, Stone, & Shay, 2014).

Engaging in collaborative problem solving can also be helpful when working with reluctant or resistant clients (Trotter, 2015). Collaborative problem solving involves soliciting members' views and definitions of their problems, helping them to develop modest but highly achievable goals that they are motivated to work on, and working with members to develop strategies to achieve these goals. It is important that the goals that are developed are the members', not the worker's (Trotter, 2015).

Dramatizing naturally occurring consequences also works well with some members who are reluctant to work on problems (Newhill, 2015; Rooney, 2009; Trotter, 2015). The worker should avoid talking about abstract consequences and, instead, focus on the natural consequences that have occurred because members failed to confront their problems. For example, the worker might say: "You almost lost your license for driving while you were drunk. What would you do if they took away your license? How would you get to work? In what other ways would not being able to drive affect you?"

The worker should avoid moralizing or blaming (Hohman, 2013; Miller & Rollnick, 2013). Problem behaviors should be discussed in a direct, factual way. Whenever possible, members should be asked to describe in their own words the negative consequences that have resulted from problem behaviors. For example, the worker might divulge what members' blood-alcohol levels were at the time of their arrests for driving while intoxicated and ask them to describe what consequences they have had as a result of the arrest.

Workers should encourage resistant members to make "I" statements. Instead of allowing members to project blame onto someone else, "I" statements help members take responsibility for their feelings, thoughts, and actions.

Confrontation is sometimes necessary to help members overcome their resistance (Newhill, 2015; Rooney, 2009; Trotter, 2015). It is better for members to confront each other, rather than for the leader to confront members (Edelwich & Brodsky, 1992; Schimmel & Jacobs, 2011). The latter approach can lead members to coalesce against the leader. Also, because members' confrontations are based on members' experiences, their confrontations are often more powerful than workers' confrontations.

The leader should strive to build a group culture that encourages confrontation of members' motivation to work in the group. However, because resistant members avoid taking responsibility for their actions, it is unrealistic to expect them to confront each other initially. The worker must first model constructive confrontation.

According to Edelwich and Brodsky (1992), constructive confrontations should be (1) solicited rather than imposed, (2) done gently and with care, (3) descriptive rather than evaluative, (4) specific and concrete, (5) presented in an atmosphere of trust, and (6) timed so that the member is able to hear and experience the full effect of the interaction. Constructive confrontations should include a descriptive statement, an "I" statement, and a reference to natural consequences (Edelwich & Brodsky, 1992). For example, the worker might say: "You say that you didn't do anything and you can't understand why you're being singled out. But if I had been caught driving with a blood alcohol level as high as yours, I would have been given the same choice as you: lose my license or come here. And if I kept avoiding the consequences of my behavior, I'd have problems on the job, at home, and with the law—as you are having."

To build a group culture in which confrontation of resistance and avoidance of problems is normative among members rather than solely emanating from the leader to members, it can be helpful to include former members or members with greater longevity in the group. Members who have already confronted and grappled with their own resistance can discuss their initial reluctance to participate in the group and how the group enabled them to work through their resistance and confront their problems. For example, it is helpful to have more experienced members talk about how avoiding problems does not help and how facing up to problems is the first step to doing something about them. To create empathy and to help members take responsibility for their actions, Rooney and Chovanec (2004) point out that it can also be helpful to invite victims to group meetings. These individuals can talk about the experience of victimization and its impact on them.

Even though constructive confrontations can help overcome members' resistance to working in the group, it is important to remember that reluctant and resistant members will continue to experience obstacles to goal achievement as they attempt to develop and implement treatment plans. These obstacles can reduce their motivation, which makes them reluctant to continue to work to accomplish specific goals. Methods designed to help members change their beliefs and make the external environment more responsive are described in Chapter 10.

Although all the tactics mentioned can be helpful when working with resistant clients, the most important thing the worker can do is maintain a therapeutic stance. It is essential for workers to avoid personalizing oppositional behavior. Also, one must avoid retaliating, threatening, or levying overly punitive sanctions. Instead, the worker should be patient and compassionate, keep a sense of humor, and avoid feeling omnipotent, which is believing that one can help anyone, all the time.

Monitoring and Evaluating the Group's Progress

Monitoring and evaluating progress provides feedback for workers and members, which is useful in developing, modifying, and changing treatment plans. It is also helpful in maintaining the functioning of the group as a whole. Monitoring and evaluating are important ongoing processes that should occur throughout the life of a group.

One of the most common methods of obtaining feedback from members during the middle stage of a group's development is to give members a session evaluation form (such as that shown in Chapter 14, Figure 14.3) at the end of each group session. Although the format of session evaluation questions (close-ended, Likert-type questions and open-ended questions) remains fairly standard from group to group, the content of questions varies. Changing the content of questions provides workers with the specific information they need about a particular group's work.

How frequently should session evaluation forms be administered? In some groups, they can be used at the end of each session. Workers who are not familiar with using session evaluation forms sometimes wonder how they will be received by members, but brief forms that take only a few minutes to fill out are not a burden for members to complete. In fact, members often enjoy the chance to let the worker know what they like and dislike about the group.

In other groups, workers may prefer to evaluate the group's progress after every second or third session. The exact frequency of monitoring and evaluating ultimately depends on the need for ongoing feedback about the group's development. Verbal evaluations are often used as a substitute for written evaluations, but anonymous written evaluations may offer better feedback because they can offer a measure of confidentiality not available through verbal evaluations.

Other frequently used methods of monitoring and evaluating include having members self-monitor their behaviors and having others who are familiar with the members' concerns (such as other workers or family members) report progress to the worker. These and other assessment, monitoring, and evaluation methods are described in Chapters 8 and 14. The actual methods used for obtaining feedback are, however, not as important as whether the feedback is systematically solicited, collected, and acted on. Obtaining feedback allows workers to fine-tune a group as it progresses through the middle stage. It is also a signal to members that their opinions are valued and that their ideas and concerns will be analyzed and acted on. For these reasons, monitoring and evaluating a group's progress is an essential worker activity during the middle stage of group development.

? Assess your understanding of working with reluctant or resistant group members by taking this brief quiz.

Case Example

As Jim planned for the middle stage of his group for men who were physically abusive to their partners, he grew increasingly concerned about how he was going to help overcome their resistance to participating in the group. As a condition of their probation, members were mandated to attend a 10-session group that had both an educational and a rehabilitative focus. Jim's responsibility was to conduct the group and write individual progress reports for the probation department.

During the initial two meetings, members spent a great deal of time objecting to being mandated to attend the group. Several members noted that although the probation department required them to be there, they felt little obligation to participate in discussions. Others stated that they were thinking of dropping out. Jim knew that these statements represented initial resistance to being mandated for treatment. Jim also recognized that these members, who once exercised control over their relationships through violence, were now in a position of being controlled through the legal process. Because domestic violence often involves power and control, the involuntary status of the membership was particularly difficult for members to accept.

During the first session, Jim allowed members to express their feelings and to ventilate. He also pointed out their ambivalence about dealing with the problems that had caused their situation. He hoped that by doing this he could overcome some of the initial resistance and help members accept the purpose of the group. Although this helped somewhat, several members continued to demonstrate verbal and nonverbal expressions of resentment and anger about being required to attend the group. However, Jim asked members to talk about what the consequences of nonattendance might be. This discussion helped reinforce and make more vivid a member's recognition that, if they chose not to attend, they would have their probation revoked and be jailed. Through discussing possible consequences, members seemed to become more resigned to their attendance, although they continued to show some resentment about having to discuss what they considered to be private matters.

During the second session, Jim helped some members to overcome resistance by reframing their situations. Jim assured the members that they had rights and choices about attending the group. He suggested that although they were ordered by the court to attend, they had also actively chosen to obey this mandate. He gave them positive feedback for making this choice and suggested that now that they had made this decision, they might as well decide to make the best possible use of the group. By avoiding threats, moralizing, and blaming, Jim secured the initial participation of the members.

As the group entered the middle stage, Jim sensed that the men were beginning to accept their involuntary status as members. However, when he suggested that members begin to discuss what individual goals they might want to accomplish in the group, he was again met with silence and nonverbal communications that suggested to him that members were not willing to move into the middle (i.e., work) phase of the group. A few members eventually noted that they felt they could handle their problems by themselves and were reluctant to discuss their personal situations with other members. Jim stated that sometimes he thought that, as a man, he was expected always to be in control of his feelings and be competent enough to handle his own problems. He asked members if they sometimes felt this way too. One member agreed that this seemed to be true for him, and then several other members nodded in agreement. This led to some meaningful discussion about role expectations but it did not seem to help members identify individual goals for changing their feelings and behaviors.

By modeling nonjudgmental and accepting behavior, Jim helped members talk briefly about their relationships with their partners. Jim noted that most of the members verbalized a strong need for having power and control in their relationships with their partners. He wondered out loud whether members were reluctant to have their assumptions about relationships challenged. He acknowledged members' feelings and beliefs, but at the same time, he challenged members to rethink how they viewed their relationships. He speculated that this might be one of the reasons that members were unwilling to discuss individual goals for themselves. Although some members still blamed their partners for the violence, for the most part, they responded well to Jim's honest and authentic confrontations.

Jim used two techniques that gradually helped members respond to his demand for work. First, he gave members a copy of the "Power and Control Wheel," which illustrates how domestic violence centers around power and control. He discussed some of the theoretical aspects of the cycle of domestic violence. It took some discussion for members to understand the point of view expressed in this material, but Jim could see that it was sinking in. Second, he discussed how he had helped members of other groups like this to have more satisfying relationships with their partners. He noted that success and better relationships were both possibilities if members committed themselves to working hard in the group. He again assured members that he would be supportive of their efforts, but that they needed to take the first step by thinking about their individual goals. The introduction of new information that challenged members' beliefs, accompanied by the instillation of hope, eventually helped members overcome their resistance to moving into deeper aspects of their problems. By the end of the fourth session, members had developed individual goals they could work on for the rest of the group sessions. In later sessions, resistance reemerged again. For example, some members had great difficulty accepting that they needed to change some of their thoughts and behaviors. Other members had difficulty at work or in other environments that contributed to their resistance to investing themselves in change efforts.

The sessions were difficult ones because of the different types and levels of resistance in the group. Nevertheless, Jim's understanding about involuntary group members and about resistance within the group helped him to avoid taking the resistance he encountered personally. Jim continued to struggle, however, both with his own strong feelings about violence and working with men who had dysfunctional beliefs about relationships and with the group's constant testing of his ability to be accepting and nonjudgmental. He discussed these feelings and how he was handling them with his supervisor.

SUMMARY

The middle stage of treatment groups is the period in which members focus on the goals they have contracted to achieve in the group. This chapter focuses on seven fundamental tasks that all workers perform while leading treatment groups during their middle stage. The first task is to prepare for group meetings. The second task includes determining the optimal amount of group structure to help members meet their needs. The third task, involving and empowering group members, includes building on members' strengths and their commitment to the group as a whole. The fourth task, helping members to achieve agreed upon goals, includes (1) keeping members aware of goals they have contracted to achieve, (2) developing treatment plans, (3) overcoming obstacles to members' work on treatment plans, and (4) helping members carry out their treatment plans. The fifth task includes using empirically based treatment methods when they are available so that workers can become effective evidence-based practitioners. The sixth task, working with reluctant and resistant group members, includes a discussion of constructive uses of confrontation. The chapter concludes by focusing on the tasks of monitoring and evaluating the group's progress.

Treatment Groups: Specialized Methods

This chapter focuses on specialized intervention methods for individual group members, the group as a whole, and the group's external environment. Even though this chapter sequentially presents interventions at the three levels, in actual practice, interventions at one level often affect other levels. As the group unfolds, the skilled worker moves easily among all the levels by combining interventions for the individual member, the group as a whole, and the group's environment to help members reach their treatment goals.

Overreliance on Specialized Methods

Before reviewing the specialized middle-stage skills presented in this chapter, it is important for beginning group workers to be aware that learning specialized strategies and techniques is not the complete answer to becoming a skilled and effective group worker. Many experienced workers have noted the tendency of new workers to overvalue highly technical and specialized techniques as the key to effective clinical work (Boyd-Franklin, Cleek, Wofsy, & Mundy, 2013). Learning a wide variety of specific techniques is certainly helpful but working with people in treatment groups also requires excellent interpersonal skills, and the ability to guide group dynamics to harness the power of the group for therapeutic purposes. Gaining a therapeutic alliance with each member based on trust, humility in the human condition, and respect for the dignity and worth of every group member is critical for any specialized technique to work effectively. Similarly, fostering therapeutic group dynamics empowers all members to help themselves learn new coping and problem solving skills. They enable members to engage in empathic self-reflection with the support of fellow members who understand the self-esteem eroding challenges of experiencing painful, stigmatizing, and traumatic life events. Therefore, focusing on therapeutic group dynamics is also essential when using advanced techniques.

There are long-standing and continuing efforts by leading group work scholars to identify change mechanisms and therapeutic factors in groups (for example, Barlow, 2013; Burlingame,

MacKenzie, & Strauss, 2004; Burlingame, Strauss, & Joy, 2013; Kivlighan & Kivlighan, 2014; Yalom, 2005). Some of the therapeutic factors that have been identified include:

- Cohesion
- Instillation of hope
- Universality (i.e., feeling that one is not alone with one's problems)
- Feedback about group behavior and its relationship to family of origin issues and deeply held cognitive schema
- Altruism and mutual aid
- Interpersonal bonding and the formation of trusting relationships,
- Imitative behaviors
- Ventilation and catharsis
- Radical acceptance (i.e., the ability to acknowledge, live with, and come to peaceful terms with difficult events that can't be changed)
- Existential factors, such as acquiring new or altered belief systems, frames of reference, personal meaning, spirituality, and worldviews
- Improved communication and social skills
- The obtaining of new information and resources

A substantial body of research exists about therapeutic factors. This research incudes clinical observations from group practice (Yalom, 2005), qualitative interviews of practitioners (Ogrodniczuk, Piper, Joyce, Lau, & Sochting, 2010), and quantitative research (for reviews, see Barlow, 2013; Burlingame, 2010; Burlingame, Strauss, & Joyce, 2013; Burlingame, Whitcomb, & Woodland, 2014; Kivlighan & Kivlighan, 2014). Measurement instruments and other methodological innovations have been created to study these therapeutic factors empirically (Burlingame, 2010; Burlingame, Strauss, & Joyce, 2013; Joyce, MacNair-Semands, Tasca, & Ogrodniczuk, 2011; Lese & MacNair-Semands, 2000; Norcross, 2011, 2014). Therefore, there is a greater evidence-base linking these factors to positive outcomes in groups than ever before (Norcross, 2011; Norcross & Beutler, 2014). A thorough discussion and critique of the empirical literature on therapeutic factors is beyond the scope of this book. Still, when focusing on middle-stage skills, new workers who want to engage in evidence-based practice should keep in mind the importance of developing therapeutic alliances with group members and the power of group dynamics to heal (see, for example, Gelso & Harbin, 2007; Joyce, Piper, & Ogrodniczuk, 2007). This evidence should not be neglected in the quest to apply specialized techniques and strategies in a rote fashion. This caveat should be kept in mind when reviewing and using the specialized techniques and strategies presented in the remainder of this chapter.

INTERVENING WITH GROUP MEMBERS

When intervening with individual group members, the worker may select from:

- Intrapersonal interventions that focus on members' cognition and affects, that is, their thoughts, beliefs, values, feelings, sensations, and emotions
- Interpersonal interventions that focus on members' relationships with others within and outside the group
- Environmental interventions that seek to change or modify the psychosocial and physical space in which members function

Intrapersonal interventions are particularly appropriate when an assessment has determined that a member's bio-psychosocial development may have helped to contribute to dysfunctional or irrational belief systems. Interpersonal interventions are particularly useful when an assessment has determined that members need further development of their skills in relating to others. Environmental interventions are particularly useful when an assessment determines that a member lacks material resources to ameliorate a problem or when the environment is impeding a member's ability to accomplish a goal.

Intrapersonal Interventions

Since the beginnings of group work practice, workers with psychodynamic orientations have focused most interventions in treatment groups on the intrapersonal aspects of group members' behavior. In recent years, there has also been a growing interest in techniques to intervene in the covert, intrapersonal lives of group members using cognitive and cognitive-behavioral therapy (CBT) approaches to practice (Beck, 2011; Bieling, McCabe, & Antony, 2006; Chacko et al., 2014; Craske, 2010; Dobson, 2010; Ellis & Joffe-Ellis, 2011; Gopalan et al., 2014; Heimberg & Becker, 2002; Kazantzis, Reinecke, & Freeman, 2010; McKay, Abramowitz, & Taylor, 2010; Reinecke, Dattilio, & Freeman, 2006; Segal, Williams, & Teasdale, 2013; Sheldon, 2011; Wenzel, 2013; Wenzel, Liese, Beck, & Friedman-Wheeler, 2012; White & Freeman, 2000; Wright, Basco, & Thase, 2006). These approaches to practice have been found to be efficacious in clinical trials and hence fit in with the increasing emphasis in social work on evidence-based practice.

Some of the newer intervention approaches, such as Acceptance and Commitment Therapy (ACT), Dialectical Behavior Therapy (DBT), and Emotion Focused Therapy (EFT), are multicomponent interventions that have also been found to be very effective for emotional regulation and behavior change (see, for example, Gross, 2014; Kazantzis, Reinecke, & Freeman, 2010; Lynch & Cuper, 2010; Roemer & Orsillo, 2014; Waltz & Hayes, 2010). ACT is based on a careful functional and contextual analysis of verbal behavior (Harris, 2009; Hays, Strosahl, & Wilson, 2011). It focuses on six core processes: (1) acceptance, (2) cognitive diffusion, (3) being present, (4) self in context, (5) values, and (6) committed action. It is often used with members who have anxiety disorders, chronic pain, depression, psychotic symptoms, and substance abuse disorders. DBT is a comprehensive cognitive behavioral treatment developed for individuals with severe mental disorders, such as borderline personality disorder (BPD) and suicidal behavior (Linehan, 2015). These are individuals with pervasive emotion dysregulation (Neacsiu, Bohus, & Linehan, 2014). The main components of DBT are (1) mindfulness, (2) distress tolerance, (3) emotion regulation, and (4) interpersonal effectiveness. Versions of DBT have been subsequently used to treat other disorders with emotional dysregulation, such as eating disorders, depression, and other personality disorders (Lynch & Cuper, 2010). DBT changes (1) vulnerability to emotional cues, (2) emotional response tendencies, (3) emotional responses, and the (4) emotional aftermath of reactivity to emotional stress (Dimeff & Koerner, 2007; Linehan, 2015; Neacsiu, Bohus, & Linehan, 2014; McKay, Wood, & Brantley, 2007). EFT focuses on coaching clients to work through feelings that can lead to dysfunctional thoughts and actions (Greenberg, 2015).

Before using specific therapies, however, group workers should be aware of the overall process of helping members make intrapersonal changes. This process includes helping members to:

- Identify and discriminate among thoughts, feelings, and behaviors
- Recognize associations between specific thoughts, feelings, and behaviors
- Analyze the rationality of thoughts and beliefs
- Change distorted or irrational thoughts and beliefs

Identifying and Discriminating

The first step in any intrapersonal intervention is to help members accurately identify thoughts, feelings, and behaviors and to discriminate among them. Some members have great difficulty putting their subjective thoughts and feelings into words. But without clearly identifying a member's thoughts and feelings for the rest of the group, it is not possible to help the member cope with and change automatic thoughts and other covert processes.

When helping members identify and discriminate behaviors from thoughts and feelings, members should be encouraged to describe behaviors in specific, observable terms as if a camera was taking a picture of the event and members were bystanders observing the behaviors. Sometimes, members have a difficult time describing the thoughts or feelings that accompany behaviors. For example, it is common for group members to respond to a question about what they are feeling with a description of a behavior or a thought. This response is particularly true of men, who are taught as they are growing up that expressing feelings is a feminine, not masculine, trait. This is illustrated in the following case.

Case Example   Describing Feelings

In response to a question about what he was feeling, an obviously angry group member stated, "I'm not feeling anything." When the worker responded that people are always feeling something, no matter how slight, the member said, "I'm feeling that your interpretation of my behavior is not correct." This statement was, of course, a thought, not a feeling. The statement also reflected the difficulty this member had in acknowledging this feeling. The worker had several choices at this point. The worker could wait for the group to talk about how they experienced this member's behavior. She could ask the group how they perceived the member. The worker's experiences suggested that in adult groups, members are often reluctant to express how they perceive others without prompting. Therefore, the worker chose to conduct a go-round asking members, in turn, to talk about the perceptions they felt comfortable enough to disclose. Then, the worker led the group in a discussion about how feelings are expressed and how they are perceived. The worker also helped the member to consider the feedback he received from the group. As the group continued, additional feedback was given and he became more aware of how he expressed feelings and was perceived by others.

To help members who have difficulty discriminating feelings from thoughts, the worker can have the member get feedback from the group. In the previously described situation, for example, the member went around the group and asked the other members how they perceived he was feeling. Responses expressing that he appeared to be angry gradually indicated to the member that he was not in touch with his feelings. Sometimes it is necessary to have members practice discriminating thoughts from feelings in several situations inside and outside the group before they are able to identify and separate them correctly. Using a specially designed log book or journal, members can record the situation or activating event, the thought or belief, and the behavioral or emotional consequences. Often, dysfunctional or distorted thoughts are instantaneous and automatic because they are so ingrained. Identifying the thought or belief can help members be aware of when they occur and their consequences. It can also be helpful to gradually connect automatic dysfunctional or distorted ingrained beliefs about themselves that cognitive behaviorists call core beliefs or cognitive schema, and psychodynamic and interpersonal practitioners conceptualize as coping mechanisms left over from early childhood trauma.

ACT, DBT, and EFT all attempt to help members identify and discriminate between thoughts and feelings but also focus on the context surrounding the behavior. ACT uses metaphors to help group members accept and break out of self-defeating thought patterns. DBT uses (1) exercises to increase distress tolerance and soothe the pain, (2) mindfulness skills to help group members focus more effectively, (3) emotion regulation skills including radical acceptance to calm and uplift members, and (4) interpersonal effectiveness skills training to empower members. Exercises for each of these four areas can be found in Dimeff and Koerner (2007), McKay, Wood, and Brantley (2007), and Linehan (2015). EFT focuses on identifying, experiencing, exploring, accepting, interpreting, and transforming dysfunctional emotions and thoughts so that they lead to more effective coping behaviors and skills.

Recognizing Associations

The second step in intrapersonal interventions is to help members recognize that there is an association among thoughts, feelings, and behaviors. For example, if a man thinks someone is deliberately following him as he walks home one evening, he is likely to feel apprehensive and behave accordingly. He may look over his shoulder or walk on the well-lighted side of a street. Similarly, if a woman thinks she is not skillful at a particular task, she is likely to feel incompetent and is less likely to continue to work on the task if she encounters difficulty than if she thinks that she can perform the task adequately.

For members to alter associations among thoughts, feelings, and behaviors, they must be aware of their existence. Awareness can be accomplished through a self-monitoring process. Members are asked to monitor particular thoughts and the feelings and behaviors that occur immediately following them. The group helps members look for patterns of association among particular thoughts, feelings, and behaviors. Sometimes members may clearly remember specific thoughts and their associated feelings and behaviors, and it may not be necessary to spend time monitoring them before reporting them to the group. This is often the case with automatic thoughts that constantly recur to members (Beck, 2011; Dobson, 2010; Freeman, Pretzer, Fleming, & Simons, 2004; Sheldon, 2011; Wenzel, 2013; Wenzel, Liese, Beck, & Friedman-Wheeler, 2012; Young, Rygh, Weinberger, & Beck, 2014).

Data about thoughts, feelings, and behaviors collected either prospectively or retrospectively should be discussed in the group. Such a discussion usually reveals that specific thoughts are exacerbating or maintaining unwanted feeling states and behavior patterns, as the following example illustrates.

Case Example   Tracking Thoughts, Feelings, and Resulting Behaviors

After keeping a log for a week to track how her thoughts and feelings affected her behavior, an anxious group member found that her thoughts were focused on her belief about her "inability to do anything right." She realized that this "froze" her so that she was unable to complete her work assignments on time. By discussing her thoughts in the group, she became aware that automatic thoughts and core beliefs about herself led to her fears and her anxiety about her performance on the job. This, in turn, distracted her from her work, which led her to feel more anxious and to become even less productive. Both consequences (i.e., being distracted and unproductive) further reinforced her beliefs that she would not be able to complete her assignments, that she could not do anything right, and that she was a failure. Data from the member's log led to a group discussion of this cycle and what to do about it.

This example reveals that thoughts can lead to feelings and behavior, but it is also possible that particular cues or signals can lead to thoughts, which can, in turn, lead to feelings and behavior. For example, a cue for an anxiety-producing thought might be the approach of a person of the opposite sex in a singles bar. The approach signals the person who begins to think anxiety-producing thoughts, such as "I hope he doesn't come over here" and "I won't know what to say." The thoughts can then lead to feelings of anxiety and to avoidance behavior. Such a sequence of events can become habituated, and thus a particular cue or even the thought of the particular cue can lead to the entire sequence of dysfunctional thoughts, feelings, and behaviors. This type of contextual functional analysis is particularly prominent in EFT.

The second step in the process of intrapersonal interventions, therefore, also includes helping members become aware of internal cues, such as muscle tension or butterflies in the stomach, and external cues, such as the approach of a person, that trigger a sequence of events. In long-term treatment focused on personality change, workers may want to help members gain insight into the historical determinants of the cues. Once members are aware of the cues that trigger an association between thoughts, feelings, and behavior, they are ready to move to the next step in the process.

Analyzing the Rationality of Thoughts and Beliefs

The third step in intrapersonal intervention is to help members analyze the rationality of the thoughts and beliefs that maintain or exacerbate dysfunctional feelings and behavior patterns. Epictetus wrote in *The Enchiridion*: "Men are not disturbed by things but by the views taken of them." According to many cognitive psychologists, dysfunctional and irrational thoughts and beliefs arise from erroneous or misleading interpretations of events, which may, in turn, come from long-standing cognitive schema or core beliefs (Ellis & Joffe-Ellis, 2011; DiGiuseppe, 2010; Freeman et al., 2004; Meichenbaum, 2014; Young, Rygh, Weinberger, & Beck, 2014). Group members engage in faulty thinking patterns and cognitive distortions that fall into three broad types: (1) making faulty inferences about an observation or behavior, (2) attributing responsibility or control to some erroneous source, and (3) evaluating the inferences and controlling sources as having terrible consequences. Some of the common cognitive distortions are listed here.

Cognitive Distortions
- Overgeneralize from an event
- Selectively focus on portions of an event
- Take too much responsibility for events that are beyond their control
- Think of the worst possible consequence of future events
- Engage in either-or dichotomous thinking
- Assume that because certain events have led to particular consequences in the past they will automatically lead to the same consequences if they occur in the future

Sometimes corrective information and feedback are sufficient to change thoughts and beliefs based on incomplete or incorrect information. For example, some teenage girls believe that they will not become pregnant if they have sexual intercourse only once or twice. With proper information, however, beliefs about the result of sexual activity can be changed.

Ellis (1962) was one of the first to suggest that faulty interpretations occur because of irrational beliefs and ideas people have about the way things should operate in their world. For example, members may believe that they must be thoroughly "competent, adequate, and achieving in all possible respects if they are to consider themselves worthwhile" (Ellis, p. 63). Ellis lists 11 common irrational ideas that affect members' interpretations of events. These beliefs are usually based on absolutist thinking, rather than on well-reasoned, logical interpretations or elaborations from factual evidence. Words such as *should, ought*, and *must* are cues to the existence of absolutist thinking, which may lead to irrational or erroneous interpretations of events. For example, a group member might believe that to consider himself worthwhile he must be competent in all possible respects. When his performance falls short of his unrealistically high standards, he becomes depressed.

From a psychodynamic point of view, the worker may also want to explore with members how what they learn from their families of origin contributes to their current thoughts and beliefs about themselves (Rutan, Stone, & Shay, 2014). In this framework, thoughts and beliefs are shaped early in life by relationships with mothers, fathers, and other primary caretakers. The worker's role is to help members explore how these early relationships affect their current functioning. The insight gained from this exploration can then be used by group members to examine current coping strategies. This, in turn, can lead to a reduction in coping strategies that are no longer effective, and toward new coping skills that are more responsive to the current situation. In a similar way, CBT posits that entrenched cognitive schema and core beliefs play an important role in the formation of thoughts, feelings, and beliefs about oneself, and that changing these can have a profound effect on how one thinks, feels, and acts (see, for example, Beck, 2011; Meichenbaum, 2014; Wenzel, 2013; Wenzel, Liese, Beck, & Friedman-Wheeler, 2012).

ACT and DBT add mindfulness skills to the repertoire of CBT skills that can be used to analyze the rationality of beliefs and thoughts (Bien, 2006; Boyd-Franklin, Cleek, Wofsy, & Mundy, 2013). ACT and DBT do not emphasize disputing irrational thoughts and beliefs as done in rational emotive therapy (Ellis & Joffe-Ellis, 2011). Instead, mindfulness meditation skills are practiced to distract and clear the mind from dysfunctional self-talk and to focus on more soothing thoughts and images. The worker leads members in brief focusing exercises using cognitive imagery, breathing, body awareness, and other mindfulness meditation techniques (Brown, Creswell, & Ryan, 2015; Stahl & Goldstein, 2010; McKay, Wood, & Brantley, 2007; Rogers & Maytan, 2012; Segal, Williams, Teasdale, & Kabat-Zin, 2012). Lengthier meditation activities delivered by the worker or by CD or DVD are also used in some groups (see, for example, Kabat-Zinn, 2002).

Mindfulness skills require group members to focus on a particular thought and to come back to that thought whenever their minds drift from it. Group members may also be asked to focus on their breath and do deep breathing while they are focused on the thought. Alternatively, meditation can be done by asking members to focus on a favorite natural setting, or on a mantra that one repeats to oneself. Many different foci can be used, but commonly used natural settings are beaches, mountains, or waterfalls. Between meetings, mindfulness exercises may be done as often as required to stabilize and regulate emotion (see, for example, Brown, Cresswell, & Ryan, 2015).

Changing Thoughts, Beliefs, and Feeling States

The fourth step in intrapersonal interventions is to help members change irrational or distorted thoughts, beliefs, and associated feeling states. Several techniques that have been developed for this purpose are listed here along with a brief description of their use in group treatment.

Cognitive Restructuring. *Cognitive restructuring* is a term first used by Mahoney (1974) to refer to a group of techniques that focus on correcting cognitive distortions and deprecating self-talk. Over three decades ago, Yost, Beutler, Corbishley, and Allender (1985) reported using cognitive restructuring techniques effectively when working with groups of depressed older adults, but these techniques are still used widely today (see, for example, Beck, 2011; Meichenbaum, 2014). Some cognitive restructuring techniques are also designed to expose faulty logic in group members' thought patterns and to help them replace irrational thought processes with logical, rational patterns of thought (see, for example, Ellis & Joffe-Ellis, 2011; Wenzel, 2013; Wenzel et al., 2012).

Mahoney (1995a, 1995b) has pointed out that belief systems are formed through the course of development as individuals interact with their social environment. Thus, beliefs may not be "faulty" or "irrational" but constructed from unique social experiences and the processing of these experiences that continually occurs within each individual. For example, Smucker and colleagues (1999) described how childhood trauma experiences can affect adult survivors.

Group work can help members become more aware of the factors that shape and maintain belief systems and how these factors might be modified through new experiences within and outside the group. For example, Bauer and McBride (2003) helped members who suffered from bipolar disorders to identify the thoughts, feelings, and behaviors they experienced while being in the depressed phase of their disorders. They then helped members to develop personal depression profiles and personal care plans to control re-occurring "breakthrough" symptoms that are common with this type of mental disorder.

ACT and DBT use other cognitive restructuring techniques, such as acceptance and meditation, to help members think in new ways. Group members often have thoughts, behaviors, and coping skills that were functional in the past but that no longer lead to workable solutions (Hayes, Strosahl, & Wilson, 2011). Once members are aware of how to focus thoughts through meditation, they are better able to understand the control strategies that they have used to avoid examining their own thoughts. ACT teaches members to accept the reality of coping skills, patterns, and control strategies that are no longer effective and may have caused problems and pain, and to commit themselves to replacing them with new effective ones. In a similar fashion, DBT describes practicing radical acceptance, which is tolerating something without judging or trying to change it (McKay, Wood, & Brantley, 2007). Group members accept themselves as they are and strongly commit themselves to new ways of thinking, feeling, and acting based on self-acceptance. By accepting themselves as they are, members are restructuring the way they think and emote about themselves and others, and this, in turn, leads to behavior change.

The worker can help members change belief systems by pursuing the activities listed here.

Changing Belief Systems

- Have members examine the experiences on which thoughts and beliefs are based.
- Help members examine the way past experiences were construed.
- Help members consider the impact of their construction of experiences in their current lives.
- Help members get feedback from others in the group about alternative ways of construing and responding to experiences.
- Practice new ways of responding both cognitively and behaviorally that will enhance members' current coping abilities.
- Prepare coping statements as reminders to practice alternative ways of responding to distorted thoughts.
- Use paper or electronic records to keep track of cognitive and emotional distortions and methods that proved successful to counteract them that can be shared during meetings.

Through a combination of group discussion, analysis, and action, members help each other gain insight into their attributions concerning previous events and the effects of their construction of events in their current lives. ACT refers to this as discovering and building awareness of the self, and defusing the self so that one can look as an observer at oneself (Hayes, Strosahl, & Wilson, 2011). DBT refers to this as being mindful, in the present, and committed to action to make things better (Lynch & Cooper, 2010; Linehan, 2015). EFT refers to this as interpreting and transforming feeling and thoughts. These therapeutic approaches are aimed at cognitive unfreezing of ingrained thoughts and beliefs so that they can be replaced with healthier core beliefs.

Cognitive Self-Instruction. Cognitive self-instruction refers to helping members use internal dialogues and covert self-statements for solving problems and coping with difficult life events. Children and adults can use the technique to replace dysfunctional internal dialogues with self-statements that help them solve a problem. For example, instead of a member's saying to herself, "I can't do this," she can learn to say, "I'll try to do it the best

I can" or "I'll bet my answer is as good or better than anyone else's," and "First I'll examine all the data and then I'll think of the possible solutions."

Cognitive self-instructions can be used to prepare for a particular situation or to help a member perform effectively during a situation (Beck, 2011; Meichenbaum, 2014). For example, to prepare for a situation, a member might say, "When I talk to Sally, I'll tell her directly that I can't do it. If she tries to persuade me, I'll just repeat that I've decided not to do it." While in a particular situation, a member might say, "I'm in control" or "I can do this." Internal dialogues are important mediators of effective problem solving. Poor problem solvers tend to repeat dysfunctional self-statements, which make them give up more quickly and get blocked more easily in problem-solving efforts than persons whose self-statements encourage active problem-solving efforts. Research evidence supports the effectiveness of CBT for replacing dysfunctional self-statements with statements that support healthy functioning (Beck, 2011; Meichenbaum, 2014; Sheldon, 2011).

ACT, DBT, and EFT also attack dysfunctional inner dialogues with cognitive self-instruction, but unlike CBT, they place more emphasis on the acceptance of intrusive and maladaptive thoughts. Energy that was used to control rather than accept these thoughts and feelings is freed up and committed to the practice of a variety of coping strategies. For example, DBT teaches group members to use distress tolerance skills such as distraction, living in the present moment, relaxing, thinking self-encouraging coping thoughts, soothing, and improving the current moment (McKay, Wood, & Brantley, 2007; Linehan, 2015). ACT focus on freeing up energy through acceptance to enable a commitment to new beliefs and values. Group workers using EFT encourage members to identify, accept, and explore negative emotions and thoughts, interpreting and transforming them into more positive ones (Greenberg, 2015). Because these are newer techniques, there is currently much less evidence for their effectiveness than there is for CBT.

Thought Stopping. Some group members have difficulty controlling maladaptive or self-defeating thoughts and internal dialogues. The thought-stopping technique is a way to help members reduce these thoughts (Antony & Roemer, 2011; Davis, Eshelman, & McKay, 2008; Kazdin, 2013). While the member is concentrating on a thought, the worker suddenly and emphatically says, "Stop." This procedure is repeated several times. The member gradually begins to think "Stop" and to remember the worker's voice saying "Stop" whenever the obtrusive thought occurs. Variations of the technique include having members pinch themselves when obtrusive thoughts occur, having them replace obtrusive thoughts with covert dialogues and images that are not self-defeating, and having members meditate on a particular scene or phrase when obtrusive thoughts occur.

Reframing. Reframing is a cognitive technique used to help group members see situations or problems from another point of view. It means "to change the conceptual and/or emotional setting or viewpoint in relation to which the situation is experienced and to place it in another frame which fits the facts of the same concrete situation equally well or even better, and thereby changes its entire meaning" (Watzlawick, Weakland, & Fisch, 1974, p. 95).

For example, a member who complains that he is afraid to ask a coworker to dinner might be helped to reframe the situation as one in which he is sparing himself and his coworker from possible romantic entanglements that may interfere with job performance.

In another case, a single parent who is angry at her former husband for encouraging their child to fight back when teased may be helped to reframe the situation as one in which her former husband is helping the child develop and maintain a male identity.

Once a member experiences a problem from a new perspective, the positive aspects of the situation are highlighted and the negative aspects of the situation have a better chance of being changed. The woman, for example, may then thank her former husband for staying involved with their child and suggest some other ways that the husband might help the child, such as how to settle disputes without fighting. The male group member may develop a platonic friendship with his coworker.

Reframing can also be used to help a member experience a problem or concern as an asset (Lynch & Cuper, 2010; Waltz & Hayes, 2010). For example, in a situation in which a member's spouse does not want to have sexual relations, the problem can be viewed as a helpful sign that something is wrong in their relationship.

Visualization and Cognitive Imagery Techniques. Everyone daydreams, has memories of certain places, people, and things. Visualization encourages group members to focus on a particular image that is relaxing for them (Stahl & Goldstein, 2010). This is illustrated in the following case example.

Case Example   Using Visualization and Cognitive Imagery

Group members were asked to imagine themselves on a beach, sitting on a bench near a pond, or in a park. When visualizing the scene, members were asked to involve all their senses. The worker began by helping members visualize their favorite beach. Members were asked to envision the boats, trees, and the cloud formations that they could see in their minds' eyes. They were also asked to feel the sunlight hitting their body, to hear the sound of the waves, and to smell and taste the salt air and the other aromas they remember. As they were visualizing the scene, members were asked to say things to themselves that reduced tension, such as "The sun feels good and I am feeling at peace with myself and the world around me."

When using visualization in a group, workers should guide the group through a particular visualization. Have the group members sit in a relaxing position and close their eyes. Set the scene and gradually add details. While doing this, ensure that members remain in a relaxed state and that they are able to imagine the situation vividly. Members should be instructed to signal the worker immediately if their anxiety increases or if the cognitive image they are visualizing fades. To help produce vivid imagery, the worker should recite a richly detailed image while members are in a relaxed state with their eyes closed. If workers have access to an audiotape with sounds from the scene, such as waves, breezes blowing, and so forth, they can use it to enhance the experience. Once the visualization is complete, workers can do a group go-round asking members what scene they imagined, why they find it especially relaxing, and how they might use visualization at home between sessions. Between meetings, workers should ask group members to practice using their own favorite visualization, adding details, sounds, colors, smells, and tastes as they go along.

Flooding and implosion are two other cognitive imagery techniques used to extinguish excessive and unproductive reactions to feared or anxiety-provoking events

(Kazdin, 2013). In *implosion*, the member is asked to imagine the most extreme version of a feared event or stimulus within the protected environment of the group. Thus, if a group member experiences anxiety when thinking about asking someone for a date, the member would be asked to imagine that person saying no and making a disparaging remark such as "I wouldn't go out with someone like you" or "You're not sophisticated enough for me." Because the member will not experience any horrible consequences from such a rebuff, he or she will overcome the fear associated with the possible consequences of asking for a date. Members often react to this technique with comments such as "That wasn't so bad" or "I didn't like the reaction I received, but I learned that I could live with it. I won't be so afraid of the consequences the next time."

Flooding is a procedure similar to implosion except that the member is asked to imagine the actual feared event rather than an extreme or exaggerated version of it. Feedback from other group members can be used to help the member see that although reactions may, at times, be unpleasant, they can be handled without great difficulty. The member learns how others cope with unpleasant reactions and develops personal methods for coping.

Research evidence on flooding and implosion suggests that *in vivo* exposure to the situation or event is more successful than imagined exposure (Kazdin, 2013). In group treatment, a role-play exercise may be used to expose members to the feared situations. After members practice handling the situation in the group, they can be assigned the task of experiencing the situation outside the group. Because duration of exposure is also associated with treatment outcomes, members should be encouraged to lengthen their exposure and practice flooding and implosion frequently.

Imagery techniques are used widely in ACT and DBT. In ACT, imagery is conjured up by stories that contain metaphors, paradoxes, and other verbal strategies to break through dysfunctional thought patterns. In ACT, dysfunctional thought patterns are called unworkable because they do not lead to actions to improve a member's situation (Waltz & Hayes, 2010). In DBT, imagery techniques are used when learning mindfulness, emotional regulation, distress tolerance, and interpersonal effectiveness skills (Linehan, 2015). Imagery skills are used to soothe and distract group members experiencing painful thoughts and emotions, to change thinking patterns, and to encourage radical acceptance. They may also be used to help members take action to change unhelpful control strategies and replace them with positive coping skills that are more helpful in the present moment (Lynch & Cuper, 2010).

Deep Breathing.   One of the simplest yet most effective strategies for reducing tension is deep breathing. Although deep breathing can be done almost anywhere and in any position, Davis, Eshelman, and McKay (2008) recommend that members do it while sitting or lying down with their feet slightly apart. The basic procedure starts with members inhaling slowly and deeply through the nose and exhaling through the mouth. The idea is to take long slow breaths focusing on the air as it goes into the member's nose, fills up the abdomen, and then is released again through the nose. Members are asked to meditate on their breath going slowly in and out as they become more relaxed. They are asked to repeat the deep breathing about five times. Members can combine deep breathing with words. For example, each time members take in a breath they can say "I am" and when they exhale "relaxing." There are many alternatives to this simple deep breathing procedure. For example, Davis, Eshelman, and McKay (2008) suggest an alternative breathing procedure in which members sit in a comfortable position, rest the index and second finger of their right hand on their forehead, and close their right nostril with their thumb. After inhaling through their left nostril, members are asked to close their left nostril with their ring finger and open their right nostril by removing their thumb and exhale through their right nostril. Next, they are asked to inhale through their right nostril, close their right nostril with their thumb, and open their left nostril. Then, they are asked to exhale through their left nostril and then inhale through their left nostril. Members are asked to repeat the procedure several times and encouraged to practice it at home.

Davis, Eshelman, and McKay (2008) also give instructions for breath retraining or controlled breathing to avoid panic breathing. People who panic often gasp for breath, holding on to it, and then follow it with shallow breathing or hyperventilation. To avoid this, they suggest that at the first sign of nervousness or panic, members should exhale first and then breathe in and exhale through their nose. When members exhale they should make sure their exhalation is longer than their inhalation. One way to ensure this is to count to three while inhaling slowly, and then count to four while exhaling. Members can slow their breathing even further by counting to four while inhaling and counting to five while exhaling. While exhaling, and counting, members are encouraged to focus on their breath going in and out. Gradually they may also want to say while inhaling "I am" and while exhaling "relaxing."

When practicing deep breathing in a group setting, all members usually do it together. In fact, it is quite common to start children, teen, and adult groups with a quick deep breathing exercise. This eases the transition from the previous setting and sets the tone for calm, focused interactions. Following the practice, a group go-round can be used so that each person can talk about how it felt for them and where and when they might use it in between sessions. Workers may find that some members say they have used deep breathing before and found it helpful. Workers can encourage these members to describe their experiences, asking if they count breaths, say anything to themselves, or do any other variation on the technique.

Progressive Muscle Relaxation. This technique combines cognitive instructions with physical activities to relieve stress and help group members overcome anxiety. The premise is that muscle tension is related to anxiety and stress. Helping members reduce muscle tension, therefore, helps relieve anxiety.

Case Example   Deep Breathing

With members seated in comfortable chairs or reclining on the floor, the worker explains the entire progressive muscle relaxation procedure to them. Members should be as comfortable as possible throughout the procedure. In a calm, hypnotic voice, the worker (or an audiotaped voice) repeats the relaxation instructions that include tensing and relaxing each major muscle group in the body. For example, the worker might say, "Stretch your arms out next to you [or on your lap, if seated]. Make a fist with both hands as hard as you can. Feel the tension and tightness in your hands. Keep your hands clenched [10 seconds]. Now relax. Just let your hands rest against the floor [or on your lap, if seated]. Notice how the tension and tightness are leaving your hands. Notice how the feelings of tension are being replaced by warm feelings of relaxation and comfort. Notice how your hands feel now compared with when you were tensing them."

Each muscle group is tensed and relaxed in this manner. Instructions for the entire relaxation procedure are not given here, but they are available in several excellent sources (Bernstein, Borkovek, & Hazlett-Stevens, 2000; Davis, Eshelman, & McKay, 2008; Lazarus, 2000). CDs and DVDs are available from many print and Internet sources.

Although progressive muscle relaxation is most often used in individual treatment, it can be used in groups. The major drawback in using this technique in group treatment is that it requires cooperation from every member. One member who distracts the group can ruin the effect of the procedure for everyone else. Sometimes the distraction may be unintentional, such as when a member falls asleep and begins to snore. In other situations, the distraction may be intentional. For example, a member who is not motivated may laugh or joke during the first tension-release cycle and thereby distract other group members.

To use relaxation effectively, the entire procedure should be explained before beginning. To reduce intentional distractions, members should have the opportunity to voice any questions or any reluctance about using the procedure before beginning. Practicing on one set of muscles and asking members about their reactions is also recommended before beginning the entire procedure the first time. To reduce unintentional distractions, members should be given a signal to let the group leader know if they are having a problem. For example, a member might not be able to relax or, in rare cases, may become more tense. The member uses the signal to get individual attention from the worker. The relaxing nature of the procedure, dim lights, and comfortable position sometimes causes members to fall asleep and the resulting rhythmic breathing or snoring may be distracting to others. Such unintentional distractions can be reduced if the worker explains that sleeping members will be awakened by a touch on the hand or arm.

Other relaxation procedures can be used as a substitute for progressive muscle relaxation, but all require some lifestyle changes (Barlow, Rapee, & Perini, 2014). For example, some members may prefer deep breathing, meditation, or yoga. Although developed from differing theoretical orientations, all can achieve a similar result: a relaxed group member. Therefore, it is a good idea for the group worker to offer a menu of choices for how to relax that will fit the lifestyles and preferences of different group members.

Systematic Desensitization.   This technique requires the worker to help members construct a hierarchy of situations or scenes that are feared. Starting with the least feared situation and progressing to the most feared situation, members are asked to imagine each situation while they are in a state of deep relaxation induced by progressive muscle relaxation. A hierarchy of situations should consist of at least 10 scenes that cause the member to experience gradually increasing levels of anxiety, as the following case example illustrates.

Case Example   Systematic Desensitization Hierarchy

A hierarchy for a member who has been too fearful to date consists of (1) thinking about a prospective dating partner, (2) considering asking that person for a date, (3) planning where to go on the date, (4) planning how to ask the person for a date, (5) approaching the person to ask for a date, (6) starting a conversation, (7) asking the person for a date, (8) driving to the person's house, (9) walking up to the person's home, and (10) going out with the person. The member worked through the hierarchy slowly, only progressing when he felt comfortable at each step.

Depending on the extent and the intensity of the anxiety, hierarchies may contain many more scenes. Scenes should not jump too quickly from a low to a high level of anxiety. For very fearful members, it is often necessary to construct hierarchies with as many as 20 or 30 scenes.

Once the members are helped to construct their own hierarchies (even if each member has the same phobia, individual hierarchies differ), the progressive muscle relaxation technique is used to induce a state of relaxation. The members are then asked to imagine the first scene on their hierarchy as if they were actually involved in it for about 10 seconds. If members experience anxiety, they are instructed to signal by raising a finger. Members experiencing anxiety are told to stop imagining the scene and helped to return to their former state of relaxation. When they are fully relaxed, they can imagine the scene again.

At this point, desensitization proceeds at the pace of the slowest group member unless some provision is made for members to complete their hierarchies at their own pace. One method to overcome this problem is to have members work in pairs to help each other work through the hierarchy each has developed. The worker should not allow members to work on their hierarchies for more than 30 minutes because the desensitization procedure is quite demanding, both in terms of continuously visualizing scenes and in remaining in a deeply relaxed state. If members do not complete their hierarchies during one meeting, they can begin the next meeting with the next to last scene they completed successfully in the previous meeting. Systematic desensitization is particularly effective for treatment groups composed of members with phobias, and may be helpful in conjunction with other treatments for panic attacks and symptoms related to trauma such as Post Traumatic Stress Disorder.

Mindfulness Meditation. Mindfulness meditation is a deceptively simple technique to explain. Group members choose a particular focal point and allow other thoughts to float by their consciousness like clouds. The focal point may be the breath as in deep breathing or it may be a particular thought, such as an object like a leaf in a stream, a beautiful mountain ledge, or a pool next to a waterfall. According to mindfulness therapy, our intelligence has two distinct functions. The first is to divide things up and categorize them. The second function is to connect and see similarities (Bien, 2006). The first function predominates in Western culture but is no less important than the second function. Mindfulness meditation emphasizes the second function so that we see how things are related, interconnected, and interdependent (Brown, Cresswell, & Ryan, 2015).

When we meditate even for a few minutes we become an observer of our thoughts as they pass through our consciousness and we do nothing to interfere with them except refocus on our breath, a beautiful mountain, a waterfall, a beach, or whatever we are using as a focal point. This reduces tension because we can't focus on anxiety-producing situations or other negative thoughts for too long before returning to the focal point. It also enables us to see our situation as a neutral observer. Once we are able to observe our situation as a neutral observer, we can see it more clearly. We can then decide deliberately to take action to do something about the way we view ourselves or our situation.

Mindfulness meditation leads to letting go and letting ourselves be with our current selves (Bien, 2006; Brown, Cresswell, & Ryan, 2015). There is a peacefulness that builds up in learning to take a few minutes to focus our thoughts while we are in a relaxed state of mind. We can remember these feelings and the behaviors that go along with the meditative state as we go about our daily activities.

We are not "doing nothing" when we meditate. Rather we are actively and deliberately focusing on our focal point. Exercises in the form of meditating on a story with metaphorical characteristics or meditating on a visualization can help us to achieve a peaceful mind. Both ACT and DBT call for giving up control of the past, a willingness to accept our past without resentment or anger, and without trying to hold onto it.

DBT also emphasizes being mindful in daily life and having a daily mindfulness regime. This might include mindful breathing, doing tasks mindfully, and wise-mind meditation. Wise-mind meditation is being mindful of the emotions as well as the facts of a situation, making decisions that feel right at a core level of values, and examining the results of the decisions we make (McKay, Wood, & Brantley, 2007; Linehan, 2015). There has been great interest in the use of mindfulness meditation for many types of problems. Some good sources for additional reading include: Bowen, Chawla, and Marlatt (2011); Brown, Creswell, and Ryan (2015); Stahl and Goldstein (2010); Rogers and Maytan, (2012); Segal, Williams, Teasdale, and Kabat-Zinn (2012); Sundquist et al., (2014). The evidence-base for the effectiveness of mindfulness therapy is growing (see, for example, Piet & Hougaard, 2011).

Interpersonal Interventions

Group work is an especially appropriate modality for dealing with interpersonal problems. Used effectively, the group can become a natural laboratory for examining and improving the relationships members have with one another. Unlike individual treatment, a group offers members the opportunity to demonstrate their interpersonal skills and receive feedback from a variety of people. Members can serve as models of particular interpersonal skills and can play various roles in situations acted out in the group.

Interpersonal behaviors can be learned indirectly by listening to others describe how to behave in a situation. But behaviors are more effectively learned (1) vicariously, by watching what other people do or say, and (2) directly, by repeating and practicing new behaviors. When learned directly, a new behavior is usually performed on a trial-and-error basis until it is performed appropriately.

Learning a new behavior by hearing it described is often imprecise and is fraught with potential misinterpretation. Therefore, behavior is most adequately taught by having a member watch someone else perform it correctly and having the member practice the new behavior in a role-play exercise.

Many workers tend to allow the group to spend too much time discussing how to behave without actually helping members practice new behaviors, perhaps because of the contrived nature of role-play situations, and some members' resistance to role playing. The learning that occurs from watching a model and rehearsing a new behavior, compared with merely talking about how to perform a new behavior, suggests that both modeling and role-play techniques should be used more frequently by workers helping members learn new or improved interpersonal behaviors. For example, DBT focuses on basic and advanced interpersonal effectiveness skills training as one of its components. Role playing can help this component to be effective.

Learning by Observing Models

Several factors affect the extent to which behaviors are learned by observing others (Bandura, 1977). Workers should understand the process underlying observational learning so that they can use modeling to help members solve interpersonal problems and learn new interpersonal skills.

Figure 10.1 illustrates the major components of observational learning. Performance of the modeled behavior depends on:

- The level of attention or awareness of the observer
- The extent to which the observer retains what is seen
- The observer's abilities to perform the observed behavior
- The extent to which the observer is motivated to perform the behavior

The attention of a member who observes a model is important because, although behavior may be learned without one's awareness, attention is always selective and is greatly facilitated by focusing on what is being observed. The worker can help focus awareness by calling members' attention to particular aspects of a model's behavior. For example, a member who is learning to be more assertive may be asked to pay particular attention to the facial expressions, body positions, and voice tones of a member who is modeling an assertive response.

Attention is also enhanced by the attractiveness of the model. For example, a member is more likely to pay attention to a group member who is held in high regard than to a member who has low status in the group. Members are also likely to be more attentive

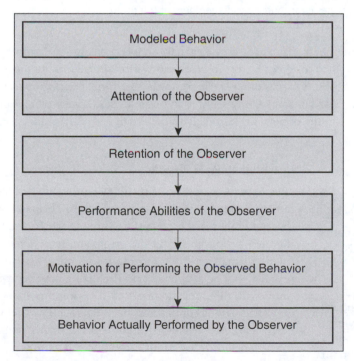

Figure 10.1
The Process of Observational Learning

to models who are similar to themselves. Thus, workers should try to match the characteristics of models to the members who are observing them. That is why it is often helpful to bring in role models who have completed group treatment successfully and can talk about the obstacles they faced before becoming successful, and how they maintained gains made during their time in the group.

Retention processes are also important in learning an observed behavior. In addition to developing images of the behavior that can be easily retrieved from a member's memory, retention is often facilitated if the model explains the covert and overt processes he or she goes through before performing a behavior. Explanations help the member develop a cognitive structure in which to organize perceptual images. As can be seen in the following case, explaining general principles also provides an organizing framework that the member can use in different situations encountered in the future.

Case Example   Learning New Behaviors

When modeling an assertive behavior, a worker helped members to understand how internal monologues and dialogues can facilitate an assertive response. For example, she explained that she makes self-statements, such as "I have a right to tell the person . . ." She explained that those kinds of self-statements encourage assertiveness and that self-statements that focus on why an assertive response should not be made contribute to a lack of assertiveness. The worker also explained general principles that she keeps in mind when responding to situations that require an assertive response. For example, she explained that she makes direct statements, explaining her needs or perceptions, and making a clear statement or a request of the person with whom she is interacting. The members of the group were then encouraged to describe situations where they would like to be more assertive and to practice these and other strategies contributed by all members of the group.

Group members may know how to behave in interpersonal situations but may not be motivated to do so. What factors increase motivation? Behaviors are more likely to be imitated if the observer sees others being rewarded for similar performances (Antony & Roemer, 2011; Kazdin, 2013). Conversely, if an observer sees others being sanctioned for a given behavior, the observer is less likely to behave in a way that may result in similar sanctions.

Intervention

Behavior: Critically choose and implement interventions to achieve practice goals and enhance capacities of clients and constituencies

Critical Thinking Question: Role playing can help group members learn new behaviors. How can groups use role playing during the middle stage of an anger management group?

Learning by Role Playing

New behaviors are often difficult to perform in real life situations until they are practiced a number of times. The best way to ensure that a member is able to perform a behavior correctly is to have the member perform it in the group and receive feedback about the performance. Video recording a member's performance can provide very helpful feedback. Practicing new behaviors several times with different members, and asking members to practice them with friends or partners between meetings, helps to solidify newly learned behaviors, overcome performance fears, and make the new behavior feel more automatic and natural.

Role playing is a powerful tool for assessment and behavior change. As shown in Table 10.1, role-playing techniques increase

Table 10.1   Uses of Unstructured Role-Play Procedures

Procedure	Awareness/Understanding	Behavior Change
A. Primary Role-Play Procedures		
1. Own role	Demonstrates and clarifies members' behavior, their role in interpersonal interactions, and their concerns and problems Facilitates members' insight into their own feelings, thoughts, and behaviors Identifies situational cues to facilitate differential responses Identifies members' problems and concerns	Allows members to practice new behaviors Reduces members' performance anxiety Prepares members for obstacles and setbacks
2. Role reversal	Stimulates empathy for another person whose role is being enacted by the protagonist Increases members' awareness of cognitive and affective aspects of other people Objectifies and clarifies the situational context of members' own behaviors	Encourages spontaneity and participation Facilitates changes in members' expectations of others Facilitates change in members' behavior Improves empathic skills
3. Autodrama/ monodrama/ chairing	Same as for own role and role-reversal procedures Identifies and clarifies members' own feelings at deeper levels than own-role or role-reversal procedures Increases members' awareness of their own self-talk	Same as for own role and role-reversal procedures Facilitates learning of adaptive self-talk Enables changes on deeper, more complex levels than own-role or role-reversal procedures
4. Sculpting/ choreography (Action sociogram)	Stimulates members' awareness and discussion of their own behavior and the group's interaction patterns	Facilitates changes in members' attitudes, behaviors, and interaction patterns
B. Supplementary Role-Play Procedures		
1. On-the-spot interview	Identifies and clarifies members' thoughts and feelings while they are in a role Connects thinking and feeling to behaviors in a role	Provides practice in self-awareness and self-talk
2. Soliloquy	Same as on-the-spot interview procedure but less structured	Same as on-the-spot interview procedure
3. Doubling	Helps members verbalize and express covert thoughts, feelings, and behaviors Same as on-the-spot interview procedure Identifies new behaviors for acquisition	Same as on-the-spot interview procedure Gives permission and support for members' owning their own thoughts, feelings, and behaviors Facilitates expression of feelings Promotes members' skill in using feelings as cues for appropriate responses Allows members to practice their self-expression skills

Table 10.1   (Continued)

Procedure	Awareness/Understanding	Behavior Change
4. Mirror	Promotes members' knowledge of the consequences of their own behavior on others Enables self-confrontation	Provides members the opportunity to practice new behaviors Enables feedback and reinforcement when learning new behaviors Facilitates learning of self-disclosure skills
5. Sharing	Universalizes members' experiences Models self-disclosure	Provides support and confirmation of members' experiences, abilities, etc.

members' awareness and understanding of their interpersonal skills and produce behavior changes by providing members with corrective feedback and the opportunity to practice improved responses in the sheltered environment of the group.

Role-playing techniques can be structured, semi-structured, or unstructured. Structured procedures use predetermined scripts or vignettes developed by the leader, and members act out prescribed roles believed to be important by the leader. For example, children with autistic spectrum disorders in a social skills group were asked to role play friendly greetings, and how to ask a teacher for help. The worker used an evidence-based field tested curriculum that described these and other social skills role plays.

Semi-structured role plays enable the worker and the members to be spontaneous. During psychodrama, for example, there is a warm-up period followed by the action, and then a period for closure (Duffy, 2008; McHenry & McHenry, 2015). Within this structure, there is plenty of freedom for the worker and the group members to shape the content. Some psychodrama techniques such as the "magic shop" employ structure and spontaneity at the same time (Verhofstadt-Deneve, 2000). The basic structure in the "magic shop" is that members who volunteer to participate have to buy psychological qualities or characteristics that they feel they lack. The types of qualities that are bought, and the type of payment made to purchase the qualities, are unique to the members engaged in the role play, but the group can profit from a discussion of the choices no matter what choices members make.

Unstructured role-play procedures are listed in Table 10.1. The procedures are developmental and open-ended to allow spontaneous, emerging processes of learning and problem solving. Unstructured role-play procedures can be further divided into primary and secondary procedures. Primary role-play procedures can be used alone to accomplish particular purposes; secondary procedures are used in conjunction with primary procedures to extend their effect and widen their scope (Duffy, 2008; Blatner, 1996; McHenry & McHenry, 2015).

Primary Role-Play Procedures

Own Role. In the own-role procedure, a member uses his or her experiences and plays the protagonist. Other roles are played by the worker or other group members who may represent people, feeling states, thoughts, or objects. The own-role technique is particularly useful in assessing a member's interpersonal skills because it allows the worker and other group members to observe how the protagonist acts in a particular situation.

The own-role procedure is also helpful as a means for members to practice new behaviors. Supportive procedures, such as the soliloquy, the on-the-spot interview, or doubling can be used to increase a member's awareness of behavior while performing the role of protagonist.

Role Reversal. In role reversal, a group member acts as the protagonist by taking on the role of another person. For example, a husband may act in the role of his spouse. The procedure enables a member to experience a situation from another's point of view. Role reversal is particularly useful for teaching empathy, especially if it is used with doubling or soliloquy. It helps to clarify situations and to increase members' self-awareness. It also increases the spontaneity, flexibility, and openness of the member playing the protagonist's role. Variations of this procedure include substitute role playing (playing a symbolic, substitute role) and role distance (playing an emotionally distant role).

Autodrama, Monodrama, and Chairing. A procedure in which a group member plays multiple roles is variously called autodrama, monodrama, and chairing (Blatner, 1996). The multiple roles represent the different ways members view themselves or the different ways others view a member. The procedure is usually conducted using one or more empty chairs, each representing a role, a character part, or a personality aspect. The member switches from one chair to another in changing roles. When occupying each chair, the person initiates and maintains a dialogue with the other chairs that represent other aspects of the person's self.

The technique is particularly useful in helping members become aware of the various roles they play and their effects on each other. It is also useful in helping members assess internal dialogues and self-talk, such as irrational beliefs and devaluating self-statements. Therefore, the procedure can be used effectively in cooperation with cognitive restructuring procedures to practice adaptive self-statements and self-instructions that aid effective problem solving. Self-role and double chairing are other names for this procedure.

Sculpting and Choreography. Also called action sociogram, variations of the sculpting and choreography technique are psychodrama and sociodrama (Blatner, 1996; Moreno, 1946). In this procedure, a member, as protagonist, is directed to sculpt or position himself or herself and other group members in a drama that represents a symbolic or real situation in the member's life. The protagonist explains each person's role, and the worker directs the action, which can last for an extended period of time.

The dramatic enactment is designed to expose intense feelings and conflicts in a member's life and thus it can be used as an assessment device by the worker. Another benefit of the technique is that it immerses the whole group in intense participatory involvement leading to in-depth self-disclosure and enactment of crucial concerns and issues. In addition to the self-awareness this technique produces, the procedure helps the protagonist understand the importance of others in personal life situations. Although there is little empirical evidence for the efficacy of the technique, clinical reports and experience suggest that the cathartic experience and heightened awareness that result from participating in a dramatic enactment can lead to changes in members' thoughts, feelings, behaviors, attitudes, and interaction patterns.

The psychodrama variation of the technique focuses on the internal, psychological status of the actors. The sociodrama variation emphasizes the social and environmental aspects of the protagonist's situation. For an excellent, in-depth explanation of these procedures, see Blatner (1996).

Supplementary Role-Play Procedures

On-The-Spot Interview. On-the-spot interviewing involves stopping the role-play action before it is finished and interviewing one or more actors. The worker asks specific, detailed questions designed to elicit particular thoughts and feelings at that point in the role play. The procedure is designed to increase a member's awareness of cognitive, affective, and behavioral aspects of a role performance. It identifies self-statements and self-talk that are dysfunctional and self-devaluating. It also teaches self-observation and enhances self-awareness.

Soliloquy. The soliloquy procedure involves stopping the role-play action and asking an actor to disclose what he or she is thinking or feeling. Unlike the on-the-spot interview, in which the actor is asked specific, closed-ended questions, soliloquy questions are open ended and encourage the member to engage in a monologue that discloses in-depth thoughts and feelings. The procedure is particularly useful for increasing a member's self-awareness.

Doubling. The doubling procedure uses a group member to act as the alter ego or inner voice of the protagonist. To emphasize identification with the protagonist, the double is required to speak in the first person, for example, saying, "I feel . . ." or "I think . . ." Variations on the procedure are the "divided double" and the "multiple double." In the divided double, the alter ego speaks for different parts of the protagonist's inner self. The multiple double calls for two or more actors to speak for different aspects of the protagonist's self. To validate the truth of a double's statements in offering inferences, interpretations, or alternative reactions, the protagonist is sometimes asked to repeat and accept or reject the double's statements.

The doubling procedure can serve several important functions. It helps make role plays more dramatic and produces more in-depth experiences. It facilitates understanding and self-awareness of the protagonist's behavior. In addition to fostering insight, it gives permission for the protagonist to acknowledge repressed or taboo thoughts and feelings. It also increases the emotional sensitivity and self-expression of the protagonist. The procedure is often used in conjunction with own-role, chairing, and sculpting procedures.

Mirror. In the mirror procedure, a group member reenacts a role-played performance for the protagonist. Other members can verify the accuracy of the replay. The procedure may also be used in an exaggerated, amplified, and stereotypical manner to emphasize particular aspects of the protagonist's behavior.

The procedure is useful as a confrontational technique to help protagonists gain awareness of their behaviors. It is an excellent substitute for videotape feedback when videotape equipment is unavailable. The procedure is particularly useful in conjunction with modeling, coaching, and prompting to provide feedback to a member attempting to learn a new behavior. It is also a way of involving other group members in a member's situation to facilitate their empathy and their skills in self-expression.

Sharing. The sharing procedure is often used at the close of role-play action. Group members give members who have role played feedback about their performances. The procedure is designed to provide supportive feedback to the member who risked himself or herself in revealing a difficult situation by acting as the protagonist in the role play. It also enables members to share their own reactions and feelings to the role play.

? Assess your understanding of intrapersonal and interpersonal interventions carried out in the middle stage by taking this brief quiz.

Environmental Interventions

Environmental interventions help members to modify or change the psychosocial and physical situations in which they live. Environmental interventions consist of:

- Connecting members to concrete resources
- Expanding members' social networks
- Modifying the contingencies that result when members perform desired behaviors
- Planning physical environments to facilitate members' goal achievement

Connecting Members to Concrete Resources

To connect clients to concrete resources, the worker first identifies the member's need and then assesses the member's ability and motivation to follow through and obtain the resource. For a highly motivated, well-functioning group member, the worker may be able to act as a broker to identify a contact person at the appropriate resource and give the member general information about what to expect when contacting the resource. The worker verifies that the member has obtained the needed resource at the next group session.

In some treatment groups, such as those composed of severely disabled psychiatric patients or older people with dementia, workers may have to take additional steps to ensure that members obtain the resources they need. For example, it may take some time to prepare members for a referral because of their lack of motivation or their failure to recognize their need for services. It may also be necessary to contact family members or guardians to help prepare them for a referral. In addition, medical disabilities may limit or prevent members from contacting resources without assistance. Transportation may have to be arranged, and the worker, an aide, or a volunteer may have to accompany the member to the resource. It may also be necessary to teach members the skills necessary to obtain a needed resource. For example, an unemployed group member might need to learn interviewing and resume-writing skills before beginning a job search. Some of the steps for making an effective referral for impaired group members are presented below.

Making Referrals on Behalf of Group Members with Severe Disabilities
- Thoroughly prepare the member for the referral. Review the reasons for the referral, how it is expected to help the member, and how it will help members to achieve individual and group goals.
- Carefully consider members' ability to access and engage the referral source.
- Arrange for escort services, transportation, or other resources that will ensure that members reach the referral source.
- Help members with the skills and support systems to obtain and utilize referrals.

- Check to see that members have reached referral sources and that they are meeting the members' needs.
- With the consent of members, involve family or trusted individuals in the decision to seek a referral, and the choice of the referral source.
  - Help family members and trusted individuals to become advocates and brokers for members, helping them to obtain needed resources while maintaining and respecting their autonomy.

Expanding Members' Social Networks

Another type of environmental intervention consists of helping socially isolated members expand their social networks by gaining needed support from others (Forse & Degenne, 1999). The first step in expanding a member's social network is to analyze the member's current social relationships. Figure 10.2 illustrates the social network of Tom, a socially isolated member of a support group for people who have recently separated. The diagram indicates that Tom has only two active social relationships. Tom's

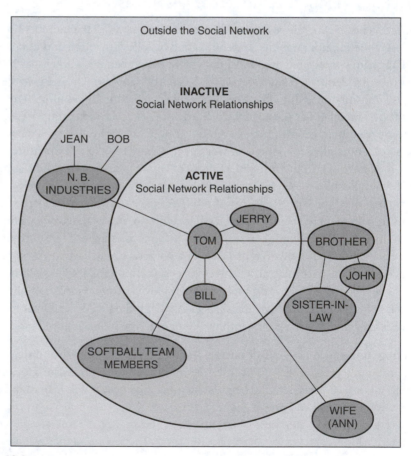

Figure 10.2
A Social Network Chart

other network relationships are inactive. He no longer plays with the softball team; he no longer sees Jean or Bob, with whom he used to be friendly; and because his brother lives nearly 1,000 miles away, they rarely see one another.

Diagramming a member's social network on a flip chart or blackboard can stimulate group discussion about ways to expand the network. This is illustrated in the following case example.

Case Example   Diagramming a Member's Social Network

After examining the chart shown in Figure 10.2, several group members suggested that Tom renew former network relationships that lapsed after his marriage. To do this, Tom rejoined the softball team and renewed his friendships with Jean and Bob. Tom was also encouraged to join Parents without Partners, a self-help group that sponsors many social, recreational, and educational events in his community. In a subsequent group meeting Tom reported making several new friends in this organization and that he had also begun dating someone that he met during a dinner sponsored by the organization. He also mentioned that he had become friendly with several members of the softball team and that one person invited him to join a bowling league.

Analyzing one group member's social network can stimulate other members to consider their own networks. Examining Figure 10.2 might cause members to become aware that they could also benefit from expanding their own social relationships. For example, after confirming that group members wanted to become more involved with one another, the worker suggested that members exchange telephone numbers and choose one person to call during the week. By scheduling one meeting at a member's home and supporting members' suggestions that they get together informally after the meeting, the worker encouraged the members to form a supportive social network for one another. As the members began to meet regularly, it became apparent that child care responsibilities limited many of the members' abilities to socialize, so members with children decided to help each other with child care, thereby freeing each other to engage in social activities. Thus, through a worker's intervention efforts and the mutual-aid properties of the group, members' social networks were expanded.

Another strategy that can be used to expand members' social networks is to ask them during the first group meeting if they would like to exchange telephone numbers and e-mail addresses. If all members give their permission, and if between-meeting contact is not contraindicated for therapeutic reasons, a list of telephone numbers and e-mail addresses of all group members can be shared during the second meeting. The worker can also facilitate members' contacting each other between meetings by helping members choose a partner who they will call or e-mail during the week. Clinical experience suggests that, for this to be effective, it is often helpful for the pair to pick a time to call and who will make the call. It is also helpful to briefly discuss the calls or e-mails during subsequent group meetings.

Contingency Management Procedures

So that members can maintain their successes between group sessions, it is often necessary to modify or change the rewards and punishments they receive for behaving in ways that are not consistent with their treatment goals. This procedure is sometimes called *contingency management* because the rewards or punishments that are contingent on the performance of a behavior are modified to increase or decrease the probability that a behavior will be performed in the future (Antony & Roemer, 2011; Kazdin, 2013; Sheldon, 2011).

Contingencies that increase the probability that a member will perform a behavior are called *reinforcers*. Typical positive reinforcers include social rewards that are verbal, such as praise, and nonverbal, such as a smile, a pat on the back, and similar signs of approval. Positive reinforcers also include tangible rewards, such as money and food.

Negative reinforcers also increase behaviors. But unlike positive reinforcers that increase behavior through rewards, negative reinforcers increase behavior by giving someone attention or some other reward for doing something that is inappropriate. To decrease unwanted behaviors, the worker can either ignore the behavior or can administer some kind of sanction or punishment. Often, inappropriate behaviors will extinguish themselves if they are simply ignored or not reinforced. This works when the member in question is seeking attention for an inappropriate behavior. However, it will not work if the inappropriate behavior is self-reinforcing. Then, the worker may have to apply a sanction. Social disapproval or denial of a tangible reward can then be used to try to distinguish an unwanted behavior. For example, a member of an inpatient group for people suffering from severe and persistent mental disorders may lose the privilege to go to a "movie night" with other residents because he did not follow group rules about confidentiality. Workers, however, should emphasize the use of positive reinforcers that members enjoy receiving rather than sanctions that are unpleasant and often result in deleterious side effects, such as anger. In addition to causing anger and resentment, sanctions, such as taking "movie night" away, do not address the problem (why the breach of confidentiality occurred, for example), and they do not reinforce those behaviors that would avoid future breaches of confidentiality.

In general, workers should encourage the use of positive reinforcers to encourage therapeutic behaviors; inattention, ignoring, or other extinction procedures that are used to discourage behaviors that do not help the group reach agreed-upon goals. Often, it is sufficient to reward a desired behavior and ignore an undesirable behavior. Although positive reinforcers are preferred whenever possible, in some circumstances punishments may be imposed for failure to comply with group rules. For example, the members of a children's group decided together that those who came late to group meetings would clean up after snacks were served.

Punishments should not be imposed unilaterally by the worker. The group as a whole should decide on a policy, that is, the type of punishment (social disapproval or removal from the group) and the circumstances in which sanctions will be applied. The resulting policy should be applied uniformly. Also, some of the undesirable side effects of punishment procedures are avoided when members impose their own punishments, sometimes referred to as *response costs*.

The worker should help the group develop realistic rules that are not too restrictive. Sometimes members develop unrealistically harsh rules to govern behavior in the group. William Golding's novel, *Lord of the Flies*, is a literary example of how groups can decide on rules for behavior and punishments that are too severe. It is common for members of children's groups, for example, to develop group rules that, left unchallenged, lead to severe punishment. For example, in one group, members decided that anyone caught laughing should be thrown out of the group. In such cases, the worker should intervene and help the group develop less severe sanctions for misbehavior.

When using contingency management procedures, the worker should begin by helping members identify the rewards and punishments they receive for performing desired and undesired behaviors. Contingencies are identified by monitoring the consequences resulting from the performance of a particular behavior. If contingencies do not act to increase desired behavior and decrease undesired behavior, the worker can help the member modify them. Sometimes members may be able to administer their own rewards. For example, members may be encouraged to praise themselves for performing a certain behavior—to take themselves out for a good meal or buy a new piece of clothing. Such self-reinforcement procedures have been shown to be effective in helping members control their own behaviors and feel better about themselves (Neacsiu, Bohus, & Linehan, 2014). Behaviors are also frequently self-reinforcing, so that changes in behavior are sustained by the approval of others, improved feelings about oneself, and so forth.

It can be helpful to involve other group members or significant others in members' lives in modifying the contingent rewards and punishments members receive for performing desired and undesired behaviors. Family members and friends can help provide an environment that promotes therapeutic goals. For example, a wife or husband may compliment the spouse for positive changes. A mother or father may praise their daughter for helping her little brother with his homework.

To formalize an agreement about what behaviors to reinforce, a verbal or written contingency contract can be developed. The following list specifies the points that should be covered in these contracts.

What Contingency Contracts Should Specify
- What specific behaviors will be performed?
- Who will perform the behaviors?
- How will the behaviors be reinforced?
- Who will administer the reinforcement?

For example, the father of an adolescent group member may agree to take his son on a fishing trip if his son agrees to attend classes without misbehaving for two weeks. Although developing a written contingency contract may strike some individuals as too rigid or formal, it should be recognized that written agreements have the advantage of avoiding confusion later when individuals may have different recollections of the nature of an agreement.

There are many different types of contingency contracts. As mentioned, members may administer their own rewards and punishments in self-administered contingency contracts. Contracts may be made between the group member and significant others, between two group members, or between all group members and the worker. Contracts may also be reciprocal; that is, parties to the contract reward each other for performing desired behaviors. Reciprocal contracts are particularly useful in couples' groups because spouses can reinforce each other for performing desired behaviors. By using contingency management procedures, the worker helps members perform desired behaviors by changing the environmental consequences that result when a behavior is performed. Too often, workers intervene effectively in the group to help members reach desired goals but fail to pay attention to what will happen when members try to perform desired behaviors outside the group. Contingency management procedures are a useful way to extend therapeutic interventions beyond the boundaries of group sessions. Yost and colleagues (1985), for example, described how contingency management procedures can be used to help group members who are depressed to engage in pleasurable activities that help to reduce depression. Martell, Dimidjian, and Lewinshon (2010) described how pleasurable events can be used to increase activity. Behavioral activation is one of several evidence-based interventions for depression (for a review see Dimidjian, Martell, Herman-Dunn, & Hubley, 2014; Forsman, Nordmyr, & Wahlbeck, 2011; Mazzucchelli, Kane, & Rees, 2009). Problem Solving Therapy is another evidence-based intervention that reduces stress and pathology by increasing positive problem-solving attitudes and skills including the use of pleasurable activities (Bell & D'Zurilla, 2009; Nezu, Nezu, & D'Zurilla, 2010).

Some individuals react negatively to contingency contracts because they are perceived as manipulative, artificial, or as relying exclusively on extrinsic rather than intrinsic motivation. It is important to remember that contingency contracts are *voluntary* and *explicit* agreements between two or more parties. Coercive, exploitative, and underhanded attempts to control behavior have no place in the design or the execution of contingency contracts. It is true that contingency contracts specify artificial arrangements of rewards and punishments, but they should be prepared with consideration of the naturally occurring consequences that will sustain the behavior over the long term. For example, in the situation described previously, although the father will not be able to take his son on a fishing trip each time the son behaves well for a two-week period in school, it is anticipated that by behaving well, the son will stop receiving negative feedback from teachers, administrators, and peers and will start enjoying school. Therefore, the artificial arrangement of contingencies will be replaced with naturally occurring contingencies such as praise from the teacher and good report cards. The extrinsic rewards for behaving well will be replaced, over the long term, by intrinsic rewards such as feeling competent, well liked, or self-confident.

Modifying Physical Environments

Helping members modify their physical environments is another type of environmental intervention. Although often given little consideration, the physical environment has a profound effect on the problems and concerns that members experience. Environmental stimuli can make it easier or more difficult for a member to accomplish treatment goals. For example, members of a weight-loss group find that it is more difficult to lose weight if their refrigerators are stocked with fattening foods than if their refrigerators contain only those items that are a part of the diet that members agreed on. Similarly, it is difficult for a member of an inpatient psychotherapy group who is about to be discharged to learn independent living skills in an institutional environment that does not allow the person to cook, clean, or shop.

To the extent possible, workers should help members modify physical environments so they promote goal achievement. In general, physical environments should give members the opportunity to practice the skills they are learning in the group. Members who are learning skills for independent living, for example, should have the opportunity to practice as many of the skills as feasible in the institutional setting in which they live. Physical environments should reduce barriers that are likely to impede a member's attempts to accomplish a goal. For example, a member who is attempting to stop drinking should remove all alcohol from his or her home.

Environmental interventions should be proactive as well as reactive; that is, in addition to ensuring that an environment does not provide unwanted stimuli, the worker should help members modify environments so that they encourage goal-directed behavior. A member who is attempting to lose weight may, for example, place a calorie chart on his refrigerator door to help him plan meals. A member of a parenting group may place a monitoring chart in her child's room. Each time the child behaves correctly, gold stars are placed on the chart. When a certain number of stars accumulate, they can be redeemed for a trip to the zoo or extra play time with Mom or Dad. In both cases, modifications of the environment stimulate efforts toward goal achievement.

In inpatient settings, environmental modifications can include a restructuring of the entire milieu. For example, Tuten, Jones, Schaeffer, and Spitzer (2012) describe a comprehensive behavioral approach for treating substance use disorders, and Swenson, Witterholt, and Bohus (2007) describe how to implement DBT on inpatient psychiatric units.

> **?** Assess your understanding of environmental interventions carried out with group members by taking this brief quiz.

INTERVENING IN THE GROUP AS A WHOLE

Workers select the group as a whole as the focus of interventions when they decide that the group process should be altered to help members achieve their goals. In this way, the group becomes the means as well as the context of treatment. As discussed in Chapter 3, four areas are critical to the effective functioning of any group: (1) communication and interaction patterns, (2) cohesion, (3) social integration, and (4) culture. These are the primary areas in which the worker intervenes when selecting the group as a whole as the focus of interventions.

Because most group dynamics have developed before the middle stage begins, the worker's task during this stage is to maintain and enhance dynamics that are contributing to the group's success and intervene to change dynamics that are interfering with the group's development. Experienced workers realize the power that group dynamics have in leading to successful group outcomes, and this has been supported by numerous recent reviews of the literature (see, for example, Barlow, 2013; Barlow, Rapee, & Perini, 2014; Burlingame, 2010; Burlingame, Strauss, & Joyce, 2013; Burlingame, Whitcomb, & Woodland, 2014; Forsyth, 2014).

Changing Communication and Interaction Patterns

The worker may intervene to change the frequency, duration, distribution, or content of the communication and interaction patterns occurring in a treatment group. The frequency of interactions a member initiates in a group is important because it is difficult, if not impossible, to assess and treat a member who remains relatively silent throughout the group. Members must actively participate if they are to benefit from group treatment.

Shulman (2016) points out that what silent members really fear is being confronted with their silence. Therefore, it is more helpful to prompt such members to speak with statements such as, "What do you think about what _____ is saying?" or "You have some experience with this _____, what do you think?" rather than to confront the members with data that suggest they are not participating frequently enough.

Another way to increase participation is to praise members when they add to the group's discussion. Positive comments such as "That was really helpful" or "I see that you understand what _____ is saying" can be used to show quiet group members that their contributions are valued. Positive reinforcement procedures have been demonstrated to be effective in several studies that have examined methods to increase members' participation in groups (Rose, 1989). Other techniques to increase the frequency of communication include asking members to lead the group discussion on a certain topic and going around the group and eliciting members' thoughts and comments on a particular topic, so that those who tend to be silent do not feel singled out.

Workers also may wish to change the duration of a member's communications in the group. This is particularly true for very talkative members who dominate the group's discussions. Sometimes simply pointing out that other members of the group need time to participate is sufficient to limit a talkative member's communications. For others, it is necessary to develop a contingency contract in which members agree to ignore the talkative member when the member talks for more than a specified length of time. Alternatives to this procedure include interrupting the member after he or she talks for a certain amount of time as well as reminding the member with a nonverbal cue that he or she is talking too much.

Workers may also want to change the distribution of communication and interaction patterns. Ideally, each member of the group should have an opportunity to participate. Although some group members may be more involved in a particular discussion than other members, communications should be distributed fairly evenly among all members over the course of several meetings. Workers should prevent situations in which they are doing most of the communicating or situations in which members direct most of their comments to the worker rather than to each other. Workers may also want to intervene when members of subgroups interact primarily with one another rather than with everyone. The most successful interventions for changing the distribution of communication patterns include cues to help members remain aware of their inappropriate communications, and prompts and positive reinforcement to help them change these patterns.

The content of the messages sent and received in the group is just as important as the frequency, duration, and distribution of group members' communications. Workers should be particularly concerned about the task orientation and the tone of the messages communicated in the group. Workers should intervene when communications are not task relevant or when they are excessively negative. Of course, some group discussion will not be task relevant. Joking, small talk, and interesting but irrelevant stories often make the group more attractive. Members have a need to express their own identity in the group and to satisfy socio-emotional needs that might not be directly relevant to the topic of the group. However, task-irrelevant discussions should not be allowed to take much of the group's time. Members come to treatment groups for particular purposes, and too much irrelevant conversation interferes with their ability to achieve goals, which ultimately leads to their dissatisfaction with the group.

Usually, it is sufficient to point out excessive digressions to the group and call the group's attention back to the session's agenda and the goals that should have been briefly mentioned at the beginning of the meeting. In some cases, however, such intervention may not be sufficient to help the group return to a task-centered discussion. The group's digression may signify a test or a challenge to the worker's authority, dissatisfaction with the content outlined in the session agenda, or an indication that group members are too fearful or anxious to discuss a particular topic. In such cases, it is helpful for the worker to point out a personal hypothesis about the reasons for the group's digression. Through discussion and feedback, the worker can help members to decide on how best to renew their focus on the group's goals. This process may make members aware that they are avoiding a difficult issue that they need to discuss. In other cases, it may lead to changes in the worker's style or the session's agenda.

Workers should also be concerned about the tone of the messages conveyed in the group. Frequent put-downs; excessive negative comments without suggestions for improvement; and infrequent occurrences of supportive, warm, or reinforcing comments make the group unattractive for its members. To change the tone of messages being communicated in the group, workers can act as models by making supportive comments. Workers can also show their disapproval of negative comments by ignoring them or by suggesting that the member who makes the negative comment accompany it with a positive comment. Exercises designed to help members give positive feedback can also be helpful. For example, a worker might say, "I've noticed we make a lot of comments about what a person does wrong during our role plays. How about for the next role play, each member will identify at least one thing that the person does well."

Changing the Group's Attraction for Its Members

There is a consensus in group work literature (see Chapter 3) that cohesiveness and interpersonal attraction have many beneficial effects on group functioning. Group cohesion is built in a warm, caring, and empathic group environment. The worker can foster the development of this type of environment by actively listening to members, validating their experiences, and affirming their attempts to cope with the situations confronting them (Norcross, 2011). By modeling genuine concern and interest in each member's experiences, the leader encourages members to tune in to each other's needs and to reach out in supportive, mutually helping interactions.

Cohesion and interpersonal attraction can also be stimulated by acknowledging members' efforts to support each other and by praising members for their active and constructive participation in the group. Thus, in addition to modeling concern and interest, the leader should take an active stance in guiding the group to increased cohesion and intimacy. Appropriate self-disclosures and revelations that deepen the group experience and make it more meaningful and more profound should be encouraged. Similarly, gentle and caring confrontations that encourage members to get in touch with their strengths or realize overlooked possibilities and alternative perspectives should be invited.

Physical arrangements can also make a difference in building group cohesion. Groups tend to be more cohesive and attractive when they are relatively small and there is plenty of interaction that is distributed fairly evenly throughout the group. In small groups in which there is considerable interaction, members have the feeling that their ideas are being heard and considered; in large groups and groups with poorly distributed communication patterns, members who are not a part of the "inner circle" of decision makers often feel that their ideas and suggestions are not being given sufficient attention. Suggestions for redistributing communication patterns can also be helpful to make a group more attractive.

Simple creature comforts can also make a difference in the attractiveness of the group. Refreshments such as coffee and doughnuts can be offered, and socializing over coffee during a break in a long session or immediately after a short session helps reduce the exclusive problem focus of groups and allows members to get to know each other as ordinary people rather than as clients. In addition, for some group members, refreshments and snacks can be strong incentives for participating in a group, particularly for children and psychiatric inpatients because their access to snacks is often limited.

Other ways to increase the attractiveness of a group include dispensing rewards such as a weekend pass as an incentive for participation in a group, planning interesting program activities and outings for the agenda of future group meetings, encouraging members to select topics for group discussion, and ensuring that members continue to make progress toward their treatment goals.

As the group becomes more cohesive, some members may fear becoming overly dependent on the group. The leader should encourage members to talk about these feelings and ease their concerns by indicating that such feelings are commonly experienced in groups when cohesion and intimacy increase. Acknowledging the support and security that the group provides and also acknowledging members' efforts to maintain their autonomy and their ability to function independently can help allay members' fears.

Fears about becoming overly dependent sometimes have their roots in problems with members' ability to develop intimate relationships. Intimacy implies vulnerability. When members disclose personal, emotionally charged issues that they may not have been able to talk about with others, they are exposing their vulnerability to the group. Members may have had previous unsatisfactory experiences in revealing emotionally charged issues to persons with whom they felt intimate. Thus, it is natural for members to feel ambivalent about sharing personal issues with the group. It is helpful for the leader to point this out so that all members of the group will be more likely to respond in a sensitive and caring way to fledgling attempts to self-disclose personal issues. Leaders should also make clear that they will protect members by blocking critical, insensitive comments and by encouraging supportive and caring interactions. The following case example illustrates this point.

Case Example   Supporting Members' Self Disclosures

In a support group for recently widowed persons, a member who had not talked a great deal broke her silence by stating that she felt that her situation was very different from the situations described by other members. Another member of the group asked her what she meant. She stated that unlike the other members of the group, "she was relieved that her husband had died, and she did not miss him." A member of the group jumped in and said that that was a terrible thing to say. The worker, sensing that this could stop the member from disclosing anything else, asked the gentleman who had responded to the woman who had made the disclosure to hold off in making a judgment about the statement until the member could elaborate and fully explain what she meant. The member then went on to say that this was a second marriage for her. She had had a very difficult relationship with her second husband, including much verbal abuse, and during his long illness he was "miserable to be with." She also said that he suffered during his long illness with throat cancer, and that "no one should go through that much pain, not even him." The worker asked other members if they had any similar feelings. One woman said that her husband died from complications related to Alzheimer's disease, and that for many years he was "not himself." She said that she also felt a sense of relief when he died, but felt guilty about saying that. She thanked the original member for self-disclosing her feelings, because it made it easier for her to self-disclose. The group member who had originally responded negatively then jumped in stating that he was wrong, and that if her husband "was miserable anyway," that it was probably good that "the Lord decided to take him." Other members then stepped in to talk about how difficult it was to care for their spouses before they died. For example, one member picked up the angry feelings expressed by the person who first self-disclosed by stating, "It was really hard not to lose my temper. I lost it all the time. I felt guilty about that, I still do."

There are times when a worker does not want to increase a group's cohesion. For example, cohesion should not be increased in groups in which harmful norms have been established. Classic research by Feldman, Caplinger, and Wodarski (1983), for example, found that in groups composed solely of antisocial boys, interpersonal integration, defined as the reciprocal liking of the boys in a group for one another, was negatively associated with treatment outcomes. In these groups, cohesion apparently resulted in peer pressure to conform to harmful group norms. Thus, antisocial behaviors were reinforced rather than extinguished by group treatment. Prevention efforts to stop youth from joining gangs is another example that is very pertinent for group work practitioners (see, for example, Berlatsky, 2015; Howell & Griffiths, 2016).

Using Social Integration Dynamics Effectively

When it is present, social integration can enhance the functioning of the group as a whole, but when it is absent it can lead to the demise of the group. Social integration is promoted through norms, roles, and status hierarchies. These group dynamics can be viewed both as social controls and as methods of enhancing the integration of individual group members and the cohesion of the group as a whole. Without social controls, group interaction would become chaotic and unpredictable, and the group would soon cease functioning. But in groups in which social controls are too strong, members soon feel restricted and coerced. They tend to rebel against the control or refuse to attend future meetings. Instead of achieving social integration, members feel devalued and lack commitment to the group and to each other.

Workers who command the admiration and respect of group members encourage norms, roles, and status hierarchies that foster the interpersonal integration of each member into the life of the group. Personal characteristics, such as an empathic and warm demeanor; a sense of humor; sensitivity; insight; and the ability to remain calm, collected, and professional in difficult situations encourage members to follow the worker's guidance and leadership. Similarly, specialized knowledge and the judicious use of wisdom gained from personal and professional experience help to increase the potency of the worker. Potent workers are self-confident but able to admit mistakes. They lead by example, not by applying social sanctions or by attempting to control, dominate, or manipulate the group. They tend to ignore rather than to sanction deviant behavior exhibited by group members, preferring instead to acknowledge and praise positive contributions and to set a tone and an atmosphere that encourage members to support and uplift one another. These are the characteristics of transformational leaders previously discussed in Chapter 4.

During the middle stage of treatment groups, the effective worker helps the group develop norms, roles, and status hierarchies that integrate members' activities for goal achievement. Both normative integration (members' acceptance of group norms) and functional integration (members' assuming roles and activities that contribute to the group's work) are positively associated with beneficial group outcomes (Forsyth, 2014). One step that can help members to become normatively and functionally integrated into a group is to prevent domination of the group by one or more members who have a great deal of social power and who do not use it for therapeutic purposes. For example, in a classic study by Felman, Caplinger, and Wodarski (1983), the socially dominant members in groups for youth with antisocial behavior problems subverted therapeutic group norms and resisted efforts to promote prosocial behavior change.

When facilitating normative integration, potent workers help members adhere to therapeutic group norms and change norms that are interfering with the group accomplishing its goals. For example, in a group that has developed a norm that members are not to be verbally abusive with one another, a member who becomes verbally abusive may be asked to leave the group until he or she can regain control.

In other situations, the worker can encourage and protect members who are deviating from harmful group norms. For example, a worker supports and encourages a member of a couples' group who begins to describe problems in the couple's sexual relations, a topic that has not been previously discussed by group members. The worker's role in one situation with problematic social integration norms is illustrated in the following case example.

Case Example   Intervening When Scapegoating Is a Problem in a "Banana Splits" Group

In the middle stage of a "Banana Splits" support group for young adolescents whose parents were separating or divorcing, the worker noticed that a lot of negative attention and comments were being focused on one member, Billy. This had been happening increasingly over the past three sessions. The worker decided to intervene by first asking the whole group if they had noticed that a lot of attention was being devoted to Billy. Two members spoke up making harsh statements about Billy's looks and behavior. The worker then said that he thought the negative comments made to, and about, Billy were a problem for the whole group. She talked about the positive aspects of the group and the fact that they had decided to help each other get through the school year and how the comments toward Billy were interfering with the positive supportive atmosphere. The worker then asked members if they were willing to do an experiment. After noting the positive responses from members, the worker asked the whole group to close their eyes and think about how they would feel if they were in "Billy's shoes." After a few minutes, the worker encouraged members to talk about what they had thought and felt during the brief meditation. A number of members commented how they felt bad for Billy although some said "he deserved it." The worker continued to encourage members to talk about the scapegoating of Billy and its effect on the group as a whole. When this was completed, the worker asked each member to say something that they would like to see Billy change, but also one nice thing that they had noticed about him. The worker asked Billy to consider the feedback, and the group went back to work on issues related to their emotional reactions to their parents' relationships. The worker noticed in the remainder of the meeting and in the next group meetings, that the scapegoating stopped. In fact, the worker observed that members seemed to be nicer to Billy in the group and at other times during the school day. She also asked to meet with Billy briefly to go over his feelings about the whole interaction in the group and the things he wanted to change about his own interpersonal style that might help him get along better with his classmates.

Workers should also help members playing other roles to become more functionally integrated in the group. As mentioned in Chapter 8, some members take on deviant group roles, such as the "group jester" or the "isolate." It is the worker's responsibility either to help the member assume a more functional role or to help the group modify its processes to find a useful role for the member. For example, the jester might be encouraged to take on a more functional role, such as expressing thoughts, feelings, or concerns about a particular problem.

Changing Group Culture

Another aspect of group dynamics that workers should consider during the middle stage of treatment groups is the culture that has developed in the group. Does the culture help the group achieve its goals? If not, one way to change the group's culture is to challenge commonly accepted beliefs and ideas held by members. This is illustrated in the following case.

Case Example   Changing Group Culture

In a group of abusive parents, the worker wanted to change a group culture that discouraged the expression of intense emotions and feelings. First, the worker pointed out that feelings were rarely expressed during group sessions. Next, the worker invited the group to discuss this observation. Several members indicated that they were afraid they might lose control of their actions if they showed these feelings. The worker suggested a series of role-play exercises designed to help the members gradually express more intense emotions. During these exercises, members learned that they could express feelings without losing control. As the group progressed, members acknowledged that allowing feelings to become pent up until they exploded was much less healthful for themselves and their families than learning to express feelings before they built up. The worker then helped the group to discuss tension and how it builds in the body. This was followed by a discussion about what coping mechanisms members used to deal with stress and what other coping strategies might be adopted. Relaxation and mindfulness meditation was brought up as possible coping strategies by several members.

Another way workers can change the existing group culture is to point out its dominant features and areas that appear to be taboo or not able to be discussed. When this is done, members often indicate that they had wanted to discuss taboo areas in previous group meetings but feared the group would not be receptive. These members can then be encouraged to express their thoughts and feelings on the taboo subject. In other instances, role-play exercises can be used to stimulate the group's consideration of an area that was formerly taboo.

A third way to change the culture established in a group is for the worker to develop a contingency contract with members. This procedure was used successfully in working with adolescents in a group home. The contract specified that if a member was supportive and helpful to other members who disclosed personal problems and concerns during three of five group meetings each week, the member would have access to special rewards, such as a trip to a sports event or tickets to a movie. The contract helped change the group culture from one in which members were ridiculed for expressing personal issues to one in which members supported and encouraged personal disclosures.

A similar procedure was used in a children's group. Peer pressure had created an environment in which members were teased for participating in role play and program activities. The worker developed a contingency contract using a point system. Points accumulated for participating in role plays were used at the end of the group meeting to obtain special refreshments, games, or small toys. The incentive system was effective in encouraging the children to participate in role-play exercises designed to teach them problem-solving skills.

> **?** Assess your understanding of interventions used in the group as a whole by taking this brief quiz.

CHANGING THE GROUP ENVIRONMENT

The material resources provided for group work services, the types of clients eligible for services, and the service technologies and ideologies endorsed by the agency all have a bearing on the services the group worker offers. Group services are also influenced by interagency linkages and by the community's response to the problems and concerns of persons who seek group treatment. In this section, suggestions are made about ways to:

- Increase social service agency support for group work services
- Develop links to interagency networks
- Increase community awareness of social problems that could be treated through group work services

Policy Practice

Behavior: Assess how social welfare and economic policies impact the delivery of and access to social services

Critical Thinking Question: Social service organizations' policies are important for establishing and maintaining group work services. How can groups exert influence on the policy-making processes of the organization sponsoring a group?

Increasing Agency Support for Group Work Services

Before intervening to increase support for group work services, workers must first have a thorough understanding of their organization. Like people, organizations have unique histories that influence their continued growth and development. It is often helpful to trace the development of treatment group services within an organization to learn about the changes and innovations that have taken place over time. This process can help the worker understand the rationale for current clinical services, the agency's responsiveness to proposals for change, and the ways in which previous proposals for change were incorporated into the agency's structure. A historical perspective helps the worker avoid making a proposal for increased support for group work services on the basis of a rationale that has been rejected in the past. It also helps to give the worker an understanding of the long-term development of the agency, an understanding that is likely to be shared by administrators whose support for innovations in clinical programming is essential (Breshears & Volker, 2013; Tropman, 2014).

Before proposing an increase in support for group work services, the worker should have a grasp of the current needs and future development plans of the agency. A proposal for group work services should be structured in such a way that it clearly shows how new or increased services will meet the current needs and future developments anticipated by the agency's administrators and board members. The proposal should emphasize the distinct advantages of group work services. For example, it may be possible to show that treatment groups are a cost-effective alternative to individual treatment services (see the cost–benefit analysis example in Chapter 14). Because most agencies want to get the most out of their resources by serving as many clients as possible for as little cost as possible, group treatment services may be an attractive alternative to individual treatment services.

A well-developed proposal itself is not enough to guarantee that an agency will increase its support for group work services. Workers also should know how to proceed within their agencies to get proposed changes accepted. Workers should be aware of several organizational factors that help to predict the degree of resistance that can be expected to a change proposal. These factors include:

- The extent of the proposed change
- The value orientation and decision-making style of the administrator responsible for deciding whether to accept the proposal
- The administrative distance between the practitioner and the decision maker
- The agency's investment in the status quo

The worker can, for example, expect greater resistance to a proposal for a basic change in the agency's services, such as a change from individual treatment to group treatment in all clinical programs, than to a modest proposal for group services to a specific client group.

The rationale for a proposal is also important in terms of the resistance it will encounter. An administrator who is concerned about saving money will probably be less inclined to accept a proposal that requires new funding than a proposal that is expected to reduce costs. Workers should try to present multiple rationales for group work services. For example, the worker might cite relevant research about the type of group being proposed, suggest how desired individual and group outcomes might be achieved, and describe how the group work service may reduce agency costs or increase reimbursement for clinical services.

The more levels of approval—that is, the further a proposal must go from the originator to final administrative approval—the greater the likelihood of resistance. If a group worker's proposal requires approval from administrators who are at a much higher level in the bureaucratic structure, the worker will have to elicit the support of supervisors who can argue for the proposal when it reaches higher levels of review. Even with support from supervisors, proposals are more likely to be altered the higher they go in the bureaucracy.

Resistance may also be encountered if the worker is proposing changes that reverse or negate program components or services that have received substantial support in the past. Agencies are not likely to abandon funded commitments in favor of a new proposal unless the proposal can be proved to be quite exceptional.

Once the worker has anticipated the resistance a proposal may encounter, support to overcome this resistance can be developed. Group motivational interviewing techniques presented by Wagner and Ingersoll (2013) suggest involving resistant coworkers in the proposal's development. Because they have had a hand in shaping the proposal, initially reluctant coworkers can usually be counted on for support in later negotiations. It is especially important to allow administrators who will be deciding whether to accept the proposal and persons who will be responsible for carrying out the proposal to have input into its development. During its development, a proposal may be revised several times to gain the support of critics who have reservations about the proposed changes. By the time it is ready for final consideration, the proposal is likely to have gone through several levels of review in which important participants have become sensitized to its benefits and their own questions or concerns have been addressed. These and other techniques for overcoming resistance are presented by Tropman (2014) and Trotter (2015).

During each stage of review, it is important for the worker to provide evidence for the effectiveness of the proposed group. Providing information about successful group programs in similar organizations is one way to accomplish this. Information about successful group programs that are similar to the proposed group can be obtained through personal and professional contacts with government and nongovernment organizations, literature reviews, conferences, listservs, trade journals and similar sources, and by searching the Internet.

Intervention

Behavior: Use inter-professional collaboration as appropriate to achieve beneficial practice outcomes

Critical Thinking Question: Collaboration among service providers results from common interests. How could workers use group work methods to link service providers and enhance collaborations?

Links with Interagency Networks

Interventions in a group's environment include establishing links between agencies. Interagency links can be established by identifying and contacting workers in other agencies who work with similar populations or deal with similar social service problems. After informal telephone discussions are initiated, a planning meeting should be scheduled.

Interagency links can have several benefits. When other agencies are aware of particular types of group services offered by an agency, they may refer clients for treatment. For example, if a worker at a community agency is aware that a battered women's shelter offers support groups for women, the worker can refer women who would otherwise not receive services to this agency.

Agency networks help identify needs for particular services. In a meeting of workers from several agencies, for example, it became apparent to a group worker from a family service agency that no services existed for treating men who battered their wives. After carefully documenting the need in other agencies, a group work service was established for this population by the family service agency.

Interagency networks also help avoid duplication of services. Competition between agencies can be avoided by preventing the development of duplicate services existing elsewhere in the community and by facilitating the development of services when gaps in service delivery exist. Workers who cultivate interagency links can share the knowledge and practice experience they have gained from working with specific client groups and learn from the experiences of group workers in other agencies. In this way, knowledge can be pooled, and mistakes made by one worker can be avoided by others.

Interagency networks are useful in lobbying for new group work services. For example, in a meeting of workers from a number of community agencies, it became apparent that additional services were needed to prevent criminal activity among unemployed youths. Although no worker was able to do anything about this problem alone, together they put enough pressure on the city's youth services program to obtain funding for a half-time group worker for the local community center.

Increasing Community Awareness

Ultimately, group work services depend on the support of local community residents. Residents' awareness of the social problems that exist in their communities, and their belief that group work services can help maintain adequate social functioning and alleviate social problems, are essential. Group workers have a responsibility to bring community problems to the attention of local officials and civic organizations and to make them aware of how group work services can help to alleviate their problems.

A variety of methods can be used to raise a community's awareness of social problems and increase its commitment to group work services. Needs assessments (see Chapter 14) are especially effective for documenting the need for additional services. Agency statistics about the number of clients not served because of a lack of resources or a lack of available services can also be useful. To call attention to community problems, workers can testify at legislative hearings, they can become members of local planning bodies, or they can help to elect local officials who are supportive of the community's social service needs. Only through such efforts will group work services remain available to persons who need them.

A group worker's skills can also be used to organize clients so that they can lobby on their own behalf for needed services. For example, an outpatient group in a community mental health center in a poor urban area was composed entirely of women who were receiving Aid to Families with Dependent Children (AFDC) benefits. It became apparent that many of the women's problems were tied to the subsistence-level benefits they received as well as to the environmental conditions in which they lived. The worker informed the women of a national welfare rights coalition and helped them form a local rights group. Although this effort did not make a tremendous or immediate change in their life circumstances, it did give the women a constructive way to voice their complaints and lobby for changes in their community. It helped them to overcome what Seligman (1975) called "learned helplessness" in his classic book on this topic.

> **?** Assess your understanding of methods of changing the group environment by taking this brief quiz.

Case Example

Diana instituted several groups as part of the Mental Health Association's Assertive Community Treatment Program. The mission of this program was to actively reach out to persons who lived in the community and experienced a variety of severe and persistent mental health problems, particularly schizophrenia. Employment, with accompanying case management and family support counseling, was strongly associated with successful treatment outcomes.

One of Diana's groups was aimed at empowering members by helping them build the interpersonal and problem-solving skills necessary for successfully finding and keeping employment. The group also served as a support system for members as they attempted to find and keep jobs in the community. The members of the group were adult men and women who lived in either the association's community residences or at home with their families.

The group had been together for several weeks. Members had worked through the beginning stage of group development, despite a difficult "storming" period during which several members had expressed some discomfort with the level of disclosure in the group. Following this, Diana was successful in helping each member articulate and set individual goals to work on during the group. Diana encouraged them to help each other and the group as a whole to achieve the goals they had agreed to accomplish.

Diana guided the group in its middle phase by introducing some structure into meetings. She divided work done during group meetings into two time periods. During the first part of the meeting, members engaged in structured role plays and program activities aimed at increasing their readiness for seeking employment. These activities helped members learn new skills that would help them do job searches and make initial contacts with employers. They also practiced interpersonal skills by doing mock employment interviews with each other. After each interview, members gave and received feedback from each other and from Diana. They also learned to use modeling and rehearsal to develop better interviewing skills. During the second part of the meeting, members had open discussion time, when they could share their successes and concerns about securing and maintaining employment. During this part of the group session, members were able to provide mutual aid and support to each other. Diana found that structuring the time during sessions and using exercises and role plays were helpful for reinforcing job readiness skills. These activities also bolstered members' confidence in the effectiveness of the group.

Diana gave individual attention and encouragement to members and expressed her belief in their strengths and capacities, helping members feel validated as individuals and as members. Getting members involved in the group also meant helping them to feel they had a stake in the work of the group. For example, she would ask the group as a whole to plan activities they thought would be helpful. She also encouraged them to fully participate in these activities and to try new experiences in the protective environment of the group.

Diana also helped remind members of their individual goals by utilizing individual contracts between members and the group. For example, one of the members mentioned that she had difficulties in working with older persons in her previous work environment. As part of her individual contract, this member agreed to talk to three older persons in her neighborhood and report back to the group about her experiences. Another member who had a history of being late for previous jobs was asked to keep track of when he woke up and to make notes about his morning routine. These notes were used during group problem solving to make suggestions about how this member could become more organized and punctual.

As each session began, Diana had a brief check-in period during which members reviewed what they had done between sessions and reported on any homework they had to complete from the previous session. She asked members to talk about how they were progressing in meeting their individual goals. She also discussed and demonstrated ways for them to monitor their progress. She used effective modeling skills to show members how to give each other positive reinforcement when they made progress on their goals.

Work with the group was not always easy. Diana found herself helping members deal with setbacks that stemmed from interpersonal difficulties. Some of these obstacles to achieving goals were related to difficulties members had in forming mutually supportive relationships. Diana helped the group discuss how best to achieve good social relationships with others. She also helped members see how some of their social behaviors might interfere with their job search efforts. Discussion with members about these issues proved useful in helping her to design role plays and rehearsals to build members' social and interpersonal skills.

SUMMARY

This chapter focuses on specialized intervention methods that can be used during the middle stage of treatment groups. The methods are commonly used to intervene at the level of (1) the group member, (2) the group as a whole, and (3) the environment in which the group functions. Interventions at the level of the group member can be subdivided into those that deal with (1) intrapersonal, (2) interpersonal, and (3) environmental concerns. Interventions in the group as a whole can be subdivided into those that focus on (1) communication and interaction patterns, (2) attraction for its members, (3) social integration, and (4) culture.

The chapter concludes with an examination of interventions to change the environment in which a group functions, an important, but often neglected, area of group work practice. Discussion of interventions in this portion of the chapter includes ways to (1) increase agency support for group work services, (2) develop links to interagency networks, and (3) increase community awareness of social service problems that can be alleviated by group treatment.

Task Groups: Foundation Methods

This chapter focuses on the foundation skills, procedures, and methods used in task groups during their middle stage. It describes the importance of task groups for clients, organizations, communities, and the activities that group workers engage in to facilitate these groups effectively. The chapter concludes with a six-step problem-solving model that can be used when working with all the types of task groups described in Chapter 1.

THE UBIQUITOUS TASK GROUP

Although it has been pointed out that meetings are ubiquitous, it has also been noted that many people find them "boring" or even "awful" (Tropman, 2014, p. 1). Yet, participation in the decisions that affect our lives is characteristic of a democratic society, and social service agencies could not function without committees, treatment conferences, teams, boards, and other task groups. The good news is that there are ways to make meetings effective, efficient, and interesting. These methods will be described in this chapter.

Social workers are also often called on to chair meetings in social service organizations and host settings, such as schools, or mental health organizations. Social workers are frequently designated as team leaders in interdisciplinary settings because social work functions include coordination, care management, and concern for the bio-psychosocial-cultural functioning of the whole person. Workers are also asked to "staff" task groups that are led by other professionals, such as physicians or managers with business or public administration degrees. The staff person plays a key supportive role by helping the group clarify its goals and carry out its work (Tropman, 2014). The duties and roles of a staff person are quite varied and can include serving as a resource person, consultant, enabler, analyst, implementer, tactician, catalyst, and technical adviser. Despite the importance and widespread use of task groups in social service agencies, with a few notable exceptions (for example, Ephross & Vassil, 2005; Tropman, 2014), the human services have paid little attention to how to lead them effectively.

Task groups can be a source of frustration for their participants when they function ineffectively. Meetings that are not well run are boring and unsatisfying for members and often suffer from a lack of participation and interest. Although task group meetings are often seen as a chore to be endured by members for the good of the organization, well-run meetings can be a positive experience. They help draw people together by creating effective teamwork in which ideas are shared, feelings are expressed, and support is developed. There are few experiences in the workplace to equal the sense of cohesion, commitment, and satisfaction that members feel when their ideas have been heard, appreciated, and used to resolve a difficult practice or program issue or to form the basis for a new organizational practice or policy.

LEADING TASK GROUPS

To lead task groups effectively during the middle stage, it is important to stay focused on the purposes and functions that the group is expected to accomplish. Task groups are often "charged" with a specific purpose either by an administrator or as a result of the bylaws governing the organization. For example, the bylaws of an organization may call for a personnel committee, a grievance committee, or a fundraising committee. In his classic text on leading task groups, Maier (1963) suggested that the underlying primary purposes of task groups are problem solving and decision making. Other important purposes of task groups include keeping members informed and involved, empowering members, and monitoring and supervising their performance. For example, a staff meeting of a social service agency might be used for informational purposes, for advice or suggestions given to an administrator about policies and practices, or to review treatment plans or entire programs of the organization.

To accomplish these objectives during the middle stage of task groups, workers are called on to help with a variety of activities including the following:

- Leading meetings
- Sharing information, thoughts, and feelings about concerns and issues facing the group
- Involving members and helping them feel committed to the group and the agency in which they work
- Facilitating fact-finding about issues and concerns facing the group
- Dealing with conflict
- Making effective decisions
- Understanding the political ramifications of the group
- Monitoring and evaluating the work of the group
- Problem solving

Intervention

Behavior: Critically choose and implement interventions to achieve practice goals and enhance capacities of clients and constituencies

Critical Thinking Question: Important work gets done during the middle stage. What types of activities characterize work with task groups during this time?

Leading Meetings

At the beginning of a meeting, the worker is responsible for several tasks. The worker begins by introducing new members and distributing handouts not included with the material distributed before the meeting. Before working on agenda items, the worker should make a brief opening statement about the purpose of the meeting. In this statement, the worker may want to call members' attention to previous meetings and to the mandate of the group as a way to indicate that the meeting will undertake a necessary and important function related to the overall objectives of the group. Making members aware of the overall objectives of the group and the salience of particular agenda items to be considered that day is important for maintaining members' interest and willingness to work during the meeting.

The worker should seek members' approval of written minutes that were distributed before the meeting and request that members raise any questions, changes, or amendments they would like to enter into the minutes. After the minutes are approved, the worker should make announcements and call on group members to make designated reports. Reports should be brief and to the point. Members should verbally summarize written reports that have been circulated with the agenda rather than reading them verbatim, because reading lengthy reports can be boring and result in loss of interest and attention of other members.

During the middle portion of the meeting, the worker's task is to help the group follow its agenda. Whatever the purpose of a specific meeting, the middle portion is the time when the group accomplishes much of its most difficult work. To avoid getting stuck on one item of business in meetings that have extensive agendas, details of particular items should be worked out before the meeting. If this is not possible, Tropman (2014, p. 46) suggests that the group should agree "in principle" on overall objectives and goals about a particular task and then charge a subcommittee or an individual group member with working out the details and bringing them back to the group at a later meeting for discussion.

The worker should model the behavior that is expected of all members. A worker who shows respect, interest, integrity, and responsibility will convey these feelings to members. By encouraging equitable participation, the expression of minority-group opinions and an appreciation of all sincere contributions to the group's work, the worker sets a positive example for group members to follow. The worker should act more as a servant of the interests of the whole group than as a master who imposes his or her will on it. By demonstrating that the good of the whole group is foremost when conducting the group's business, the worker gains the respect of members. Authority, control, and discipline should be used only to reduce threats to the group's effective functioning, not to impose the worker's wishes on the group. As members perceive that the worker is committed to accomplishing the group's common objective, the worker will gain the cooperation and the admiration of group members.

Another leadership task is to ensure that the pace of the meeting leaves enough time to accomplish the items specified in the agenda. Time management avoids rushing through important decisions because members are pressed for time at the end of a meeting. Members also become frustrated when they are expected to present or discuss ideas but have no time to do so because the group has spent too much time on earlier agenda items. It is the responsibility of the leader to make sure that the number of agenda items is manageable. Items sometimes take longer to discuss than anticipated, so it is good practice to plan extra time into an agenda. When too many agenda items are submitted for a meeting, the worker should rank the items for importance. Items that are assigned a low priority should be postponed to a later meeting.

Before adjourning, the worker should carry out several actions. These are summarized in the following list.

Ending Meetings
- Summarize the meeting's accomplishments.
- Praise members for their efforts.
- Identify issues and agenda items that need further attention.
- Mention where the meeting has placed the group in terms of its overall schedule.
- Mention major topics for the next group meeting.
- Summarize as clearly as possible the tasks that members agreed to accomplish before the next meeting.

These strategies help to clarify responsibilities, reduce confusion, and increase the probability that members will complete assignments that were agreed to during earlier portions of the group's discussion.

Leading meetings includes planning ahead. Two major tasks to accomplish between meetings are (1) seeing that decisions and tasks decided on at the previous meetings are carried out, and (2) preparing for the next meeting. The worker can do the first task by reading the minutes of previous meetings. Properly kept minutes include summaries of actions taken, tasks that were assigned, and the time frame for reporting back to the group. It is also helpful for the worker to make brief notes during a meeting or soon after the meeting ends about any decisions made that need to be followed up before the next meeting. Tropman (2014) also suggests that leaders should encourage members to carry out assigned tasks and facilitate their work when necessary. For example, the worker might meet with subcommittees of the larger group to provide information or guidance as they carry out their functions.

Between meetings, leaders should also develop and maintain close contacts with supervisors, keeping them apprised of group developments. Supervisors may also want leaders to apprise other administrators, governing bodies, or other internal and external constituencies that may be affected by the group's work. As the spokesperson for the group, the worker should keep in mind that he or she represents the group's public image. A worker should express the officially accepted opinions of the committee, not personal views. The worker should not enter into private agreements or commit to decisions or positions that have not been discussed and accepted by the group. In all but emergency situations, the worker should convene the group and consult with it before making decisions. The only exception is when the group, the agency, or a regulatory body has empowered the leader to act independently without first consulting with the group.

The second major task of the worker between meetings is to prepare for the next group meeting. When there is a written agenda for each meeting, the worker or the member designated as the group's secretary should send a memo to each group member soon after a meeting to request agenda items well ahead of the next meeting. This process allows enough time for the agenda and background information or position papers to be completed and sent to members so they can be read before the next meeting. Meeting agendas should be established to facilitate discussion. One effective framework is illustrated in the following meeting agenda outline.

> **Meeting Agenda Outline**
> - Examine and approve (with any corrections) brief, relevant minutes from the last meeting
> - Make information announcements
> - Vote to include special agenda items
> - Work on less controversial, easier items
> - Work on difficult items
> - Break
> - Work on "for discussion only" items
> - Consider any special agenda items if there is sufficient time
> - Summarize
> - Adjourn

In preparing for the next meeting, the worker should also organize opening remarks and administrative summaries to be presented. Special care should be taken in preparing for meetings that do not have a written agenda. In such instances, the worker should be clear about how to direct the meeting, what tasks the group will work on, and what goals are to be achieved.

Part of the worker's responsibility in preparing for a meeting is assessing the group's functioning. Questions such as "What is the group's relationship with its outside environment?" "Has the group been functioning smoothly?" "What norms, roles, and interaction patterns have developed in the group?" can stimulate the worker to consider how best to prepare for the next meeting.

In many task groups, the worker acts as both the leader and staff person. However, if a separate staff person is available to a task group, that person can prepare background reports and memos that analyze the group's options, develop resources, set up the meeting arrangements, and attend to other group needs.

Sharing Information

Another important activity of the leader during the middle stage is to help members share information, thoughts, and feelings with one another. For example, medical social workers from different community hospitals organize into an informal support group. Once each month, the group meets to share information about their work and new techniques for working with people in medical settings.

Teams, committees, delegate councils, and boards use group meetings as a means for members to share their concerns, their experiences, their perspectives, and their expertise. This is an important activity because, as a result of highly differentiated work roles, contact among workers in many agencies is infrequent. Job assignments, such as individual treatment sessions and home visits, limit opportunities for communication among workers.

Case Example   A Home Health-Care Team

In a community health-care team serving homebound older people, home health-care aides met with their supervisor every two weeks to discuss the situations of the frail older people with whom they were working. The meetings were also used to discuss psychological, social, medical, and other community services the aides might use to help maintain the independent function of those with whom they were working. Because the workers spent so much time away from the office, the team meetings also had the secondary objective of helping the workers to get to know each other and to identify with the organization with which they were working.

Social issues and problems often affect the whole community, and task groups can bring workers from different agencies together. A group meeting is a convenient way for them to share unique viewpoints and differing perspectives on issues, problems, or concerns they face in their own agencies. By providing a forum for sharing knowledge and resources, interagency task groups encourage cooperative and coordinated problem solving.

Open communication and unimpeded sharing of information are prerequisites for task groups to accomplish their objectives. Effective communication within the group and between the group and the organization are often mentioned as key elements of effective teamwork (see, for example, Franz, 2012; Levi, 2014; Salas, Tannenbaum, Cohen & Latham, 2013; and Thompson, 2014). Empirical findings regarding group productivity and group processes confirm that how information is communicated and used in a group has an important effect on the quality and the quantity of a group's productivity (Forsyth, 2014).

The first step in aiding effective communication and sharing information is to ensure that all members have a clear understanding of the topic being discussed and the task facing the group. To stimulate all members' participation in the discussion, the topic must be relevant. If members have little interest in the topic and no stake in the outcome, there is little reason for them to participate. In many groups, members become bored, disinterested, and dissatisfied because they do not understand the importance of a particular topic. The leader should help each member see the relevance and importance of issues as they are brought before the group. When it is clear that a discussion topic is relevant to only a few members of a task group, the worker should consider forming a subgroup to meet separately from the larger group and have the subgroup provide a brief report of its deliberations and recommendations at a later meeting of the entire group. Focusing and summarizing are also important skills for task group leaders. Focusing can be accomplished by suggesting that the group discuss one issue at a time, by pointing out that the group has digressed from the discussion topic and by making task-relevant statements. Effective workers often have self-imposed rules limiting their communications early in group meetings to allow members the maximum opportunity to participate in the discussion. Often, a few brief summaries and comments that focus the discussion are all that is needed by the worker early in the group's work.

Another method of establishing open communication channels and promoting information-sharing among all group members is to ensure equitable participation in the group. Some members may have more information on a given topic, and, if that is the case, it is reasonable that they contribute more than others. However, some members are naturally talkative and others shy or reticent. Quieter members often do not like to be singled out by the leader. Instead, it is a good practice to use go-rounds and subgroups to help these members participate. The leader can also interrupt long monologues by verbose members by asking them to summarize briefly or suggest that they give others a chance to reply. The leader can also paraphrase a particularly cogent point that talkative members make and ask others to respond. In this way, overly talkative and quiet members are not offended by what might otherwise be viewed as a controlling leader.

Case Example   The Go-Round Procedure

In a go-round, each group member is asked to present one idea or one piece of information. Going around the group, members take turns presenting one idea. This procedure is continued, and each member takes as many turns as needed to share all their ideas with the group. Members who do not have additional ideas simply pass their turn. The go-round is completed when all members have shared all their ideas.

The go-round, or round robin procedure as it is sometimes called, has several advantages over unstructured, interactive communication procedures. All members have an equal opportunity to participate. Because only one idea is presented at a time, the procedure avoids the boredom that often results when one member enumerates several ideas one after another. By continuing to go around the group until all ideas are heard and by asking members to pass if they do not have any new information to present, a norm is established for sharing as many ideas as possible.

In large task groups, however, round robin procedures are often too time-consuming. Unless the group is divided into subgroups, the procedure is not useful. To facilitate equitable participation in large groups, the worker should consider using parliamentary procedures (Robert & Robert, 2011). These procedures provide for orderly and structured participation in large groups. Group workers and members, however, should be aware that parliamentary procedures are subject to manipulation by members who are familiar with their complexities. By trading favors for votes before a meeting and calling for votes with few members present, parliamentary procedures can be used to subvert majority rule. Despite these disadvantages, *Robert's Rules of Order* can be helpful in ensuring equitable participation in large meetings. They are described in Chapter 12.

Enhancing Involvement and Commitment

A third important activity during the work stage of task groups is to help members feel that they are a vital part of their agency and the task groups that it sponsors. Because much of any organization's work is done by individuals, there is a danger that staff can become isolated and alienated from an organization. Task groups provide support for their members and a sense of belonging that reduces alienation. For example, a worker in an outreach program for the frail elderly spends much time working with the frail elders who comprise the caseload. Monthly team meetings with other outreach workers provide support and recognition for the worker.

Helping members become involved through their participation in a task group benefits both the organization and its employees. Task groups provide an organized means of developing, implementing, and getting employees to follow policies, procedures, and goals of the agency. They allow employees an opportunity to influence the policies and procedures developed by the agency, which, in turn, helps to make the agency responsive to the needs of its workers. Task groups also help to organize, coordinate, and channel employees' input by clearly delineating how a task group fits into the overall structure of an agency—to whom the group reports and what authority and power the group has to develop or change agency policies. Employees' input can be organized and channeled appropriately.

Several steps can be taken to help task group members feel their input is vital to the agency's sound functioning.

Helping Members Feel Involved

- Emphasize the importance of the group's work, its relationship to the organization's purpose, and administrative structure.
- Assign members specific roles in the group.
- Invite members' input into the agenda and the decision-making process of the group.
- Encourage members to participate in the decision-making process of the group.

To help members feel involved, state the purpose of the group and explain how the group fits into the agency's administrative and decision-making structure. Clarify the duties, responsibilities, authority, and power that result from membership in the group. Emphasize that members are of vital importance to effective agency functioning. Invite members to develop and submit agenda items for future group meetings. Circulating the agenda and any background papers before a meeting can help members prepare their thoughts and concerns before the meeting. This increases the chances that members will participate and share their thoughts about agenda items during the meeting. If the sponsor of the group is willing, have members participate in as many decisions affecting them as possible. This increases motivation and interest in the group (Forsyth, 2014). As the following case example illustrates, it is also important to gain the whole group's cooperation in problem solving.

Case Example   Problem Solving in a Psychiatric Team

The leader of a psychiatric team in an inpatient setting for adolescents noticed that the team had trouble discussing problems about the way it functioned with teenagers who were aggressive or violent. Instead of singling out any team members, the leader reframed the problem as one shared by all members of the team. The leader mentioned that all members of the team would benefit from coming up with new ways to handle these adolescents. After an extensive discussion, new rules for handling aggressive and violent outbursts were decided upon. The team also came up with the idea of having in-service training by someone who specialized in dealing with problems of aggressive and violent adolescents.

Developing Information

A fourth activity of the worker during the middle stage of task groups is to help members generate information and develop creative alternatives for responding to difficult issues and problems facing the group. Although task groups are often thought to be particularly effective for sharing information and developing creative ideas, the available

Intervention

Behavior: Critically choose and implement interventions to achieve practice goals and enhance capacities of clients and constituencies

Critical Thinking Question: Workers often help members find creative solutions to problems. What can the worker do to encourage creative solutions during group work?

evidence suggests that ordinary interactive group discussions often inhibit rather than increase the disclosure of information, ideas, and creative solutions (Forsyth, 2014; Kahneman, 2011).

Group Factors that Inhibit Ideas and Creativity

- Status-conscious group members feel intimidated by members with higher status. Lower-status members tend to share less information and avoid making suggestions that offend higher-status members.
- Norms and social pressures for conformity tend to limit the expression of new and creative ideas.
- Groups have the advantage of the variety of opinions and knowledge offered by all members, but group members may censor controversial opinions.
- Covert judgments are often made but not expressed openly in groups. Members, therefore, become concerned about the effects their self-disclosures will have on future interactions with group members.
- Interacting groups tend to reach premature solutions without considering all available evidence.

Despite these factors, leaders can help members to present new ideas and generate creative solutions in many ways. First, clearly indicate to all members that their input is welcome. This means that the worker must be able to address the members' expressed and hidden concerns about sanctions that may result from expressing sensitive or controversial ideas in the group. If the worker cannot guarantee freedom from sanctions, he or she should try to be as clear as possible about the boundaries of the discussion. For example, it might be possible for committee members to discuss new policies regarding service delivery, but it might not be acceptable for them to criticize existing supervisory staff that has to follow current policy guidelines. When sanctions are possible from individuals outside the group, the worker can encourage the group to consider keeping their discussions confidential. If lower-status members fear reprisals from higher-status members, the worker can discuss the use of sanctions with higher-status members before the group meeting and gain their cooperation in refraining from applying them. The worker can also suggest that higher-status and lower-status members discuss this issue in the group.

Feedback can both help and hinder the group's development of information and creative solutions. It is commonly thought that all feedback is useful because it helps group members detect and correct errors in information processing, but this is not true in all circumstances. In the early phase of developing information and forming creative solutions, evaluative feedback can have the effect of suppressing further suggestions (Forsyth, 2014; Kahneman, 2011). Members fear their ideas may be evaluated negatively and that this will reflect on their competence and their status in the organization. Under these circumstances, few members risk making suggestions, giving opinions, or volunteering information that will not be readily accepted. To encourage free discussion, creative ideas, and new insights about a problem or issue, the worker should ask members to refrain from evaluating ideas early in the group's discussion.

Several other steps can also be taken to help the group develop information and creative ideas to solve a problem.

Developing Information and Creative Ideas

- Encourage the group to develop norms that promote free discussion of ideas.
- Point out group pressures that inhibit members' free discussion.
- Model an open exchange of ideas by presenting creative, controversial, and thought-provoking ideas.
- Encourage members to continue to share unique ideas by praising those who present innovative suggestions.
- Encourage members to share minority opinions early in the group's discussion so that they can be given full consideration.
- Help the group separate information and idea-generating steps from decision-making steps.

When these suggestions are implemented, groups can develop more creative solutions than they would under ordinary conditions.

Dealing with Conflict

It is unlikely that all members of a task group will immediately agree on all aspects of the work of the group. Therefore, it is important for workers to realize that conflicts occur even in effective task groups (Forsyth, 2014; Franz, 2012; Levi, 2014; Thompson, 2014). Conflicts often emerge at the end of the beginning stage or beginning of the middle stage of the group as members feel more comfortable with their participation in the group.

It is important for leaders of task groups to make a distinction between task conflict and relationship conflict. *Task conflict* is based on members' differing opinions about ideas, information, and facts presented during the task group's work. This type of conflict is often helpful to the development of the group because it stimulates healthy dialogue, the development of solutions that encompass different points of view, and the careful analysis of proposed solutions. *Relationship conflict* is based on the emotional and interpersonal relationships among members within and outside of the group. This type of conflict is rarely helpful to the development of the group. In general, relationship conflict is more difficult to resolve than task conflict because it is resistant to persuasive reasoning.

Certain personality characteristics have also been associated with productive and nonproductive conflict. For example, a win-win orientation is often associated with productive conflict, whereas a zero-sum orientation is often associated with nonproductive conflict (Jehn & Chatman, 2000; Franz, 2012; Thompson, 2014). Similarly, rigidity is associated with conflict escalation, and flexibility is associated with the ability to change perceptions and to accommodate differing points of view (Forsyth, 2014).

Some workers have difficulty dealing with conflict. They avoid, ignore, or minimize it, hoping it will go away. These strategies are generally counterproductive. Avoiding conflict rarely leads to satisfying and meaningful dialogue about the issues facing the group. Most often, when conflicts are avoided, members get the message that they should not express their true feelings and that an honest sharing of information and opinions should be sacrificed so that the group can function "harmoniously." When conflicts are ignored, they often smolder until a particular interaction or event causes them to intensify and erupt. At other times, conflicts subside, but one or more group members are left feeling they have lost the battle. Neither outcome is desirable. Timely intervention into group processes can often help to defuse conflicts, as illustrated in the following case example.

Case Example Leadership During a Conflict

The worker leading a treatment conference in a mental health center noticed that a subgroup of members was not participating as expected. The worker commented on this and discovered that subgroup members were quiet because they disagreed with the opinions of the more vocal majority. The worker helped the subgroup and the other members to resolve their differences by pointing out the conflict. However, instead of pointing out points of agreement and disagreement, the worker facilitated a discussion of the key elements of the treatment situation and what they all hoped to accomplish. She helped the group to come to consensus about these key elements and to understand the differing points of view as all contributing to achieving these key elements. As differences continued to arise, she also acted as a mediator to help the minority and majority subgroups to negotiate differences by keeping in mind the key elements they all wanted to achieve.

The following procedures describe how task and relationship conflicts can be handled in a productive and satisfying manner by group workers.

Handling Conflict in Groups
- View conflict as a natural and helpful part of group development.
- Help members recognize the conflict.
- Encourage group norms of openness and respect for others' viewpoints.
- Encourage group members to suspend judgment until they have listened to the entire group discussion.
- Encourage members to view issues in new ways, to understand situations from other members' vantage points, and to be flexible in their own views of a situation.
- Help members avoid focusing on personality conflicts or personal differences. Instead, help members express the facts and preferences underlying their alternative viewpoints and opinions.
- Emphasize factors that promote consensus in the group discussion.
- Develop information and facts about the situation and seek expert judgments to help resolve conflicting information.
- Follow orderly, preplanned steps for considering alternatives and deciding on solutions.
- Use decision criteria that are mutually agreed on by group members.
- Clarify and summarize the discussion frequently so that all members have a similar understanding of what is being discussed and the decision criteria that will be used.
- Be sensitive to members' personal concerns and needs in developing solutions and arriving at a decision.
- Remain neutral in the conflict and ask questions that seek clarification whenever possible.

In the text *Getting to Yes*, Fisher, Ury, and Patton (2012) suggest that the worker should help members (1) separate the person from the issue or problem being addressed, (2) focus on interests or attributes of the problem rather than on members' positions on the issue, (3) generate a variety of possible options before deciding what to do, and (4) insist that the decision about how to proceed be based on some objective standard.

Probably the single most important step in dealing with conflicts in a group is to help members view disagreements as opportunities to gather information and to share views and opinions, rather than as personal attacks or as threats to authority or position. Help members to recognize the legitimacy of others' interests (Barsky, 2014). As a role model, it is important for the leader to welcome differing viewpoints and to encourage the members to do the same. Also, it is helpful to (1) ask members to elaborate on the thinking that led to their viewpoints, (2) suggest that other members listen carefully and ask questions before they react, and (3) highlight points of consensus and mutual interest as they arise.

Another step in dealing with conflict involves helping members avoid turning conflicts into personal attacks. Workers should ask members to be respectful of others' perspectives and opinions and keep their comments focused on the issues rather than on members' personal characteristics. They should encourage members to make "I" statements and to avoid "you" statements that attack other members or subscribe motives to their behavior. Workers should also not react to outbursts or encourage members to defend their positions. Instead, workers should help members in a conflict describe their interests, values, fears, and goals or objectives. This is illustrated in the following case.

Case Example   Ways of Handling Conflicts

Consider the following two ways of handling a conflict. In the first version, a member of a committee defends her position opposing the development and implementation of a new program by saying, "I don't want my staff to take on this proposed new program because they are already overworked. We were asked just last month to take on more work. I just don't think it is fair to ask us again. What about Joe's department [referring to another member of the committee who is not present]? Why can't Joe and his staff handle this? Joe's not that busy!" In the second version, the member defends her position by using "I" statements. "My interests are in ensuring that the workers in my department don't get so overloaded with work that quality and morale goes down. I appreciate your faith in my department, but I fear that my already overworked staff will become overwhelmed. My objective is to ensure that the workers in my department don't get so burned out that they just throw up their hands and stop trying to do a quality job." The first version could be viewed as a personal attack on Joe, who is likely to learn about the member's comments and become angry. The second version uses "I" statements and avoids personalizing the issue. Notice that the second statement lends itself to further discussion and negotiation. For example, the leader might ask the member to describe the workload of her department and how it has changed over the past year. If the workload has increased and concerns about an overload are warranted, the leader might facilitate a discussion among group members about options for getting the work accomplished.

Another useful procedure for dealing with conflict is to help members look beyond their particular positions on an issue and to understand what others hope to accomplish (Barsky, 2014). The worker should encourage members who are having a conflict to state their concerns and their priorities as concretely as possible, but discourage them from defending their positions. Instead, the worker can encourage members to ask questions of each other and to put themselves in each other's positions. The worker should point out shared interests and mutual gains. For example, the worker might point out that all department heads have a stake in ensuring that the members of one department do not become so overloaded that they cannot do a good job. The following case example points out how this can be accomplished.

Case Example Conflict Resolution

In the committee where the member is worried about a work overload, the leader might say, "Mary, I understand your concern for your people. They have been working hard. We are all worried about it. Everyone here, and many others, have a stake in your group not getting bogged down, because without the programming your group is doing, none of the other groups could complete their assignments. Let's go around the group and see if we can get some suggestions and ideas about how we could get this new work accomplished without just expecting Joe's group to do it all. I will give you a minute or two to think about it, I will start with the first idea, and then we can go around the group starting with Tom to get everybody's ideas. Okay?"

The worker can help members to reach consensus by agreeing in principle to mutually acceptable goals. As many solutions as possible for achieving the goals should be generated. For example, the committee members might agree that Joe's group should

> ? Assess your understanding of issues involved in leading task groups during the middle stage by taking this brief quiz.

not be asked to take on all the new work, and that the work should be divided up and given to several departments to complete, but first, the worker should ask members to express their preferences for particular options. If a single option is not preferred by all parties, the worker should negotiate a solution by combining options that include some gains and some sacrifices on the part of all parties to the conflict.

Making Effective Decisions

Facilitators of task groups are often called on to help members make effective decisions. For example, a board president helps the board of directors decide whether to expand their agency's geographical service area. A community organizer helps a neighborhood association decide whether to establish a neighborhood watch group to address the crime rate in the community. The leader of an executive council helps the group determine who will be promoted within the organization.

Although groups are often used to make decisions, evidence about their effectiveness is mixed. Groups are better than individuals at influencing opinions and obtaining commitments from members. However, for other types of problems, groups may not be any more effective than individuals, and sometimes may be less efficient than individuals working alone (Forsyth, 2014). In summarizing the literature that has compared the problem-solving activities of task groups with the activities of individuals, Hare and colleagues (1995) drew the following conclusions.

Problem Solving: Groups Versus Individuals

- Groups are superior to individuals in solving manual problems such as puzzles, particularly when the problem can be subdivided so that each person can use personal expertise to work on a problem component. The superiority of groups has been less consistently documented when the task to be accomplished is of a more intellectual nature, such as a logic problem.

- Although groups are better than the average individual, they are not better than the best individual. Therefore, a group of novices may perform worse than one expert.
- Groups have the advantage of the variety of opinions and knowledge offered by the members, but group members may censor controversial opinions.
- When groups solve intellectual tasks, members' rational, information-processing orientation may be impeded by socioemotional concerns.
- Because task groups require members to deliberate until they reach a decision, the decisions made in task groups may be more costly than decisions made by one or more individuals working alone.

To improve group decision making, workers should help members avoid the phenomenon known as *group think* (Janis, 1972). Group think occurs when group contagion takes over and members fail to express their own thoughts and feelings. Instead, they go along with the predominant sentiment of the group. This phenomenon has been recognized for many years. For example, more than 100 years ago, LeBon (1910) referred to *group mind*, a state in which members allow an emotion generated from their participation in a group to dominate their intellectual powers. Similarly, more than 90 years ago, Freud (1922) wrote about the power that the group has over an individual's ego. Stoner (1968) also found that groups sometimes engage in riskier decisions than individuals would make by themselves. He referred to this as the *risky shift*, and it is easy to see this phenomenon operating in gangs, cults, and terrorist and fundamentalist groups. Group think continues to be an important topic in the group dynamics literature (Forsyth, 2014). For example, it can be used to examine the coercive power and the malevolent authority of cults and gangs (Berlatsky, 2015; Howell & Griffiths, 2016).

Several steps can be taken to help members avoid group think. Norms and a group climate that encourages free and open discussion of ideas tend to discourage conformity to very conservative or radical ideas. Procedures that clarify how a group will use information and arrive at a decision also tend to reduce conformity as illustrated in the case example.

Case Example   Avoiding "Group Think"

In a family service agency, the personnel committee was charged with the hiring of a new clinical supervisor. Many applications were received for the position, and a cursory review suggested that many appeared to be well qualified. However, some of the members of the committee favored one particular applicant and other members started to agree, mentioning the skills of this person. The leader cautioned the group against deciding before giving all candidates careful consideration. In order to avoid deciding on one applicant before carefully considering all others, the leader suggested that the group come up with a set of decision criteria that they could apply evenly to all candidates. The leader indicated that these decision criteria should include all the factors that the members of the committee felt were important for the new clinician to possess. The committee came up with criteria that included clinical and supervisory experience, ability to speak Spanish, and familiarity with the type of psychotropic medications typically used by clients of family service agencies.

To arrive at a group decision, a procedure for choosing among alternatives is needed. Most groups make decisions using consensus, compromise, or majority rule. In certain situations, each procedure can result in quite different decisions. To avoid the suspicion that a particular decision-making procedure is being chosen to influence a decision about a particular issue, a method of choosing among alternatives should be agreed on as early as possible in a task group's deliberations.

Consensus is often considered the ideal way to select among alternatives because all group members commit themselves to the decision. When reviewing conditions for effective work with groups, Susskind and Cruikshank (2006) suggest that helping a group achieve consensus reduces conflict within the group and makes the group more effective. Consensus does not, however, necessarily imply agreement on the part of all group members but rather that individuals are willing to go along with the group's predominant view and carry it out in good faith. Although other decision-making procedures are quicker, reaching consensus often brings considerable support for a decision because members are more likely to cooperate in implementing decisions that they have thoroughly discussed and agreed on. Consensus is sometimes difficult to achieve in groups. It can be time-consuming because each alternative must be discussed thoroughly, along with dissenting viewpoints.

When issues are controversial and there is much dissenting opinion, it is often possible to reach consensus by modifying original proposals and reaching a compromise. To develop amendments to proposals that are acceptable to all group members, the discussion of each alternative should focus on the reasoning behind members' objections to the alternative. This process helps all group members identify the acceptable and unacceptable parts of each alternative. After a discussion of all the alternatives, the acceptable parts of several alternatives can often be combined into one solution that is acceptable to most, if not all, members.

Majority rule is a frequently used procedure to decide between alternatives in task groups because it is less time-consuming than consensus or compromise procedures, and when the vote is done by secret ballot, it protects the confidentiality of members. Majority rule is an excellent procedure for deciding routine and relatively minor questions. However, because a significant minority may not agree with the final outcome, majority rule is a less-appealing procedure when the issue is important and when the support and cooperation of the entire group are needed for successful implementation. For important decisions, a two-thirds majority vote is an alternative to simple majority rule. A two-thirds majority vote ensures at least substantial support for a decision made by the group.

> **?** Assess your understanding of the process involved in making effective decisions by taking this brief quiz.

Understanding Task Groups' Political Ramifications

Task groups have political functions that are frequently overlooked by beginning group workers because of naiveté or discomfort with the notion of behaving in a political fashion. Yet, workers should understand these political functions to be effective.

Social workers should be also aware that often there are stakeholders and constituencies with political agendas and interests in task groups' work. Effective task group leaders are aware of these stakeholders and constituencies, their influence, and how best to relate to them.

Rather than viewing political behavior as symptomatic of a character defect, it may be better viewed "as the quest of the mature personality for the resources needed to affect increasingly larger areas of one's world" (Gummer, 1987, p. 36). Although the overt exercise of power is generally frowned on in our society, there are many symbolic ways that task groups help managers exercise their power and position within an organization. In a power-oriented analysis of task groups, Gummer (1987) focused on four elements: (1) the physical setting, (2) membership, (3) the agenda, and (4) procedural rules.

In regard to the physical setting, consider the symbolic meaning of the meeting location. For example, is the meeting taking place in a neutral place or in a place that is "owned" by the leader or a particular member? Is the meeting taking place in a symbolic setting, such as an outreach office or a new building to symbolize the importance of the setting? There also may be symbolism attached to how the meeting room is arranged. For example, does the setting promote work or comfort? Are chairs set up around a table with paper, pencils, overhead projectors, and other work-oriented aids? Or is the setting filled with couches, soft chairs, food, and other items that convey a relaxed, informal atmosphere?

Who is invited to participate in a meeting is also important from a political perspective. Participation in meetings is the organizational equivalent of enfranchisement. Inclusion in certain organizational groups and exclusion from others is often used to delineate one's organizational position. Determining who can participate is an important source of power because it is a concrete reminder of the power hierarchy. For example, the character of a task group might be changed when consumers are included on advisory boards. Similarly, the substantive deliberations of a committee examining staffing ratios and workloads is likely to change when both nonprofessional and professional staff are included in the meetings.

Meeting agendas can also be used for political purposes. Power can be exercised by confining the scope of decision making to issues where managers are willing to give up control. The ordering of items on the agenda may also be used for political purposes. For example, the leader or certain members may take a long time to discuss several trivial issues at the beginning of a meeting as a way to leave little time to work on issues that they would rather not address. Similarly, how agenda items are presented often has political ramifications. Politically oriented individuals who want certain items tabled, defeated, or changed encourage their selected colleagues to present issues in the broadest and most controversial terms possible so that the specifics of the issue are not discussed. Conversely, items that these members would like to see acted on and accepted by the group are presented as specifically and non-controversially as possible.

Procedures governing how the group conducts its business can also be developed with political purposes in mind. In democratic organizations it is expected that, at a minimum, procedural rules should (1) provide task group members with sufficient time to deliberate the issues the group is charged to address and (2) provide for adequate representation of minority opinions. However, procedural rules can be manipulated by politically minded individuals. For example, important decisions may be deferred to the executive committee of an organization rather than taken up during a staff meeting. Similarly, the membership of a nominating subcommittee or a finance subcommittee may be stacked so as to include members who are known to favor the wishes of the organization's director.

Monitoring and Evaluating

The worker is also often called on to help task groups monitor and evaluate their efforts. Monitoring by the group leader should focus on both group processes and group

Evaluation

Behavior: Select and use appropriate methods for the evaluation of outcomes

Critical Thinking Question: Goal achievement is essential. How can the worker monitor the functioning of the group during the middle stage?

outcomes. The leader monitors group processes to ensure that they are leading to a satisfying experience for group members while at the same time facilitating the group's work. The dual focus on members' satisfaction and goal accomplishment has long been identified as an effective means of working with task groups (Bales, 1954, 1955). It continues to be an important focus for the leadership of task groups in contemporary society (Forsyth, 2014).

For effective monitoring and evaluation during the middle stage, task groups must be clear about their mandate from the agency and the ethical, moral, and legal obligations as expressed by regulatory agencies, professional societies, legislative bodies, and the larger society. Sometimes these items are clearly specified in the bylaws of the sponsoring organization. Sometimes, however, task groups develop their own set of standards, rules, or guidelines that can be used to monitor and evaluate their performance. An example presented in the following case illustrates this function of a board.

Case Example   Development of an Institutional Research Review Board

A large, nonprofit social service agency decided to encourage evaluations of several of its service programs. To ensure that the research would serve a useful purpose, protect the rights and the confidentiality of their clients, and meet state and federal rules and regulations, an institutional research review board was formed. The first meeting of this group focused on reviewing the procedures of similar review boards at other agencies and examining state and federal regulations. The group then prepared guidelines governing its own operation and guidelines for researchers to use when preparing proposals to be reviewed by the board. The guidelines were, in turn, modified and ratified by the executive staff and the board of the social service agency.

To fulfill their monitoring and evaluating functions adequately, task groups develop feedback mechanisms to help them obtain information about the results of a decision and take corrective actions when necessary. The type of feedback useful to a task group depends greatly on the group's mandate and the monitoring and evaluating required in the particular situation. A board, for example, may require periodic reports from the agency director, the director of clinical services, the agency executive, and the coordinator of volunteer services. In addition, the board may review program statistics, quarterly financial statements from a certified accountant, and reports from funding sources about the performance of the agency. In other cases, a task group may use formal data-gathering procedures to perform its monitoring and evaluation functions. A discussion of these methods is presented in Chapter 14.

Problem Solving

Problem solving has been given more consideration in the group work literature than any other function of task groups. Task groups spend much time performing other functions, but problem solving is often seen as a task group's major function. The next section describes a six-step, problem-solving model that can be used effectively in a variety of task groups.

A MODEL FOR EFFECTIVE PROBLEM SOLVING

The effectiveness of problem-solving efforts depends on the extent to which an optimal solution is developed and implemented. Effective problem solving involves six steps:

1. Identifying a problem
2. Developing goals
3. Collecting data
4. Developing plans
5. Selecting the best plan
6. Implementing the plan

As shown in Figure 11.1, the steps are not discrete. In practice, they tend to overlap. For example, preliminary goals are often discussed during problem identification, and goals are modified and refined as data collection continues.

Problem-solving processes are used repeatedly by groups as they conduct their business. A task group may have to use two or more cycles of a problem-solving process to accomplish a single task. The process is represented in Figure 11.2.

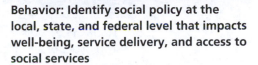

Policy Practice

Behavior: Identify social policy at the local, state, and federal level that impacts well-being, service delivery, and access to social services

Critical Thinking Question: Local, state, and federal social policies have important implications for group work. How can task groups such as social action groups, coalitions, or delegate councils affect these policies?

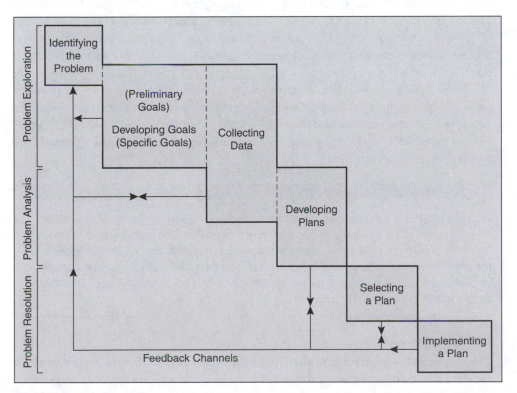

Figure 11.1
The Problem-Solving Process in Task Groups

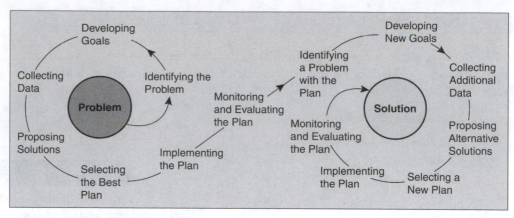

Figure 11.2
Two Cycles of a Problem-Solving Process

Identifying a Problem

How a problem is identified and defined is crucial to effective problem solving. It affects what data will be collected, who will work on the problem, what alternatives will be considered, and who will be affected by the problem's resolution. When they are first identified, problems are often unclear and muddled. For example, the staff of a social service agency perceives a problem in serving a large group of Mexican Americans who live in the area. The problem could be defined in several ways, including (1) not having Spanish-speaking workers, (2) not conducting any outreach efforts to this population, (3) having a poor public image with Mexican Americans in the community, (4) not having the financial resources to develop programs, and (5) providing the wrong services to meet the needs of the population.

Several steps can be taken to help a group define a problem to promote problem solving. These include: (1) clarify the boundaries of the problem, (2) seek out members' perceptions of the problem and their expectations about how it will be solved, (3) develop a problem-solving orientation, (4) define a solvable problem, and (5) specify the problem as clearly as possible.

Case Example   Problem Solving

An adult protective services team spends three meetings developing a plan for emergency evening coverage for all clients on team members' caseloads. The plan is then implemented for three months on a trial basis. After the trial period, the team may reconsider aspects of the plan. Using the problem-solving process a second time, the team decides on a modified version of the plan that includes greater cooperation with police and emergency health and mental health providers in the county.

Clarifying Boundaries

The first issue that confronts workers and members as they define the boundaries of a problem is how to handle large problems that may have several interrelated components. One method of handling a large problem is to set boundaries. Boundaries refer to the extent and scope of a problem or issue facing the group. Defining clear boundaries helps problem solvers focus and clarify their thoughts and suggestions about a problem, which leads to more effective solutions.

When setting boundaries, workers are in a delicate position. On the one hand, the worker usually wants the group to be creative and consider all the relevant options for problem resolution. On the other hand, the worker is often in a better position than is any other group member to recognize what is politically, economically, and organizationally feasible. The following case example illustrates this point.

Case Example   Setting Boundaries

In a community group working on ways to increase services for Mexican Americans, the worker informs members that potential solutions to the problem should not commit the agency sponsoring the group to new services that require additional funding this year. The worker goes on to explain how funding for new programs is obtained and that all funds requested for the current fiscal year are already committed to other projects. The worker continues to explain that although the proposed solutions should not require new funds, the group might consider making recommendations to the agency's administrative staff about seeking additional funding during the next fiscal year.

Early in problem solving, boundaries should be as broad and as flexible as possible but workers should point out the boundaries and specified limits set out by the sponsor of the group. Without guidelines, the group may arrive at a solution that is unacceptable to persons who will implement it. Members who spent time and energy developing an unwelcome solution will feel frustrated, disappointed, and even betrayed by the sponsor.

Members' Perceptions and Experiences

If the members of a group are to be satisfied with the group's problem-solving process and committed to the solution that is reached, their views about problems facing the group should be respected. There is no better way to show respect than to solicit their views and ensure that they are given a fair hearing (Hohman, 2013). Failure to clarify members' expectations and perceptions about a problem can lead to difficulties later in the group's problem-solving process. Hidden agendas can develop, in part, because unclarified expectations are acted on by members. An open discussion of members' perceptions and expectations about what is possible given the mandate of the group from administrators or other sponsors can form the basis for mutually agreed-on goals.

Problem-Solving Orientation

During the process of identifying a problem, it is important for the worker to help members use critical thinking skills (Gambrill, 2009, 2013). This includes recognizing problems that need attention and being willing to work on them. It is sometimes difficult for task groups to confront and work on problems facing them. For example, a team in a psychiatric hospital may avoid discussing problems in its own functioning for fear that the discussion will be viewed as an attack on individual members. In this case, the team leader should facilitate the development of a group climate that encourages problems to be viewed as shared concerns whose resolution will benefit all team members. In situations where conflicts are severe, an outside consultant who is an expert on team building may be needed. For advice about team building and working with difficult groups, see Franz

(2012); Levi (2014); Salas, Tannenbaum, Cohen, and Latham (2013); Schuman (2010); and Thompson (2015).

When developing a problem-solving orientation within the group, workers should help members reduce their tendency to make immediate and automatic responses. Frequently, members suggest solutions without carefully considering the problem. Ineffective problem solvers are impulsive, impatient, and quick to give up (Forsyth, 2014). Therefore, workers should encourage members to stop and think about the problem, collect evidence, and analyze alternative solutions using critical thinking skills before deciding what to do next (Gambrill, 2009, 2013).

There should be sufficient time during a meeting agenda to grapple with difficult problems. According to Tropman (2014), difficult items should be placed in the middle portion of the agenda. At this point, members are at the peak of their (1) psychological focus, (2) physiological awareness, (3) attention, and (4) attendance. Easier items should be placed earlier in the agenda. Because they require less energy, items for discussion should be placed at the end, when members have little energy for problem solving.

Defining a Solvable Problem

Groups are sometimes blocked in their problem-solving ability because they fail to frame the problem correctly (Forsyth, 2014; Tropman, 2014). Group members may fail to identify the correct actors, the correct systems, or the correct obstacles that constitute the problem situation. In the early stages of problem solving, the group should be tentative and flexible with its problem definition so that it can be modified when new data are collected. For example, consider the previous case example about setting boundaries. Defining the problem as a lack of service hours for Mexican Americans suggests the possibility of modifying service delivery patterns, whereas defining it as a lack of knowledge and expertise about Mexican American clients suggests the possibility of learning more about Mexican Americans.

To help the group obtain a new perspective on a problem, the worker can use the reframing technique described in Chapter 10 and illustrated in the following example.

Case Example   Reframing

Some of the members of the committee considering services for Mexican Americans are not convinced that services for this population are lacking. The worker asked members to imagine going to an agency where no one speaks English and where all workers and most clients have different cultural backgrounds from their own. The exercise encouraged skeptical members to reconsider their stand on the question of whether something should be done to improve services for Mexican Americans.

Reframing may also be done by focusing on the positive aspects of a problem. For example, a problem that is experienced as anxiety-provoking may be reframed as one that motivates the group to improve a situation. In these ways, members' motivation to solve problems can be increased.

Specifying the Problem

Having a clearly defined and mutually understood problem is essential if members are to work effectively together. When problems are first expressed in a meeting, they are often stated as partially formulated concerns. For example, a committee member might say: "I get a sense that some of our staff may be having difficulty with the new re-cord-keeping system." Many terms in this statement are vaguely defined. Terms such as "get a sense," "some of our staff," and "difficulty" can have different meanings for each member of the group. Workers should help members clarify vague or ambiguous terms. For exam-ple, "some of our staff" could be clarified to indicate that three members of the commu-nity team and one member of the day treatment team expressed concerns that the new record-keeping forms took too long to fill out. Further, the phrase "took too long to fill out" should be clarified so that it becomes clear what it is the group is being asked to consider and "having difficulty" could mean "cannot complete the case record in the 15 minutes allocated for that purpose" or could mean "being asked to collect data that are not needed to work with clients." Using critical thinking skills by collecting data and analyzing it can also be very helpful for problem solving (Gambrill, 2009, 2013).

After the group has clarified the problem, the worker should summarize it in a clear, brief statement. Ideally, the problem should be defined in a way that has the same meaning for all members. Objective terms with clear, observable referents help mem-bers arrive at a common understanding of the situation. When summarizing, the worker should restate the boundaries of the problem and the group's role and authority, such as advisory, fact finding, or decision making.

Developing Goals

The second step in the problem-solving process is goal setting. Tentative goals are for-mulated soon after the problem has been identified and aid in data collection because they help shape the scope of the information to be collected. Goals are often modified and specified as information is accumulated. Initial goals may sometimes be abandoned entirely, with new goals developed on the basis of the data accumulated. Workers should help members share their problem-solving perspectives and make sure that each member's perspective is heard.

Case Example   Specifying a Problem

The worker stated that it had come to her attention that several members expressed having a hard time with the new record-keeping system that had recently become required. She asked for members to provide as specific feedback as possible about the record-keeping system. Several members gave their opinions. However, because the worker wanted to get everyone's feedback, she went around the group and asked members to state their experiences with the new system. She wrote the comments on an easel so that all members could see the different and similar comments she wrote on the paper. After all the members had a chance to give their opinions, the worker noted that she was not in a position to change the new record-keeping system by herself, but that she would take all the comments that had been written down and share them with her supervisor. She promised to report the extent of concern expressed by the members and report back to the group the next time they met. At the next meeting, the worker reported that the supervisor was going to bring the concerns of the group to the execu-tive committee and that the supervisor had asked her to come to the meeting and also to invite one member of the staff to attend. The group then spent time deciding on which member would represent them at the executive committee meeting and listed a number of points about the new record-keeping system that the representative could make at the meeting.

Goal statements should be as clear and specific as possible. Desired changes in problem situations should be stated as objective tasks. For example, goals to increase services to the Mexican Americans mentioned in a previous example might include (1) providing eight hours of training for each outreach worker during the next six months, (2) increasing the number of Mexican Americans served by the agency from an average of 3 per month to 15 per month by the next fiscal year, (3) translating program brochures into Spanish within three months, and (4) printing 400 bilingual Spanish-English brochures at the beginning of the next fiscal year. Each goal is specific and easily understood.

Group workers can use several other principles for developing effective goals. These are presented in the following list.

Principles for Developing Goals
- Goals should be consistent with the group's mandate, its overall objectives, and the values that have been agreed on by the group as a whole.
- Goals should be framed by the worker to gain the maximum commitment, cooperation, and investment of all group members.
- Goals should be realistic and attainable through the resources available to the group and its members.
- Goals should be time limited.
- The goal-setting process should set a supportive, encouraging climate for goal attainment.

At the end of the goal-setting process, it is important for the worker to summarize the goals that have been decided on by the group and to review each member's role in their achievement. This includes being clear about the time frame for accomplishing goals and about the mechanisms for reporting their achievement to the group.

Collecting Data

Data collection is concerned with generating ideas and sound evidence. It should be kept separate from analyzing facts and making decisions, because analyses and evaluations tend to inhibit idea generation and the collection of unbiased data. Groups sometimes arrive at hasty, ill-conceived solutions because they rush to implement initial ideas without carefully exploring the situation, the obstacles to problem resolution, and the ramifications of a proposed solution.

Knowing the history of the problem often helps the group develop a longitudinal perspective on the problem's development and course. Comparing the state of affairs before and after a problem has occurred can often point to potential causes and possible solutions. While gathering data about the history of the problem, the group should become familiar with previous attempts to solve it. This information can help the group avoid repeating past failures.

Conditions that can help to create a group climate that encourages members to share information and views about a problem include the following.

Principles for Sharing Information
- Maintain the group's openness to speculation.
- Encourage an open search for all pertinent data.
- Encourage all group members to present their ideas.

- Demonstrate genuine appreciation for differences.
- Refrain from evaluation.
- Express communications nonjudgmentally, genuinely, without the intent of controlling others, and as an equal rather than a superior contribution.

Facilitating this type of communication in a group increases problem exploration and contributes to high-quality solutions. However, members occasionally can become stuck in the ways they explore and review a problem. To develop new approaches, members should be encouraged to (1) view problems flexibly, (2) expand the way information is collected and combined, (3) recognize and fill gaps in available information, and (4) generate new ideas by viewing situations from alternative perspectives.

Two problem-solving perspectives are particularly helpful. One perspective relies on inductive and deductive reasoning. Evidence and reason are used in a logical fashion until a solution is reached. Solutions are grounded in facts that are built one on another in an orderly, systematic, and linear fashion. The other perspective is characterized by the use of analogies, metaphors, similarities, contrasts, and paradoxes. Seemingly disparate facts, thoughts, and ideas are put together in new and creative ways. Analogies, for example, help bring out similarities between objects or situations that were previously considered to be different. For example, solutions found to be helpful in analogous situations might be tried by group members in their current problem-solving situation.

> **?** Assess your understanding of identifying problems, goals, and data in problem solving by taking this brief quiz.

Developing Plans

During planning, the worker calls on members to organize, analyze, and synthesize facts, ideas, and perspectives generated during problem exploration. It can be difficult for members to keep a large amount of information in mind as they attempt to develop alternative solutions. Displaying information on a flipchart or a blackboard can help members view the full range of information that has been collected. Ordering and clarifying the information generated by the group can also be helpful. Useful techniques for doing this are presented in the following list.

Handling Information Generated by the Group
- Separate relevant from irrelevant facts.
- Combine similar facts.
- Identify discrepancies.
- Look for patterns across different facts.
- Rank facts from most important to least important.

During the process of organizing data, members should be encouraged to develop as many alternative solutions as possible. Because critical and evaluative comments tend to inhibit the production of creative ideas, workers should caution members not to criticize each other's solutions as they are presented.

Selecting the Best Plan

After all members have presented their alternatives, the group should review each one. The review helps to clarify any misunderstandings. It can also encourage members to discuss how they would overcome possible obstacles and challenges that may be encountered if the alternative were implemented. Members should also be encouraged to consider the overall likelihood that a plan will resolve the problem in a manner that is valued by all group members.

To select the best plan, groups often rely on the expertise of their own members to develop decision criteria. This is frequently done by having members rate the advantages and the disadvantages of each alternative. Alternatives may be combined or modified to maximize advantages and minimize disadvantages. As members decide among alternatives, the leader can remind them of the group's mandate, its goals, and the ideal situation they would like to see if the problem were resolved successfully. Members may also want to consider other factors, such as the benefits and costs of implementing alternative solutions, the comfort and ease with which particular solutions are likely to be implemented, and the political ramifications of alternative solutions. The most effective solution to a problem may not be the most desirable solution if it is too costly or if it is likely to offend, inconvenience, or otherwise upset persons who will be asked to implement it.

Sometimes, groups rely on experts to develop decision criteria as illustrated in the following example.

Case Example   Decision Criteria for Solving a Problem

A committee formed by the health department of a large state was charged with selecting and recommending funding for six health maintenance organizations (HMOs) to serve medically underserved areas. The committee assembled a panel of health care services experts to advise them about important issues to consider about the delivery of health care to underserved areas. The panel of experts helped the committee to develop four criteria for deciding among the programs that applied for funds to establish HMOs in the medically underserved areas of the state. These criteria included (1) the number of physicians per 1,000 people, (2) the percentage of families in the area with less than $12,000 annual family income, (3) the infant mortality rate in the area, and (4) the percentage of the area's population over age 65. The group then went on to recommend to the health department six applicants that best fit the criteria.

Implementing the Plan

Excellent decisions can be worthless if they are not implemented properly, so task groups should consider implementation issues as they proceed with the problem-solving process. Input from persons who will be influential in implementing the plan should be solicited and considered as early as possible. The group should also consider the support needed from constituencies outside the group. It is especially important to seek the support of persons who will be accountable for the decision and with the authority to implement it. For example, the committee that decided to improve outreach efforts to Mexican Americans by training staff and publicizing agency programs in the community sought the cooperation of the board of directors, the agency's executive director, the directors of programs responsible for implementing staff training and publicity campaigns, all the direct service staff who were going to be involved in the program, and the leaders of the Mexican American community.

It is often helpful to delineate steps in the implementation sequence and to develop a timeline. Objectives can be specified for each step, and the group can obtain periodic feedback about implementation progress. With a large plan, a division of labor is often helpful—each member may be assigned specific responsibilities. Feedback channels should be established to keep the group informed of the solution's utility in terms of its expected outcome. Feedback can be used to overcome obstacles, stabilize change, and meet the challenges of a continually changing environment.

Implementing the proposed solution also includes identifying, contacting, and utilizing available resources. A heterogeneous group can be advantageous in this process because of the resources a diverse membership brings to the group. There may also be a need for training to educate persons about implementing strategies and to prepare members for opposition. Obstacles may include inertia, passive resistance, or active attempts to block implementation of a proposed solution.

When seeking the support of others, members may have to educate people about the value of a new approach to a problem. Motivating people to cooperate with the implementation of a decision is not an easy task. Persuasion, lobbying, and other tactics may be necessary to gain support for the proposed solution (Pyles, 2013; Rothman, Erlich, & Tropman, 2007). Strategies to overcome inertia and resistance are described at the end of the next chapter.

> **?** Assess your understanding of how to develop, select, and implement a plan for effective problem solving by taking this brief quiz.

Case Example

Lola's supervisor reviewed her accomplishments as a group leader in preparation for her annual review. Two years ago, Lola was assigned to chair the organization's long-range planning committee. Lola felt she had been an active group leader. Lola lived in a rural part of West Virginia called Blair County. She worked for Join Together, an outreach and community development organization. The organization's long-range planning committee was composed of representatives from all levels of the organization, including administration, client services, program development, and finance. Over the course of her tenure as leader, the group had achieved a high level of functioning. Lola's supervisor identified several activities and skills that helped the group function effectively and achieve its purpose.

Lola spent a good deal of time preparing for group meetings. In addition to reviewing and monitoring the work of the subcommittees, she researched issues for future meetings, prepared an agenda, and made numerous personal contacts with group members. Lola hoped that her level of activity between meetings served as a model for all members. After evaluating the amount of work done by members outside of meetings, Lola's supervisor concluded that her modeling behavior had helped to establish a group norm of hard work.

One of the most impressive aspects of the group meetings was the sharing of information that occurred among members. Lola encouraged all members to keep the group updated on existing programs and ideas for new services. Between meetings Lola shared important information with all members of the committee. At the beginning of each meeting, members shared updates and suggestions with each other. Lola's supervisor noted to herself that through this process, the group had achieved a high level of communication and interaction. Members were familiar and comfortable with the roles they played in the group. Her assessment was that these factors fostered group cohesiveness and raised the productivity of group members.

Lola also helped the group develop a clear structure for the monthly meetings. She helped establish clear procedures for developing information, solving problems, and making decisions. She encouraged members to participate actively during meetings by modeling good member skills, such as listening, asking good questions, and giving support. She also helped members feel that their feedback and recommendations were taken seriously by the organization. Lola worked carefully with the administrators to ensure that group deliberations would be influential on the future directions of organizational policy and programs. Group members felt empowered by this knowledge.

Lola's organizational skills helped the group adopt a clear structure for solving problems and making decisions. She helped the group decide on a standard format for problem solving. For example, when faced with having to decide how to find funding for a new volunteer outreach program in the local school, the group followed the steps of identifying the problem, setting goals, collecting data, developing plans, and selecting and implementing the best plan. The group learned and relied on this format in many of its problem-solving discussions. During decision-making activities, Lola suggested clear guidelines about how to proceed. These were discussed, modified, and adopted by the group. She encouraged the group to develop decision criteria and procedures before making important decisions. Although this took some time, Lola's organizational skills helped the group decision-making process become easier and more systematic. Lola was also good at helping the group build consensus by finding common interests and points of agreement. Consensus building helped members be more committed to the group decision.

Lola spent time monitoring and evaluating the group. She devoted a regular portion of each meeting agenda to discussions of members' efforts and their effectiveness. She also developed a survey form to obtain members' feedback about her leadership skills and for gathering suggestions about how the group could be improved. Lola shared the results of the survey with members and incorporated members' suggestions into the work of the group.

The long-range planning committee had some history of disagreements and conflicts. Several of the members had strong personalities. Others felt that their departments should have more control over the projects chosen for future funding and implementation. Lola's greatest difficulty was her ability to deal with the conflicts that arose in the group. Her supervisor noted that she seemed uncomfortable with conflict in the group. She suggested that Lola listen carefully to both sides of the discussions and remain neutral in the face of pressure to agree with one side or the other. Lola helped the group recognize that some disagreements about issues were healthy for group discussions. Lola's supervisor suggested that she help the group differentiate these substantive conflicts from affective conflicts, in which members personalized conflicts with other members. At different times, Lola helped the group resolve both types of conflicts. Still, she worked hard to more fully develop her skills of listening, mediating, negotiating, and compromising.

As Lola's supervisor reflected on the group's accomplishments, she noted that Lola had guided the group by providing it with many of the elements it needed to function effectively. Lola felt a sense of pride in knowing that she had used her talents and skills to guide the development of an effective task group. Through her efforts, the group identified several service needs and helped to implement programs for persons living in rural West Virginia.

SUMMARY

This chapter focuses on the foundation skills, procedures, and methods needed to work effectively with task groups. Task groups have an important place in all human service organizations. Each day, meetings take place that have an important effect on what services are provided and how they are delivered. Social workers and other helping professionals are frequently called on to chair or staff committees, teams, and other task groups. When meetings are well run, members become a satisfied and cohesive team committed to achieving its objectives. Poorly run meetings, however, often lead to boredom and frustration.

During the work stage of task groups, the worker is often called on to engage in the following activities: (1) preparing for group meetings, (2) helping members share information, (3) helping all members get involved in the work of the group, (4) helping members develop ideas and information, (5) dealing with conflict, (6) helping members make effective decisions, (7) understanding the political ramifications of task groups, (8) monitoring and evaluating, and (9) problem solving.

Problem solving is probably the single most important function of task groups. The chapter concludes with a six-step, problem-solving model: (1) identifying a problem, (2) developing goals, (3) collecting data, (4) developing plans, (5) selecting the best plan, and (6) implementing the plan. In practice, these steps overlap and they are interconnected by feedback channels. Task groups repeat variations of problem-solving processes during the life of the group as they perform their functions and work on the tasks that confront them.

Task Groups: Specialized Methods

This chapter describes specialized methods for helping organizational and community groups accomplish their goals during the middle stage. The first section describes methods for helping small and large organizational groups accomplish their objectives. The second section describes methods for helping community groups accomplish their objectives. A brief introduction of each method is followed by a description of the procedures necessary to implement the method, its recommended uses, and evidence about its effectiveness.

SMALL ORGANIZATIONAL GROUPS

Brainstorming

Brainstorming is probably the best known of the specialized methods presented in this chapter. The primary purpose of brainstorming is to increase the number of ideas generated by members. Elements of brainstorming, such as suspending judgment of ideas, have long been recognized as effective techniques, but Osborn (1963) was the first to develop a systematic set of rules for generating creative ideas, which he called *brainstorming*. The method is still widely used today (see, for example, Franz, 2012; Harrington & Mignosa, 2015; Levi, 2014; Thompson, 2014; Unger, Nunnally, & Willis, 2013).

During brainstorming, the total effort is directed toward creative thinking rather than to analytical or evaluative thinking. Analytical and evaluative thinking can reduce the ability to generate creative ideas. Members are concerned about their status in a group, and if they expect critical judgments about their thoughts and ideas, they are not likely to express them. Analytical and evaluative thinking can also serve as a social control mechanism. Members who continue to present ideas that are viewed critically are likely to be sanctioned. Members may also screen out potentially creative, but controversial, ideas before they are ever expressed. By attempting to reduce analytical and evaluative thinking, brainstorming encourages free disclosure of ideas.

Procedures

Brainstorming includes determining the problem, discussing the different parts of the problem, generating ideas about the different aspects of the problem, and selecting the best ideas for further discussion and implementation (Basadur, Basadur, & Licina, 2012; Deuja, Kohn, Paulus, & Korde, 2014). Brainstorming can be conducted in any size group. It is unclear if larger groups (15 or more members) are better than smaller groups for idea generation (Paulus, Kohn, Arditti, & Korde, 2013). The procedure can be conducted in a short period of time (15 to 30 minutes), but longer meetings may produce higher quality ideas because those presented later in the brainstorming session build on the ones presented earlier (Kohn, Paulus, & Choi, 2011; Paulus, Kohn, & Arditti, 2011). Therefore, leaders who encourage members to extend the idea generation period can improve brainstorming results (Franz, 2012).

Procedures for Brainstorming
- *Freewheeling* is welcomed. Members are encouraged to express all their ideas, no matter what they are. Members should not hold back on ideas that might be considered wild, repetitious, or obvious.
- Criticism is ruled out. Members are asked to withhold analyses, judgments, and evaluations about any ideas presented during the idea-generating process. Members should not try to defend or explain their ideas.
- Quantity is encouraged. Good ideas can emerge at any time during the method.
- Combining, rearranging, and improving ideas are encouraged. Often called *hitchhiking*, this technique calls on group members to build on ideas that have already been expressed. Members can combine or modify ideas and suggest how other members' ideas can be improved.

At the beginning of the meeting, the worker explains the problem to be brainstormed and the four brainstorming procedures. A warm-up period of 10 to 15 minutes is helpful to familiarize members with the procedure and to help them learn to express and hear ideas without criticism. Acclimation to brainstorming and training in freewheeling idea generation has been shown to improve brainstorming results (Paulus & Coskun, 2012; Paulus, Kohn, & Arditti, 2011). Even when some members of the group have used brainstorming procedures previously, the warm-up time gives all members an opportunity to prepare to change routine patterns of analyzing and evaluating ideas. During this time, the worker can model appropriate behavior and make some suggestions about procedures to increase creativity and stop production blocking, such as encouraging members to continue to share or to work alone and generate ideas in silence when the worker suspects that verbal or nonverbal cues may be inhibiting members (Alencar, 2012; De Dreu, Nijstad, Bechtoldt, & Baas, 2011; Kahneman, 2011; Paulus, Dzindolet, & Kohn 2011; Putnam & Paulus, 2009).

During the brainstorming procedure, it is helpful to write members' ideas on a flip chart or a whiteboard so that all group members can view all ideas. Having a co-leader record ideas is particularly helpful because it is difficult for the leader to train members, record ideas, and model appropriate behavior at the same time. Ideas should be recorded by using the words of the speaker as much as possible. Key words should be abstracted so suggestions fit on a sheet of newsprint or a whiteboard.

The interaction pattern in the group should encourage the free flow of ideas. Members can be asked to offer one idea at a time to allow everyone to have a turn presenting ideas. The worker encourages members to continue until all ideas are exhausted. Sometimes groups run out of ideas or repeat similar ideas without pursuing new or alternative thinking patterns. At this point, instead of closing a session, the worker should read ideas from the list to stimulate thinking, focus the group's attention on unexplored areas of the problem by using prompts, and pick out one or two ideas around which the group may want to generate additional ideas. Throughout the process, the worker should (1) express interest in the ideas as they are presented, (2) urge members to continue to produce creative ideas, and (3) help the group elaborate on ideas that have already been presented (Unger, Nunnally, & Willis, 2013).

The worker should not try to have the group evaluate ideas immediately after the brainstorming procedure. Waiting a day or longer allows members to think of new ideas to add to the list and allows time for them to return to an analytical way of evaluating ideas. Once the meeting has ended, the worker should ensure that members are not blamed or sanctioned for the ideas they have expressed. If they are, brainstorming will not succeed in future meetings. Forsyth (2014) also recommends the following steps to ensure effective brainstorming.

Making Brainstorming Effective
- Do not deviate from the four previously described procedures.
- Pay careful attention to each member's contributions.
- Use both group and individual brainstorming during the same session.
- Go slowly and take rest periods.
- Facilitate persistence and motivation especially later in the session.
- Use electronic brainstorming software to minimize idea production blocking.

Uses

Brainstorming procedures are useful under certain conditions. Brainstorming should be done in groups that have already defined a problem. In many respects, brainstorming can be used as a substitute for the methods described in the Developing Plans section of the problem-solving model described in Chapter 11. Brainstorming procedures are particularly appropriate if the problem the group is working on is specific and limited in range (Paulus, Kohn, & Arditti, 2011; Kohn et al., 2011). Therefore, the leader should consider partializing larger problems into smaller categories and doing sequential brainstorming (Baruah & Paulus, 2011; Deuja et al., 2014). The following example shows how brainstorming can be used in groups to accomplish organizational goals.

Case Example   Brainstorming in an Organizational Setting

When a board of directors of a social service organization began a search for a new executive director, the board president decided to involve line staff in the hiring process. The president convened a diverse group of staff members to brainstorm ideas about what qualities a new executive director should demonstrate. Members of the brainstorming group were encouraged to think of as many positive qualities as they could, and each was asked to contribute creative ideas. When they were finished, the board president prompted members to generate additional ideas by mentioning aspects of an executive director's job that did not appear to be fully considered. The board president prepared a written report from the ideas listed by staff and on flip chart pages used during the brainstorming session. The written report was presented to the board of directors for their consideration. The board decided to appoint a subcommittee to lead the search. The subcommittee considered the ideas generated by the focus group meeting of the line staff along with all the others gathered from various constituencies, and reported their findings and recommendations during a subsequent board meeting.

Brainstorming methods are useful when the group wants to generate as many ideas as possible. Brainstorming, therefore, should not be used when the group faces a technical problem that requires systematic, organized thinking. Implicit in the brainstorming approach is the notion that the problem can have varied solutions. In many situations, groups confront problems that can be solved several ways, but sometimes problems have only one right answer. In these situations, brainstorming is not appropriate, and other techniques presented later in this chapter should be used instead.

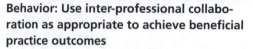

Intervention

Behavior: Use inter-professional collaboration as appropriate to achieve beneficial practice outcomes

Critical Thinking Question: Brainstorming is a common practice in groups. When is it appropriate to use this technique?

Effectiveness

There is evidence that brainstorming is effective for generating creative ideas (see, for example, De Dreu et al., 2011; Forsyth, 2014; Kohn, Paulus, & Choi, 2011; Paulus & Brown, 2007; Paulus & Coskun, 2012; Paulus, Dzindolet, & Kohn, 2011; Paulus, Kohn, & Arditti, 2011). It has been found that members of brainstorming groups are more satisfied and more effective when they are carefully trained in the procedure and practice it before beginning to use it (Ferreira, Antunes, & Herskovic, 2011; Paulus & Coskun, 2012; Paulus, Dzindolet, & Kohn, 2011). It has also been shown that brainstorming is more effective when large ideas are divided into categories, and separate brainstorming is done for each category (Baruah & Paulus, 2011; Deuja et al., 2014). Brainstorming is also more effective when warm-up sessions help members to be as motivated and as effective at processing shared ideas as possible (Baruah & Paulus, 2008, 2009; De Dreu et al., 2011; Paulus & Brown, 2007). Therefore, motivation and effective processing skills should be part of any warm-up or training session.

Brainstorming generates ideas from a wide base because it encourages all group members to participate fully. The method also tends to establish members' commitment to the idea that is ultimately decided on because members have helped shape it. Other benefits of brainstorming in groups are presented in the following list.

Benefits of Brainstorming
- Dependence on an authority figure to come up with problem-solving ideas is reduced.
- Open sharing of ideas is encouraged.
- Members can build on others' ideas.
- A maximum output of ideas occurs in a short period of time.
- Members' ideas are posted immediately for everyone to see.

- Ideas are generated internally rather than imposed from outside the group, which increases the feeling of accountability.
- Brainstorming is enjoyable and self-stimulating.

Despite its benefits, brainstorming is not without drawbacks. It is not easy to achieve an atmosphere in which ideas are generated freely. Brainstorming can initially cause discomfort to members who are not used to freely sharing their ideas, and it breaks norms that ordinarily protect members from making suggestions that may result in overt or covert sanctions. In fact, these norms may be very difficult to change and there is evidence that brainstorming alone, both initially and periodically during meetings, is more effective than group brainstorming (Mullen, Johnson, & Salas, 1991; Paulus & Nijstad, 2003; Putnam & Paulus, 2009).

Other factors also may reduce the efficacy of brainstorming procedures. For example, although the warm-up period is essential for optimal performance during brainstorming, warm-ups require time that may not be available. Inertia may also interfere with brainstorming because the technique requires a change from ordinary group procedures. The worker may not feel justified in imposing the procedure on reluctant or skeptical members who are unaware of its benefits. Although brainstorming has many potentially beneficial effects, if it is to be used effectively, members must be motivated to use it, and workers must apply it correctly.

Variations on Brainstorming

Reverse Brainstorming

Reverse brainstorming is a procedure that can be used to list the negative consequences of actions quickly and thoroughly. Group members are asked, "What might go wrong with this idea?" Reverse brainstorming is useful after a variety of ideas have been generated, and members narrow the ideas to a few top choices. Members then brainstorm about the consequences of carrying out each alternative. After the group identifies potential obstacles to problem solving, the worker then can lead members in a discussion of the ways to overcome them. Therefore, reverse brainstorming can help groups to present the ideas that are likely to be the most appealing, and to be ready with thoughtful responses if decision makers raise implementation issues.

Trigger Groups and Brainwriting

The trigger group procedure uses the early findings of Taylor, Berry, and Block (1958) and Dunnette, Campbell, and Joastad (1963), who discovered that brainstorming is more effective when it is done by individuals working alone than by individuals interacting in groups. In a trigger group, each individual works alone for 5 to 10 minutes to develop a list of ideas and suggestions. Members then read their lists to the group. The group takes about 10 minutes to clarify, add to, or combine ideas that each member has presented. As in brainstorming, suggestions are made without criticism. After all members have presented their ideas, the group decides together on criteria for evaluating the ideas. Ideas are then screened by the group, one at a time, to arrive at a single solution to a problem.

This approach allows members to work independently to develop ideas without verbal or nonverbal evaluative comments from other group members. Also, as each member reads, it focuses the attention of the entire group on the ideas of one individual, which gives members a feeling that their ideas are heard, understood, and carefully examined. It gives each member an opportunity to receive constructive comments from all group members. Trigger groups are best when conducted with five to eight members because the time necessary to develop ideas, to brainstorm, and to critically evaluate each individual's ideas can be prohibitive in larger groups. The more modern adaptation, *brainwriting*, calls for members to pass the ideas they generated in silence to the members seated to their right (Scholtes, Joiner, & Streibel, 2003; Franz, 2012). These members then can take a few minutes to add ideas and pass the list to the next person on their right in the group. This continues until all members have had an opportunity to hitchhike or piggyback on everyone else's ideas in silence. Variations on this procedure include (1) placing ideas generated silently into the center of a meeting table and having others pick them out at random and add their ideas, and (2) using post-it notes to write ideas and place them on meeting room walls so that others can add to them (Levi, 2014). Only after silent idea generation is completed can the group discuss combining, categorizing, and prioritizing ideas.

Focus Groups

Focus groups are designed to collect in-depth, qualitative information about a particular service or topic of interest. The emphasis is on facilitating members' discussion of a subject until viewpoints are fully understood and points of agreement and disagreement become clear. The strength of focus groups is their ability to explore topics and generate hypotheses through the explicit use of group interaction (Hennink, 2014; Kamberelis, & Dimitriadis, 2013; Krueger, Richard, & Casey, 2015; Stewart & Shamdasani, 2015). They are also used to clarify and enrich data collected during surveys or other research methods. Focus groups are often associated with business marketing research where they are used to solicit opinions and reactions to new products or services. However, they were used as early as World War II in the social sciences to examine the effectiveness of wartime propaganda (Merton & Kendall, 1946). Today, they are used by many organizations where social workers practice to gather information for many purposes.

Procedures

Focus group meetings consist of a semi-structured group interview and discussion with 6 to 12 group members. Meetings typically last one to two hours. The worker's task is to lead the semi-structured interview, keeping the group on track and making sure that all members have a chance to share their opinions. They gently direct the group to discuss topics of interest to the sponsor. Workers probe superficial answers, encouraging elaboration and exploration while at the same time helping the group to move on when a particular topic is exhausted.

Aaker, Kumar, Leone, and Day (2013) have presented four key elements to the success of a focus group: (1) planning a specific agenda, (2) recruiting and screening appropriate participants, (3) effective moderation during meetings, and (4) clear and detailed analysis and interpretation of the results. Planning the agenda begins by carefully considering the purpose for the group and the topics to be covered. Because focus groups are meant to encourage in-depth discussion, it is important to maintain the focus by not exploring too many topics. The worker should develop a series of relevant questions for which responses are sought. From these questions, a discussion guide is prepared. The guide is an outline that helps ensure that specific issues are covered. The discussion guide should proceed in a logical order from general to specific areas of inquiry. Although all topics should be covered, the guide is not meant to be a rigid template for the conduct of group meetings. If a question does not generate useful, non-repetitive information, the facilitator should move on to the next question or probe. Similarly, new or interesting ideas that emerge from the interaction between members should be pursued using paraphrasing, follow-up prompts, and additional questions.

Careful screening of participants is crucial to the success of a focus group. Focus group participants should be interested in the topic to be discussed and opinions about it. They should have enough characteristics in common so that they will feel comfortable interacting. To get a broad, in-depth understanding of a subject, it is important to select individuals with a wide range of experience and diverse opinions. Because individuals who have participated in previous focus groups may dominate the discussion, they are generally excluded from participation. Also, it is preferable to recruit individuals who do not know one another. Relatives, friends, and neighbors tend to talk to each other rather than to the whole group, and, because of the presence of individuals they know, they are sometimes less open about their true opinions.

Because positive, freewheeling group interaction can help reticent participants express in-depth opinions and discuss all aspects of a particular topic, effective leadership is essential in focus groups. Leaders should be familiar with the topic to be discussed and sensitive to the verbal and nonverbal cues given off by participants. Aaker, Kumar, Leone, and Day (2013) suggest that focus group leaders should have the ability to (1) establish rapport quickly, (2) listen carefully to each member's opinions, (3) demonstrate a genuine interest in each member's views, (4) avoid jargon and sophisticated terminology that may turn off members, (5) flexibly implement the discussion guide, (6) sense when a topic is exhausted or when it is becoming threatening, (7) know what topic to introduce to maintain a smooth flow of the discussion, and (8) facilitate group dynamics that encourage the full participation of all members and avoid domination by talkative members.

Focus groups often yield a wealth of disparate comments and opinions. To prepare reports and to do qualitative analyses of the data derived from a focus group meeting, it is useful to have an audiotape or videotape of group meetings. Reports of focus group meetings should capture the diverse opinions that are expressed as well as any consensus that is achieved. It is also useful to categorize members' comments in a manner that relates the comments to the specific hypotheses or questions that the focus group was intended to address.

Uses

Focus groups can be used for many purposes, some of which are listed here.

> **Uses of Focus Groups**
> - Generating hypotheses about the way individuals think or behave that may be tested quantitatively at a later point
> - Obtaining in-depth information about a topic
> - Generating or evaluating impressions and opinions about the services an organization offers or plans to offer

- Overcoming reticence to obtaining personal views and opinions
- Generating information to help develop client-satisfaction questionnaires and other types of questionnaires
- Providing in-depth analysis and interpretation of previously collected data and the findings of previously reported studies

Focus groups are particularly well suited for gathering in-depth data about the attitudes and opinions of participants (Krueger, Richard, & Casey, 2015; Stewart & Shamdasani, 2015). This is illustrated in the following case.

Case Example   Using a Focus Group in the Community

The director of a community mental health clinic was concerned about her agency's ability to reach out and effectively serve Native American communities in the large rural area served. During a weekly executive committee meeting, it was decided to recruit a focus group of Native American leaders to explore their communities' perceptions of the mental health center and its services. Following a carefully planned agenda and using a structured interview guide, the group leader helped the focus members identify and elaborate on their perceptions of the agency and its strengths and weaknesses in serving Native Americans. The group leader prepared a written report summarizing the focus group findings for the executive committee. The report spurred the executive committee to plan a larger needs assessment project. The goal of this project was to develop recommendations about improving service delivery to Native Americans for the consideration of the board of directors of the agency.

Although the information derived from focus groups is excellent for developing hypotheses and for exploring issues in-depth, caution should be exercised when using the information as the sole basis for making important decisions affecting large groups of individuals. Because a limited number of participants can be included in focus groups, the data derived may not be as representative of a larger population as data derived from a well-designed survey.

Effectiveness

Focus groups are considered to be a qualitative research method because they yield rich descriptions of participants' attitudes and opinions about targeted topics. They can yield new insights and ideas and lend support or contradict commonly accepted notions and ingrained beliefs. They are also frequently used to help understand the nuances and boundaries of problems or issues so that social workers can have a better idea about how to construct needs assessments, in-depth individual interviews, surveys, and other quantitative methods to gather more reliable data about particular populations of interest. Focus groups are more flexible than many other methods of collecting data. Leaders can pursue particular comments made by members with probes that ask for additional information, and invitations to elaborate. Another advantage is that they can help participants become actively engaged with the sponsoring organization in efforts to improve group work and other services.

Sometimes, focus groups are thought of as a quick, inexpensive way of collecting data, but considerable time and expense can be involved in recruiting participants and in analyzing the large amount of data that comes from these meetings (Rubin & Babbie, 2014;

Monette, Sullivan, DeJong, & Hilton, 2014). Therefore, group workers can be helpful to organizations' administrators by gently pointing out the hidden costs and time-consuming nature of focus groups. Another disadvantage of focus groups is that the data collected may not be generalizable to a larger target population. Workers can be helpful by pointing out the select nature of the individuals who participate in focus groups and the small sample sizes. Conformity, group think, the risky shift, and other group dynamics discussed in Chapter 3 may affect the data that is obtained from focus group meetings. Therefore, workers with experience in leading groups are often better at leading focus groups than other staff. It is also important to recognize that results from focus groups may not be clear or quantifiable, and sharp discrepancies in the data from different participants may be difficult to interpret (Rubin & Babbie, 2014; Monette, Sullivan, DeJong, & Hilton, 2014). Most experts also agree that the effectiveness of focus groups depends heavily on the moderator's ability to facilitate the discussion (Aaker et al., 2013; Hennink, 2014; Kamberelis & Dimitriadis, 2013; Krueger, Richard, & Casey, 2015; Stewart & Shamdasani, 2015).

Despite these limitations, with adequate preparation and a skillful moderator, focus groups can provide an effective and efficient method for collecting in-depth, qualitative data about the thoughts and opinions of consumers of health and social services. For more information about conducting focus groups, see Aaker, Kumar, Leone, and Day (2013); Hennink (2014); Kamberelis and Dimitriadis (2013); Krueger, Richard, and Casey (2015); or Stewart and Shamdasani (2015).

 Assess your understanding of specialized methods that facilitate generating ideas and information in task groups by taking this brief quiz.

Nominal Group Technique

The nominal group technique (NGT) is different from traditional interacting approaches to solving problems in task groups. The technique was developed in the late 1960s by Andre Delbecq and Andrew Van de Ven as they studied program planning groups in social service agencies and the operation of committees and other idea-aggregating and decision-making groups in business and industry (Delbecq, Van de Ven, & Gustafson, 1986). Since its development, the technique has been used extensively in health, social service, industrial, educational, and governmental agencies as an aid to planning and managing programs (see, for example, Andersen & Fagerhaug, 2000; Levi, 2014; Thompson, 2015).

Research-Informed Practice

Behavior: Use and translate research evidence to inform and improve practice, policy, and service delivery

Critical Thinking Question: The Nominal Group Technique (NGT) minimizes group interaction. What negative aspects of groups can be overcome using NGT?

Procedures

An NGT meeting should have six to nine group members. Larger groups should be separated into two or more smaller groups. Because participants are required to write and because ideas are presented on a flip chart, group members should be seated around a U-shaped table. A flip chart with newsprint should be placed at the open end of the U. Supplies that are needed include a flip chart, felt-tip pen, roll of tape, index cards, worksheets, and pencils. A summary of NGT procedures follows.

> **Procedures for Using NGT**
> - Developing a clear statement of the problem
> - Round robin recording of ideas generated by group members

- Hitchhiking: generating new ideas from ideas already listed
- Serial discussion to clarify ideas
- Preliminary ordering of ideas by importance
- Choosing highest priority ideas and ranking in order of priority
- Discussion of ranked ideas

Before an NGT meeting, the worker should develop a clear statement of the problem in cooperation with the sponsoring agency. At the beginning of the group, the worker states the purpose of the meeting. Then the worker hands out lined paper with the problem statement written at the top, reads the problem statement, and asks all members to take five minutes to list their ideas or responses to the problem. Ideas and responses should be written in brief phrases, without verbal or nonverbal communication with other group members. To give the members some notion of what types of responses are being asked for, workers may want to prepare some sample ideas or responses as models. While group members are working, the leader also writes ideas in silence and ensures that members of the group do not interact with one another.

The next step is a round robin recording of ideas generated by each group member. The ideas are listed on a flip chart that is visible to all group members. The worker asks one member for an idea, writes it on the flip chart, and then goes around the group by asking each person in turn for one idea. Members are encouraged to use ideas already on the chart to stimulate their thinking and add on their worksheets ideas that they did not think of during the silent period. When a member has no new ideas, the member passes and allows the next group member to present an idea until everyone is finished.

The ideas should be recorded as rapidly as possible in members' own words. During the round robin, members should not critique, elaborate on, or defend ideas. Completed sheets from a flip chart should be taped to a flat surface in view of all group members.

The third step is a serial discussion to clarify the ideas that have been presented. Items from the flip chart are taken in order and discussed for two or three minutes. Each member who expressed an idea is encouraged to explain briefly the evidence and the logic used in arriving at it. At this point, members are free to express their agreement or disagreement with the idea and to discuss its relative importance. Although evaluative comments are welcome, the group should not be allowed to focus on any one idea for a long period of time or to get into a debate over the merits of a particular idea.

The fourth step is a preliminary ordering of the importance of the ideas that have been listed. Each member is asked to work independently in selecting from the list a predetermined number of the ideas with the highest priority. The number of items selected varies, depending on the length of the list, but should include about one-quarter to one-half of the original ideas. Members write their choices on index cards and hand them to the worker. The number of votes that each idea receives from all members is recorded next to the item. This process helps individual members obtain feedback about ideas that are highly regarded by their fellow members.

Each member is then asked to choose five highest-priority ideas from the narrowed-down list. The members rank the ideas on a scale of 5 = highest priority to 1 = lowest priority. The idea and its rank order are then placed on an index card. One index card is used for each idea. The cards are collected and the rank orders are tallied by writing them next to their corresponding ideas on the flip chart. After all ranks have been tallied, the mean rank for each idea is determined by adding the numbers (ranks) next to each item and dividing by the number of group members. The group may want to discuss the ranks and take a second vote when there are large discrepancies among members' rating patterns. To avoid this being viewed as a way to manipulate the group process, it is recommended that before beginning NGT, the group as a whole should decide under what circumstances a second vote will be taken.

Uses

NGT was created to "increase rationality, creativity, and participation in problem-solving meetings associated with program planning" (Delbecq et al., 1986, p. 1). It is designed to prevent group processes that inhibit interaction (Van de Ven & Delbecq, 1971). These inhibiting influences are presented in the following list.

> **Factors Inhibiting Group Interaction**
> - The pursuit of a single thought pattern for a long time period
> - Members relying on other group members to do the work, i.e., social loafing
> - Covert judgments that may or may not be expressed
> - Status hierarchies and differentials preventing participation by low-status members
> - Group pressure for conformity, such as members participating only to the extent that they feel equally competent to other members
> - Dominant or talkative group members
> - Reaching quick decisions without fully exploring the problem by information gathering and fact finding

Case Example   Nominal Group Technique

A multiservice community agency was facing a fiscal crisis. The executive council charged with tightening and balancing the budget by the board of directors decided to use NGT to generate ideas for saving money. The executive director led the council in this effort by first asking that each member work alone and write down creative ideas for saving money in the budget. In round robin fashion, each member was then asked to present one idea at a time to the group until all ideas were presented and recorded on a flip chart. Next, the executive director led the group in very brief discussions of the pros and cons of each suggested savings method. Then, she asked each member to independently rank each item in order of its value to the savings effort. These rankings were then used during a brief group discussion that focused on eliminating ideas that were not rated highly ranked by any member. Also during the discussion, whenever possible, similar money savings ideas were combined. Then, the members were asked to rank the five highest-priority suggestions. These ideas were studied more closely for their impact on the budget by the management of the agency. During the next board meeting, these and other recommendations were presented to the board for approval as part of the overall plan to balance the budget and restore the agency to fiscal health.

Effectiveness

Delbecq, Van de Ven, and Gustafson (1986) developed NGT by combining the positive aspects of noninteracting nominal groups and interacting problem-solving groups. NGT

(1) stimulates members' active participation because it requires members to work both in silence and interactively, (2) avoids dominance by strong personalities and enables minority opinions to be expressed, (3) prevents premature decision making, and (4) structures the process so that all members participate and feel that their views and opinions are given equal weight in the solution (Van de Ven & Delbecq, 1971). NGT builds consensus by giving each group member an equal opportunity to express ideas and participate in reaching a decision. By structuring the interaction, NGT reduces the domination of a few members and makes full use of the creative capabilities and pooled wisdom of all group members. This, in turn, helps to ensure a broad base of support for any decision made by the group.

NGT is based on social science findings about task groups that have been accumulated over decades of research. Each step is designed to make use of these findings. Delbecq, Van de Ven, and Gustafson (1986) reported that NGT incorporates the following research-based findings to increase decision-making accuracy.

Procedures to Increase Judgment Accuracy
- Having members make independent judgments
- Expressing judgments mathematically by ranking or rating items
- Using the arithmetic mean of independent judgments to form the group's decision
- Having members make decisions anonymously
- Using feedback about preliminary judgments for final voting

The NGT technique uses these research findings in its decision-making step by taking the mean rating of independent rank-order judgments that have been placed on anonymous index cards. There is also some limited empirical evidence that NGT is more effective than interacting group methods for idea generation, problem solving, and consensus building (Toseland, Rivas, & Chapman, 1984; Van de Ven, 1974), and members are more satisfied with their participation in NGT groups than in untrained groups (Kramer, Kuo, & Dailey, 1997).

NGT has some limitations. It takes a considerable amount of time to arrive at a decision (experience suggests at least two hours in most cases). This can present an obstacle for some task groups that have many decisions to make and must complete their work in a short time frame. Therefore, NGT is often reserved for important decisions. It is less frequently used for routine decisions that may not require the precision afforded by this method.

Another limitation is that the group process is highly structured, which some members may find too restrictive. One study found that members of NGT groups were less satisfied than members of less structured groups using a problem-solving approach (Toseland, Rivas, & Chapman, 1984). NGT may also raise members' suspicions about being manipulated. For example, having the worker rather than group members define the problem and having the worker or a powerful group member influence voting procedures by calling for a second vote may feel constricting or even manipulative to members who are used to having more freedom during freely interacting problem-solving and decision-making groups. Although consensus is built by including all members in every step of the decision making process, NGT uses voting to make final decisions, which is not recommended for building consensus (Forsyth, 2014).

Multi-attribute Utility Analysis

Multi-attribute Utility Analysis (MAU) uses decision rules to specify the relationships between attributes of a problem. The decision rules that are derived from the process promote rational and transparent decision making and enable sponsors and oversight bodies to understand the basis for judgments. For social group workers without statistical backgrounds, MAU can be a bit complicated to understand. Still, it is presented in this chapter because it is very effective for helping groups make sound, rational decisions, especially when important policy decisions are being made or when decision-making processes may be scrutinized. It helps members avoid conflict by focusing on the reasoning behind their choices, rather than by them defending particular choices without sharing their underlying reasoning. Also, MAU is well suited to intranet and Internet decision making in virtual meetings, which are efficient in large multisite organizations or when interagency decisions are needed. Virtual meetings are likely to become more common in the next decade (see Chapter 7).

Procedures

A group's use of MAU begins by having each member work alone, either in individual meetings between each member and the worker or in a nominal group meeting in which all members work separately on instructions given by the worker. During this time, the problem and its alternative solutions are explained to members. For example, members are informed that their group has been appointed to decide among applicants for the position of assistant program director. The worker helps group members clarify their thinking about the problem. Specifically, the worker helps each member determine the attributes that are thought to be relevant to making a decision. As presented in Figure 12.1, a member might decide that the attributes he or she considers important for the position of assistant program director include (1) amount of supervisory experience, (2) amount of clinical experience, (3) level of management skills, and (4) extent that the candidate likes to develop new and innovative service programs. Alternatively, the attributes might be developed through a brainstorming or NGT process.

The worker also helps each member specify the levels of each attribute by deciding on (1) the minimal criteria for a solution, (2) any constraints on the solution, (3) the utility function that accompanies each attribute, and (4) the weight placed on each attribute and its accompanying utility function. For example, members might decide that minimal criteria for the assistant program director's position include three years of supervisory experience and five years of clinical experience. The members also decide that the candidate must have an MSW or an MPA degree.

The utility function of each attribute specifies its relationship to the overall solution—that is, how levels of an attribute are related to a particular solution. Figure 12.1 presents one member's utility functions for the four attributes mentioned previously. The utility functions indicate that as the amount of supervisory experience increases, satisfaction with the candidate increases until the candidate has more than 10 years of experience, at which time the members' satisfaction with the candidate declines. At this point, the member's utility function indicates that she thinks candidates would have too much supervisory experience for the position.

For the clinical experience attribute, a utility function with a similar form occurs, except that satisfaction with a candidate increases until the candidate has more than

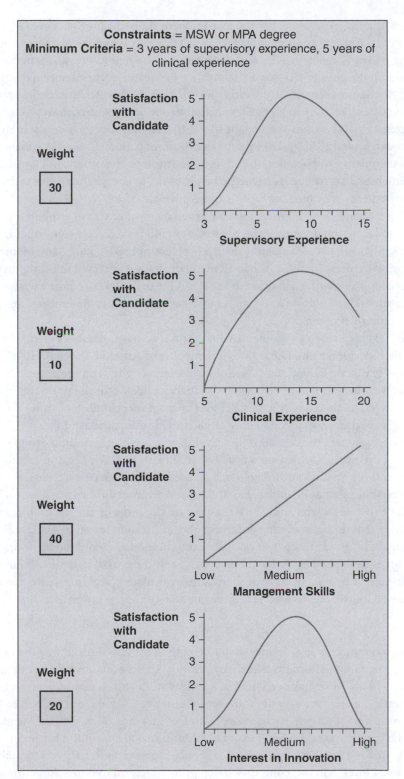

Figure 12.1
A Group Member's Decision Rules for Choosing Among Applicants for
Assistant Program Director

15 years of clinical experience. For the management skills attribute shown in Figure 12.1, the utility function shows an ascending linear relationship, which suggests that the higher the score on a management skills test and interview, the higher the satisfaction with the candidate. In the case of developing innovative programs, a curvilinear relationship is present; that is, candidates who are either low or high on this attribute are less preferred than candidates who have moderate inclination to develop new programs.

Figure 12.1 also shows the weight that a group member gave to each attribute. Weights can be assigned by dividing 100 points among all attributes in a manner that reflects the relative importance of each in proportion to the others. In Figure 12.1, the management skills attribute is assigned a weight of 40, making it four times as important as clinical experience, which has been assigned a weight of 10.

The procedure of establishing minimal criteria, constraints, and attributes with their weights and functional forms is the basis of a member's decision rule—that is, how a group member will use information about a problem to make a judgment. Members develop their own decision rules. When all members have completed this task, they share their decision rules with each other. It is helpful for the worker to post each member's decision rules side by side on a flip chart or whiteboard so that all members can see how their decision rules compare.

The next step when using the MAU method is to have members discuss the logic behind their decision rules. During this unstructured discussion, the only "rule" is to focus on the reasoning behind the choice of attributes, weights, and functional forms. For example, members should not discuss individual candidates for the position, but would be encouraged to discuss why a member gave management skills four times the weight of clinical experience when considering candidates for this particular job.

Members discuss the decision rules until they agree on a common group rule that satisfies all members. Consensus is usually not difficult to reach because members find it easier to agree on how information will be used than on specific alternatives. Once a group decision rule has been decided, it is a routine procedure to see how each alternative (in this case, a job candidate) is ranked on the basis of the decision rule. First, alternatives that do not meet the criteria or the constraints set up by the decision rule are eliminated. The next step is to calculate each alternative's score on the decision rule. Each score is multiplied by that attribute's weight, and the total score is summed across each attribute. A total score on each alternative is calculated. The alternative that is rated the highest based on the decision rule is the one selected by the group as its final decision.

Uses

MAU is used primarily as a decision-making method for choosing among distinct alternatives or for ranking numerous cases by priority. The method should not be used for generating ideas. MAU has been used in a variety of health, social service, and mental health settings (see, for example, Carretero-Gomez & Cabrera, 2012; Clark & Unruh, 2009; Dolan, 2010; Peacock, Richardson, Carter, & Edwards, 2006; Stoner, Meadan, Angell, & Daczewitz, 2012; Weiss, Edwards, & Mouttapa, 2009). In the future, it is likely that an increasing number of large human service organizations, particularly at the state and national level, will use computer-based group decision making, sometimes called *electronic brainstorming* or *electronic group decision support systems*, to enhance the quality of group decision making. For more information about electronic brainstorming and computer-assisted group decision support systems, see Bose (2015), Dzindolet, Paulus, and Glazer (2012), Paulus et al. (2013), or Thompson (2015).

Effectiveness

MAU is the most rational and technical method discussed in this chapter for making decisions in task groups. It attempts to order and systematize information by identifying important decision making attributes and assigning each a weight and a functional relationship to the overall decision. There is empirical evidence for the effectiveness of this method (for reviews, see Cabrera & Raju, 2001; Roth, Bobko, & Mabon, 2001). By providing for a thorough discussion of each individual's decision rules instead of a more traditional discussion of alternative choices, the group achieves consensus about how information will be used to make a decision. MAU helps to eliminate the polarization that often takes place when members try to defend their choices of alternative solutions. Once the group decides on a decision rule, all alternatives are rated according to that rule. In this way, MAU is an impartial and transparent method. Because members have had a chance to influence the decision rule, the choice that is made by the group reflects the input of all members and, therefore, is likely to have the cooperation and commitment of all members when it is implemented.

The primary drawback to MAU is that it is a technical method limited to making decisions between clear, established alternatives. When decisions between clearly delineated alternatives are crucial and consensus is important, MAU should be considered the method of choice for problem-solving groups. However, MAU should be used only by a trained worker who has both conceptual and practical experience in developing decision rules. In addition, MAU is not useful for generating ideas or alternative solutions but can be used after alternatives have been developed by brainstorming or other methods.

Quality Improvement Groups

Following trends in business and industry, continuous quality improvement (CQI) has become increasingly popular in health and human services. Groups are used extensively in CQI. In fact the literature is replete with many different names for quality improvement groups, including Quality Circles (QCs), Learning Collaboratives, Quality Improvement Teams (QITs), Continuous Quality Improvement Work Groups, and Self-Managed Work Teams (see, for example, Clark & Unruh, 2009; Davis et al., 2012, 2014; Dresser et al., 2009; Strating & Nieboer, 2013; Nadeem et al., 2014; Nolan, 2014; Lewis, Packard, & Lewis, 2012; Murphy, 2015; Neck & Houghton, 2006; Patti, 2009; Paul, Smith, & Blumberg, 2010; Strating & Nieboer, 2013).

QCs are small groups of employees who get together voluntarily, elect a leader, and identify and solve problems they have in completing their work assignments in a particular department or other settings. The intent is not only to improve quality but also to prevent workers from becoming alienated from the process and place of their work. Self-Managed Work Teams extend the concept of QCs by taking responsibility for all the work functions assigned to them and may use QC techniques as a way to ensure the quality

Intervention

Behavior: Critically choose and implement interventions to achieve practice goals and enhance capacities of clients and constituencies

Critical Thinking Question: Private industry uses group methods for problem solving. What types of problems lend themselves to solutions using task groups in social work?

of their work. They are often associated with organizations that are attempting to reduce hierarchical management. For more about these groups see Neck and Houghton (2006).

In contrast to QCs and Self-Managed Work Teams, QITs and Continuous Quality Improvement Work Teams frequently consist of employees from different organizational levels and a variety of departments or functions within the organization. Members are often selected by management, and membership on the team is often required. Also, the projects the teams work on are often selected and approved by management.

Learning Collaboratives are relatively new phenomena. They can occur in a single organization or include members from other organizations. Their purpose is to improve usual care by sharing and disseminating evidence-based practices and by using quality improvement methods. They sometimes work at multiple levels in the same organization or across organizations to improve the quality of care. For example, a mental health Learning Collaborative may hold seminars focused on evidence-based practices for different mental health problems and also join with organizations focused on substance abuse or developmental disabilities to plan comprehensive treatment approaches for dually diagnosed consumers. Although Learning Collaboratives are growing in mental health and other practice fields, there is still very little information about their makeup, methods, or effectiveness (see, for example, Nadeem et al., 2014 or Strating & Nieboer, 2013). Because more is known about QCs and QITs, the remaining portion of this section will focus on these groups.

Procedures

Organizations generally have a coordinator for all CQI activities. This individual's role is to ensure that (1) training is provided, (2) there is coverage when facilitators are sick or take personal leave, and (3) each circle or team has a way of communicating suggestions about problem solving to top-level management. QCs and QITs generally consist of six to eight employees who meet regularly (e.g., weekly, monthly) to identify and solve problems that they face individually or as a larger work force. In QCs, a facilitator is selected by the membership; in QITs, this member may be appointed. Often the facilitator is a mid-level manager who serves as the link between the QC or QIT and upper management. To ensure that QCs and QITs run smoothly and effectively, facilitators should be trained in group dynamics and leadership skills. During meetings, the facilitator uses group dynamics, problem solving, brainstorming, and other procedures to facilitate an in-depth discussion and analysis of the topic or issue being addressed by the group.

QCs operate on the basis of core principles rather than specific steps or procedures. These principles are presented in the following list.

QC Core Principles
- Commitment from top-level management to the process
- A commitment to provide training for members of QCs in brainstorming, problem solving, and information technology to gather evidence-based procedures
- Voluntary membership in QC groups
- A focus on problems identified by workers rather than by management
- The selection of leadership and the ownership of the QC process by line staff
- A focus on data-based problem solving
- A focus on solving problems in ways that benefit both line workers and management

Unlike QCs, QITs use the following specific steps for quality improvement: (1) understanding the opportunity or problem, (2) defining the specific target for improvement, (3) designing strategies to reach the target, (4) designing data-acquiring strategies, (5) designing a process to use the data, and (6) determining how the project will be managed. QCs are often used for idea generation and for improving the work environment, whereas QITs emphasize systematic, data-based, problem-solving strategies for improving the quality of services delivered by an organization.

Uses

The primary purpose of QCs and QITs is to improve the quality of the service delivered to consumers. Thus, QCs and QITs are two ways for management and line staff to demonstrate their commitment to delivering health and social services in the most effective manner.

Case Example   A Quality Improvement Team

In a multiservice agency serving developmentally disabled adults, staff members became increasingly aware that clients often have multiple service providers. In these situations, problems often arose in the coordination of service plans among all the providers. In a QIT meeting, staff decided to review a selected number of consumer files to obtain data about the number of providers, and how services were currently coordinated. The QIT group used these data as the basis for recommendations about the design of a new care management system.

QCs and QITs have several benefits including encouraging workers to solve problems that interfere with their job satisfaction and performance, and gaining a greater sense of control and autonomy. In turn, workers are likely to feel better about their work, and more committed to it.

Effectiveness

Many writers have claimed that QCs and QITs improve services and workers' morale by reducing vertical and horizontal demarcations of power (see, for example, Harrington & Mignosa, 2015). Despite these assertions, there is not yet a great deal of high quality empirical evidence about the effectiveness of quality improvement groups in social service organizations, and little is even known about the extent of use of the different types of quality improvement groups mentioned in this section. Therefore, this is an area that could benefit from additional research.

> **?** Assess your understanding of specialized methods that promote rational decision making in groups by taking this brief quiz.

LARGE ORGANIZATIONAL GROUPS

Parliamentary Procedure

Parliamentary procedure is a framework for guiding decision making and problem solving in large task groups. It has been developed over time in many different settings to meet the needs of a variety of task groups. Although there are some commonly accepted rules, there is no single body of laws that is universally accepted as parliamentary procedure.

Parliamentary procedure originated in 1321 in the English Parliament. From these roots, Thomas Jefferson developed a *Manual of Parliamentary Practice* in 1801 for use in Congress, and in 1845, Luther Cushing formulated a manual for use in lay, as well as legislative, assemblies (Robert & Robert, 2011). Today, *Robert's Rules of Order* is the set of parliamentary procedures most frequently followed by task groups (Robert & Robert, 2011).

Procedures

In parliamentary meetings, the activity of the group is determined by motions brought by group members.

Classes of Motions in Parliamentary Procedures

- *Privileged motions* deal with the agenda of the group meeting as a whole. They do not have a relationship with the business before the group and include motions such as adjournment and recess.
- *Incidental motions* are concerned with procedural questions relating to issues *on the floor*. Some examples are a *point of order* and a *point of information*.
- *Subsidiary motions* assist in the handling and disposal of motions on the floor. Motions to table, postpone, or amend are subsidiary motions.
- *Main motions* introduce the central, substantive issues for group consideration. There can be no pending motions when a main motion is proposed. Examples of main motions are reconsideration of an issue previously disposed of and resuming consideration of a tabled motion.

All motions made from the floor follow procedures governing the introduction of that type of motion. It is the chairperson's job to ensure that the rules and procedures are followed. Although the chairperson is supposed to remain neutral during group deliberations, the person can influence the group's work in a variety of ways. Group members must be recognized by the chair before they can make a motion. The chairperson rules on questions of procedure that arise during a meeting and also organizes the meeting by ordering the agenda items and specifying the amount of time available to discuss each item.

Robert's Rules of Order provides a method for prioritizing motions during parliamentary meetings. Table 12.1 shows the priority that each motion takes during a meeting.

Table 12.1   Procedures for Acting on a Motion During a Parliamentary Meeting

Type of Motion	Priority of the Motion	Can the Speaker Be Interrupted?	Does the Motion Need a Second?	Is the Motion Debatable?	Can the Motion Be Amended?	Vote Needed to Adopt the Motion
Privileged Motions						
Set the time of adjournment	1	N	Y	N	Y	Majority
Call for adjournment	2	N	Y	N	N	Majority
Call for recess	3	N	Y	N	Y	Majority
Question of privilege	4	Y	N	N	N	Chair's decision
Call for prescheduled items of business	5	Y	N	N	N	No vote

Table 12.1 (Continued)

Type of Motion	Priority of the Motion	Can the Speaker Be Interrupted?	Does the Motion Need a Second?	Is the Motion Debatable?	Can the Motion Be Amended?	Vote Needed to Adopt the Motion
Incidental Motions						
Point of order	6	Y	N	N	N	Chair's decision
Request for information	6	Y	N	N	N	No vote
Call for a revote	6	N	N	N	N	No vote
Appeal the chair's decision	6	Y	Y	N	N	Majority
Object to consideration of a motion	6	Y	N	N	N	2/3
Call to suspend the rules	6	N	Y	N	N	2/3
Request to withdraw a motion	6	Y	Y	N	N	Majority
Subsidiary Motions						
Table a motion	7	N	Y	N	N	Majority
Call for immediate vote	8	N	Y	N	N	2/3
Limit/extend debate	9	N	Y	N	N	2/3
Postpone the motion	10	N	Y	Y	Y	Majority
Refer the motion to a subcommittee	11	N	Y	Y	Y	Majority
Amend the motion	12	N	Y	Y	Y	Majority
Postpone the motion indefinitely	13	N	Y	Y	N	Majority
Main Motions						
General main motion	14	N	Y	Y	Y	Majority
Reconsider a motion already voted on	14	Y	Y	Y	Y	2/3
Rescind a motion under consideration	14	N	Y	Y	Y	2/3
Resume consideration of a tabled motion	14	N	Y	N	N	Majority
Set a special order of business	14	N	Y	Y	Y	2/3

Although main motions contain the essential business of the parliamentary meeting, they receive the lowest priority because privileged motions govern how all agenda items are considered, and incidental and subsidiary motions are always made in reference to a main motion. Therefore, these motions are given a higher priority than main motions. For further information about parliamentary meetings, see *Robert's Rules of Order Newly Revised* (Robert & Robert, 2011), and for other ways of running meetings to reach consensus, see *Breaking Roberts' Rules* (Susskind & Cruikshank, 2006).

Uses

Parliamentary procedure is often used in large groups because it provides a well-defined structure to guide group process. The rules of parliamentary procedure help ensure a high level of order and efficiency in task group meetings when many agenda items are discussed. Order and efficiency are achieved through rules that demand consideration of one issue at a time. The rules prescribe the way in which issues are brought before the group, processed by the group, and disposed of by the group. In a meeting of a delegate council composed of representatives from many social service agencies, for example, parliamentary procedure can be used to lend order to how representatives interact. Thus, with many members representing the diverse interests of several agencies, meetings are run in a formal manner, and members are generally guaranteed a structured means by which they can bring their interests, motions, and agenda items to the large group.

Parliamentary procedure is especially useful for considering well-developed agenda items that need some discussion and debate and a relatively speedy decision by an entire task group. Parliamentary procedure is a formal and technically precise set of rules that is widely used but has a tendency to squelch directness, openness, and vitality (Forsyth, 2014). Thus, the procedure should not be used as a substitute for brainstorming or problem solving done by subcommittees of the larger task group.

Effectiveness

The long history of using parliamentary procedure in important decision-making bodies throughout the Western world testifies to its usefulness in providing a structure for task group meetings. By limiting and focusing the deliberations of a task group to one solution at a time, discussion and debate are facilitated, and motions are dealt with expeditiously. Clearly specified rules lead to an orderly and systematic consideration of each agenda item. Rules that remain consistent throughout the life of a group assure members that there is an established order that they can rely on for fair and equitable treatment when sensitive or controversial issues are presented.

Parliamentary procedure also protects the rights of the minority. For example, it takes only two members to introduce a main motion, one to state the motion and another to second the motion. Some motions can be made by a single member. Every group member is given an equal opportunity to participate. Majority rights are also protected because a quorum is needed to conduct a meeting, and majority rule is relied on for all decisions.

Parliamentary meetings have several disadvantages. Meetings are subject to manipulation by members who are familiar with parliamentary procedures. Members who are less familiar with the procedures may be reluctant to speak or be unsure of when or how to raise an objection to a motion. Another limitation is that private deals may be made outside a meeting to gain a member's support for an agenda item in a forthcoming meeting. Private deals circumvent the intent of parliamentary procedure, which is based on openly debating the merits of a proposal. They also tend to enforce the will of powerful members who offer attractive incentives to members who support their positions on particular agenda items.

Parliamentary meetings have other limitations. The procedure encourages debate, which can lead to polarization of members' opinions. Also, members often try to defend their positions rather than understand the logic behind opposing viewpoints. Perhaps the most important limitation of parliamentary procedure is that it is not well suited for problem solving, especially when the problem is complex, muddled, or not fully understood. A large task group using parliamentary procedure does not usually attain the level of interaction, the depth of communication, or the flexibility necessary to explore alternative solutions that may be necessary to resolve difficult problems. Large task groups should conduct most problem-solving efforts in subcommittees that report back to the larger group. The larger group can then debate the merits of a proposed solution and reach a decision based on majority rule.

Phillips' 66

Phillips' 66 was developed to facilitate discussion in large groups (Phillips, 1948). Originally, Phillips' 66 referred to a technique of dividing a large group or audience into groups of six and having each group spend six minutes formulating one question for the speaker. The method has been expanded to include many different ways to facilitate communication in large groups. For example, members of the larger group may be asked to form smaller groups and discuss different aspects of a problem. Each group is asked to designate a recorder who uses a flip chart or other method to display the results of the subgroup's work. Then, the recorder or another member reports a summary of the subgroup's work when the larger group reconvenes.

Procedures

Phillips' 66 should be used only after clear instructions are given to members about what they will be doing during the procedure, especially because once the large group has broken down into smaller groups, the sudden change from the structure and control of a large group meeting can cause confusion. If the groups are not clear about their direction, they may flounder or begin to work on something other than what was assigned by the leader.

To reduce the chances for confusion, the worker should ensure that each group is clear about the problem or task it is facing. Problem statements, tasks, and goals should be specific. When they are broad and nonspecific, the small groups have to spend time refining them, which may lead to work that is quite different from what the worker had intended. Members should also be clear about their assignments. They should understand what subgroup they belong to, what the group is supposed to do, what should be contained in the recorder's report, how much time they have, and where and when the subgroup is supposed to meet.

The size of the subgroups and the amount of time each subgroup spends together depend on the situation. The original design of six-member groups meeting for six minutes may be appropriate in some situations but not in others. Generally, at least 20 to 30 minutes are required for a large group to break down into smaller groups and accomplish any meaningful work. Subgroups should be separated so members can hear each other and conduct their work. However, in a large meeting room, it is not necessary to ask members to talk quietly. The noise and activity of other groups can be contagious and thus spur all groups to work harder (Maier, 1963).

In very large meetings, having each subgroup report back to the larger group may be monotonous and time-consuming. Alternatives include limiting the reporting time to a few minutes for each subgroup, having each subgroup report on a portion of the discussion, and having each subgroup prepare a brief written report that can be shared after the meeting.

Phillips' 66 can be combined with a procedure known as *idea writing* (Moore, 1994). When participants break into small groups, each member can be given a sheet of paper with a triggering question or item to which the member should respond in writing. After approximately five minutes, members place their sheets in the center of the group. Each member then selects another member's sheet and responds in writing for approximately 5 to 10 minutes to the initial idea prepared by the first member. This process is repeated until all members have prepared written responses on every idea sheet. Members may react by writing what they like and dislike about the previous ideas and reactions and can offer suggestions for improvement. After this process is completed, members find their original sheets and read their ideas and other members' reactions to them. The members of the small group then discuss the ideas that emerge from the written interaction, and the group facilitator summarizes the discussion on a flip chart. When the larger group reconvenes, the small-group facilitator can use information on the flip chart to present a summary of the small group's ideas.

Another way to use Phillips' 66 is to have each of the smaller groups who have worked on ideas on a flip chart, tear off their pages and tape them to the walls around the room. Then members of the larger group can go around and select their top two or three favorite ideas by placing a tally mark next to the items of their choice on the sheets hanging on the walls. Then, when the group reconvenes, the marks can be tallied, and the larger group can decide to work on one or more of the ideas that were given the most checkmarks by members of the entire group.

Uses

Although most problem-solving activities take place in small task groups, occasionally there is a need for large groups, such as members of a social agency or a delegate assembly, to engage in problem-solving discussions. Parliamentary procedure, in which the chair must recognize individual speakers from the floor, is not designed for large problem-solving discussions. It is designed for debating the merits of proposals and voting on alternatives that are already well developed. Phillips' 66 can be used as an alternative method for problem solving in large task groups. For example, during an in-service training program covering management skills, the group trainer asks the large group to divide into smaller groups and answer the question, "What makes a good manager?" Members of the small groups work to develop a short list of answers to the question within a limited period of time. When the large group reconvenes, each group reports its answers, and the material is used by the trainer in the didactic presentation and in group discussion following the presentation.

It can be difficult to hold the attention of all members when individual members are speaking. It is also difficult to encourage shy members to express themselves, particularly if they have minority opinions. Using Phillips' 66, the worker can involve all members in a group discussion. The small size of the groups makes it easier for shy members to express themselves. Also, members can choose to participate in groups that are focused on topics of particular interest to them. Reporting ideas generated by subgroups back to the larger assembly ensures that input from all members is considered in the problem-solving process. Overall, Phillips' 66 is a useful method that overcomes the limitations of parliamentary procedure when large groups are called on to solve problems.

Effectiveness

Phillips' 66 is a practical, commonsense procedure for facilitating discussion and problem solving in large groups. Although there is little empirical evidence about its effectiveness, its effective use has been reported in several sources (Gulley, 1968; Maier, 1963; Stattler & Miller, 1968). When applied correctly, Phillips' 66 can be used in a variety of situations. However, poor planning, confused or nonspecific instructions, or a muddled explanation of the goals of the procedure can turn a large task group meeting into disorganization and chaos.

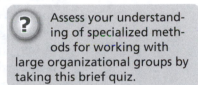

? Assess your understanding of specialized methods for working with large organizational groups by taking this brief quiz.

METHODS FOR WORKING WITH COMMUNITY GROUPS

Work with community groups such as social action groups, coalitions, and delegate councils involves many of the methods and skills described throughout this text. For example, community groups frequently use brainstorming and other problem-solving methods to generate ideas and address issues during meetings. Work with community groups is distinguished from other forms of group work practice by special emphasis on the following: (1) mobilizing individuals to engage in collective action, (2) building the capacity of the group and its members to effect community change, and (3) planning and organizing social action strategies. The remainder of this chapter focuses on these three aspects of practice with community groups.

Mobilization Strategies

Whether working with social action groups, coalitions, or delegate councils, a primary task of the worker is to mobilize individual members to action. The worker is a catalyst who stimulates interest in community problems and motivates members to work together (Hardina, 2013; McKnight & Plummer, 2015; Pyles, 2013; Walls, 2015). When engaging in mobilization efforts, the worker identifies and works with several constituencies, including the individuals who are experiencing the problem, community leaders, informal and formal community groups and organizations, and larger social institutions. For example, to mobilize a coalition to prevent domestic violence, a worker meets with victims of domestic violence, women's groups, the staff of domestic violence shelters, dispute resolution centers, police departments, family courts, and departments of social services, as well as with ministers, priests, rabbis, and local politicians.

An important initial step in any mobilization effort is to become familiar with the perceptions of community members about the issues the community group will attempt to address (McKnight & Plummer, 2015). It is often helpful to begin by meeting with civic and religious leaders and with community activists. These individuals can provide a helpful overview of the community's past responses to the issue and to similar issues. However, it is also essential to meet with as many community residents as possible.

McKnight and Plummer (2015) emphasize the importance of getting to know the community where any mobilization strategies will occur. Person-to-person contact with community residents helps build community groups and organizations in which each member feels valued (Pyles, 2013). When meeting with community residents, the worker should avoid telling residents why they should be concerned about a particular issue or problem. A more effective strategy is to ask them to describe their problems and concerns and validate and affirm the issues they raise by mentioning how their views are consistent with views of other community residents. In this way, community residents begin to get a sense that it is their issues, not the worker's issues, that will be addressed through collective action. Hardina (2013) suggests that after one-on-one interviews are conducted, it is helpful to meet with community residents in groups. Hardina (2013) also notes that group dialogue can be fostered in many different ways. For example, she mentions using the nominal group technique, focus groups, study circles, and larger community forums to help mobilize community residents.

As workers become familiar with communities, they should identify key individuals, community groups, and organizations that might be willing to help with mobilization efforts. To determine the extent to which individuals, groups, and organizations can help, the worker should evaluate their positions within the power structure of the community (McKnight & Plummer, 2015; Walls, 2015). The worker should then consider how forming a partnership with particular individuals and groups may help or hinder mobilization efforts. Often, the worker decides to form partnerships with a wide range of individuals, community leaders, and organizations. However, the worker should also be careful about involving individuals or organizations who do not share compatible goals or who have such a negative reputation in the community that they might damage the group's effort. Therefore, a careful analysis of community power structures is essential for effective mobilization efforts (Hardina, 2013; Kuyek, 2011).

Meyer (2013) notes that members are motivated to become part of coalitions to preserve what they have had or to promote new or different ways of behaving toward community residents. When something that is important is at risk, community members are motivated to form social action groups and larger coalitions to preserve what is dear to them. Members of social action groups and coalitions are also motivated by the opportunity to make better lives for themselves, their families, and others in their community (Meyer, 2013). Mobilization involves consciousness raising and empowerment. Working with individual citizens, community leaders, and formal and informal organizations, the worker attempts to bring a single issue or a group of related issues to greater public awareness. Consciousness raising may be done in several ways.

Strategies for Raising Public Awareness
- Meeting with community residents
- Making presentations to civic and religious organizations

- Testifying at public hearings
- Publicizing the issue through local newspapers, radio or television stations, and websites
- Demonstrating, picketing, and boycotting

The goal of consciousness-raising efforts is to encourage community members to gain a renewed sense of individual and community pride and to join forces to improve their community. McKnight and Plummer (2015) point out that consciousness raising involves helping community residents to realize that the way things are is not a result of fate or their own failings, but rather social structures that promote the status quo. With this new awareness, residents are then encouraged to stand up for themselves.

Mobilization to action involves helping members understand the power of collective action against injustices and inequities. Helping individuals vent their frustration and anger by public declarations and acting against those causing the problem can sometimes resolve individual problems (Rubin & Rubin, 2008). However, individual actions are easily ignored, dismissed, or punished by persons in power. Therefore, the goal of the worker should be to help individuals understand the value of pooling their efforts so they can exert sufficient influence to effect change.

One way to accomplish this goal is to highlight the incentives for collective action. Individuals become actively involved in a community group if they think they have something to gain, if they think they can contribute, and if they believe in the goals of the group. According to Rubin and Rubin (2008), the worker can use a variety of material incentives, such as improved income or better housing; solidarity incentives, such as the enjoyment of belonging to the group; and expressive incentives, such as the excitement and satisfaction of articulating opinions and values.

Mobilization to action also involves engaging in action projects that build interest and commitment in a community (Hardina, 2013; Pyles, 2013; Rubin & Rubin, 2008). A good way to begin is to identify a project or activity that is relatively easy and leads to an immediate success. For example, a social action group, a coalition, or even a delegate council might sponsor a community forum to which they invite local politicians and the news media. Similarly, a "community education day" might be planned at a shopping mall, a "teach-in" might be scheduled at a school, or a rally might be organized in a public square. Later, when members have experienced the initial successful completion of a project, they can be encouraged to tackle larger projects, such as a community survey or an extensive lobbying effort, that require more effort and resources.

Capacity-Building Strategies

Capacity building means helping community groups develop the ability and the resources to successfully tackle one issue or a set of issues. Community development and other forms of community work are a form of capacity building (Hardina, 2013; Pyles, 2013). Group workers facilitate the formation of groups of involved citizens in private, voluntary, and public settings for the purpose of social action (McKnight & Plummer, 2015; Pyles, 2013). This process of community development involves

Assessment

Behavior: Collect and organize data and use critical thinking to interpret information from clients and constituencies

Critical Thinking Question: Groups are important parts of communities. How can the worker help group members use capacity-building strategies?

the locating and bringing together of local assets in the community, including but not limited to groups (Pyles, 2013).

The worker plays the role of coordinator in helping members gather data and build resources. A first step in capacity building is to help group members become as knowledgeable as possible about the issues they are addressing. Workers should facilitate exchanges of information among members about the issues facing groups and about ways to accomplish particular objectives.

In many instances, the worker and the members will not have enough information about a problem. In these situations, the worker should encourage groups to gather data before proceeding. Original data can be gathered through community surveys or focused interviews with key informants (Hardina, 2013). The worker might also help members gain access to public records and reports as the following case example illustrates.

Case Example   Organizing in a Community

Several workers from a large family service agency decided that they would like to do something to reduce urban blight in the catchment area served by their agency. After talking with community leaders and other key stakeholders, the workers were able to identify a significant number of community residents who expressed interest in organizing a neighborhood association. The workers called a meeting with community leaders, neighborhood small business owners, other key stakeholders, and interested citizens, to discuss how to begin. The social action group decided to collect data to help them apply for funding. They decided that (1) city building department files could be used to gather data on building-code violations, (2) police department records could be used to collect data on the number and type of crimes in a particular neighborhood, (3) the county clerk's office could be used to gather data on property ownership, and (4) the department of public welfare and the local community development agency could be used to obtain estimates of poverty rates, and the homeless population. In this way, the social action group began to build a database to be used for an application for seed funding from the United Way and a local foundation to obtain the necessary resources for beginning and sustaining a vibrant neighborhood association.

A second step in capacity building involves helping the group or coalition become familiar with the structures within a community that can aid change efforts. It is important to identify individuals with the power to bring about needed changes within a community and determine to whom these individuals report. The worker also can help the group identify and contact religious and civic organizations that may be interested in joining forces to work on a particular issue, analyze the strengths and weaknesses of opponents to change, or decide what tactics might be used to change opponents' minds (Hardina, 2013). For example, would a landlord be most vulnerable to a rent strike, to moral pressure from a church group, or to having housing-code violations strictly enforced?

A third step is to help the group learn how to influence local government. The worker can help group members identify policy makers and bureaucrats who might support group efforts to have existing laws enforced or to introduce new legislation to address a particular issue. The worker can help the group develop a clear position on the issues with as much supporting documentation as available. To the extent possible, the group might form a partnership with legislators and bureaucrats so they can collaborate on the change effort. Rubin and Rubin (2008) note that legislators are receptive to ideas that make them look active, creative, and effective. The worker can help legislators and bureaucrats place the issue on the agenda by testifying at public hearings and by using lobbying efforts.

A fourth step in capacity building is to help the group make an inventory of its existing resources and identify resources needed to accomplish particular goals. In this way, members are empowered to use their own resources to help them tackle the problems they are facing as a community. For example, the group may find it needs legal advice. Can a lawyer be identified who would be willing to work with the group? Similarly, the group may want to publish a fact sheet or a brochure for a lobbying effort. Can a business or community organization that would be willing to help the group design or print the brochure be identified? An important role of the worker is to help the group locate resources to accomplish its objectives. For more information about capacity building through the formation of coalitions, see Feinberg, Bontempo, and Greenberg (2008), Mattessich, Murray-Close, and Monsey (2008), Meyer (2013), or Zakocs and Edwards (2006).

Social Action Strategies

According to Harrison and Ward (1999), social action has two central characteristics. First, it promotes the capacity of all people to take action to improve their situation. Second, this action is based on open participation, when people working collectively in groups explore underlying social issues and take action to alleviate problems. Self-management and empowerment are essential ingredients. There is no victim blaming or a focus on deficits. Instead, workers facilitate members' skills, helping them to take action for themselves. Although there are a number of theories and ideas about how to organize (see Pyles, 2013), social action is based on the idea that the people who are most affected by a problem are in the best position to articulate their experiences and to define and implement solutions. A variety of social action strategies can be used to help community groups accomplish their objectives during the middle stage. These include political advocacy, negotiation, legal strategies including legal and regulatory suits, asset-based community development, direct action, and alternative community and cultural development strategies (Hardina, 2013; Pyles, 2013; Rubin & Rubin, 2008; Walls, 2015).

Many forms of political activity are available to community groups, such as those that follow.

Community Group Political Activity
- Organizing voter registration drives
- Nominating and working on the campaigns of public officials
- Developing and supporting referendums, propositions, and other grass-roots efforts to bypass legislators and get proposals directly on the ballot
- Lobbying and advocating positions
- Participating in public hearings
- Monitoring compliance with laws by bureaucratic and regulatory agencies

Although political action strategies are designed to get persons in power to pay attention to the goals of a community group, legal action strategies are designed to force politicians and bureaucrats to take action on issues supported by a community group or a coalition of community groups. Political action strategies can have sweeping and binding effects, but they are often expensive and time-consuming. Sometimes, the threat of legal action by a single counsel on retainer can create some action. More often, however, legal action requires a professional staff, a large budget, and a great deal of patience. Although coalitions of community groups and community groups affiliated with national organizations can use legal strategies effectively, political action strategies and direct action strategies are often preferred.

Direct action strategies include rallies, demonstrations, marches, picketing, sit-ins, vigils, blockades, boycotts, slowdowns, strikes, and many other forms of non-violent and violent protest. Direct action strategies allow members to ventilate frustration and anger, but they can be counterproductive. Negative publicity, fines, physical injury, fines, imprisonment, physical injury, and time lost at work are just a few of the possible consequences. Thus, direct action strategies should not be undertaken without careful thought and preparation, and then only if it is clear that safer political and legal strategies are unlikely to achieve the desired objective. It is also important to keep in mind that the threat of direct action is often as terrifying as the action itself. Therefore, if a community group is serious about engaging in a direct action strategy, it is often wise to publicize the group's intent and the specific steps that an opponent can take to avoid the action.

In his text, *Rules for Radicals*, Alinsky (1971) developed a number of pragmatic rules for choosing among different action strategies. For example, he suggested picking a direct action strategy that enjoys wide support among members. He also suggested picking a strategy that emphasizes the weaknesses of the opponent. Thus, a rally that gets widespread news coverage might be particularly effective against an opponent concerned about negative publicity, but an economic boycott might be more effective against a corporation under pressure from shareholders to increase profits.

When selecting a social action strategy, there is a generally accepted protocol that should be adhered to when carrying out work with community groups. Less-intrusive and more cooperative strategies should be tried before disruptive or conflict-oriented strategies are engaged. Collaboration and negotiation strategies should be employed before conflict strategies. Collaboration means that in attempting to effect some change in a target system, the worker tries to convince the target system that change is in the best interests of all involved. In negotiation, the worker and the target system both give and receive something in the process of change. The process of bargaining involves a good faith *quid pro quo* arrangement and assumes that each party will make some change desired by the other.

Should collaboration and negotiation fail to achieve a desired change, the group may be forced to engage in conflict strategies. In any case, the worker should always help group members use each of the three strategies in a constructive and an ethical fashion.

The worker should carefully guard against a group choosing conflict as an initial strategy because of the perception that the strategy will result in change more quickly or because members wish to carry out personal retribution. For more information about working with community groups, see Hardina (2013), McKnight and Plummer (2015), Pyles (2013), Walls (2015), and Wells-Wilbon (2016).

> **?** Assess your understanding of specialized methods for working with community groups by taking this brief quiz.

Case Example

Funding sources for the AIDS Outreach Association were so impressed with Nora's research and documentation that they approved a budget allocation for hiring four people to fill newly created case-management positions. Because of the importance of this new initiative, Nora wanted to have input from all constituencies within the organization. Therefore, she formed an *ad hoc* committee composed of supervisors, program directors, and two consumers to assist in the recruitment and selection procedures and processes.

During the first meeting of the committee, Nora discussed the development and implementation of the purpose of the group and its charge. She noted that the group would be responsible for deciding what skills would best fit the position and for rating and ranking job candidates. During this first session, the group discussed the tasks, activities, and services that case managers would be providing to consumers. The first session ended with a list of potential duties that could be assigned to the new employees.

One week later, Nora convened the group for the second time. The group members tried to design a procedure for screening candidates but were unable to focus on what criteria would guide the selection process. There were lots of ideas, but the group could not seem to keep track of them. Nora suggested that the group take a short break. When group members returned, Nora placed a flip chart at the head of the table. She suggested that members use brainstorming techniques to generate ideas about the skills and attributes needed for the job. She explained that in brainstorming, members should develop as many ideas as possible without evaluating the importance of the ideas. In other words, members were asked to come up with as many ideas as possible and not to critique any ideas until the idea-generation phase of the process was complete. As each member contributed an idea, it was recorded on the flip chart. At the end of the brainstorming session, Nora took all the criteria that had been listed and rearranged them into a comprehensive list. She was amazed at the number of criteria the group had generated.

Armed with many creative ideas for how to rate candidates, the group now faced the task of reducing the list to the most important set of criteria. Nora suggested that the group use elements of the nominal group technique (NGT) to identify important criteria. She guided the group members in a review of the list of criteria, and she asked members to write their top choices on a piece of paper, ranking their choices from highest to lowest. During this process members were asked to refrain from discussing their choices with each other. Next, Nora asked members to present their highest-ranked ideas in round robin fashion, going around the group until all members had contributed their choices for the five highest criteria. Nora used this list to sort criteria into categories. She then asked members to take turns discussing their choices with the rest of the group. Following the discussion, Nora asked members to vote on a consolidated list of criteria by assigning values to their top five choices within each category. After this was done, Nora tallied up the numerical ratings and listed the top five criteria as determined by the vote of each group member. These included amount of experience working with persons with AIDS, knowledge about AIDS, knowledge of the service system, interpersonal skills, and potential for developing new programs. The group agreed that these would be the criteria that they would use to screen and rank job applicants. They ended the group meeting by developing a position description using the criteria and directed Nora to advertise the position in two local newspapers.

Some weeks later, Nora convened the group to discuss their next task. Since the last meeting, the positions had been advertised, and a number of applications had been sent to the organization. The group's next task was to screen the candidates and to rate them according to the criteria the group had established.

At first, members rushed into the task of discussing individual candidates without establishing ground rules for how to proceed. Nora suggested that the group use a more organized approach to the process, namely, multiattribute utility (MAU) analysis. This required the group to review and specify the criteria they had previously decided on to rank candidates, to specify minimum and optimum levels of qualifications for the job, and to systematically rate candidates according to the decision criteria. Although some members were skeptical in the beginning of this procedure, they soon found that using this method enabled them to systematically review each job candidate. At the close of this procedure, members were able to rank the top candidates for the open positions. To ensure that consensus about the ranking of the top candidates was achieved, a final round of discussion followed the group's ranking process. The committee ended its work by presenting the chief executive officer of the AIDS Outreach Association with a ranked list of candidates to be interviewed for the new positions.

SUMMARY

A variety of methods have been developed in industry, business administration, and human service organizations to help task groups accomplish their goals during the middle stage. This chapter examines some of the most widely used methods: (1) brainstorming, (2) reverse brainstorming, (3) trigger groups, (4) focus groups, (5) the nominal group technique, (6) social judgment analysis, (7) quality circles, and (8) quality improvement teams. The chapter also includes descriptions of methods, such as parliamentary procedure and Phillips' 66, that can be used to lead large task groups.

The second section of the chapter describes specialized methods for helping community groups accomplish their objectives during the middle stage. This section focuses on three methods for helping community groups achieve their objectives: (1) mobilizing individuals to engage in collective action, (2) building the capacity of the group and its members to effect community change, and (3) social action strategies.

Ending the Group's Work

- Explain the factors that influence group endings
- Compare the variables that affect planned and unplanned terminations
- Identify the techniques for ending group meetings
- Describe the steps involved in ending the group as a whole

The ending stage, a critical part of group work practice, has been given little attention in the literature since a special issue of the International Journal of Group Psychotherapy was published in 1996. The skills workers use in the ending stage determine, in part, the success of the entire group experience. In this stage, workers and members form their lasting impressions of the group. An otherwise satisfying and effective group can be ruined by a worker who is not skillful at ending the group's work.

During the ending stage, the group's work is consolidated. In task groups, the decisions, reports, recommendations, and other products of the group as a whole are completed, and consideration is given to how the results of the work can best be implemented. In treatment groups, the changes made by individual group members are stabilized, and plans are made for maintaining these gains after the group ends. In groups in which members' self-disclosure has been high, it is necessary to help members work through their feelings about terminating their relationships with the worker and with each other. It is also a time when workers confront their own feelings regarding ending their work with a particular group. This chapter examines the tasks and skills involved in ending individual group meetings and ending the work of the group as a whole.

FACTORS THAT INFLUENCE GROUP ENDINGS

Endings vary depending on whether a group has an open or closed membership policy. In closed groups, unless there are unplanned terminations, all members end at the same time. In these groups, the worker can help all members to deal with common issues and feelings that arise as the group draws to a close. Open groups present a more difficult challenge for the worker. Some members may be experiencing reactions to termination, but others may experience reactions common to the beginning stage of the group. In open groups, the worker should individualize work with each member. However, because each member will eventually experience disengagement from the group, the worker can use the reactions of members who are terminating to help members who will experience similar reactions in the future.

Endings also vary according to the attraction of the group for its members. In groups that members find attractive, endings may not be viewed as a positive event. Conversely, if group meetings are viewed as something to be endured, news of the last meeting may be received with relief.

In addition, endings vary depending on whether the group is a treatment group or a task group. In many therapy groups and support groups, for example, members reveal intimate details of their personal lives. They let down their defenses and become vulnerable as they share concerns and issues that are important to them. In these types of groups, mutual aid and support develop as members deepen relationships with one another and the worker. They come to trust each other and to rely on the therapeutic advice and suggestions given by the worker and fellow members.

THE PROCESS OF ENDING

In therapy, support, and growth groups, termination may be accompanied by strong emotional reactions. However, in educational and socialization groups, termination rarely results in the expression of strong emotional reactions.

Terminating the relationships that may have influenced the members of treatment groups is quite different from terminating the relationships formed in task groups. In task groups, members' self-disclosure is generally at a relatively low level. Because the focus of these groups is on a product, such as a report or the development of a plan of action, members often look forward to the end of a group with a sense of accomplishment or with relief that their work is finished. Because they have not let down their defenses or shared their personal concerns to any great extent, there is rarely an intense emotional reaction to ending. Also, members of task groups may work together again on other committees, teams, or councils. Therefore, the endings of task groups do not have the same sense of finality as do endings of treatment groups.

In the task group literature, the focus is on the skills the leader uses to end individual group meetings rather than on how the leader ends the entire group experience (Tropman, 2014). This focus contrasts sharply with treatment group literature that generally focuses on ending work with the group rather than ending work in a particular meeting.

> **?** Assess your understanding of the factors that influence endings in group work practice by taking this brief quiz.

PLANNED AND UNPLANNED TERMINATION

At the beginning of closed, time-limited groups, workers and members decide how many times the group will meet. At the beginning of other groups where there is no fixed number of meetings, terminations can result from a variety of factors that are not under workers' control, such as when a person leaves an inpatient or residential setting.

In other situations, the worker should discuss with members how termination should occur. For example, the worker may ask for a two-meeting notice. The extra week can be used to integrate the changes that are made and to plan for the future. It also discourages members from ending without notice.

Member Termination

Sometimes members stop attending before the planned ending date. Unplanned termination of membership is a relatively common experience. Review studies have found unplanned termination rates of about 30 percent (Barlow, 2013; Burlingame, Strauss, & Joyce, 2013).

Case Example   Premature Termination

In a group for separated and divorced persons, three people did not return to the second group meeting. When they were contacted, it was found that one person lived 40 miles from where the group met and, after driving home on foggy rural roads after the first group meeting, had decided not to return. Another member's job had unexpectedly changed and required the person to be at work during the group's meeting times. It was learned from the third person's employer that one of his children had experienced a serious accident. The member called two weeks later to explain that "I have been running between the hospital and my responsibilities to the other two [children]."

In treatment groups in which participation is voluntary, a reduction in membership sometimes occurs after the first or second meeting of a group. After the initial drop, groups often develop a stable core of members who continue until the group ends.

When leading groups, workers sometimes find themselves asking rhetorically, "What have I done to cause members to fail to return to the group?" In follow-up contacts with members who terminated prematurely, many workers find they did not cause premature termination.

There is also empirical data that indicates that workers may not be responsible for some unplanned terminations. For example, when evaluating a smoking-cessation group treatment program, it was found that members left treatment prematurely for a variety of reasons (Toseland, Kabat, & Kemp, 1983). Several were dissatisfied with their group or their group's leader, but others left for reasons unrelated to their treatment experience. Although it is commonly assumed that dropouts are treatment failures, in evaluating eight smoking-cessation groups, it was found that one of seven dropouts left treatment prematurely because he had stopped smoking and believed he no longer needed treatment. Another dropout quit smoking before a follow-up evaluation. Thus, it is important to realize that unplanned termination of members may be the result of their lack of interest or motivation, particular life circumstances, or other factors beyond the control of the worker that have little or nothing to do with a worker's leadership skills. Toseland and colleagues (1997), for example, found that attendance at group meetings by older adults in nursing homes was greatly affected by their health status.

Research-Informed Practice

Behavior: Use and translate research evidence to inform and improve practice, policy, and service delivery

Critical Thinking Question: Members often drop out of groups. What do research findings suggest about how the group worker might prevent premature termination?

Yalom (2005) lists nine factors that may cause group members to drop out of treatment prematurely. Yalom points out that some members leave because of faulty selection processes and others as the result of flawed therapeutic techniques (Yalom, 2005). These factors are presented in the following list.

Factors Leading to Termination
- External factors, such as scheduling conflicts and changes in geographical location
- Group deviancy, such as being the richest group member, the only unmarried member, and the like
- Problems in developing intimate relationships
- Fear of emotional contagion
- Inability to share the worker's time
- Complications arising from concurrent individual and group therapy
- Early provocateurs
- Inadequate orientation to therapy
- Complications arising from subgrouping

However, sometimes members do drop out as a result of their dissatisfaction with the group or its leader. For example, in therapy and growth-oriented groups in which confrontation is used as a therapeutic technique, members occasionally become so angry when confronted with an emotionally charged issue that they threaten to terminate. To prevent premature termination, Barlow (2013) and Walsh (2010) suggest using a careful pregroup screening interview to select members who have the capacity to benefit from the group. It is not always possible, however, to screen out members whose defensiveness, anger, and impulsivity may cause them to abruptly leave a group. Therefore, some workers also specify in the initial contract that members must give two weeks' notice before leaving the group so that members have a chance to rethink their decisions.

Pregroup training has also been found to be an effective way to prevent premature dropouts from therapy groups (Barlow, 2013; Burlingame, Strauss, & Joyce, 2013; Mangione, Forti, & Lacuzzi, 2007). The most common form of pregroup training is for the worker to meet with individual members to thoroughly review group procedures and processes (see also Chapter 6). Pregroup training can also take many other forms, such as listening to or viewing recordings of similar groups, sitting-in on a group, and talking with members or the worker about where the group is in its developmental stage. Piper, Debbane, Bienvenu, and Garant (1982) found a reduction of 13 percent to 30 percent in the dropout rate attributed to the successful management of anxiety and the development of interpersonal bonds that resulted from a pregroup training program. Many other studies have been conducted over the past 20 years about the benefits of pregroup training, which seems to work by reducing the ambiguity and uncertainty in beginning group meetings. For a summary of these studies, and the findings from them, see Barlow (2013) or Mangione, Forti, and Lacuzzi (2007).

When workers take the time to explore members' reasons for terminating, the data gathered can help reduce premature terminations in subsequent groups. Sometimes, for example, workers learn that arranging for child care while the group is in session helps reduce the number of dropouts. Arranging transportation to and from the group may also help. At other times, workers may find that there are ways they can improve their own skills to prevent members from dropping out of the group. For example, they may learn to be more gentle or tentative when they use confrontation methods. A survey of 275 workers who were members of the American Group Psychotherapy Association engaged in long-term group work found that the top reason for unplanned termination was that the member was asked to leave because of disruptive behavior (33 percent). This was followed by 29 percent being asked to leave the group because there was a poor fit or match between the group and a member. Other reasons included client threatening to the group (20 percent), member not committed to the group (19 percent), disruptive dual relationships with another member of the group (16 percent), and the group was not appropriate for the member (18 percent). It should be noted that these figures are based on a low response rate to the survey (11 percent), and over half of the respondents being in private practice and leading mostly long-term groups (Mangione, Forti, & Iacuzzi, 2007).

Occasionally, an entire group may end prematurely. Just as there are many reasons for the premature termination of individuals, there are also many reasons for the premature termination of groups. A group that begins with a small number of members may lose several members and thus be unable to continue functioning effectively. Groups may not receive sufficient support from their sponsoring agencies to continue functioning, or groups may be unable or unwilling to respond to external pressure to change their functioning.

Groups may also end prematurely as a result of internal dysfunction. For example, communication and interaction patterns may be poorly distributed and cause subgrouping, scapegoating, or domination by a few members. The group may lack sufficient attraction for its members and, therefore, may fail to coalesce or function as a cohesive unit. Social controls, such as norms, roles, status hierarchies, and power, may cause severe tension and conflict when some members rebel against the control of the worker or other members. Lack of appropriate social controls may cause chaos or an aimless drift that eventually leads to dissolution of the group as a whole. Members may also have great difficulty deciding on common values, preferences, ways of working together, or other aspects of the group's culture.

Whenever workers confront the possibility that a group may end prematurely, they should carefully examine the factors that are contributing to the problem. It is often possible to trace a group's dysfunction back to the planning stage. Careful examination of the factors that contributed to a group's demise can help workers avoid such pitfalls in future groups.

Worker Termination

Although rarely mentioned in the literature, there are times when workers have to terminate their work with a group. Probably the most common reason for worker termination is that students leave at the end of their field placements, but change of employment or shifting job responsibilities also lead to worker termination. In a study of two groups in which workers terminated their participation, Long, Pendleton, and Winter (1988) found that the

Ethical and Professional Behavior

Behavior: Make ethical decisions by applying the standards of the NASW Code of Ethics, relevant laws and regulations, models for ethical decision-making, ethical conduct of research, and additional codes of ethics as appropriate to context

Critical Thinking Question: Group workers sometimes leave their groups. What ethical issues should be considered when a worker starts the termination process?

termination of the worker led to testing of the new worker and to a reorganization of the group's processes and structures.

Several steps can be taken to reduce the disruption that can be caused by worker termination in an ongoing group.

Steps to Reduce Disruption

- Group members should be told as early as possible when termination will occur.
- The reasons for termination should be shared with the group, and members should be encouraged to discuss their feelings frankly.
- Unfinished business should be completed.
- The new worker should be introduced to the group and, if possible, co-lead the group for a while with the terminating worker.

? Assess your understanding of the variables that affect planned and unplanned termination by taking this brief quiz.

ENDING GROUP MEETINGS

Scheidel and Crowell (1979) list four generic worker tasks in ending group meetings: (1) closing the group's work, (2) arranging another meeting, (3) preparing a summary or report of the group's work, and (4) planning future group actions. In preparing to close, the worker should help the group keep to its agenda. The worker should ensure that all items of business and all members' concerns are given sufficient attention, but the group should not be allowed to spend too much time discussing one item of business or one member's concerns. To move the group along, the worker can do the following:

- Keep members focused on the topic of discussion.
- Limit the time that each member has to discuss an issue.
- Summarize what has been said.
- Obtain closure on each issue or concern as it is discussed.

In closing the group's work, the worker should avoid bringing up new issues, concerns, or items of business. Instead, the ending of a session is a good time to engage in a process of reflection. This process entails (1) focusing on the session, (2) looking back on what transpired to see what it meant for members, (3) analyzing the significance of what occurred, and (4) examining what members can take away from the discussions and put into practice in their own lives. It is also a good time to identify unfinished work and to think about work that should be accomplished in future sessions (Birnbaum & Cicchetti, 2000). A discussion of what was accomplished and what needs to be done in future sessions lends continuity to the group. Enabling members to have a role in setting the agenda for future sessions and to give feedback about the group experience empowers them (Birnbaum, Mason, & Cicchetti, 2002). It provides an opportunity for members to express their satisfaction and sense of accomplishment with what occurred in the meetings, as well as any concerns they have about how the group is functioning. Birnbaum and Cicchetti (2000) point out that it is helpful for group leaders to invite members to raise discrepant points of view during ending discussions. Leaders who solicit discrepant viewpoints and feelings about how the group is going can help group members to express and resolve conflicts before they can become inflamed. At the same time, soliciting different points of view can help members to discuss group processes as well as the content of group meetings. In this way, members of the group take increasing responsibility for both the content and the process of future group meetings.

Despite efforts to structure the agenda to ensure that there is enough time to discuss important issues at the end of a meeting, Shulman (2016) points out that members occasionally raise "doorknob" issues just before ending. If consideration of these issues can be postponed, they are best handled during the next meeting when they can be given fuller consideration. When discussion of an important issue cannot be postponed, the worker should ask group members whether they prefer to continue the discussion for a brief period. If not, the issue may be taken up outside the group by the worker and any interested members.

In closing the group's work, the worker should also help members resolve any remaining conflicts. Resolving conflicts helps members to work in harmony for the decisions reached by the group as a whole. In addition, the worker may want to discuss the strengths and weaknesses of the working relationship that has developed among members during the group meeting, particularly if the group will work together in the future.

During the ending minutes, the worker should help the group plan for future meetings. When considering whether to meet again, it is helpful to review and summarize the group's work. A summary of the group's activities during the meeting clarifies issues that have been resolved and points out issues that remain unresolved. A clear summary of the group's progress is a prerequisite for arranging another meeting. Summaries also remind members of the activities or tasks they have agreed to work on between meetings and help the worker become aware of items that should be included in the agenda for the next meeting.

If a group has completed action on a particular task, the final minutes can also be used to ensure that all members understand and agree to the oral or written information that will be presented at the conclusion of a group's work. Some task forces may prepare extensive written reports of their findings and conclusions. In these groups, it is not productive to prepare the report during the group meeting. The closing minutes can be used to formulate and highlight the major conclusions to be enumerated in the report, to assign members responsibility for preparing major sections of the report, and to develop a mechanism for obtaining approval from members before disseminating the report.

The endings of group meetings can also be used to plan future group actions. However, because planning action steps is time-consuming, plans are usually developed during the middle of a group meeting. At the ending of a meeting, plans are summarized, and members select (or are assigned) tasks to carry out.

The worker should help members maintain their motivation, commitment, and responsibility to implement and carry out the tasks they have agreed to complete between meetings. To help members maintain their motivation, the worker should praise members for their work in the group and for their willingness to commit themselves to tasks outside the meeting. The worker may also want to mention any benefits that will accrue to members for maintaining their commitment to the plans and activities they have agreed to complete.

> **?** Assess your understanding of the techniques for ending group meetings by taking this brief quiz.

ENDING THE GROUP AS A WHOLE

A variety of tasks are associated with ending a group as a whole:

- Learning from members
- Maintaining and generalizing change efforts
- Reducing group attraction and promoting the independent functioning of individual members
- Helping members deal with their feelings about ending
- Planning for the future
- Making referrals
- Evaluating the work of the group

With the exception of evaluating the work of the group, which is discussed in Chapter 14, the remaining portion of this chapter examines each ending task and the skills and techniques the worker can use to facilitate the effective ending of a group. Many of these tasks may be carried out simultaneously. The specific order in which each task is completed depends on the group the worker is leading.

Learning from Members

In the last session of a group, in addition to any formal evaluation procedures, workers should give members a chance to describe what it was like for them to be in the group. One way to do this is a final group go-round where each member gets a chance to say what they enjoyed about the group, what they learned, and how they will use what they learned in the future. Members should be encouraged to talk about what they think could be improved in future groups. All members should also have a discussion of what they learned from one another. It is also an important time to give individual members a chance to give some final feedback to other members whom they would especially like to thank for their contributions to the group. Workers can make a statement about what they learned from individual members and what individual members contributed to the group. Workers should also give positive but realistic feedback about what each member accomplished and what each member should remember about their resiliency and strengths, and how they can use them in the future to work on any issues that arise after the group ends. If there are no follow-up group sessions planned, it can also be useful to schedule individual follow-up meetings with members a month or two after the group ends to get additional feedback from them about the group experience, to praise them for any changes in their lives that they have started or sustained, and to help them with any problems or issues that may have arisen since the last group meeting.

Maintaining and Generalizing Change Efforts

After treatment plans have been developed and carried out, workers should ensure that the changes that have been achieved are maintained and generalized to other important aspects of members' lives. Evaluations of results of therapeutic interventions suggest that positive changes are often difficult to maintain over time. For example, in an evaluation of two different group intervention programs for caregivers of the frail elderly, it was found that some of the positive changes found immediately after group intervention were not sustained at one year (Labrecque, Peak, & Toseland, 1992; Toseland, 1990).

Positive changes are even harder to maintain in group treatment programs that are focused on individuals with addictive disorders. For example, in an evaluation of a group treatment program for smokers, it was found that although more than 60 percent of members who attended the program initially stopped smoking, the cessation rate had dropped to 36 percent after three months (Toseland, Kabat, & Kemp, 1983). Results obtained for a variety of other addictive disorders, such as narcotics use, alcohol use, and overeating, show similarly high relapse rates (Boyd-Franklin, Cleek, Wofsy, & Mundy, 2013; Chiauzzi, 1991; Marlatt, 1996; Marlatt & Barrett, 1994; Vaillant, 1995). Maintenance is also difficult to achieve in working with antisocial group members, such as juvenile delinquents, and in working with group members who have severe psychological disorders.

Both novice and experienced workers often mistakenly believe that changes in specific behaviors can be taken as a sign of generalized improvement in a member's level of functioning. These workers do little to ensure that specific behavior changes generalize to related, but untreated, behaviors. Results of a variety of different treatment programs have shown, however, that therapeutic changes occurring in specific behaviors do not always generalize to similar behaviors performed by a member in other contexts (Masters, Burish, Hollon, & Rimm, 1987). For example, a parent may learn how to reduce a child's temper tantrums, but this success may not affect the parent's ability to help the child play cooperatively with other children.

Although some people seek group treatment only for changes in specific behaviors, most people enter group treatment with the expectation that there will be a generalized improvement in their life situations. Therefore, it is important for workers to help members generalize changes achieved in specific behaviors and performed in particular situations to related behaviors performed in other contexts. With the notable exception of Rose (1989, 1998), little has been written about these topics in group work. Almost all the theoretical and clinical work on maintenance and generalization of change has come from the literature on behavior modification and learning theory. The literature suggests several things workers can do to help members maintain and generalize the changes they have achieved.

Maintaining and Generalizing Changes
- Helping members work on relevant situations
- Helping members develop confidence in their abilities
- Using a variety of different situations and settings in helping members learn new behaviors
- Using a variety of naturally occurring consequences
- Extending treatment through follow-up sessions
- Preventing setbacks in an unsympathetic environment
- Helping members solve problems independently by providing a framework for organizing data and solving problems that can be used in many different situations

Relevant Situations

To achieve long-lasting changes that will generalize to similar situations in members' lives, the concerns and issues worked on in the group should be a relevant and realistic sample of concerns and issues experienced by members in their daily lives. Sometimes members become distracted by issues that are not central to their concerns, a possible sign that the members are avoiding difficult issues and the changes they necessitate. The worker can help by drawing members' attention back to the central concerns that brought them together as a group.

In other cases, the situations discussed may be highly specific and individual. Although it is important to be as specific and concrete as possible when developing treatment plans, it is also important to ensure that situations that are relevant to all group members are included in the group's work so that members are prepared for situations they are likely to encounter in the future.

Although group meetings should provide a protected environment in which members receive support, encouragement, and understanding, the group should also be a place in which members can get honest feedback about how their behavior is likely to be seen outside the group. Members should be encouraged to try out new behaviors in the group, but they should not be misled into thinking they will receive the same level of support and encouragement for trying new behaviors outside the group. In short, although the group should provide a supportive and caring atmosphere in which to work, the group should help members understand, cope with, and prepare for reactions likely to be experienced outside the group.

Helping Members Develop Confidence

Many treatment groups spend much time discussing members' problems and concerns as well as their inappropriate ways of handling situations. Although ventilating thoughts and feelings may be therapeutic, Lee (2001) points out that too much time in treatment is often spent on the negative aspects of members' problems and not enough time is spent empowering members and building their self-confidence. Lee suggests that emphasis on negative thoughts, feelings, and experiences reinforces the members' tendency to continue to express these problems outside the group.

As the group progresses, workers should encourage members to focus on adaptive alternatives to the problematic situations they are experiencing. If members dwell on poor performances and inhibiting thoughts in the group, they are less likely to feel confident about their abilities to cope with or resolve the problems they experience in their daily lives. Although it is not possible or desirable to avoid discussions of problems in treatment groups, workers should help members become more aware of their own abilities. Members should be encouraged to use their abilities and their resources to resolve the problematic situations they encounter as they prepare for leaving the group (Saleebey, 2013). Program activities, role plays, and exercises are particularly useful in helping members to become more aware of their strengths and to build confidence in their ability to solve problems. This process, in turn, will help members gain confidence in their abilities to continue to function adaptively after they leave the group.

Case Example An Adolescent Group

A worker in a day treatment program asked members of her group to think about a situation when they were scared or anxious about their performance, but when they actually got into the situation it worked out well. The worker then asked each member, in turn, to describe the situation and what happened. After each member shared, the worker asked the group what they had learned from these experiences and how they could use them in the future to develop confidence in their abilities to get through difficult situations.

Using a Variety of Situations and Settings

Another aspect of maintaining and generalizing change is preparing members for different situations that may interfere with their abilities to maintain the changes they have made. Although preparations for maintaining changes are emphasized during ending-stage meetings, such activities should be given attention throughout members' participation in a group. Issues and concerns brought to group treatment are rarely, if ever, confined to one situation or setting in a member's life. A member who experiences communication difficulties, for example, often experiences them in many situations with different people. Therefore, it is helpful in treatment groups to have members practice responses with different members in a variety of situations. Because of the availability of group members who will respond differently from one another, group treatment is ideally suited for this purpose. Bandura's (1977) research confirms that the use of multiple models (group members) promotes generalization of treatment effects.

Easier situations should be role-played before more difficult situations. What constitutes an easy or a difficult situation varies from person to person, so the worker should assess each person's needs when developing a hierarchy of situations to work on in the group. Once a member demonstrates the ability to handle a variety of situations in the group, the member should be encouraged to get additional practice by trying new ways of behaving between meetings.

Program activities can also be used to simulate situations that may be encountered outside the group. For example, children referred to a group because they have difficulty playing with classmates can be encouraged to participate in team sports in which cooperative play is essential; long-term psychiatric patients may be encouraged to prepare and participate in a group dinner as a way of practicing skills that will help them when they are placed in a community residence.

Using Naturally Occurring Consequences

Although it is often difficult to make changes initially, changes are maintained and generalized by the resulting positive consequences. For example, although losing weight is initially uncomfortable, loss soon results in positive compliments from peers and feeling better about oneself. To maintain and generalize behavior changes, the worker should help group members experience the positive consequences of changes as soon as possible and maintain the positive consequences for as long as possible.

Case Example   An End Smoking Group

Once members have decided to stop smoking they should be encouraged to seek out the reactions of family members and friends about their decision. Members might talk with these individuals and think to themselves about the benefits of quitting. They might talk and think about the following: (1) they will save money by not buying cigarettes, (2) their breath will no longer smell like stale cigarettes, (3) their clothes, their home, and their car will no longer smell like cigarette smoke, (4) food will taste better, (5) they will have increased lung capacity and greater vitality and endurance while walking and climbing stairs,

(6) they will no longer live in smoke-filled rooms with the dangers of secondhand smoke, and (7) they may feel better and live longer. Members should be encouraged to replace urges to smoke with thoughts of the previously mentioned soon-to-be expected positive effects of quitting. With members' permission, the worker can also contact significant others in members' lives and ask them to continue to reinforce the ex-smoker's resolve not to smoke after the group ends. The worker can also discuss with members the possibility of setbacks and relapse and how to return to being a nonsmoker.

One method is to help members focus on positive rather than negative consequences. Another way to enhance naturally occurring contingencies is to help members modify environmental consequences so that behavior change is more readily maintained and generalized. For example, a buddy system may be established so that group members receive positive feedback for changes between group sessions. Group members may be asked to modify friendship patterns, social activities, or their home environment in ways that provide positive consequences for changes they have made through their efforts in the group. By enhancing and highlighting naturally occurring positive consequences and by reducing negative consequences, initial changes can be maintained and generalized.

Follow-Up Sessions

Another way to help ensure that treatment results are maintained and generalized is to provide members the opportunity to meet together for follow-up sessions after the completion of a formal group treatment program. For example, a time-limited, outpatient psychotherapy group might meet for twelve weekly sessions and then for six follow-up sessions at one-month intervals. After this time, two quarterly meetings during the rest of the year might complete the treatment contract.

Follow-up sessions reinforce members' commitment to maintaining changes. They remind members of the changes that have taken place in their lives since they began treatment. Members can share similar experiences about their difficulties in maintaining changes and trying to generalize changes to new situations and new life experiences.

Follow-up sessions are generally not used to introduce members to new material. Instead, they are used as an opportunity for members to share their experiences since the previous meeting. Members should be encouraged to discuss new problem situations they have encountered and to describe how they have handled these situations. The emphasis should be on helping members identify the coping skills they have developed to maintain changes achieved during treatment.

Follow-up sessions are particularly helpful for members who have difficulty maintaining treatment gains. Members can discuss the circumstances surrounding particular relapses and consult the group worker and other members about how best to handle these occurrences. The additional support provided by follow-up sessions is often sufficient to help members overcome brief relapses that might otherwise turn into treatment failures.

The popularity of self-help groups can, in part, be attributed to the flexible, open-ended, long-term membership that is encouraged in many of these groups. Self-help groups often have a small group of members who regularly attend meetings, along with many other members who attend as needed (Toseland & Hacker, 1982). For self-help group participants who have attended sessions regularly in the past, occasional attendance at future meetings can maintain treatment gains and gradually reduce dependency on the group.

Preventing Setbacks in Unsympathetic Environments

Even when careful attention has been given to the environment that a member faces outside the group, the support, trust, and sharing found in well-functioning treatment groups is rarely duplicated in the members' home or community environments. Members should be prepared to face possible setbacks in the unsympathetic environment they are likely to experience outside the group. Rose (1989) suggests that the experiences of the worker in leading previous groups, as well as the experiences of former group members, are useful in developing vignettes that describe realistic and typical situations group members are likely to encounter outside the group. During the final few group sessions, members should discuss how to respond to such situations and practice responses with one another by using modeling, role play, rehearsal, and coaching.

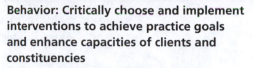

Behavior: Critically choose and implement interventions to achieve practice goals and enhance capacities of clients and constituencies

Critical Thinking Question: Unsympathetic environments are often identified as causing relapses and setbacks. How can the worker help members decrease the effects of pernicious environments so that gains in the group can be maintained?

Because members are likely to experience situations that threaten their treatment gains soon after changes are initiated, members should be encouraged to describe such situations in the group sessions. It is especially important to examine likely triggers for relapses and to plan for how to avoid or cope with them when they occur (Boyd-Franklin, Cleek, Wofsy, & Mundy, 2013). In this way, all group members become exposed to a variety of situations and reactions to changes, and they can learn to handle reactions before the situations occur in their own lives.

Members may encounter difficult situations any time of the day or night. Because the group worker may not be available to members at those times, the worker should inform members about how to contact on-call workers, emergency hotlines, and other 24-hour services.

The difficulty of maintaining changes among members with drug, alcohol, and other addictive behavior problems suggests a need for intensive and extensive treatment. One way to augment group treatment with a professional worker is to link members to self-help groups. Alcoholics Anonymous groups, for example, often meet each evening, or at least several times each week and can provide members with an alternative to spending their evenings in a neighborhood bar or drinking alone at home. These groups also encourage recovering alcoholics to form close relationships with new members, which provides new members with models of sobriety and encourages the development of a network of supportive relationships. Similarly, organizations such as Recovery, Inc., Parents without Partners, Parents Anonymous, and Gamblers Anonymous help members with other types of problems and concerns to become involved with a network of people to whom they can turn at particularly difficult times. Safety plans and relapse prevention plans can also be put in place during the ending part of the group, and reminders about them and other helping resources can be placed in prominent places in members' homes so they are available after the group ends.

Members of task groups can also benefit from preparing for an unsympathetic environment. Plans, reports, and other products of a task group's work may encounter resistance as they are considered by others outside the group. Resistance is especially likely when the products of a task group are controversial or have negative implications for a particular program, an entire organization, or a social service delivery system. Also, resistance is more likely to be encountered when proposals must go through several levels of review before they are approved (Tropman, 2014). Therefore, it is important for task group members to anticipate resistance to implementing the group's work and to plan strategies to counteract the resistance.

Helping Members Solve Problems Independently

No matter how many different situations are discussed and practiced within a group, it is not possible to cover the full range of situations that members may experience outside a group. Therefore, during the group, members should learn how to solve their own problems independently. This gradually lessens the need for continued treatment. Teaching problem-solving skills should begin as early as possible in the group experience and be given particular emphasis in the last few meetings.

Throughout the group treatment process, workers can support independent functioning by building members' confidence in their existing coping skills and by helping members develop and rely on new coping skills. Workers should also teach members the principles underlying the intervention methods used in the group. Workers sometimes fail to teach members the underlying therapeutic principles of an intervention because they think professional knowledge should not be shared with clients, group members may not be able to understand therapeutic principles, or members may misuse the information they receive. Most group members who enter treatment voluntarily are eager to learn more about ways to cope with their concerns. For example, having members of an assertion-training group read *Your Perfect Right* (Alberti & Emmons, 2008), having members of a parent-training group read *Parents Are Teachers* (Becker, 1971), or having members of a weight-loss group read *Slim Chance in a Fat World* (Stuart & Davis, 1972) helps them learn basic principles that they can use as they encounter situations not discussed in the group.

Some treatment approaches, such as Albert Ellis' *rational-emotive therapy* (Ellis, 1962, 1992, 2002; Ellis & Joffe-Ellis, 2011), encourage workers to help members understand the basic principles underlying their treatment approaches. Workers who use other treatment approaches should also consider spending time teaching members the basic principles underlying therapeutic interventions. When teaching members, workers should translate technical terms into jargon-free explanations, especially if members use English as a second language.

Having members summarize what they have learned in the group and deduce general principles from the summaries are other effective ways to help members see how principles can be applied to other situations. For example, in summarizing what they have learned, members of a couples' group became aware of general principles regarding communication, such as maintaining eye contact to show that they are listening, summarizing the core content of messages to ensure understanding, and using "I" messages to communicate their feelings and thoughts.

Reducing Group Attraction

In addition to helping members maintain and generalize the changes they have made in a group, the ending stage should help members become less dependent on the group. This goal can be achieved by helping members rely on their own skills and resources as well as on sources of support outside the group. Planning for termination should begin with workers' awareness of their own feelings about terminating with individual members and with the group as a whole. Particularly in support groups and therapy groups, it is not uncommon for workers to become emotionally attached to individual members or to the group as a whole. Workers should be careful not to foster dependence. They should carefully assess whether they are being overly protective of members or covertly or overtly undermining members' efforts to function without the group. Supervision can be useful in helping workers examine their feelings about terminating.

To ensure that members are prepared for ending, it is good practice to begin discussions of termination at least four sessions before the planned termination date. Members should be fully involved in planning for termination. Program activities can be used effectively at the end of a group to help members prepare for termination (Nitza, 2014). Workers should describe the ideas they have about program activities for ending the group, solicit members' feedback, and ask for additional suggestions. Appropriate program activities for ending a group include the following principles.

Principles for Program Activities
- Demonstrate or encourage reflection about the skills members have learned in the group.
- Encourage members to express their feelings about the group and each other.
- Focus on future activities.
- Encourage participation in activities outside of the group.

For example, getting together for a dinner is a program activity that is commonly used at the ending of a group. Planning for a dinner encourages both individual and group-oriented participation. During the dinner, members often discuss the things they have learned in the group, their feelings about ending, and their plans for the future.

Endings are often marked by ceremonies. Program activities, such as having a party or a potluck dinner, awarding certificates of merit, or having each member say or write something special about other members, can be viewed as ceremonies that signify the end of the group. Barlow, Blythe, and Edmonds (1999) have developed a series of exercises that can be done in the last meetings of a group. These include exercises that are focused on ending the group on a positive note, celebrating the ending of a group, summarizing progress, reflecting on what has been accomplished, and thinking about the future. Used creatively, ceremonies can also help to maintain and generalize changes made by members. One example of the creative use of ceremonies and program activities is illustrated in the following case.

Group attraction can be reduced in other ways. Members can be encouraged to summarize their accomplishments and discuss why they no longer need the group. They can celebrate their successes and talk about what they have accomplished. Workers should be positive and upbeat, giving praise for members' accomplishments and celebrating successes along with members. Workers should express confidence in members, noting their resiliency, capacity, strengths, and ability to maintain changes in the future (Saleebey, 2013).

Case Example   Maintaining Changes

In the next-to-last session of a weight-loss group, members were asked to write themselves two letters, each containing (1) their feelings about being overweight, (2) how good it felt to be losing weight, and (3) a reiteration of their commitment to continue losing weight. The self-addressed letters were mailed by the worker after the group had ended at three-week intervals as a reminder to members of their commitment to losing weight and maintaining weight losses. In the last session of the group, the worker arranged for members to meet at a local restaurant and participate in cooking a meal that reinforced useful nutritional knowledge members had learned from participating in the group. During the dinner, members were asked to evaluate the overall group and discuss how they would modify their eating behaviors in the future.

Meetings can be scheduled less frequently or for shorter periods of time to reduce the importance of the group for members. Workers can encourage members to become involved in outside activities that compete with the group for members' time and energy. Volunteering is one way to accomplish this goal. Such activities can also support members and help them maintain changes. Members can also be encouraged to participate in self-help groups.

In task groups, there is less concern about reducing attraction to the group. In standing committees, membership is usually for a particular term, and members are often happy to be finished at the end of their service period. Similarly, in *ad hoc* groups that have endings, members are often glad that they have succeeded in accomplishing whatever tasks they were charged with completing and are happy to be finished. In *ad hoc* groups, however, it is important for the worker to make sure that members are aware of the steps that need to be taken after the group ends to follow through with tasks that will make the group a success. Therefore, in these groups during the ending phase, workers should encourage and remind members to follow-up to make sure the group is successful. Sometimes, follow-up meetings are needed to determine how plans are being implemented and to make adjustments as needed.

Feelings About Ending

The feelings that members and workers have about ending are related to the relationships that have developed in the group. Feelings about ending are also affected by whether the group is planned to be time-limited or open-ended, how long the group meets, the nature of the group's work (e.g., primarily task or socio-emotional), the intensity of the relationships that develop among members, and the extent to which the ending is associated with a sense of progress, achievement, or graduation (Germain & Gitterman, 2008). After examining reactions to termination, Fortune and colleagues (Fortune, 1987; Fortune, Pearlingi, & Rochelle, 1992) concluded that the strongest reactions were positive affect, positive flight to constructive outside activities, and objective evaluations of treatment goals and processes.

Many positive feelings can result from a skillfully facilitated group ending.

Positive Feelings About Ending
- A feeling of empowerment and potency as members realize they are capable of accomplishing goals

- A feeling of independence resulting from being in greater control of their own lives
- A sense of satisfaction and pride in successfully completing the group experience
- A feeling of usefulness resulting from helping other members during group interactions
- A feeling of confidence that problems can be coped with or solved

At the same time, however, members may experience negative feelings about the ending of a group. A common reaction is denial (Levine, 2012). Not wanting to show that they will miss the worker or others in the group, members sometimes ignore workers' attempts to prepare them for ending by changing the topic of discussion or by indicating that they are looking forward to ending. Other common reactions are feelings of disappointment, powerlessness, abandonment, or rejection. Members may act out these feelings by becoming angry or hostile. In other cases, they may engage in regressive behavior that exhibits the symptoms or problems they had when they first entered the group (Malekoff, 2014). Other reactions include emotional or psychological clinging to the worker, acting out, and devaluing the group experience or the skill of the worker (Malekoff, 2014).

More often, members simply wish they could continue with the warm, supportive relationships they have found in the group. Therefore, they may experience a sense of loss and accompanying sadness at the ending of the group. Members may also question their ability to maintain changes without the help of the group.

As mentioned earlier, workers are not immune to reactions to ending a group. Some of these reactions follow.

Worker Reactions to Group Termination
- Pride and accomplishment in the members' success
- Pride in worker's own therapeutic skills
- Sadness, sense of loss, or ambivalence about no longer working with the members
- Doubt or disappointment about the members' progress or ability to function independently
- A re-experiencing of their own losses
- Relief, doubt, or guilt about their therapeutic effectiveness

Workers should be aware of their own reactions to ending to fully appreciate the difficulties that members may be experiencing. If workers are not aware of their own feelings, they may withdraw emotionally or they may encourage the dependence of members and prolong treatment beyond what is needed. Workers may also want to share their reactions as a way of helping members identify and express their own feelings and reactions.

It is helpful to begin termination several meetings before the end of the group. As members begin to react to ending, the worker can point out that conflicting or ambivalent feelings during this stage are common. Members should be encouraged to discuss their conflicting and ambivalent feelings.

Workers can help members with their negative emotional and behavioral reactions to ending by developing increased awareness of the connection between their feelings and behaviors and the termination process. It is also helpful to encourage members to discuss the coping abilities and other gains they have achieved as a result of being in the group. The worker can prepare members for ending by clarifying what the role of the worker and the sponsoring agency will be in helping members maintain gains after the group ends.

Planning for the Future

In time-limited groups, some members may wish to contract for additional services. When considering new services, the worker should help members clarify (1) their continuing needs, (2) the goals they hope to achieve, (3) the duration of the new service period, and (4) any appropriate modifications of the original contract. Re-contracting should occur when there is a clear need for additional services and when members are highly motivated to achieve additional goals or to continue work on original goals that they have only partially completed. Occasionally, all members of a group may express interest in continuing to meet. In such cases, the worker may re-contract for additional meetings with all members or may encourage members to meet on their own without the worker.

When workers encourage members to continue to meet on their own, they are participating in the development of a self-help group. The worker helps groups continue to meet by developing natural leadership and by helping with any resources that may be needed (Toseland & Coppola, 1985). Rather than total independence, many new self-help groups prefer continuing contact, guidance, and leadership from the worker until the new group has been firmly established. Many existing self-help groups have been started by professional workers in this manner (Toseland & Hacker, 1982). The worker can continue to assist self-help groups after they have developed by (1) providing material support to maintain the group, (2) referring clients to the group, and (3) acting as a consultant to the group.

In rare instances, the members of a group may wish to continue meeting because they are unable to terminate the group in a positive and responsible fashion. The group may develop a culture that supports members' dependency rather than preparing them for independent functioning in the environment outside the group. When this occurs, the worker should explore this with the group and begin to help members become more independent. This can be accomplished by focusing on empowerment and strengths-based practice, and having members increase supportive activities outside the group.

Sometimes the ending of a group may result in no further contact with members. However, workers are rarely sure that members will not need services in the future. Changing life situations, new crises, or relapses may cause members to seek help again. The worker should discuss how members can seek additional services if they are needed. In some agencies, the worker may explain that he or she has an open-door policy, so that members who need additional services can contact the worker directly. In other agencies, the policy may be for former clients to apply for services in the same manner that new clients apply. Taking this step clarifies the position of the worker and the agency with regard to how members can obtain any additional services that may be needed.

The worker should plan for the future with each member. Plans should include the support systems and resources that will be available after the group ends. Workers should also encourage members to use their own skills, resources, and strengths to meet their needs by expressing confidence in members' abilities, encouraging them to try new skills outside the group, and repeating successful skill-building activities and role plays so members develop feelings of mastery and self-confidence.

In some situations, preparation for the future may involve planning with others for continuing treatment for members. For example, in preparing for the ending of the children's group, the worker should contact the children's parents to review each child's progress and to plan for additional services. In groups in which members are participating in other agency services, such as individual counseling, the worker should contact the member's case manager or primary worker to evaluate the member's progress in the group and to plan for additional services. Similarly, in residential and inpatient settings, the ending of a group may not signify the end of service. The worker should meet with other staff, perhaps in a case conference or team meeting, to report progress and to plan for the future needs of members. For example, there is likely to be a transition to one or more new groups in an outpatient or aftercare setting.

Members who prematurely terminate from groups should not be forgotten when plans for future service needs are made. Without follow-up contact, dropouts may feel abandoned. Their failure to continue with a particular group may signify to them that their situation is hopeless. Therefore, dropouts from treatment should be contacted whenever possible. One of the primary objectives of a follow-up contact is to motivate persons who terminate prematurely to seek further treatment if it is needed. The worker can inquire about difficulties the former members may be having in continuing to attend group meetings and may suggest ways to overcome these impediments. During this process, the worker should identify any needs that former group members have for continuing service and refer them to appropriate resources and services.

Making Referrals

During the ending stage of group work, workers frequently connect members to other services or resources. In some cases, members may be transferred to workers in the same agency. In other cases, referrals may be made to workers in other agencies.

A referral should be made only after the worker and the member have appraised the member's need for additional services or resources. If the member is motivated to seek additional services, the referral can proceed. If the member is not motivated to seek additional services, but the worker's assessment suggests that additional services may be beneficial, the worker should proceed by helping the member explore reasons for resistance.

Whenever possible, the member should be helped to use informal, natural helping systems. If these types of systems are unavailable or are judged to be inadequate, the member should be referred to professional helping resources. Before making a referral, the worker should discuss the reasons for the referral with the member and answer any questions the member has. It is often helpful to find out whether the member has had any prior contact with the referral source or has heard anything about the source. Members' impressions and previous experiences with particular

Intervention

Behavior: Apply knowledge of human behavior and the social environment, person-in-environment, and other multidisciplinary theoretical frameworks in interventions with clients and constituencies

Critical Thinking Question: Group workers should have knowledge of the social service system. What should the worker do when making a referral?

referral sources can be influential in determining whether members will follow through and use the resources to which they are referred.

In preparing to make effective referrals, workers should become familiar with available community resources. They should also get to know a particular contact person in frequently used referral sources. It is also helpful to be familiar with basic information about referral sources to share with members who are being referred, such as information about eligibility requirements, the waiting time for service, the business hours of the agency, and the type of service provided. Such information will prepare the member for what to expect when contacting the referral source and will avoid members' developing expectations that will not be met. Because it may be difficult for workers to be familiar with all community resources that are available in an area, agencies should maintain up-to-date files with basic information about such resources and services.

When making a referral, the worker should write the name of the agency, the contact person, and the agency's address on a card to give to the member. In some cases, referral sources may have forms that have to be filled out before a member can be seen. Often, release forms need to be signed by the member so that information in a member's file can be sent to the referral source. Information should never be sent without a signed release form from the member. Because many members never reach referral resources and services, it is helpful for the worker to use the following referral principles.

Referral Principles
- Call the contact person while the member is with the leader.
- Emphasize that the member is expected at the referral source.
- Provide instructions for getting to the referral source.
- Assist with transportation if necessary.
- Check to make sure that disabilities or other obstacles do not prevent a successful referral.
- Check to ensure that the member reached the referral source and received the needed information or services.

Members also should be instructed to contact the worker if they fail to get what they need from the referral sources. Members who are severely impaired may need help in getting to referral sources. The worker, a volunteer, or a case aide may have to accompany the member during the first visit. A referral may fail for a number of reasons.

Failure of Referrals
- The referral source has had a change in policy; for example, eligibility requirements may have become more stringent.
- The member lacks motivation or desire.
- The member lacks the skill necessary to obtain the needed resources.
  - The worker has given the member incorrect information or insufficient help to contact the referral source.

> **?** Assess your understanding of the steps involved in ending the group as a whole by taking this brief quiz.

Follow-up contacts allow workers to assess why members did not obtain needed services or resources. They also allow workers to plan with members about how to obtain needed resources and services in the future.

Case Example

As the facilitator of a staff support group for hospice workers, Carla was familiar with the needs of the group members. She had been hired two years ago to conduct weekly sessions of the group so that the staff could have an opportunity to discuss their feelings and the stress associated with working with the terminally ill. But Carla faced a new challenge when Nick, the new executive director, informed her that the group would have to be discontinued because of cost constraints. Although Nick had insisted that she give the group only one week's notice before it ended, Carla had been able to negotiate for three more group sessions.

Carla pondered the group's situation and wondered how the members would take the news. As hospice workers, the group members faced endings with their clients every day. Now, the group members would have to deal with the ending of the group and the dissolution of an important support system. Although group members had achieved high levels of cohesiveness and mutual aid in the group, Carla feared that ending the group would detrimentally affect staff morale and the quality of their work.

Carla outlined some of the goals she hoped to accomplish in the next three sessions. She wanted to present the news about discontinuing the group in as positive a way as possible. Members would need time to adjust to the idea of ending the group, so she planned on telling the group during the next meeting. She also wanted to help members maintain some of the gains they had accomplished through the group, particularly those that helped them deal with the stress of their work. At the same time, she wanted to help members reduce their reliance on the group for formal support and find sources of support outside of the group. Finally, she hoped that the members would be able to spend time evaluating the effectiveness of the group. These were formidable goals for the group's last sessions.

The ending of the group was announced at the next meeting. Carla took a supportive but matter-of-fact approach to making the announcement. Despite her own feelings about the actions of the new executive director, she refrained from blaming him for ending the group. By doing this she hoped to redirect some of the members' energies into accomplishing as much as they could in the next three sessions. However, members spent a good deal of time expressing strong feelings about ending the group. Several were angry and others expressed a sense of sadness and loss. Some members wondered how they would be able to deal with the stress of their jobs without the support of the group. Carla allowed a good deal of time for members to ventilate.

As members came to accept the ending of the group, Carla made some suggestions about how to proceed. She challenged group members to discuss how the group had helped them. Despite some early resistance, members were able to discuss the benefits they had obtained by participating in the group. Several were quite articulate about how, as a result of their group participation, they had accomplished personal changes that helped them deal with the emotional impact of their work. Carla used the discussions to encourage members to maintain these changes after the group ended. She then suggested that members come to the next group session prepared to discuss how they could get personal and emotional support from sources outside the group. Members accepted this homework assignment and the session ended.

During the next session, members began by revisiting their reactions to the ending of the group. Members expressed feelings of anger, loss, grief, and frustration. Carla again allowed them time to ventilate and work through these feelings. She pointed out that in a symbolic way, the ending of the group would mirror the dying, death, and grief process so familiar to the members in their everyday work at the hospice. She observed that members needed time to work through their own sense of loss over ending the group.

Later in the session, Carla reviewed each member's suggestions about how to find support outside of the group. As a result of this discussion, the group decided to develop a buddy system in place of the weekly group. Relying on this system, members could systematically exchange feelings and experiences related to their work. Carla suggested that the support system would allow members to become more independent from the group and more focused on other sources of support. She emphasized that the development of the buddy system demonstrated members' ability to create a new way to obtain support. Then, as the meeting ended, she reviewed and reinforced some of the capacities and skills members had demonstrated during previous group sessions when describing how they coped with emotionally challenging patient care situations.

Carla was totally surprised by the group's last meeting. She had expected that the beginning of the last session would be somber because of the strong emotional bonds among members and the feelings they had expressed about ending. On her arrival, however, she was greeted with a chocolate cake, refreshments, and a nicely wrapped present from the group. Members expressed their gratitude to Carla for her strong leadership and support. Carla gratefully accepted the members' comments and asked if the group could finish its formal discussions and then move on to its party.

Members mentioned that they were more resigned to ending the group. They expressed fewer feelings of anger and more feelings of sadness during this last session. Members also discussed their favorite memories of the group and how the group had benefited them. Finally, Carla asked members to evaluate the effectiveness of the group by completing a short questionnaire with open-ended questions. After completing the questionnaire, members discussed plans for the future. Although the last session went well, it was a bittersweet experience.

SUMMARY

The ending stage is a critical time in the life of a group. During the ending stage, the work of the group is consolidated and lasting impressions are made about the efficacy of the entire group experience. Endings can either be planned or unplanned. Unfortunately, in many voluntary groups, unplanned terminations are fairly common. This chapter makes suggestions about how to facilitate planned endings and what to do when members terminate before the planned ending of a group.

Procedures for facilitating endings vary, depending on the type of group being led. In task groups and treatment groups in which members have not been encouraged to self-disclose or form supportive relationships, endings are less emotionally charged than are endings in groups in which considerable self-disclosure has taken place and in which members depend on one another for help with their personal concerns and problems. Other variations in group endings depend on whether the group has an open or closed membership policy, is short-term or long-term, and is attractive or unattractive to its members.

Major tasks in ending a meeting of a group include (1) closing the work, (2) arranging another meeting, (3) preparing a summary or a report of the group's work, and (4) planning for future group actions. Major tasks in ending the group as a whole include (1) maintaining and generalizing change efforts, (2) evaluating the work of the group, (3) reducing group attraction and promoting independent member functioning, (4) helping members with their feelings about the ending, (5) planning for the future, and (6) making effective referrals. This chapter examines the skills and strategies needed to carry out each of these tasks.

Evaluation

Evaluation is the process of obtaining formative, summative, or evaluative information about the group. Workers can use formative information for planning a new group or an entire group work service. They can use summative information for documenting services and monitoring members' and groups' progress toward goals. Evaluative information can be used to identify and document the effectiveness and efficiency of workers' efforts to reach members' and groups' goals. All three types of information are essential for effective group-work practice. The remainder of this chapter focuses on conducting evaluations to collect and utilize this information.

Workers can use informal or formal measures to obtain such information. To conduct an informal evaluation a worker might ask members to fill out anonymously a five question written progress form at the end of every fourth meeting. In contrast, to complete a formal evaluation, a worker might collect information systematically using preplanned reliable and valid measurement devices before, during, and after the group has met. This chapter explores many ways to obtain information about a group and guides workers' decisions about what evaluation methods might be most useful in various situations.

Increasingly in social work and allied disciplines, there has been a push toward accountability and evidence-based practice. Evaluations to monitor whether clients are being served in an ethical and timely fashion are now mandated by many accrediting and funding organizations. Increasingly, there are requirements to go beyond merely counting numbers of clients served to measuring and documenting the efficacy of services. To get reimbursed for services, there has also been a growing push by managed care companies and other funders for workers to demonstrate that they are using empirically based practice guidelines and the best available evidence (Barlow, 2013; Boyd-Franklin, Cleek, Wofsy, & Mundy, 2013). This evidence is generated through evaluation research.

The push for evaluating practice has occurred even though practitioners often encounter obstacles when trying to fulfill obligations for accountability. First, workers often perceive a lack of relevance of evaluation information for enhancing outcomes that they

LEARNING OUTCOMES

- Explain why evaluation is important in group work.
- Acquire skills in designing evaluations for planning, developing, and monitoring a group.
- Demonstrate skills in designing evaluations for measuring effectiveness and efficiency in group practice.
- Identify evaluation measures that are particularly appropriate to group work practice.

CHAPTER OUTLINE

perceive as having already been achieved. In treatment groups, workers often get immediate verbal and nonverbal feedback from group members about their satisfaction with
services. In task groups, they often think they know whether the group has achieved its
goals because of the feedback they receive from the members of the group and administrators, or others who are the beneficiaries of the group's work. This can lead group
workers to question the need for any additional evaluation. Second, in many practice
settings there are severe time constraints, with workers being asked to do more with
the same or shrinking resources. Managers often strive to maximize client contact hours
so that workers can increase their billable hours to public and private health insurance
funders, or to fulfill contractual obligations for services already funded by public or
private sources. At the same time, documentation demands have increased, often forc-
ing workers to scramble to comply with "paperwork" requirements while meeting the
growing demands of clients' needs. Third, in some social service settings group workers
still do not have ready access to computers, databases, or other tools that are needed to
help them evaluate their practice or to research evidence-based guidelines and practices.
Fourth, in everyday practice, group workers often encounter individuals with complex,
multifaceted bio-psycho-social problems. Evidence bases may not seem very relevant or
helpful, and workers often do not know how to evaluate these complex cases.

   Although there are obstacles, there are many encouraging recent developments including the following: (1) computers and many other devices for connecting to the Internet are
becoming much more widely available in social service organizations, (2) electronic reporting
systems with user-friendly interfaces are being developed, (3) the number and availability of
evidence-based practice guidelines, treatment manuals, and field-tested curricula is growing,
and (4) scholars are creating and enhancing easy-to-use databases for evidence-based and
research-informed practice. For example, practice guidelines for the treatment of depression
indicate that the most effective method for treating it is a combination of pharmacotherapy
and psychotherapy (American Psychiatric Association, 2013), and several evidence-based treatments such as cognitive behavioral, behavioral activation, and problem solving therapies are
available for group workers to use in groups for members who suffer from depression.

   The push toward accountability and empirically based group work practice has led to a
larger evidence base for practice. Reviews by Barlow (2013); Burlingame, Strauss, and Joyce
(2013); Burlingame, Whitcomb, and Woodland (2014); Macgowan, (2008) and others show
that group work research has continued to expand over the last decade. Reviews are now
beginning to examine questions about what specific problems group work is most effective
for addressing (see, for example, Barlow, 2013; Burlingame, Strauss,
& Joyce, 2013). There is also beginning to be research on how to
tailor evidence-based interventions for new populations (Chen,
Reid, Parker, & Pillemer, 2012). Moreover, there is an increasing
amount of Internet resources for identifying evidence-based, research-supported, group interventions (see, for example, Johnson,
2008; Macgowan, 2008). Overall, evidence-based group work practice includes the best available empirical evidence, but also critical
thinking and clinical expertise along with the needs, values, and
preferences of clients (Kazdin, 2008). For a very thoughtful discussion of evidence-based practice from the practitioner's viewpoint,
see Boyd-Franklin, Cleek, Wofsy, and Mundy (2013).

Research-Informed Practice

**Behavior: Use and translate research
evidence to inform and improve practice,
policy, and service delivery.**

Critical Thinking Question: Group workers
are accountable for providing the most
effective services possible. How can
evidence-based practice improve group
work service delivery?

WHY EVALUATE? THE GROUP WORKER'S VIEW

When evaluating their work with a particular group, workers should consider the resources they have available for conducting an evaluation. For example, it is important to assess the encouragement they will receive from their agency for evaluating their own practice. It is also important to consider the time they have available for an evaluation. Matching resources and available time with an appropriate method for evaluating their practice is essential.

Reasons for Conducting Evaluations

In addition to organizational, funding, regulatory, and other requirements, workers often want feedback about their leadership of groups. Some of the benefits of evaluation for group workers are presented here.

Benefits of Evaluations
- Evaluations can satisfy workers' curiosity and professional concerns about the effects of specific interventions they perform while working with a group.
- Information from evaluations can help workers improve their leadership skills.
- Evaluations can demonstrate the usefulness of a specific group or a specific group work method to an agency, a funding source, or society.
- Workers can assess the progress of individual group members and see whether the whole group is accomplishing agreed-on purposes and goals.
- Evaluations allow group members and others who may be affected to express their satisfactions and dissatisfactions with a group.
- Workers can gather knowledge that can be shared with others who are using group methods for similar purposes and in similar situations.
- Workers can systematize the informal hypothesis-generating and hypothesis-testing processes they routinely engage in as they practice.
- Evaluations can examine the cost-effectiveness of group work services.

Organizational Encouragement and Support

To evaluate their practice with a group, workers should begin by assessing the willingness of their organization or agency to provide the resources to conduct an evaluation. Some organizations do little or nothing to encourage evaluations. Agency norms, peer pressure, or administrative directions may suggest to workers that other tasks are more important than evaluating their practice. In other cases, high caseloads may inhibit workers' abilities to evaluate their practice.

Without active encouragement by an organization's administrators, workers are left to rely on their own motivations for evaluating their work with a group. Organizations can increase workers' opportunities for evaluation by including evaluation tasks as a part of workers' practice responsibilities, by providing the time for evaluations, and by encouraging workers to discuss evaluations during regularly scheduled staff meetings. Partnerships can also be developed among university faculty and agencies that enable and promote evidence-based group work practice.

Rather than requiring workers to fill out forms and records that they do not use and often do not see again after administrative processing, organizations can instead help by developing and implementing information systems that can be used by workers to evaluate their practice. A well-designed information and evaluation system can provide feedback for group work practitioners and agency administrators.

Time Considerations

Workers should consider how much time they have available to conduct an evaluation. Most workers collect some information about the groups they lead, and this information can often be the basis for an evaluation if it is collected correctly. Little additional time may be needed for evaluation beyond the time necessary to make modifications in the original data-collection system.

In other situations, workers may want information that is not routinely collected. They should estimate the amount of time it will take them to collect, organize, and analyze the additional information. They can then compare the time needed for the evaluation with the time they have available and decide whether the evaluation is feasible.

Group workers also need to think clearly about the purpose and usefulness of any evaluation information they decide to collect. When workers have valid reasons for evaluating their practice, they may be able to persuade their organization to allow them sufficient time to conduct a particular evaluation or to include some form of evaluation into their routine practice. This is particularly true when a worker is developing a new, innovative program to achieve the goals the organization has set as a priority for service delivery.

Selecting a Data Collection Method

After determining how much time is available for an evaluation, workers should consider how to match their information needs and available time to an appropriate evaluation method. This chapter reviews the major types of evaluations. Workers must also decide what data-collection instruments they will use in conjunction with a particular evaluation method. The major types of data-collection instruments used by group workers follow.

Data Collection Instruments
- Progress notes
- Self-reports or personal interview data from workers, members, and observers
- Questionnaires
- Analysis of reports or other products of a group's work
- Review of CDs and DVDs of group meetings
- Observational coding schemes
- Role play or *in vivo* performance tests
- Reliable and valid scales

These data-collection instruments can be used with any of the major types of evaluation methods. Some measures, however, are frequently associated with one type of evaluation. For example, progress notes are often used in monitoring evaluation methods, whereas reliable and valid scales are more frequently used in effectiveness and efficiency evaluations.

EVALUATION METHODS

Workers can use four types of evaluations for groups: (1) planning, (2) monitoring, (3) developing, and (4) effectiveness and efficiency. Workers can use many different types of evaluation methods to obtain information about the process or the outcome of a group. The choice of a research method depends on factors, such as available time and support, but also on the workers' objective. For example, a review of databases (Barlow, 2013; Johnson, 2008; Macgowan, 2008) or participatory action research (Chevalier & Buckles, 2013; Lawson, Caringi, Pyles, Jurkowski, & Bozlak, 2015; Schneider, 2014) might be good choices when developing a new group or a new group work service, whereas experimental design or single-system research might be better choices for evaluating effectiveness (Barlow, 2013; Forsyth, 2014; Macgowan & Wong, 2014).

Regardless of the type of evaluation methods employed, workers can use evaluations to receive feedback about their practice. Instead of viewing practice evaluations as useless administrative requirements that add to the burden and pressure of seeing as many people as possible, workers should try to reframe evaluations as a way to help themselves become more effective and to develop new knowledge that can be shared with others.

> **?** Assess your understanding of why evaluation is important in group work by taking this brief quiz.

EVALUATIONS FOR PLANNING A GROUP

Evaluations used for planning a group are seldom mentioned in the group work literature. This section discusses two important evaluation methods for planning: (1) obtaining program information, technical data, and materials for specific groups that the worker is planning to lead, and (2) conducting needs assessments to determine the feasibility of organizing a proposed group.

Obtaining Program Information

The worker can often benefit from information about methods previously used in working with similar groups. Workers may be able to obtain some information from colleagues or from workers in other agencies in which similar groups have been conducted. Workers may also find it useful to utilize the sources listed here.

Ways to Obtain Program Information
- Examine records from previous groups that focused on similar concerns.
- Attend workshops and conferences where group workers share recent developments in the field.
- Review relevant journals and books using computerized or manual search procedures.
- Read the minutes of previous group meetings.
- Read the bylaws of the sponsoring organization.
- Read any operating procedures that may exist from previous meetings of the task group.
- Be clear about the charges and responsibilities of the group.

- Obtain information about how similar objectives and goals were accomplished in other organizations and by other task groups.
- Attend meetings of groups working on similar concerns.

Library literature searches have been made much easier and much less time-consuming in recent years by the availability of online computerized databases. Two databases that are particularly relevant to social group workers are Social Work Abstracts Plus and PSYCLIT (psychology). Also, group workers in health settings may find MEDLINE (medicine) useful; group workers in school settings may find ERIC (education) useful; and group workers in forensic settings may find NCJRS (National Criminal Justice Reference Service) useful. All of the previously mentioned databases are to search for journal articles. To search for books the World Cat database can be used. Google and Google Scholar may be even more readily available for those who do not have access to the previously mentioned databases.

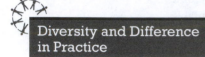

Diversity and Difference in Practice

Behavior: Present themselves as learners and engage clients and constituencies as experts of their own experiences

Critical Thinking Question: Assessing community needs is important. How can the worker assess the need for group work in particular cultural communities?

Needs Assessment

Workers might also find it useful to have some information about potential members of a proposed group as illustrated in the following case. This information might include (1) potential members' willingness to attend the group, (2) their motivations for attending, and (3) their capabilities for helping the group achieve its purposes. In treatment groups, workers may want to conduct a needs assessment by asking other workers whether clients with whom they work might be appropriate for the group or whether workers have received requests for a particular group service they have been unable to meet.

Data from community needs assessments designed for multiple purposes can be useful in obtaining information about potential group members. Contacting people or organizations in the community may also provide access to potential members. When workers have identified the clients, they can contact them directly by a personal interview, a telephone call, or a letter. Toseland (1981) has described methods of reaching out to clients in more detail.

In some task groups, membership may result from elections, appointments, or the person's position in an organization. A planning evaluation can familiarize a worker with the bylaws of the organization that governs standing committees and any rules and regulations governing *ad hoc* task groups' composition and operation. Planning evaluations can also help a worker collect information and assess the potential contributions that particular members can make in helping the group achieve its objectives (Tropman, 2014). For a board, this might include, for example, inviting the participation of a lawyer, an accountant, fundraisers, or other members who can help the group achieve its objectives. For more information about conducting planning evaluations, see Rossi, Freeman, and Lipsey (2004).

Case Example   Evaluating the Need for a Group

In order to assess the need for a support group for teen parents, the worker began by consulting existing research from several government organizations, including the local Department of Health and the state Department of Children and Family Services. Data suggested that the incidence and prevalence of teen parenting was particularly high in the local community. The worker also conducted "key informant" interviews with community leaders and executive directors of several local social service organizations. Information obtained during the interviews confirmed the results found in the initial analysis of existing data. In addition, several interviewees suggested that they would be interested in referring potential members to the group; the worker sent them copies of a survey designed to obtain information about the number of potential referrals to the group and any other information about the interests and motivations of potential members.

EVALUATIONS FOR MONITORING A GROUP

Monitoring refers to keeping track of the progress of group members and group processes. Monitoring is discussed in Chapter 8 as an assessment device, but it can also be used to evaluate group work practice. Monitoring methods have received more attention in the group work literature than has any other type of evaluation method. Monitoring is the least demanding and most flexible of the evaluation procedures described in this chapter. It can be useful for obtaining information for process or outcome evaluations.

Monitoring Methods

The first step in the monitoring process is to decide what information to collect. For example, persons who work with therapy groups designed for clients with psychological disorders may be interested in monitoring changes in individual members over the course of the group on the five axes presented in the *Diagnostic and Statistical Manual of Mental Disorders* (American Psychiatric Association, 2013). A worker asked to lead an interdepartmental committee of a large public welfare agency may be interested in monitoring the extent to which individual committee members complete assigned tasks.

Whatever information group workers decide to collect, they must be clear about how they define it so it can be monitored with appropriate measures. Concepts that are ambiguous or unspecified cannot be measured accurately.

The next step in monitoring is to decide how the needed information will be collected. Data can be collected by administering questionnaires; by asking for verbal feedback about the group from members; by observing the group; or by recording information about the group through written records, audio recordings using a CD, or video recordings using a DVD of group sessions.

In treatment groups, members may be asked to record information about their own behavior or the behavior of other group members. Self-monitoring methods include (1) counting discrete behaviors; (2) keeping a checklist, a log, or a diary of events that occur before, during, and after a behavior or a task that is being monitored; and (3) recording ratings of feeling states on self-anchored rating scales. These types of monitoring methods are described in Chapter 8 because they are often used for assessment. As illustrated in the following sections, in the monitoring process, collecting data can be the task of the worker or of the group members.

Monitoring by the Group Worker

One of the easiest methods of monitoring a group's progress is to record the activities that occur during each meeting. This form of record-keeping involves writing or dictating notes after a meeting (Garrett, 2005). The worker may use a process-recording method of monitoring or a summary-recording method. Process recordings are narrative, step-by-step descriptions of a group's development. They can help a worker analyze the interactions that occur during a group meeting. However, they are time-consuming and, therefore, are used rarely by experienced group workers. They are, however, useful in the training and supervision of beginning group workers because they provide rich detail and give trainees an opportunity to reflect on what occurs during group meetings.

Summary recording is less time-consuming, more selective, and more focused than process recording. Summary recording focuses on critical incidents that occur in a group and involves using a series of open-ended questions, which are used for monitoring a group's progress after each group session. Figure 14.1 is an example of a summary recording form used to record a meeting of a family life education group for foster parents.

When using either summary or process recordings, it is important for the worker to record the information as soon as possible after the meeting so that events are remembered as accurately as possible. The meaning of the open-ended summary-recording questions should be as clear as possible so that workers' recordings are consistent from group to group. Ambiguous questions open to several interpretations should be avoided. The amount of time required for summary recordings depends on the number of questions to which the worker responds and the amount of analysis each question requires. The next case provides an example of how a group recording form can be employed.

Case Example   Using a Summary Recording

In a family life education group for foster parents, the worker wanted to systematically analyze whether the group was achieving its goals. Using a group recording form after each weekly meeting, the worker noted who was present, and wrote down the goals of the group and any changes in them, the activities that occurred to accomplish the goals, and the quality of the interaction. She also recorded her analysis of how well the group worked toward achieving its overall purpose that week. After several sessions, she reviewed the summary recordings to ascertain how well the group was achieving its purpose. Based on her weekly analyses of meetings, the worker concluded that although members appeared to be learning a lot about family life, they had failed to create significant supportive relationships with each other. Based on these conclusions, the worker increased program activities that provided members with opportunities to develop closer, more supportive relationships.

The open-ended questions of summary-recording devices sometimes fail to focus or define the recorded information sufficiently, especially when the worker wants similar information about all clients. Summary-recording devices are usually not designed to connect the group worker's activities to specific goals and outcomes.

Recording systems, such as the problem-oriented record (Kane, 1974), have been designed to overcome this problem. In the problem-oriented record-keeping system, problems to be worked on by the group are clearly defined, goals are established, and data are collected and recorded in relation to each specified problem. The system enables workers to show how group work interventions designed to accomplish a certain goal are

```
Group name: _____     Beginning date: _____

Worker's name: _____   Termination date: _____

Session number: _____  Date of session: _____

Members present: _____
_____
_____
_____

Members absent: _____
_____
_____

Purpose of the group: _____
_____

Goals for this meeting: _____
_____
_____

Activities to meet these goals: _____
_____
_____
_____

Worker's analysis of the meeting: _____
_____
_____
_____
_____

Plan for future meetings: _____
_____
_____
_____
_____
```

Figure 14.1
Group Recording Form

connected to a specific assessment of the problem and are now being used in electronic medical records in many countries (see, for example, Uto, Iwaanakuchi, Muranaga, & Kuamoto, 2013). Audio and video recordings of group meetings can be used as substitutes for summary recordings, and they can be used to improve practice as the following case example illustrates.

Case Example   Improving Co-leadership

Bonnie and Fred decided to videotape a new employment skills group they were co-leading in a day treatment program for persons recently discharged from inpatient mental health settings. With the members' written permission, they recorded the meetings and reviewed the recordings between meetings. The review and subsequent discussion helped them to identify ways they might improve their leadership of future meetings.

Although time-consuming to review, workers may also want to use audio or video recordings to obtain feedback about their leadership of groups. Recordings have the advantage of providing an accurate, unedited record of the meeting. In therapy groups, portions of audio and video recordings can be played back to provide immediate feedback for members. Experience suggests that this is a powerful intervention that can be very helpful to members' change efforts. We have also found that members of psycho-educational groups often like to get copies of recordings so they are able to review the content of the meetings at home.

In educational and other groups, DVDs can be used to demonstrate appropriate behavior and critique inappropriate behavior. Video recording using a DVD is especially useful during program activities, such as role playing, that are designed to increase skills or change behavior patterns. Video feedback helps members review their behavior during role-play practices to discuss alternative ways of behaving. For example, members of an assertion training group might watch recordings of themselves in a situation requiring an assertive response. They may analyze voice tone, facial expressions, body posture, and the verbal interactions that occurred. CDs and DVDs provide the worker with a permanent record that can be shared with the group, with supervisors, or in educational workshops.

There are some disadvantages to taping a group. A recording's absolute quality makes it difficult for members to make statements off the record, which may inhibit the development of trust in the group. The worker may not find it necessary or even desirable to have the level of detail provided by a recording. The worker may have to spend too much time reviewing irrelevant portions of a recording to find information that could have been obtained quickly if brief, summary recordings had been used instead. However, if a worker is interested in monitoring the group's interaction patterns in a thorough and precise fashion or if an entire transcript of the group session is needed, audio or video recordings are ideal.

Sometimes it is desirable to use specialized coding systems when the worker wishes to obtain a detailed and accurate picture of group processes for research. Coding systems can be used by one or more raters of audio or video recordings to determine the frequency or type of group interaction, and properties of groups such as cohesion. Coding systems are described in comprehensive reviews of group process instruments (Barlow, 2013; Macgowan, 2008; Sandano, Guyker, Delucia-Waack, Cosgrove, Altaber, & Amos, 2014; Schwartz, Wald, & Moravec, 2010).

In task groups, the minutes of a meeting serve as the record of the group's business. They are often the official record of the proceedings of a group. Minutes are prepared from notes taken during the meeting by a person designated by the worker or elected by the group's membership. A staff person, the secretary of the group, or another person may take notes regularly. Sometimes, members rotate the task. The minutes of each meeting are usually distributed to members before the next meeting and are approved by members, with any revisions, during the first part of the next meeting.

Research-Informed Practice

Behavior: Use practice experience and theory to inform scientific inquiry and research

Critical Thinking Question: Self-monitoring is one way to gather data about members' behavior between meetings. How can the worker help members construct self-monitoring measures?

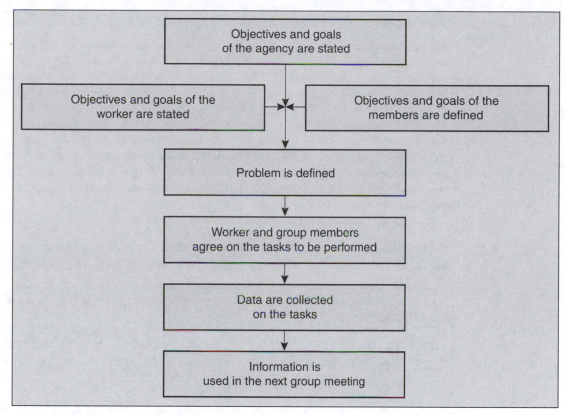

Figure 14.2
The Self-Monitoring Process

Monitoring by Group Members

The most common use of monitoring by group members occurs in treatment groups in which individual members keep a record of their behavior between group meetings and report back on the behaviors during the next meeting. An illustration of the steps in the self-monitoring procedure appears in Figure 14.2. During this procedure, the worker and the group members together decide (1) what data to collect, (2) when to collect the data, (3) how much data to collect, (4) how to collect the data, and (5) when the information collected by members should be analyzed by the group. As these questions are discussed and answered, the worker reviews each member's monitoring plan.

Members can also monitor a group's progress at the end of each meeting or at intervals during the life of the group. Members may use a short questionnaire devised for this purpose, or they can discuss the group's performance orally with the worker. Monitoring of this type encourages members to provide periodic feedback that can be used by workers to improve their practice throughout the life cycle of a group.

Group members also benefit from self-monitoring procedures. Members can share ideas about the group's performance and how it might be improved, which gives them a sense of control and influence over the group's progress and increases their identification with the group's purposes. Also, members who believe their ideas are valued, respected, and listened to are more likely to feel satisfied with their participation in the group. See, for example, the following case example.

Case Example   Monitoring the Progress of a Single Parent's Group

In an educational group for single parents, the worker asked each member to complete a session evaluation form during the last five minutes of each meeting. The form was composed of short, closed-ended questions using a Likert scale, as well as open-ended questions designed to obtain qualitative data about member satisfaction with the group meetings (see Figure 14.3). At several intervals during the life of the group, the worker did a quantitative analysis of members' ratings on the level of helpfulness of information obtained from the group sessions as well as members' satisfaction with the group and with its leader. These data indicated a steady positive progression in how members valued the information they received and how they rated the group and the leader. Data collected about what members liked most and least about each session suggested that members particularly disliked some of the guest speakers brought in by the leader and preferred sessions where they could practice child management skills.

Verbal evaluations of a group's performance do not provide a permanent record. An evaluation form consisting of closed-ended, fixed-category responses and open-ended

---

Was the information presented about child development helpful to you in understanding your child's behavior?

4	3	2	1
Very Helpful	Somewhat Helpful	A Little Helpful	Not at All Helpful

What information did you find most helpful? _____

_____

_____

Rate the effectiveness of the leader in this group session.

4	3	2	1
Very Effective	Somewhat Effective	A Little Effective	Not at All Effective

What did you find most helpful about the group during this session? _____

_____

_____

What did you find least helpful about the group? _____

_____

_____

Overall, rate your satisfaction with today's group meeting.

4	3	2	1
Very Satisfied	Somewhat Satisfied	A Little Satisfied	Not at All Satisfied

Additional comments: _____

_____

_____

Figure 14.3
Session Evaluation Form

items can be used if the worker, group members, or the agency want written feedback about the group. Figure 14.3 shows a session evaluation form developed by a worker leading a group for single parents. The form contains several easily understood closed- and open-ended questions. The closed-ended questions are Likert-type scales that require respondents to record their opinions on an ordered scale. Because the same scale values are used for all group members, responses made by each member can be compared with one another. Open-ended items are designed to allow each member to reply uniquely; responses may vary considerably from member to member.

In task groups, members often make oral reports of their progress. Although the reports are often not considered to be evaluation devices, they are an important means by which the worker and the members monitor the group's work. At the completion of a task group, minutes, documents, final reports, and other products that result from the group's efforts can also be used to evaluate the success of the group.

In treatment groups, an important indicator of the group's performance is the completion of contracts that individual members make with the group or the worker about tasks to be done during the week to resolve a problem or change a particular behavior. Another indicator is the completion of between-session tasks. Rose (1989) calls the completion of between-session tasks the "products of group interaction." He suggests that the rate of completion of tasks is an important indicator of the success of the group.

EVALUATIONS FOR DEVELOPING A GROUP

A third method of evaluating group work practice, developmental evaluation, is useful for the worker who is interested in preparing new group work programs, developing new group work methods, or improving existing group programs. Developmental research, as it has been called by Thomas (1978), is similar to research and development in business and industry. It allows practicing group workers to create and test new group work programs.

The process of developmental evaluation includes developing, testing, evaluating, modifying, and reevaluating intervention methods as new groups are offered. Developmental evaluations are especially appealing for workers who offer the same or similar group programs repeatedly because the evaluations require workers to evaluate group programs in a sequential manner. A developmental evaluation occurs as successive group programs are offered.

Unlike monitoring evaluations that are relatively easy for group workers to conduct, developmental evaluations are rather complex. They require careful thought, planning, and design by the worker. The steps for conducting a developmental evaluation are presented in the following list.

Steps in a Developmental Evaluation
- Identifying a need or problem
- Gathering and analyzing relevant data
- Developing a new group program or method
- Evaluating the new program or method
- Modifying the program or method on the basis of the data obtained

As shown in Figure 14.4, the process may be conducted several times as new group programs are offered and evaluated by the worker. Although developmental research

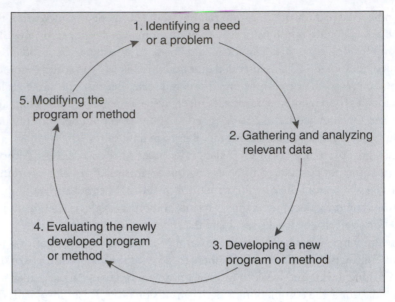

Figure 14.4
Steps in the Developmental Research Process

requires careful thought as well as time and energy, it yields improvements in programs and methods that can make group work practice more effective and more satisfying.

When developing and evaluating a new group program or a new group method, the worker can select from a variety of research designs, depending on the type of program or method being developed and the context in which the evaluation will occur. Single-system methods and case study methods are particularly useful for developmental evaluations. Although quasi-experimental design methods are also frequently used in developmental research, in this chapter the methods are described in relation to effectiveness and efficiency evaluations because they are also frequently used in evaluations of group outcomes (Thyer, 2012).

> ? Assess your understanding of evaluations for planning, developing, and monitoring a group by taking this brief quiz.

Single-System Methods

Single-system methods (often called single-subject designs) have been developed to evaluate data collected over time from a single system such as a group. They are included in the section on evaluations for developing a group because they are often used to get feedback on a new intervention, and less frequently on the effectiveness of a group work service. If a single-subject method determines that the new intervention is effective, this intervention can be evaluated in larger effectiveness or efficiency evaluations described later in this chapter.

The data obtained by using single-system designs may include information about a single group member or the group as a whole. Single-system methods compare data collected before, during, and after an intervention is made in the group. Information collected before an intervention is often called "baseline" data.

As shown in Figure 14.5, a change in level or in the slope of the data collected may occur after the intervention. Observations before and after the intervention are

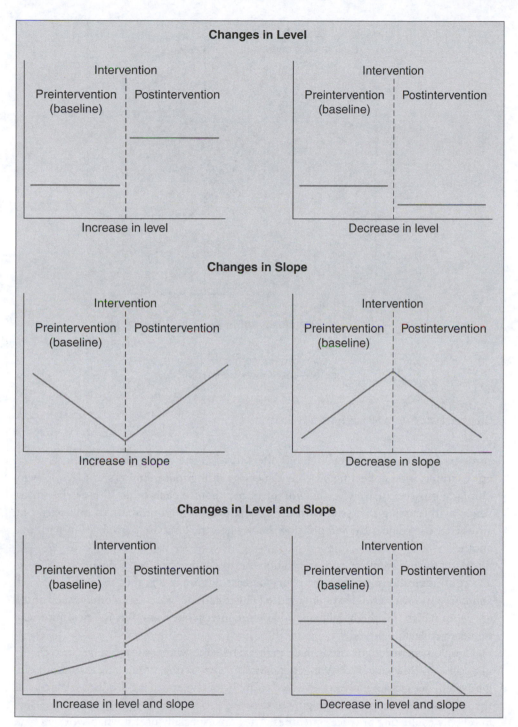

Figure 14.5
Changes in Baseline Data after an Intervention in a Group

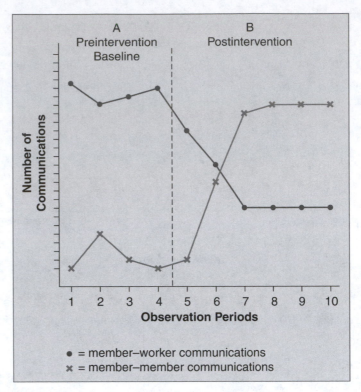

Figure 14.6
Graphed Data from a Single-System Evaluation

compared to see how the change has affected what the group worker is measuring. For example, after collecting baseline data and finding that members of a group were talking almost exclusively to the worker rather than to each other, the worker intervenes by discussing the issue with the group, prompting members to talk with one another more frequently, and praising them when they initiate conversation with one another.

After the intervention, communications between members and the worker decrease, and communications between members increase. Figure 14.6 graphs the results of such an intervention. The single-system method illustrated in Figure 14.6 is often called an *AB design*, in which A is the baseline period before intervention and B is the post-intervention data-collection period.

Single-system designs also include multiple baseline, withdrawal, reversal, and changing criterion (Macgowan & Wong, 2014; Smith, 2012; Wong, 2010). These types of single-system designs are more complicated to apply for the practicing group worker than is the AB baseline-intervention design, but they are also more effective than the AB design in reliably evaluating practice outcomes. They are especially useful when workers have the time, energy, interest, and resources to test the efficacy of a new or alternative intervention to improve practice. For additional information about single-system methods, see Bloom, Fisher, and Orme (2009); Kratochwill and Levin (2010); Mattaini (2010); Macgowan and Wong, (2014); Monette, Sullivan, DeJong, and Hilton (2014); Nugent (2010); Wong (2010).

Case Study Methods

Case studies rely on precise descriptions, accurate observations, and detailed analyses of a single example or case. Case studies were developed by researchers interested in qualitative research methods. Because group workers are accustomed to keeping records and analyzing their work in detail, these methods may have more appeal for some group workers than the quantitatively oriented, single-system research methods.

As with single-system methods, case study methods are based on intensive analysis of a single case. Therefore, the data collected may not be as internally or externally valid as data collected using classic control-group designs. Nevertheless, the strengths of case studies are that they can provide a clear, detailed, and vivid description of the processes and procedures of a group in action, and they are often more feasible to apply in practice settings than in control-group designs.

Case study methods include participant and nonparticipant observation, case comparison, ethnographic, focus groups, and narrative inquiry (Flyvbjerg, 2011; Kamberelis & Dimitriadis, 2013; Krueger, Richard, & Casey, 2015; Marshall & Rossman, 2011; Padgett, 2008; Stewart, 2014; Stewart & Shamdasani, 2015; Smith, 2012; Wells, 2011). The following example illustrates the use of case study methods.

Case Example   Using Case Study Methods

A group worker who was planning on leading a health and wellness group for cardiac patients found it useful to "sit in" on several other wellness groups conducted in the community. She obtained permission to observe several groups in hospital and nonhospital settings and was able to record some of these using a DVD. Using case study methods to analyze the content of the video recordings as well as her own notes made from observing each group, she concluded that most of the groups not only provided important education information, but also provided a strong sense of "universality" among members, that is, helping members to understand that they were not unique or alone in experiencing particular problems. She also concluded that members provided a strong component of mutual aid to each other in these groups. She used this information to develop a new group in her own setting.

Using a case comparison method, a worker who has developed a group program for alcoholics may want to compare the program with similar programs, perhaps those offered by Alcoholics Anonymous and a county alcoholism program. A comparison of the three programs along pre-specified dimensions created by the worker to answer specific information needs could lead to innovations in the worker's program. The worker may also want to conduct focus group interviews with individuals who have participated in each program to determine the most- and least-valued features of each program. These features could then be evaluated for their efficacy, as described in the process shown in Figure 14.4.

Group workers might also want to use case study methods in working with task groups. For example, a worker might want to use nonparticipant observation to compare the methods that other day-treatment mental health agencies use when reviewing clients in treatment-team meetings.

Both single-system methods and case study methods offer workers the opportunity to continually develop and improve their practice. Rigorous application of these methods may require that workers spend time designing and implementing evaluation methods and collecting data that are not routinely available. The worker must decide whether the extra effort spent in organizing and carrying out a developmental evaluation is worth the new or improved programs that may result.

Participatory Action Research Methods (PARS)

PARS is an approach to developing and monitoring groups that relies on a partnership between group workers and community stakeholders. All members of a PARS team are treated equally, with everyone having a voice in the development and implementation of the group work service. Group workers who use PARS follow three basic principles: (1) involve all stakeholders in the definition of the problem or goal and the way it will be addressed by the group work service, (2) implement the service while getting the highest quality feedback possible, and (3) use the feedback in an iterative cycle to improve the service as it continues in the field setting. To get the highest quality feedback possible, the worker may involve a researcher and use any number of quantitative or qualitative research methods. The worker and any researchers are treated as equal members of the team along with consumers, funders, and other stakeholders. PARS is consistent with social work values because it is dedicated to the full involvement of the consumers of the group work service, and to all other stakeholders. Like any other evaluation method, PARS faces obstacles, such as the active and full involvement of community stakeholders, especially when funding is not available for their participation. Nevertheless, it is a method that fits very well with the movement toward consumer-driven services and should be given serious consideration when developing a group work service, engaging community members in social action and coalition groups, and monitoring the impact of a group work service. For additional information about PARS see Chevalier and Buckles (2013); Lawson, Caringi, Pyles, Jurkowski, and Bozlak (2015); McNiff (2013); or Schneider (2014).

EVALUATIONS FOR DETERMINING EFFECTIVENESS AND EFFICIENCY

Effectiveness evaluations focus on the extent to which a group accomplishes its objectives. They give workers the opportunity to gain objective feedback about the helpfulness of the methods being used and the outcomes achieved. Efficiency evaluations compare the benefits of a group program with its cost. They attempt to place a monetary value on the outcomes of a group and to compare this cost with the costs incurred by conducting a group.

Effectiveness and efficiency evaluations rely on experimental and quasi-experimental designs, reliable and valid measures, and statistical procedures to determine the significance of an intervention on the outcome of task or treatment groups. Compared with the other types of evaluations mentioned in this chapter, effectiveness and efficiency evaluations are less flexible, more technically complex, and more difficult to conduct. Because of the nature of the methods employed and the precision and rigor necessary to apply them, a flexible and cooperative setting is needed to conduct effectiveness and efficiency evaluations. The sponsoring agency must be willing to supply the needed resources and the technical assistance necessary for conducting such evaluations.

One method for evaluating outcomes that is less difficult to apply than many other effectiveness evaluation methods is called *goal attainment scaling* (Kiresuk & Sherman, 1968; Kiresuk, Smith, & Cardillo, 1994; Turner-Stokes, 2009). Using this method, the worker can obtain information about the achievement of goals by individual group members or the group as a whole. An example of goal attainment scaling is shown in Figure 14.7.

Members and the group leader can work together to develop outcome measures for each scale level. For example, a group may decide that the most unfavorable outcome for the problem of depression is suicide. Similarly, the group may decide that the most favorable outcome for loss of appetite is to eat three meals a day and to snack between meals. After work on the problem areas is completed, goal attainment can be measured by using the scales that have been developed for each problem area. In the example in Figure 14.7, goal attainment is indicated by a box around the actual outcome. For the problem of anxiety, the outcome was one self-rated occurrence of feeling anxious each day. This outcome was given a score of 4.

As shown in Figure 14.7, it is possible to weigh each scale differentially so that attaining more important goals receives greater emphasis in the overall evaluation than does attaining less important goals. Thus, the goal attainment score of 4 obtained for the problem of anxiety is multiplied by its weight of 5 to yield a goal attainment score of 20. Even though the goal attainment score on the problem area of depression is a 3, after it is multiplied by its weight (25), the weighted goal attainment score for the problem of

Scale Levels	Problem Areas		
	Anxiety	Depression	Loss of Appetite
1. Most unfavorable expected outcome	Four or more self-rated occurrences of feeling anxious each day	Suicide	Refuses to eat any daily meals
2. Less than expected outcome	Three self-rated occurrences of feeling anxious each day	One or more attempts at suicide	Eats one meal each day
3. Expected outcome	Two self-rated occurrences of feeling anxious each day	No attempt at suicide, discusses feelings of depression	Eats two meal each day
4. More than expected outcome	One self-rated occurrence of feeling anxious each day	No attempt at suicide, discusses possible causes of depression	Eats three meals each day
5. Most favorable expected outcome	No self-rated occurrence of feeling anxious each day	No attempt at suicide, identifies two causes for depression	Eats three meals a day and snacks between meals
Weight	5	25	5
Goal Attainment Score	4	3	3
Weighted Goal Attainment Score	20	75	15

Figure 14.7
Example of Goal Attainment Scaling

depression (75) is much greater than that obtained on the problem of anxiety (20). Goal attainment scores on each scale can be added together to form a composite score for individual or group goal attainment.

Although goal attainment scaling has received some methodological criticism (Seaberg & Gillespie, 1977), the procedure remains an important tool for group workers to consider when conducting effectiveness evaluations.

A variation on goal attainment scaling that has been used successfully in several studies of the effectiveness of group treatment is the pressing problem index (Toseland, Labrecque, Goebel, & Whitney, 1992; Toseland et al., 2001; Toseland, McCallion, Smith, & Banks, 2004). During the intake interview, potential group members are asked to describe several problems they would like to work on in the group. These problems, plus any other problems known to commonly affect the individuals targeted for the intervention, are listed in an inventory of pressing problems. Before meeting and again at the end of the group, participants are asked to rate the stress caused by each pressing problem and their efficacy in coping with the problem. Change in stress and efficacy in coping with the pressing problems are assessed by adding up the responses to all pressing problems at each time of measurement.

Effectiveness evaluations rely on experimental and quasi-experimental designs to determine whether a group accomplishes its objectives. A true experimental design employs random assignment of participants to treatment and control groups. It compares the treatment and control groups on specific outcome variables to measure differences between treatment and control group subjects. In quasi-experimental designs, participants are not randomly assigned to treatment and control groups (Thyer, 2012). It is often difficult to assign subjects randomly to treatment and control groups in practice settings. Therefore, quasi-experimental designs are often used in effectiveness evaluations, even though they are subject to possible biases because non-randomly assigned subjects are more likely to be nonequivalent on important variables that may affect the outcome variables being measured.

It is especially difficult to conduct adequate effectiveness evaluations in group research projects. To do valid statistical analyses of data from experimental designs, the data collected from each member must be independent of any influence from other members. Researchers testing the effectiveness of group treatment sometimes assume that individual group members are the unit of analysis. However, individual members are not independent of one another in a group setting because they are affected by other members of the group. For example, while members are taking a questionnaire, a lawn mower might go past the window and disturb all members of the group. Members' scores are not totally independent of one another; that is, the lawn mower affects all members in some manner. One way to overcome this problem for individual outcomes such as a change in depression is to ensure that all evaluation instruments are given to group members on a one-to-one basis outside of the group meeting. However, when studying the effects of group processes such as cohesion, members' observations are not independent because cohesion affects all members in the same group in similar ways. The only solution to this problem is to use group level data from many groups, and treat the group rather than the individual member as the unit of analysis.

The requirement for independent observations is often violated by researchers interested in group-level phenomena, such as cohesion and leadership. Tasca, Illing, Ogrodniczuk, and Joyce (2009) have pointed out that some statistical procedures, such as analysis of variance (ANOVA), are not robust to this violation, which can lead to serious overestimates of the effectiveness of group procedures. Because there must be a relatively large number of units of analysis to obtain valid statistical comparisons of a group-level phenomenon, effectiveness evaluations of group work practice require that a relatively large number of groups be measured. Evaluating large numbers of groups is often difficult to do in practice settings because of the limitations on resources, group participants, and competent group leaders. For these reasons, alternatives to using the group as the unit of analysis have been proposed (Bonito, 2002; Brower, Arndt, & Ketterhagen, 2004; Magen, 2004; Tasca, Illing, Ogrodniczuk, & Joyce, 2009).

Efficiency evaluations can be complex and time-consuming, but they can also be useful to persons who want to assess whether their programs are cost-effective. For example, a nonprofit health agency employs a group worker to conduct a smoking-cessation group program. The worker conducts an effectiveness evaluation and finds that 60 percent of the group members became nonsmokers after the group program. The worker also collects data about the costs of the program and the costs to employers who have employees who smoke. These data provide the basis for the worker's efficiency evaluation.

Figure 14.8 shows the worker's calculations and illustrates that at a success rate of 50 percent, the smoking-cessation group program saves the employer $174 each year, beginning one year after the program ends. Savings to the employer last for as long as the employee remains with the company as a nonsmoker. Because the smoking-cessation program has a success rate of 60 percent, employers who have long-term employees

Costs of Smoking to the Employer per Employee per Year	
Insurance:	
Health	320.00
Fire	20.00
Workers' compensation and other accidents	0.00
Life and disability	35.00
Other:	
Productivity	189.00
Absenteeism	110.00
Smoking effects on nonsmokers	140.00
Total cost of smoking	$814.00
Per Employee Cost of the Smoking-Cessation Program	
Smoking-cessation program	$140.00
Employee time to complete the program	200.00
Total Cost for Each Employee	$340.00
Total Cost of Achieving One Nonsmoker	
(based on a projected success rate of 50%)	$680.00
Savings to Employers	
Total cost of smoking	$854.00
Total cost of the smoking-cessation program	−680.00
	$174.00

Figure 14.8
An Efficiency Evaluation of a Group Program for Smoking Cessation

are likely to save more than $174 each year for each employee who participates in the smoking-cessation program. This information would be helpful to the nonprofit health agency in motivating large employers whose workers' average length of employment exceeds one year to offer smoking-cessation group programs to their employees.

A description of the methodology for effectiveness evaluations can be found in Babbie (2015); Fraser, Richman, Galinsky, and Day (2009); Solomon, Cavanaugh, and Draine, (2009); or Rossi, Freeman, and Lipsey (2004), and a description of efficiency evaluations can be found in Drummond, Sculpher, Torrance, O'Brien, and Stoddart (2005) or Levin and McEwan (2001). Group workers should have a basic understanding of these methods to be able to assess the efficacy of their own practice and to be able to critically evaluate methodologies used in published reports about the effectiveness and efficiency of group work methods and group programs.

? Assess your understanding of evaluations for measuring effectiveness and efficiency in group practice by taking this brief quiz.

Ethical and Professional Behavior

Behavior: Use technology ethically and appropriately to facilitate practice outcomes

Critical Thinking Question: Group services should be evaluated. What parts of the *NASW Code of Ethics* require professional social workers to evaluate their practice?

EVALUATION MEASURES

The four broad types of evaluation methods provide a framework that workers can use to collect information for planning, monitoring, developing, or assessing the efficacy or efficiency of their practice with a group. In applying these methods, workers can choose from a variety of measures to collect the necessary information for an effective evaluation. Numerous measures have been developed for evaluating group work practice; some specifically focus on properties of the group as a whole, and others may be useful to the worker in evaluating changes in members of specific groups. Decisions about which measures to use depend on (1) the objectives of the evaluation, (2) properties of the measures being considered for use, (3) the form in which the data will be collected, and (4) what constructs will be measured.

Choosing Measures

The first and most essential step in choosing appropriate measures is to decide on the objectives of the evaluation. Clarifying the information that is needed, who will use the information, and what the information collected will be used for can help the worker choose the appropriate measures for the evaluation. For example, if the worker is interested in obtaining feedback from members about their satisfaction with a particular group, the worker may be less concerned about the reliability and validity of a measure than about the difficulties members might experience in providing the information. The worker may also be concerned about members' reactions to the evaluation and the time needed to administer it, particularly if the worker has a limited amount of group time available for conducting an evaluation.

The worker should be familiar with two properties of measures that govern the quality of the data to be collected. *Reliability* refers to the extent to which an instrument measures the same phenomenon in the same way each time the measure is used. A reliable measure is consistent. When measuring the same variable, it yields the same score each time it is administered. *Validity* refers to the extent to which a data-collection instrument measures what it purports to measure. A valid measure is one that yields a true or actual representation of the variable being measured. The ideal situation is for a group worker to use a reliable and valid measure that has already been constructed. When such measures exist, they are generally superior to measures developed quickly by the worker without regard to reliability or validity.

Constructing reliable and valid measures takes a considerable amount of time. Workers should decide what level of measurement precision and objectivity is needed when deciding how much time to spend constructing and validating a measure. For additional information about constructing reliable and valid measures, see, Rao and Sinharay (2007), or Salkind and Rasmussen (2007).

Another consideration in choosing appropriate evaluation measures is to decide what form of data collection would be most useful to the group worker and most convenient for group members. Data can be collected by interviewing members, by written response to a questionnaire, or by audio or video recordings. The data-collection form that will be most helpful to the worker depends on how the data will be used and the extent to which group members are willing and able to cooperate with the data-collection procedures used. In evaluating group work with children, older people, and disabled people, for example, audio and video recordings responses can overcome the difficulties that some individuals might have when asked to make written responses.

The worker must also decide how a particular property or concept will be measured. For example, after deciding that the objective of an evaluation is to test the effectiveness of a particular group, the worker must decide whether information is sought about changes in the behavior, cognition, or emotions of individual group members. In task groups, the worker may want to measure both the extent to which a group completes its tasks and the quality and the quantity of the products or tasks achieved.

When one conducts evaluations, it is often helpful to have multiple measures of the property being measured. When measuring the effectiveness of a group program for drug abusers, for example, the worker might want to measure reductions in drug intake, changes in self-concept, and changes in beliefs about the effects of drug abuse. Multiple measures, such as blood tests, attitude scales, and a questionnaire concerning information about drug use, might be useful in assessing the group's effectiveness in helping members become drug free.

Types of Measures

A wide variety of reliable and valid measures are available for group workers to use when they are evaluating individual outcomes for members of specific groups (Corcoran & Fischer, 2013; Kramer & Conoley, 1992; Sandano et al., 2014; Simmons & Lehmann, 2012). These sources include self-report measures, observational measures, and measures of the products of group interaction. In the description of each type of measure, the text indicates particular measures that have often been used in evaluations of group work.

Self-Report Measures

Perhaps the most widely used evaluation measures are written and oral self-reports, in which group members are asked to respond to questions about a particular phenomenon. Although they may focus on any phenomenon, self-report measures are particularly useful in measuring intrapersonal phenomena, such as beliefs or attitudes, that cannot be measured directly by observational measures. Group workers can also construct their own self-report measures for specialized situations in which no published self-report measures exist. However, it is difficult to construct a reliable and valid self-report measure. Fortunately, a variety of published self-report measures are available, including measures of anxiety, depression, assertiveness, self-concept, and locus of control. Six published measures that may be of particular interest to group workers are the (1) Group Atmosphere Scale (Silbergeld, Koenig, Manderscheid, Meeker, & Hornung, 1975), (2) Hemphill's Index of Group Dimensions (Hemphill, 1956), (3) Hill Interaction Matrix (Hill, 1977), (4) Curative Factors Scale (Lieberman, Yalom, & Miles, 1973; Stone, Lewis, & Beck, 1994), (5) Therapeutic Factors Inventory (Lese & MacNair-Semands, 2000), and (6) Group Engagement Scale (Macgowan, 2000).

The Group Atmosphere Scale (GAS) was designed to measure the psychosocial environment of therapy groups. It consists of 12 subscales: (1) aggression, (2) submission, (3) autonomy, (4) order, (5) affiliation, (6) involvement, (7) insight, (8) practicality, (9) spontaneity, (10) support, (11) variety, and (12) clarity. Each subscale contains 10 true-false items. The GAS has been assessed to have acceptable reliability and validity (Silbergeld et al., 1975).

Hemphill's Index of Group Dimensions measures 13 properties of groups: (1) autonomy, (2) control, (3) flexibility, (4) hedonic tone, (5) homogeneity, (6) intimacy, (7) participation, (8) permeability, (9) polarization, (10) potency, (11) stability, (12) stratification, and (13) viscidity. The measure consists of 150 items to which group members respond on a five-point scale from definitely true to mostly false.

The Hill Interaction Matrix is a self-report measure in which a group leader, a group member, or an observer responds to 72 items about group process. The measure is designed to discriminate between types of group interactions on two dimensions: the content discussed and the level and type of work occurring in the group.

Yalom's Curative Factors Scale is a widely used, 14-item measure that assesses 12 therapeutic dimensions in treatment groups: (1) altruism, (2) catharsis, (3) cohesiveness, (4) existentiality, (5) family re-enactment, (6) guidance, (7) hope, (8) identification, (9) interpersonal input, (10) interpersonal output, (11) self-understanding, and (12) universality. Stone, Lewis, and Beck (1994) have reported some psychometric properties of the instrument.

The original Therapeutic Factors Inventory is a 99-item scale that measures Yalom's (2005) therapeutic factors. It contains 11 subscales that measure (1) altruism, (2) catharsis, (3) cohesiveness, (4) corrective enactment of the primary family group, (5) development of socializing techniques, (6) existential factors, (7) imitative behavior, (8) imparting information, (9) instillation of hope, (10) interpersonal learning, and (11) universality. The scale has been updated and now includes only 19 items (Sodano et al., 2014), and research is ongoing (see, for example, Kivlighan & Kivlighan, 2014).

The Group Environment Scale (GES) is another instrument for measuring group conditions (Moos, 1986). The GES is a 90-item true-false measure that consists of three domains: relationship, personal growth, and system maintenance/system change. The relationship domain measures cohesion, leader support, and expressiveness. The personal growth domain measures independence, leader support, and expressiveness. The system maintenance/system change domain measures order and organization, leader control, and innovation. Data are provided on the reliability and validity of the scale which has been used with 148 task and treatment groups (Moos, 1986).

Macgowan (2000) has also developed the Groupwork Engagement Measure (GEM), which is conceptualized as measuring seven dimensions: (1) attendance, (2) contributing, (3) relating to the worker, (4) relating to members, (5) contracting, (6) working on one's own problems, and (7) working on others' problems (Macgowan & Levenson, 2003). The GEM has 37 items scored on five-point scales from 1 ("rarely or none of the time") to 5 ("most or all of the time"). The psychometric properties of the GEM have been established in several studies (Macgowan, 1997, 2000; Macgowan & Levenson, 2003; Macgowan & Newman, 2005).

Observational Measures

Unlike self-report measures that rely on the accuracy of a respondent's memory, observational measures use independent, objective observers to collect data as they occur or as they are replayed from video or audio recordings. Although observational measures are less susceptible to biases and distortions than are self-report measures, observational measures are used less frequently than self-report measures because they require the availability of one or more trained observers to collect the data. The observers code discrete group interactions into categories that are mutually exclusive and exhaustive; that is, during each observation period, only one observation is recorded, and it can be recorded in only one category.

The most well-known observational measure for groups is called Bales' Interaction Process Analysis (Bales, 1950). This observational index consists of 12 categories. Interactions are coded by assigning each person a number. For example, when an interaction occurs from member 1 to member 4 or from member 3 to member 1, the interaction is marked 1-4 or 3-1 in the appropriate category. With well-trained observers, Bales' Interaction Process Analysis can be a useful tool for the evaluation of group interactions.

Bales (1980) and Bales, Cohen, and Williamson (1979) have developed a measure called Systematic Multiple Level Observation of Groups (SYMLOG). As explained in Chapter 8, SYMLOG is a method for analyzing the overt and covert behaviors of group members. With SYMLOG, a three-dimensional graphic presentation or field diagram of the interaction of group members is made. Through the field diagram, group members can analyze the way they interact with one another to improve the ability of the group to accomplish its tasks. An example of the use of SYMLOG for assessing group functioning can be found in Chapter 8. As an evaluation tool, SYMLOG can be used to measure several variables affecting both the socio-emotional and the task aspects of members' behavior in groups.

Other observational measures have also been used for evaluating changes in a group over time. For example, Moreno's (1934) scales of sociometric choice and sociometric preference, described more fully in Chapter 8, assess relationships among members of a group by having each member rank other members on certain dimensions, such as their preference for working with other group members or their liking for other group members.

Products of Group Interaction

A worker may be able to measure the products of group interaction in a simple and straightforward manner. In task groups, products of the group's work are often tangible. For example, a team may develop a written document that governs how services will be delivered to clients. The work of a delegate council may be evaluated by the number of agenda items it acts on during its monthly meeting. In both instances, group products can be used for purposes of evaluation. In treatment groups, products of group inter-action may also be useful measures. Rose (1989) suggests that measurable products of group interaction include behavior change, the number of between-meeting tasks gener-ated at a group meeting, and the number of tasks actually completed.

Evaluation measures from which workers can choose when evaluating their practice with a group range from measures consisting of a few open-ended questions made by a worker who wants to get some feedback from group members to sophisticated observa-tional measures requiring highly trained observers. Workers develop or select measures in relation to the evaluation design they are going to use and, ulti-mately, in relation to the information they hope to obtain. Although selecting appropriate measures and implementing effective evaluations is time-consuming for the practicing group worker, it is often well worth the effort because it may result in improved service and in new and innovative group programs.

> **?** Assess your under-standing of evaluation measures appropriate to group work practice by taking this brief quiz.

Case Example

Despite telling his group work students always to monitor and evaluate their practice with groups, Bob knew that they would be caught in the classic practitioner's dilemma. The demands of service delivery would make it difficult for them to spend the time and resources needed to formally evaluate their work with groups. He was surprised, however, when a former student returned with good news about research funding and a request for help. Maureen had been awarded a demonstration grant of $5,000 to develop an evaluation of her violence reduction group. In addition, the state's education department suggested that if her research project was successful, Maureen could apply for a much larger grant to implement and evaluate additional groups. She hoped that Bob could give her some helpful ideas for a research design.

Maureen's violence reduction group was aimed at sensitizing elementary students to the types of violence in their school environment and helping them find nonviolent ways of behaving. It had an educational component that consisted of a series of standardized lessons about violence. In addition, it had a growth component in which members learned new ways of handling themselves when confronted with anger from their peers.

Based on her conversations with Bob, Maureen decided to use the Achenbach Child Behavior Checklist (Achenbach, 1991) in her evaluation because it had been found to be a reliable and valid measure of children's behavior by researchers who had examined its psycho-metric properties. Although there is both a parent and a teacher version of the Achenbach Child Behavior Checklist, she decided to use only the parent form because she was concerned that teachers were too busy to spend the time to fill out the form for each student involved in the project. Instead, she designed a short questionnaire aimed at collecting feedback from teachers about students' behaviors in the classroom.

Maureen decided to use a partial-crossover control group design to evaluate the impact of the group. She would start a new group from the waiting list and use some of the students who were still on the waiting list as a control group. In a partial-crossover design, after the intervention is conducted with the experimental group, the control group is then offered the intervention.

Although the design would provide good information about the effectiveness of the group, it posed several ethical issues. First, Maureen had to secure written permission from the parents of the children who would participate in both the experimental and control groups. Second, Maureen had to discuss and justify the use of the waiting list as a control group with the children's parents and with school administrators. Confidentiality and volun-tary participation were also issues. As a result of her discussions with students, parents, and administrators, Maureen secured permission to proceed with the research.

To help ensure the equivalence of the experimental and control groups, Maureen randomly assigned students on the waiting list to either of the two groups. When the groups were composed, she asked the parents of children in both groups to fill out the behavior checklist. This measurement served as a pretest for both the experimental and control groups and provided important baseline information. She triangulated these data with information obtained from teachers who filled out the short questionnaire she had developed. Maureen then conducted the violence reduction sessions with the experimental group. At the end of the group, she again administered the Achenbach checklist to parents of children in the experimental and control groups and again collected data from teachers. She then compared the pretest and posttest results for both groups. Students in the experimental group achieved positive movement on their checklist scores whereas scores for the control group members did not change significantly. Using the control group scores as a second pretest, Maureen then ran the violence reduction group for the members of the control group. Posttest scores for this crossover group were significantly higher than their pretest scores.

The parents of students who participated in Maureen's violence reduction groups reported fewer incidents of acting out behavior of a violent nature, especially related to school. In addition, teachers reported that students who participated in the violence reduction groups had more control over their feelings of anger and used more positive measures for mediating their personal disputes in the classroom.

Maureen spent a good deal of time preparing a final report on her research project. She made sure to document both the results of her findings as well as the nature of the intervention that took place within the violence reduction groups. School administrators were pleased at the outcome of her evaluation efforts. With a sense of pride and gratefulness, Maureen sent a copy of the final report to her former research teacher with a note of thanks for helping her with the project. She later learned that her research report was the highlight of the state education department's review panel's deliberations on funding new initiatives aimed at reducing violence in schools.

SUMMARY

Evaluation is the method by which practitioners obtain information and feedback about their work with a group. In the current age of accountability and fiscal constraints by which difficult program choices are made, evaluation methodologies are useful tools for practitioners. This chapter discusses some reasons that group workers may choose to use evaluation methods in their practice.

Practitioners are often faced with a dilemma when considering whether to evaluate their practice. They must decide whether the demands of serving clients are compatible with developing and conducting evaluations. This chapter describes the strengths and weaknesses of a number of evaluation methods that may be used in differing practice situations and settings.

Four broad types of evaluation methods are evaluations for (1) planning a group, (2) monitoring a group, (3) developing a group, and (4) testing the effectiveness and efficiency of a group. These methods are used with a variety of evaluation measures to help practitioners develop, test, and implement more effective group work methods. Evaluation methods can also be combined with knowledge accumulated from practice experiences (sometimes referred to as *practice wisdom*) to improve the methods used by group workers to meet a variety of needs in diverse practice settings.

Standards for Social Work Practice with Groups[1]

Association for the Advancement of Social Work with Groups, Inc., an International Professional Organization (AASWG)

PURPOSE

These Standards represent the perspective of the Association for the Advancement of Social Work with Groups, Inc., on the value, knowledge, and skill base essential for professionally sound and effective social work practice with groups and are intended to serve as a guide to social work practice with groups.

INTRODUCTION

The Standards focus on central distinguishing concepts of social work with groups and highlight the unique perspective that social group workers bring to practice. By design, the Standards are general rather than specific and descriptive rather than prescriptive. They are applicable to the wide range of groups encountered by social group workers in a variety of practice settings. These groups include, among others, treatment, support, psycho-educational, task, and community action groups. The Standards draw heavily on the Code of Ethics from the National Association of Social Work (United States), group theory from the social sciences, knowledge of individuals and the environment, the historical roots of social group work practice, current practice with groups, and practice research. Thus, they are based on practice wisdom, theories of group work practice, and empirical evidence. They emphasize the understanding and use of group processes and the ways members help one another to accomplish the purposes of the group. The role of the worker, as articulated in the Standards, reflects the values of the social work profession generally as well as the unique features associated with social work with groups.

Overview of the Standards

Various comprehensive perspectives of social work practice provide a broad underpinning of the values and knowledge bases of social group workers' practice. Values and types of knowledge that have particular relevance for group work practice are addressed in Section I. Sections II through IV identify the required knowledge and major worker

Source: Reprinted with the permission of AASWG.

tasks and skills in each of the phases of group work practice, from planning to ending. These sections are structured around the understanding, also, that groups change and evolve over time, thus requiring changes in the worker's tasks and responsibilities. For example, certain worker actions enable group members to start to work together in a new group; other actions enable members who have already developed relationships to engage in work to achieve the purpose of the group. Thus, as the groups develop, the nature of the workers' responsibilities will change.

The stages and the associated tasks described in these Standards are guides for practice. They represent the wisdom that has been acquired from practice, theory, and research. However, each group is unique, and practitioners must apply these standards in terms of their appropriateness for each group and its particular members.

Section V examines ethical considerations for social group work practice.

SECTION I CORE VALUES AND KNOWLEDGE

The group worker should understand the history of group work and the evolving visions of group workers as they face the challenges posed by each historical era. During this evolution, the following values emerged as those that are essential to the practice of group work.

A. Core Values

1. **Respect for persons and their autonomy.** In view of the equality of persons, people are to be treated with respect and dignity. In group deliberations no one person should be more privileged in a group than other persons, not a worker, a group member, nor the agency director. In a group this occurs when a worker helps each member to appreciate the contributions of the other members so that everyone's ideas are heard and considered. This principle is stated while recognizing that the worker, by virtue of his or her position in the agency and his or her expertise, is likely to have a great deal of influence. This requires the worker to use his or her influence prudently and transparently.

   A major implication of this principle is a respect for and a high value placed on diversity in all of its dimensions, such as culture, ethnicity, gender, sexual orientation, physical and mental abilities, and age.

2. **The creation of a socially just society.** The group offers an opportunity to live and practice the democratic principles of equality and autonomy, and the worker should use his/her knowledge and skills to further this. The worker should be mindful of the quest for a society that is just and democratically organized, one that ensures that the basic human needs of all its members are met. This value is presented to the group whenever this is appropriate and reinforced when members articulate it.

B. Core Knowledge

There are special areas of knowledge that enable group workers to more ably serve the group. This includes knowledge of the history and mission of our profession as it impacts group work with poor people, minorities, and other disenfranchised people. Understanding when group work is the practice of choice is important. The skills needed to carry out the professional mission emerge from our values and knowledge and requires specialized education.

1. **Knowledge of Individuals**

   a. The nature of individual human growth and behavior, utilizing a bio-psycho-social perspective and a "person in environment" view. The forces impacting the person and the group are important factors in group work assessment and intervention. This includes viewing the member in the context of the group and of the community.

   b. The familial, social, political, and cultural contexts that influence members' social identities, interactional styles, concerns, opportunities, and the attainment of their potentials.

   c. The capacity of members to help one another and to change.

   d. The capacity of members to contribute to social change in the community beyond the group.

   e. Competency-based assessment.

   f. The group worker places an emphasis on members' strengths, in addition to their concerns. The worker also must understand protective and risk factors that affect individuals' need for services and their ability to act.

   g. The worker has an appreciation and understanding of such differences as those due to culture, ethnicity, gender, age, physical and mental abilities, and sexual orientation among members and between members and him/herself that may influence practice.

2. **Knowledge of Groups and Small Group Behavior**

   a. The worker understands that the group is an entity separate and distinct from the individual members. The group has its own dynamics, culture, and other social conditions.

   b. The worker understands that the group consists of multiple helping relationships, so that members can help one another to achieve individual goals and pursue group goals. This is often referred to as "mutual aid."

   c. The democratic process in groups occurs as the members evolve a sense of "ownership" of the group in which each member's contribution to the group is solicited and valued.

   d. The group can develop in such a way that members, individually and collectively, are empowered to act on their own behalf as well as on behalf of the group.

   e. Groups can develop goals that members are committed to pursuing. These goals may be for individual member growth, group development, and/or social change.

   f. Group members as well as the group-as-a-whole can seek changes in the social environment.

   g. The phases of group development influence change throughout the life of the group.

   h. Group processes and structures encompass all transactions that occur within the group and give meaningfulness to the life of the group. These consist of such conditions as roles, norms, communications, the expression of affect, and the nature of interaction patterns. These shape and influence individual member behavior as well as the development of the group and also determine whether and how the group will accomplish its purposes. The members can come to understand how group processes and structures shape and influence both individual member behavior as well as the development of the group.

i. Groups are formed for different purposes and goals (e.g., education problem solving, task accomplishment, personal change, social action), and this influences what the worker does and how the group accomplishes its goals, as well as the nature of the contract between the worker and members, among the members, and between the group and the sponsoring organization.

3. **Knowledge of the Function of the Group Worker**

a. The worker promotes individual and group autonomy.

b. The worker helps the group members to select means of achieving individual and group purposes.

c. The worker's assessments and interventions are characterized by flexibility, sensitivity, and creativity.

d. The worker should have a clear understanding of the stages of group development and the related group character, members' behaviors and tasks, and worker tasks and skills that are specific to each stage.

e. Practice should be based on currently available knowledge and research and represent contemporary practice principles.

f. The worker has responsibility for ongoing monitoring and evaluation of the success of the group in accomplishing its objectives through personal observation, as well as collecting information in order to assess outcomes and processes. The worker seeks the involvement of the members in the process of evaluation. Specifically, this means that members should be involved in evaluation of outcomes throughout the life of the group. Workers should systematically evaluate the achievement of goals. The worker should be knowledgeable about methods of evaluation of group work and ways of measuring or otherwise determining the accomplishment of group and individual goals. The worker should use all available evidence regarding effectiveness of particular interventions for different kinds of groups.

g. The worker should maintain appropriate records of group processes and outcomes and ensure the confidentiality of these.

h. The worker should have a commitment to supporting research on group work and to disseminating knowledge about effective practices through professional meetings, education, and scholarship.

i. The worker adheres to professional, ethical, and legal requirements generally associated with social work practice as well as those specifically associated with social work with groups. The worker seeks to prevent any action in the group that may harm any member.

j. Workers should have a commitment to engage in reflective practice in which they assess their own practice and seek supervision and/or consultation in order to enhance their practice.

SECTION II PRE-GROUP PHASE: PLANNING, RECRUITMENT, AND NEW GROUP FORMATION

A. Tasks and Skills

1. The worker should identify aspirations and needs of potential group members as perceived by members, worker, and agency.

2. The worker should obtain organizational support for and affirmation of the group.

3. The worker should select the group type, structure, processes, and size that will be appropriate ones for attaining the purposes of the group.

4. The worker should reach out to and recruit potential group members.

5. The worker should obtain consent from potential members and relevant others as required by ethical guidelines and organizational requirements.

6. The worker should clarify potential group members' goals and expectations of the group work service and use this information to assess prospective members' potential investments in the pursuit of group goals. The worker should help members specify these goals in terms that can lead to the determination of their attainment.

7. The worker should establish an appropriate meeting place and meeting time that will be conducive to members' comfort, safety, and access to the group.

8. The worker should prepare members for the group in ways that are appropriate. This will differ depending on the extent to which the group is intended to attain individual goals or to accomplish task purposes in the agency and community. The worker should be empathic in identifying members' feelings and reactions to joining the group.

9. The worker should know how to select members for the group in relationship to principles of group composition, although this principle may not apply to some task groups in which other bodies determine the group's membership.

10. The worker should develop a clear statement of group purpose that reflects member needs and agency mission and goals. This is often done cooperatively with the group members.

11. The worker should consider potential contextual, environmental, and societal impacts on the group.

12. The worker, as appropriate, should explain group purposes and processes to non-members, such as other agency personnel, relevant community entities, and parents or referring agencies in the case of groups promoting individual change.

13. The worker should consider issues of group content as well as the use of activities, supplies needed, and resources.

14. The worker should identify methods that will be used to track group progress (e.g., group progress notes, formal and informal evaluations).

15. After each session, the worker should debrief and plan with the co-facilitator (if there is one) and arrange for consultation and/or supervision on a regular basis. If there is a co-facilitator, they should consider together the implications of their similarities and differences with respect to such issues as approaches, styles, and communication.

B. **Required Knowledge**

1. Organizational mission and function and how these influence the nature and development of the group work service.
2. Social and institutional barriers that may impact the development of group work service.
3. How to assess the impact on the group of the community and agency context.
4. Issues associated with group composition (e.g., gender, education, socio-economic status, previous group experience, occupation, race, ethnicity, age, and presenting problems).
5. The influence of cultural factors on potential members' lives and their ways of engaging in group interactions and relationships with others, the agency, and the worker.
6. The importance of diversity in relationship to how a group attains its goals.
7. The theoretical approaches utilized by group workers and how to select those most appropriate and effective for the proposed group.
8. Issues associated with group structure (e.g., group size, length of sessions, duration of the group, meeting place, open or closed to new members, resources, supplies, and transportation).
9. The impact of human development/life cycle factors on potential members' needs and abilities and group goals.
10. Types of groups, such as task groups, treatment groups, psycho-educational groups, socio-recreational groups, and their applicability to individual, organizational, and community needs.
11. Issues related to group content, such as discussion processes, and purposeful use of activities and simulations. Such issues include how these kinds of content are affected by stage of group development, capacities of members, and the purposes of the group.
12. Contracting procedures including the identification and clarification of group purpose and behavioral standards and norms needed to actualize group goals as determined by potential members, the worker, and the agency.
13. Recruitment procedures, such as community outreach and referral processes.
14. How to identify and develop resources required for group functioning.
15. Group monitoring and evaluation procedures (e.g., group progress notes, pretest-posttest measures, questionnaires) to track worker interventions, group progress, and the group work service.
16. The importance of consultation and supervision in enhancing the quality of group work service.

SECTION III GROUP WORK IN THE BEGINNING PHASE

A. **Tasks and Skills**

1. **Task: Establishing a Beginning Contract** The worker and members collaboratively develop a beginning contract for work that identifies tasks to be

accomplished, goals to be achieved, and the process by which the work is to occur. The worker identifies the community's and/or agency's stakes in the group, the group purpose and process, and clarifies worker and member roles. Confidentiality and limits thereof are clearly identified. The worker assists members in identifying and clarifying individual goals and group goals. The worker helps the members to link individual goals with group purposes. The worker invites full participation of all members and solicits member feedback on the progress of the group. The worker employs special skills in working with mandated members and understands the impact on group dynamics of member's mandated status.

2. **Task: Cultivating Group Cohesion** The worker establishes rapport with individual members and the group as a whole. The worker also aids the group members in establishing relationships with one another so as to promote group cohesion. The worker highlights member commonalities, links members to one another, and encourages direct member-to-member communication.

3. **Task: Shaping Norms of Participation** The worker seeks to aid the group in establishing norms for participation that promote safety and trust, facilitate a culture of work, and cultivate mutual aid. The worker is active in modeling these norms and instructing members when needed about productive group participation. The worker appreciates the impact of various psychological, sociocultural, and environmental forces on these norms. The worker promotes group exploration of nonproductive norms when these arise. The worker demonstrates respect for sociocultural differences, promotes autonomy and self-determination, and encourages member empowerment.

B. Required Knowledge

1. An understanding of the dynamic interaction between the community, agency, group, and individual members of the group with which he/she is working.
2. The relevant theories and evidence-based practices regarding the developmental, psychosocial, and clinical needs of the group members and how this informs beginnings.
3. The group type and technology being employed and the ways such may impact group functioning in the beginning stage.
4. The characteristics and needs of the beginning stage of group development and the related skills. Knowledge is needed regarding such variations as working with mandated members, replacing a previous worker, and receiving new members into an ongoing group.

SECTION IV GROUP WORK IN THE MIDDLE PHASE

A. Group Tasks and Worker Skills/Actions:

1. Task: Assist group to make progress on individual and group goals. When group goals are a major focus, as in task and community groups, the worker encourages individual members to use their skills in pursuit of group goals.

Skills/Actions:

a. Reinforce the connection between individual concerns/needs and group goals.

b. Offer programmatic ideas and activities that support group purpose and assist in helping members achieve individual and group goals.

c. Assess progress toward individual and group goals.

d. Identify difficulties and obstacles that interfere with the group and its members' abilities to reach their goals.

e. If obstacles are related to the specific needs of an individual member, when appropriate offer individual time, outside of group.

f. Ensure that the group has attended to any special needs of individual members (e.g., physical, cognitive, language, or cultural needs).

g. Assist members to engage in problem solving, in making choices and decisions, and in evaluating potential outcomes of decisions.

h. Summarize sessions with the group.

i. Plan next steps with the group.

j. Re-contract with members, if needed, to assist in achieving individual and group goals.

2. **Task: Attend to Group Dynamics/Processes**

Skills/Actions:

a. Support members to develop a system of mutual aid.

b. Clarify and interpret communication patterns among members, between members and worker, and between the group and systems outside the group.

c. Model and encourage honest communication and feedback among members and between members and workers.

d. Review group values and norms.

e. Assist members to identify and articulate feelings.

f. Assist members to perceive verbal and nonverbal communication.

g. Help members mediate conflict within the group.

h. Assist members to make connections with other group members that may continue after the group ends, if this is appropriate.

i. Use tools of empowerment to assist members to develop "ownership" of the group.

Tasks:

1. Assist members to identify and access resources from inside and outside the group.

2. Includes knowledge, skills, and other resources of group worker, group members, and sources outside the group.

3. Ensure that workers are using the best possible practice techniques in facilitating the group.

Skills/Actions:

1. Use group approaches appropriate to the populations served and the tasks undertaken as demonstrated in the literature, worker and agency experience, and other sources of professional knowledge.

2. Use record-keeping techniques to monitor leadership skills and group process.
3. Access and use supervision.

B. Required Knowledge

1. Group dynamics.
2. Role theory and its application to members' relationships with one another and the worker.
3. Communication theory and its application to verbal and nonverbal interactions within the group and between the group and others external to the group.
4. Problem-solving processes in groups.
5. Conflict resolution in groups.
6. Organizational theories.
7. Community theories.
8. Developmental theories.
9. Evaluation theories and methods.
10. The impact of diversity: class, race, gender, sexual orientation, and ability status.
11. Knowledge about the group's relations with its environment.
12. Specific knowledge of issue being addressed in the group.
13. Awareness of self.

SECTION V GROUP WORK IN THE ENDING PHASE

A. Tasks and Skills

1. Prepare members for the group's ending in advance.
2. In a direct practice group, help members identify gains they have made and changes that have resulted from their participation in the group. In a task group, members may discuss what they have learned from this experience that will be useful to them in other task groups. This involves a consideration of how achieving group goals will contribute to the functioning of the organization and/or community.
3. Discuss the impact of the group on systems outside of the group (e.g., family, organization, community).
4. Discuss the movement the group has made over time.
5. Identify and discuss direct and indirect signs of members' reactions to ending.
6. Share worker's feelings about ending with the group.
7. Assist members in sharing their feelings about ending with one another and with the worker.
8. Systematically evaluate the achievement of individual and group goals. Routine and systematic evaluation of the group experience could/should occur over time rather than in the ending stage alone.
9. Help members make connections with other agencies and programs as appropriate.
10. Assist members in applying new knowledge and skills to their daily lives.

11. Encourage members to give feedback to the worker on the worker's role and actions in the group.

12. Help members apply new knowledge and skills to their activities outside of the group.

13. Prepare record material about the group for the agency, for individual members, and for referrals as needed.

B. Required Knowledge

1. Group dynamics related to endings. These will be different depending on the type of group (e.g., long-term, short-term, open-ended, single-session). There are also special issues when a member or worker ends the group but parts of the group continue or there is a new worker.

2. Formal and informal resources that maintain and enhance members' growth.

3. Influence of past losses and separation in lives of members and the worker on endings.

4. Agency policies related to worker maintaining connections following the ending of a group or member service.

5. Various forms of evaluation, formal and informal, and of evaluation measures, both qualitative and quantitative.

SECTION VI ETHICAL CONSIDERATIONS

National and/or regional social work organizations typically have codes of ethics to which social workers must adhere. For example, social group workers in the United States of America are expected to be knowledgeable about and responsive to the ethical mandates of the social work profession, as explicated in the National Association of Social Workers (NASW) Code of Ethics. While the entire code is important, some items have particular relevance to social group work.

Similarly, Canadian social workers must follow the Canadian Association of Social Workers Code of Ethics (2005). The expectation of AASWG is that social workers will respect the code of ethics relevant to their locations of practice wherever in the world that may be as long as it is respectful of all persons.

Other social work ethical guides exist and may be more relevant for specific countries. Each needs to be considered in the context of work with groups and may call for some modifications or additions that reflect the unique situations of group work.

A. Elements of Ethical Practice in Social Group Work

1. Knowledge of and use of best practices that reflect the state of the art; knowledge of research evidence regarding social work with groups.

2. A basic discussion with prospective members of informed consent and an explanation of what group work offers and requires of the members individually and as a group.

3. Maximizing member choice and minimizing coercive processes by members or worker to the extent possible. Emphasizing member self-determination and empowerment of the group.

4. Discussion of the importance, limits, and implications of privacy and confidentiality with the members.
5. Helping the group maintain the purposes for which it was formed, allowing for changes as mutually agreed upon.
6. Helping each member as required within the parameters of the group's purpose, including individual meetings when appropriate.
7. Clarifying the decision-making process.
8. Clarifying how members may be chosen for or excluded from the group.
9. Maintaining group records and storing them in a secure location.

B. Ethical Issues in the Use of New Techniques

As new techniques are used, such as those based on electronic communications, workers should pay attention to ethical issues, practice skills, and knowledge and evaluation of these techniques. The following is a general statement with reference to electronic communications:

Increasingly, practice with groups of all kinds is being done by utilizing technologies, such as computer and telephone facilities. Professional associations are assessing both effectiveness and ethical issues.

Issues such as member interaction, decision-making, group structure, mutual aid, and, particularly, confidentiality are of vital concern.

Worker competency may require new skills and knowledge, not only in technology use, but also in communication techniques.

Clearly these technologies are likely to be extremely valuable for all persons seeking resources, as well as for the profession's ability to share information about practice including emerging approaches. In the meantime, workers contemplating their use should consider the appropriate codes of ethics as a guide and document all of their processes related to such work.

NOTES

1. The terms "social group work," "social work with groups," and "group work" are used interchangeably in these Standards.
2. In the NASW Code current at the time of approval of these Standards, these sections include the Preamble and Ethical Principles 1.01, 1.02, 1.05 1.06, 1.07, 2.06, 3.02, 3.07, 3.09, and 4.01.

REFERENCES

National Association of Social Workers (approved 1996, revised 1999) Code of Ethics for Social Workers, Washington, DC: NASW.
Canadian Association of Social Workers/Association Canadienne des
Travailleuses Sociaux (2005) Code of Ethics, Ottawa. CASW/ACTS.
January 2006, first printing
July 2006, second printing

Group Announcements

SUPPORT GROUP FOR NEW PARENTS

You are invited to join a support group of parents who have children from ages 6 months to 2 years. The group will discuss concerns identified by its members including such possible issues as infant care, sharing household responsibilities, disciplining your child, toilet training, and child-care resources.

Sponsor

Greenwich Community Mental Health Center
49 Cambridge Avenue
Greenwich, NY
(212) 246-2468

Group Leaders

George Oxley, ACSW, clinic director
Marybeth Carol, BSW, clinic social worker

Membership

Open to all parents with children from ages 6 months to 2 years

Dates and Times

March–April–May, Thursday evenings from 7:30 to 9:30 P.M.

Child Care

Parents are encouraged to bring their children to the center. Child care will be available from human service interns of Hudson Center Community College.

Cost

Enrollment fee for the three-month group, total $90.00 per couple, payable monthly
For further information, call Mr. Oxley or Ms. Carol at (212) 246-2468.

YOUTH CENTER INTEREST MEETING

The residents of the Johnsonville, Pittstown, and Valley Falls area are invited to discuss the proposed establishment of a youth center for these communities. Issues to be discussed include cost of service, fundraising, need for service, and support for such a service.

Sponsor

Rensselaer Council of Community Services

Meeting Place

Johnsonville Firehouse

Date and Time

Thursday, March 25, from 7 to 9 P.M.

Further Information

Call Jim Kesser, ACSW
(212) 241-2412

Refreshments will be served.

Outline for a Group Proposal
Treatment/Task

Abstract

Short statement summarizing major points of group

Purpose

Brief statement of purpose
How the group will conduct its work
Job description of the worker

Agency Sponsorship

Agency name and mission
Agency resources (physical facilities, financial, staff)
Geographic and demographic data on agency

Membership

Specific population for the group
Why population was chosen

Recruitment

Methods to be used

Composition

Criteria for member inclusion/exclusion
Size, open or closed group, demographic characteristics

Orientation

Specific procedures to be used

Contract

Number, frequency, length, and time of meeting

Environment

Physical arrangements (room, space, materials)
Financial arrangements (budget, expense, income)
Special arrangements (child care, transportation)

An Example of a Treatment Group Proposal

ADOLESCENT DISCHARGE GROUP

The Children's Refuge Home

Abstract

This is a proposal for a social skills training group for adolescents who are about to be released into the community from the Children's Refuge Home.

Purpose

The group will discuss what each member expects to be doing on release to the community. The group will reinforce social learning that has taken place during the residential placement and will help members learn new social skills that will be needed to successfully relate to parents, siblings, teachers, and employers. Role playing, behavior rehearsal modeling, and reinforcement will be employed as methods of teaching social skills.

Agency Sponsorship

The Children's Refuge Home (CRH), a residential treatment facility for delinquent youth, serves teenage boys who cannot live at home because of law-breaking activities. About 200 boys reside here in 15 cottages. The agency has a 200-acre campus with an on-campus school. Staff ratio is about one staff member per four boys; direct-care staff include child-care workers, social workers, nursing staff, psychologists, psychiatrists, and clergy.

Membership

Approximately 10 boys are released to the community each month. The discharge group will be composed from a population of boys for whom discharge is planned within the next three months.

Recruitment

Because this group represents a new service for the institution, members will be recruited by asking cottage parents for volunteers from their respective cottages. An announcement will be printed and delivered to the senior cottage parents for all cottages. In addition, teachers and social workers will be contacted to suggest possible candidates for the group.

Composition

The group will be composed of six to eight boys from 12 to 14 years of age who antici-pate discharge from CRH within the next three months. In addition, this first group will include only children who will be returning to natural parents or relatives rather than to foster care or group homes. The group will be closed and will not add new members because it is important that social skills be learned in a gradual and cumulative fashion.

Orientation

Each member will be interviewed by the leaders. During this interview, the members will view a video on group treatment for children, and the details of the tape will be dis-cussed to demonstrate how group meetings will be conducted.

Environment

The ideal location for this group is the diagnostic classroom within the campus school. Proximity to video recording equipment is necessary so group members can record and view role plays. A small budget is required ($120) for proposed field trips, for charts and materials for listing skills and posting individual and group progress, and for refreshments after meetings. Additional expenses include two color DVD's ($60). Special arrangements will have to be made so that each member's afterschool recreation schedule is free for Monday afternoon meeting times.

An Example of a Task Group Proposal

TASK FORCE ON RESEARCH UTILIZATION IN PROBATION

Abstract

This is a proposal for establishing an interagency task force to study how research and research procedures are used in three county probation offices. The group will issue a report with recommendations for increasing research use in probation settings.

Purpose

This group will be formed to study the use of research in county probation offices. The group will meet to discuss the results of surveys taken on each probation office regarding the extent to which probation workers use published research to inform their practice and the extent to which they conduct research in conjunction with their practice. The group will be convened by Robert Rivas, ACSW, at Siena College.

Agency Sponsorship

The task force will be sponsored by the tri-county consortium of probation agencies. The Rockwell County agency will provide physical facilities for meetings. Financial costs will be shared by all county agencies.

Membership

Each county agency will nominate three representatives to attend meetings to ensure equal representation among agencies.

Recruitment

Mailings will be sent to all agency directors. Members of the tri-county association will be informed by an announcement in the newsletter. Each agency director will be requested by letter to appoint three representatives to the task force.

Composition

The task force will require that each agency appoint one representative from each of the following categories: probation administrator, probation supervisor (or senior officer), and probation officer. The task force will include nine representatives from agencies and two research consultants from local colleges. All members of the task force should have some knowledge about research methods. This will be a closed group, although interested people may attend specific meetings after obtaining permission from the group's leader.

Orientation

The group will be given several research reports to read to prepare for discussions. The group leader will contact each member individually to get ideas for composing an agenda.

Contract

The task force will meet once a month for six sessions. Meetings will last for three hours and will take place every fourth Monday of the month from 9 A.M. to noon. The group will be required to compose and issue a preliminary report on research use within one month after the final meeting.

Environment

The Rockwell County agency will provide the use of its staff meeting room, which is equipped with tables and blackboards, for the group's work. Copying facilities will be provided by Rockwell County, and each county will be billed for one-third of the expenses (limit $30.00 per county). About $100 will be required to prepare and distribute the task force's final report and recommendations (contributed by the county association). Agency directors for each county have been requested to provide travel allowance (25 cents a mile) for all travel in conjunction with the work of the task force.

References

Chapter 1

Abramson, J. (1989). Making teams work. *Social Work with Groups, 12*(4), 45–63. doi:10.1300/J009v12n04_04

Abramson, J. S. (2002). Interdisciplinary team practice. In A. R. Roberts & G. J. Greene (Eds.), *Social workers' desk reference* (pp. 44–50). New York, NY: Oxford University Press.

Abramson, J. S., & Bronstein, L. R. (2004). Group process dynamics and skills in interdisciplinary teamwork. In C. D. Garvin, L. M. Gutierrez, & M. J. Galinsky (Eds.), *Handbook of social work with groups* (pp. 384–399). New York, NY: Guilford Press.

Association for the Advancement of Social Work with Groups, Inc. (2013). Standards for social work practice with groups, second edition. *Social Work with Groups, 36*(2–3), 270–282. doi:10.1080/01609513.2012.759504

Barlow, S. (2013). *Specialty competencies in group psychology*. New York, NY: Oxford University Press.

Bell, J. (1981). The small group perspective: Family group-therapy. In E. Tolson & W. Reid (Eds.), *Models of family treatment* (pp. 33–51). New York, NY: Columbia University Press.

Bergeron, L. G., & Gray, B. (2003). Ethical dilemmas of reporting suspected elder abuse. *Social Work, 48*(1), 96–105. doi:10.1093/sw/48.1.96

Berlastsky, N. (2015). *Gangs*. Fenington Hills, MI: Greenhaven Press.

Boyd, N. (1935). Group work experiments in state institutions in Illinois. In *Proceedings of the National Conference of Social Work* (p. 344). Chicago, IL: University of Chicago Press.

Boyd-Franklin, N., Cleek, E., Wofsy, M., & Mundy, B. (2013). *Therapy in the real world*. New York, NY: Guilford Press.

Brown, L., Feinberg, M., Shapiro, V., & Greenberg, M. (2015). Reciprocal relations between coalition functioning and the provision of implementation support. *Prevention Science, 16*(1), 101–109. doi:10.1007/s11121-013-0447-x

Bruner, M., & Spink, K. (2011). Effects of team building on exercise adherence and group task satisfaction in a youth activity setting. *Group Dynamics, Theory, Research, and Practice, 15*(2), 161–172. doi:10.1037/a0021257

Burlingame, G., Fuhrium, A., & Mosier, J. (2003). The differential effectiveness of group psychotherapy: A meta-analytic perspective. *Group Dynamics: Theory, Research, and Practice, 7*(1), 3–12. doi:10.1037/1089-2699.7.1.3

Burlingame, G., MacKenzie, K., & Strauss, B. (2004). Small group treatment: Evidence for the effectiveness and mechanisms of change. In M. J. Lambert (Ed.), *Bergin and Garfield's handbook of psychotherapy and behavior change* (5th ed., pp. 647–696). Hoboken, NJ: Wiley.

Burlingame, G., Strauss, B., & Joyce, A. (2013). Change mechanisms and effectiveness of small group treatments. In M. J. Lambert (Ed.), *Bergin and Garfield's handbook of psychotherapy and behavior change* (6th ed., pp. 640–689). Hoboken, NJ: Wiley.

Burlingame, G., Whitcomb, K., & Woodland, S. (2014). Process and outcome in group counseling and psychotherapy. In J. Delucia-Waack, C. Kalodner, & M. Riva (Eds.), *Handbook of group counseling & psychotherapy* (2nd ed., pp. 55–68). Thousand Oaks, CA: Sage Publications.

Callen, J., Klein, A., & Tinkelman, D. (2010). The contextual impact of nonprofit board composition and structure on organizational performance: Agency and resource dependence perspectives. *Voluntas, 21*(1), 101–125.

Chen, M., & Rybak, C. (2004). *Group leadership skills*. Belmont, CA: Brooks/Cole.

Cheung, M. (2014). *Therapeutic games and guided imagery* (Vol. II). Chicago, IL: Lyceum.

Conrad, W., & Glenn, W. (1976). *The effective voluntary board of directors: What it is and how it works*. Chicago, IL: Swallow Press.

Corey, M., Corey, G., & Corey C. (2014). *Groups: Process and practice* (9th ed.). Belmont, CA: Brooks/Cole.

Council on Social Work Education. (2015). Educational Policy and Accreditation Standards. Alexandria Virginia, CSWE.

Dolgoff, R., Harrington, D., & Loewenberg, F. (2012). *Ethical decisions for social work practice* (9th ed.). Belmont, CA: Brooks/Cole.

Drews, A., & Schaefer, C. (2010). *School-base play therapy* (2nd ed.). New York, NY: Wiley.

Fallon, A. (2006). Informed consent in the practice of group psychotherapy. *International Journal of Group Psychotherapy, 56*(4), 431–454. doi:10.1521/ijgp.2006.56.4.431

Feinberg, M., Bontempo, D., Greenberg, M. (2008). Predictors and level of sustainability of community prevention coalitions. *American Journal of Preventive Medicine, 34*(8), 495–501. doi:10.1016/j.amepre.2008.01.030

Forsyth, D. R. (2014). *Group dynamics* (6th ed.). Belmont, CA: Wadsworth Cengage Learning.

Gitterman, A., & Shulman, L. (Eds.). (2005). *Mutual aid groups, vulnerable populations, and the life cycle* (3rd ed.). New York, NY: Columbia University Press.

Glassman, U., & Kates, L. (1990). *Group work: A humanistic approach*. Newbury Park, CA: Sage Publications.

Gort, M., Broekhuis, M., & Regts, G. (2013). How teams use indicators for quality improvement – A multiple-case study on the use of multiple indicators in multidisciplinary breast cancer teams. *Social Science & Medicine, 96,* 69–77. doi:10.1016/j.socscimed.2013.06.001

Greenberg, M., Feinberg, M., Meyer-Chilenski, S., Spoth, R., & Redmond, C. (2007). Community and team member factors that influence the early phase functioning of community prevention teams: The PROSPER project. *Journal of Primary Prevention, 28*(6), 485–504. doi:10.1007/s10935-007-0116-6

Gruenfeld, D. (Ed.). (1998). *Research on managing groups and teams, Vol. 1.* Stamford, CT: JAI Press.

Hackman, J. R. (2002). *Leading teams: Setting the stage for great performances.* Boston, MA: Harvard Business School Press.

Haines, R. (2014). Group development in virtual teams: An experimental reexamination. *Computers in Human Behavior, 39*(C), 213–222. doi:10.1016/j.chb.2014.07.019

Hardina, D. (2013). *Interpersonal social work skills for community practice.* New York, NY: Springer Publishing Company.

Hare, A. P., Blumberg, H. H., Davies, M. F., & Kent, M. V. (1995). *Small group research: A handbook.* Norwood, NJ: Ablex.

Harpine, E. (2008). *Group intervention in schools.* New York, NY: Springer Publishing Company.

Heinemann, G. Z., & Zeiss, A. (2002). *Team performance in health care: Assessment and development.* New York, NY: Kluwer Academic/Plenum Publishers.

Howe, F. (2002). *Fund-raising and the nonprofit board member* (3rd ed.). Washington, DC: National Center for Nonprofit Boards.

Howell, J., & Griffiths, E. (2016). *Gangs in America's communities.* Thousand Oaks, CA: Sage Publications.

Hughes, S., Lakey, B., Bobowick, M., & National Center for Nonprofit Boards (U.S.). (2007). *The board building cycle: Nine steps of finding, recruiting, and engaging nonprofit board members* (2nd ed.). Washington, DC: Board Source.

Hyde, B. (2013). Mutual aid group work: Social work leading the way to recovery-focused mental health practice. *Social Work with Groups, 36*(1), 43–58.

Jaskyte, K. (2012). Boards of directors and innovation in nonprofit organizations. *Nonprofit Management & Leadership, 22*(4), 439–459. doi:10.1002/nml.21039

Kirschenbaum, H. (2013). *Values clarification in counseling and psychotherapy.* New York, NY: Oxford University Press.

Kivlighan, D. M., & Tarrant, J. M. (2001). Does group climate mediate the group leadership-group member outcome relationship? A test of Yalom's hypotheses about leadership priorities. *Group Dynamics: Theory, Research, and Practice, 5*(3), 220–234. doi:10.1037/1089-2699.5.3.220

Klein, A. (1972). *Effective group work.* New York, NY: Associated Press.

Klein, C., Diaz Granados, D., Salas, E., Le, H., Burke, S., Lyons, R., & Goodwin, G. (2009). Does team building work? *Small Group Research, 40*(2), 181–222. doi:10.1177/1046496408328821

Konopka, G. (1983). *Social group work: A helping process* (3rd ed.). Englewood Cliffs, NJ: Prentice Hall.

Kosters, M., Burlingame, G., Nachtigall, C., & Straus, B. (2006). A meta-analytic review of the effectiveness of inpatient group psychotherapy. *Group Dynamics: Research, Theory, and Practice, 10*(2), 146–163. doi:10.1037/1089-2699.10.2.146

Kurtz, L. F. (2004). Support and self-help groups. In C. D. Garvin, L. M. Gutierrez, & M. J. Galinsky (Eds.), *Handbook of social work with groups* (pp. 139–159). New York, NY: Guilford Press.

Kurtz, L. F. (2014). *Recovery groups.* New York, NY: Oxford University Press.

Kyrouz, E., Humphreys, K., & Loomis, C. (2002). A review of research on the effectiveness of self-help mutual aid groups. In B. J. White & E. Madara (Eds.), *The self-help sourcebook: Your guide to community and online support groups* (7th ed., pp. 193–217). Denville, NJ: St. Clare's Health Services.

Lakin, M. (1991). Some ethical issues in feminist-oriented therapeutic groups for women. *International Journal of Group Psychotherapy, 41*(2), 199–215.

Lasky, G. B., & Riva, M. T. (2006). Confidentiality and privileged communication in group psychotherapy. *International Journal of Group Psychotherapy, 56*(4), 455–476. doi:10.1521/ijgp.2006.56.4.455

LeCroy, C. (2008). (Ed.). *Handbook of evidence-based treatment manuals for children and adolescents* (2nd ed.). New York, NY: Oxford University Press.

Lemieux-Charles, L., & McGuire, W. (2006). What do we know about health care team effectiveness? A review of the literature. *Medical Care Research Review, 63*(3), 263–300.

Levi, D. (2014). *Group dynamics for teams* (4th ed.). Thousand Oaks, CA: Sage Publications.

Levine, J. (2012). *Working with people: The helping process* (9th ed.). Boston, MA: Allyn & Bacon.

Macgowan, M. J. (2008). *A guide to evidence-based group work.* New York, NY: Oxford University Press.

MacKenzie, K. R. (1990). *Introduction to time-limited group psychotherapy.* Washington, DC: American Psychiatric Press.

MacKenzie, K. R. (1996). Time-limited group psychotherapy. *International Journal of Group Psychotherapy, 46*(1), 41–60.

Maguire, L. (1991). *Social support systems in practice: A generalist approach.* Silver Spring, MD: National Association of Social Workers Press.

McKnight, J. S., & Plummer, J. M. (2015). *Community organizing: Theory and practice.* New York, NY: Pearson.

McRoberts, C., Burlingame, G. M., & Hoag, M. J. (1998). Comparative efficacy of individual and group psychotherapy: A meta-analytic perspective. *Group Dynamics: Theory, Research and Practice, 2*(2), 101–117. doi:10.1037/1089-2699.2.2.101

McWhirter, P., & Robbins, R. (2014). Group therapy with native people. In J. Delucia-Waack, C. Kalodner, & M. Riva (Eds.), *Handbook of group counseling & psychotherapy* (2nd ed., pp. 370–382). Thousand Oaks, CA: Sage Publications.

Meyer, C. J. (2013). A new perspective on coalitions: What motivates membership? *Group Dynamics: Theory, Research, and Practice, 17*(2), 124–135. doi:10.1037/a0031346

Miller, G. A. (2012). *Group exercises for addiction counseling.* Hoboken, NJ: Wiley.

Misurell, J., & Springer, C. (2013). Developing culturally responsive evidence-based practice: A game-based group therapy program for child sexual abuse (CSA). *Journal of Child and Family Studies, 22*(1), 137–149. doi:10.1007/s10826-011-9560-2

Mondros, J., & Wilson, S. (1994). *Organizing for power and empowerment.* New York, NY: Columbia University Press.

Nash, M. (2011). *Developing language and communication skills through effective small group work* (3rd ed.). New York, NY: Routledge.

Newstetter, W. (1948). The social intergroup work process. In *Proceedings of the National Conference of Social Work* (pp. 205–217). New York, NY: Columbia University Press.

Norcross, J., Campbell, L., Grohol, J., Santrock, J., Selagea, F., & Sommer, R. (2013). *Self-help that works* (4th ed.). New York, NY: Oxford University Press

Pelletier, S. (2012). High-performing committees: What makes them work? *Association of Governing Boards of Universities and Colleges*, 20(3), 5–15.

Penarroja, V., Orengo, V., Zornoza, A., & Hernandez, A. (2013). The effects of virtuality level on task-related collaborative behaviors: The mediating role of team trust. *Computers in Human Behavior*, 29(3), 967–974. doi:10.1016/j.chb.2012.12.020

Perkins, D. F., Feinberg, M. E., Greenberg, M. T., Johnson, L. E., Chilenski, S. M., Mincemoyer, C. C., & Spoth, R. L. (2011). Team factors that predict to sustainability indicators for community-based prevention teams. *Evaluation Program Planning*, 34(3), 283–291. doi:10.1016/j.evalprogplan.2010.10.003

Powell, T. (1987). *Self-help organizations and professional practice*. Silver Spring, MD: National Association of Social Workers Press.

Putnam, R. D. (2000). *Bowling alone: The collapse and revival of American community*. New York, NY: Simon & Schuster.

Pyles, L. (2013). *Progressive community organizing: A critical approach for a globalizing world* (2nd ed.). New York, NY: Routledge.

Ramirez, C. (2014). *Teams: A competency-based approach*. New York, NY: Routledge.

Ratts, M., & Pedersen, P. (2014). *Counseling for multiculturalism and social justice: Integration, theory, and application* (4th ed). Alexandria, VA: American Counseling Association.

Reamer, F. G. (2001). *The social work ethics audit: A risk-management tool*. Washington, DC: NASW Press.

Reamer, F. G. (2006). *Ethical standards in social work: A review of the NASW Code of Ethics* (2nd ed.). Washington, DC: NASW Press.

Riessman, F. (1965). The "helper" therapy principle. *Social Work*, 10, 27–32.

Roback, H., Moore, R., Bloch, F., & Shelton, M. (1996). Confidentiality in group psychotherapy: Empirical findings and the law. *International Journal of Group Psychotherapy*, 46(1), 117–135.

Roback, H., Ochoa, E., Bloch, F., & Purdon, S. (1992). Guarding confidentiality in clinical groups: The therapist's dilemma. *International Journal of Group Psychotherapy*, 42(1), 81–103.

Rokeach, M. (1968). *Beliefs, attitudes and values: A theory of organization and change*. San Francisco, CA: Jossey-Bass.

Rose, S. (1998). *Group therapy with troubled youth*. Thousand Oaks, CA: Sage Publications.

Rose, S. D. (2004). Cognitive-behavioral group work. In C. D. Garvin, L. M. Gutierrez, & M. J. Galinsky (Eds.), *Handbook of social work with groups* (pp. 111–135). New York, NY: Guilford Press.

Rose, S., & LeCroy, C. (1991). Group treatment methods. In F. Kanfer & A. Goldstein (Eds.), *Helping people change* (4th ed., pp. 422–453). New York, NY: Pergamon Press.

Rothman, J. C. (2013). *From the front lines: Student cases in social work ethics* (4th ed.). Boston, MA: Allyn & Bacon Pearson Education.

Saksa, J., Cohen, S., Srihari, V., & Woods, S. (2009). Cognitive behavior therapy for early psychosis: A comprehensive review of individual vs. group treatment studies. *International Journal of Group Psychotherapy*, 59(3), 357–383. doi:10.1521/ijgp.2009.59.3.357

Scholtes, P., Joiner, B., & Streibel, B. (2003). *The team handbook* (3rd ed.). Madison, WI: Oriel Incorporated.

Shulman, L. (2016). *The skills of helping individuals, families, groups and communities* (8th ed.). Itasca, IL: F. E. Peacock.

Slavson, S. R. (1945). *Creative group education*. New York, NY: Association Press.

Slavson, S. R. (1946). *Recreation and the total personality*. New York, NY: Association Press.

Smith, A. (1935). Group play in a hospital environment. In *Proceedings of the National Conference of Social Work* (pp. 372–373). Chicago, IL: University of Chicago Press.

Smokowski, P. R., Rose, S. D., & Bacallao, M. L. (2001). Damaging experiences in therapeutic groups: How vulnerable consumers become group casualties. *Small Group Research*, 32(2), 223–251. doi:10.1177/104649640103200205

Springer, C., Misrell, J., & Hiller, A. (2012). Game-based cognitive-behavioral therapy (GB-CBT) group program for children who have experienced sexual abuse: A three-month follow-up investigation. *Journal of Child Sexual Abuse*, 21(6), 646–664. doi:10.1080/10538712.2012.722592

Staples, L. H. (2004). Social action groups. In C. D. Garvin, L. M. Gutierrez, & M. J. Galinsky (Eds.), *Handbook of social work with groups* (pp. 344–383). New York, NY: Guilford Press.

Steinberg, D. (2014). *A mutual-aid model social work with groups* (3rd ed.). Oxford, UK: Routledge.

Strozier, R. (1997). Group work in social work education. What is being taught? *Social Work with Groups*, 20(1), 65–77. doi:10.1300/J009v20n01_06

Sue, D. W., & Sue, D. (2013). *Counseling the culturally diverse: Theory and practice* (6th ed.). New York, NY: Wiley.

Toseland, R., & Hacker, L. (1982). Self-help groups and professional involvement. *Social Work*, 27(4), 341–347.

Toseland, R., & Hacker, L. (1985). Social workers' use of groups as a resource for clients. *Social Work*, 30(3), 232–239.

Toseland, R., Ivanoff, A., & Rose, S. (1987). Treatment conferences: Task groups in action. *Social Work with Groups*, 10(2), 79–94. doi:10.1300/J009v10n02_08

Toseland, R., Palmer-Ganeles, J., & Chapman, D. (1986). Teamwork in psychiatric settings. *Social Work*, 31(1), 46–52.

Toseland, R., Rossiter, C., Peak, T., & Smith, G. (1990). Comparative effectiveness of individual and group interventions to support family caregivers. *Social Work*, 35(3), 209–219.

Toseland, R., & Siporin, M. (1986). When to recommend group treatment: A review of the clinical and research literature. *International Journal of Group Psychotherapy*, 36(2), 171–201.

Tropman, J. (2014). *Effective meetings: Improving group decision-making* (4th ed.). Thousand Oaks, CA: Sage Publications.

Tropman, J., & Harvey, T. (2009). *Nonprofit governance: The why, what, and how of nonprofit boardship*. Chicago, IL: University of Chicago Press.

Waldo, C. (1986). *A working guide for directors of not-for-profit organizations*. New York, NY: Quorum Books.

Walls, D. (2015). *Community organizing*. Cambridge, UK: Polity Press.

Walsh, J. (2010). *Psychoeducation in mental health*. Chicago, IL: Lyceum Books.

White, B. J., & Madara, E. (Eds.). (2002). *The self-help sourcebook: Your guide to community and online support groups* (7th ed.). Denville, NJ: St. Clare's Health Services.

Whittingham, M., & Capriotti, G. (2009). The ethics of group therapy. In J. Allen, E. Wolf, & L. Vandecreek (Eds.), *Innovations in clinical practice: A 21st century sourcebook* (pp. 173–188). Sarasota, FL: Professional Resources Press.

Wilson, G. (1976). From practice to theory: A personalized history. In R. W. Roberts & H. Northen (Eds.), *Theories of social work with groups* (pp. 1–44). New York, NY: Columbia University Press.

Winer, M., & Ray, K. (2009). *Collaboration handbook: Creating, sustaining, and enjoying the journey* (2nd ed.). St. Paul, MN: Amherst Wilder Foundation.

Yalom, I. (2005). *The theory and practice of group psychotherapy* (5th ed.). New York, NY: Basic Books.

Yang, E., Foster-Fishman, P., Collins, C., & Ahn, S. (2012). Testing a comprehensive community problem-solving framework for community coalitions. *Journal of Community Psychology, 40*(6), 681–698. doi:10.1002/jcop.20526

Zakocs, R., & Edwards, E. (2006). What explains community coalition effectiveness? A review of the literature. *American Journal of Preventive Medicine, 30*(4), 351–361. doi:10.1016/j.amepre.2005.12.004

Chapter 2

Addams, J. (1909). *The spirit of youth and the city streets.* New York, NY: Macmillan.

Addams, J. (1926). *Twenty years at Hull House.* New York, NY: Macmillan.

Alissi, A. S. (2001). The social group work tradition: Toward social justice in a free society. *Social Group Work Foundation Occasional Papers,* Paper 1. Retrieved from: http://digitalcommons.uconn.edu/sw_op/1

Allport, F. (1924). *Social psychology.* Boston, MA: Houghton Mifflin.

American Association of Group Workers. (1947). *Toward professional standards.* New York, NY: Association Press.

Anderson, J. (1979). Social work practice with groups in the generic base of social work practice. *Social Work with Groups, 2*(4), 281–293. doi:10.1300/J009v02n04_03

Antony, M. M., & Roemer, L. (2011). *Behavior therapy.* Washington, DC: American Psychological Association.

Asch, S. (1952). *Social psychology.* Englewood Cliffs, NJ: Prentice Hall.

Asch, S. (1955). Opinions and social pressures. *Scientific American, 193*(5), 31–35. doi:10.1038/scientificamerican1155-31

Bales, R. (1950). *Interaction process analysis: A method for the study of small groups.* Reading, MA: Addison-Wesley.

Bales, R. (1954). In conference. *Harvard Business Review, 32,* 44–50.

Bales, R. (1955). How people interact in conference. *Scientific American, 192*(3), 31–35. doi:10.1038/scientificamerican0355-31

Bales, R., Cohen, S., & Williamson, S. (1979). *SYMLOG: A system for the multiple level observations of groups.* New York, NY: The Free Press.

Balgopal, P., & Vassil, T. (1983). *Groups in social work: An ecological perspective.* New York, NY: Macmillan.

Bandura, A. (1977). *Social learning theory.* Englewood Cliffs, NJ: Prentice Hall.

Barlow, S. (2013). *Specialty competencies in group psychology.* New York, NY: Oxford University Press.

Beck, J. (2011). *Cognitive therapy: Basics and beyond* (2nd ed.). New York, NY: Guilford Press.

Bieling, P. J., McCabe, R. E., & Antony, M. M. (2006). *Cognitive-behavioral therapy in groups.* New York, NY: Guilford Press.

Bion, W. (1991). *Experiences in groups and other papers.* London: Routledge.

Blau, P. (1964). *Exchange and power in social life.* New York, NY: Wiley.

Bowman, L. (1935). Dictatorship, democracy, and group work in America. In *Proceedings of the National Conference of Social Work* (p. 382). Chicago, IL: University of Chicago Press.

Boyd, N. (1935). Group work experiments in state institutions in Illinois. In *Proceedings of the National Conference of Social Work* (p. 344). Chicago, IL: University of Chicago Press.

Boyd, N. (1938). Play as a means of social adjustment. In J. Lieberman (Ed.), *New trends in group work* (pp. 210–220). New York, NY: Association Press.

Brackett, J. (1895). The charity organization movement: Its tendency and its duty. In *Proceedings of the 22nd National Conference of Charities and Corrections* (p. 86). Boston, MA: G. H. Ellis.

Breton, M. (1994). On the meaning of empowerment and empowerment-oriented social work practice. *Social Work with Groups, 17*(3), 23–37. doi:10.1300/J009v17n03_03

Breton, M. (1995). The potential for social action in groups. *Social Work with Groups, 18*(2/3), 5–13. doi:10.1300/J009v18n02_02

Breton, M. (1999). The relevance of the structural approach to group work with immigrant and refugee women. *Social Work with Groups, 22*(2–3), 11–29. doi:10.1300/J009v22n02_03

Brill, N. (1976). *Team-work: Working together in the human services.* Philadelphia, PA: J. B. Lippincott.

Brown, L. (1991). *Groups for growth and change.* New York, NY: Longman.

Buckman, R., Kinney, D., & Reese, A. (2008). Narrative therapies. In N. Coady & P. Lehmann (Eds.), *Theoretical perspectives for direct social work practice* (pp. 369–400). New York, NY: Springer Publishing Company.

Burlingame, G. (2010). Small group treatments: Introduction to special edition. *Psychotherapy Research, 20*(1), 1–7. doi:10.1080/10503301003596551

Burlingame, G., Strauss, B., & Joyce, A. (2013). Change mechanisms and effectiveness of small group treatments. In M. J. Lambert (Ed.), *Bergin and Garfield's handbook of psychotherapy and behavior change* (6th ed., pp. 640–689). Hoboken, NJ: Wiley.

Cartwright, D. (1951). Achieving change in people. *Human Relations, 4*(4), 381–392. doi:10.1177/001872675100400404

Cartwright, D., & Zander, A. (Eds.). (1968). *Group dynamics: Research and theory* (3rd ed.). New York, NY: Harper & Row.

Cohen, M. B., & Mullender, A. (1999). The personal in the political: Exploring the group work continuum from individual to social change goals. *Social Work with Groups, 22*(1), 13–31. doi:10.1300/J009v22n01_02

Conyne, R. (Ed.). (2010). *The Oxford handbook of group counseling.* New York, NY: Oxford University Press.

Cooley, D. (1909). *Social organization.* New York, NY: Charles Scribner's Sons.

Cox, E. (1988). Empowerment of the low income elderly through group work. *Social Work with Groups, 11*(4), 111–119. doi:10.1300/J009v11n04_10

Cox, E., & Parsons, R. (1994). *Empowerment-oriented social work practice with the elderly.* Pacific Grove, CA: Brooks/Cole.

Coyle, G. (1930). *Social process in organized groups.* New York, NY: Richard Smith.

Coyle, G. (1935). Group work and social change. In *Proceedings of the National Conference of Social Work* (p. 393). Chicago, IL: University of Chicago Press.

Coyle, G. (1937). *Studies in group behavior.* New York, NY: Harper & Row.

Coyle, G. (1938). Education for social action. In J. Lieberman (Ed.), *New trends in group work* (pp. 1–14). New York, NY: Association Press.

Delucia-Waack, J., Kalodner, C., & Riva, M. (Eds.). (2014). *Handbook of group counseling & psychotherapy* (2nd ed.). Thousand Oaks, CA: Sage Publications.

Dluhy, M. (1990). *Building coalitions in the human services.* Newbury Park, CA: Sage Publications.

Douglas, T. (1979). *Group process in social work: A theoretical synthesis.* New York, NY: Wiley.

Early, B. (1992). An ecological-exchange model of social work consultation with the work group of the school. *Children and Schools, 14*(4), 207–214. doi:10.1093/cs/14.4.207

Ellis, A. (1992). Group rational-emotive and cognitive-behavior therapy. *International Journal of Group Psychotherapy, 42*(1), 63–82.

Empey, L., & Erikson, M. (1972). *The Provo experiment: Impact and death of an innovation.* Lexington, MA: Lexington Books.

Ephross, P. H., & Vassil, T. (2005). *Groups that work* (2nd ed.). New York, NY: Columbia University Press.

Fatout, M., & Rose, S. (1995). *Task groups in the social services.* Thousand Oaks, CA: Sage Publications.

Feldman, R., & Wodarski, J. (1975). *Contemporary approaches to group treatment: Traditional, behavior modification and group-centered.* San Francisco, CA: Jossey-Bass.

Feldman, R., Caplinger, T., & Wodarski, J. (1983). *The St. Louis conundrum: The effective treatment of antisocial youth.* Englewood Cliffs, NJ: Prentice Hall.

Follett, M. P. (1926). *The new state: Group organization, the solution of popular government.* New York, NY: Longmans, Green.

Forsyth, D. R. (2014). *Group dynamics* (6th ed.). Belmont, CA: Wadsworth Cengage Learning.

Freud, S. (1922). *Group psychology and the analysis of the ego.* London: International Psychoanalytic Press.

Garvin, C. (1997). *Contemporary group work* (3rd ed.). Boston, MA: Allyn & Bacon.

Germain, C., & Gitterman, A. (2008). *The life model of social work practice* (3rd ed.). New York, NY: Columbia University Press.

Gitterman, A., & Shulman, L. (Eds.). (2005). *Mutual aid groups, vulnerable populations, and the life cycle* (3rd ed.). New York, NY: Columbia University Press.

Glassman, U., & Kates, L. (1990). *Group work: A humanistic approach.* Newbury Park, CA: Sage Publications.

Granvold, D. (2008). Constructivist theory and practice. In N. Coady & P. Lehmann (Eds.), *Theoretical perspectives for direct social work practice* (pp. 401–428). New York, NY: Springer Publishing Company.

Gummer, B. (1991). A new managerial era: From hierarchical control to "collaborative individualism." *Administration in Social Work, 15*(3), 121–137. doi:10.1300/J147v15n03_08

Gummer, B., & McCallion, P. (Eds.). (1995). *Total quality management in the social services: Theory and practice.* Albany, NY: State University of NY, University at Albany, School of Social Welfare, Professional Development Program of Rockefeller College.

Hare, A. P. (1976). *Handbook of small group research* (2nd ed.). New York, NY: Free Press.

Homans, G. (1950). *The human group.* New York, NY: Harcourt Brace Jovanovich.

Homans, G. (1961). *Social behavior: Its elementary forms.* New York, NY: Harcourt Brace Jovanovich.

Jennings, H. (1947). Leadership and sociometric choice. *Sociometry, 10*(1), 32–49. doi:10.2307/2785559

Jennings, H. (1950). *Leadership and isolation* (2nd ed.). New York, NY: Longman.

Johnson, D., & Johnson, F. (2013). *Joining together: Group theory and group skills* (11th ed.). Boston, MA: Pearson Education.

Kaduson, H. G., & Schaefer, C. E. (2015). *Short-term play therapy for children* (3rd ed.). New York, NY: Guilford Press.

Kalodner, C., Coughlin, J., & Seide, M. (2014). Psychoeducational and counseling groups to prevent and treat eating disorders and disturbances. In J. Delucia-Waack, C. Kalodner, & M. Riva (Eds.), *Handbook of group counseling & psychotherapy* (2nd ed., pp. 484–494). Thousand Oaks, CA: Sage Publications.

Kauff, P. (2012). Psychoanalytic group psychotherapy. In J. Kleinberg (Ed.), *The Wiley-Blackwell handbook of group psychotherapy* (pp. 13–32). Chichester, England: Wiley-Blackwell.

Kazdin, A. (2013). *Behavior modification in applied settings* (7th ed.). Long Grove, IL.: Waveland Press.

Keller, T., & Dansereau, F. (1995). Leadership and empowerment: A social exchange perspective. *Human Relations, 48*(2), 127–146. doi:10.1177/001872679504800202

Kellner, M. H. (2001). *In control, a skill-building program for teaching young adolescents to manage anger.* Champaign, IL: Research Press.

Kiesler, S. (1978). *Interpersonal processes in groups and organizations.* Arlington Heights, IL: AHM.

Klein, A. (1953). *Society, democracy and the group.* New York, NY: Whiteside.

Klein, A. (1970). *Social work through group process.* Albany: School of Social Welfare, State University of New York at Albany.

Klein, A. (1972). *Effective group work.* New York, NY: Associated Press.

Klein, R. H., Bernard, H. S., & Singer, D. L. (Eds.). (2000). *Handbook of contemporary group psychotherapy: Contributions from object relations, self psychology, and social systems theories.* Madison, CT: International Universities Press.

Kleinberg, J. (Ed.). (2012). *The Wiley-Blackwell handbook of group psychotherapy.* Chichester, England: Wiley-Blackwell.

Knottnerus, J. (1994). Social exchange theory and social structure: A critical comparison of two traditions of inquiry. *Current Perspectives in Social Theory,* (Suppl. 1), 29–48.

Konopka, G. (1949). *Therapeutic group work with children.* Minneapolis: University of Minnesota Press.

Konopka, G. (1954). *Group work in the institution.* New York, NY: Association Press.

Langelier, C. A. (2001). *Mood management: A cognitive-behavioral skills building program for adolescents: Leader's manual.* Thousand Oaks, CA: Sage Publications.

Lawson, H. A., Caringi, J. C., Pyles, L., Jurkowski, J., & Bozlak, C. (2015). *Participatory action research.* New York, NY: Oxford University Press.

Lazell, E. W. (1921). The group treatment of dementia praecox. *Psychoanalytical Review, 8,* 168–179. Retrieved from: https://archive.org/details/psychoanalyticr04usgoog

Leahy, R. (1996). *Cognitive therapy: Basic principles and applications.* Northvale, NJ: Jason Aronson.

LeBon, G. (1910). *The crowd: A study of the popular mind.* London: George Allen & Unwin Ltd.

LeCroy, C. (2008). (Ed.). *Handbook of evidence-based treatment manuals for children and adolescents* (2nd ed.) New York, NY: Oxford University Press.

Lee, J. (2001). The empowerment group: The heart of the empowerment approach and an antidote to injustice. In J. Parry (Ed.), *From prevention to wellness through group work* (2nd ed., pp. 290–320). New York, NY: Columbia University Press.

Leszcz, M. (1992). The interpersonal approach to group psychotherapy. *International Journal of Group Psychotherapy, 42*(1), 37–62.

Leszcz, M., & Malat, J. (2012). The interpersonal model of group psychotherapy. In J. Kleinberg (Ed.), *The Wiley-Blackwell handbook of group psychotherapy* (pp. 33–58). Chichester, England: Wiley-Blackwell.

Levi, D. (2014). *Group dynamics for teams* (4th ed.). Thousand Oaks, CA: Sage Publications.

Lewin, K. (1946). Behavior as a function of the total situation. In L. Carmichael (Ed.), *Manual of child psychology* (pp. 791–844). New York, NY: Wiley. doi:10.1037/10756-016

Lewin, K. (1947). Frontiers in group dynamics. *Human Relations, 1*(1), 2–38. doi:10.1177/001872674700100103

Lewin, K. (1948). *Resolving social conflict: Selected papers on group dynamics.* New York, NY: Harper & Row.

Lewin, K. (1951). *Field theory in social science.* New York, NY: Harper and Row.

Lewin, K., Lippitt, R., & White, R. (1939). Patterns of aggressive behavior in experimentally created "social climates." *Journal of Social Psychology, 10*(2), 271–299. doi:10.1080/00224545.1939.9713366

Lippitt, R. (1957). Group dynamics and the individual. *International Journal of Group Psychotherapy, 7*(10), 86–102.

Macgowan, M. J., & Pennell, J. (2001). Building social responsibility through family group conferencing. *Social Work with Groups, 24*(3–4), 67–87.

Maloney, S. (1963). *Development of group work education in social work schools in U. S.* Unpublished doctoral dissertation, Case Western Reserve University, School of Applied Social Science, Cleveland, OH.

Marmarosh, C., Dunton, E., & Amendola, C. (2014). *Groups: Fostering a culture of change.* Thousand Oaks, CA: Sage Publications.

Marsh, L. C. (1931). Group treatment of the psychoses by the psychological equivalent of the revival. *Mental Hygiene, 15,* 328–349.

Marsh, L. C. (1933). An experiment in group treatment of patients at Worchester State hospital. *Mental Hygiene, 17,* 396–416.

Marsh, L. C. (1935). Group therapy and the psychiatric clinic. *Journal of Nervous & Mental Disorders, 82,* 381–393. doi:10.1097/00005053-193510000-00002

McCaskill, J. (1930). *Theory and practice of group work.* New York, NY: Association Press.

McGrath, J. (1984). *Groups: Interaction and performance.* Englewood Cliffs, NJ: Prentice Hall.

McGrath, J., Arrow, H., & Berdahl, J. (2000). The study of groups: Past, present, and future. *Personality and Social Psychology Review, 4*(1), 95–105.

Middleman, R. (1980). The use of program: Review and update. *Social Work with Groups, 3*(3), 5–23. doi:10.1300/J009v03n03_02

Middleman, R. (1982). *The non-verbal method in working with groups: The use of activity in teaching, counseling, and therapy* (Enlarged Ed.). Hebron, CT: Practitioners Press.

Middleman, R., & Wood, G. (1990). Reviewing the past and present of group work and the challenge of the future. *Social Work with Groups, 13*(3), 3–20. doi:10.1300/J009v13n03_02

Mills, T. (1967). *The sociology of small groups.* Englewood Cliffs, NJ: Prentice Hall.

Mondros, J., & Wilson, S. (1994). *Organizing for power and empowerment.* New York, NY: Columbia University Press.

Moreno, J. (1934). *Who shall survive?* Washington, DC: Nervous and Mental Diseases.

Mullender, A., & Ward, D. (1991). *Self-directed groupwork: Users take action for empowerment.* London: Whitney & Birch.

Newstetter, W., Feldstein, M. J., & Newcomb, T. M. (1938). *Group adjustment: A study in experimental sociology.* Cleveland, OH: School of Applied Social Sciences, Western Reserve University.

Nixon, H. (1979). *The small group.* Englewood Cliffs, NJ: Prentice Hall.

Nosko, A., & Breton, M. (1997–1998). Applying strengths, competence and empowerment model. *Groupwork, 10*(1), 55–69.

Olsen, M. (1968). *The process of social organization.* New York, NY: Holt, Rinehart & Winston.

Papell, C. (1998). Thinking about thinking about group work: Thirty years later. *Social Work with Groups, 20*(4), 5–17. doi:10.1300/J009v20n04_02

Papell, C., & Rothman, B. (1962). Social group work models: Possession and heritage. *Journal of Education for Social Work, 2*(2), 66–77.

Papell, C., & Rothman, B. (1980). Relating the mainstream model of social work with groups to group psychotherapy and the structured group approach. *Social Work with Groups, 3*(2), 5–23. doi:10.1300/J009v03n02_02

Parsons, R. (1991). Empowerment: Purpose and practice principle in social work. *Social Work with Groups, 14*(2), 7–21. doi:10.1300/J009v14n02_02

Parsons, T. (1951). *The social system.* New York, NY: Free Press.

Parsons, T., Bales, R., & Shils, E. (Eds.). (1953). *Working papers in the theory of action.* New York, NY: Free Press.

Pernell, R. (1986). Empowerment and social group work. In M. Parnes (Ed.), *Innovations in social group work* (pp. 107–118). New York, NY: Haworth Press.

Piper, W., Ogrodniczuk, J., & Duncan, S. (2002). Psychodynamically oriented group therapy. In F. W. Kaslow & J. J. Magnavita (Vol. Ed.), *Comprehensive handbook of psychotherapy. Volume 1: Psychodynamic/object relations* (pp. 457–479). New York, NY: Wiley.

Putnam, R. D. (2000). *Bowling alone: The collapse and revival of American community.* New York, NY: Simon & Schuster.

Pyles, L. (2013). *Progressive community organizing: A critical approach for a globalizing world* (2nd ed.). New York, NY: Routledge.

Raczynski, K., & Horne, A. (2014). Psyhoeducational and counseling groups for bullying. In J. Delucia-Waack,

C. Kalodner, & M. Riva (Eds.), *Handbook of group counseling & psychotherapy* (2nd ed., pp. 495–505). Thousand Oaks, CA: Sage Publications.

Redivo, M., & Buckman, R. (2004). T.E.A.M. program. *Journal of Systemic Therapies, 23*(4), 52–66. doi:10.1521/jsyt.23.4.52.57842

Redl, F. (1942). Group emotion and leadership. *Psychiatry, 5*(4),573–596. doi:10.1521/00332747.1942.11022422

Redl, F. (1944). Diagnostic group work. *American Journal of Orthopsychiatry, 14*(1), 53–67. doi:10.1111/j.1939-0025.1944.tb04850.x

Reid, K. (1981). *From character building to social treatment: The history of the use of groups in social work.* Westport, CT: Greenwood Press.

Reid, W. J. (1997). Research on task-centered practice. *Social Work Research, 21*(3), 132–137. doi:10.1093/swr/21.3.132

Richmond, M. (1917). *Social diagnosis.* New York, NY: Russell Sage Foundation.

Riess, H., & Dockray-Miller, M. (2002). *Integrative group treatment for bulimia nervosa.* New York, NY: Columbia University Press.

Roethlisberger, F., & Dickson, W. (1939). *Management and the worker.* Cambridge, MA: Harvard University Press.

Roethlisberger, F., & Dickson, W. (1975). A fair day's work. In P. V. Crosbie (Ed.), *Interaction in small groups* (pp. 85–94). New York, NY: Macmillan.

Roffman, R. (2004). Psychoeducational groups. In C. D. Garvin, L. M. Gutierrez, & M. J. Galinsky (Eds.), *Handbook of social work with groups* (pp. 160–175). New York, NY: Guilford Press.

Rose, S. (1989). *Working with adults in groups: A multi-method approach.* San Francisco, CA: Jossey-Bass.

Rose, S. (1998). *Group therapy with troubled youth.* Thousand Oaks, CA: Sage Publications.

Rose, S. D. (2004). Cognitive-behavioral group work. In C. D. Garvin, L. M. Gutierrez, & M. J. Galinsky (Eds.), *Handbook of social work with groups* (pp. 111–135). New York, NY: Guilford Press.

Rose, S., & Edleson, J. (1987). *Working with children and adolescents in groups.* San Francisco, CA: Jossey-Bass.

Rutan, J. (1992). Psychodynamic group psychotherapy. *International Journal of Group Psychotherapy, 42*(1), 19–36.

Rutan, J., Stone, W., & Shay, J. (2014). *Psychodynamic group psychotherapy* (5th ed.). New York, NY: Guilford Press.

Schermer, V., & Rice, C. (2012).Towards an integrative intersubjective and relational group psychotherapy. In J. Kleinberg (Ed.), *The Wiley-Blackwell handbook of group psychotherapy* (pp. 59–88). Chichester, England: Wiley-Blackwell.

Schilder, P. (1937). The analysis of ideologies as a psychotherapeutic method, especially in group treatment. *American Journal of Psychiatry, 93*, 601–615.

Schwartz, W. (1966). Discussion of three papers on the group method with clients, foster families, and adoptive families. *Child Welfare, 45*(10), 571–575.

Schwartz, W. (1976). Between client and system: The mediating function. In R. Roberts & H. Northen (Eds.), *Theories of social work with groups* (pp. 171–197). New York, NY: Columbia University Press.

Schwartz, W. (1981, April). *The group work tradition and social work practice.* Paper presented at Rutgers University, School of Social Work, New Brunswick, NJ.

Schwartzberg, S., & Barnes, M. (2010). The functional group model. In J. Kleinberg (Ed.), *The Wiley-Blackwell handbook of group psychotherapy* (pp. 139–168). Chichester, England: Wiley-Blackwell.

Shaw, C. (1930). *The jack roller.* Chicago, IL: University of Chicago Press.

Shaw, M. (1976). *Group dynamics: The psychology of small group behavior.* New York, NY: McGraw-Hill.

Sheldon, B. (2011). *Cognitive-behavioural therapy: Research and practice in health and social care* (2nd ed.). Abingdon, England: Routledge.

Shepard, C. (1964). *Small groups: Some sociological perspectives.* San Francisco, CA: Chandler.

Sherif, M. (1936). *The psychology of social norms.* New York, NY: Harper & Row.

Sherif, M. (1956). Experiments in group conflict. *Scientific American, 195*(5), 54–58. doi:10.1038/scientificamerican1156-54

Sherif, M., & Sherif, C. (1953). *Groups in harmony and tension: An introduction of studies in group relations.* New York, NY: Harper & Row.

Sherif, M., White, J., & Harvey, O. (1955). Status in experimentally produced groups. *American Journal of Sociology, 60*, 370–379. doi:10.1086/221569

Shils, E. (1950). Primary groups in the American army. In R. Merton & P. Lazarsfeld (Eds.), *Continuities in social research* (pp. 16–39). New York, NY: Free Press.

Shulman, L. (2016). *The skills of helping individuals, families, groups and communities* (8th ed.). Itasca, IL: F. E. Peacock.

Singh, C., & Salazar, C. (2010). The roots of social justice in group work. *Journal of Specialists in Group Work, 35*(2), 97–104. doi:10.1080/01933921003706048

Slavson, S. R. (1939a). *Character education in a democracy.* New York, NY: Association Press.

Slavson, S. R. (1939b). Democratic leadership in education. *The Group, 2*, 1–2.

Slavson, S. R. (1940). Group psychotherapy. *Mental Hygiene, 24*, 36–49.

Smith, A. (1935). Group play in a hospital environment. In *Proceedings of the National Conference of Social Work* (pp. 372–373). Chicago, IL: University of Chicago Press.

Steinberg, D. (2014). *A mutual-aid model social work with groups* (3rd ed.). Oxford, UK: Routledge.

Stouffer, S. (1949). *The American soldier, combat and its aftermath.* Princeton, NJ: Princeton University Press.

Syz, H. C. (1928). Remarks on group analysis. *American Journal of Psychiatry, 85*, 141–148.

Taylor, N., & Burlingame, G. (2001). A survey of mental health care provider and managed care organization attitudes toward, familiarity with, and use of group psychotherapy. *International Journal of Group Psychotherapy, 51*(2), 243–263. doi:10.1521/ijgp.51.2.243.49848

Taylor, R. (1903). Group management. *Transactions of the American Society of Mechanical Engineers, 24*, 1337–1480.

Thibaut, J., & Kelley, H. (1959). *The social psychology of groups.* New York, NY: Wiley.

Thrasher, F. (1927). *The gang.* Chicago, IL: University of Chicago Press.

Toseland, R., & Rivas, R. (1984). Structured methods for working with task groups. *Administration in Social Work, 8*(2), 49–58. doi:10.1300/J147v08n02_05

Toseland, R., Naccarato, T., & Wray, L. (2007). Telephone groups for older persons and family caregivers. *Clinical Gerontologist, 31*(1), 59–76. doi:10.1300/J018v31n01_05

Trecker, H. (1956). *Group work in the psychiatric setting.* New York, NY: William Morrow.

Trecker, H. (1980). Administration as a group process: Philosophy and concepts. In A. Alissi (Ed.), *Perspectives on social group work practice* (pp. 332–337). New York, NY: Free Press.

Triplett, N. (1898). The dynamogenic factors in pacemaking and competition. *American Journal of Psychology, 9*(4), 507–533. doi:10.2307/1412188

Tropman, J. (2014). *Effective meetings: Improving group decision-making* (4th ed.). Thousand Oaks, CA: Sage Publications.

Tropp, E. (1968). The group in life and in social work. *Social Casework, 49,* 267–274.

Tropp, E. (1976). A developmental theory. In R. Roberts & H. Northen (Eds.), *Theories of social work with groups* (pp. 198–237). New York, NY: Columbia University Press.

Velasquez, M., Maurer, G., Crouch, C., & DiClemente, C. (2001). *Group treatment for substance abuse: A stages-of-change therapy manual.* New York, NY: Guilford Press.

Vinter, R. (Ed.) (1967). *Readings in group work practice.* Ann Arbor: Campus Publishing.

Vorrath, H. H., & Brendtro, L. K. (1985). *Positive peer culture* (2nd ed.). Chicago, IL: Aldine.

Walsh, J. (2013). *Theories for direct social work practice* (3rd ed.). Belmont, CA: Wadsworth Cengage Learning.

Wasserman, H., & Danforth, J. (1988). *The human bond: Support group and mutual aid.* New York, NY: Springer Publishing Company.

Waterman, J., & Walker, E. (2009). *Helping at-risk students: A group counseling approach for grades 6–9* (2nd ed.). New York, NY: Guilford Press.

Weissman, H. (Ed.). (1969). *Individual and group services in the mobilization for youth experiment.* New York, NY: Association Press.

Wender, L. (1936). The dynamics of group psychotherapy and its application. *Journal of Nervous & Mental Disorders, 84,* 54–60. doi:10.1097/00005053-193607000-00005

Western, D. (2013). *Gender-based violence and depression in women: A feminist group work response.* New York, NY: Springer Publishing Company.

White, J. R., & Freeman, A. (Eds.). (2000). *Cognitive-behavioral group therapy for specific problems and populations.* Washington, DC: American Psychological Association. doi:10.1037/10352-000

Whyte, W. (1943). *Street corner society.* Chicago, IL: University of Chicago Press.

Wyss, D. (1973). *Psychoanalytic schools: From the beginning to the present.* New York, NY: Jason Aronson.

Yalom, I. (2005). *The theory and practice of group psychotherapy* (5th ed.). New York, NY: Basic Books.

Yan, M. C. (2001). Reclaiming the social in social group work: An experience of a community center in Hong Kong. *Social Work with Groups, 24*(3/4), 53–65.

Yuki, M., & Brewer, M. (Eds.). (2014). *Culture and group processes.* New York, NY: Oxford University Press.

Chapter 3

American Foundation for the Blind. (n.d.). *Statistical Snapshots.* Retrieved October 26, 2015, from http://www.afb.org/info/blindness-statistics/2

Anderson, J., & Carter, R. W. (2003). *Diversity perspectives for social work practice: Constructivism and the constructivist framework.* Boston, MA: Allyn & Bacon.

Asch, S. (1952). *Social psychology.* Englewood Cliffs, NJ: Prentice Hall.

Asch, S. (1955). Opinions and social pressures. *Scientific American, 193*(5), 31–35. doi:10.1038/scientificamerican1155-31

Asch, S. (1957). *An experimental investigation of group influence.* Paper presented at the Symposium on Preventative and Social Psychiatry, Walter Reed Army Institute of Research, Washington, DC.

Back, K. (1951). Influence through social communication. *Journal of Abnormal and Social Psychology, 46*(1), 9–23. doi:10.1037/h0058629

Bales, R. (1950). *Interaction process analysis: A method for the study of small groups.* Reading, MA: Addison-Wesley.

Bandura, A. A. (1997a). *Self-efficacy: Exercise and control.* New York, NY: Freeman.

Bandura, A. A. (1997b). *Self-efficacy in changing societies.* New York, NY: Cambridge University Press.

Barker, V., Abrams, J., Tiyaamornwong, V., Seibold, D., Duggan, A., Park, H., & Sebastian, M. (2000). New contexts for relational communications in groups. *Small Group Research, 31*(4), 470–503. doi:10.1177/104649640003100405

Budman, S., Soldz, S., Demby, A., Davis, M., & Merry, J. (1993). What is cohesiveness? An empirical examination. *Small Group Research, 24*(2), 199–216. doi:10.1177/1046496493242003

Burlingame, G., McClendon, D., & Alonso, J. (2011). Cohesion in group therapy. *Psychotherapy, 48*(1), 34–42. doi:10.1037/a0022063

Burnes, T., & Ross, K. (2010). Applying social justice to oppression and marginalization in group process: Interventions and strategies for group counselors. *The Journal for Specialists in Group Work, 35*(2), 169–176. doi:10.1080/01933921003706014

Carletta, J., Garrod, S., & Fraser-Krauss, H. (1998). Placement of authority and communication patterns in workplace groups. *Small Group Research, 29*(5), 531–559. doi:10.1177/1046496498295001

Cartwright, D. (1968). The nature of group cohesiveness. In D. Cartwright & A. Zander (Eds.), *Group dynamics: Research and theory* (3rd ed., pp. 91–109). New York, NY: Harper & Row.

Coyle, G. (1930). *Social process in organized groups.* New York, NY: Richard Smith.

Coyle, G. (1937). *Studies in group behavior.* New York, NY: Harper & Row.

Dion, K., Miller, N., & Magnan, M. (1971). Cohesiveness and social responsibility as determinants of group risk taking. *Journal of Personality and Social Psychology, 20*(3), 400–406. doi:10.1037/h0031914

Elliott, H. (1928). *Process of group thinking.* New York, NY: Association Press.

Evans, C., & Dion, K. (1991). Group cohesion and performance. *Small Group Research, 22*(2), 175–186. doi:10.1177/1046496491222002

Festinger, L. (1950). Informal social communication. *Psychological Review, 57*(5), 271–282. doi:10.1037/h0056932

Forsyth, D. R. (2014). *Group dynamics* (6th ed.). Belmont, CA: Wadsworth Cengage Learning.

Galinsky, M., & Schopler, J. (1977). Warning: Groups may be dangerous. *Social Work, 22*(2), 89–94. doi:10.1093/sw/22.2.89

Galinsky, M., & Schopler, J. (1989). Developmental patterns in open-ended groups. *Social Work with Groups, 12*(2), 99–114. doi:10.1300/J009v12n02_08

Garland, J., Jones, H., & Kolodny, R. (1976). A model of stages of group development in social work groups. In S. Bernstein (Ed.), *Explorations in group work* (pp. 17–71). Boston, MA: Charles River Books.

Gibson, A. (1999). *Project-based group work facilitator's manual: Young people, youth workers, and projects.* Bristol, PA: Jessica Kingsley Publications.

Gray-Little, B., & Kaplan, D. (2000). Race and ethnicity in psychotherapy research. In C. R. Snyder & R. Ingram (Eds.), *Handbook of psychological change* (pp. 591–613). New York, NY: Wiley.

Gully, S., Devine, D., & Whitney, D. (1995). A meta-analysis of cohesion and performance: Effects of level of analysis and task interdependence. *Small Group Research, 26*(4), 497–520. doi:10.1177/1046496495264003

Hare, A. P., Blumberg, H. H., Davies, M. F., & Kent, M. V. (1995). *Small group research: A handbook.* Norwood, NJ: Ablex.

Hartford, M. (1971). *Groups in social work.* New York, NY: Columbia University Press.

Hearing Loss Association of America. (n.d.). *Basic facts about hearing loss.* Retrieved October 26, 2015, from http://hearingloss.org/content/basic-facts-about-hearing-loss

Henry, S. (1992). *Group skills in social work: A four-dimensional approach* (2nd ed.). Itasca, IL: F. E. Peacock.

Hohman, M. (2012). *Motivational interviewing in social work practice.* New York, NY: Guilford Press.

Hopps, J., & Pinderhughes, E. (1999). *Group work with overwhelmed clients.* New York, NY: Free Press.

Hornsey, M., Dwyer, L., Oei, T., & Dingle, G. (2009). Group processes and outcomes in group psychotherapy: Is it time to let go of "cohesiveness"? *International Journal of Group Psychotherapy, 59*(2), 267–278. doi:10.1521/ijgp.2009.59.2.267

Janis, I. (1972). *Victims of group think.* Boston, MA: Houghton Mifflin.

Kiesler, S. (1978). *Interpersonal processes in groups and organizations.* Arlington Heights, IL: AHM.

Klein, A. (1972). *Effective group work.* New York, NY: Associated Press.

Kleinberg, J. (Ed.). (2012). *The Wiley-Blackwell handbook of group psychotherapy.* Chichester, England: Wiley-Blackwell.

Levi, D. (2014). *Group dynamics for teams* (4th ed.). Thousand Oaks, CA: Sage Publications.

Lewin, K. (1947). Frontiers in group dynamics. *Human Relations, 1*(1), 2–38. doi:10.1177/001872674700100103

Lieberman, M., Yalom, I., & Miles, M. (1973). *Encounter groups: First facts.* New York, NY: Basic Books.

Macgowan, M. J. (2000). Evaluation of a measure of engagement for group work. *Research in Social Work Practice, 10*(3), 348–361. doi:10.1093/acprof:oso/9780195183450.001.0001

Macgowan, M. J. (2008). *A guide to evidence-based group work.* New York, NY: Oxford University Press.

MacKenzie, K. R. (1994). Group development. In A. Fuhriman & G. M. Burlingame (Eds.), *Handbook of group psychotherapy* (pp. 223–268). New York, NY: Wiley.

Matsukawa, L. A. (2001). Group therapy with multiethnic minorities. In W. Tseng & J. Streltzer (Eds.), *Culture and psychotherapy: A guide to clinical practice.* Washington, DC: American Psychiatric Publishing Inc.

Milgram, S. (1974). *Obedience and authority.* New York, NY: Harper and Row.

Miller, W., & Rollnick, S. (Eds.). (2013). *Motivational interviewing: Helping people for change* (3rd ed.). New York, NY: Guilford Press.

Moscovici, S. (1985). *The age of the crowd: A historical treatise on mass psychology.* New York, NY: Cambridge University Press.

Moscovici, S. (1994). Three concepts: Minority, conflict, and behavioral styles. In S. Moscovici, M. Faina, & A. Maass (Eds.), *Minority influence* (pp. 235–251). Chicago, IL: Nelson-Hall.

Moscovici, S., & Lage, E. (1976). Studies in social influence: III. Majority versus minority influence in a group. *European Journal of Social Psychology, 6*(2), 149–174. doi:10.1002/ejsp.2420060202

Moscovici, S., Lage, E., & Naffrechoux, M. (1969). Influence of a constant minority on the responses of a majority in a color perception task. *Sociometry, 32*(4), 365–380. doi:10.2307/2786541

Mullen, B., & Cooper, C. (1994). The relationship between cohesiveness and performance: An integration. *Psychological Bulletin, 115*(2), 210–227. doi:10.1037/0033-2909.115.2.210

Napier, R., & Gershenfeld, M. (1993). *Groups: Theory and experience* (5th ed.). Boston, MA: Houghton Mifflin.

Newcomb, T. M. (1943). *Personality and social change.* New York, NY: Dryden.

Northen, H. (1969). *Social work with groups.* New York, NY: Columbia University Press.

Pepitone, A., & Reichling, G. (1955). Group cohesiveness and the expression of hostility. *Human Relations, 8*(3), 327–337. doi:10.1177/001872675500800306

Pescosolido, A. T. (2001). Informal leaders and the development of group efficacy. *Small Group Research, 32*(1), 74–93. doi:10.1177/104649640103200104

Pescosolido, A. T. (2003). Group efficacy and group effectiveness: The effects of group efficacy over time on group performance and development. *Small Group Research, 34*(1), 20–42. doi:10.1177/1046496402239576

Pooler, D., Qualls, N., Rogers, R., & Johnson, D. (2014). An exploration of cohesion and recovery outcomes in addiction treatment groups. *Social Work with Groups, 37*(4), 314–330. doi:10.1080/01609513.2014.905217

Prapavessis, H., & Carron, A. (1997). Cohesion and work output. *Small Group Research, 28*(2), 294–301. doi:10.1177/1046496497282006

Prochaska, J., DiClimente, C., & Norcross, C. (1992). In search of how people change. *American Psychologist, 41*(4), 1102–1114. doi:10.1037/0003-066X.47.9.1102

Sarri, R., & Galinsky, M. (1985). A conceptual framework for group development. In M. Sundel, P. Glasser, R. Sarri, & R. Vinter (Eds.), *Individual change through small groups* (2nd ed., pp. 70–86). New York, NY: Free Press.

Schachter, S. (1959). *The psychology of affiliation.* Stanford, CA: Stanford University Press.

Schiller, L. (1995). Stages of development in women's groups: A relational model. In R. Kurland & R. Salmon (Eds.), *Group work practice in a troubled society* (pp. 117–138). New York, NY: Haworth Press.

Schopler, J., & Galinsky, M. (1990). Can open-ended groups move beyond beginnings? *Small Group Research, 21*(4), 435–449. doi:10.1177/1046496490214001

Seashore, S. (1954). *Group cohesiveness in the industrial work group.* Ann Arbor: University of Michigan Press.

Shaw, M. (1964). Communication networks. In L. Berkowitz (Ed.), *Advances in experimental social psychology* (Vol. 1, pp. 111–149). New York, NY: Academic Press.

Shaw, M. (1976). *Group dynamics: The psychology of small group behavior*. New York, NY: McGraw-Hill.

Sherif, M. (1936). *The psychology of social norms*. New York, NY: Harper & Row.

Silver, W. B., & Bufiano, K. (1996). The impact of group efficacy and group goals on group task performance. *Small Group Research, 27*(3), 345–472. doi:10.1177/1046496496273001

Smith, P. (1978). Group work as a process of social influence. In N. McCaughan (Ed.), *Group work: Learning and practice* (pp. 36–57). London: George Allen & Unwin.

Smokowski, P. R., Rose, S. D., & Bacallao, M. L. (2001). Damaging experiences in therapeutic groups: How vulnerable consumers become group casualties. *Small Group Research, 32*(2), 223–251. doi:10.1177/104649640103200205

Smokowski, P. R., Rose, S. D., Todar, K., & Reardon, K. (1999). Post-group casualty-status, group events and leader behavior: An early look into the dynamics of damaging group experiences. *Research on Social Work Practice, 9*(5), 555–574. doi:10.1177/104973159900900503

Spink, K., & Carron, A. (1994). Group cohesion effects in exercise classes. *Small Group Research, 25*(1), 26–42. doi:10.1177/1046496494251003

Stockton, R., Rohde, R., & Haughey, J. (1992). The effects of structured group exercises on cohesion, engagement, avoidance, and conflict. *Small Group Research, 23*(2), 155–168. doi:10.1177/1046496492232001

Sue, D. W., & Sue, D. (2013). *Counseling the culturally diverse: Theory and practice* (6th ed.). New York, NY: Wiley.

Thibaut, J., & Kelley, H. (1954). Experimental studies of group problem-solving process. In G. Kindzey (Ed.), *Handbook of social psychology* (Vol. 2, pp. 735–785). Reading, MA: Addison-Wesley.

Thibaut, J., & Kelley, H. (1959). *The social psychology of groups*. New York, NY: Wiley.

Toseland, R., Decker, J., & Bliesner, J. (1979). A community program for socially isolated older persons. *Journal of Gerontological Social Work, 1*(3), 211–224. doi:10.1300/J083V01N03_04

Trecker, H. (1972). *Social group work: Principles and practices*. New York, NY: Association Press.

Tropman, J. (2014). *Effective meetings: Improving group decision-making* (4th ed.). Thousand Oaks, CA: Sage Publications.

Tuckman, B. (1965). Developmental sequence in small groups. *Psychological Bulletin, 63*(6), 384–399. doi:10.1037/h0022100

Wech, B., Mossholder, K., Steel, R., & Bennett, N. (1998). Does work group cohesiveness affect individuals' performance and organizational commitment? A cross-level examination. *Small Group Research, 29*(4), 472–494. doi:10.1177/1046496498294004

Wheelan, S. (1994). *Group processes: A developmental perspective*. Boston, MA: Allyn & Bacon.

Widmeyer, W., & Williams, J. (1991). Predicting cohesion in a coacting sport. *Small Group Research, 22*(4), 548–570. doi:10.1177/1046496491224007

Worchell, S. (1994). You can go home again: Returning group research to the group context with an eye on developmental issues. *Small Group Research, 25*(2), 205–223. doi:10.1177/1046496494252004

Yalom, I. (2005). *The theory and practice of group psychotherapy* (5th ed.). New York, NY: Basic Books.

Yuki, M., & Brewer, M. (Eds.). (2014). *Culture and group processes*. New York, NY: Oxford University Press.

Chapter 4

Alimo-Metcalfe, B., & Alban-Metcalfe, R. (2001). The development of a new transformational leadership questionnaire. *Journal of Occupational and Organizational Psychology, 74*(1), 1–27. doi:10.1348/096317901167208

Avolio, B., Walumbwa, F., & Weber, T. (2009). Leadership: Current theories, research, and future directions. *Annual Review of Psychology, 60*, 421–449. doi:10.1146/annurev.psych.60.110707.163621

Aronson, H., & Overall, B. (1966). Treatment expectations of patients in two social classes. *Social Work, 11*, 35–41. doi:10.1093/sw/11.1.35

Bandura, A. A. (1995). *Exercise of personal and collective efficacy in changing societies*. New York, NY: Cambridge University Press. doi:10.1017/CBO9780511527692.003

Bandura, A. A. (1997b). *Self-efficacy in changing societies*. New York, NY: Cambridge University Press.

Barlow, S. (2013). *Specialty competencies in group psychology*. New York, NY: Oxford University Press.

Barlow, C., Blythe, J., & Edmonds, M. (1999). *A handbook of interactive exercises for groups*. Boston, MA: Allyn & Bacon.

Bass, B. M. (1985). *Leadership and performance beyond expectations*. New York, NY: Free Press.

Bass, B. M. (1998). *Transformational leadership: Industry, military, and educational impact*. Mahwah, NJ: Erlbaum.

Bass, B. M., & Avolio, B. J. (1990a). The implications of transactional and transformational leadership for individual, team, and organizational development. In R. W. Woodman & W. A. Passmore (Eds.), *Research in organizational change and development*. Greenwich, CT: JAI Press.

Bass, B. M., & Avolio, B. J. (1990b). *Manual for the multifactor leadership questionnaire*. Palo Alto, CA: Consulting Psychologists Press.

Bass, B. M., & Avolio, B. J. (1993). Transformational leadership: A response to critiques. In M. M. Chemers & R. Ayman (Eds.), *Leadership theory and research: Perspectives and directions*. San Diego, CA: Academic Press.

Bauman, S. (2010). Group leader style and functions. In R. Conyne (Ed.), *The Oxford handbook of group counseling* (pp. 325–345). New York, NY: Oxford University Press.

Bednar, K., & Kaul, T. (1994). Experimental group research: Can the cannon fire? In A. Bergen & S. Garfield (Eds.), *Handbook of psychotherapy and behavior change* (4th ed., pp. 631–663). New York, NY: Wiley.

Brabender, V., & Fallon, A. (2009). *Group development in practice*. Washington, DC: American Psychological Association.

Brown, N. (2010). Group leadership teaching and training: Methods and issues. In R. Conyne (Ed.), *The Oxford handbook of group counseling* (pp. 346–369). New York, NY: Oxford University Press.

Browning, L. (1977). Diagnosing teams in organizational settings. *Group and Organization Studies, 2*(2), 187–197. doi:10.1177/105960117700200205

Burlingame, G., Whitcomb, K., & Woodland, S. (2014). Process and outcome in group counseling and psychotherapy. In J. Delucia-Waack, C. Kalodner, & M. Riva, (Eds.), *Handbook of group counseling & psychotherapy* (2nd ed., pp. 55–68). Thousand Oaks, CA: Sage Publications.

Chemers, M. M. (2000). Leadership research and theory: A functional integration. *Group Dynamics: Theory, Research, and Practice, 4*(1), 27–43. doi:10.1037/1089-2699.4.1.27

Chen, M., & Rybak, C. (2004). *Group leadership skills*. Belmont, CA: Brooks/Cole.

Davis, F., & Lohr, N. (1971). Special problems with the use of co-therapists in group psychotherapy. *International Journal of Group Psychotherapy, 21*(2), 143–158.

Davis, I. (1975). Advice-giving in parent counseling. *Social Casework, 56*(6), 343–347.

Dienesch, R. M., & Liden, R. C. (1986). Leader-member exchange model of leadership: A critique and further development. *Academy of Management Review, 11*, 618–634. doi:10.2307/258314

Dies, R. (1994). Therapist variables in group psychotherapy research. In A. Fuhriman & G. M. Burlingame (Eds.), *Handbook of group psychotherapy* (pp. 114–154). New York, NY: Wiley.

Egan, G. (2013). *The skilled helper* (10th ed.). Pacific Grove, CA: Brooks/Cole.

Emrick, C. D., Lassen, C. L., & Edwards, M. T. (1977). Nonprofessional peers as therapeutic agents. In A. Gurman & A. Razin (Eds.), *Effective psychotherapy: A handbook of research* (pp. 120–161). New York, NY: Pergamon Press.

Etzioni, A. (1961). *A comparative analysis of complex organizations on power, involvement and their correlates*. New York, NY: Free Press.

Ewalt, P., & Kutz, J. (1976). An examination of advice giving as a therapeutic intervention. *Smith College Studies in Social Work, 47*(1), 3–19. doi:10.1080/00377317609516494

Forsyth, D. R. (2014). *Group dynamics* (6th ed.). Belmont, CA: Wadsworth Cengage Learning.

Fortune, A. (1979). Communication in task-centered treatment. *Social Work, 24*(5), 390–397. doi:10.1093/sw/24.5.390

French, J., & Raven, B. (1959). The bases of social power. In D. Cartwright (Ed.), *Studies in social power*. Ann Arbor: Institute for Research, University of Michigan.

Galinsky, M., & Schopler, J. (1981). Structuring co-leadership in social work training. *Social Work with Groups, 3*(4), 51–63. doi:10.1300/J009v03n04_08

Garvin, C. (1997). *Contemporary group work* (3rd ed.). Boston, MA: Allyn & Bacon.

Gelso, C., & Harbin, J. (2007). Insight, action, and the therapeutic relationship. In L. G. Castonguay & C. E. Hill (Eds.), *Insight in psychotherapy* (pp. 293–311). Washington, DC: American Psychological Association.

Germain, C., & Gitterman, A. (2008). *The life model of social work practice* (3rd ed.). New York, NY: Columbia University Press.

Gitterman, A., & Shulman, L. (Eds.). (2005). *Mutual aid groups, vulnerable populations, and the life cycle* (3rd ed.). New York, NY: Columbia University Press.

Goldstein, H. (1983). Starting where the client is. *Social Casework, 64*(5), 267–275.

Goldstein, H. (1988). A cognitive-humanistic/social learning perspective on social group work practice. *Social Work with Groups, 11*(1–2), 9–32. doi:10.1300/J009v11n01_02

Graen, G., & Schiemann, W. (1978). Leader-member agreement: A vertical dyad linkage approach. *Journal of Applied Psychology, 63*(2), 206–212. doi:10.1037/0021-9010.63.2.206

Hare, A. P., Blumberg, H. H., Davies, M. F., & Kent, M. V. (1995). *Small group research: A handbook*. Norwood, NJ: Ablex.

Harel, Y., Shechtman, Z., & Cutrona, C. (2011). Individual and group process variables that affect social support in counseling groups. *Group Dynamics: Theory, Research, and Practice, 15*(4), 297–310. doi:10.1037/a0025058

Heap, K. (1979). *Process and action in work with groups*. Elmsford, NY: Pergamon Press.

Joyce, A., Piper, W., & Ogrodniczuk, J. (2007). Therapeutic alliance and cohesion variables as predictors of outcome in short-term group psychotherapy. *International Journal of Group Psychotherapy, 57*(3), 269–296. doi:10.1521/ijgp.2007.57.3.269

Karakowsky, L., & McBey, K. (2001). Do my contributions matter? The influence of imputed expertise of member involvement and self-evaluations in the work group. *Group Organization & Management, 26*(1), 70–92. doi:10.1177/1059601101261005

Kaul, T., & Bednar, R. (1994). Pretraining and structure: Parallel lines yet to meet. In A. Fuhriman & G. M. Burlingame (Eds.), *Handbook of group psychotherapy* (pp. 155–188). New York, NY: Wiley.

Kivlighan, D., & Kivlighan, M. (2014). Therapeutic factors: Current theory and research. In J. Delucia-Waack, C. Kalodner, & M. Riva (Eds.), *Handbook of group counseling & psychotherapy* (2nd ed., pp. 46–54). Thousand Oaks, CA: Sage Publications.

Kivlighan, D. M., & Tarrant, J. M. (2001). Does group climate mediate the group leadership-group member outcome relationship? A test of Yalom's hypotheses about leadership priorities. *Group Dynamics: Theory, Research, and Practice, 5*(3), 220–234. doi:10.1037/1089-2699.5.3.220

Kottler, J. A., & Englar-Carlson, M. (2015). *Learning group leadership: An experiential approach* (3rd ed.). Thousand Oaks, CA: Sage Publications.

Lewin, K., & Lippitt, R. (1938). An experimental approach to the study of autocracy and democracy: A preliminary note. *Sociometry, 1*, 292–300. doi:10.2307/2785585

Lewin, K., Lippitt, R., & White, R. (1939). Patterns of aggressive behavior in experimentally created "social climates." *Journal of Social Psychology, 10*(2), 271–299. doi:10.1080/00224545.1939.9713366

Lieberman, M., & Golant, M. (2002). Leader behaviors as perceived by cancer patients in professionally directed support groups and outcomes. *Group dynamics: Theory, Research and Practice, 6*(4), 267–276. doi:10.1037//1089-2699.6.4.267

Lonergan, E. C. (1989). *Group intervention* (3rd ed.). Northvale, NJ: Jason Aronson.

Luke, M. (2014). Effective group leadership skills. In J. Delucia-Waack, C. Kalodner, & M. Riva (Eds.), *Handbook of group counseling & psychotherapy* (2nd ed., pp. 107–119). Thousand Oaks, CA: Sage Publications.

Luke, M., & Hackney, H. (2007). Group coleadership: A critical review. *Counselor Education and Supervision, 46*(4), 280–293. doi:10.1002/j.1556-6978.2007.tb000032.x

Marmarosh, C., Dunton, E., & Amendola, C. (2014). *Groups: Fostering a culture of change*. Thousand Oaks, CA: Sage Publications.

Marshall, W., & Burton, D. (2010). The importance of group processes in offender treatment. *Aggression and Violent Behavior, 15*(2), 141–149. doi:10.1016/j.avb.2009.08.008

Mayer, J., & Timms, N. (1970). *The client speaks: Working class impressions of casework*. New York, NY: Atherton Press.

McClane, W. (1991). The interaction of leader and member characteristics in the leader-member exchange model of leadership. *Small Group Research, 22*(3), 283–300. doi:10.1177/1046496491223001

Middleman, R. (1978). Returning group process to group work. *Social Work with Groups, 1*(1), 15–26. doi:10.1300/J009v01n01_03

Middleman, R., & Wood, G. (1990). Reviewing the past and present of group work and the challenge of the future. *Social Work with Groups, 13*(3), 3–20. doi:10.1300/J009v13n03_02

Miles, J., & Kivlighan, D. (2010). Co-leadership similarity and group climate in group interventions: Testing the co-leadership, team cognition-team diversity model. *Group Dynamics: Theory, Research, and Practice, 14*(2), 114–122 doi:10.1037/a0017503

Nixon, H. (1979). *The small group.* Englewood Cliffs, NJ: Prentice Hall.

Nosko, A., & Wallace, R. (1997). Female/male co-leadership in group. *Social Work with Groups, 20*(2), 3–16. doi:10.1300/J009v20n02_02

Ogrodniczuk, J., Joyce, A., & Piper, W. (2007). Effect of patient dissatisfaction with the therapist on group therapy outcomes. *Clinical Psychology and Psychotherapy, 14*(2), 126–134. doi:10.1002/cpp.526

Okech, J. E. (2008). Reflective practice in group co-leadership. *The Journal for Specialists in Group Work, 33*(3),236–252. doi:10.1080/01933920802196138

Okech, J. E., & Kline, W. B. (2006). Competency concerns in group co-leader relationships. *The Journal for Specialists in Group Work, 31*(2), 165–180. doi:10.1080/01933920500493829

Paquin, J., Kivlighan, D., & Drogosz, L. (2013). Person-group fit, group climate and outcomes in a sample of incarcerated women participating in trauma recover groups. *Group Dynamics: Theory, Research, & Practice, 17*(2), 95–109. doi:10.1037/a0032702

Piper, W. (1994). Client variables. In A. Fuhriman & G. M. Burlingame (Eds.), *Handbook of group psychotherapy* (pp. 83–113). New York, NY: Wiley.

Pyles, L. (2013). *Progressive community organizing: A critical approach for a globalizing world* (2nd ed.). New York, NY: Routledge.

Reid, W. J. (1997). Research on task-centered practice. *Social Work Research, 21*(3), 132–137. doi:10.1093/swr/21.3.132

Reid, W. J., & Shapiro, B. (1969). Client reactions to advice. *Social Service Review, 43*(2), 165–173.

Riva, M. (2014a). An overview of current research and best practices for training beginning group leaders. In J. Delucia-Waack, C. Kalodner, & M. Riva (Eds.), *Handbook of group counseling & psychotherapy* (2nd ed., pp. 120–133). Thousand Oaks, CA: Sage Publications.

Riva, M. (2014b). Supervision of group counseling. In J. Delucia-Waack, D. Gerrity, C. Kalodner, & M. Riva (Eds.). *Handbook of group counseling & psychotherapy* (pp. 370-382). Thousand Oaks, CA: Sage Publications.

Rivas, R., & Toseland, R. (1981). The student group leadership evaluation project: A study of group leadership skills. *Social Work with Groups, 4*(3/4), 159–175.

Rose, S. (1989). *Working with adults in groups: A multi-method approach.* San Francisco, CA: Jossey-Bass.

Sarason, I., & Sarason, B. (2009). Social support: Mapping the construct. *Journal of Social and Personal Relationships, 26*(1), 113–120. doi:1177/0265407509105526.

Saleebey, D. (Ed.). (2013). *The strengths perspective in social work practice* (6th ed.). Boston, MA: Pearson, Allyn & Bacon.

Shulman, L. (2014). Unleashing the healing power of the group. In J. Delucia-Waack, C. Kalodner, & M. Riva (Eds.), *Handbook of group counseling & psychotherapy* (2nd ed., pp. 120–133). Thousand Oaks, CA: Sage Publications.

Shulman, L. (2016). *The skills of helping individuals, families, groups and communities* (8th ed.). Itasca, IL: F. E. Peacock.

Smith, M., Tobin, S., & Toseland, R. (1992). Therapeutic processes in professional and peer counseling of family caregivers of frail elderly. *Social Work, 37*(4), 345–351.

Smokowski, P. R., Rose, S. D., & Bacallao, M. L. (2001). Damaging experiences in therapeutic groups: How vulnerable consumers become group casualties. *Small Group Research, 32*(2), 223–251. doi:10.1177/104649640103200205

Sosik, J., & Jung, D. (2002). Work group characteristics and performance in collectivistic and individualistic cultures. *Journal of Social Psychology, 142*(1), 5–23. doi:10.1080/00224540209603881

Stockton, R., Morran, K., & Chang, S. (2014). An overview of research and best practices for training beginning group workers. In J. Delucia-Waack, D., Kalodner, & M. Riva (Eds.), *Handbook of group counseling & psychotherapy* (2nd ed., pp. 146–149). Thousand Oaks, CA: Sage Publications.

Tasca, G., & Lampard, A. (2012). Reciprocal influence of alliance to the group and outcome in day treatment for eating disorders. *Journal of Counseling Psychology, 59*(4), 507–517.

Thorndike, R. (1938). On what type of task will a group do well? *Journal of Abnormal and Social Psychology, 33*(3), 409–413. doi:10.1037/h0062321

Toseland, R. (1995). *Group work with the elderly and family caregivers.* New York, NY: Springer Publishing Company.

Toseland, R. (2009). *Instructors manual and test bank for Toseland and Rivas.* Boston, MA: Allyn & Bacon.

Toseland, R., Rivas, R., & Chapman, D. (1984). An evaluation of decision making in task groups. *Social Work, 29*(4), 339–346.

Tropman, J. (2014). *Effective meetings: Improving group decision-making* (4th ed.). Thousand Oaks, CA: Sage Publications.

Trotzer, J. (2010). Personhood of the leader. In R. Conyne (Ed.), *The Oxford handbook of group counseling* (pp. 287–307). New York, NY: Oxford University Press.

Ward, D. (2014). Effective processing in groups. In J. Delucia-Waack, C. Kalodner, & M. Riva (Eds.), *Handbook of group counseling & psychotherapy* (2nd ed., pp. 84–94). Thousand Oaks, CA: Sage Publications.

Wright, M. (2002). Co-facilitation: Fashion or function? *Social Work with Groups, 25*(3), 77–92. doi:10.1300/J009v25n03_06

Yalom, I. (2005). *The theory and practice of group psychotherapy* (5th ed.). New York, NY: Basic Books.

Yukl, G. (2012). *Leadership in organizations* (8th ed.). Upper Saddle River, NJ: Prentice Hall.

Chapter 5

Abernethy, A. (2012). A spiritually informed approach to group psychotherapy. In J. Kleinberg (Ed.), *The Wiley-Blackwell handbook of group psychotherapy* (pp. 681–706). Chichester, England: Wiley-Blackwell.

Akinsulure-Smith, A. (2009). Brief psychoeducational group treatment with re-traumatized refugees and asylum seekers. *Journal for Specialists in Group Work, 34*(2), 137–150. doi:10.1080/01933920902798007

Appleby, G., Colon, E., & Hamilton, J. (2011). *Diversity, oppression, and social functioning: Person-in-environment assessment and intervention* (3rd ed.). Boston, MA: Allyn & Bacon.

Aponte, J., Rivers, R., & Wohl, R. (2000). *Psychological interventions and cultural diversity* (2nd ed.). Boston, MA: Allyn & Bacon.

Atkinson, D., & Lowe, S. (1995). The role of ethnicity, cultural knowledge, and conventional techniques in counseling and psychotherapy. In J. Ponterotto, J. Casas, L. Suzuki, & C. Alexander (Eds.), *Handbook of multicultural counseling* (pp. 387–414). Thousand Oaks, CA: Sage Publications.

Barlow, S. (2013). *Specialty competencies in group psychology*. New York, NY: Oxford University Press.

Brown, A., & Mistry, T. (1994). Group work with mixed membership groups: Issues of race and gender. *Social Work with Groups, 17*(3), 5–21. doi:10.1300/J009v17n03_02

Brown, B. M. (1995). A bill of rights for people with disabilities in group work. *Journal for Specialists in Group Work, 20*(2), 71–75. doi:10.1080/01933929508411328

Burnes, T., & Ross, K. (2010). Applying social justice to oppression and marginalization in group process: Interventions and strategies for group counselors. *Journal for Specialists in Group Work, 35*(2), 169–176. doi:10.1080/01933921003706014

Burwell, N. (1998). Human diversity and empowerment. In H. W. Johnson, et al. (Eds.), *The social services: An introduction* (5th ed., pp. 357–370). Itasca, IL: Peacock Press.

Crethar, H., Torres, R., & Nash, S. (2008). In search of common threads: Linking multicultural, feminist, and social justice counseling paradigms. *Journal of Counseling and Development, 86*(3), 269–278. doi:10.1002/j.1556-6678.2008.tb00509.x

D'Andrea, M. (2004). The impact of racial-cultural identity of group leaders and members: Theory and recommendations. In J. L. Delucia-Waack, D. A. Gerrity, C. R. Kalodner, & M. T. Riva (Eds.), *Group counseling and psychotherapy* (pp. 265–282). Thousand Oaks, CA: Sage Publications.

D'Andrea, M. (2014). Understanding racial/cultural identity development theories to promote effective multi-cultural group counseling. In J. Delucia-Waack, C. Kalodner, & M. Riva (Eds.), *Handbook of group counseling & psychotherapy* (2nd ed., pp. 196–208). Thousand Oaks, CA: Sage Publications.

Davis, L., Galinsky, M., & Schopler, J. (1995). RAP: A framework for leadership of multiracial groups. *Social Work, 40*(2), 155–165. doi:10.1093/sw/40.2.155

Davis, L., & Proctor, E. (1989). *Race, gender and class: Guidelines for practice with individuals, families and groups*. Englewood Cliffs, NJ: Prentice Hall.

Debiak, D. (2007). Attending to diversity in group psychotherapy: An ethical imperative. *International Journal of Group Psychotherapy, 57*(1), 1–12. doi:10.1521/ijgp.2007.57.1.1

Delucia-Waack, J., Kalodner, C., & Riva, M. (Eds.). (2014). *Handbook of group counseling & psychotherapy* (2nd ed.). Thousand Oaks, CA: Sage Publications.

Devore, W., & Schlesinger, E. (1999). *Ethnic-sensitive social work practice* (5th ed.). Boston, MA: Allyn & Bacon.

Diaz, T. (2002). Group work from an Asian Pacific Island perspective: Making connections between group worker ethnicity and practice. *Social Work with Groups, 25*(3), 43–60. doi:10.1300/J009v25n03_04

dickey, l., & Loewy, M. (2010). Group work with transgendered clients. *Journal for Specialists in Group Work, 35*(3), 236–245. doi:10.1080/01933922.2010.492904

Diller, J. (2015). *Cultural diversity: A primer for the human services* (5th ed.). Belmont, CA: Wadsworth.

Dinges, N., & Cherry, D. (1995). Symptom expression and use of mental health services among ethnic minorities. In J. Aponte, R. Rivers, & J. Wohl (Eds.), *Psychological interventions and cultural diversity* (pp. 40–56). Boston, MA: Allyn & Bacon.

Earley, P. R., & Randel, A. (1997). Self and other: "Face" and work group dynamics. In C. Granrose & S. Oskamp (Eds.), *Cross-cultural work groups: An overview* (pp. 113–133). Thousand Oaks, CA: Sage Publications.

Ellis, S., Simpson, C., Rose, C., & Plotner, A. (2014). Group counseling services for people with disabilities. In J. Delucia-Waack, C. Kalodner, & M. Riva, (Eds.), *Handbook of group counseling & psychotherapy* (2nd ed., pp. 264–276). Thousand Oaks, CA: Sage Publications.

Finn, J., & Jacobson, M. (2008). *Just practice: A social justice approach to social work* (2nd ed.). Peosta, IA: Eddie Bowers.

Flores, M. (2000). La familia Latina. In M. Flores & G. Carey (Ed.), *Family therapy with Hispanics: Toward appreciating diversity*. Boston, MA: Allyn & Bacon.

Forsyth, D. R. (2014). *Group dynamics* (6th ed.). Belmont, CA: Wadsworth Cengage Learning.

Garland, J., Jones, H., & Kolodny, R. (1976). A model of stages of group development in social work groups. In S. Bernstein (Ed.), *Explorations in group work* (pp. 17–71). Boston, MA: Charles River Books.

Goto, S. (1997). Majority and minority perspectives on cross-cultural interactions. In C. Granrose & S. Oskamp (Eds.), *Cross-cultural work groups: An overview* (pp. 90–112). Thousand Oaks, CA: Sage Publications.

Gray-Little, B., & Kaplan, D. (2000). Race and ethnicity in psychotherapy research. In C. R. Snyder & R. Ingram (Eds.), *Handbook of psychological change* (pp. 591–613). New York, NY: Wiley.

Green, J. (1999). *Cultural awareness in the human services: A multi-ethnic approach* (3rd ed.). Boston, MA: Allyn & Bacon.

Hays, P. (2007). *Addressing cultural complexities in practice: Assessment, diagnosis, and therapy* (2nd ed.). Washington, DC: American Psychological Association.

Hays, P., Arredondo, S., Gladding, R., & Toporek, R. (2010). Integrating social justice in group work. *Journal for Specialists in Group Work, 35*(2), 177–206.

Hogan-Garcia, M. (2013). *The four skills of cultural diversity competence: A process for understanding and practice* (4th ed.). Belmont, CA: Wadsworth.

Holmes, L. (2002). Women in group and women's groups. *International Journal of Group Psychotherapy, 52*(2), 171–188. doi:10.1521/ijgp.52.2.171.45495

Horne, S., Levitt, H., Reeves, T., & Wheeler, E. (2014). Group work with gay, lesbian, bisexual, transgender, queer, and questioning clients. In J. Delucia-Waack, C. Kalodner, & M. Riva, (Eds.), *Handbook of group counseling & psychotherapy* (2nd ed., pp. 253–263). Thousand Oaks, CA: Sage Publications.

Johnson, D. W. (2014). *Reaching out: Interpersonal effectiveness and self-actualization* (11th ed.). Boston, MA: Allyn & Bacon.

Koss-Chioino, J. (2000). Traditional and folk approaches among ethnic minorities. In J. Aponte, R. Rivers, & J. Wohl (Eds.), *Psychological interventions and cultural diversity* (2nd ed., pp. 149–166). Boston, MA: Allyn & Bacon.

Kurtz, L. F. (2014). *Recovery groups*. New York, NY: Oxford University Press.

Lev, A. I. (2009). The ten tasks of the mental health provider. Recommendations for revision of the World Professional Association for Transgender Health Standards of Care. *International Journal of Transgenderism, 11*(2), 74–99. doi:10.1080/15532730903008032

Lum, D. (2004). *Social work practice and people of color: A process-stage approach* (5th ed.). Belmont, CA: Brooks/Cole.

Lum, D. (Ed.). (2005). *Cultural competence, practice stages, and client systems.* Belmont, CA: Brooks/Cole.

Lum, D. (Ed.). (2011). *Culturally competent practice: A framework for understanding diverse groups and justice issues* (4th ed.). Sacramento, CA: Thomson, Brooks/Cole.

Mallon, G. (2008). (Ed.). *Social work practice with lesbian, gay, bisexual, and transgender people* (2nd ed.). New York, NY: Routledge.

Maznevski, M., & Peterson, M. (1997). Societal values, social interpretation, and multinational teams. In C. Granrose & S. Oskemp (Eds.), *Cross-cultural work groups: An overview* (pp. 61–89). Thousand Oaks, CA: Sage Publications.

McGrath, P., & Axelson, J. (1999). *Accessing awareness & developing knowledge: Foundations for skill in a multicultural society* (3rd ed.). Pacific Grove, CA: Brooks/Cole.

McLeod, P., Lobel, S., & Cox, T. (1996). Ethnic diversity and creativity in small groups. *Small Group Research, 27*(2), 248–264. doi:10.1177/1046496496272003

McRoy, R. (2003). Cultural competence with African Americans. In D. Lum (Ed.), *Culturally competent practice: A framework for understanding diverse groups and justice issues.* Sacramento, CA: Thomson Brooks/Cole.

McWhirter, P., & Robbins, R. (2014). Group therapy with native people. In J. Delucia-Waack, C. Kalodner, & M. Riva (Eds.), *Handbook of group counseling & psychotherapy* (2nd ed., pp. 370–382). Thousand Oaks, CA: Sage Publications.

Misurell, J., & Springer, C. (2013). Developing culturally responsive evidence-based practice: A game-based group therapy program for child sexual abuse (CSA). *Journal of Child and Family Studies, 22*(1), 137–149. doi:10.1007/s10826-011-9560-2

Moreno, C. L., & Guido, M. (2005). Social work practice with Latino Americans. In L. Doman (Ed.), *Cultural competence, practice stages, and client systems* (pp. 88–111). Belmont, CA: Thomson Brooks/Cole.

Nystrom, N. M. (2005). Social work practice with lesbian, gay, bisexual, and transgender people. In L. Doman (Ed.), *Cultural competence, practice stages, and client systems* (pp. 203–229). Belmont, CA: Thomson Brooks/Cole.

Orasanu, J., Fischer, U., & Davison, J. (1997). Cross-cultural barriers to effective communication in aviation. In C. Granrose & S. Oskamp (Eds.), *Cross-cultural work groups: An overview* (pp. 134–162). Thousand Oaks, CA: Sage Publications.

Parrillo, V. (2014). *Strangers to these shores: Race and ethnic relations in the United States* (11th ed.). Boston, MA: Allyn & Bacon.

Pearson, V. (1991). Western theory, Eastern practice: Social group work in Hong Kong. *Social Work with Groups, 14*(2), 45–58. doi:10.1300/J009v14n02_04

Pillari, V. (2002). *Social work practice: Theories and skills.* Boston, MA: Allyn & Bacon.

Pinderhughes, E. B. (1995). Empowering diverse populations: Family practice in the 21st century. *Families in Society, 76*, 131–140.

Pure, D. (2012). Single-gender or mixed-gender groups: Choosing a perspective. In J. Kleinberg (Ed.), *The Wiley-Blackwell handbook of group psychotherapy.* Chichester, England: Wiley-Blackwell.

Ratts, M., Anthony, L., & Santos, K. (2010). The dimensions of social justice model: Transforming traditional group work into a socially just framework. *Journal for Specialists in Group Work, 35*(2), 160–168. doi:10.1080/01933921003705974

Ratts, M., & Pedersen, P. (2014). *Counseling for multiculturalism and social justice: Integration, theory, and application* (4th ed). Alexandria, VA: American Counseling Association.

Ritter, K. (2010). Group counseling with sexual minorities. In R. Conyne (Ed.), *The Oxford handbook of group counseling.* New York, NY: Oxford University Press.

Rivera, E., Fernandez, I., & Hendricks, A. (2014). Psychoeducation and counselling with Latinos/as In J. Delucia-Waack, C. Kalodner, & M. Riva, (Eds.), *Handbook of group counseling & psychotherapy* (2nd ed., pp. 242–253). Thousand Oaks, CA: Sage Publications.

Rothman, J. C. (2008). *Cultural competence in process and practice: Building bridges.* Boston, MA: Allyn & Bacon Pearson Education.

Saleebey, D. (Ed.). (2013). *The strengths perspective in social work practice* (6th ed.). Boston, MA: Pearson, Allyn & Bacon.

Schiller, L. (1995). Stages of development in women's groups: A relational model. In R. Kurland & R. Salmon (Eds.), *Group work practice in a troubled society* (pp. 117–138). New York, NY: Haworth Press.

Schiller, L. (1997). Rethinking stages of development in women's groups: Implications for practice. *Social Work with Groups, 20*(3), 3–19. doi:10.1300/J009v20n03_02

Schriver, J. (2011). *Human behavior and the social environment* (5th ed.). Boston, MA: Allyn & Bacon.

Shea, M., Cachelin, F., Uribe, L., Striegel, R., Thompson, D., & Wilson G. (2012). Cultural adaptation of a cognitive behavior therapy guided self-help program for Mexican American women with binge eating disorders. *Journal of Counseling & Development, 9*(3), 308–318. doi:10.1002/j.1556-6676.2012.00039.x

Smith, L. C., & Shin, R. Q. (2008). Social privilege, social justice, and group counseling: An inquiry. *The Journal for Specialists in Group Work, 33*(4), 351–366. doi:10.1080/01933920802424415

Steen, S., Shi, Q., & Robbins, R. (2014). Group counseling for African Americans: Research and practice considerations. In J. Delucia-Waack, C. Kalodner, & M. Riva (Eds.), *Handbook of group counseling & psychotherapy* (2nd ed., pp. 370–382). Thousand Oaks, CA: Sage Publications.

Sue, D. W., & Sue, D. (2013). *Counseling the culturally diverse: Theory and practice* (6th ed.). New York, NY: Wiley.

Walters, K., Longres, J., Han, C., & Icard, D. (2003). Cultural competence with gay and lesbian persons of color. In D. Lum (Ed.), *Culturally competent practice: A framework for understanding diverse groups and justice issues* (pp. 310–342). Sacramento, CA: Thomson Brooks/Cole.

Watson, W., Johnson, L., & Merritt, D. (1998). Team orientation, self-orientation, and diversity in task groups: Their connection to team performance over time. *Group & Organization Management, 23*(2), 161–188. doi:10.1177/1059601198232005

Weaver, H. (1999). Indigenous people and the social work profession: Defining culturally competent services. *Social Work, 44*(3), 217–225. doi:10.1093/sw/44.3.217

Weine, S., Kulauzovic, Y., Klebic, A., Besic, S., Mujagic, A., Muzurovic, J., Spahovic, D., Sclove, S., Pavkovic, I., Feetham, S., & Rolland, J. (2008). Evaluating a multiple-family group access intervention for refugees with PTSD. *Journal of Marital and Family Therapy, 34*(2), 149–164. doi:10.1111/j.1752-0606.2008.00061.x

Western, D. (2013). *Gender-based violence and depression in women: A feminist group work response.* New York, NY: Springer Publishing Company.

Williams, O. (1994). Group work with African-American men who batter: Toward more ethnically sensitive practice. *Journal of Comparative Family Studies, 25*(1), 91–103.

Yuki, M., & Brewer, M. (Eds.). (2014). *Culture and group processes.* New York, NY: Oxford University Press.

Chapter 6

Barlow, S. (2013). *Specialty competencies in group psychology.* New York, NY: Oxford University Press.

Blouin, J., Schnarre, K., Carter, J., Blouin, A., Tener, L., Zuro, C., & Barlow, J. (1995). Factors affecting dropout rate from cognitive-behavioral group treatment for bulimia nervosa. *International Journal of Eating Disorders, 17*(4), 323–329. doi:10.1002/1098-108X(199505)17:4<323::AID-EAT2260170403>3.0.CO;2-2

Brabender, V., & Fallon, A. (2009). *Group development in practice.* Washington, DC: American Psychological Association.

Burlingame, G., Cox, J., Davies, R., Layne, C., & Gleave, R. (2011). The group selection questionnaire: Further refinements in group member selection. *Group Dynamics: Theory, Research, and Practice, 15*(1), 60–74. doi:org/10.1037/a0020220

Burnes, T., & Ross, K. (2010). Applying social justice to oppression and marginalization in group process: Interventions and strategies for group counselors. *Journal for Specialists in Group Work, 35*(2), 169–176. doi:10.1080/01933921003706014

Conyne, R. (Ed.). (2010). *The Oxford handbook of group counseling.* New York, NY: Oxford University Press.

Coulson, N., & Greenwood, N. (2011). Families affected by childhood cancer: An analysis of the provision of social support within online support groups. *Child Care Health and Development, 38*(6), 870–877. doi:10.1111/j.1365-2214.2011.0136.x

Forsyth, D. R. (2014). *Group dynamics* (6th ed.). Belmont, CA: Wadsworth Cengage Learning.

Fukkink, R., & Hermanns, J. (2009). Children's experiences with chat support and telephone support. *Journal of Child Psychology and Psychiatry, 50*(6), 759–766. doi:10.1111/j.1469-7610.2008.02024.x

Galinsky, M., & Schopler, J. (1989). Developmental patterns in open-ended groups. *Social Work with Groups, 12*(2), 99–114. doi:10.1300/J009v12n02_08

Glueckauf, R. L., & Ketterson, T. U. (2004). Telehealth interventions for individuals with chronic illness: Research review and implications for practice. *Professional Psychology: Research and Practice, 35*(6), 615–627. doi:10.1037/0735-7028.35.6.615

Glueckauf, R. L., & Loomis, J. S. (2003). Alzheimer's caregiver support online: Lessons learned, initial findings and future directions. *NeuroRehabilitation, 18*(2), 135–146. Retrieved from: http://iospress.metapress.com/content/etxhn7tpn46dy-2qr/?p=f02026fc736c4929a230992af5e4d623&pi=5

Glueckauf, R. L., & Noel, L. T. (2011). Telehealth and family caregiving: Developments in research, education, policy and practice. In R. Toseland, D. Haigler, & D. Monahan *Education and support programs for caregivers* (pp. 85–106). New York, NY: Springer Publishing Company.

Glueckauf, R. L., Nickelson, D., Whitton, J., & Loomis, J. S. (2004). Telehealth and healthcare psychology: Current developments in telecommunications, regulatory practices, and research. In R. G. Frank, A. Baum, & J. L. Wallander (Eds.), *Handbook of clinical health psychology: Models and perspectives in health psychology* (Vol. 3, pp. 377–411). Washington, DC: American Psychological Association.

Glueckauf, R. L., Pickett, T. C., Ketterson, T. U., Loomis, J. S., & Rozensky, R. H. (2003). Preparation for the delivery of telehealth services: A self-study framework for expansion of practice. *Professional Psychology: Research and Practice, 34*(2), 159–163. doi:10.1037/0735-7028.34.2.159

Golkaramnay, V., Bauer, S., Haug, S., Wolf, M., & Kordy, H. (2007). The exploration of the effectiveness of group therapy through an internet chat as aftercare: A controlled naturalistic study. *Psychotherapy and Psychosomatics, 76*(4), 219–225. doi:10.1159/000101500

Haas, L., Benedict, J., & Kobos, J. (1996). Psychotherapy by telephone: Risks and benefits for psychologists and consumers. *Professional Psychology: Research and Practice, 27*(2), 154–160. doi:10.1037/0735-7028.27.2.154

Haberstroh, S., & Moyer, M. (2012). Exploring an online self-injury support group: Perspectives from group members. *Journal for Specialists in Group Work, 37*(2), 113–132. doi:10.1080/01933922.2011.646088

Janis, I. (1982). *Groupthink* (2nd ed.). Boston, MA: Houghton Mifflin.

Keats, P., & Sabharwal, V. (2008). Time-limited service alternatives: Using the therapeutic enactment in open group therapy. *Journal of Specialists in Group Work, 33*(4), 297–316. doi:10.1080/01933920802424357

Kelleher, K., & Cross, T. (1990). *Teleconferencing: Linking people together electronically.* Norman: University of Oklahoma Press.

Kiesler, S. (1978). *Interpersonal processes in groups and organizations.* Arlington Heights, IL: AHM.

LeCroy, C. (Ed.). (2008). *Handbook of evidence-based treatment manuals for children and adolescents* (2nd ed.). New York, NY: Oxford University Press.

MacNair-Semands, R. (2002). Predicting attendance and expectations for group therapy. *Group Dynamics, Theory, Research, 6*(3), 219–228. doi:10.1037/1089-2699.6.3.219

Maheu, M., Whitten, P., & Allen, A. (2001). *E-Health, telehealth, and telemedicine: A guide to start-up and success.* San Francisco, CA: Jossey-Bass.

Martindale-Adams, J., Nichols, L., Burns, R., & Malone, C. (2002). Telephone support groups: A lifeline for isolated Alzheimer's disease caregivers. *Alzheimer's Care Quarterly, 3*(2), 181–189.

McKenna, K. Y. A., & Bargh, J. (1999). Causes and consequences of social interaction on the Internet: A conceptual framework. *Media Psychology, 1*(3), 249–269.

McKenna, K. Y. A., & Bargh, J. (2000). Plan 9 from cyberspace: The implications of the Internet for personality and social psychology. *Personality and Social Psychology Review, 4*(1), 57–75. doi:10.1207/S15327957PSPR0401_6

McKenna, K. Y. A., & Green, A. S. (2002). Virtual group dynamics. *Group Dynamics: Theory, Research, and Practice, 6*(1), 116–127. doi:10.1037/1089-2699.6.1.116

McKenna, K. Y. A., Green, A. S., & Gleason, M. E. J. (2002). Relationship formation on the Internet: What's the big attraction? *Journal of Social Issues, 58*(1), 9–31. doi:10.1111/1540-4560.00246

Merchant, N. M., & Yozamp, C. J. (2014). *Groups in community and agency settings.* Thousand Oaks, CA: Sage Publications.

National Board For Certified Counselors (NBCC) (2012). *Policy regarding the provision of distance professional services.* Retrieved from: http://www.NBCC.org.

Nickelson, D. (2000). Telehealth, health care services, & health care policy: A plan for action in the new millennium. *New Jersey Psychologist, 50*(1), 24–27.

Oei, T. K., & Kazmierczak, T. (1997). Factors associated with dropout in a group cognitive behaviour therapy for mood disorders. *Behavior Research and Therapy, 35*(11), 1025–1030. doi:10.1016/S0005-7967(97)00060-0

Oravec, J. (2000). Online counseling and the Internet: Perspectives for mental health care supervision and education. *Journal of Mental Health, 9*(2), 121–135. doi:10.1080/09638230050009122

Owen, J., Goldstein, M., Lee, J., Breen, N., & Rowland, J. (2010). Use of health-related online support groups: Population data from the California health interview survey complementary and alternative medicine study. *Journal of Computer-mediated Communication, 15*(3), 427–446. doi:10.1111/j.1083-6101.2010.01501.x

Page, B. (2010). Online groups. In R. Conyne (Ed.), *The Oxford handbook of group counseling* (pp. 520–533). New York, NY: Oxford University Press.

Postmes, T., Spears, R., & Lea, M. (1999). Social identity, normative content, and "deindividuation" in computer-mediated groups. In N. Ellemers, R. Spears, & B. Doosje (Eds.), *Social identity: Context, commitment, content* (pp. 164–183). Malden, MA: Blackwell Publishers.

Postmes, T., Spears, R., Sakhel, K., & de Groot, D. (2001). Social influence in computer-mediated communication: The effects of anonymity on group behavior. *Personality and Social Psychology Bulletin, 27*(10), 1243–1254. doi:10.1177/01461672012710001

Riper, H., Spek, V., Boon, B., Conjin, B., Kramer, J., Martin-Abello, K., & Smit, F. (2011). Effectiveness of e-self-help interventions for curbing adult problem drinking: A meta-analysis. *Journal of Medical Internet Research, 13*(2), e42. doi:10.2196/jmir.1691

Riva, M. T., Lippert, L., & Tackett, M. J. (2000). Selection practices of group leaders: A national survey. *Journal for Specialists in Group Work, 25*(2), 157–169. doi:10.1080/01933920008411459

Rooney, R. (2009). *Strategies for work with involuntary clients* (2nd ed.). New York, NY: Columbia University Press.

Rosswurm, M., Larrabee, J., & Zhang, J. (2002). Training family caregivers of dependent elderly adults through on-site and telecommunications programs. *Journal of Gerontological Nursing, 28*(7), 27–38.

Schopler, J., & Galinsky, M. (1984). Meeting practice needs: Conceptualizing the open-ended group. *Social Work with Groups, 7*(2), 3–21. doi:10.1300/J009v07n02_02

Schopler, J., & Galinsky, M. (1990). Can open-ended groups move beyond beginnings? *Small Group Research, 21*(4), 435–449. doi:10.1177/1046496490214001

Schopler, J., Galinsky, M., & Abell, M. (1997). Creating community through telephone and computer groups: Theoretical and practice perspectives. *Social Work with Groups, 20*(4), 19–34. doi:10.1300/J009v20n04_03

Shulman, L. (2016). *The skills of helping individuals, families, groups and communities* (8th ed.). Itasca, IL: F. E. Peacock.

Siegel, J., Dubrovsky, V., Kiesler, S., & McGuire, T. (1986). Group processes in computer-mediated communication. *Organizational Behavior and Human Decision Processes, 37*(2), 157–187. doi:10.1016/0749-5978(86)90050-6

Smith, T., & Toseland, R. (2006). The evaluation of a telephone caregiver support group intervention. *Gerontologist, 46*(5), 620–629. doi:10.1093/geront/46.5.620

Smokowski, P. R., Galinsky, M., & Harlow, K. (2001). Using technologies in groupwork, Part II: Technology-based groups. *Groupwork, 13*(1), 6–22.

Spek, V., Cuijpers, P., Nyklicek, I., Riper, H., Keyzer, J., & Pop, V. (2007). Internet-based cognitive behaviour therapy for symptoms of depression and anxiety: A meta-analysis. *Psychological Medicine, 37*(3), 319–328. doi:10.1017/S003329706008944

Spek, V., Nyklicek, I., Cuijpers, P., & Pop, V. (2007). Predictors of outcomes of group and internet-based cognitive behavior therapy. *Journal of Affective Disorders, 105*(1–3), 137–145. doi:10.1016/j.jad.2007.05.001

Stein, L., Rothman, B., & Nakanishi, M. (1993). The telephone group: Accessing group service to the homebound. *Social Work with Groups, 16*(1/2), 203–215.

Tasca, G., Ramsay, T., Corace, K., Illing, V., Bone, M., Bissada, H., & Balfor, L. (2010). Modeling longitudinal data from a rolling therapy group program with membership turnover: Does group culture affect individual alliance? *Group Dynamics: Theory, Research, & Practice, 14*(2), 151–162. doi:10.1037/a0018778

Toseland, R., & Rizzo, V. (2004). What's different about working with older people in groups? Journal of Gerontological Social Work, 44(1/2), 5–23. doi:10.1300/1j083v44n01_02

Toseland, R., Naccarato, T., & Wray, L. (2007). Telephone groups for older persons and family caregivers. *Clinical Gerontologist, 31*(1), 59–76. doi:10.1300/J018v31n01_05

Tourigny, M., & Hebert, M. (2007). Comparison of open versus closed group interventions for sexually abused adolescent girls. *Violence and Victims, 22*(3), 334–349. doi:10.1891/088667007780842775

Tropman, J. (2014). *Effective meetings: Improving group decision-making* (4th ed.). Thousand Oaks, CA: Sage Publications.

Turner, H. (2011). Concepts for effective facilitation of open groups. *Social Work with Groups, 34*(3–4), 246–256. doi:10.1080/01609513.2011.558822

Weinberg, H. (2001). Group process and group phenomena on the Internet. *International Journal of Group Psychotherapy, 51*(3), 361–378. doi:10.1521/ijgp.51.3.361.49881

Wiener, L. S., Spencer, E. D., Davidson, R., & Fair, C. (1993). Telephone support groups: A new avenue toward psychosocial support for HIV-infected children and their families. *Social Work with Groups, 16*(3), 55–71. doi:10.1300/J009v16n03_05

Yalom, I. (2005). *The theory and practice of group psychotherapy* (5th ed.). New York, NY: Basic Books.

Chapter 7

Bales, R. (1950). *Interaction process analysis: A method for the study of small groups.* Reading, MA: Addison-Wesley.

Bales, R. (1955). How people interact in conference. *Scientific American, 192*(3), 31–35. doi:10.1038/scientificamerican0355-31

Barlow, S. (2013). *Specialty competencies in group psychology.* New York, NY: Oxford University Press.

Bauer, M. M., & McBride, L. (2003). *Structured group psychotherapy for bipolar disorder: The life goals program* (2nd ed.). New York, NY: Springer Publishing Company.

Bieling, P. J., McCabe, R. E., & Antony, M. M. (2006). *Cognitive-behavioral therapy in groups*. New York, NY: Guilford Press.

Edelwich, J., & Brodsky, A. (1992). *Group counseling for the resistant client: A practical guide to group process*. New York, NY: Lexington Books.

Egan, G. (2013). *The skilled helper* (10th ed.). Pacific Grove, CA: Brooks/Cole.

Forsyth, D. R. (2014). *Group dynamics* (6th ed.). Belmont, CA: Wadsworth Cengage Learning.

Frank, J. (1961). *Persuasion and healing: A comparative study of psychotherapy*. New York, NY: Schocken Books.

Fuhriman, A., & Burlingame, G. (1994). Group psychotherapy: Research and practice. In A. Fuhriman & G. M. Burlingame (Eds.), *Handbook of group psychotherapy* (pp. 3–40). New York, NY: Wiley.

Garland, J., Jones, H., & Kolodny, R. (1976). A model of stages of group development in social work groups. In S. Bernstein (Ed.), *Explorations in group work* (pp. 17–71). Boston, MA: Charles River Books.

Garvin, C., Guiterrez, L., & Galinsky, M. (2004). *Handbook of social work with groups*. New York, NY: Guilford Press.

Gitterman, A., & Shulman, L. (Eds.). (2005). *Mutual aid groups, vulnerable populations, and the life cycle* (3rd ed.). New York, NY: Columbia University Press.

Glassman, U., & Kates, L. (1990). *Group work: A humanistic approach*. Newbury Park, CA: Sage Publications.

Goldstein, A. P. (2001). *Reducing resistance: Methods for enhancing openness to change*. Champaign, IL: Research Press.

Hays, S., Strosahl, K., & Wilson, K. (2011). *Acceptance and commitment therapy* (2nd ed.). New York, NY: Guilford Press.

Levi, D. (2014). *Group dynamics for teams* (4th ed.). Thousand Oaks, CA: Sage Publications.

Linehan, M. (1993). *Cognitive-behavioral treatment of borderline personality disorders*. New York, NY: Guilford Press.

Linehan, M. (2015). DBT skills training manual. New York, NY: Guilford Press.

LeCroy, C. (Ed.). (2008). Handbook of evidence-based treatment manuals for children and adolescents (2nd ed.) New York, NY: Oxford University Press.

Levine, B., & Gallogly, V. (1985). *Group therapy with alcoholics: Outpatient and inpatient approaches*. Newbury Park, CA: Sage Publications.

Lynch, T., & Cuper, P. (2010). Dialectical behavior therapy. In N. Kazantzis, M. Reinecke, & A. Freeman (Eds.), *Cognitive and behavioral theories in clinical practice*. New York, NY: Guilford Press.

Macgowan, M. J. (2008). *A guide to evidence-based group work*. New York, NY: Oxford University Press.

Maxwell, H., Taswca, G., Gick, M., Ritchie, K., Balfour, L., & Bissada, H. (2012). The impact of attachment anxiety on interpersonal complementarity in early group therapy interactions among women with binge eating disorder. *Group Dynamics: Theory, Research, & Practice.* 16(4), 255–271. doi:10.1037/a0029464

McKay, M., Gopalan, G., Franco, L., Dean-Assael, K., Chacko, A., & Jackson, J. (2011). A collaboratively designed child mental health service model: Multiple family groups for urban children with conduct difficulties. *Research on Social Work Practice, 21*(6), 664–674. doi:10.1177/1049731511406740

McKay, M., & Paleg, K. (Eds.). (1992). *Focal group psychotherapy*. Oakland, CA: New Harbinger.

McKay, M., Wood, J., & Brantley, F. (2007). *The dialectical therapy skills workbook*. Oakland, CA: New Harbinger Publications.

Miller, W., & Rollnick, S. (Eds.). (2013). *Motivational interviewing: Helping people change* (3rd ed.). New York, NY: Guilford Press.

Munzer, J., & Greenwald, H. (1957). Interaction process analysis of a therapy group. *International Journal of Group Psychotherapy, 7*, 175–190.

Neacsiu, A. D., Bohus, M., & Linehan, M. M. (2014). Dialectical behavior therapy: An intervention for emotion dysregulation. In J. J. Gross (Ed.), *Handbook of emotion regulation* (2nd ed., pp. 491–507). New York, NY: Guilford Press.

Paquin, J., Kivlighan, D., & Drogosz, L. (2013). Person-group fit, group climate and outcomes in a sample of incarcerated women participating in trauma recover groups. *Group Dynamics: Theory, Research, & Practice, 17*(2), 95–109. doi:10.1037/a0032702

Pearson, V. (1991). Western theory, Eastern practice: Social group work in Hong Kong. *Social Work with Groups, 14*(2), 45–58. doi:10.1300/J009v14n02_04

Passi, L. (1998). *A guide to creative group programming in the psychiatric day hospital*. New York, NY: Haworth Press.

Prochaska, J., DiClimente, C., & Norcross, C. (1992). In search of how people change. *American Psychologist, 41*(4), 1102–1114. doi:10.1037/0003-066X.47.9.1102

Rooney, R. (2009). *Strategies for work with involuntary clients* (2nd ed.). New York, NY: Columbia University Press.

Rooney, R. H., & Chovanec, M. (2004). Involuntary groups. In C. D. Garvin, L. M. Gutierrez, & M. J. Galinsky (Eds.), *Handbook of social work with groups* (pp. 212–226). New York, NY: Guilford Press.

Rose, S. (1989). *Working with adults in groups: A multi-method approach*. San Francisco, CA: Jossey-Bass.

Rose, S. (1998). *Group therapy with troubled youth*. Thousand Oaks, CA: Sage Publications.

Saleebey, D. (Ed.). (2013). *The strengths perspective in social work practice* (6th ed.). Boston, MA: Pearson, Allyn & Bacon.

Schimmel, C., & Jacobs, E. (2011). When leaders are challenged: Dealing with involuntary members in groups. *The Journal for Specialists in Group Work, 36*(2), 144–158. doi:10.1080/0193392 22.2011.562345

Schwartz, W. (1971). On the use of groups in social work practice. In W. Schwartz & S. Zalba (Eds.), *The practice of group work* (pp. 3–24). New York, NY: Columbia University Press.

Shapiro, J., Peltz, L., & Bernadett-Shapiro, S. (1998). *Brief group treatment for therapists and counselors*. Florence, KY: Wadsworth.

Shulman, L. (2014). Unleashing the healing power of the group. In J. Delucia-Waack, C. Kalodner, & M. Riva (Eds.), *Handbook of group counseling & psychotherapy* (2nd ed., pp. 120–133). Thousand Oaks, CA: Sage Publications.

Shulman, L. (2016). *The skills of helping individuals, families, groups and communities* (8th ed.). Itasca, IL: F. E. Peacock.

Steinberg, D. (2014). *A mutual-aid model social work with groups* (3rd ed.). Oxford, UK: Routledge.

Tropman, J. (2014). *Effective meetings: Improving group decision-making* (4th ed.). Thousand Oaks, CA: Sage Publications.

Trotter, C. (2015). *Working with involuntary clients: A Guide to Practice* (3rd ed.). New York, NY: Routledge.

Walsh, J. (2010). *Psychoeducation in mental health*. Chicago, IL: Lyceum Books.

Waltz, T., & Hays, S. (2010). Acceptance and commitment therapy. In N. Kazantzis, M. Reinecke, & A. Freeman (Eds.), *Cognitive and behavioral theories in clinical practice.* New York, NY: Guilford Press.

Welo, B. K. (2001). *Tough customers: Counseling unwilling clients* (2nd ed.). Upper Marlboro, MD: Graphic Communications.

White, J. R., & Freeman, A. (Eds.). (2000). *Cognitive-behavioral group therapy for specific problems and populations.* Washington, DC: American Psychological Association. doi:10.1037/10352-000

Yalom, I. (1983). *Inpatient group psychotherapy.* New York, NY: Basic Books.

Yalom, I. (2005). *The theory and practice of group psychotherapy* (5th ed.). New York, NY: Basic Books.

Chapter 8

Achenbach, T. (1997). *Child behavior checklist.* Burlington, VT: University Medical Education Associates.

American Psychiatric Association. (2013). *Diagnostic and statistical manual of mental disorders* (5th ed.). Arlington, VA: American Psychiatric Publishing.

Anderson, N., & West, M. (1998). Measuring climate for work group innovation: Development and validation of the team climate inventory. *Journal of Organizational Behavior, 19*(3), 235–258.

Bales, R. (1980). *SYMLOG: Case study kit.* New York, NY: Free Press.

Bales, R., Cohen, S., & Williamson, S. (1979). *SYMLOG: A system for the multiple level observations of groups.* New York, NY: Free Press.

Barlow, S. (2010). Evidence bases for group practice. In R. Conyne (Ed.), *The Oxford handbook of group counseling* (pp. 207–230). New York, NY: Oxford University Press.

Barlow, S. (2013). *Specialty competencies in group psychology.* New York, NY: Oxford University Press.

Bloom, M., Fisher, J., & Orme, J. (2009). *Evaluating practice: Guidelines for the accountable professional* (6th ed.). Boston, MA: Allyn & Bacon.

Budman, S., Demby, A., Feldstein, M., Redondo, J., Scherz, B., Bennett, M., Koppenall, G., Daley, B., Hunter, M., & Ellis, J. (1987). Preliminary findings on a new instrument to measure cohesion in group psychotherapy. *International Journal of Group Psychotherapy, 37*(1), 75–94.

Budman, S., Soldz, S., Demby, A., Davis, M., & Merry, J. (1993). What is cohesiveness? An empirical examination. *Small Group Research, 24*(2), 199–216.

Carless, S. D., & De Paola, C. (2000). The measurement of cohesion in work teams. *Small Group Research, 31*(1), 71–88. doi:10.1177/104649640003100104

Chapman, C., Baker, E., Porter, G., Thayer, S., & Burlingame, G. (2010). Rating group therapist interventions: The validation of the group psychotherapy intervention rating scale. *Group Dynamics: Theory, Research, and Practice, 14*(1), 15–31. doi:10.1037/a0016628

Corcoran, J., & Walsh, J. (2015). *Mental health in social work.* Boston, MA: Pearson.

Corcoran, K., & Fischer, J. (2013). *Measures for clinical practice and research: A sourcebook* (5th ed.). (Vol. 1, Couples, Families, and Children & Vol. 2, Adults). New York, NY: Oxford University Press.

Cox, M. (1973). The group therapy interaction chronogram. *British Journal of Social Work, 3,* 243–256. Retrieved from: http://bjsw.oxfordjournals.org/content/3/2/243.full.pdf+html

Crano, W., & Brewer, M. (1973). *Principles of research in social psychology.* New York, NY: McGraw-Hill.

Delucia-Waack, J. (1997). Measuring the effectiveness of group work: A review and analysis of process and outcome measures. *Journal for Specialists in Group Work, 22*(4), 277–293. doi:10.1080/01933929708415531

Forsyth, D. R. (2014). *Group dynamics* (6th ed.). Belmont, CA: Wadsworth Cengage Learning.

Fuhriman, A., & Barlow, S. (1994). Interaction analysis: Instrumentation and issues. In A. Fuhriman & G. M. Burlingame (Eds.), *Handbook of group psychotherapy* (pp. 191–222). New York, NY: Wiley.

Fuhriman, A., Drescher, S., Hanson, E., Henrie, R., & Rybicki, W. (1986). Refining the measurement of curativeness: An empirical approach. *Small Group Behavior, 17*(2), 186–201. doi:10.1177/104649648601700204

Fuhriman, A., & Packard, T. (1986). Group process instruments: Therapeutic themes and issues. *International Journal of Group Psychotherapy, 36*(3), 399–525.

Gambrill, E. (2009). *Critical thinking for helping professionals: A skills-based workbook.* New York, NY: Oxford University Press.

Garvin, C. (1997). *Contemporary group work* (3rd ed.). Boston, MA: Allyn & Bacon.

Gazda, G., & Mobley, J. (1981). INDS-CAL multidimensional scaling. *Journal of Group Psychotherapy, Psychodrama and Sociometry, 34,* 54–73.

Goldfried, M., & D'Zurilla, T. (1969). A behavioral-analytic model for assessing competence. In C. D. Spielberger (Ed.), *Current topics in clinical and community psychology* (Vol. 1, pp. 151–196). New York, NY: Academic Press.

Hill, W. (1965). *Hill interaction matrix* (Rev. ed.). Los Angeles, CA: Youth Studies Center, University of Southern California.

Hopwood, C., & Bornstein, R. (Eds). (2014). *Multimethod clinical assessment.* New York, NY: Guilford Press.

Horwitz, A., & Wakefield, J. (2007). *The loss of sadness: How psychiatry transformed normal sadness into depressive disorder.* New York, NY: Oxford University Press.

Horwitz, A., & Wakefield, J. (2012). *All we have to fear: Psychiatry's transformation of natural anxieties into mental disorders.* New York, NY: Oxford University Press.

Johnson, J., Pulsipher, D., Ferrin, S., Burlingame, G., Davies, D., & Gleave, R. (2006). Measuring group processes: A comparison of the GCQ and the CCI. *Group Dynamics, Theory, Research, and Practice, 10*(2), 136–145. doi:10.1037/1089-2699.10.2.136

Johnson, L., & Yanca, S. (2010). *Social work practice: A generalist approach* (10th ed.). Boston, MA: Allyn & Bacon.

Joyce, A., MacNair-Semands R., Tasca, G., & Ogrodniczuk, J. (2011). Factor structure and validity of the Therapeutic Factor Inventory – Short Form. *Group Dynamics: Theory, Research, and Practice, 15*(3), 201–219. doi:10.1037/a0024677

Kirk, S., Gomory, T., & Cohen, D. (2013). *Mad science: Psychiatric coercion, diagnosis and drugs.* New Brunswick, NJ: Transaction Publications.

Kirk, S., & Kutchins, H. (1999). Making us crazy. *DSM: The psychiatric bible and the creation of mental disorders* (2nd ed.). London: Constable.

Kirst-Ashman, K., & Hull, G. (2012). *Understanding generalist practice* (6th ed.). Belmont, CA: Brooks Cole.

Kottler, J. A., & Englar-Carlson, M. (2015). *Learning group leadership: An experiential approach* (3rd ed.). Thousand Oaks, CA: Sage Publications.

Lese, K., & MacNair-Semands, R. (2000). The therapeutic factors inventory: Development of a scale. *Eastern Group Psychotherapy Society, 24*(4), 303–317. doi:10.1023/A:1026616626780

Levi, D. (2014). *Group dynamics for teams* (4th ed.). Thousand Oaks, CA: Sage Publications.

Macgowan, M. J. (2008). *A guide to evidence-based group work.* New York, NY: Oxford University Press.

Macgowan, M. J., & Levenson, J. S. (2003). Psychometrics of the group engagement measure with male sex offenders. *Small Group Research, 34*(2), 155–160.

Macgowan, M. J., & Newman, F. (2005). Factor structure of the group engagement measure. *Social Work Research, 29*(2), 107–118. doi:10.1093/swr/29.2.107

MacKenzie, K. R. (1983). The clinical application of a Group Climate measure. In R. R. Dies & K. R. MacKenzie (Eds.), *Advances in group psychotherapy: Integrating research and practice* (pp. 159–170). New York, NY: International Universities Press.

MacKenzie, K. R. (1990). *Introduction to time-limited group psychotherapy.* Washington, DC: American Psychiatric Press.

Malekoff, A. (2014). *Group work with adolescents* (3rd ed.). New York, NY: Guilford Press.

Moos, R. H. (1986). *Group environment scale manual* (2nd ed.). Palo Alto, CA: Consulting Psychologists Press.

Moreno, J. (1934). *Who shall survive?* Washington, DC: Nervous and Mental Diseases.

Newhill, C. (2015). *Interventions for serious mental disorders.* Boston, MA: Pearson.

Ramirez, C. (2014). *Teams: A competency-based approach.* New York, NY: Routledge

Reder, P. (1978). An assessment of the group therapy interaction chronogram. *International Journal of Group Psychotherapy, 28*(2), 185–194.

Rubin, H., & Rubin, I. (2008). *Community organizing and development* (4th ed.). New York, NY: Macmillan.

Selltiz, C., Wrightsman, L., & Cook, S. (1976). *Research methods in social relations* (3rd ed.). New York, NY: Holt, Rinehart & Winston.

Shulman, L. (2016). *The skills of helping individuals, families, groups and communities* (8th ed.). Itasca, IL: F. E. Peacock.

Silbergeld, S., Koenig, G., Manderscheid, R., Meeker, B., & Hornung, C. (1975). Assessment of environment-therapy systems: The group atmosphere scale. *Journal of Consulting and Clinical Psychology, 43*(4), 460–469. doi:10.1037/h0076897

Sodano, S., Guyker, W., Delucia-Waack, J., Cosgrove, H., Altabef, D., & Amos, B. (2014). Measures of group process, dynamics, climate, behavior, and outcome: A review. In J. Delucia-Waack, C. Kalodner, & M. Riva (Eds.), *Handbook of group counseling & psychotherapy* (2nd ed., pp. 159–177). Thousand Oaks, CA: Sage Publications.

Spielberger, C., Gorsuch, R., Lushene, R., Vagg, P., & Jacobs, G. (1983). *Manual for the stait-trait anxiety inventory.* Palo Alto, CA: Consulting Psychologists Press.

Strauss, B., Burlingame, G., & Bormann, B. (2008). Using the CORE-R battery in group psychotherapy. *Journal of Clinical Psychology: In Session, 64*(11), 1225–1237. doi:10.1002/jclp.20535

Toseland, R., Rossiter, C., Peak, T., & Hill, P. (1990). Therapeutic processes in support groups for caregivers. *International Journal of Group Psychotherapy, 40*(3), 279–303.

Ward, D. (2014). Effective processing in groups. In J. Delucia-Waack, C. Kalodner, & M. Riva (Eds.), *Handbook of group counseling & psychotherapy* (2nd ed., pp. 84–94). Thousand Oaks, CA: Sage Publications.

Chapter 9

Akinsulure-Smith, A. (2009). Brief psychoeducational group treatment with re-traumatized refugees and asylum seekers. *Journal for Specialists in Group Work, 34*(2), 137–150. doi:10.1080/01933920902798007

Bandura, A. (1977). *Social learning theory.* Englewood Cliffs, NJ: Prentice Hall.

Barlow, S. (2010). Evidence bases for group practice. In R. Conyne (Ed.), *The Oxford handbook of group counseling* (pp. 207–230). New York, NY: Oxford University Press.

Barlow, S. (2013). *Specialty competencies in group psychology.* New York, NY: Oxford University Press.

Beck, J. (2011). *Cognitive therapy: Basics and beyond* (2nd ed.). New York, NY: Guilford Press.

Black, B. M., Weisz, A. N., Mengo, C. W., & Lucero, J. L. (2015). Accountability and risk assessment: Members' and Leaders' Perspectives about Psychoeducational Batterers' Group. *Social Work with Groups, 38*(2), 136–151. doi:10.1080/01609513.2014.923363

Blatner, H. (1996). *Acting-in: Practical applications of psychodramatic methods* (3rd ed.). New York, NY: Springer Publishing Company.

Bowen, S., Chawla, N., Marlatt, A. G. (2011). *Mindfulness-based relapse prevention for addictive behaviors: A clinician's guide.* New York, NY: Guilford Press.

Boyd-Franklin, N., Cleek, E., Wofsy, M., & Mundy, B. (2013). *Therapy in the real world.* New York, NY: Guilford Press.

Burlingame, G. (2010). Small group treatments: Introduction to special edition. *Psychotherapy Research, 20*(1), 1–7. doi:10.1080/10503301003596551

Burlingame, G., Strauss, B., & Joyce, A. (2013). Change mechanisms and effectiveness of small group treatments. In M. J. Lambert (Ed.), *Bergin and Garfield's handbook of psychotherapy and behavior change* (6th ed., pp. 640–689). Hoboken, NJ: Wiley.

Burlingame, G., Whitcomb, K., & Woodland, S. (2014). Process and outcome in group counseling and psychotherapy. In J. Delucia-Waack, C. Kalodner, & M. Riva (Eds.), *Handbook of group counseling & psychotherapy* (2nd ed., pp. 55–68). Thousand Oaks, CA: Sage Publications.

Cooley, L. (2009). *The power of groups: Solution-focused group counseling in schools.* Thousand Oaks, CA: Corwin.

Corvo, K., Dutton, D., & Chen, W. (2008). Toward evidence-based practice with domestic violence perpetrators. *Journal of Aggression, Maltreatment, and Trauma, 16,* 111–130.

Courtois, C., & Ford, J. (2013a). *Treatment of complex trauma: A sequenced, relationship-based approach.* New York, NY: Guilford Press.

Courtois, C., & Ford, J. (Eds.). (2013b). *Treating complex traumatic stress disorders: An evidence-based guide.* New York, NY: Guilford Press.

Crenshaw, D. A., Brooks, R., & Goldstein, S. (Eds.). (2015). *Play therapy interventions to enhance resilience.* New York, NY: Guilford Press.

Crenshaw, D. A., & Stewart, A. L. (Eds.). (2015). *Play therapy: A comprehensive guide to theory and practice.* New York, NY: Guilford Press.

Edelwich, J., & Brodsky, A. (1992). *Group counseling for the resistant client: A practical guide to group process.* New York, NY: Lexington Books.

Ellis, A., & Joffe-Ellis, D. (2011). *Rational emotive behavior therapy.* Washington, DC: American Psychological Association.

Fall, K., & Howard, S. (2012). *Alternatives to domestic violence: A homework manual for battering intervention groups* (3rd ed.). Philadelphia, PA: Taylor & Francis.

Franklin, C., Trepper, T. S., Gingerich, W. J., & McCollum, E. E. (Eds.). (2012). *Solution-focused brief therapy: A handbook of evidence-based practice.* New York, NY: Oxford University Press.

Gondolf, E. W. (2011). The weak evidence for batterer program alternatives. *Aggression and Violent Behavior, 16*(4), 347–353. doi:10.1016/j.avb.2011.04.011

Glassman, U., & Kates, L. (1990). *Group work: A humanistic approach.* Newbury Park, CA: Sage Publications.

Greene, G. J., & Lee, M. Y. (2011). *Solution-oriented social work practice: An integrative approach to working with client strengths.* New York, NY: Oxford University Press.

Hamberger, L. K., Lohr, J. M., Parker, L. M., & Witte, T. (2009). Treatment approaches for men who batter their partners. In C. Mitchell & D. Anglin (Eds.), *Intimate partner violence: A health-based perspective* (pp. 459–472). New York, NY: Oxford University Press.

Herman, K., Rotunda, R., Williamson, G., & Vodanovich, S. (2014). Outcomes from a Duluth model batterer intervention program at completion and long term follow-up. *Journal of Offender Rehabilitation, 53,* 1–18. doi:10.1080/10509674.2013.861316

Hohman, M. (2013). *Motivational interviewing in social work practice.* New York, NY: Guilford Press.

Joyce, A., Piper, W., & Ogrodniczuk, J. (2007). Therapeutic alliance and cohesion variables as predictors of outcome in short-term group psychotherapy. *International Journal of Group Psychotherapy, 57*(3), 269–296. doi:10.1521/ijgp.2007.57.3.269

Kaduson, H. G., & Schaefer, C. E. (2015). *Short-term play therapy for children* (3rd ed.). New York, NY: Guilford Press.

Kastner, J. W., & May, W. (2009). Action-oriented techniques in adolescent group therapy. *Group, 33*(4), 315–327.

Kazantzis, N., Reinecke, M., & Freeman, A. (2010). *Cognitive and behavioral theories in clinical practice.* New York, NY: Guilford Press.

LeCroy, C. (Ed.). (2008). *Handbook of evidence-based treatment manuals for children and adolescents* (2nd ed.). New York, NY: Oxford University Press.

Lefley, H. (2009). *Family psychoeducation for serious mental illness.* New York, NY: Oxford University Press.

Macgowan, M. J. (2008). *A guide to evidence-based group work.* New York, NY: Oxford University Press.

McKay, M., Gopalan, G., Franco, L., Dean-Assael, K., Chacko, A., & Jackson, J. (2011). A collaboratively designed child mental health service model: Multiple family groups for urban children with conduct difficulties. *Research on Social Work Practice, 21*(6), 664–674. doi:10.1177/1049731511406740

Miller, G. A. (2012). *Group exercises for addiction counseling.* Hoboken, NJ: Wiley.

Mills, L. G., Barocas, B., & Ariel, B. (2013). The next generation of court-mandated domestic violence treatment: A comparison study of batterer intervention and restorative justice programs. *Journal of Experimental Criminology, 9*(1), 65–90. doi:10.1007/s11292-012-9164-x

Miller, W., & Rollnick, S. (Eds.). (2013). *Motivational interviewing: Helping people for change* (3rd ed.). New York, NY: Guilford Press.

Muroff, J., Underwood, P., & Steketee, G. (2014). *Group treatment for hoarding disorder: Therapist guide.* New York, NY: Oxford University Press.

Nason-Clark, N., & Fisher-Townsend, B. (2015). *Men Who Batter.* New York, NY: Oxford University Press.

Newhill, C. (2015). *Interventions for serious mental disorders.* Boston, MA: Pearson.

Norcross, J., Campbell, L., Grohol, J., Santrock, J., Selagea, F., & Sommer, R. (2013). *Self-help that works* (4th ed.). New York, NY: Oxford University Press

Rapp, C., & Goscha, R. (2012). *The strengths model: A recovery-oriented approach to mental health services* (3rd ed.). New York, NY: Oxford University Press.

Riessman, F. (1965). The "helper" therapy principle. *Social Work, 10*(2), 27–32.

Rooney, R. (2009). *Strategies for work with involuntary clients* (2nd ed.). New York, NY: Columbia University Press.

Rooney, R. H., & Chovanec, M. (2004). Involuntary groups. In C. D. Garvin, L. M. Gutierrez, & M. J. Galinsky (Eds.), *Handbook of social work with groups* (pp. 212–226). New York, NY: Guilford Press.

Rutan, J., Stone, W., & Shay, J. (2014). *Psychodynamic group psychotherapy* (5th ed.). New York, NY: Guilford Press.

Saleebey, D. (Ed.). (2013). *The strengths perspective in social work practice* (6th ed.). Boston, MA: Pearson, Allyn & Bacon.

Saunders, D. G. (2008). Group interventions for men who batter: A summary of program descriptions and research. *Violence and Victims, 23*(2), 156–172. doi:10.1891/0886-6708.23.2.156

Schimmel, C., & Jacobs, E. (2011). When leaders are challenged: Dealing with involuntary members in groups. *Journal for Specialists in Group Work, 36*(2), 144–158. doi:10.1080/01933922.2011.562345

Seligman, L. (2014). *Selecting effective treatments* (4th ed.). San Francisco, CA: Jossey-Bass.

Shulman, L. (2016). *The skills of helping individuals, families, groups and communities* (8th ed.). Itasca, IL: F. E. Peacock.

Substance Abuse and Mental Health Services Administration. (2012). *Substance abuse treatment: Group therapy inservice training.* HHS Publication No. (SMA) SMA-11-4664. Rockville, MD: Substance Abuse and Mental Health Services Administration. Retrieved from: http://store.samhsa.gov/shin/content//SMA12-3991/SMA12-3991.pdf

Trotter, C. (2015). *Working with involuntary clients: A guide to practice* (3rd ed.). New York, NY: Routledge.

Tuten, L. M., Jones, H. E., Schaeffer, C. M., & Stitzer, M. L. (2012). *Reinforcement-based treatment for substance use disorders.* New York, NY: Springer Publishing Company.

Wagner, C., & Ingersoll, K., with Contributors. (2013). *Motivational interviewing in groups.* New York, NY: Guilford Press.

Walsh, J. (2010). *Psychoeducation in mental health.* Chicago, IL: Lyceum Books.

Webb, N. (2015). *Play therapy with children and adolescents in crisis* (4th ed.). New York, NY: Guilford Press.

Wenzel, A., Liese, B. S., Beck, A. T., & Friedman-Wheeler, D. G. (2012). *Group cognitive therapy of addictions.* New York, NY: Guilford Press.

White, B. J., & Madara, E. (Eds.). (2002). *The self-help sourcebook: Your guide to community and online support groups* (7th ed.). Denville, NJ: St. Clare's Health Services.

Yeager, K., & Roberts, A. (2015). *Crisis intervention handbook* (4th ed.). New York, NY: Oxford University Press.

Chapter 10

Antony, M. M., & Roemer, L. (2011). *Behavior therapy*. Washington, DC: American Psychological Association.

Bandura, A. (1977). *Social learning theory*. Englewood Cliffs, NJ: Prentice Hall.

Barlow, D. H., Rapee, R. M., & Perini, S. (2014). *10 steps to mastering stress: A lifestyle approach* (Updated Ed.). New York, NY: Oxford University Press.

Barlow, S. (2013). *Specialty competencies in group psychology*. New York, NY: Oxford University Press.

Bauer, M. M., & McBride, L. (2003). *Structured group psychotherapy for bipolar disorder: The life goals program* (2nd ed.). New York, NY: Springer Publishing Company.

Beck, J. (2011). *Cognitive therapy: Basics and beyond* (2nd ed.). New York, NY: Guilford Press.

Bell, A. C., & D'Zurilla, T. J. (2009). Problem-solving therapy for depression: A meta-analysis. *Clinical Psychology Review, 29*(4), 348–353. doi:10.1016/j.cpr.2009.02.003

Berlatsky, N. (2015). *Gangs*. Fenington Hills, MI: Greenhaven Press.

Bernstein, D. B., Borkovek, T., & Hazlett-Stevens, H. (2000). *New directions in progressive relaxation training: A guidebook for helping professionals*. Westport, CT: Praeger.

Bieling, P. J., McCabe, R. E., & Antony, M. M. (2006). *Cognitive-behavioral therapy in groups*. New York, NY: Guilford Press.

Bien, T. (2006). *Mindful therapy: A guide for therapists and helping professionals*. Boston, MA: Wisdom Publishing.

Blatner, H. (1996). *Acting-in: Practical applications of psychodramatic methods* (3rd ed.). New York, NY: Springer Publishing Company.

Bowen, S., Chawla, N., & Marlatt, A. G. (2011). *Mindfulness-based relapse prevention for addictive behaviors: A clinician's guide*. New York, NY: Guilford Press.

Boyd-Franklin, N., Cleek, E., Wofsy, M., & Mundy, B. (2013). *Therapy in the real world*. New York, NY: Guilford Press.

Breshears, E., & Volker, R. (2013). *Facilitative leadership in social work practice*. New York, NY: Springer Publishing Company.

Brown, K. W., Creswell, J. D., & Ryan, R. M. (Eds.). (2015). *Handbook of mindfulness: Theory, research, and practice*. New York, NY: Guilford Press.

Burlingame, G. (2010). Small group treatments: Introduction to special edition. *Psychotherapy Research, 20*(1), 1–7. doi:10.1080/10503301003596551

Burlingame, G., MacKenzie, K., & Strauss, B. (2004). Small group treatment: Evidence for the effectiveness and mechanisms of change. In M. J. Lambert (Ed.), *Bergin and Garfield's handbook of psychotherapy and behavior change* (5th ed., pp. 647–696). Hoboken, NJ: Wiley.

Burlingame, G., Strauss, B., & Joyce, A. (2013). Change mechanisms and effectiveness of small group treatments. In M. J. Lambert (Ed.), *Bergin and Garfield's handbook of psychotherapy and behavior change* (6th ed., pp. 640–689). Hoboken, NJ: Wiley.

Burlingame, G., Whitcomb, K., & Woodland, S. (2014). Process and outcome in group counseling and psychotherapy. In J. Delucia-Waack, C. Kalodner, & M. Riva, (Eds.), *Handbook of group counseling & psychotherapy* (2nd ed., pp. 55–68). Thousand Oaks, CA: Sage Publications.

Chacko, A., Gopalan, G., Franco, L., Dean-Assael, K., Jackson, J., Marcus, S., & McKay, M. (2014). Multiple family group service model for children with disruptive behavior disorders: Child outcomes at post-treatment.

Journal of Emotional and Behavioral Disorders, 23(2), 67–77. doi:10.1177/1063426614532690

Craske, M. G. (2010). *Cognitive-behavioral therapy*. Washington, DC: American Psychological Association.

Davis, M., Eshelman, E., & McKay, M. (2008). *The relaxation and stress reduction workbook* (6th ed.). Oakland, CA: New Harbinger.

DiGiuseppe, R. (2010). Rational-emotive behavior therapy. In N. Kazantzis, M. Reinecke, & A. Freeman (Eds.), *Cognitive and behavioral theories in clinical practice* (pp. 115–147). New York, NY: Guilford Press.

Dimeff, L., & Koerner, K. (Eds.). (2007). *Dialectical behavior therapy in clinical practice*. New York, NY: Guilford Press.

Dimidjian, S., Martell, C. R., Herman-Dunn, R., & Hubley, S. (2014). Behavioral activation for depression. In D. H. Barlow (Ed.), *Clinical handbook of psychological disorders: A step-by-step treatment manual* (5th ed., pp. 353–393). New York, NY: Guilford Press.

Dobson, K. (2010). *Handbook of cognitive-behavioral therapies* (3rd ed.). New York, NY: Guilford Press.

Duffy, T. (2008). Psychodrama. In A. Strozier & J. Carpenter (Eds.), *Introduction to alternative and complementary therapies* (pp. 129–152). New York, NY: Haworth Press

Ellis, A. (1962). *Reason and emotion in psychotherapy*. Secaucus, NJ: Lyle Stuart.

Ellis, A., & Joffe-Ellis, D. (2011). *Rational emotive behavior therapy*. Washington, DC: American Psychological Association.

Feldman, R., Caplinger, T., & Wodarski, J. (1983). *The St. Louis conundrum: The effective treatment of antisocial youth*. Englewood Cliffs, NJ: Prentice Hall.

Forse, M. D., & Degenne, A. (1999). *Introducing social networks*. Thousand Oaks, CA: Sage Publications.

Forsman, A. K., Nordmyr, J., & Wahlbeck, K. (2011). Psychosocial interventions for the promotion of mental health and the prevention of depression among older adults. *Health Promotion International, 26*(S1), i85–i107. doi:10.1093/heapro/dar074

Forsyth, D. R. (2014). *Group dynamics* (6th ed.). Belmont, CA: Wadsworth Cengage Learning.

Freeman, A., Pretzer, J., Fleming, J., & Simons, K. (2004). *Clinical applications of cognitive therapy* (2nd ed.). New York, NY: Plenum.

Gelso, C., & Harbin, J. (2007). Insight, action, and the therapeutic relationship. In L. G. Castonguay & C. E. Hill (Eds.), *Insight in psychotherapy* (pp. 293–311). Washington, DC: American Psychological Association.

Gopalan, G., Chacko, A., Franco, L., Dean-Assael, K. M., Rotko, L. E., Marcus, S. M., & McKay, M. (2014). Multiple family groups for children with disruptive behavior disorders: Child outcomes at 6-month follow-up. *Journal of Child and Family Studies*. doi:10.1007/s10826-014-0074-6

Greenberg, L. S. (2015). *Emotion-focused therapy: Coaching clients to work through their feelings* (2nd ed.). Washington, DC: American Psychological Association.

Gross, J. J. (Ed.). (2014). *Handbook of emotional regulation* (2nd ed.). New York, NY: Guilford Press.

Harris, R. (2009). *ACT made simple*. Oakland, CA: New Harbinger.

Hayes, S., Strosahl, K., & Wilson, K. (2011). *Acceptance and commitment therapy* (2nd ed.). New York, NY: Guilford Press.

Heimberg, R. B., & Becker, R. (2002). *Cognitive-behavioral group therapy for social phobia*. New York, NY: Guilford Press.

Howell, J., & Griffiths, E. (2016). *Gangs in America's communities*. Thousand Oaks, CA: Sage Publications.

Joyce, A., MacNair-Semands, Tasca, G., & Ogrodniczuk J. (2011). Factor structure and validity of the Therapeutic Factor Inventory- Short Form. *Group Dynamics: Theory, Research, and Practice, 15*(3), 201–219. doi:10.1037/a0024677

Joyce, A., Piper, W., & Ogrodniczuk, J. (2007). Therapeutic alliance and cohesion variables as predictors of outcome in short-term group psychotherapy. *International Journal of Group Psychotherapy, 57*(3), 269–296. doi:10.1521/ijgp.2007.57.3.269

Kabat-Zinn, J. (2002). *Guided mindfulness meditation.* (4 CD set running time 23/4 hours) Boulder, CO: Sounds True.

Kazdin, A. (2013). *Behavior modification in applied settings* (7th ed.). Long Grove, IL: Waveland Press.

Kivlighan, D., & Kivlighan, M. (2014). Therapeutic factors: Current theory and research. In J. Delucia-Waack, C. Kalodner, & M. Riva (Eds.), *Handbook of group counseling & psychotherapy* (2nd ed., pp. 46–54). Thousand Oaks, CA: Sage Publications.

Kazantzis, N., Reinecke, M., & Freeman, A. (2010). *Cognitive and behavioral theories in clinical practice.* New York, NY: Guilford Press.

Lazarus, J. (2000). *Stress relief & relaxation techniques.* Oakland, CA: New Harbinger Publications.

Lese, K., & MacNair-Semands, R. (2000). The therapeutic factors inventory: Development of a scale. *Eastern Group Psychotherapy Society, 24*(4), 303–317. doi:10.1023/A:1026616626780

Linehan, M. (2015). *DBT skills training manual.* New York, NY: Guilford Press.

Lynch, T., & Cuper, P. (2010). Dialectical behavior therapy. In N. Kazantzis, M. Reinecke, & A. Freeman (Eds.), *Cognitive and behavioral theories in clinical practice* (pp. 218–243). New York, NY: Guilford Press.

Mahoney, M. J. (1974). *Cognitive and behavior modification.* Cambridge, MA: Ballinger Books.

Mahoney, M. J. (Ed.). (1995a). *Cognitive and constructive psychotherapies: Theory, research and practice.* New York, NY: Springer Publishing Company.

Mahoney, M. J. (Ed.). (1995b). *Constructive psychotherapy.* New York, NY: Guilford Press.

Martell, C., Dimidjian, S., & Lewinsohn, P. (2010). Behavioral activation therapy. In N. Kazantzis, M. Reinecke, & A. Freeman (Eds.), *Cognitive and behavioral theories in clinical practice* (pp. 193–217). New York, NY: Guilford Press.

McHenry, B., & McHenry, J. (2015). *What therapists say and why they say it: Effective therapist responses and techniques* (2nd ed.). New York, NY: Routledge.

McKay, D., Abramowitz, J. S., & Taylor, S. (Eds.). (2010). *Cognitive-behavioral therapy for refractory cases: Turning failure into success.* Washington, DC: American Psychological Association.

McKay, M., Wood, J., & Brantley, F. (2007). *The dialectical therapy skills workbook.* Oakland, CA: New Harbinger Publications.

Meichenbaum, D. (2014). *Cognitive-behavior modification: An integrative approach.* New York, NY: Springer-Verlag.

Moreno, J. (1946). *Psychodrama* (Vol. 1). Boston, MA: Beacon Press.

Norcross, J. C. (Ed.). (2011). *Psychotherapy relationships that work: Evidence-based responsiveness* (2nd ed.). New York, NY: Oxford University Press.

Norcross, J. C., & Beutler, L. E. (2014). In D. H. Barlow (Ed.), *Clinical handbook of psychological disorders: A step-by-step treatment manual* (5th ed., pp. 617–639). New York, NY: Guilford Press.

Neacsiu, A. D., Bohus, M., & Linehan, M. M. (2014). Dialectical behavior therapy: An intervention for emotion dysregulation. In J. J. Gross (Ed.), Handbook of emotion regulation (2nd ed., pp. 491–507). New York, NY: Guilford Press.

Nezu, A., Nezu, C., & D'Zurilla, T. (2010). Problem-solving therapy. In N. Kazantzis, M. Reinecke, & A. Freeman (Eds.), *Cognitive and behavioral theories in clinical practice* (pp. 76–114). New York, NY: Guilford Press.

Norcross, J. C., & Beutler, L. E. (2014). Evidence-base relationships and responsiveness for depression and substance abuse. In D. H. Barlow (Ed.), *Clinical handbook of psychological disorders: A step-by-step treatment manual* (5th ed., pp. 617–639). New York, NY: Guilford Press.

Ogrodniczuk, J., Piper, W., Joyce, A., Lau, M., & Sochting, I. (2010). A survey of Canadian Group Psychotherapy Association members' perceptions of psychotherapy research. *International Journal of Group Psychotherapy, 60*(2), 159–176.

Piet, J., & Hougaard, E. (2011). The effect of mindfulness-based cognitive therapy for prevention of relapse in recurrent major depressive disorder: A systematic review and meta-analysis. *Clinical Psychology Review, 31*(6), 1032–1040. doi:10.1016/j.cpr.2011.05.002

Reinecke, M., Dattilio, M., & Freeman, A. (2006). *Cognitive therapy with children and adolescents* (2nd ed.). New York, NY: Guilford Press.

Roemer, L., & Orsillo, S. M. (2014). An acceptance-based behavioral therapy for generalized anxiety disorder. In D. H. Barlow (Ed.), *Clinical handbook of psychological disorders: A step-by-step treatment manual* (5th ed., pp. 206–236). New York, NY: Guilford Press.

Rogers, H., & Maytan, M. (2012). *Mindfulness for the next generation: Helping emerging adults manage stress and lead healthier lives.* New York, NY: Oxford University Press.

Rose, S. (1989). *Working with adults in groups: A multi-method approach.* San Francisco, CA: Jossey-Bass.

Rutan, J., Stone, W., & Shay, J. (2014). *Psychodynamic group psychotherapy* (5th ed.). New York, NY: Guilford Press.

Segal, Z., Williams, M., & Teasdale, J. (2013). *Mindfulness-based cognitive therapy for depression* (2nd ed.). New York, NY: Guilford Press.

Segal, Z. V., Williams, M. G., Teasdale, J. D., & Kabat-Zinn, J. (2012). *Mindfulness-based cognitive therapy for depression: A new approach to preventing relapse* (2nd ed.). New York, NY: Guilford Press.

Seligman, M. (1975). *Helplessness: On depression, development, and death.* San Francisco, CA: W. H. Freeman.

Sheldon, B. (2011). *Cognitive-behavioural therapy: Research and practice in health and social care* (2nd ed.). Abingdon, England: Routledge.

Shulman, L. (2016). *The skills of helping individuals, families, groups and communities* (8th ed.). Itasca, IL: F. E. Peacock.

Smucker, M., Dancu, C., & Foa, E. (1999). *Cognitive behavioral treatment for adult survivors of childhood trauma: Imagery rescripting and reprocessing.* Northvale, NJ: Jason Aronson.

Stahl, B., & Goldstein, E. (2010). *A mindfulness-based stress reduction workbook.* Oakland, CA: New Harbinger Publications.

Sundquist, J., Lilja, A., Palmer, K., Memon, A. A., Wang, X., Johansson, L. M., & Sundquist, K. (2014). Mindfulness group therapy in primary care patients with depression, anxiety, and stress and adjustment disorders: Randomised controlled trial. *British Journal of Psychiatry, 206*(2), 128–135. doi:10.1192/bjb.bp.114.150243

Swenson, C., Witterholt, S., & Bohus, B. (2007). Dialectical behavior therapy on inpatient units. In L. Dimeff & K. Koerner (Eds.), *Dialectical behavior therapy in clinical practice* (pp. 69–111). New York, NY: Guilford Press.

Tropman, J. (2014). *Effective meetings: Improving group decision-making* (4th ed.). Thousand Oaks, CA: Sage Publications.

Trotter, C. (2015). *Working with involuntary clients: A Guide to Practice* (3rd ed.). New York, NY: Routledge.

Tuten, L. M., Jones, H. E., Schaeffer, C. M., & Stitzer, M. L. (2012). *Reinforcement-based treatment for substance use disorders.* New York, NY: Springer Publishing Company.

Verhofstadt-Deneve, L. (2000). The "Magic Shop" technique in psychodrama: An existential–dialectical view. *International Journal of Action Methods: Psychodrama, Skill Training, and Role Playing, 53*(1), 3–15.

Wagner, C., & Ingersoll, K., with Contributors. (2013). *Motivational interviewing in groups.* New York, NY: Guilford Press.

Waltz, T., & Hayes, S. (2010). Acceptance and commitment therapy. In N. Kazantzis, M. Reinecke, & A. Freeman (Eds.), *Cognitive and behavioral theories in clinical practice.* New York, NY: Guilford Press.

Watzlawick, P., Weakland, J., & Fisch, R. (1974). *Change: Principles of problem formation and problem resolution.* New York, NY: W. W. Norton.

Wenzel, A. (2013). *Strategic decision making in cognitive behavioral therapy.* Washington, DC: American Psychological Association.

Wenzel, A., Liese, B. S., Beck, A. T., & Friedman-Wheeler, D. G. (2012). *Group cognitive therapy of addictions.* New York, NY: Guilford Press.

White, J. R., & Freeman, A. (Eds.). (2000). *Cognitive-behavioral group therapy for specific problems and populations.* Washington, DC: American Psychological Association. doi:10.1037/10352-000

Wright, J., Basco, M., & Thase, M. (2006). *Learning cognitive behavior therapy: An illustrated guide.* Washington, DC: American Psychiatric Publishing.

Yalom, I. (2005). *The theory and practice of group psychotherapy* (5th ed.). New York, NY: Basic Books.

Yost, E., Beutler, L., Corbishley, M., & Allender, J. (1985). *Group cognitive therapy: A treatment approach for depressed older adults.* Elmsford, NY: Pergamon Press.

Young, J. E., Rygh, J. L., Weinberger, A. D., & Beck, A. T. (2014). Cognitive therapy for depression. In D. H. Barlow (Ed.), *Clinical handbook of psychological disorders: A step-by-step treatment manual* (5th ed., pp. 275–331). New York, NY: Guilford Press.

Chapter 11

Bales, R. (1954). In conference. *Harvard Business Review, 32,* 44–50.

Bales, R. (1955). How people interact in conference. *Scientific American, 192*(3), 31–35. doi:10.1038/scientificamerican0355-31

Barsky, A. (2014). *Conflict resolution for the helping professions.* New York, NY: Oxford University Press.

Berlatsky, N. (2015). *Gangs.* Fenington Hills, MI: Greenhaven Press.

Ephross, P. H., & Vassil, T. (2005). *Groups that work* (2nd ed.). New York, NY: Columbia University Press.

Fisher, R., Ury, W., & Patton, B. (2012). *Getting to yes: Negotiating agreement without giving in* (3rd ed.). London, England: Random Business Books.

Forsyth, D. R. (2014). *Group dynamics* (6th ed.). Belmont, CA: Wadsworth Cengage Learning.

Franz, T. M. (2012). *Group dynamics and team interventions: Understanding and improving team performance.* Malden, MA: Wiley-Blackwell.

Freud, S. (1922). *Group psychology and the analysis of the ego.* London, England: International Psychoanalytic Press.

Gambrill, E. (2009). *Critical thinking for helping professionals: A skills-based workbook.* New York, NY: Oxford University Press.

Gambrill, E. (2013). *Social work practice: A critical thinker's guide* (3rd ed.). New York, NY: Oxford University Press.

Gummer, B. (1987). Groups as substance and symbol: Group processes and organizational politics. *Social Work with Groups, 10*(2), 25–39. doi:10.1300/J009v10n02_04

Hare, A. P., Blumberg, H. H., Davies, M. F., & Kent, M. V. (1995). *Small group research: A handbook.* Norwood, NJ: Ablex.

Hohman, M. (2013). *Motivational interviewing in social work practice.* New York, NY: Guilford Press.

Howell, J., & Griffiths, E. (2016). *Gangs in America's communities.* Thousand Oaks, CA: Sage Publications.

Hughes, S., Lakey, B., Bobowick, M., & the National Center for Nonprofit Boards (U.S.). (2007). *The board building cycle: Nine steps of finding, recruiting, and engaging nonprofit board members* (2nd ed.). Washington, DC: Board Source.

Janis, I. (1972). *Victims of group think.* Boston, MA: Houghton Mifflin.

Jehn, K. C., & Chatman, J. (2000). The influence of proportional and perceptual conflict composition on team performance. *International Journal of Conflict Management, 11*(1), 56–73. doi:10.1108/eb022835

Kahnman, D. (2011). *Thinking fast and slow.* New York, NY: Free Press.

Levi, D. (2014). *Group dynamics for teams* (4th ed.). Thousand Oaks, CA: Sage Publications.

LeBon, G. (1910). *The crowd: A study of the popular mind.* London, England: George Allen & Unwin Ltd.

Maier, N. (1963). *Problem-solving discussions and conferences: Leadership methods and skills.* New York, NY: McGraw-Hill.

Pyles, L. (2013). *Progressive community organizing: A critical approach for a globalizing world* (2nd ed.). New York, NY: Routledge.

Robert, H., & Robert, S. (2011). *Robert's rules of order newly revised* (11th ed.). Philadelphia, PA: Da Capo Press.

Rothman, J., Erlich, J., & Tropman, J. (Eds.). (2007). *Strategies of community intervention* (5th ed.). Itasca, IL: F. E. Peacock.

Salas, E., Tannenbaum, S. I., Cohen, D. J., & Latham, G. (Eds.). (2013). *Development and enhancing teamwork in organizations.* San Francisco, CA: Jossey-Bass.

Schuman, S. (Ed.). (2010). *The handbook for working with difficult groups: How they are difficult, why they are difficult and what you can do about it.* San Francisco, CA: Jossey-Bass.

Stoner, J. (1968). Risky and cautious shifts in group decisions: The influence of widely held values. *Journal of Experimental Social Psychology, 4*(4), 442–459.

Susskind, L., & Cruikshank, J. (2006). *Breaking Robert's rules: The new way to run your meeting, build consensus, and get results.* New York, NY: Oxford University Press.

Thompson, L. L. (2015). *Making the team: A guide for managers* (5th ed.). Upper Saddle River, NJ: Pearson Education, Inc.

Tropman, J. (2014). *Effective meetings: Improving group decision-making* (4th ed.). Thousand Oaks, CA: Sage Publications.

Tropman, J., & Harvey, T. (2009). *Nonprofit governance: The why, what, and how of nonprofit boardship*. Chicago, IL: University of Chicago, IL Press.

Chapter 12

Aaker, D., Kumar, V., Leone, R., & Day, G. (2013). *Marketing research* (11th ed.). New York, NY: Wiley.

Alencar, E. (2012). Creativity in organizations: Facilitators and inhibitors. In M. Mumford (Ed.), *Handbook of organizational creativity* (pp. 87–111). London, UK: Academic Press.

Alinsky, S. (1971). *Rules for radicals*. New York, NY: Random House.

Andersen, B., & Fagerhaug. T. (2000). The nominal group technique. *Quality Progress*, *33*(2), 144. Retrieved from http://asq.org/quality-progress/2000/02/one-good-idea/the-nominal-group-technique.html

Baruah, J., & Paulus, P. B. (2008). Effects of training on idea generation in groups. *Small Group Research*, *39*, 523–541. doi:10.1016/j.jesp.2011.04.007

Baruah, J., & Paulus, P. B. (2009). Enhancing creativity in groups: The search for synergy. In E. A. Mannix, M. A. Neale, & J. A. Goncalo (Eds.), *Research on managing groups and teams* (Vol. 12, pp. 29–56). Bingley, UK: Emerald Group Publishing Limited.

Baruah, K., & Paulus, P. (2011). Category assignment and relatedness in the group ideation process. *Journal of Experimental Social Psychology*, *47*(6), 1070–1077. doi:10.1016/j.jesp.2011.04.007

Basadur, M., Basadur, T., & Licina, G. (2012). Organizational development. In M. Mumford (Ed.), *Handbook of organizational creativity* (pp. 667–703). London, UK: Elsevier.

Bose, U. (2015). Design and evaluation of a group support system supported process to resolve cognitive conflicts. *Computers in Human Behavior*, *49*, 303–312. doi:10.1016/j.chb.2015.03.014

Cabrera, E. F., & Raju, N. S. (2001). Utility analysis: Current trends and future directions. *International Journal of Selection and Assessment*, *9*(1/2), 92–102. doi:10.1111/1468-2389.00166

Carretero-Gomez, J. M., & Cabrera, E. F. (2012). An empirical evaluation of training using multi-attribute utility analysis. *Journal of Business and Psychology*, *27*(2), 223–241. doi:10.1007/s10869-011-9241-6

Clark, H. B., & Unruh, D. K. (Eds.). (2009). *Transition of youth & young adults with emotional or behavioral difficulties: An evidence supported handbook*. Baltimore, MD: Brookes Publishing Company.

Davis, M. V., Mahanna, E., Joly, B., Zelek, M., Riley, W., Verma, P, & Fisher, J. S. (2014). Creating quality improvement culture in public health agencies. *American Journal of Public Health*, *104*(1), e98–e104. doi:10.2105/AJPH.2013.301413

Davis, M. V., Vincus, A., Eggers, M., Mahanna, E., Riley, W., Joly, B., & Bowling, M. J. (2012). Effectiveness of public health quality improvement training approaches: Application, application, application. *Journal of Public Health Management and Practice*, *18*(1), e1–e7. doi:10.1097/phh.0b013e3182249505

De Dreu, C. K. W., Nijstad, B. A., Bechtoldt, M. N., & Baas, M. (2011). Group creativity and innovation: A motivated information processing perspective. *Psychology of Aesthetics, Creativity, and the Arts*, *5*(1), 81–89. doi:10.1037/a0017986

Delbecq, A., Van de Ven, A., & Gustafson, D. (1986). *Group techniques for program planning: A guide to nominal group and delphi processes*. Middleton, WI: Green Briar Press.

Deuja, A., Kohn, N. W., Paulus, P. B., & Korde, R. M. (2014). Taking a broad perspective before brainstorming. *Group Dynamics: Theory, Research, and Practice*, *18*(3), 222–236. doi:10.1037/gdn0000008

Dolan, J. G. (2010). Multi-criteria clinical decision support: A primer on the use of multiple-criteria decision-making methods to promote evidence-based, patient-centered healthcare. *The Patient: Patient-Centered Outcomes Research*, *3*(4), 229–248. doi:10.2165/11539470-000000000-00000

Dresser, K. L., Zucker, P. J., Orlando, R. A., Krynski, A. A., White, G., Karpur, A., & Unruh, D. K. (2009). Collaborative approach to improving quality in process, progress, and outcomes: Sustaining a responsive and effective transition system. In H. Clark & D. Unruh (Eds.), *Transition of youth and young adults with emotional or behavioral difficulties: An evidence-supported handbook* (pp. 291–321). Baltimore, MD: Brookes Publishing Company.

Dunnette, M., Campbell, J., & Joastad, K. (1963). The effect of group participation on brainstorming effectiveness for two industrial samples. *Journal of Applied Psychology*, *47*(1), 30–37. doi:10.1037/h0049218

Dzindolet, M. T., Paulus, P. B., & Glazer, C. (2012). Brainstorming in virtual teams. In C. N. Silva (Ed.), *Online research methods in urban and planning studies: Design and outcome* (pp. 138–156). Hershey, PA: IGI Global.

Feinberg, M., Bontempo, D., & Greenberg, M. (2008). Predictors and level of sustainability of community prevention coalitions. *American Journal of Preventive Medicine*, *34*(8), 495–501. doi:10.1016/j.amepre.2008.01.030

Ferreira, A., Antunes, P., & Herskovic, V. (2011). Improving group attention: An experiment with synchronous brainstorming. *Group Decision and Negotiation*, *20*, 643–666. doi:10.1007/s10726-011-9233-y

Forsyth, D. R. (2014). *Group dynamics* (6th ed.). Belmont, CA: Wadsworth Cengage Learning.

Franz, T. M. (2012). *Group dynamics and team interventions: Understanding and improving team performance*. Malden, MA: Wiley-Blackwell.

Gulley, H. (1968). *Discussion, conference and group process* (2nd ed.). New York, NY: Holt, Rinehart & Winston.

Harrington, H. J., & Mignosa, C. (2015). *Techniques and sample outputs that drive business excellence*. Boca Raton, FL: Productivity Press.

Harrison, M. W., & Ward, D. (1999). Values as context: Groupwork and social action. *Groupwork*, *11*(3), 89–103.

Hardina, D. (2013). *Interpersonal social work skills for community practice*. New York, NY: Springer Publishing Company.

Hennink, M. M. (2014). *Focus group discussions: Understanding qualitative research*. New York, NY: Oxford University Press.

Kahnman, D. (2011). *Thinking fast and slow*. New York, NY: Free Press.

Kamberelis, G., & Dimitriadis, G. (2013). *Focus groups: From structured interviews to collective conversations*. New York, NY: Routledge.

Kohn, N. W., Paulus, P. B., & Choi, Y. (2011). Building on the ideas of others: An examination of the idea combination process. *Journal of Experimental Social Psychology*, *47*, 554–561. doi:10.1016/j.jesp.2011.01.004

Kramer, M., Kuo, C., & Dailey, J. (1997). The impact of brainstorming techniques on subsequent group processes. *Small Group Research*, *28*(2), 218–242. doi:10.1177/1046496497282003

Krueger, R., Richard, A., & Casey, M. (2015). *Focus groups: A practical guide for applied research* (5th ed.). Thousand Oaks, CA: Sage Publications.

Kuyek, J. (2011). *Community organizing: A holistic approach*. Black Point, Nova Scotia: Fernwood Publishing Company.

Levi, D. (2014). *Group dynamics for teams* (4th ed.). Thousand Oaks, CA: Sage Publications.

Lewis, J. A., Packard, T. R., & Lewis, M. D. (2012). *Management of human service programs* (5th ed.). Belmont, CA: Brooks/Cole.

Maier, N. (1963). *Problem-solving discussions and conferences: Leadership methods and skills*. New York, NY: McGraw-Hill.

Mattessich, P., Murray-Close, M., & Monsey, B. (2008). *Collaboration: What makes it work?* (2nd ed.). Saint Paul, MN: Amherst H. Wilder Foundation.

McKnight, J. S., & Plummer, J. M. (2015). *Community organizing: Theory and practice*. New York, NY: Pearson.

Merton, R., & Kendall, P. (1946). The focused interview. *American Journal of Sociology, 51*(6), 541–557. doi:10.1086/219886

Meyer, C. J. (2013). A new perspective on coalitions: What motivates membership? *Group Dynamics: Theory, Research, and Practice, 17*(2), 124–135. doi:10.1037/a0031346

Monette, D., Sullivan, T., DeJong, C., & Hilton, T. (2014). *Applied social research*. Belmont, CA: Brooks/Cole.

Moore, C. (1994). *Group techniques for idea building*. Thousand Oaks, CA: Sage Publications.

Mullen, B., Johnson, C., & Salas, E. (1991). Productivity loss in brainstorming groups: A meta-analytic integration. *Basic and Applied Social Psychology, 12*(1), 3–23. doi:10.1207/s15324834basp1201_1

Murphy, B. (2015). Quality improvement. In S. Patole (Ed.), *Management and leadership – A Guide for clinical professionals* (pp. 75–90). New York, NY: Springer.

Nadeem, E., Olin, S. S., Hill, L. C., Campbell, L., Hoagwood, K. E., Horwitz, S. M., & McCue, S. (2014). A literature review of learning collaboratives in mental health care: Used but untested. *Psychiatric Services, 65*(9), 1088–1099. doi:10.1176/appi.ps.201300229

Neck, C. P., & Houghton, J. D. (2006). Two decades of self-leadership theory and research: Past developments, present trends, and future possibilities. *Journal of Managerial Psychology, 21*(4), 270–295. doi:10.1108/02683940610663097

Nolan, T. (2014). *The essential handbook for highly effective managers*. Indianapolis, IN: Dog Ear Publishing.

Osborn, A. (1963). *Applied imagination: Principles and procedures of creative problem solving* (3rd ed.). New York, NY: Charles Scribner's Sons.

Patti, R. J. (Ed.). (2009). *The handbook of human services management* (2nd ed.). Thousand Oaks, CA: Sage Publications.

Paul, S., Smith, P. K., & Blumberg, H. B. (2010). Addressing cyberbullying in school using the quality circle approach. *Australian Journal of Guidance & Counseling, 20*(2), 157–168. doi:10.1375/ajgc.20.2.157

Paulus, P. B., & Brown, V. R. (2007). Toward more creative and innovative group idea generation: A cognitive-social-motivational perspective of brainstorming. *Social and Personality Psychology Compass, 1*(1), 248–265. doi:10.1111/j.1751-9004.2007.00006.x

Paulus, P. B., & Coskun, H. (2012). Group creativity. In J. M. Levine (Ed.), *Group processes* (pp. 215–239). Amsterdam, The Netherlands: Elsevier.

Paulus, P. B., Dzindolet, M. T., & Kohn, N. W. (2011). Collaborative creativity: Group creativity and team innovation. In M. D. Mumford (Ed.), *Handbook of organizational creativity* (pp. 327–357). New York, NY: Elsevier.

Paulus, P. B., Kohn, N. W., & Arditti, L. E. (2011). Effects of quantity and quality instructions on brainstorming. *Journal of Creative Behavior, 45*(1), 38–46.

Paulus, P. B., Kohn, N. W., Arditti, L. E., & Korde, R. M. (2013). Understanding the group size effect in electronic brainstorming. *Small Group Research, 44*(3), 332–352.

Peacock, S., Richardson, J., Carter, R., & Edwards, D. (2006). Priority setting in health care using multi-attribute utility theory and programme budgeting and marginal analysis (PBMA). *Social Science & Medicine, 64*(4), 897–910. doi:10.1016/j.socscimed.2006.09.029

Phillips, J. (1948). Report on discussion 66. *Adult Education Journal, 7*, 181–182.

Putnam, V. L., & Paulus, P. B. (2009). Brainstorming, brainstorming rules and decision making. *Journal of Creative Behavior, 43*(1), 29–40. doi:10.1002/j.2162-6057.2009.tb01304.x

Pyles, L. (2013). *Progressive community organizing: A critical approach for a globalizing world* (2nd ed.). New York, NY: Routledge.

Robert, H., & Robert S. (2011). *Robert's rules of order newly revised* (11th ed.). Philadelphia, PA: Da Capo Press.

Roth, P. L., Bobko, P., & Mabon, H. (2001). Utility analysis: A review and analysis at the turn of the century. In N. Anderson, D. S. Ones, H. K. Sinangil, & C. Viswesvaran (Eds.), *Handbook of industrial, work & organizational psychology* (Vol. 1, pp. 363–384). Thousand Oaks, CA: Sage Publications.

Rubin, H., & Rubin, I. (2008). *Community organizing and development* (4th ed.). New York, NY: Macmillan.

Rubin, A., & Babbie, E. R. (2014). *Research methods for social work* (8th ed.). Belmont, CA: Brooks/Cole.

Scholtes, P., Joiner, B., & Streibel, B. (2003). *The team handbook* (3rd ed.). Madison, WI: Oriel Incorporated.

Stattler, W., & Miller, N. (1968). *Discussion and conference* (2nd ed.). Englewood Cliffs, NJ: Prentice Hall.

Stewart, D., & Shamdasani, P. (2015). *Focus groups: Theory and practice* (3rd ed.). Los Angeles, CA: Sage Publications.

Stoner, J. B., Meadan, H., Angell, M. E., & Daczewitz, M. (2012). Evaluation of the parent-implemented communication strategies (PiCS) project using the Multiattribute Utility (MAU) approach. *Educational Assessment, Evaluation and Accountability, 24*(1), 57–73. doi:10.1007/s11092-011-9136-0

Strating, M. H., & Nieboer, A. P. (2013). Explaining variation in perceived team effectiveness: Results from eleven quality improvement collaboratives. *Journal of Clinical Nursing, 22*(11–12), 1692–1707. doi:10.1111/j.1365-2702.2012.04120.x

Susskind, L., & Cruikshank, J. (2006). *Breaking Robert's rules: The new way to run your meeting, build consensus, and get results*. New York, NY: Oxford University Press.

Taylor, D., Berry, P., & Block, C. (1958). Does group participation when using brainstorming facilitate or inhibit creative thinking? *Administrative Science Quarterly, 3*(1), 23–47. doi:10.2307/2390603

Thompson, L. L. (2015). *Making the team: A guide for managers* (5th ed.). Upper Saddle River, NJ: Pearson Education, Inc.

Toseland, R., Rivas, R., & Chapman, D. (1984). An evaluation of decision making in task groups. *Social Work, 29*(4), 339–346.

Unger, R., Nunnally, B., & Willis, D. (2013). *Designing the conversation: Techniques for successful facilitation*. Berkeley, CA: New Riders.

Van de Ven, A. (1974). *Group decision making and effectiveness: An experimental study*. Kent, OH: Kent State University Press.

Van de Ven, A., & Delbecq, A. (1971). Nominal versus interacting group processes for committee decision-making effectiveness. *Academy of Management Journal, 14*(2), 203–212. doi:10.2307/255307

Walls, D. (2015). *Community organizing*. Cambridge, UK: Polity Press.

Weiss, J. W., Edwards, W., & Mouttapa, M. (2009). The puzzle of adolescent substance initiation. In J. W. Weiss & D. J. Weiss (Eds.), *A science of decision making: The legacy of Ward Edwards* (pp. 439–450). New York, NY: Oxford University Press.

Zakocs, R., & Edwards, E. (2006). What explains community coalition effectiveness? A review of the literature. *American Journal of Preventive Medicine, 30*(4), 351–361. doi:10.1016/j.amepre.2005.12.004

Chapter 13

Alberti, R., & Emmons, M. (2008). *Your perfect right* (9th ed.). San Luis Obispo, CA: Impact Press.

Bandura, A. (1977). *Social learning theory*. Englewood Cliffs, NJ: Prentice Hall.

Barlow, C., Blythe, J., & Edmonds, M. (1999). *A handbook of interactive exercises for groups*. Boston, MA: Allyn & Bacon.

Barlow, S. (2013). *Specialty competencies in group psychology*. New York, NY: Oxford University Press.

Becker, W. (1971). *Parents are teachers*. Champaign, IL: Research Press.

Berne, E. (1961). *Transactional analysis in psychotherapy*. New York, NY: Ballantine Books.

Birnbaum, M. C., & Cicchetti, A. (2000). The power of purposeful sessional endings in each group encounter. *Social Work with Groups, 23*(3), 37–52. doi:10.1300/J009v23n03_04

Birnbaum, M. M., Mason, S., & Cicchetti, A. (2002). Impact of purposeful sessional endings on both the group and the practitioner. *Social Work with Groups, 25*(4), 3–19. doi:10.1300/J009v25n04_02

Boyd-Franklin, N., Cleek, E., Wofsy, M., & Mundy, B. (2013). *Therapy in the real world*. New York, NY: Guilford Press.

Budman, S., Simeone, P., Reilly, R., & Demby, A. (1994). Progress in short-term and time-limited group psychotherapy: Evidence and implications. In A. Fuhriman & G. M. Burlingame (Eds.), *Handbook of Group Psychotherapy* (pp. 319–339). New York, NY: Wiley.

Burlingame, G., Strauss, B., & Joyce, A. (2013). Change mechanisms and effectiveness of small group treatments. In M. J. Lambert (Ed.), *Bergin and Garfield's handbook of psychotherapy and behavior change* (6th ed., pp. 640–689). Hoboken, NJ: Wiley.

Chiauzzi, E. J. (1991). *Preventing relapse in the addictions: A biopsychosocial approach*. New York, NY: Pergamon Press.

Ellis, A. (1962). *Reason and emotion in psychotherapy*. Secaucus, NJ: Lyle Stuart.

Ellis, A. (1992). Group rational-emotive and cognitive-behavior therapy. *International Journal of Group Psychotherapy, 42*(1), 63–82.

Ellis, A., & Joffe-Ellis, D. (2011). *Rational emotive behavior therapy*. Washington, DC: American Psychological Association.

Fieldsteel, N. D. (1996). The process of termination in long-term psychoanalytic group therapy. *International Journal of Group Psychotherapy, 46*(1), 25–39.

Fortune, A. (1987). Grief only? Client and social worker reactions to termination. *Clinical Social Work Journal, 15*(2), 159–171. doi:10.1007/BF00752909

Fortune, A., Pearlingi, B., & Rochelle, C. (1992). Reactions to termination of individual treatment. *Social Work, 37*(2), 171–178. doi:10.1093/sw/37.2.171

Germain, C., & Gitterman, A. (2008). *The life model of social work practice* (3rd ed.). New York, NY: Columbia University Press.

Labrecque, M., Peak, T., & Toseland, R. (1992). Long-term effectiveness of a group program for caregivers of frail elderly veterans. *American Journal of Orthopsychiatry, 62*(4), 575–588. doi:10.1037/h0079385

Lee, J. (2001). The empowerment group: The heart of the empowerment approach and an antidote to injustice. In J. Parry (Ed.), *From prevention to wellness through group work* (2nd ed., pp. 290–320). New York, NY: Columbia University Press.

Levine, J. (2012). *Working with people: The helping process* (9th ed.). Boston, MA: Allyn & Bacon.

Long, K., Pendleton, L., & Winter, B. (1988). Effects of therapist termination on group processes. *International Journal of Group Psychotherapy, 38*(2), 211–223.

Malekoff, A. (2014). *Group work with adolescents* (3rd ed.). New York, NY: Guilford Press.

Mangione, L., Forti, R., & Lacuzzi, C. (2007). Ethics and endings in group psychotherapy: Saying good-bye and staying well. *International Journal of Group Psychotherapy, 57*(1), 25–40.

Marlatt, G. (1996). Taxonomy of high-risk situations for alcohol relapse: Evolution and development of a cognitive-behavioral model. *Addiction, 91*(supplement), S37–S49.

Marlatt, G., & Barrett, K. (1994). Relapse prevention. In M. Galanter & H. D. Kleber (Eds.), *The American Psychiatric Press textbook of substance abuse treatment* (pp. 285–299). Washington, DC: American Psychiatric Press.

Masters, J., Burish, T., Hollon, S., & Rimm, D. (1987). *Behavior therapy: Techniques and empirical findings* (3rd ed.). San Diego, CA: Harcourt Brace Jovanovich.

Meichenbaum, D. (2014). *Cognitive-behavior modification: An integrative approach*. New York, NY: Springer-Verlag.

Nitza, A. (2014). Selecting and using program activities. In J. Delucia-Waack, C. Kalodner, & M. Riva, (Eds.), *Handbook of group counseling & psychotherapy* (2nd ed., pp. 95–106). Thousand Oaks, CA: Sage Publications.

Piper, W., Debbane, E., Bienvenu, J., & Garant, J. (1982). A study of group pretraining for group psychotherapy. *International Journal of Group Psychotherapy, 32*(3), 309–325.

Rose, S. (1989). *Working with adults in groups: A multi-method approach*. San Francisco, CA: Jossey-Bass.

Rose, S. (1998). *Group therapy with troubled youth*. Thousand Oaks, CA: Sage Publications.

Saleebey, D. (Ed.). (2013). *The strengths perspective in social work practice* (6th ed.). Boston, MA: Pearson, Allyn & Bacon.

Scheidel, T., & Crowell, L. (1979). *Discussing and deciding: A deskbook for group leaders and members*. New York, NY: Macmillan.

Shulman, L. (2016). *The skills of helping individuals, families, groups and communities* (8th ed.). Itasca, IL: F. E. Peacock.

Stuart, R., & Davis, B. (1972). *Slim chance in a fat world*. Champaign, IL: Research Press.

Toseland, R. (1990). Long-term effectiveness of peer-led and professionally led support groups for family caregivers. *Social Service Review, 64*(2), 308–327. doi:10.1086/603765

Toseland, R. (1995). *Group work with the elderly and family caregivers.* New York, NY: Springer Publishing Company.

Toseland, R., & Coppola, M. (1985). A task-centered approach to group work with the elderly. In A. Fortune (Ed.), *Task-centered practice with families and groups* (pp. 101–114). New York, NY: Springer Publishing Company.

Toseland, R., Diehl, M., Freeman, K., Manzanares, T., Naleppa, M., & McCallion, P. (1997). The impact of validation therapy on nursing home residents with dementia. *Journal of Applied Gerontology, 16*(1), 31–50. doi:10.1177/073344689701600102

Toseland, R., & Hacker, L. (1982). Self-help groups and professional involvement. *Social Work, 27*(4), 341–347.

Toseland, R., Kabat, D., & Kemp, K. (1983). An evaluation of a smoking cessation group program. *Social Work Research and Abstracts, 19*(1), 12–20. doi:10.1093/swra/19.1.12

Toseland, R., Labrecque, M., Goebel, S., & Whitney, M. (1992). An evaluation of a group program for spouses of frail, elderly veterans. *Gerontologist, 32*(3), 382–390. doi:10.1093/geront/32.3.382

Tropman, J. (2014). *Effective meetings: Improving group decision-making* (4th ed.). Thousand Oaks, CA: Sage Publications.

Vaillant, G. (1995). *The natural history of alcoholism revisited.* Cambridge, MA: Harvard University Press.

Walsh, J. (2010). *Psychoeducation in mental health.* Chicago, IL: Lyceum Books.

Yalom, I. (2005). *The theory and practice of group psychotherapy* (5th ed.). New York, NY: Basic Books.

Chapter 14

Achenbach, T. (1991). *Manual for the child behavior checklist: 4–18 and 1991 profile.* Burlington, VT: University Associates in Psychiatry.

American Psychiatric Association. (2013). *Diagnostic and statistical manual of mental disorders* (5th ed.). Arlington, VA: American Psychiatric Publishing.

Bales, R. (1950). *Interaction process analysis: A method for the study of small groups.* Reading, MA: Addison-Wesley.

Bales, R. (1980). *SYMLOG: Case study kit.* New York, NY: Free Press.

Bales, R., Cohen, S., & Williamson, S. (1979). *SYMLOG: A system for the multiple level observations of groups.* New York, NY: Free Press.

Barlow, S. (2013). *Specialty competencies in group psychology.* New York, NY: Oxford University Press.

Bloom, M., Fisher, J., & Orme, J. (2009). *Evaluating practice: Guidelines for the accountable professional* (6th ed.). Boston, MA: Allyn & Bacon.

Bonito, J. (2002). The analysis of participation in small groups: Methodological and conceptual issues related to interdependence. *Small Group Research, 33*(4), 412–438. doi:10.1177/104649640203300402

Boyd-Franklin, N., Cleek, E., Wofsy, M., & Mundy, B. (2013). *Therapy in the real world.* New York, NY: Guilford Press.

Brower, A. M., Arndt, R. G., & Ketterhagen, A. (2004). Very good solutions really do exist for group work research design problems. In C. D. Garvin, L. M. Gutierrez, & M. J. Galinsky (Eds.), *Handbook of social work with groups* (pp. 435–446). New York, NY: Guilford Press.

Burlingame, G., Strauss, B., & Joyce, A. (2013). Change mechanisms and effectiveness of small group treatments. In M. J. Lambert (Ed.), *Bergin and Garfield's handbook of psychotherapy and behavior change* (6th ed., pp. 640–689). Hoboken, NJ: Wiley.

Burlingame, G., Whitcomb, K., & Woodland, S. (2014). Process and outcome in group counseling and psychotherapy. In J. Delucia-Waack, C. Kalodner, & M. Riva, (Eds.), *Handbook of group counseling & psychotherapy* (2nd ed., pp. 55–68). Thousand Oaks, CA: Sage Publications.

Chen, E., Reid, M., Parker, S., & Pillemer, K. (2012). Tailoring evidence-based interventions for new populations: A method for program adaptation through community engagement. *Evaluation Health Profession, 36*(1), 73–92. doi:10.1177/0163278712442536

Chevalier, J., & Bukles, D. (2013). *Participatory action research: Theory and methods for engaged inquiry.* New York, NY: Routledge.

Corcoran, J. (2011). *Mental health treatment for children and adolescents.* New York, NY: Oxford University Press.

Corcoran, K., & Fischer, J. (2013). *Measures for clinical practice and research: A sourcebook* (5th ed.). (Vol. 1, Couples Families and Children & Vol. 2, Adults). New York, NY: Oxford University Press.

Drummond, M., Sculpher, M., Torrance, G., O'Brien, B., & Stoddart, G. (2005). *Methods for the economic evaluation of health care programmes* (3rd ed.). Oxford, UK: Oxford University Press.

Flyvbjerg, B. (2011). Case study. In N. Denzin & Y. Lincoln (Eds.), *The Sage handbook of qualitative research* (4th ed., pp.301–316). Thousand Oaks, CA, Sage Publications.

Forsyth, D. R. (2014). *Group dynamics* (6th ed.). Belmont, CA: Wadsworth Cengage Learning.

Fraser, M., Richman, J., Galinsky, M., & Day, S. (2009). *Intervention research: Developing social programs.* New York, NY: Oxford University Press.

Garrett, K. (2005). School social workers' evaluations of group work practices. *Children and Schools, 27*(4). 247–252. doi:10.1093/cs/27.4.247

Hemphill, J. (1956). *Group dimensions: A manual for their measurement.* Columbus, OH: Monographs of the Bureau of Business Research, Ohio State University.

Hill, W. (1977). Hill interaction matrix (HIM): The conceptual framework, derived rating scales, and an updated bibliography. *Small Group Behavior, 8*(3), 251–268. doi:10.1177/104649647700800301

Johnson, J. (2008). Using research-supported group treatments. *Journal of Clinical Psychology: In session, 64*(11), 1206–1224. doi:10.1002/jcplp.20532

Kamberelis, G., & Dimitriadis, G. (2013). *Focus groups: From structured interviews to collective conversations.* New York, NY: Routledge.

Kane, R. (1974). Look to the record. *Social Work, 19*(4), 412–419. doi:10.1093/sw/19.4.412

Kazdin, A. (2008). Evidence-based treatment and practice: New opportunities to bridge clinical research and practice and improve patient care. *American Psychologist, 63*(3), 146–159.

Kiresuk, T., & Sherman, R. (1968). Goal attainment scaling: A general method for evaluating comprehensive community mental health programs. *Community Mental Health Journal, 4*(6), 443–453. doi:10.1007/BF01530764

Kiresuk, T., Smith, A., & Cardillo, J. (1994). *Goal attainment scaling: Applications theory and measurements.* Hillsdale, NJ: L. Erlbaum Associates.

Kivlighan, D., & Kivlighan, M. (2014). Therapeutic factors: Current theory and research. In J. Delucia-Waack, C. Kalodner, & M. Riva (Eds.), *Handbook of group counseling & psychotherapy* (2nd ed., pp. 46–54). Thousand Oaks, CA: Sage Publications.

Kramer, J., & Conoley, J. (1992). *Eleventh mental measurement yearbook.* Lincoln, NE: Buros Institute of Mental Measurements.

Kratochwill, T., & Levin. J. (2010). Enhancing the scientific credibility of single-case intervention research: Randomization to the rescue. *Psychological Methods, 15*(2), 124–144. doi:10.1037/a0017736

Krueger, R., Richard, A., & Casey, M. (2015). *Focus groups: A practical guide for applied research* (5th ed.). Thousand Oaks, CA: Sage Publications.

Lawson, H. A., Caringi, J. C., Pyles, L., Jurkowski, J., & Bozlak, C. (2015). *Participatory action research*. New York, NY: Oxford University Press.

Lese, K., & MacNair-Semands, R. (2000). The therapeutic factors inventory: Development of a scale. *Eastern Group Psychotherapy Society, 24*(4), 303–317. doi:10.1023/A:1026616626780

Levin, H. M., & McEwan, P. (2001). *Cost-effectiveness analysis: Methods and applications*. Thousand Oaks, CA: Sage Publications.

Lieberman, M., Yalom, I., & Miles, M. (1973). *Encounter groups: First facts*. New York, NY: Basic Books.

Macgowan, M. J. (1997). A measure of engagement for social group work: The groupwork engagement measure (GEM). *Journal of Social Service Research, 23*(2), 17–37. doi:10.1300/J079v23n02_02

Macgowan, M. J. (2000). Evaluation of a measure of engagement for group work. *Research in Social Work Practice, 10*(3), 348–361. doi:10.1093/acprof:oso/9780195183450.001.0001

Macgowan, M. J. (2008). *A guide to evidence-based group work*. New York, NY: Oxford University Press.

Macgowan, M. J., & Levenson, J. S. (2003). Psychometrics of the group engagement measure with male sex offenders. *Small Group Research, 34*(2), 155–160. doi:10.1177/1046496402250498

Macgowan, M. J., & Newman, F. (2005). Factor structure of the group engagement measure. *Social Work Research, 29*(2), 107–118. doi:10.1093/swr/29.2.107

Macgowan, M. J., & Wong, S. (2014). Single-case designs in group work: Past applications, future directions. *Group Dynamics, 18*(2), 138–158. doi:10.1037/GDN000003

Magen, R. (2004). Measurement issues. In C. D. Garvin, L. M. Gutierrez, & M. J. Galinsky (Eds.), *Handbook of social work with groups* (pp. 447–460). New York, NY: Guilford Press.

Marshall, C. R., & Rossman, G. (2011). *Designing qualitative research*. (5th ed.). Thousand Oaks, CA: Sage Publications.

Mattaini, M. (2010). Single-system studies. In B. Thyer (Ed.), *The handbook of social work research methods* (pp. 241–273). Thousand Oaks, CA: Sage Publications.

McNiff, J. (2013). *Action research: Principles and practice* (3rd ed.). Milton Park, Abingdon, England: Routledge.

Monette, D., Sullivan, T., DeJong, C., & Hilton, T. (2014). *Applied social research*. Belmont, CA: Brooks/Cole.

Moos, R. H. (1986). *Group environment scale manual* (2nd ed.). Palo Alto, CA: Consulting Psychologists Press.

Moreno, J. (1934). *Who shall survive?* Washington, DC: Nervous and Mental Diseases.

Nugent, W. (2010). *Analyzing single system data*. New York, NY: Oxford University Press.

Padgett, D. (2008). *Qualitative methods in social work research: Challenges and rewards* (2nd ed.). Thousand Oaks, CA: Sage Publications.

Rao, C., & Sinharay, S. (2007). *Psychometrics*. Amsterdam, The Netherlands: Elsevier North-Holland.

Rose, S. (1989). *Working with adults in groups: A multi-method approach*. San Francisco, CA: Jossey-Bass.

Rossi, P., Freeman, H., & Lipsey, M. (2004). *Evaluation: A systematic approach* (7th ed.). Thousand Oaks, CA: Sage Publications.

Salkind, N., & Rasmussen, K. (2007). *Encyclopedia of measurement and statistics*. Thousand Oaks, CA: Sage Publications.

Sandano, S., Guyker, W., Delucia-Waack, J., Cosgrove, H., Altaber, D., & Amos, B. (2014). Measures of group process, dynamics, climate, behavior, and outcome: A review. In J. Delucia-Waack, C. Kalodner, & M. Riva (Eds.), *Handbook of group counseling & psychotherapy* (2nd ed., pp. 159–177). Thousand Oaks, CA: Sage Publications.

Schneider, J. (2014). *Participatory action research from A to Z: A comprehensive guide*. Bonita Springs, FL: Principal Investigators Association.

Schwartz, J., Wald, M., & Moravec, S. (2010). Assessing groups. In R. Conyne (Ed.), *The Oxford handbook of group counseling* (pp. 245–259). New York, NY: Oxford University Press.

Seaberg, J., & Gillespie, D. (1977). Goal attainment scaling: A critique. *Social Work Research and Abstracts, 13*(2), 4–9. doi:10.1093/swra/13.2.4

Silbergeld, S., Koenig, G., Manderscheid, R., Meeker, B., & Hornung, C. (1975). Assessment of environment-therapy systems: The group atmosphere scale. *Journal of Consulting and Clinical Psychology, 43*(4), 460–469. doi:10.1037/h0076897

Smith, J. (2012). Single-case experimental designs: A systematic review of published research and currect standards. *Psychological Methods, 17*(4), 510–550. doi:10.1037/a0029312

Solomon, P., Cavanaugh, M., & Draine, J. (2009). *Randomized controlled trials: Design and implementation for community-based psychosocial interventions*. New York, NY: Oxford University Press.

Stewart, A. (2014). Case study. In J. Mills & M. Birks (Eds.), *Qualitative methodology: A practical guide* (pp. 145–160). London, England: Sage Publications.

Stewart, D., & Shamdasani, P. (2015). *Focus groups: Theory and practice* (3rd ed.). Los Angeles, CA: Sage Publications.

Stone, M., Lewis, C., & Beck, A. (1994). The structure of Yalom's Curative Factors Scale. *International Journal of Group Psychotherapy, 44*(2), 239–245.

Tasca, G., Illing, V., Ogrodniczuk, J., & Joyce, A. (2009). Assessing and adjusting for dependent observations in group treatment research using multilevel models. *Group Dynamics: Theory, Research, & Practice, 13*(3), 151–233. doi:10.1037/a0014837

Thomas, E. (1978). Generating innovation in social work: The paradigm of developmental research. *Journal of Social Services Research, 2*(1), 95–115. doi:10.1300/J079v02n01_08

Thyer, B. (2012). *Quasi-experimental research designs*. New York, NY: Oxford University Press.

Toseland, R. (1981). Increasing access: Outreach methods in social work practice. *Social Casework, 62*(4), 227–234. doi:10.1177/002087288803100103

Toseland, R., Labrecque, M., Goebel, S., & Whitney, M. (1992). An evaluation of a group program for spouses of frail, elderly veterans. *Gerontologist, 32*(3), 382–390.

Toseland, R., McCallion, P., Smith, T., & Banks, S. (2004). Supporting caregivers of frail older adults in an HMO setting. *American Journal of Orthopsychiatry, 74*(3), 349–364. doi:10.1037/0002-9432.74.3.349

Toseland, R., McCallion, P., Smith, T., Huck, S., Bourgeois, P., & Garstka, T. (2001). Health education groups for caregivers in an HMO. *Journal of Clinical Psychology*, *57*(4), 551–570. doi:10.1002/jclp.1028

Tropman, J. (2014). *Effective meetings: Improving group decision-making* (4th ed.). Thousand Oaks, CA: Sage Publications.

Turner-Stokes. L. (2009). Goal attainment scaling (GAS). *Clinical Rehabilitation*, *23*(4), 362–370. doi:10:1177/02692155081011742

Uto, Y., Iwaanakuchi, T., Muranaga, F., & Kumamoto, I. (2013). Development of the electronic patient record system based on problem oriented system. *Studies in Health Technology and Informatics*, *192*, 1036. doi:10.3233/978-1-61499-289-9-1036

Wells, K. (2011). *Narrative inquiry*. New York, NY: Oxford University Press.

Wong, S. E. (2010). Single-case evaluation designs for practitioners. *Journal of Social Service Research*, *36(3)*,248–259. doi:10.1080/01488371003707654

Author Index

M

Subject Index

U

Ubiquitous task group, 336–337
Universality, 200
Universalizing, 108

V

Valence, 62
Validity, 438
Values, 5–11
Video groups, 192
Visualization, 305
Visualization and cognitive imagery techniques, 305–306

W

Work, 94
Worker observation, 242
Worker roles
    advocate, 287
    broker, 287
    educator, 287
    enabler, 287
    mediator, 287
World War II, 46
Written contracts, 180
Written group proposal, 186
Written proposal, 186–193